W9-APG-506

White Rose Blooms in Wisconsin

Kevin Barrett, Jim Fetzer & The American Resistance

Also by Mike Palecek:

Fiction:

SWEAT: Global Warming in a small town, and other tales from the great American Westerly Midwest
Joe Coffee's Revolution
The Truth
The American Dream
Johnny Moon
KGB
Terror Nation
Speak English!
The Last Liberal Outlaw
The Progressive Avenger
Camp America
Twins
Iowa Terror
Guests of the Nation Looking For Bigfoot
A Perfect Duluth Day
American History 101: Conspiracy Nation Revolution
One Day In The Life of Herbert Wisniewski
Operation Northwoods: . . . the patsy
Red White & Blue

Non-Fiction:

Cost of Freedom (with Whitney Trettien and Michael Annis)
Prophets Without Honor (with William Strabala)
The Dynamic Duo: White Rose Blooms in Wisconsin (with Chuck Gregory)
And I Suppose We Didn't Go To The Moon, Either? (with Jim Fetzer)
Nobody Died At Sandy Hook (with Jim Fetzer)
And Nobody Died in Boston, either (with Jim Fetzer)
America was Nuked on 9/11 (with Jim Fetzer)

White Rose Blooms in Wisconsin

Kevin Barrett, Jim Fetzer & The American Resistance

Mike Palecek and Chuck Gregory, Editors

MOON ROCK BOOKS

Save the World/Resist the Empire Series

The Dynamic Duo: White Rose Blooms in Wisconsin
And I suppose we didn't go to the Moon, either?
Nobody Died at Sandy Hook
And Nobody died in Boston, either

Mike Palecek, Jim Fetzer
Series Editors

White Rose Blooms in Wisconsin
Mike Palecek and Chuck Gregory, Editors

ISBN 978-0978818678

Order more copies of *White Rose Blooms in Wisconsin* from

MOON ROCK BOOKS,
6256 Bullet Drive,
Crestview, FL 32536
or MoonRockBooks.com.

White Rose Blooms in Wisconsin is an edited and revised version of T*he Dynamic Duo: White Rose Blooms in Wisconsin,* which makes the book more accessible by standardizing its page size and adding a number of photos, diagrams and other images to enhance the presentation of the life and accomplishments of Kevin Barrett and Jim Fetzer, who represent "the American resistance" to creeping fascism in the United States, which, alas, continues to this day. This is the Moon Rock Books edition.

MOON ROCK BOOKS
6256 Bullet Drive,
Crestview, FL 32536
www.MoonRockBooks.com

Cover design and layout by Ole Dammegård

Dedicated to those hundreds of people,
in Biloxi, Baraboo, Barstow, Butte, Bancroft and Brooklyn,
those people who, on Nov. 22, or Nov. 23, or Nov. 24, 1963,
or sometime during the following week, on a long or short walk,
or at the kitchen table pouring Froot Loops for the kids or for themselves
– those first persons who sat upright in bed at 2:35 a.m. and said,
"This is bullshit."

You know who you are.

The White Rose (German: die Weiße Rose) was a non-violent, intellectual resistance group in Nazi Germany, consisting of students from the University of Munich and their philosophy professor. The group became known for an anonymous leaflet and graffiti campaign, lasting from June 1942 until February 1943, that called for active opposition to dictator Adolf Hitler's regime.

The six most recognized members of the group were arrested by the Gestapo and beheaded in 1943. The text of their sixth leaflet was smuggled by Helmuth James Graf von Moltke out of Germany through Scandinavia to the United Kingdom, and in July 1943 copies of it were dropped over Germany by Allied planes, retitled "The Manifesto of the Students of Munich."

Another member, Hans Conrad Leipelt, who helped distribute Leaflet 6 in Hamburg, was executed on January 29, 1945, for his participation. Today, the members of the White Rose are honoured in Germany amongst its greatest heroes, since they opposed the Third Reich in the face of almost certain death.

- Wikipedia

[Thank You]

I would like to thank Jim Fetzer and Kevin Barrett for saying yes to this project.

I would like to thank Chuck Gregory for joining in, and also for saving us when it looked like we might self-destruct.

I say thank you to Joe Fraser, who helped us with the interior photos and cover design. Also, my daughter, Emily, who took the original cover design and pointed us in a new direction.

Thanks to Scott Lederer for taking the cover bowling alley photo.

Thanks to Jim Fosdick, the bowler in the background, for being a part of the cover photo shoot.

And to Jim, Kevin, Chuck for letting me do my thing, with the cover ideas and the overall concept for this book.

To Kevin and Jim for being Ph.Ds willing to wear black masks in a Wisconsin bowling alley with a dozen white roses sitting between you.

And thanks again to Chuck, for working with us as designer, editor, publisher. Can you imagine a "real" publisher in America actually taking time with a book like this, which is to say a real book, in America, in 2013? I cannot. And so, Chuck Gregory is actually what a real publisher is in America today. He is not on Broadway. He is in a small apartment in Fort Lauderdale, doing book work and the like on a poverty income. Telling the truth the hard way, because there is no other way. Benjamin Franklin and Penn Jones Jr. would be proud of CWG Press.

Without Jim, without Kevin, without Chuck, any one of them, there would be no book.

Thanks also to the many writers who allowed us to use their work in this book, also to those who agreed to tell us all just what Jim Fetzer and Kevin Barrett mean to them.

And thanks again, to Fetzer and Barrett, for just doing it.

You don't see the likes of them every day.

People who get it and who go for it, and for so long, and so hard.

A friend of mine once told me, in relation to practicing the violin: “The only encouragement you will ever get is to quit.”

Well, no doubt many have felt that in relation to working with all these issues in America.

We thank them for not quitting.

And today, especially we thank Jim Fetzer and Kevin Barrett.

You guys are great. You have fought the good fight.

Very cool.

- Mike Palecek

Table of Contents

Foreword

> "A whole new form of government is going to take over the country."
>
> \- Jack Ruby

That's what it was, wasn't it?

We hoped and waited for something like what we had been born with, as if it were always there, but it was gone.

We started out spoiled, all this stuff going on, running full-blast, riding a bike down the street with no hands, arms out-stretched.

We didn't even see the wall.

The U.S. has lost its way.

It should have been evident with LBJ, then Nixon, and we should have really realized it with Ford, but really all we wanted to do was live our lives and have fun and happy children so, well, there was Reagan and Clinton and Carter and Bush and another Bush and now Obama.

And it's almost so obvious now that we can't really ignore it.

But we will ignore it as long as we possibly can.

We will ignore it.

Can you imagine John F. Kennedy trying to convince us that killing by drones is okay or that the government is spying on us pretty much 24/7/365 and that we should just get used to it?

It's a species difference between Obama and Kennedy. Kennedy and Clinton, the two Bushes, do not occupy the same phylum.

What we really need is a manifesto or a great novel that will once and for all show us what we already know.

What we knew in our hearts in 1963 and every year and day since then.

Yep, it's about all the lies. And it would probably be about money, too, because that's always in there.

Torture and Waco and Oklahoma City and 9/11 and Sandy Hook, Tucson, Aurora, and there would be a lot more names of cities in there, Memphis and the Ambassador Hotel pantry and Dallas, and see, you already know what I'm talking about. I just have to say the towns.

And now "drones" is a big word in our culture.

And all you have to say is "drones" and everyone knows what you mean. And Iraq, Afghanistan, El Salvador, Libya.

All you have to say is those names and people know what you mean.

And, oh, yeah, Fallujah.

And there should be this essay or this novel that's not too long, or maybe really long like a Russian novel that when we read it, we would all say, oh, yeah, that's just how it is.

And then Obama would be in jail.

And Bush would be in jail.

And Clinton would be in jail.

And there would be a big hearing in Washington.

And it would mean something.

And it would be on TV every afternoon.

And at the end of it all these men and women, oh, yeah, Condoleeza too, would be shown being taken to prison, just ducking their heads into the backseat of a police car, by an overhead special copter-cam.

And then they would bring in all the high school history books and start going through them and start putting in the right stuff.

They'd put big teacher red pen marks through all the made-up shit like the moon and the Pearl Harbor attack and WMD and anthrax and the Gulf of Tonkin and Wellstone's plane crash and put in the real stuff, the stuff they had in these other books in these big old cardboard boxes that they never were going to show us – like the old photos in grandma's closet with her and grandpa drinking beer and smoking cigarettes sitting on top of the ol' Model A.

And the late night comedians would talk about real stuff, like the crap that used to be in the high school history books and about how they used to talk about how one truck bomb did that to the Murrah Building and how they used to say that jet fuel took down those big NYC buildings and how we used to say a whole airplane disappeared into that little hole in the Pentagon and that little hole in the ground in Pennsylvania.

They'd say jokes about that stuff just as easily as Bob Hope used to talk about golf and airplane food and we all thought it was the funniest crap ever.

They would start talking about a whole bunch of stuff after that big meeting, things they never talked about before, because once you get talking, other things come to mind, like the minimum wage, the climate, the environment, doctor bills, things to help people live better.

Then some people would say, hey, you know what else we could do?

They'd go fix up the old school in the middle of town and put in new sidewalks in the neighborhood around that old school. They would start tearing down the county jail and the prison in town, brick by brick.

And then, all because of this one novel that said things everybody already knew, a bunch of people would walk to the CIA building and the FBI building and the Homeland Security Building and they would walk right in, because they paid for this piece of crap building anyway, and then they would walk over to the fence with the razor wire and they would cut it down and they would help the people through and they would put up this homemade sign, maybe with cardboard and crayons and tack it up on a stick or a branch or a shovel and it would say "America" on it.

That's what might all happen as soon as the person is born who will write this manifesto or clear, concise, inexpensive novel that will tell us all the things we already know.

And all we have to do now is wait.

In the preface for my novel *The American Dream* I talk about my parents, Milosh and Isabel. They were Czech and Irish. They moved to Norfolk from Winner, South Dakota when Dad got his big break to be an engineer for the Chicago & Northwestern Railroad.

They grabbed each other in the South Dakota wind and held on. They were true believers in the American dream, I suppose, though they would not have put it that way.

More likely they just believed in working and going to church and mowing the lawn and taking care of your car and watching the ball game or *Bonanza* if it was on.

Dad spent part of his career on the Long Pine run, staying overnight at the motel near the tracks and fishing for trout. He brought fish home and maybe a foul ball from the amateur games in Winner when he got a chance to go there and see his brother Jimmy, home from the Pacific war, now with a wife and his own family. Another brother, Albert, served with Patton and later went to South Omaha to work in a box factory. Frank went to California. Molly just went away. Dad didn't go to the war because his job with the railroad was considered vital to the war effort.

They said Dad was good enough at shortstop to go pro, but he didn't. Maybe he had to work. He hauled cases at the pop factory before the C&NW. They did the best they could. It's sad, a sad state of affairs for a whole nation.

Everyone does the best he can and we end up bombing Hiroshima. Dad cuts the lawn each Saturday morning on his one chance to rest and there go a thousand people in Chile, mowed down by our own CIA.

Mom calls us in to supper and poof! Laos is toast.

Us kids sneak outside for another round of playing after supper. We play hide and seek, catch lightning bugs, tell ghost stories and leave the screen door open just a peep.

A couple hundred intelligent poor people in El Salvador are hustled out of their beds and shot.

In Norfolk the media was *The Norfolk Daily News*, WJAG Radio and the *Omaha World-Herald*.

There is no way for someone just growing up, or someone who has not been much of anywhere else to know that those outlets distort the news. They tell the story in the way they want it to be told.

We suffered and bled along with the perils of Otis The Drunk, but did not have a clue about the people being murdered by our own government in Chile. And nobody told us. We weren't supposed to know.

There really is no way of knowing – not some fat kid who only has eyes for Strawberry Swirl – that what is on TV is not great and true and the only real reality worth understanding.

It wasn't until I left Norfolk, to go to the seminary in Minnesota, then Washington, D.C., then New York, later prison, that I began to understand what a warped vision and body my upbringing had saddled me with.

Later on, I even questioned Johnny Carson himself.

I studied the JFK assassination and learned that attorney Jim Garrison had been a guest on The Tonight Show talking about his investigation. I listened to the recording on the internet — of Carson grilling Garrison.

I found Carson's address and wrote to him, asking him, Norfolkan-to-Norfolkan.

March 2, 2001
Johnny Carson
c/o Carson Productions Group
3110 Main St.
Suite 200
Santa Monica, CA 90405

Mr. Carson:

Hello.

I am originally from Norfolk, Nebr., graduated from NHS in 1973. Recently I had a chance to listen to the tape of your interview with attorney Jim Garrison. I don't recall watching the live interview, but very well could have as watching your show before bed was our regular routine, as it was for many others.

As a fellow Norfolkan, I am curious as to why you treated Garrison as you did. I probably will not get the chance to contact you twice, so I will be frank right away. You sounded as if you were acting as a spokesman for someone else. Really. Were you protecting the real killers of Kennedy?

Of course, you were. What else can I say, but that it is obvious now with almost forty years of perspective. The Warren Commission was a joke and Garrison as on to something. Something frightening to be sure. But why did you have so much allegiance to the plotters and none to your dead president? Because he could not pay your from the grave? Is it as simple as that?

Thanks in part to you we have been forced to live in Disneyland since 1963, where everything is unreal, everything entertainment and illusion.

Please tell me, as I will never know myself: Is wealth

and power worth the sublimation of the truth?

Thank you for your time.
Sincerely,
Mike Palecek

Johnny Carson's Response

March 9, 2001

Mike Palecek
702 6th Avenue
Sheldon, Iowa 51201

Dear Mr. Palecek,

I'm sending you a copy of a letter I recently received to make you aware that some ignorant asshole is sending out letters over your signature.

You should look into this.

Sincerely,
Johnny Carson

We Have A Dream ...

... of bringing the United States politicians, journalists and generals who have brought about this long ten-year war and debacle to trial and putting them on TV just like O.J., every afternoon so every American can watch just like the McCarthy Hearings and the JFK funeral procession.

What we need is a New American Dream.

Not of new homes and toasters and microwaves, but of becoming the type of country we always thought we were.

And part of that is becoming the quality of people who are capable of telling the truth.

Right now we live on lies. We subsist on lies, but it's not really living. We lie to ourselves about how we deserve this country and we deserve to shut others out after we took the land from others.

We lie to ourselves and our children about all aspects of our history.

The New American Dream means never having to say some question or idea is not valid. We are allowed to ask any questions that we have ... there are no wrong questions.

There is no hidden black military budget, there are no UFO files Americans cannot see, no JFK documents that will not be opened during our lifetimes, no destroyed RFK murder photos by the L.A. police, no evidence from Ground Zero taken away before we can even look at it – we are not the Soviet Union of the 1960s – this is supposed to be America. That is our dream, to become America, The New America, the real hope of the world.

I believe that 9/11 was an inside job.

Bush, Cheney, Rice, Powell, Rumsfeld, Ashcroft, Obama, Bill Clinton, Hillary Clinton, Joe Biden.

They all know that and yet they refuse to acknowledge what they know. They kill and continue to kill. They allow others to die and continue to send others to their deaths for a lie. What we need in America is a Truth Commission like they had in South Africa to heal their broken country.

Our country is surely broken as well.

We need a Truth Commission. We need to put certain people on the stand and we need to be allowed to ask questions.

We are not even allowed to ask questions.

Those who are supposed to ask questions for us refuse to do so. Can you honestly say that Brian Williams or Matt Lauer or Katie Couric or Amy Goodman or Jon Stewart or *The New York Times* or the *Minneapolis Star-Tribune* asks the questions that need to be asked?

The United States of America is also supposed to be based on the Constitution. It is not based on the Constitution. The president does not ask anyone before he goes to war, bombing, killing people.

It is rather based on those in power being focused like a laser beam not on truth and social justice and doing the right thing – which is why we voted for them – but rather on doing whatever it takes for them to remain in power. It is based rather on the shooting of Jack Kennedy from perhaps as many as six vantages in Dealey Plaza. That is the Big Boom – The Big Boom Theory of the creation of this country.

Before that instant we had a chance to fight poverty and racism and war, get the truth, the truth about whatever, because before that moment everything seemed bright and possible, even probable.

But after that Big Boom, the dustbowl clouds of power and greed and violence came out and blotted the sun. The United States of America is not based in the Constitution or the teachings of Jesus as we proclaim that it is. It is based on the collaboration of the U.S. Army, FBI, CIA and Memphis police to murder Martin Luther King.

It is also based on the shooting of Robert Kennedy from behind his right ear, rather than from the front where Sirhan Sirhan was standing.

We do not make cars anymore in America but we do psy-ops like the Greeks and Romans did philosophy, astronomy and speeches and literature.

These Great Misdeeds are where we honed our master craft, where those who rule founded this country, where our gears, our tool and die were cast.

Forget about the Liberty Bell.

Forget about Mount Rushmore.

Forget about the Grand Canyon.

They are as much window dressing as CNN or NBC News or National Public Radio.

The Lorraine Motel in Memphis is our true Plymouth Rock.

Dallas' Dealey Plaza is our real Mount Rushmore.

The Ambassador Hotel pantry is our actual Grand Canyon.

Waco is our Arlington Cemetery.

Oklahoma City is our Yellowstone Park.

The woods near Eveleth, Minnesota where Paul Wellstone's plane went down are our National Mall. And with the confidence and experience gained in the 1960s our actual Founding Fathers, whoever they are, were able to tack on a Bill of Rights to their version of the Constitution on Sept. 11, 2001. ...

... We have fake history.

Our junior high and high school history books should be in italics, handed out by the teacher on the first day with a wink: Remember the Maine – Pearl Harbor – Gulf of Tonkin – Waco – Oklahoma City bombing – moon landings – stolen elections.

Because we accepted the Warren Commission we got the "9/11 What Controlled Demolition Commission" and our children will get the "XYZ Non-Investigation by Rich People Covering Up For Other Rich People."

I believe 9/11 was an inside job.

They got the new Pearl Harbor they wanted to invade Iraq and take the oil.

The troops are not protecting us. That is someone's spin on the day's news, somebody's advertising slogan, someone else's sermon.

The troops serve the empire. They are not heroes. They kill and plunder for the empire.

The heroes in our country are the protesters, the ones who go face to face with the empire, those who have occupied, those pounding on missiles with household hammers, those who have stood up in public meetings and shouted at the liars, those writers and little radio show hosts almost nobody knows about.

The Obama election, believing in Hope. I had hope. I had hope that we might enter a brand-new period of openness, no wrong questions, Truth – becoming the type of people, nation that we always thought we were.

It didn't happen. And we have to ask ourselves why?

It's one of those questions that we are allowed to ask — that we should ask.

You have to know that Barack Obama knows the whole truth about the 9/11 attacks. He is complicit. He has lied. He continued the wars in Iraq and Afghanistan based on a lie. And he knows he is lying.

He lied right to our faces on national television when he said that Osama bin Laden had been killed ... and buried at sea. ... Osama bin Laden was buried at sea ... and Jessica Lynch was rescued heroically, the U.S.A. does not torture, Iraq had weapons of mass destruction, George Bush won the 2000 election, see, there is a plane there in that hole in Shanksville, it went all the way into that hole and no, there is no blood and no bodies and no luggage scattered ... or plane parts ... and Osama bin Laden ... was buried at sea. ...

Can you believe the Warren Commission? I mean believe that it really happened, and we did not have riots because of it, but rather we just say, oh, well ... and so ...

Bush fought the 9/11 commission.

He did not want to testify alone. Was the commission meeting in the dark, with spiders?

After 9/11 all the propaganda to promote the war – terror alerts – where did those go? Osama Bin Laden tapes in the middle of the afternoon on Fox and CNN and NBC ... 9/11 Commission, finally, and then what a supreme joke that was and we settled for it. Building 7 – controlled demolition – where's the plane in the Pentagon – Shanksville – dancing Israelis? ... And still the Bushes ride in a golf cart down the third baseline waving to the crowd and are greeted by cheers rather than tomatoes, fists and handcuffs ... Karl Rove, Donald Rumsfeld, Dick Cheney walk free ... Condoleeza Rice teaches at Stanford rather than being locked up forever in one of these high-tech concentration camps we have, like in Florence, Colorado, and shuffling off to the shower each morning wearing ankle shackles and a waist chain and fluorescent orange pajamas ... for the rest of their lives.

If we're going to have these insane places, we might as well put the worst of the worst there, and that would be George and George Bush, Dick Cheney, Karl Rove, Condoleeza Rice, Donald Rumsfeld and whatever other dozens have conspired, continue to conspire, to overthrow this country – who know the truth and don't tell the rest of us: FBI director Moeller, General Tommy Franks and all the other generals who acted as commentators on NPR and Fox, ensuring us that the coming war was so cool, so good, so right.

And now we have how many hundreds of thousands of dead human beings in Iraq and Afghanistan.

Just people who were living their lives and found themselves in the way of the American quest for gold, for dominance.

And the thousands of young Americans who have died or had their lives ruined because of a lie, a huge, amazing lie, perpetrated by men and women we asked in good faith to lead us on our way.

Bush, Obama ... Card, Clinton, Fleischer ...

Wolfowitz, Aschcroft, Pearl, O'Reilly, Hannity, Couric, Lauer, Williams, Rather, Jennings, Brokaw, Limbaugh, Blitzer, Sawyer, Rivera, all those names, who, if history ever rights itself, will be synonymous with Goebbels, Goering, Himmler.

Back when I was a kid growing up in Nebraska, we thought Lyndon Johnson was just a big, boring dude.

Well, we all need to read: *LBJ, The Mastermind of JFK's Assassination*, by Phillip F. Nelson. It turns out that the vice-president of the United States might have planned and carried through the murder of John F. Kennedy.

Maybe he did. Maybe he was just a part of it.

But even so.

Never in 100 years would my hometown newspaper, radio station, teachers, coaches, or parents have let us even consider such a thing.

The term "grassy knoll" was said with the same sneer that "liberal" gets today and even today, almost 50 years later, that seems like a garbled term to pronounce.

All the while we pointed fingers at the Soviet Union, declaring them a closed society and pointing back at ourselves, boasting forever of a free and open society.

We are anything but, have been anything but.

The ones who ruled the Soviet Union, well, they had nothing on the ones who rule us.

Yes, these successful lies are more profound than anything else in World History, ever. It's just all so very well done. It's who we are.

And so the most profound, big thing about this big thing called America is that it is a highly successful lie.

And you can say that's conspiracy tinfoil, to think like that, about the Bushes and the assassinations and such, but I say it's just paying attention.

Remember the Anthrax Letters, which said "Are You Afraid?" Those were not written with a rock and chisel like Fred Flintstone from the recesses of some cave in Afghanistan. Those letters came from persons within our own government.

Like a horror movie and the killer is in the same house with us.

These killers are right here, with us and "they" want us to be afraid.

We cannot be afraid.

> "... the great city sprawls with people, some smartly dressed, many of them shabby, a few beautiful but most not, all reduced by the towering structures around them to the size of insects, but scuttling, hurrying, intent in the milky morning sun upon some plan or scheme or hope they are hugging to themselves, their reason for living another day, each one of them impaled live upon the pin of consciousness, fixed upon self-advancement and self-preservation. That, and only that."
>
> - John Updike, *The Terrorist*

That's perhaps the human condition.

... forced to find a reason for living another day, impaled live upon the pin of consciousness ... to become fixed upon self-advancement and self-preservation.

But the human condition also means knowing when there is something wrong, something not quite right and having the spirit to refuse to live like that, to live within a lie.

That's why so many people have worked for so long, for ten years, twenty, thirty, forty, fifty years, against all sorts of obstacles, to find the truth, to make this the country and we the people we always assumed we were.

Common people, educated people, who have set this puzzle down, spread it out over the whole kitchen table and began working on it, for years and years.

New people drift in the door and take their place. People like Kevin Barrett and Jim Fetzer, who have been working non-stop for years and years to give us that New American Dream.

They are not afraid.

We take courage from their example.

We also cannot be afraid.

AN INTERNATIONAL SYMPOSIUM

DEBUNKING THE "WAR ON TERROR": THREE PERSPECTIVES

To view Part 1 (Fetzer)

The "war on terror" has been justified by 9/11, by religious and moral arguments, and by political persuasion. These speakers will address the crucial arguments for war: Have we been told the truth about 9/11? Do religion and morality support these wars? Does an analysis of the political language employed to justify them reveal a hidden agenda? They will demonstrate that the "war on terror" is a complete and unjustifiable fraud.

EXPERT SPEAKERS and POLITICAL COMMENTATORS:

Ken O'Keefe (Ireland/Palestine), Master of Ceremonies

James Fetzer (US), Founder, Scholars for 9/11 Truth "Are wars in Iraq and Afghanistan justified by 9/11?"

Kevin Barrett (US), Co-Founder, Muslims for 9/11 Truth "Islam, Neoconservatism, and the Unwarranted 'War on Terror'"

Gilad Atzmon (UK), Jazz Musician and Political Commentator "From Promised Land to Promised Planet: Zionism and Neoconservatism"

6:30-9:30 PM, 14 JULY 2010, FRIENDS HOUSE
(OPPOSITE EUSTON STATION)

ADMISSION: £5 ON DOOR FROM 6:00 PM

Jim organized a symposium, "Debunking the War on Terror", at Friend's House in London, UK, on 14 July 2010 with Gilad Atzmon joining him and Kevin as speakers and Ken O'Keefe as Master of Ceremonies.

The Dynamic Duo:
White Rose Blooms in Wisconsin
Kevin Barrett, Jim Fetzer & The American Resistance
by Mike Palecek
edited by Chuck Gregory

The front cover of the original CWG Press edition of The Dynamic Duo *(2013)*

"How difficult it is to escape the dread consequences of a regime's calculated and incessant propaganda ... how useless it was even to try to make contact with a mind which had become warped and for whom the facts of life had become what Hitler and Goebbels, with their cynical disregard for the truth, said they were."

— William Shirer, *The Rise And Fall Of The Third Reich*

The White Rose resistance.

The American resistance.

Both grow out of necessity.

Somebody had to do it. No doubt it would fall to somebody. No doubt somebody will do something.

Right?

Yes, probably, but up close it comes down to someone, some living, breathing, thinking, feeling person beginning to understand, and then ... beginning to do something.

Beginning to put self behind, career behind, safety behind.

Kevin Barrett and Jim Fetzer donned the name "The Dynamic Duo" when they hosted a radio show together.

Like the people in The White Rose resistance movement in Nazi Germany who fought with words, by distributing leaflets, by expressing their opinion, Fetzer and Barrett do the same as they fight along with others against the American Empire whose existence can no longer be denied.

There is something that burns in the heart of people like these – Jim Fetzer, Kevin Barrett, Sophie Scholl, Hans Scholl, Alex Schmorell, Willi Graf, Christoph Probst, Kurt Huber – a fire that cannot ever really be extinguished.

Ridicule will not put it out, ignorance cannot put it out, suffering shall not put it out. It is an eternal flame that burns in the heart of people like these.

And we may take great comfort in knowing that the same thing that is within them is inside each of us, too.

ISBN 978-0-9788186-7-8

CWG Press

$18.95

9 780978 818678 >

The back cover of the original CWG Press edition of The Dynamic Duo *(2013)*

[Chapter 1] The Dynamic Duo

> "Let's face the fact, this country needs a revolution every bit as much as Hasni Mubarak's Egypt needed a revolution. The question is, what will it take?"
>
> - Kevin Barrett

Our history stems from that day, from that place.

From Nov. 22, 1963, about 12:30 p.m.

Dallas, Texas. Memphis. Los Angeles. Oklahoma City. New York City. Washington, D.C. Eveleth, Minnesota.

Aurora. Sandy Hook. Boston.

Fallujah. Kabul. Kandahar.

And whatever is happening right now.

What is coming.

Unless we stop it.

Us.

You. Me.

We.

Who was really behind the anthrax attacks?

Isn't it important? At least as important as Paul Revere's ride? Or a cracked bell?

Have you ever Googled "JFK assassination" at 11:30 at night, maybe after a couple of drinks, and then found yourself still on the computer in the living room when the family is getting up for school and work?

I used to make a wish upon a star, daydream that when I die, I would ask, the very first thing after I set down my suitcases, "Who killed JFK?"

But now, thanks to the tears and sweat and blood of Jim Fetzer, Kevin Barrett and many others, I can save that wish, keep that "one big question" for something else, because I already know, that one.

Jim Fetzer and Kevin Barrett do not face being beheaded by a guillotine in the basement of the county building on the corner of Main and First, not that we know of, if someone finds out about their writings or hears their radio shows or sees them speak at a public gathering.

That is not the American means of beheading. An American cuts off your head at your neck by taking away the ball, it's his anyway, not allowing you to play, by rolling his eyes at you as you pass on the street, as he passes the stuffing across the Thanksgiving table, interviews you on national television.

You may live here, die here, you will be free to do what you want, say what you want, but we will speak no more about you.

That is how it has gone all these years in America, at least since Nov. 23, 1963.

But still there are those who care enough to try a full-court hook shot with time running out.

And they are heroes whether that shot goes in or not.

The White Rose students wrote leaflets, words, and distributed them and were considered worthy of decapitation by the government.

Jim Fetzer and Kevin Barrett write and speak, making their education, experience, ideas and opinions available to as many people as they can.

And no doubt they are also known and reviled by those in power.

They are a face of the resistance in America, which does exist, in many forms.

The resistance in America has a long and storied history from the Wobblies and Socialists and all those who fought and died and wrote and spoke and suffered and sang and shouted, for workers rights, against war, women's rights, for the earth, since the first white man stepped foot on this land, nudged the white man standing next to him, and said that this was now their land.

And all the way up from Ammon Hennacy, Dorothy Day, Peter Maurin, Emma Goldman, so many names unknown to American school children and now American adults.

Up through the now-famous resisters of the 1960s, famous because of their acts and courage and also because the American media at that time was not yet so much a part of the state, not yet Tass and Isvestia.

But those holes in the wall were soon filled in.

We do not know of the Plowshares Heroes.

We do not know the names Helen Woodson, Carl Kabat, Larry Cloud Morgan, Paul Kabat, Frank Cordaro, John LaForge, Barb Katt, many, many others.

Why aren't the blue-collar words of Phil Berrigan etched below his smiling statue in Washington, D.C. that tourists can climb on, sit on, take their photos, and the poetry of his brother Daniel etched in stone above the entrance to the Supreme Court.

There are names, many names, many faces, as ghostly and invisible as the dead faces of the brown people in El Salvador, Guatemala, Iraq, Afghanistan.

Does anyone know the names Kevin McGuire, Jean Petersen, Darrell Rupiper, Larry Rosebaugh, Roy Bourgeois, Megan Rice, Greg Boertje-Obed, Michael Walli, Brian Terrell?

No.

All are members of the American White Rose, resisters to the empire, unknown to their countrymen, yet very real.

> "This is, uh, Jim Fetzer and I'm pleased to welcome my special guest today ..."

> "This is Kevin Barrett. Welcome to another week of *Truth Jihad Radio* on the American Freedom Radio network. I'm your host, Kevin Barrett, trying to get the most important corrections to the official narrative ..."

Fetzer & Barrett.

Barrett & Fetzer.

They became *The Dynamic Duo* in order to pitch a new radio show they were starting together.

Jim makes sure that I know that he is Batman and Kevin is Robin.

"When you talk about *The Dynamic Duo*," says Jim, "I was offered five days a week and invited Kevin to join me in doing the M/F shows. He said, 'Well, I guess that makes me *The Boy Wonder*,' and I frequently made reference to him by that name."

Well, okay, but since that time it might be hard to say ...

Which is Batman?

Which is Robin?

Probably they are both, both.

Both are leaders. Neither would fit the role of a sidekick, but each is a ready, willing ally and supporter of the other.

And for sure in these times we need some heroes.

Turn on the Bat-Signal, light the searchlight.

Send out the call.

Dr. Kevin Barrett and Dr. James Fetzer are very much a part of all that, that tradition of foresight and courage and action and struggle.

Jim grew up in California, went to college at Princeton, served four years in the Marines, returned to attend graduate school at Indiana University. He then taught philosophy at the University of Kentucky and other schools, finally ending his career at the University of Minnesota-Duluth.

Along the way he wrote on many academic topics as well as beginning to make his forays into so-called conspiracy research.

He has written many articles, spoken at public gatherings, and interviewed many guests on his radio show as well as being a guest, many, many times.

To anyone who knows him, he is a fighter.

To this day, he continues to fight.

Kevin Barrett grew up in Madison, Wisconsin, earned his undergraduate degree in journalism at the University of Wisconsin, and dreamed of being a radical writer.

He eventually drove a mobile home out to San Francisco to take his turn at being the next Tom Wolfe or Hunter S. Thompson. He lived in the bus for years on the streets and beaches of the Bay Area.

While undertaking graduate studies at San Francisco State, Kevin went on junkets to Mexico and Central America, and spent a year in Seattle working for The Nuclear Freeze and getting that whole Grunge thing going.

He wrote *Dr. Weirde's Guide To Weirde San Francisco*, and did become a successful writer.

He also studied in Paris and while there he convinced the national French media he was a famous Hollywood producer, just for kicks. And there was an Amtrak train ride around America. Remember that? Three stops anywhere in the U.S. for less than $300. Well, Kevin took a trip from San Francisco to New Orleans, and during the stop in New York City he met his future wife. He would soon turn his life over to Islam.

And that historic event would help him in his present fight, his Jihad, his quest for truth, for justice, riding his cane pony at the sunset not because he believes he can reach it, but because it is there, jousting with any unlucky windmills along the way.

This is not the definitive biography of Jim Fetzer, not the last word on Kevin Barrett. It's a good try.

It is a beginning.

In preparation for writing, I take a trip from Saginaw, near Duluth, to Madison, Wisconsin. I get to Oregon, a Madison suburb, to Jim's house, just before he is to start his radio show at 5 p.m.

He greets me with a big smile and shows me around.

I have met Jim twice before. I've listened to many, many of his radio shows, been interviewed by him a few times. He is a monthly columnist on the weekly radio show that I co-host. I've read a few of his books and many of his articles.

I know that some people don't like Jim. I know that many people love him. The reason I wanted to do this book, that I asked Jim and Kevin if they would let me do this book, was because I think they are the cutting edge. They know the truth about America, and for years and years they have been doing everything they can to get the word out.

If Jim Fetzer and Kevin Barrett could host *The Nightly News* for one month our world would be changed forever. There is no question about it.

It turns out the media is that important. Information is that big a deal. You listen to Dan Rather, Peter Jennings, Tom Brokaw, Brian Williams for years, and you get Fascist America, over time.

You put Kevin Barrett and Jim Fetzer in their spot and you get Thomas Jefferson's America, Ben Franklin's, Tom Paine's.

Jim interviewed me as part of the show and as usual did most of the talking. He then took me out to a great dinner at The Outback.

He was saddened to learn that not all of the people he asked me to contact to comment on his life have responded.

We then headed out to his daughter Sarah's home to meet her and husband, Scott, who would be taking the cover photo on Saturday morning.

On the way Jim got a call from a friend in Minneapolis. Jim talked loudly, animated when the friend said Putin had said he was going to put peacekeeping troops in Syria. Jim was glad, and also proud to know that it had been his idea first. He had remarked on *Press TV* that Russia should take a stand against American and Israeli aggression in the Middle East. The idea might have come from Jim. Who knows? It is possible.

While waiting in The Outback to be seated I asked Jim if he was going to Syria, along with Kevin and Gordon Duff. I had heard about the plans. He said, no, and it seemed to me that he considered it a dangerous trip.

So, I had an idea, while being seated behind a giant can of Foster's, to ask for another, and perhaps another. Would that be enough to stack and hide behind? If need be. The kind of barricades I would prefer.

I got a feel that this might be where it's happening. History. The resistance. The revolution. While eating a blooming onion with Professor Jim Fetzer.

This biography is not symmetrical.

Maybe it started out wanting to be, but it can't.

Barrett and Fetzer are not equal halves of some American apple pie. I have tried to be fair with space and with questions, etc., but I'm pretty sure it's not exactly half and half.

In fact, I know it's not.

While sitting in the Weary Traveler café in Madison with Kevin we went over some of his scrapbook photos to see what might be included in this book.

Kevin walks with a cane now, because of hip surgery.

He has to wait for an infection to heal before the other side gets done. He talks and points and squints to see the newspaper articles across the table as I hold the book.

He talks about his students, the university, the controversy that overtook his life when he came out against the official story of 9/11 while still an instructor at the University of Wisconsin.

We look over the letters to the editor, in support and not. Kevin points out the front-page story, with his photo, in the *Chicago Tribune*, the feature stories in *The New York Times*.

He says the photographers were on his side, the writers not so much.

He points at a story in *The Badger Herald*, one of the student papers, with quotes from his former students in support of him, and asks if that can get into the book, into the record, that his students liked him, thought he was a good guy, a good teacher, that he was not a propagandist. He was a good teacher.

I look over at Kevin. He's disheveled, though he tries not to be. He's got on what I could call "church clothes" for the photo shoot. He's rugged, kind of beaten-down, though he is a big man. Since getting blacklisted from teaching, he's been struggling to make ends meet.

There are deep roots in southern Wisconsin.

Kevin's grandfather Hunk was principal of East High School in Madison on the working class side of town, and his grandmother Bee was a friend, advocate, and defender of Frank Lloyd Wright, who was not yet totally appreciated in the area for his lifestyle and belief that every American deserved a decent house and decent living, "believing in designing structures which were in harmony with humanity and its environment, a philosophy he called 'organic architecture'."

On Friday night after the Outback, after visiting Sarah and Scott, Jim and I return to his basement and walk around, looking at an array of photos to see what might be included in the book.

There will be too many.

There is a baby album, where Jim's mother has taken great care to record the big events, a lock of hair, how big, how long, when, where.

There is an Altadena kindergarten report card narrative.

"Plays well with group."

"He learned quickly where his cot and locker were located."

"Very happy with his environment most of the time."

"Jimmy only cries when there is sufficient hurt or when another child is over-aggressive with him."

Class photos. First grade, second grade.

"Can you believe," says Jim.

Third grade. Teacher Ethel Stone. 1949.

"Jim is gaining in confidence. He seems to be quite a sensitive child and could be very easily misunderstood."

"He should move away from the jungle gym and join the boys in the various games that they play."

Family vacations, Yosemite, being commissioned as a second lieutenant at Princeton.

There, there's the move to South Pasadena from La Habra, after ...

And the photos of the six-week bicycle tour of Europe at age 15 after graduating from junior high.

And the trip to Mexico between junior and senior year ...

And Japan between graduating high school and going to college ...

Jim will probably come back down here later, after I leave, and lean over these boxes, remembering, as we all do, eventually.

There is a portrait on the wall of Jim as a young professor, done by an artist at Kentucky. There are photos with Jesse Ventura and Vince Bugliosi, Dennis Kucinich, a talented drawing done by Chauncey Holt, an original painting, etc., etc. We look through military photos, old journals, an autobiography Jim wrote in the ninth grade.

We talk about the photos.

I ask questions. Jim has the answers.

Chauncey Holt was one of the three tramps. Woody Harrelson's dad was also one. "Woody knows that." The tramps were being set up to be the patsies if Lee Oswald didn't pan out. The shooting was set for the speech at the Trade Mart if Dealey Plaza didn't work, and then later at LBJ's ranch that night if need be.

"Yeah, yeah, yeah," Jim says when I ask something.

His voice goes high when he's excited or amused. He laughs hardest when the joke is on himself.

And then we sit down for an hour interview until midnight, to wrap-up, put a bow around it, to the night, to Jim's interview portion of the book.

On that Saturday morning I am having my coffee and looking over Jim's photos.

Jim is on his computer on the opposite end of the table. He gets a phone call and begins talking loudly with someone regarding a submission to the *Veterans Today* website that Jim needs to okay in his capacity as editor.

In the meantime Jan is talking to me about the various cruises she has taken to Europe. I'm hearing Jim in one ear and St. Petersburg in the other. Jan doesn't seem to hear Jim.

I leave myself an hour to go pick up Kevin for the cover photo shoot, then head out toward Lone Rock.

I begin thinking that it's going to be a short jaunt, because we need to get to the Badger Bowl by eleven.

But it's kind of a long drive along West 14 through the river valley, through Cross Plains, Black Earth, Arena, Spring Green.

Kevin, Fatna, Hakim and Karim live back in the woods, in a cabin, with a cabin mosque in the front yard, and wood, gardens, an old tree house.

I go inside to get Kevin, greet Hakim, and ask to use the restroom.

It's a compost toilet.

I've never seen one before.

I figure it out.

Later, in town, Kevin is scrunched inside my little Honda. We're sitting parked outside the Badger Bowl. We can't go inside, there's a rock concert in the bowling alley parking lot.

So, we're talking while we wait for Jim and Scott to find another bowling alley. Kevin points to the church lot to our right and notes that they are composting, using mulch, something like that, something I never notice or care about.

And I realize that Kevin has fought the fight, that long fight they are always talking about that's good to fight and all that. And he's still right in the middle of it.

He gives a shit about compost and ecology, and he doesn't have a TV. Years ago, when my kids were small, I carried the TV downstairs, and under great familial pressure lugged it back up probably the next day.

Kevin's TV is still down there.

Kevin, who read everything he could get his hands on in the back of the station wagon driving around the country, who as a high school student heard Mark Lane tell the truth about the JFK assassination, who studied journalism in college and wanted to be a writer like Hunter S. Thompson or Tom Wolfe, who went to San Francisco to find the sun, found Islam and love, was cursed or blessed with the real knowledge about the attacks of

Sept. 11, 2001, and has really never stopped, to this moment, seeking, trying.

Later while we are in the Weary Traveler looking over old clippings that tell about the most intense time of his life, I see that seven years ago he would not have had the cane or some of the lines in his face; he would have been able to see better and perhaps someone in this folksy restaurant would know him, maybe come over to shake his hand.

Nobody does today.

Nobody knows him.

The friend of his that runs the restaurant is not here today.

The clippings, from *The Capital Times*, *The New York Times*, the *Chicago Tribune*, lauding or lambasting Kevin Barrett for standing up to the people and government of the United States of America, kind of shrivel and yellow and just lie there.

But Kevin Barrett lives.

We talk about this book.

Kevin doesn't really like the title, too busy.

He says he would, if he were writing the book, call it something like American Dissident.

And I can see that, because I see him, across the table, in real life, three dimensions, waiters talking, people walking on the street, bikes, cars.

He is an American Dissident, like Solzhenitsyn, Scholl, Sakarov, Havel, Bonhoeffer, Mandela, Berrigan, Jagerstatter.

An American dissident.

A spotting, rare as Bigfoot. More.

Geronimo, Chavez, Hampton, Day, Fetzer, Barrett.

Kevin Barrett is living the life of an American dissident.

I ask him what he thinks his life would be like if 9/11 had never happened, or if he had never become involved as he has.

He says he thinks he would be teaching somewhere, and that would be good, but there would still be other problems in life.

Jim Fetzer is also an American dissident, though officially we don't have those here.

He began his "conspiracy career" pretty much after his regular teaching career, so he lives in Oregon, not on a mosquito reserve in the woods.

They got to Kevin Barrett while he was just beginning, so he was not able to make his money. They sought to make an example of him so that other academics would not speak out.

One might argue that it only served to make the movement larger. He scrapes by day to day, week to week, trying to dream up some writing jobs to get the four of them through. Jim pretty much has the money part of things under control, but the former Marine is still under fire, very much on the front lines. He has lectured on the JFK murder at Harvard, Yale, at Cambridge, in Buenos Aires, Duluth, Tehran, Athens.

Also at The Big Kettle Room at Tobies in Hinckley. He often lapses into "play tape, File No. 74-A" mode," when he discusses various issues, in personal conversation, on his radio show, being interviewed by others, probably because he's studied this stuff for so long. He does know his material backwards and forwards.

Jim and Jan have been married for 36 years, since the Kentucky days. Their anniversary is coming up soon. Jan will take a trip to Duluth, by herself. Jim got to go to Santa Barbara last week for a conspiracy conference, now she gets her trip.

They have one daughter of their own, one son of Jim's, two of Jan's daughters.

They moved here to Oregon after Duluth, in 2006.

They like it here.

I have not talked to Jim or Kevin's first or third grade teachers for this biography, or next-door neighbors.

I have not lifted many rugs.

I like these guys. I like who they are, what they are doing.

I don't see any like them anywhere on earth.

Anyone who knows Jim Fetzer knows that he has too much ego, is too much concerned with titles and status and how he is perceived. He is too loud and too aggressive. He is a control-type person.

And anyone who knows Jim Fetzer would also say, so what?

No doubt Jim knows all that, too. And also realizes, so what?

Because there is more there.

There is a lot there. There is heart and there is soul.

Jim laughs hard at himself along the way, something we might all learn.

There is a twinkle in his eye and an excitement in his step as he trots down the carpeted steps to do his radio show.

Jim cares. He also gives a shit.

And that counts for a lot.

He is smart. And he is tough. And he gets things done.

He's a fighter.

He cares about his wife, his son, his daughters, his son-in-law. Deeply.

He cares about me and he cares about you.

And that's a lot.

As I give Kevin a lift home from the bowling alley and the Weary Traveler and from me having to make multiple pit stops because of too much Mountain Dew to keep me awake from too many Foster's at The Outback to keep from getting shot by the Mossad aiming for Jim, Kevin talks a lot.

And it's cool, to hear him kind of let down his guard for a moment. Over the past couple of months we have done several two-hour interviews over the phone and we never really got to the friendly stage.

I mean, how can you really let your hair down when this is a person writing about you, about your life, meaning to put it all in print for all to see. But Kevin does seem happy. Seems like a man laughing who is not so used to laughing.

I also talk more than maybe I'm used to. I talk about UFOs, how I love the idea that they might be real. Kevin listens, does not roll his eyes, as far as I can tell.

When I give him the chance, he talks about a trip to Iran and having stayed in a nice hotel in Tehran, and how it will be nice to have a couple months off from the radio show grind where he had to come up with seven guests every week, and about a trip he is planning with one of his sons to New Hampshire.

And also about his wife and how they have been all over, back and forth and back again, to San Francisco, Morocco, Lone Rock, another place I can't remember, seeking to be happy, seeking to be free of mosquitoes or missing the mosquitoes, trying to get away from crazy Truthers, getting to kind of like those Truthers.

Seeking fulfillment and truth in the spirit of Hunter S. Thompson, finding God in Islam, truth, jihad, justice, all that stuff.

It's a journey.

And Kevin Barrett is on it.

He has taken up his satchel, his backpack, gotten on his bike, his bus, his horse and headed on down the road.

The Midwest 9/11 Truth Conference

Jim organized The Midwest 9/11 Truth Conference with Stephen Francis, which was held in Champaign-Urbana, IL, 22 September 2013, where they were joined by Wayne Madsen.

[Chapter 2] Jim: La Habra Heights, Pasadena, Princeton, Quantico

> "This is a total character collapse of a country that was supposed to be so far above this loathsome act. You become the thing you hate. And Friday, we did. We became the Germany of 1939."
>
> - Jimmy Breslin, *Newsday*

JIM:

[Do you ever wonder, like late at night after you have written something, why am I doing this? Or, am I wrong? Or, I wish I had not done that.]

No.

[Where do you come from?]

Born in Pasadena, Dec. 6, 1940.

My Dad always talked about my having been born a year and a day before Pearl Harbor.

He served in the Army and actually had a background in finance and accounting but he was not a CPA.

He spent much of the latter years of his life working for the Department of Social Welfare in Los Angeles.

His mother, Julia, had a masters degree at a time when women didn't even go to college and his father, Henry Fetzer, Sr. , had a J.D. from Northwestern or an LLB – I think everyone now gets a J.D. – and had a successful practice in Pasadena, and it was in fact when they were living in Pasadena that he met my mother and her brothers, with whom he had a lot of interaction.

The oldest brother was Jerry Waterhouse, and then there was Eleanor and her younger sister, Betty, and then the younger brother, Johnny.

The boys had a club called Los Aventureos, or The Adventurers, and they'd do mountain climbing and go to Yosemite and Lake Arrowhead and all that kind of stuff, and I think Eleanor always wanted to join it, but it was just basically considered to be a guys' thing.

They had another friend by the name of Bill Scott who would end up spending decades in the Merchant Marines and whom after Henry and Eleanor divorced, she would marry, so Bill Scott Sr. would be her second husband, to whom she was married when we were living out in La Habra Heights, which is a rather desolate area in southern California.

We lived at the end of an unfinished road when I was eleven and my only full-brother, Phil, was nine, and she and Bill had a son, Bill Jr. , who is my closest relative, absent my half-sister, because my father would remarry a woman by the name of Marguerite Boyce, whose parents had been missionaries to India. And while that sounds like a very self-sacrificing life, actually they received such a stipend from the Assemblies of God Church that they had an estate in India and servants. So when my stepmother, Marguerite, married Henry, she had never ironed a shirt, cooked a meal and whatnot. They would have four boys and a girl, Mark, Tom, Julia, and Hal, where Mark was born, and Marguerite was pregnant with Tom when Eleanor took her own life.

I believe she did so out of despair that she'd made a terrible mistake in divorcing my father and she had discovered that Bill Scott wasn't the romantic figure she had thought.

He was very much of a hermit, whereas my mother was a very social person and really craved social interaction.

He wanted to live in an extremely remote area where almost all the homes were separated by a quarter mile or more, mostly avocado orchards, orange groves, lemon groves and the like.

She had written Henry letters suggesting she'd like a reconciliation, and he was supposed to write back and say life begins at forty.

He not only did not write back, but he actually brought Marguerite out to introduce her to Eleanor as his fiancée. And I think that precipitated the decline that led to her death.

I mean, the night before she died, when she tucked me into bed, she said, if anything ever happens, she wanted me to promise I'd look after Phil. I said, of course, you know. But what about Billy?

She said, No, no, no, Billy's got his father to look after him. I said, is anything wrong!

No, no, everything's fine.

But of course, something was wrong, terribly wrong.

It was the next day when I'd been out playing when no one else was home that I came back to discover that she was lying prostrate on the bed, surrounded by dark, brown vomitus. I didn't really know what to do.

I wanted to call a doctor but she said no. I wanted to call some neighbors, Gracie and Chet Hyatt, and she said no.

It was so silly. I asked her if I could turn on the television. Eventually she said, okay, I could tell Gracie and Chet, so I raced out of the house, I said, don't worry Mommy, I'll be right back, and I raced down through the avocado grove and through the lemon grove and up through their avocado grove to find them.

I tried to call them but it was busy, and Gracie was on the phone, so I said, hurry, hurry, Mommy's sick, Mommy's sick, so they left me there and went up to the house to look after Eleanor, and it was hours I was sitting there.

I was sitting in the house not knowing if she was dead or alive, and I dare say, in retrospect, I've come to appreciate how profound that uncertainty was in its effects upon my life, because thereafter when I would be in situations where something was at stake and there was uncertainty, I would precipitate decisions even if they were negative decisions, so I wouldn't have to bear the uncertainty.

It's really astonishing to me to appreciate how profound was the impact.

When Phil and I came to South Pasadena where Henry was living with Marguerite they thought we should become involved in some kind of, you know, church program.

There was a Congregational Church very nearby, but the Episcopal Church was across town and they liked the Episcopal Church better so Phil and I began going to the Episcopal Church.

In fact it was junior high and high school, the only time in my life that I was involved in organized religion because Bill and Eleanor weren't religious.

They took me once to a Quaker Church and asked me if I liked it. I said it was okay but did I want to go back, no, I wasn't particularly desirous of doing that; so I actually grew up in a non-religious environment.

But I got involved in the Episcopal Church there. I mean, I wound up serving as an acolyte, I sang in the choir, I became president of the Young People's Fellowship, I gave sermons on Youth Sunday, and between my graduation from high school and entrance to college I actually was a delegate from the 14th World Convention on Christian Education to the International Christian Convention held in Tokyo that year.

I was at the time the treasurer of the Young People's Fellowship for the Episcopal Diocese of Los Angeles. My brother, Phil, would exceed even that, because he'd become the president of the Young People's Fellowship, so here he was president over hundreds of thousands of Episcopalians in Los Angeles County.

I liked junior high and high school. I was never that great a student, but I always scored well on aptitude tests. I'd say by the time I graduated from high school I still had only like a B+ average probably.

I was never driven academically, but I had high test scores – in the GRE, 650 math, 770 verbal, 890, advanced philosophy – and great letters of recommendation.

But it was interesting that Princeton sent an early admissions advisor who interviewed students on campus. They were doing this all over the country.

So I had an interview, but I didn't think much about it, and one day when I got home, my Dad, as I recall, said I ought to apply to Princeton because I'd already been admitted. So, I contemplated four different schools, Berkeley, Pomona, Princeton, and, gad, what was the other school?

It might have been Stanford, but it might also have been UCLA, because both of my parents graduated from UCLA. In any case I only applied to Berkeley and to Princeton, so Berkeley was my fallback if somehow things didn't work out at Princeton, but of course, they did, and I was admitted into the Navy ROTC program.

The Navy agreed to provide four years of college education in return for my agreeing to serve four years as a commissioned officer in the Navy or the Marine Corps. And because I thought if I were going to be in a military organization I wanted it to be a real one, I preferred the Marine Corps. And then I was accepted in that program at Princeton so that when I graduated I was commissioned as a second lieutenant. Princeton was perfect for me. It was all men at the time.

And although I didn't know it at the time, while I was majoring in philosophy, Princeton was ranked number one in the world in math, in physics, and in philosophy. And I did an undergraduate thesis for the most influential philosopher of science in the world among professional philosophers by the name of Carl G. Hempel.

I would eventually edit a collection of his works and a collection of essays about his work for Oxford University Press. But at the time I had no anticipation of my future.

While I was in the Marine Corps I debated between becoming an attorney or going on in graduate school. I eventually reasoned through that, if I became an attorney, I'd gravitate to criminal law, and that I'd regard myself as my client's employee. While I'd make a lot of money, if I lost cases, I'd feel great anguish about it, and I really wouldn't have a lot of time to do the things I wanted to do, not even to spend all that money I'd make. So I preferred to pursue a Ph.D., and because I was interested in philosophy of science I entered one of two programs in the United States at Indiana University.

Hempel had recommended studying with his leading critic, a fellow by the name of Wesley Salmon, and I wound up doing my dissertation for Wesley Salmon on probability and explanation.

Work which I dare say has been considered the definitive treatment of the problems involved in the nature of laws and the interpretation of probability as a physical magnitude, and how the conditions of adequacy that must be satisfied for explanations, scientific explanations, to be successful. In the process, I was revising and refining Hempel's own criteria where he was the leading theoretician of explanation in the world. And, umm, I would eventually publish my first book, *Scientific Knowledge*, in 1981, on an NSF grant. I was actually then a visiting associate professor; I was hired for my first position at the University of Kentucky as an assistant professor.

I published a lot. I was very popular with students.

I received the first Distinguished Teaching award, but I'd been four years in the Marine Corps, ya know. I'd spent thirteen months in the Far East; I wasn't in Vietnam, but I was involved in training operations in Korea, Formosa, and the Philippines, based in Okinawa.

[Chapter 3] Kevin: Madison General, Pewaukee, Newport Beach ...

What did you learn in school today, dear little boy of mine?
I learned that Washington never told a lie
I learned that soldiers seldom die
I learned that everybody's free
That's what the teacher said to me
And that's what I learned in school today
That's what I learned in school
What did you learn in school today, dear little boy of mine?
I learned that policemen are my friends
I learned that justice never ends.
- Tom Paxton, *What Did You Learn In School Today?*

Dr. Kevin Barrett:

Was born in Madison, Wisconsin in 1959, at Madison General Hospital, has a sister [Tara] who is a Ph.D. in forestry who works for the forest service and has taught at universities, and a brother [Bruce] who is an M.D., family practice, also a Ph.D. in anthropology. Bruce has studied eccinacia and the common cold, and more recently, the health benefits of exercise and meditation.

The family moved to Newport Beach in 1964, then back to Wisconsin in 1969. Kevin graduated from Pewaukee High School in 1976 and earned a B.A. in journalism from UW-Madison in 1981.

Kevin is the oldest.

[So, you put the pressure on them to succeed, then.]

Not really.

Actually I've never been particularly interested in career success.

When I was in high school I had some spiritual experiences and then I kind of fell in love with certain kinds of writing and realized I wanted to be a writer. I got this idea that you couldn't really be an honest writer if you cared about career success, so I kind of became a bohemian writer, an artist type.

I stayed away from success pretty successfully for a while.

That was my biggest success.

[Writing for the high school paper]

I did have one article that caused a big stink.

And that involved getting my two marijuana dealing friends, hippie friends in the school, to go unannounced to the police chief's office in Pewaukee, Wisconsin with hand-rolled cigarettes in our mouths that looked like joints and asked him for a lighter to begin the interview.

It was actually a pretty good article. And then at the next election for the editor of the paper the students who worked for the paper wanted me to be editor so I won this election in a landslide, but the adviser, this kind of nerdy, English-teaching guy named Willis Harrell, just kind of arbitrarily called for another election and went and drummed up some people to vote against me, so I was overthrown in a coup d'etat.

[High school years – '72-'76]

I played football the first two years in high school and then gave up as I realized that even though I really liked the games I wasn't so crazy about the practices.

I didn't like wearing a necktie on game days and it just started to seem conformist and militaristic. I didn't particularly like the coach. The coach was kind of a small, neurotic, drill sergeant kind of a guy, kind of like Sgt. Carter in *The Gomer Pyle Show*.

[Pewaukee is the world headquarters of Harken, Inc., a leading manufacturer of sailboat and yacht hardware sold worldwide. Harken shares its building with North Sails, which Kevin's father, Peter, helped grow to become the world's leading sailmaker.]

My father was Peter Barrett.

He was a graduate student when I was born, and he was teaching, a teaching graduate assistant, a graduate student in engineering and law.

In 1960 he went to the Olympics in Italy, sailing the Finn, which is the most physically demanding small racing sailboat.

And then in 1964 he returned to represent the United States in the Olympics, this time in Tokyo, Japan, and he won a silver medal, and he became legendary by dropping out of a race in which he believed that he had fouled somebody.

If you bump somebody and it's your fault then you're out of the race – it goes down on your scores as a last place finish. His shoulder brushed against another guy's mast, which normally isn't a foul – hardly any sailboat racers call it on themselves, usually they call it on the other guy, but he called it on himself and dropped out of the race.

But the way he dropped out was, he first sailed the rest of the race and he would have won, but before he crossed the finish line he turned and sailed away, because he knew he'd fouled this guy and the guy didn't even know it.

And had he just ignored the foul, he would have won the gold medal, so he became kind of legendary in sailing for that and developed a reputation for being very ethical. And that's when he met Lowell North, who had just started a sail making business in San Diego.

So we all moved out to California so my dad could start the second Sail Loft, which was near L.A., and that's why I lived in L.A. for a few years. And my dad built that business into a huge success. Within a few years it was much, much bigger than the San Diego Loft, so he became the executive vice president and for all practical purposes the grand poobah of North Sails from then on, so he was basically kind of running the company by developing new Sail Lofts and recruiting people. He grew that business into the world's leading sail maker and then sold it off.

He probably would have been fairly wealthy except that he put a huge chunk of the money he made from Sail Lofts into an attempt to take over the life jacket industry.

He built a life jacket factory, and his life jacket business sank to the bottom, so he lost a lot of the money he had made, but he definitely had an interesting life.

He died in Dec. 2000.

The stolen election and 9/11 would have been kind of hard to deal with. He was fairly good at dealing with things and his take on American politics was never quite as jaundiced as it would have been if he had to face the full reality of some of these things.

He never really figured out JFK, though I think he maybe had a few doubts, but as I recall, during the last few months of his life, from what little he saw in the newspapers, he didn't see there was a problem with that election. And of course the last thing he needed was more trauma in admitting that the whole system is terminally corrupt at that point.

[Were you close?]

Yeah, in some ways very close, in other ways, less. I don't think he really understood my sort of spiritual, creative side.

[Maybe he somehow planted your strong sense of justice in you.]

Yeah, he had very strong ethics and also he couldn't completely suppress his curiosity about the universe.

He told people that by the time he was 20 or 21 he'd figured out his philosophy of life and he just stayed with it from then on. But beneath that there was a lot of curiosity and search for adventure. I think some of it came out in these kind of adventurous pursuits that he had.

He would try everything from helicopter skiing in the mountains to different kinds of flying.

He barely survived a plane crash once with a little home-built aircraft that he drove up to Minnesota to buy and flew back to Wisconsin.

A wooden propeller splintered and so the plane went down into a lake. He was apparently pulled out of the upside-down aircraft from underwater by an athletic fisherman.

He had a bunch of other close calls as well. He went out in like 20- or 30-foot surf during a storm in the Pacific once with his catamaran sailboat, and one of these giant waves just smashed the boat to pieces. One of the pieces of the mast went through his leg. He was laid up for a long time from that.

And then on Christmas Day, in the '70s, he went ice boating. It was a very, very windy day, and once again the mast was the problem, it came down and crushed his ribs. He was laid up, unable to move for a few months from that one. He was always doing these demanding and in some cases sort of borderline masochistic adventurous pursuits.

That's one reason I think he could excel at racing the Finn sailboat, because going through all that pain of hanging out over the edge of the boat for hours on end built character, for him.

[Family travel due to sailing]

When I was a little kid we drove all over the country. Ever since I was a kid my earliest memories are being in the back of a station wagon, driving around going to some sailing event.

[And reading]

Yeah, there's nothing much else to do in the car after awhile.

I was taught to read really early. My grandparents actually, my father's parents, taught me to read when I was three I think it was, so I took to reading pretty early.

[Where were you when your father died?]

I was living in Wisconsin partly to be close to him and my other family members.

I'd been living in San Francisco, with a few travels, a year in Paris, a year in Seattle, some time in Central America, but I was mostly in San Francisco throughout early adulthood, and then when I was 35 I moved back to Madison, both to be closer to the family and also because I had a family of my own.

I wanted the grandparents to be around my new son and wife, and then also, I had come to Islam, so I thought I had better learn what I was getting myself into in more detail. I had to learn Arabic and Islamic studies, so I enrolled in a Ph.D. program at the University of Wisconsin, Madison. And so I was in Madison doing this Ph.D. from '95 to 2004, and so that's where I was at the time.

[Where were you physically when he died?]

I wasn't there right at the moment he died, but I was there not very long before that, and I saw the gasping for air and stuff. Of course, it's disturbing. It was at my brother's house.

[Tell me about your mother.]

Laurie.

She's alive and well and doing quite well in Montana, near Kalispell, summer cabin on a lake, lives otherwise in Missoula with her new husband.

She remarried several years after my dad's death. She was pretty devastated but she's actually made a good recovery. She's doing very well now.

[Her job]

She was a housewife. She went back to school, got a CPA when I was about 12 or 13. She did accounting for North Sails and also did independent accounting on the side.

[How does she handle your views, Kevin?]

Well, pretty well actually.

I guess, considering that I kind of had absolutely no interest in money and lived like a vagabond bohemian for quite awhile, and then became a famous conspiracy theorist, a famous radical Muslim conspiracy theorist, I guess she's probably handled it unusually well, far better than most American parents would.

I don't know if she really understands all of it, and she certainly doesn't want to talk that much about a lot of it.

It's not familiar to her, so she would really rather talk about something else, but she has come around to admitting that Building 7 was clearly a controlled demolition, so let's hand it to her for that.

[Brothers and sisters? What are Thanksgivings like?]

We don't necessarily see them every Thanksgiving.

It's a bit random. I tend to see my sister maybe once a year, my mom maybe three times a year. She comes to see the kids sometimes, or else we get out there. We see my brother more often because he's here in Madison.

Family conversations ... I don't know quite how to describe them.

There's a fair amount of joking around, with occasional serious conversations, but I don't think any of these people in my family are very well equipped to discuss either, you know, the kinds of religious and spiritual topics that I'm most interested in, or the kinds of creative production issues

I'm interested in, the art, poetry, literature type stuff, or even a lot of the political stuff.

You know, they're kind of orthodox, left-leaning Democrats, all Obama fans, and anything I'm going to say about these topics tends to be very emotionally disturbing to them. I've told them these things over time, and at first nobody believed it, and then starting, I believe, about 2008 or '09, my brother finally figured it out. His jaw just dropped when he looked at this three-minute video I showed him about Building 7, in particular the BBC's report of the premature collapse of Building 7.

That blew his mind, so he's basically figured it out.

Also, surgeons are smarter than family docs. He's a family doc, so when this surgeon he knows, who's also very politically connected and savvy, told him that, yeah, your brother's right about this, that I think also influenced him. And my mom, she also figured out Building 7 a few years ago, so they're learning slowly.

[Skipped first grade. Glue and scissors. How does one go about arranging that?]

It wasn't my idea.

They were putting me in first grade in Newport and thought I was reading at too high a level. They threw me into second grade.

[High school top student?]

No, not by a long shot. I think I ended up with like a B-average.

I spent a lot of my time in high school in the library, skipping classes, reading books.

We had an eccentric librarian named Charlotte Smith, who had all kinds of interesting, bizarre books like Freud, Velikovsky, *Worlds In Collision*, Kurt Vonnegut Jr., so I was reading this kind of weird stuff in the library. It was much more interesting than what was going on in the classroom.

[In your autobiography you talk a bit about your drinking habits. Did you drink in high school?]

A bit.

I remember kind of experimenting with beer when I was in high school, not liking it very much, especially at first, but then these guys were doing it and I was hanging around with them, so I would drink beer occasionally too.

I remember the high school graduation party was a big, disgustingly drunken event, and as I recall, I barely managed to get home. I can't even remember who drove.

I kind of identified for a while with the intoxicated poet tradition, the French symbolists and then rock and rollers like Jim Morrison. I kind of for a while was imagining that I would be able to be more poetically creative through some kind of ... there's a French poem, I think by Baudelaire, get drunk by whatever means, on whatever you can find, on love, on poetry, or whatever, just get drunk. So I was influenced by that, as well as the whole cultural milieu, where just about everybody drinks.

I'm glad I stopped. I virtually stopped at age 35. I pretty much totally stopped by age 40 or so. I noticed I felt a lot better.

[At UW-Madison – what was it like? Did you live on campus, at home?]

When I was at the University of Wisconsin I started out in a dormitory for my first year, and then these little rooms in rooming houses for the next couple of years, and then in a hippie co-op for my last maybe year and a half, two years.

It was an old frat house that had been transformed into a hippie co-op, called Nottingham Co-op. It was a pretty interesting place.

It's on the lake, in Madison, close to the university, and it has a tradition of kind of wild and crazy hippie behavior, so I participated in that tradition.

[What kind of writer did you want to be? Reporter?]

Like I said, I was inspired in high school by writers like Philip K. Dick and Kurt Vonnegut, and in journalism by Tom Wolfe and Hunter S. Thompson, so I really liked these kinds of writers, and I was also inspired a little bit by *The National Lampoon* magazine.

I developed a sort of dark satirical edge from reading too many *National Lampoons*.

So in college I majored in journalism, kind of thinking that well, now Tom Wolfe and Hunter S. Thompson have come along, nobody's ever going to go back to writing this boring shit that you read in the newspaper, but of course, that wasn't the case.

My first year was with *The Badger Herald*, which was the arch-conservative rival to the larger paper, which is *The Daily Cardinal*.

At that time *The Daily Cardinal* had kind of been taken over by radicals. In the '60s in Madison, you know, there was a big radical thing, basically the east coast Jewish radicals ran *The Daily Cardinal*.

Madison developed as a first-class liberal arts university because it brought in lots of extremely talented Jewish kids from the east coast, and that started back when the Ivy League had a quota on the number of Jewish kids it would allow in to the Ivy League schools, so there were a lot of Ivy League caliber Jewish kids on the east coast who couldn't get in to the Ivy League and so then their second choice became Madison.

It actually started pitching itself as sort of the Ivy League for Jews in the Midwest. So, enriched by all of these bright Jewish kids from the east coast, you know, Madison really flourished and then of course in the '60s it went crazy and became a big anti-Vietnam, leftist kind of mecca. So, *The Daily Cardinal* was influenced by that and became a pretty strong, left-wing paper, with reasonably high standards, starting in the '60s, and it was still like that when I got there.

When I started as a freshman I was only 17. And I forget how I ended up going to *The Herald* instead of *The Cardinal.* I think they asked.

Somebody asked me if I could write for *The Herald,* and said that there were free records, for anybody who would review records, so I think that was the bait. So I went down and got some free records and reviewed some records and ended up writing for the *Herald* for my first year and maybe partly into the second and then somewhere along the line I switched over to the Cardinal.

But I still remember there were some incredibly cool records I got from *The Badger Herald*, this kind of dorky, right-wing paper.

Just for example, I got the first records by Richard and Linda Thompson, and I still own one of these, that's supposedly worth hundreds of dollars.

And Richard Thompson is the coolest Muslim pop musician ever, by a mile, he's so much cooler than Cat Stevens it's not even funny, and at the time I didn't even know he was Muslim. He's an amazing performer, great guitar player, he's a gem.

And then I also got Bruce Cockburn, I think his first album, free, from *The Badger Herald*, and Bruce Cockburn is now this radical icon.

And so I was getting kind of amazingly good stuff. I'd never heard of these people at that time and I was kind of blown away at how great the Thompson album was and Bruce Cockburn, I still remember that.

In the middle of the second year I switched to *The Daily Cardinal*. I was interested in free stuff and I was able to get hold of a 35mm camera, so I became a writer and photographer and I was able to get into rock music shows free, if I would go take the picture and write up the show.

So I got to go backstage with different performers and take their pictures and get in free, so it was all a lot of fun, and part of the reason probably I didn't get better grades was because I was staying out all night with rock musicians, writing up things for the Cardinal.

I was backstage with The Ramones, ate pizza with Joey Ramone, and tried to sweet-talk his girlfriend. The Stranglers. Iggy Pop. Psychedelic Furs. I actually took magic mushrooms with certain members of that band in their hotel room. I'm sure there were a few more, but it's like they say, if you remember the '60s you weren't there, and this was true for Wisconsin in the '70s. Wisconsin was behind the times in the '60s, and didn't really get there until the '70s.

[Why is Madison liberal? Why isn't Lincoln, Nebraska liberal?]

Like I said, I think this is something we can actually thank the Jews for. Right now I have like an ADL fatwa about me, trying to make me out to be anti-Semitic because I'm very critical of Israel.

But the fact is there are a lot of good things about Jewish culture and one of them is stress on educational excellence. Madison, I think, owes its edge to these Ivy-League-caliber Jews from the east coast who started coming to Madison back in the '40s and '50s and kept on coming. Actually, it's gone away now to a certain extent.

Madison is not as good as it was.

It probably was Ivy League quality in terms of liberal arts in the '60s, but I think the powers that be saw that allowing a public university like Wisconsin to be fully funded and have all of these great liberal arts programs actually contributed to the '60s rebellion. You had all of these really bright kids, hanging around with time on their hands. So I think they decided to defund all of that stuff. They defunded the liberal arts, and that kind of changed the situation.

Madison still gets more than its share of east coast Jewish kids, but I think that percentage has gone down and the caliber has gone down. Now the Ivy League accepts as many Jews as they can take, in fact they're actually over-represented, thanks to Jewish nepotism, according to some studies.

So they don't have to come to Madison anymore, so that's one reason Madison has slipped, and then also the liberal arts were defunded by the powers that be, who decided they didn't want to be creating these radical meccas by bringing in bright kids and turning them loose.

[After graduating, were you thinking about getting a reporter job? About graduate school? What?]

No, actually I wasn't.

The thought of graduate school and teaching did not even cross my mind.

My first thought when I got into the journalism program was that I would like to go write somewhere, but then I had some disillusioning experiences and insights in terms of the career path, which wasn't all that great for journalism because everyone suddenly wanted to be a journalist after Watergate. There was a huge influx of journalism students.

Everyone wanted to be like Woodward and Bernstein, and so there was a lot of competition. When I got out it was really hard to find a job in journalism, so if you wanted to do a career in journalism the only thing open at that point was going to work at some small town paper in the middle of nowhere, working really, really hard, and then hoping you'd eventually be able to work your way up.

But for a long time you'd be doing small-town work at low pay, and now I look back at it and think that would have been kind of fun, but at the time I had such a bohemian sensibility, that the thought of working in a small town like that wasn't very appealing.

I wanted to immediately start writing like Hunter S. Thompson, so I just did freelance.

I was politically disillusioned, too.

I wrote a pretty good piece on the Kennedy assassination for one of the anniversaries, it might have been in 1979, and shopped it around. Erwin Knoll of *The Progressive* said it was a great article, but he wouldn't publish it because his policy was he wouldn't publish anything on the JFK assassination unless it has more answers than questions, and he said my article just raised more questions than answers. Well, I thought my article answered the question.

The CIA did it, you know, duh. But Erwin apparently didn't agree.

So, I was getting more disillusioned with politics as I saw that ... we all kind of hoped that Jimmy Carter's election in '76 was pointing in the right direction. But it quickly became obvious that things were not getting better.

I remember cheering for the Iranian revolution in 1979 and seeing the reaction against it, kind of realizing that the situation wasn't going to improve.

We sort of thought with all the anti-war stuff and the end of Vietnam, the end of Nixon, that things would get better, and then they didn't.

They got worse.

So I was disillusioned as far as what kind of careers were available in journalism and also politically disillusioned, and so I just said to hell with it, I'm just going to be a rebel bohemian and do what I want, write what I want.

So I worked for a while as a proofreader in Madison, for a printer called "Landmann Associates."

They did a bunch of academic journals. I bicycled across Madison to their office every day.

[Excited to have the job, the opportunity, the foot in the door? Or not?]

Not. Not at all. It was burning out my eyes.

It was kind of fun to learn the tricks of computer typesetting. This was the early stage of computer typesetting. That was kind of fun and I liked the people I worked for, but the bad thing was that it was burning out my eyeballs.

I couldn't do real reading because I was burning out my eyeballs with proofreading. It tended to be pretty small print with these academic pieces.

I saved up some money and bought a half-size 1955 Chevy school bus that had been converted to become a motor home.

So I jumped in there and drove out to San Francisco.

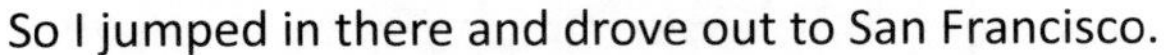

Google
Sunday, May 22nd, 07:00-08:50 am PST * 10:00-11:50 am EST * 14:00-15:50 GMT
False Flags — Defeating a "Global Gladio" Agenda
Speakers: Kevin Barrett, Richard Dolan, Chris Emery

Kevin Barrett spoke on defeating "Operation Gladio", which is also manifesting itself in America, at the Left Forum on 22 May 2016

[Chapter 4] The First White Rose Leaflet

Nothing is so unworthy of a civilized nation as allowing itself to be "governed" without opposition by an irresponsible clique that has yielded to base instinct. It is certain that today every honest German is ashamed of his government.

Who among us has any conception of the dimensions of shame that will befall us and our children when one day the veil has fallen from our eyes and the most horrible of crimes – crimes that infinitely outdistance every human measure – reach the light of day?

If the German people are already so corrupted and spiritually crushed that they do not raise a hand, frivolously trusting in a questionable faith in lawful order in history; if they surrender man's highest principle, that which raises him above all other God's creatures, his free will; if they abandon the will to take decisive action and turn the wheel of history and thus subject it to their own rational decision; if they are so devoid of all individuality, have already gone so far along the road toward turning into a spiritless and cowardly mass – then, yes, they deserve their downfall.

Goethe speaks of the Germans as a tragic people, like the Jews and the Greeks, but today it would appear rather that they are a spineless, will-less herd of hangers-on, who now – the marrow sucked out of their bones, robbed of their center of stability – are waiting to be hounded to their destruction. So it seems – but it is not so.

Rather, by means of a gradual, treacherous, systematic abuse, the system has put every man into a spiritual prison. Only now, finding himself lying in fetters, has he become aware of his fate.

Only a few recognized the threat of ruin, and the reward for their heroic warning was death.

We will have more to say about the fate of these persons. If everyone waits until the other man makes a start, the messengers of avenging Nemesis will come steadily closer; then even the last victim will have been cast senselessly into the maw of the insatiable demon.

Therefore every individual, conscious of his responsibility as a member of Christian and Western civilization, must defend himself against the scourges of mankind, against fascism and any similar system of totalitarianism. Offer passive resistance – resistance – wherever you may be, forestall the spread of this atheistic war machine before it is too late, before the last cities, like Cologne, have been reduced to rubble, and before the nation's last young man has given his blood on some battlefield for the hubris of a sub-human. Do not forget that every people deserves the regime it is willing to endure.

From Friedrich Schiller's *The Lawgiving of Lycurgus and Solon:*

Viewed in relation to its purposes, the law code of Lycurgus is a masterpiece of political science and knowledge of human nature. He desired a powerful, unassailable state, firmly established on its own principles.

Political effectiveness and permanence were the goal towards which he strove, and he attained this goal to the full extent possible under the circumstances.

But if one compares the purpose Lycurgus had in view with the purposes of mankind, then a deep abhorrence takes the place of the approbation which we felt at first glance.

Anything may be sacrificed to the good of the state except that end for which the State serves as a means.

The state is never an end in itself; it is important only as a condition under which the purpose of mankind can be attained, and this purpose is none other than the development of all of man's powers, his progress and improvement.

If a state prevents the development of the capacities which reside in man, if it interferes with the progress of the human spirit, then it is reprehensible and injurious, no matter how excellently devised, how perfect in its own way.

Its very permanence in that case amounts more to a reproach than to a basis for fame; it becomes a prolonged evil, and the longer it endures, the more harmful it is ...

At the price of all moral feeling a political system was set up, and the resources of the state were mobilized to that end.

In Sparta there was no conjugal love, no mother love, no filial devotion, no friendship; all men were citizens only, and all virtue was civic virtue.

A law of the state made it the duty of Spartans to be inhumane to their slaves; in these unhappy victims of war humanity itself was insulted and mistreated.

In the Spartan code of law the dangerous principle was promulgated that men are to be looked upon as means and not as ends – and the foundations of natural law and of morality were destroyed by that law ...

What an admirable sight is afforded, by contrast, by the rough soldier Gaius Marcius in his camp before Rome, when he renounced vengeance and victory because he could not endure to see a mother's tears! ...

The state [of Lycurgus] could endure only under the one condition: that the spirit of the people remained quiescent. Hence it could be maintained only if it failed to achieve the highest, the sole purpose of a state.

From Goethe's *The Awakening of Epimenides*, Act II, Scene 4:

SPIRITS:

Though he who has boldly risen from the abyss
Through an iron will and cunning
May conquer half the world,
Yet to the abyss he must return.
Already a terrible fear has seized him;
In vain he will resist!
And all who still stand with him
Must perish in his fall.

HOPE:

Now I find my good men
Are gathered in the night,
To wait in silence, not to sleep.
And the glorious word of liberty
They whisper and murmur,
Till in unaccustomed strangeness,
On the steps of our temple
Once again in delight they cry: Freedom! Freedom!

Please make as many copies of this leaflet as you can and distribute them.

Kevin Barrett, PhD – Lecturer on Islamic Studies, University of Wisconsin. Co-editor of *911 and American Empire (Vol II) – Christians, Jews and Muslims Speak Out* .

- **Co-founder**: Muslim-Jewish-Christian Alliance for 9/11 Truth, a group of scholars, religious leaders and activists dedicated to uniting members of the Jewish, Christian and Islamic faiths in pursuit of 9/11 truth.
- **Member:** Scientific Panel Investigating Nine-Eleven Association Statement: "We have found solid scientific grounds on which to question the interpretation put upon the events of September 11, 2001 by the Office of the President of the United States of America and subsequently propagated by the major media of western nations."
- **Member:** *Scholars for 9/11 Truth* Association Statement: "Research proves the current administration has been dishonest about what happened in New York and Washington, D.C. The World Trade Center was almost certainly brought down by controlled demolitions and that the available relevant evidence casts grave doubt on the government's official story about the attack on the Pentagon."

Jim and Kevin would become members of Patriots Question 9/11, which features hundreds of experts across different disciplines, including military officers and law-enforcement officials.

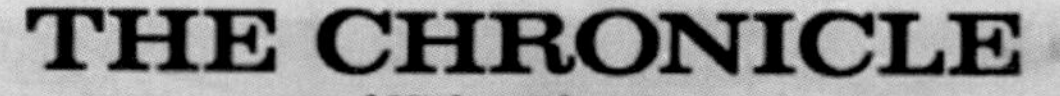

THE CHRONICLE
of Higher Education.

http://chronicle.com

June 23, 2006 • $3.75
Volume LII, Number 42

Faulkner Is of No Help in Drive to Cut College Pork

An anti-earmark lawmaker invokes the author but gets only sound and fury

BY JEFFREY BRAINARD

WASHINGTON

It isn't often that members of Congress invoke the writings of William Faulkner, but the renowned novelist figured in a debate full of sound and fury last week about earmarks, the noncompetitive grants that lawmakers secure annually for colleges and other favored constituents.

Earmarks have become a hot topic here this year because of scandals over lobbying and influence-peddling. Congressional leaders have agreed to tighten up on awarding earmarks, which legislators tuck into appropriations bills for favored constituents. And in fact, the first few appropriations bills approved by the U.S. House of Representatives for the 2007 fiscal year appear to have less earmarked money than was contained in similar bills this year.

However, as an Arizona congressman named Jeff Flake found out last week, standing between a legislator and his or her particular earmark is a different matter altogether.

Representative Flake, who was among the Republicans elected in 1994 on a platform of fiscal conservatism, has pointed out for years that spending on earmarks and the federal deficit have both spiked to record levels while Republicans have controlled Congress, despite his party's promises of restraint.

In what appears to be a first in the House, he has begun introducing amendments this year to strike specific earmarks from spending bills, including some for colleges. He's not earning many friends or allies in the process.

Mr. Flake's latest, doomed efforts came during the House's consideration of an appropriations bill to finance transportation, housing, and community-development projects (HR 5576). One of the projects he went

Continued on Page A27

Scholars on the Fringe

A handful of professors band together with those who think 9/11 was an inside job: A10

The Greed Debate

Scholars clash over whether the push for maximum shareholder returns automatically breeds corruption: **A14**

Tough Year to Be No. 1

3 higher-education leaders discuss college presidents' recent hardships: **A28**

In a Data Flood, Librarians to the Rescue

Academic archivists help scientists who are drowning in information: **A35**

Complete guide to this issue: Page A3 • The Chronicle Review: Section B • 333 job opportunities: Section C

Jim and Kevin first met at the 9/11 Truth Conference in Chicago, IL, 4-5 June 2006, which was covered by The New York Times *and by* The Chronicle of Higher Education, *which was unenthusiastic.*

[Chapter 5] More Voices

> "'What no one seemed to notice,' said a colleague of mine, a philologist, 'was the ever widening gap, after 1933, between the government and the people. Just think how very wide this gap was to begin with, here in Germany. And it became always wider. You know, it doesn't make people close to their government to be told that this is a people's government, a true democracy, or to be enrolled in civilian defense, or even to vote. All this has little, really nothing, to do with knowing one is governing.
>
> "'What happened here was the gradual habituation of the people, little by little, to being governed by surprise; to receiving decisions deliberated in secret; to believing that the situation was so complicated that the government had to act on information which the people could not understand, or so dangerous that, even if the people could not understand it, it could not be released because of national security. And their sense of identification with Hitler, their trust in him, made it easier to widen this gap and reassured those who would otherwise have worried about it.'"
>
> - Milton Mayer, 1955, *They Thought They Were Free: The Germans 1933-45*

Len Osanic and Mark Lane, *Black Op Radio*, March 21, 2013:

[LO] ... there are some people who want to do the right thing, despite public opinion. We are just appalled that some people have their heads in the sand like an ostrich and refuse to look at the details that have come forward, and they have come forward against government wishes ... and these are concerned citizens who are not paid by any governmental agency, every agency has let the American people down, and that's the sad state of affairs, that 50 years later there's no one saying, this is what happened, and let's learn from it, and here are the facts. It's taken concerned citizens to write the book.

[ML] At the time and a few years thereafter, you have to remember, if you looked into it, you're going to find people high up in the government who were involved in killing the President of the United States, and of course, their main goal was that we not know that. And it's not like the FBI wasn't interested, they were there every place I went, there was the FBI. ... I talked everywhere in America, hundreds of speeches, often two a day ... at least five times a week. I spoke at colleges, universities, law schools, everywhere. Every single time I spoke there was an FBI agent, or two agents present. I suspected that because I spoke at a Catholic women's college in Colorado one time, outside of Denver. They are all young Catholic women, except two guys in trench coats in the back row ... But that's just anecdotal. The facts are I have the documents and these are FBI reports: Mark Lane spoke here, in the San Francisco Bay area, he spoke seven times at various places, and he said pretty much the same thing each place he went.

[LO] If they spent as much time in the investigation of the crime as they are of authors who are revealing what's leaked out this would have been resolved.

[ML] There obviously will be more interest on the 50th, but what it will be and what it will result in is not clear to me. It could be the same thing we've seen all along. Which is just avoiding the facts.

[LO] Oh, yeah, the City of Dallas wants to block off the Grassy Knoll area for a whole week. Gary Mack says there's a time and a place but Nov. 22 is not it. We want to celebrate Kennedy's life that day. What are you talking about? This is the scene of the crime, the murder, on the anniversary, 50 years later. And the people who say we should open up the files are there in remembrance of the murder of their president. That is the time and day.

[ML] And the fact is, what was John Kennedy? What did he believe in? What was he doing? ... When you think about what he stood for, then you understand why they killed him. So there is a relationship between the assassination and the history of this man.

Gaeton Fonzi

[Note: The following is from a speech delivered by Gaeton Fonzi at the Third Annual "November in Dallas" conference in 1998. The speech was made as Mr. Fonzi accepted JFK Lancer's Pioneer Award for Lifetime Achievement in the Investigation of the Assassination of President John F. Kennedy]

... We must win this struggle for truth ...

Let me suggest to you tonight that it's time to go well beyond the focus of that charge. Let me suggest to you tonight that we have not only emerged victorious in that struggle, but that the truth has long ago rushed into our arms seeking our embrace. Perhaps, in fact, it got too close for us to accept it. But it was known to us from the beginning.

The truth was known to us almost immediately on that fateful day thirty five years ago when a barrage of gun fire – a barrage of gun fire – echoed through Dealey Plaza. The truth was known to us in the government's immediate designation of the assassin and the government's immediate extermination of that designated assassin.

The truth was known to us in the government's immediate actions to cover that truth, in the immediate government-generated deluge of misinformation to the public, in the government's squalid attempt at feigning a legitimate investigation. The truth was as obvious as a bright morning sun rising from the sea on a cloudless blue-sky day.

It was ours to grasp, to hold, to proclaim.

But only a few brave souls did, their voices micro-cries that were quickly muffled.

The rest of us chose not to face the truth, to avoid its harsh and terrible glare, its shocking significance and awesome implications.

We were reinforced in this decision by the media and academia, who abandoned their responsibility as society's pursuers and preservers of the truth. And so we pliantly donned the dark glasses handed to us by the government and saw the truth become a distant aspiration, deliberately shadowed with mystery and puzzlement.

And over the years the initial false question – "Who really killed President Kennedy?" – was massaged into the more durable: "We won't ever really know the truth, will we?"

I'll never forget the numbing disbelief I came away with after my interviews with Specter. Vince Salandria was right, the Warren Report was wrong, there had to have been a conspiracy.

In the article I wrote:

> It is difficult to believe the Warren Commission Report is the truth. Arlen Specter knows it. It is difficult to believe the Warren Commission Report is the truth.

I look back on that now and I think: What a cowardly way to put it. Why didn't I myself tell the absolute truth?

And the absolute truth is that the Warren Report is a deliberate lie.

The truth is that the Warren Commission's own evidence proves there was a conspiracy to murder President Kennedy.

The truth is that in covering up the criminal conspiracy to kill Kennedy, the Warren Commission itself became part of that conspiracy. And why didn't I tell the absolute truth about Arlen Specter and say that, in helping devise the single-bullet theory, he himself was a conspirator?

We were young once and not so brave.

We wanted to cling to the myth of a mystery. We wanted to hang on to the questions of motivation and parade the usual suspects and the illusion of a dilemma before the American people.

Could the Mob have killed President Kennedy? Could the KGB have killed President Kennedy? Could Castro have killed President Kennedy? Could anti-Castro Cubans have killed President Kennedy? Could the CIA have killed President Kennedy?

I suggest to you that if it ever becomes known what specific individuals comprised the apparatus that killed Kennedy, those individuals will have some association with any or all of the above. And still the emergence of such individuals, dead or alive, will add but inconsequential detail to the truth about the assassination.

Because we have known – and have long known – who killed President Kennedy.

[...] Could any but a totally controlling force – a power elite within the United States government itself – call it what you will, the military-intelligence complex, the national security state, the corporate-warfare establishment – could any but the most powerful elite controlling the U.S. government have been able to manipulate individuals and events before the assassination and then bring such a broad spectrum of internal forces to first cover up the crime and then control the institutions within our society to keep the assassination of President Kennedy a false mystery for 35 years? Where is the mystery?

Is there any doubt that the uniquely impossible – uniquely impossible – meaning it couldn't ever possibly be duplicated – is there any doubt that the uniquely impossible single-bullet theory actually is proof of a conspiracy?

Is there any doubt that Lee Harvey Oswald, quickly and deliberately portrayed by the government as a simple, superficial personality – a lone nut – was clearly a well-trained and groomed tool of the intelligence establishment?

Is there any doubt that only the power elite at the highest levels of government could have taken control of the White House Situation Room and (as Theodore S. White in his book, *The Making of a President,* reported) on the afternoon of November 22nd while Air Force One was still in the air returning to Washington, sent a message to the Presidential party that "there was no conspiracy" and that the President's assassin had been identified and arrested. This before Oswald was charged, before the Dallas Police knew anything about him, or even if he had any associates.

Is there any doubt that the power elite at the highest levels of government – and anyone who knows Washington and how it works knows that might not include those who the American electorate assume to be at the highest levels of their government – is there any doubt that the highest levels of the power elite took immediate control of the cover up and began a long-term program to deceive and confuse the American people?

Is there any doubt that the Warren Commission deliberately set out not to tell the American people the truth?

Would an innocent government react the way our government reacted if the Mafia had killed Kennedy?

Would an innocent government react the way ours did if Castro or anti-Castro Cubans or even a so-called "rogue element" within the CIA had killed Kennedy?

No matter what the concern for the reaction of the American people, an innocent government would have isolated the apparatus and used its resources to limit the focus of popular reaction. Instead, what the government did was marshal its massive national and international resources to influence and control the reaction of our nation's major media corporations, and our nation's most influential pundits and academic luminaries in support of the blatantly false *Warren Commission Report*.

Is there any doubt that only the most powerful forces could have maintained as strong and lengthy a hold in manipulating the media down through the years? Right from the beginning, the early critics of the Warren Report found themselves being immediately ground down by the country's major media.

Those of you who were involved then also remember seeing another powerful publication, *The New York Times*, immediately and vehemently endorse the Warren Commission Report even before its 26 volumes of evidence were released.

And then, years later, you saw that same newspaper use its news columns to help destroy the first chief counsel of the Assassination Committee, Richard Sprague, because he wanted to conduct a legitimate investigation.

And then, more than three decades after the event, you have seen a giant publishing company like Random House spend a million dollars in publicity to give validity to the hogwash of a Gerald Posner.

What has our reaction been to all this down through the years?

The answer is in the question. Reaction. We have been defensive in our posture and perspective. We have done hard, grinding research and then presented it as if it were another significant piece of the puzzle, hoping that someday the picture will become clear and the mysterious image will emerge whole and explicit.

We have offered the evidence we uncovered as openly and innocently as we can, hoping it was going to be judged on its substance and its validity – and seen it too often ambushed by those still intent on subverting the truth.

We have written letters to the editor believing that rational and logical retort will somehow result in the editor's publication recognizing the obvious and accept the evidence we put forth on its merits, evidence that appears to point towards solving the so-called mystery of Kennedy's assassination. And we have played into the hands of such covert illusionists as Posner by climbing into his trick-filled ring and, in critical rebuttal, actually provide credibility to his assertion that the issue of conspiracy remains a valid question.

It's time we climbed into our own ring. That's what our future demands.

Our future as researchers demands that we abandon our posture as explorers of a mystery and assume the role as re-enforcers of the foundation of truth. That, after all, is what most of us have been about.

Now from this distance, these 35 years from that awful day, we can now clearly know what we believed from the beginning. Now we know the truth. Let us shift the focus of the American people, let us lead the American people away from believing the truth to knowing the truth.

And we can do this if we are persistent and steadfast in proclaiming the truth. This, I suggest, should be our challenging cry for the future:

We know who killed President Kennedy. Why don't you?

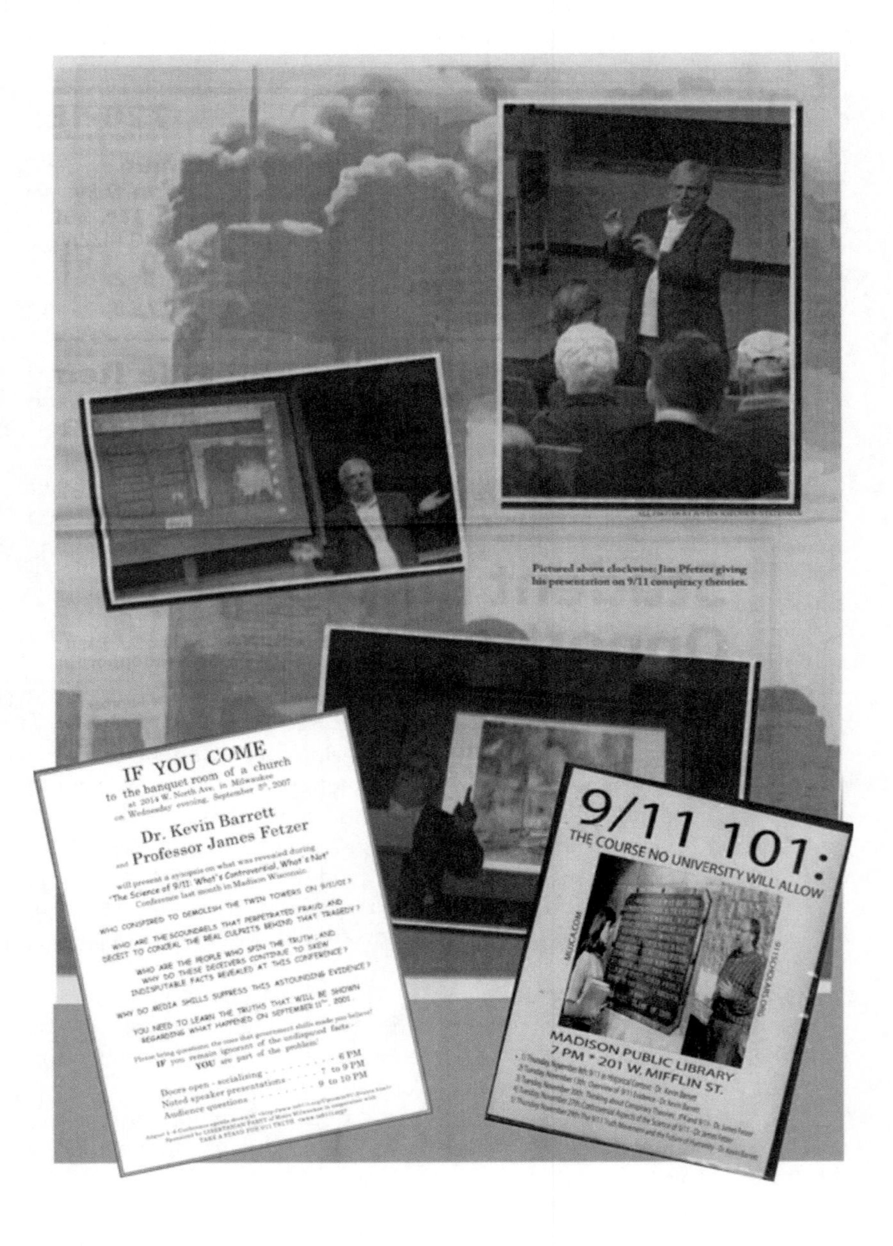
Pictured above clockwise: Jim Pfetzer giving his presentation on 9/11 conspiracy theories.
IF YOU COME
to the banquet room of a church
at 2014 W. North Ave. in Milwaukee
on Wednesday evening, September 5th, 2007
Dr. Kevin Barrett
and Professor James Fetzer
will present a synopsis on what was revealed during
"The Science of 9/11: What's Controversial, What's Not"
Conference last month in Madison Wisconsin.
WHO CONSPIRED TO DEMOLISH THE TWIN TOWERS ON 9/11/01?
WHO ARE THE SCOUNDRELS THAT PERPETRATED FRAUD AND DECEIT TO CONCEAL THE REAL CULPRITS BEHIND THAT TRAGEDY?
WHO ARE THE PEOPLE WHO SPIN THE TRUTH, AND WHY DO THESE DECEIVERS CONTINUE TO SKEW INDISPUTABLE FACTS REVEALED AT THIS CONFERENCE?
WHY DO MEDIA SHILLS SUPPRESS THIS ASTOUNDING EVIDENCE?
YOU NEED TO LEARN THE TRUTHS THAT WILL BE SHOWN REGARDING WHAT HAPPENED ON SEPTEMBER 11TH, 2001.
IF you remain ignorant of the undisputed facts -
YOU are part of the problem!
Doors open - socializing . . . . . . 6 PM
Noted speaker presentations . . . . 7 to 9 PM
Audience questions . . . . 9 to 10 PM
9/11 101:
THE COURSE NO UNIVERSITY WILL ALLOW
MADISON PUBLIC LIBRARY
7 PM * 201 W. MIFFLIN ST.

[Chapter 6] JFK

> "... Professor Jim Fetzer [...] has unarguably driven the research community through the apparently insurmountable obstacles placed before it by those who would like us to simply all go away, who like to obfuscate and prevaricate and bloviate, and finish every debate with the smug conclusion, 'We will probably never know.'"
>
> - John Costella, *The Great Zapruder Film Hoax*

KEVIN:

[1975 – While in high school in Madison, you went to hear Mark Lane speak. What drew you to that?]

I didn't know anything about it. My friend John Mensing invited me. The same guy I went to New York with when I met Fatna.

He was one of the most interesting guys in my high school. He currently lives in Japan.

John told me there was this really interesting lecturer who was saying that the JFK assassination was some kind of an inside job.

So I said, sure I'll check that out.

So we drove, I think it was he and I and a couple of other friends, four of us, I believe.

It was quite an interesting presentation and pretty compelling and the part that I found most compelling was the Zapruder film frames.

He showed the Zapruder film. Showing that Kennedy was obviously shot from the front, creating a backwards head snap and his whole brains and stuff going backwards.

And then he showed a slide of how the Zapruder film had been printed in *Life Magazine*, and they were printed in reverse order, so it looked like the head snap was going forward as if he had been shot from behind. That looked like pretty serious evidence to me that there was a huge problem, not only that it was pretty obvious that the President was shot from the front and to the right, but also that *Life Magazine* would reverse the image of the frames to conceal that fact.

If that were true then it would be obvious as far as I was concerned that there would be a huge problem and a huge cover-up.

So I kind of thought that one over and a day or two later I called up some film companies and asked to speak to their technicians and asked them about whether there could be an innocent mistake, anyway of having

an innocent mistake of printing these frames backwards. And, of course, they said, of course not. That could not happen. So at that point I was pretty sure that there was a big problem surrounding the JFK assassination, so I started reading about it and discovered there was.
[Does the Lane event represent an epiphany, a turning point in your life?]

In retrospect, it does.

Now my work is mostly around 9/11 and similar events, and the JFK assassination is the biggest single precedent for 9/11, arguably up there with Pearl Harbor, if not more of a kind of direct precedent.

So, it looks that way from this perspective.

But if 9/11 had never happened, or if I had never figured it out, and if I were off somewhere teaching North African literature and Arabic at some university, then it probably wouldn't look that way.

It would be interesting, but it wouldn't seem very life-shaping.

[Why the silence of the Kennedy family?]

I guess they're probably making a strategic calculation that that's the best move. Either that or the fear is contributing to their strategic calculation.

It's hard to tell where fear ends and strategic calculation begins.

Because if you have a well-based fear that something bad will happen if you talk about something then strategically you may choose not to talk about it. I think they did want to solve these problems, or some of them did. Bobby Kennedy ran for President with the intention of solving the crime of his brother's murder, and of course, then he was murdered. And a generation later, JFK Jr. started his magazine with the expressed intention of solving the crimes of his brother and uncle.

And once again, he was murdered. You might say that strategically it would have been smarter for them to be perfectly honest and just kind of do what I've done and just blurt everything out immediately.

And if they'd done that maybe it would have been harder to kill them. It might have been too obvious, who knows? But, for whatever reason, I think they were sort of planning to not talk about it and amass the power to do something about it.

They were going to like sneakily build up enough muscles to you know, whack the bully on the head hoping the bully wouldn't notice they were building up those muscles, but unfortunately the bully did notice and whacked them on the head first.

I think those people maybe would be better off if they just came out and spoke the truth rather than sort of strategically try to hide their knowledge of the truth as they build up power, at least that's my strategy with 9/11.

There are a lot of people who hold back on 9/11, who are very coy about the way they talk about it, who limit themselves pretty strictly.

I think they imagine that if they do that then they can sort of preserve what power they have, they can preserve their careers and their money and they'll be in a better position to try to do something about it. But I think the best strategic move is often to just wage a truth jihad like I'm doing, just go all out for truth from the get-go and let the chips fall where they may.

JIM:

[Please talk about seeing *JFK*, the movie]

I have seen it several times, but I cannot recall particulars. On the 49th observance, I was invited to a special viewing of the Director's Cut at the Roxie Theater in San Francisco, where I spoke after the film and explained what Oliver Stone had right and had wrong.

It is a great film and would have won "Best Picture" but for Jack Valenti campaigning against it.

The idea that a picture about a sadistic cannibal should have won instead of JFK is simply obscene.

He deserved it.

[Why do you refer to John Kennedy as "Jack"? I know it is a nickname for John, but is there some reason you use it, the familiar sounding "Jack."]

As a professional philosopher who has spent so much of his life devoted to abstract questions about the nature of truth, reality, probability and inference, it has astonished me that I should have come to know so much about a single historical event.

I often call him "Jack" because I feel as though I knew him.

It took me years to realize that, as a Marine Corps 2nd Lieutenant going through Basic School in Quantico, where I participated in the Basic School Marine Corps Men's Chorus, we were rushed into our dress whites and taken to an undisclosed location one evening, which turned out to be a formal event at The White House. Bright lights were in our faces, but I have no doubt that Jack and Jackie were there – and no doubt LBJ as well, who would play a pivotal role in his assassination a year later.

[Where were you when you heard about it?]

I was anchored out in Kaohsiung Harbor when JFK was assassinated. I remember the executive officer waking me at three-thirty in the morning to tell me JFK had been shot and then an hour later to tell me they'd caught the guy who'd done it and he was a Communist, which I thought then was pretty fast work, but it wasn't until I returned to the United States and began reading some of the early books about it, including one by a professor of philosophy from Haverford by the name of Josiah Thompson entitled *Six Seconds in Dallas*, that I became very interested in the case.

I would not become serious about it however until late 1992, in the wake of criticism of Oliver Stone in his film and a host of others who I already knew had done the best work on the assassination, including Mark Lane and Robert Groden and David Lifton.

There was a book out by a physician by the name of Charles Crenshaw, who had actually been present in Trauma Room I where JFK was treated and then two days later was responsible for the care of his alleged assassin Lee Oswald.

And then my wife said, you're not going to believe this, turn on the TV and watch this distinguished looking fellow standing behind the lectern bearing the logo of the American Medical Association, who was using his authority to denounce all these people who'd done work that had actually demonstrated the Warren Commission Report to be untenable. And it occurred to me if a person of his august standing were to abuse his position as editor-in-chief of the *Journal of the American Medical Association*, perhaps some of us like myself, with special background and ability, ought to become involved in this.

So I tracked down the issues of the journal, JAMA, and discovered a letter from a fellow who was resigning from the AMA over the abuse of the journal by publishing two interviews with the pathologist who'd conducted the autopsy at Bethesda as though they were science.

The letter writer was David W. Mantik. He had both a Ph.D. and an M.D., and I liked what he said, so I reached out to him and suggested we collaborate on a long article or a book.

He agreed. And shortly thereafter several others joined us, the most important of whom would be Robert B. Livingston, M.D., a world authority on the human brain who was also an expert on wound ballistics, having supervised an emergency room hospital for injured Okinawans and Japanese prisoners of war during the Battle of Okinawa.

Others included the very same Chuck Crenshaw, who had been present in Trauma Room I and then looked after Oswald two days later, and Jack White, a legendary film and photo analyst, now deceased, who became a very strong ally of mine on discussion boards and forums about JFK.

Later we were joined by a quite brilliant guy, another Ph.D. in physics, this time with a specialty in electro-magnetism, the properties of light and of images of moving objects, who would do dazzling work on the Zapruder film.

We all, David and Jack and John Costella and I, had powerful reasons to believe that the film had been altered, was not authentic. And indeed in 1996 I would organize the first Zapruder film symposium during the Dallas JFK Lancer symposium.

I brought together about fifteen experts on the film for a workshop the day before, and then the following day I had six or eight make presentations, and it was really quite sensational.

After which Josiah Thompson, who in many ways had been my idol heretofore, began attacking me savagely for suggesting the film had been faked, offering as his principal argument a timeline, a chronology of the possession of the film that he alleged provided no opportunity for that to have happened.

We knew there was evidence internal to the film that there were witnesses, as many as sixty, who reported seeing the limousine halt, slow dramatically or come to a complete halt.

We also knew others who had actually seen what they described as "the other film", which was more complete and of course included the limo stop.

We knew especially from David's studies of the medical evidence, where he discovered almost immediately that the autopsy X-rays had been altered to conceal a massive blow-out to the back of the head; when you consider the area that had been patched, I eventually discovered there was a frame that those who were altering the film had overlooked where you could actually see the blow-out, frame 374. It bore a striking resemblance to the area "P" that David had identified.

It looked rather like a cashew on its side. But where they had painted over the blowout in earlier frames in a particularly crude way, in fact a new group of Hollywood film restoration experts has confirmed how crudely it was done.

They blew it up and literally painted it over and then shrunk it back down. But then work would be done by the Assassination Records Review Board, a five-person civilian panel that was created by an act of Congress in the wake of interest generated by Oliver Stone's film *JFK*, which George H.W. Bush had adamantly opposed.

He of course was a former director of the CIA, and whom I now am convinced was deeply involved in the assassination itself. One of the most recent articles I have published about the assassination is, "Did George H.W. Bush Supervise A JFK Hit Team?" where I believe the evidence is quite powerful that he did. So we have had a succession of Presidents who would have never held that office but for the death of JFK including most obviously Lyndon Johnson, but also Richard Nixon, but also Gerald Ford, but also George Herbert Walker Bush, but also "W" , who would never have been taken seriously but for his father's role there in fact.

I'm reading a book by Cathy O'Brien, who turns out to have undergone horrific experiences as what is known technically as a mind-controlled sex slave. And her revelations are completely stunning.

I'm in the middle of this book where she talks of the abuse she suffered at the hands of some familiar figures, including, but not limited to, Gerald Ford and Dick heney and Robert Byrd. Her daughter, who was only a few years old, was taken by George H.W. Bush and abused. I am becoming convinced that stories friends of mine have told me about the pedophilia of many of our nation's leaders is becoming increasingly well-documented.

I think I'm at the point where I'm convinced of it, whereas I've always been skeptical in the past.

But the fact of the matter is that we organized this research group. After I conducted the sympo-sium, Josiah Thompson began attacking me during the course of the work done by the Assassination Records Review Board. Bush, after the law passed over his adamant opposition, refused to appoint the members, the appointments had to await the incoming Clinton administration, so there's an 18-month delay there that really gave these agencies, the FBI, the CIA, the Secret Service and so forth, the opportunity to clean up their act.

Nevertheless, we have learned especially through Douglas Horne, who became the senior analyst for military records and discovered by interviews with persons who had worked at the National Photographic Interpretation Center located in Washington, D.C., that the original, 8mm, already split film that was developed in Dallas was brought to the NPIC on Saturday. The National Photographic Interpretation Center didn't have an 8mm projector. They had to go out and have somebody open his office, his store, so they could buy one to project it.

Thus one group of employees was working on Saturday and then Sunday another, a different version, was brought from Rochester, where the CIA has a secret photographic lab known as Hawkeye Works, by an agent who identified himself as William Smith, which was a 16mm, un-split film that was substituted for the original 8mm. There are five different physical features that distinguish the films. There's just no doubt about it.

I mean, we knew from all this evidence that the film was faked, and that Josiah Thompson's argument couldn't possibly be correct, but we did not know, until The Assassination Records Review Board interviewed employees of the NPIC, where and how it had been done, the alteration.

Josiah Thompson has continued to attack me at every opportunity, but I think it's because I have shouldered the burden of presenting the arguments to the public. I'm very much at this point in time convinced that he actually had as one of his assignments maintaining the myth of the authenticity of the Zapruder film.

He's been unable to do that.

The evidence has grown massively abundant, and, there's more to say about it. Not only have I published three collections of expert studies about the assassination, *Assassination Science*, 1989, *Murder in Dealey Plaza*, 2000, and *The Great Zapruder Film Hoax*, 2003, but I also have a host of articles on *Veterans Today* about all of this, including one about Josiah Thompson in particular, entitled *JFK, The CIA and the New York Times*, that is very revealing, and a very recent one about Robert Groden, who, to my astonishment has persisted in maintaining that the Zapruder film is authentic, to this day, entitled "The JFK War: The Challenging Case of Robert Groden."

And I have a series of articles entitled *The JFK War, An Insider's Guide to Assassination Research* where I explain all the obstacles that have been thrown up and all the moves and maneuvers and many of the players who sought to defeat presenting to the public what we have discovered about the assassination of JFK. As Martin Schotz, in his book *History Will Not Absolve Us*, has observed, the objective of disinformation isn't to convince anyone one way or the other, but to create enough uncertainty that everything is believable and nothing is knowable.

But we're doing our best to make it very clear that the arguments being made by the other side really are flimsy and without merit. I've undertaken new studies with a new group of assassination researchers, including Ralph Cinque, Richard Hooke, Larry Rivera especially, but also K.D. Ruckman and Clare Kuehn, who have made contributions in a series of articles entitled *JFK Special: Oswald Was In The Doorway After All*. We reveal the government's conundrum when they discovered a famous photograph taken by AP photographer James Ike Altgens, known technically as the Altgens 6, in which you can see the presidential limousine in the foreground and in the background there is the doorway to the book depository.

You can see a Dal-Tex window from which three shots appear to have been fired, and how Lyndon's secret service detail is already reacting even though JFK's are looking around as they have no idea. We've been able to establish, principally by focusing on the clothing and the build of the individual in the doorway, that this person was not Billy Lovelady, a co-worker, who actually was wearing a short-sleeve red and white vertically striped shirt at the time and was in the doorway but to the left of the individual we're talking about.

Nor was it a man in a checkered shirt who has a much heavier build and who doesn't look anything like either Billy Lovelady or Lee Oswald. And I regard this as the single most important discovery; if I can, if we can do anything about it, this is what will pull the rug out from the government as we approach the 50th observance of the assassination of JFK.

[Why did Oswald leave the School Book Depository after the shooting?]

He explained why he left, because no more work was going to be done that day. Wasn't that obvious, right? I mean, it's an assassination, everyone's running around. There wasn't going to be any more work, so what more was there for him to do? Nothing more, so he just left.

[Did he get his gun at his apartment?]

Oh, yeah, he went back and got his jacket and the revolver.

[Why the gun?] Well, things were going on. I mean, this was getting hot. He was probably already suspecting that this might involve him in some way, shape or form, so I think getting the revolver made perfect sense. I would have done that.

He was heading to meet his contact in the movie theater. He did not go out of his way to have his encounter with Tippit. There were four shell casings found at the scene. The first officer on the scene initialed them.

They had been ejected from one or more automatics. They were automatic shell casings.

Oswald didn't even have an automatic. They were of two makes, two Western and two Remington-Rand. Aquila Clemons, sitting across the street, said two men had killed Tippit, and that neither of them looked like Oswald.

Later, as in the case with the rifle – the rifle booked in Dallas wasn't the rifle that was booked in Washington when they transferred all the evidence to Washington. And I believe the rifle booked in Dallas was the rifle found in the book depository, and the rifle booked in Washington was the one used in the Dal-Tex to fire three un-silenced shots to create the impression that three shots had been used.

It was the only weapon that was un-silenced among the six shooters. And so you make the switch. The same thing happened with Sirhan. Sirhan unloaded his weapon, .22 caliber, I think it held eight shots. There were actually as many as thirteen or fourteen shots fired altogether. Bobby was actually shot four times from behind with the same type of weapon.

He was shot behind the right ear from about an inch and a half. Thomas Noguchi, world-famous medical examiner, established all this.

It was inconsistent, however with the police account, and believe it or not it was Noguchi who was fired when it should have been the police that were indicted because it was clear they were the ones advancing the false account.

So, what happened was, Rafer Johnson had forced the weapon out of Sirhan's hand, and it was initially booked, but there was a substitution, and the substitution, as in the Oswald case, was the gun that was actually used to shoot Bobby.

[Back to Tippit. Why kill him?]

The Tippit thing is one of those slightly mysterious aspects of the case. I do believe Tippit was involved one way or another. I don't think he expected he was going to be killed, however.

And these two guys who killed him, he may have been assisting them in departing from the Dealey Plaza area or some such, but whatever, they killed him and it was used to claim that Oswald must have been guilty because he shot the police officer, but he didn't commit either crime.

[Why the silence of the Kennedy family all this time?]

Well, Teddy responded to that. A letter from Ed Hoffman, who was a deaf mute, who observed the gunmen behind the picket fence and who said ... he wrote back and said, the duly constituted authorities should handle it, because otherwise they'd be accused of having political motivation.

And I think that's right, but I think it's also true that they knew that this was a very big deal and a large-scale conspiracy, and if you weren't in a position to pursue it, there wasn't a lot you could do about it.

[Chapter 7] More: Jim, Kevin – "Are You A Liberal?"

> "I was eight years old when President John Kennedy was shot to death in Dallas in 1963. If grace favors me, I'll be 62 when documents related to the assassination are released to the public, and 84 when the Warren Commission's investigative files into the tragedy are finally opened.
> "That's a long time to wait for a chance to evaluate the purported truth.
> "It's a blot on the presumed sophistication of the people of the United States that any aspect of an event so dramatic and shocking should be kept from us. Perhaps it's true, to abuse the line from A Few Good Men yet again, that we can't handle the truth. But there cannot be genuine resolution as long as such critical information remains concealed."
>
> \- Robert Steinback, *Boston Globe*

JIM:

[The radio career. What made you want to start that?]

A fellow named Danny Romero, who was the program director for Republic Broadcasting Network, heard me give an interview, and said, I gotta have that guy on my [station], he got hold of me and offered me a radio program. That was my first radio program. That was in 2006, probably somewhere around in there.

I've had four different shows.

That first one with Republic, it didn't last terribly long, because the manager was listening to one of my programs where I was defending Hillary Clinton from criticism and attacks saying she was a lesbian, explaining that even if it were true, it shouldn't be held against her as a political figure.

And he calls me up, on the air, and he says, "Fetzer, I wanna ask you a question. I want you to tell me the truth."

I said, "Sure."

He says, "Are you a liberal?"

I had spent the very first five minutes I went on the air with this show on his network, explaining that I believed that everyone deserved representation, not just the rich, and that the Republicans were the party that thought the poor had too much money and the rich had too little.

I mean, I wanted to make it unmistakably clear that I had a political orientation. He evidently didn't listen to that first five minutes. He fired me on the spot. He put on music or who knows what for the rest of the show, about three-quarters through.

[Were your parents "liberal?"]

Oh, well, uh, yeah, more or less, but we didn't go into a lot of that. It was my own gravitation toward the obvious benefits of the equity of providing a social safety network for people who have difficult times making ends meet. I mean, I believe in Social Security, Medicare, Medicaid, unemployment insurance, workman's compensation.

These are all programs that make a capitalistic society which tends to be exploitative of workers more manageable and fair toward the employee.

[Have you ever been in a fist fight?]

That's a very interesting question.

When I was a paper boy in the ninth grade there was a fellow who was in the junior high school who was a tough. His name was Tom Corso. And for some reason, he and I ended up having a fight, and I wound up on top. I prevailed. It wasn't that I thought I was so physically adept or anything, it was just the way it played out.

And that gave me a reputation in the junior high of being a really tough guy. Well, there was another member of my class by the name of Ron Midyett, who stood about a head taller than me, who others thought, well, let's see, let's have Midyett and Fetzer have it out, so I was challenged to meet him at the baseball diamond after – I've never told anyone this story in my life – after school.

But you know I didn't have any bone to pick with Ron Midyett, so he kind of got an arm lock on me and I really wasn't resisting, so he prevailed and that was it, it didn't last five minutes.

[Fighting, in the military, not so much?]

Oh, no, no, no. I was a commissioned officer there for cryin' out loud.

[Was not in combat in the military]

Frankly, I've never regretted that I wasn't in Vietnam, because I've come to believe that it was a completely wrong war, that Americans committed a great many atrocities there, it was the wrong thing for the country to have done.

[Have you ever been to jail?]

No.

[Do you believe in heaven?]

No.

Absolutely not. I don't believe in God. I'm an agnostic.

You can't prove the existence of God. You can't prove the non-existence of God. I'm very strongly committed to reason and rationality. There's a principle enunciated by the British philosopher William Clifford, "The Ethics of Belief", that maintains always and everywhere you're not allowed to hold a belief without sufficient evidence.

I believe in "The Ethics of Belief". That is a principle to which I strive to adhere.

So, if I don't have evidence for belief, I leave it in suspense, and in the case of God, I certainly have no reason to believe in the existence of God. But I also realize you can't disprove the existence of God, and therefore my position is that of an agnostic, where I neither claim to know that He exists or that he does not exist.

[Does it scare you? The thought that there is no heaven?]

No. Not at all.

[The Beatles. You are a big fan, right?]

Well, I think the Beatles were really great for the country, because they came on in the wake of JFK's death and I think it had a tremendous benefit. I do believe they are comparable to Mozart in their best works. Everyone in my generation favored either John or Paul and I was overwhelmingly Paul.

I mean, John wasn't even in my universe. I do like some of his songs, but I'm overwhelmingly Paul McCartney.

[Plays "Day Tripper" to open and close every show. And during the breaks in the show ...]

Well, they're fairly fixed. One is "Girl," which is a John song. That's a very interesting song. I didn't even realize how much I liked it until I started listening to it. I actually did a tribute to the Beatles, which you can find in my archives. I went through the hundred best Beatle songs, picked out my favorites.

[Do you smoke?]

I smoked for about ten years.

I began at Princeton and I actually smoked in the Marine Corps, amazingly enough. I mean, it's a very physical, you know, demanding environment.

I was smoking up to four packs a day of the philosopher's cigarette, True. It was relatively mild as cigarettes go, but when you're smoking four packs a day, that's pretty much lighting one up when you're putting one out.

Now, I did that almost exactly for ten years, even through my graduate work, and in fact when I quit smoking the most difficult aspect was I'd always associated smoking with writing and being creative, so that to learn to write without smoking was a challenge. But what turned the corner for me was that my girlfriend at the time, whose name was Linda Sartorelli, was teaching a course at St. Mary's, which is the women's college for Notre Dame, in Mishawaka, Indiana. And I was visiting her and she was doing a segment on smoking and health. And I'd always had the rationale that if I smoked more I was eating less and therefore keeping my weight down.

And the book she had on smoking explained that anyone who smoked as much as I did was putting a strain on their cardiovascular system equivalent to being three hundred pounds overweight!

And the next day I had three cigarettes, the day after that one, and that was it. Which is astounding, because it really means I did have a rationale, and when that rationale was destroyed by the evidence, then I was able to modify my behavior.

Yeah, I don't know anyone else who's ever done that, but there it is.

[Exercise?]

Not as much as I should.

My physician, bless his heart, is a very famous guy. He makes appearances on NPR, he's a friend of the Dalai Lama. His name is Zorba Paster.

When I move to this nice little town of Oregon, I wind up in the health care system and my physician is Zorba Paster! So, I really like the guy. But about a year and a half ago, we were having a conversation, and we were joking about losing weight, and I said, yeah, it's really simple, you eat less and exercise more.

And he said, well, the exercise doesn't make a lot of difference. It's really eating less. And up to that point I'd been doing five thousand steps a day on this treadmill. And after he told me that, I stopped. I mean, this is insane, Mike, it's like me cutting out the smoking.

That was my rationale for exercise, I mean, maintaining my weight. He told me it was really a function of how much I ate. After about a year of that I realized that actually I really wasn't in the shape I should be. I really was maintaining my cardiovascular system.

So, I got this treadmill repaired. I actually ordered a part that I needed because it wasn't working, and installed the part, and it needed a special adjustment. I tracked down a guy who could repair it and brought him out to the house. He got it working good as new.

And I would be using it right now, but that I developed some problem in my knee that's very painful, it's like sort of a precursor to arthritis. It just has kept me off the treadmill. I was starting to do it. I was starting to work my way back up to five thousand steps, which is actually very good, but it's been delayed by several weeks, and I'm taking pain pills.

[Had cancer]

I've had cancer a couple of times.

When I was teaching at New College at the University of South Florida, I had some incredible tightening up in my lower abdomen, and I called our physician. It went away, but he was alarmed and had me see a specialist.

In fact, it was a problem with my right kidney. At the time they took me into surgery they'd already told Jan that they thought it was a tumor and she knew that kidney tumors are almost always fatal, so she wasn't very optimistic.

When they opened the kidney, however, they discovered that it was defunct. It was a dead kidney, and it was laden with uric acid crystals, so they removed the kidney and put me on a suppressor of uric acid. And, although I only have one kidney, I've been doing just fine since then. That was in like, 1983.

But, the more serious case was while we were living in Duluth. This would have been right around 1996, I'm gonna guess, about the same year that I was promoted to be Distinguished McKnight University Professor. I was diagnosed with elevated prostate, you know, and went in for all the analysis and wound up at the Mayo.

This friend of mine, David Mantik, was sending me studies about the alternative treatments, whether you wait and see, or you do the radiation therapy, or these little seeds, radioactive seeds, or you have surgery.

And I learned the probabilities of incontinence and impotence, depending on these different methods. And I went down to the Mayo and consulted the leading expert, who's performed about thirty thousand prostatectomies.

His name is Horst Zincke and he was the principal author of these studies that David Mantik had been sending to me.

I thought, well, I'm in pretty good hands, with like the world's leading expert here. He told me the problem was, with the wait-and-see, you don't know the doubling time with cancer like this, and I just placed my faith, I mean, I was convinced with David sending me all this stuff.

So, I actually had my prostate removed, and was able to survive without either incontinence or impotence. It's just not the same, but of course, I'm 72-years old, and there's some point where you're not going to be as sexually active and vigorous as you were at a younger age, and I certainly enjoyed sex at a younger age, and I'm not distressed that Jan and I have less sex now than we did thirty, twenty, fifteen years ago.

[What makes you nervous? Anything?]

Probably the only thing that ever bothers me, really, is whether I might have inadvertently done something that might have put someone else in jeopardy or harm. If I have done something and it causes someone else some kind of problem, legal, social, whatever, that is probably all that really bothers me. I've never been concerned about what might happen to me, for example, when I take strong stands about issues like these wars, 9/11, the assassination of JFK.

I've always believed in the maxim, if you can't take the heat, stay out of the kitchen, and, I mean, that doesn't bother me, that something should happen to me. But I don't like the idea of something I ever do causing harm to anyone else.

[Why not run for office?]

Yeah, I thought about it, but I'm very bad at memory with names and people. I had so many social skills when I was a younger man, when I went through Princeton, when I went in the Marine Corps, I mean I really had a lot of smooths.

But as I grew older, they became less and less important to me.

I was more and more driven by the truth, and getting the truth out, than whether or not anyone would be affected by it.

Which may be one reason today why I'm so much concerned when 9/11 Truth groups put politics ahead of science, for example.

I'm convinced that when the American people know the truth, they'll know what to do about it.

But they worry, well, if anyone hears that we think maybe no planes, which they don't even understand anyway, because it really means that all four of the crash sites were faked in different ways...

Which I can prove. But most of these people are just a bit mamby-pamby, they don't really have enough confidence, they aren't quite good enough at research, and most strikingly, they won't look at the evidence.

I am convinced that anyone who looks at the evidence I can produce will be convinced from a rational point of view, because really there's no way out. I've reasoned this through and been through this so many times.

I'm convinced that the key to exposing 9/11 as a charade is the fact that all four of the crash sites were faked.

Two of the planes weren't even in the air that day and the other two did not crash. So, what that means is, all four of the sites were either fabricated or faked.

And if the American people understood that, they would get the idea of the enormity of the lies that were told by our government.

[Favorite movie?]

Oh, one of my favorite movies is *Apocalypse Now*. I like *Lawrence of Arabia*. I love *Patton*. Those are some of my classics.

I like the original *Godfather*. There may be some movies that may be less significant, but I enjoy a lot, *Enemy of the State* I think is just a terrific film.

I like *Erin Brokovich*. There are a lot of moves I like. Jan and I really like movies a lot. But those would be some of my favorites.

And, oh, obviously, of course, *JFK*.

[Jim compared to Mozart, in the movie, *Amadeus*]

It was George Anderson, who was the assistant principal at W.D. Sugg Middle School, that invited me, asked me if I would serve as an eighth grade science teacher – they called me one day – it was a Saturday, as I recall – and said, you've got to come over and see this.

So Jan and I went over to their house, 'cause we were very good friends.

And I sat down and they started this movie. And I couldn't believe that, you know, it was me!

There I was, chasing after this young wench, crawling under a table, all this other stuff, it was just unbelievable. And that's why they had me over, Mike! They had me over 'cuz they saw me in *Amadeus*. I was the young Mozart. And I was just blown away. It was just stunning! Just really amusing.

KEVIN:

[Graduated from college, headed out west]

I saved up some money and bought a half-size 1955 Chevy school bus that had been converted to become a motor home. So I jumped in there and drove out to San Francisco.

At the time that I was working as a typesetter I was also singing in a punk band called "The Comicosmics". For that band I was just singing. I also strum chords on guitar and write songs. I did this for about a year, and then left for San Francisco in '81.

[Was it hard to make that choice, to leave Madison?]

Not really. I mean, a lot of people that I knew were doing things like that. People I knew would finish college, hang around Madison a little bit and then head off somewhere, so it was kind of normal for me to do that too, although some of the people did have jobs.

The job situation was pretty bad at that time. I think people were less career focused then than they are now.

I get the sense that all the college students are really, really concerned about what they can line up when they leave college, partly because they're drowning in debt, and I wasn't.

[The bombing in Madison]

1970. That was before I got there, but I did hear about it. Sterling Hall. I walked past it all the time. One killed. Graduate student.

["Though the bombers said afterward that they had not intended to hurt anyone, the explosion killed Robert Fassnacht, a physics researcher who was working late. Mr. Fassnacht, 33, a father of three, was, his family said afterward, against the war." – *NY Times*, July 27, 2010, "Dwight Armstrong, Who Bombed A College Building in 1970, Dies at 58"]

By the time I got to Madison that was more history than a living issue, but, after I went out to San Francisco and did all that stuff and came back to Madison for the Ph.D. program, like 15 years later, when I got back to Madison, Karl Armstrong, who was convicted of that bombing, was out selling juice in his little juice stand.

I sold food and drink at Art Fair On The Square next to Karl Armstrong in his juice stand, and got to talk with him a bunch, and speculate about whether David Fine was actually a false-flag FBI agent. ... I think it was Fine. No, Leo Burt, that's right.

There is one who disappeared like they all did after the bombing and never resurfaced, and is still on the lam, officially, and the speculation is that he's in witness protection as an agent, and that the bombing may have been partly a false-flag. And Karl sounded like he still wasn't sure whether that might not be true.

[You were interested in journalism, and journalism at that time was all about Woodward and Bernstein, Watergate. But they did not get to the point of Watergate, which was the Kennedy murder, all that was covered up, actually, right?]

Oh, yeah, sure. I actually figured that out.

That was I believe part of my 1979 article.

I know I figured it out while I was in Madison, because, I think it was Haldeman's book came out that explained the reason Nixon was going so bonkers about the Bay of Pigs Thing, and Haldeman said the Bay of Pigs Thing was the JFK assassination.

And Haldeman described having been sent by Nixon to visit Richard Helms, the head of the CIA. And the message that Haldeman had to bring to Helms from Nixon was, we've got to stop this scandal, we've got to shut up Howard Hunt, because otherwise the whole Bay of Pigs Thing could explode.

And then, according to Haldemen, Richard Helms, the head of the CIA, went bananas, went ballistic, started screaming, you go back and tell Nixon this has nothing to do with the Bay of Pigs Thing, so this is a total smoking gun.

Obviously there's a JFK aspect to Watergate, and there's a lot of different kinds of speculation about precisely what that is, but we know that JFK was killed in a conspiracy that involved CIA people, particularly anti-Castro CIA people. They hatched it at JM/WAVE CIA station in Florida. Brad Ayers has written about this.

He was there. Brad Ayers was on loan from the military to the CIA.

He actually worked with the people that he later discovered had orchestrated the killing of John F. Kennedy.

[Woodward and Bernstein]

Well, Woodward is Office Of Naval Intelligence and who knows how he's linked up with the intelligence community. ... They probably reported it exactly the way the spooks wanted it reported.

Woodward was an intelligence agent so everything he did was scripted by an intelligence agency, and he was I think the senior partner and Bernstein was just kind of going along. Bernstein was apparently relatively innocent and later started to figure things out.

He wrote a great piece in *Rolling Stone* about the CIA infiltrating the media. Of course Woodward was probably one of the people he was talking about, although I don't think he came out and said that.

[Hunter S. Thompson – killed himself?]

Well, I've heard reports that he had woken up to 9/11 Truth and that he was working on that, and if so, then I would think he was probably murdered.

It's also possible that there might be strong enough mind-control technology to induce suicides in some cases.

Now whether that would be possible with him, I don't know.

You never really know, but for me, in these cases, barring really hard evidence, it's all just guessing about probabilities, based on circumstantial evidence.

In this case it looks like there's enough circumstantial evidence that Thompson was about to get on the 9/11 case, which would have been a disaster for the 9/11 perps, because Thompson has this big audience of skeptical-type people, so if that's true, they would silence him, so I don't think that his dying violently at that moment is likely to be a coincidence.

[*The Progressive* magazine is a traditional liberal icon based in Madison. Matt Rothschild is the current editor. You have had encounters with Rothschild over his not wanting to take on 9/11. Why do so-called progressive publications, individuals, so often characteristically not want to take that next step, as with Erwin Knoll, a previous Progressive editor not wanting to publish your article on the John F. Kennedy murder by the CIA?]

I think one of the best books that takes this up is by Martin Schotz.

He was involved in trying to break the truth about the JFK assassination and he went back and wrote a great book about it, *History Will Not Absolve Us*.

He surmises that these left wing, so-called progressive media organs, like *The Progressive*, and the others, they're all basically loyal opposition, they've all got seats at the table, and telling the truth about the JFK assassination, which involved the CIA, Lyndon Johnson, and very powerful people, and showed that ultimately decisions are made in our country by these nefarious powerful forces, not by elected officials as we like to think.

It would amount to turning over the table, rather than just sitting at the table and carping.

These guys are all being paid reasonably well. They have nice lives, and they're being paid to sit there and carp. If you're a paid carper, sitting and complaining and beating your chest about relatively minor indiscretions of the empire, you can have your cake and eat it, too. You have a really nice life, materially, and, you can keep on giving your conscience a pat on the back, because you are the good guy, and so, they have it both ways, material life success, and they can keep feeling good about themselves, doing what they're doing.

Telling the truth about how power really works and how ugly it really is, would amount to overturning the table, and they wouldn't have a place anymore, if they did that.

Either the individual who did it would be deprived of his place at the table, and he would no longer have a materially comfortable life and would no longer have the opportunity to reach thousands and thousands of people with his very moralistic carping, or – who knows what might happen.

If enough of them did it, maybe we'd fix these problems, or maybe they would just overturn the table and install an outright dictatorship, which is what they seem to be doing anyway.

I don't think you have to assume that most of them, people like Matt Rothschild, etc., are conscious agents of the forces that did 9/11 and killed JFK.

I think people like Matt Rothschild are more likely psychologically blocked by these kinds of factors.

And with Rothschild and many of the others who happen to be Jewish, I think with 9/11 there's an extra factor, which is that, I think that 9/11 was essentially a Zionist coup d'etat, by hard-line neo-conservative Jewish Zionists, who wanted to change the direction of American policy in a way they thought would ensure the future survival and thriving of the state of Israel.

That's, I think, the number one reason that 9/11 happened.

And Jewish people are brought up to believe that Jews are in danger, Jews are a persecuted, under-privileged, deprived minority that's always been persecuted by the evil goys, and that the Holocaust was kind of the epitome of this long-term pattern of Jews being victimized, and that Israel is a response to that which is very heroic and which is attempting to insure Jewish survival.

So for such people the thought of Israel being really threatened is very, very frightening, and then the thought that exposing the truth of 9/11 might expose the truth of Israel being involved in 9/11, thereby putting an end to Israel, which only survives because of the massive aid it gets from the U.S., is even more frightening.

And then the thought that these evil anti-Semites, who say these terrible things, might actually be right about something, that maybe there is a lot of Jewish Zionist power out there and that many of these powerful

Jewish Zionists are outrageously immoral and using this immense power in horrifying ways, that's even more threatening to somebody like Matt Rothschild, who wants to think that he and his ethnicity are basically good guys, and indeed, persecuted good guys.

So, this totally would blow their entire worldview.

So it's even harder for Jewish people who not only have to lose their illusions about the U.S., but also have to lose their illusions about the Jewish community and Israel at the same time, and so it's twice as hard for them as for everybody else.

And so I think these are some of the reasons that the alternative media, which is dominated by Jewish people, is so slow to pick up the ball on 9/11, but Marty Schotz, who happens to be Jewish, by the way, a big JFK-truther who analyzed this, points out that it's true psychologically for everybody in the alternative media, even in the case of JFK where this sort of Zionist angle is not really obvious.

[Allen Ruff, Rainbow Books, in Madison, a progressive bookstore. What about your experiences there?]

Oh, yeah, Allen Ruff is a kind of classic, Jewish, leftwing, sort of Zionist who doesn't want to admit he's a Zionist, and I think he's part of that sort of contradiction. Intellectually, as a Communist, Allen realizes that Zionism is completely at odds with universal morality, and Marxism is a universal morality, but he still has this attachment to his people.

He actually admitted this to me once. He said something like, well, I do have some tribal affiliations to maintain.

[Can you sell books there, speak there? At Rainbow Books?]

No, no, the last time I tried to shop there, I went in and was looking at some books, and Allen came storming around the corner and shoved his face right in my face and started just screaming at me, get out of here, I don't want you in here!

The gall, to do that when he still hadn't paid me.

He still owes me today, seventy-five or a hundred bucks, for the DVDs I sold there on consignment. And I can't even go in there and look at the books.

Allen first became very angry at me before 9/11 because we were both participants in the Al-Awda list. Al-Awda is the Palestinian right of return group, and so there were certain kinds of writings that I would occasionally post to that list, and Allen would respond: this is a horrible, anti-Semitic writing. I was saying that Palestinians and everyone who cares about the Palestinian cause, should be working to educate the American people about the fact that U.S. foreign policy has been taken over by Zionists. That's why they're able to keep doing what they're doing, because the U.S. is paying for it.

And that's because of this immense Zionist political power in the U.S., and so the thing to do is go straight at it, rather than tip-toeing around this fact that Zionist Jews own half of the mainstream media, which allows them to completely control everything in mainstream media virtually.

They own virtually all of Hollywood outright, give about half of the money that's given to federal political candidates in donations.

All of this has been meticulously shown in statistics, so I was just pointing this out, saying this is not right that these Zionists have completely taken over our country, and we need to get a patriotic reaction to rise up and overthrow this. For Allen, this is terribly threatening, and it's terribly anti-Semitic. You should never talk about this Zionist political power in America because that's very anti-Semitic. So, he went ballistic on me a few times over those issues before 9/11.

And then when I started doing 9/11 Truth activism he went even more ballistic, and people kept asking for David Ray Griffin's books, starting with *The New Pearl Harbor*, in Rainbow Books, and Allen; oh, they had to stock it because people were asking for it, but he would actually go, when people wanted to buy it, he would say, don't buy that, that's no good, that's worthless.

He would try to discourage his customers from buying it, and he was also very, very unfriendly when I approached him to ask if he wanted to help with any events for 9/11 Truth.

He was extremely hostile, and that situation kind of continued, and before I introduced David Ray Griffin at his *9/11 and Empire* talk in 2005, which was broadcast live on C-Span – it was the first, big successful 9/11 Truth event anywhere really – Allen walked right up to me at the podium when I was just about to introduce Dr. Griffin and stuck his face right up next to mine and snarled at me, we're keeping a file on you, that's right, we're keeping a file on you, you better watch out.

[Dave Zweifel, editor, *Madison Capital Times*]

He published three very, very hard-hitting 9/11 Truth op-eds in the Cap Times that I wrote.

I think these were the first three hard-hitting 9/11 Truth op-eds ever published in any mainstream daily in America, and of course, right after that, their holding company put them out of business.

They were totally on board with 9/11 Truth.

[John Nichols, reporter, *Madison Capital Times*]

John Nichols, he actually confessed to me that he's understood 9/11 Truth ever since Gore Vidal wrote that Goat Song essay less than a year after it happened.

Well, he's a good example of somebody who knows. He's psychologically strong enough to figure out for himself, but he is fully aware that if he were to openly endorse it, that his career would be over ... so he's just trying to maximize the good he does in the world and maintain a decent lifestyle for himself and his family by pretty much ignoring it.

Those guys did take a certain risk in publishing my op-eds and giving me favorable coverage during the controversy in 2006 with the legislature.

Maybe that's one reason they got shut down. But John wouldn't be given the platform he has now at *The Nation* magazine, and other kinds of platforms, his book publishing, his public speaking, all of that stuff ... he wouldn't have that if he had openly come right out and said that he knew 9/11 was an inside job.

[Lee Rayburn, former Madison progressive radio show host]

He's also 9/11 Truth savvy.

He kind of officially maintains a certain ambiguity and ambivalence about it, but Lee is on board with it and also took some professional risks, had me on his show a couple of times, with relatively favorable coverage.

Same pattern – Lee Rayburn also lost his job. He was fired by Clear Channel, just like *The Capital Times* was shut down by Madison Newspapers, Inc. He lost his job at the Mic 90.3, Madison's left wing talk radio, I think because he was also doing good work on these kinds of issues.

So Lee is off somewhere else now, maybe California, John is still doing well. Dave Zweifel is still editing the weekly Cap Times, but there's obviously a message being sent when Clear Channel shuts down people like Lee Rayburn, when Madison Newspapers, Inc. shuts down the Cap Times as a daily.

They're sending a clear message, which is the same message they sent by going after me, which is, if you talk about 9/11 or anything remotely related to that or these other hot-button issues, you will never work in this town again.

[Recent hip surgery – injury due to Lyme's Disease?]

That's probably the reason.

Lyme's disease, late 1990s, diagnosed with end-stage osteoarthritis of both hips several years ago, so that's technically a totally disabling condition, so I was eligible for everything from a disabled license plate to Social Security, etc.

The side that got the surgery is much better now. The other side I have to wait. I got infected, got a staph infection during the first surgery, so that has to get completely cleared up before they do another one.

[Jon Stewart/Rachel Maddow]

I think that people like that are generally afraid to tackle subjects like 9/11 and JFK, that is, the worst crimes of the national security state and their entrenched corruption, and they're also afraid to tackle the power structure issues involving the federal reserve and the way the biggest bankers are set up to siphon all the money in the system into their own coffers.

And that structural feature of the current capitalist system has created a situation where the biggest world bankers are hiring the best technocrats, including the best assassins and mind controllers, to push for a one-world government that they would control.

This is the so-called New World Order.

Nobody on the left is allowed to talk about that, and nobody on the left is allowed to talk about the worst crimes of the national security state, and if they do talk about it, they get, well, they'll be reviled as conspiracy theorists by the equivalent of our ideological secret police, our ideological Gestapo.

They'll have their careers damaged or they'll lose their careers. It's the same situation for just about anybody who has any kind of career that's respectable or that's involved in the world of ideas. When I started working on 9/11, I took a serious risk that I wouldn't be able to continue, that my career would be stymied for talking about that issue, and of course, it was.

And the purpose of what they did to me was to try to scare away other professors who might otherwise be willing to talk about things like 9/11. So if people like Rachel Maddow and Jon Stewart, I'm sure they know that if they started talking honestly about any of these taboo issues, the ideological secret police would very likely damage their careers.

Rosie O'Donnell lost her slot on *The View* TV show; Charlie Sheen was probably given crazy pills, somebody slipped crazy pills into his drink. Jimmy Walter, a multi-millionaire who had great resources to spend on 9/11 Truth, was terrorized and attacked and driven out of the country. He lives in exile and is afraid to support 9/11 Truth with his money anymore.

So there are these kinds of consequences. It's a lot like in Stalinist Russia, if you buck the system, you'll probably be shot or sent to Siberia.

Well, it's not quite that bad here. You'll just be unemployed, starving to death and reviled. They're maybe a little bit better than the Stalinists were.

[Barbara Boxer's remark about the Wellstone killing might be a shade of that, perhaps.]

That's right.

Barbara Boxer said the Wellstone assassination was "a warning to us all."

That's how they keep their order and that's how they prevent people from taking up the hard issues and actually doing something that would change anything, because if you do that, then they come after you.

And of course, it's always been that way.

[Is there any pressure on them to say more? No. Probably not. Probably the other way around.]

That's how it works.

All of the money is behind people who do the kind of job that Rachel Maddow and Jon Stewart do.

And that money creates people like them, who stay within the limits that they stay within, and then that creates the audience.

The audience is bombarded with messages, including, I would assume, subliminal messages. Subliminal brainwashing technology is very highly advanced today.

So, you have kind of a controlled audience whose ideas and world views have been constructed by experts, and people like Jon Stewart and Rachel Maddow had better stay within those limits and play to that constructed audience and be constructed political commentators and comedians, because if they don't, then it's pretty easy for the ideological secret police to destroy their careers, to attack them, insult them, and basically cause them untold grief.

[You once said, referring to the work you do, on your radio show, something about, "if you die for a really good cause, that's the best way to get into paradise," so might as well go for it.]

It's a basic Muslim view, and I think Christians and other religious folks, presumably, have had very similar views. The Christian martyrs were quite a story in the early days of that faith in the Roman Empire as they were being devoured by lions.

And Muslims have that same idea, which I think is really tied into ethical monotheism, the belief in a single God who actually cares how we act and wants us to make good decisions rather than bad decisions, so people from that tradition have been willing to do the right thing even if it means death and going to paradise is part of that.

Now my way of translating this to people who are outside the boundaries of this discursive world view ... I think that people do have something like a life review when they die, and I've had little experiences that kind of confirm this, and other people, including atheists, have had this experience of thinking they were going to die, just as a car accident is happening, their proverbial life flashes before their eyes, and people who have had near death experiences, NDEs, have had this life review where they experience or go over everything they did in their lives. And the Koran actually tells us that your deeds are weighed on the scales.

If your good deeds outweigh your bad deeds, then you will be going to paradise, and if not, you'll fall into the gaping pit.

I think this is all very real.

It's not just sort of a social control mechanism for keeping people in line.

We have all of these near death experiences, we have Tibetan Buddhists who have gotten very good at guiding people through the dying process, avoiding the hell fire, which is basically all of their gross or base sorts of desires like greed, envy and anger, and the same deadly sins from these traditions. So the people have to let go of those things.

Which is what you do in Islam when you fully surrender to God, because Islam means surrender, then you get past these demons of anger and greed and lust and all these things and you're free and your soul ends up in a very good place. Otherwise, if you have been lying to yourself, hiding your real nature, and these kinds of selfish, base emotions are still ruling you, and in most people I think this is happening at an unconscious level, then you're in serious trouble. And so this religious worldview that says the way you live your life is absolutely crucial because you are going to be stepping off into eternity with whatever you did here.

I think it's true. I think there's even convincing evidence that it's true. You don't even have to have faith, although that probably helps.

So, for all of those reasons it's really important to strive to do good in the world.

So, I'm convinced that's true. I'm not really even sacrificing by trying to do good at the expense of my career, or what have you.

This is actually advantageous. It's just taking a slightly longer view. And these religious traditions always taught people to take that longer view.

One of the mind control techniques of modernity is to terrorize people by basically trying to hide and deny these deeper truths, so that people think this world is the only world that exists and death is the end, which makes it extremely terrifying. And so people are terrorized by death and the power of the state and its apparatus to inflict death or the humiliating little deaths.

And then they toe the line, they obey the authority, but those of us who have learned that these religious truths are really true, are free, because we no longer have to do all of the bad things and make all of the ugly little compromises that people make when they are terrorized by death and don't understand that the important thing is that eternity that awaits us after death.

So, I don't think I'm really doing anything very heroic by trying to do good, and there are a lot of people out there like that.

Mother Theresa wasn't heroic.

She was just doing what was the right thing for her in the long run. The reason for all these rules is that they are set up to make things best for you.

[Do you think you could do what you are doing if you had not converted to Islam?]

Probably not.

I might have done some of it, because I grew up with respect for strong ethics.

My father's giving up that gold medal at the Olympics, to do what he felt was the right thing and call a foul on himself that nobody else saw, was an influence on me, and also his general kind of rigorous ethics. He had a side of him that was very rigorously ethical. That was an influence on me.

And for that reason, once I learned about the JFK assassination when I was about fifteen years old, I couldn't let go of that.

How could anyone live with themselves, knowing that this coup d'etat, this brutal execution of the President by the secret government had happened?

How could anybody just let that go and not work to try to do something about it? So I learned about it and tried to spread the word about that, although not as a full-time occupation by any means, before I was Muslim.

And I also spent a year knocking on doors for The Nuclear Freeze in the mid-80s and that was before I was Muslim. So I don't think it's impossible to do good deeds even though you are sort of spiritually confused and exploring the world, but this 9/11 thing is so intense and I got railroaded into doing this as a full-time job; it's become kind of a big part of my identity, when people see me I'm this figure of 9/11 Truth.

That would have been grueling, more grueling than it is by far, if I hadn't accepted Islam and had some of my final questions about how the universe works cleared up by Islam.

[You seem to have a bring-it-on attitude. Do you see that in yourself?]

Sure. Yeah. I was kind of personally offended by 9/11, even more so than with the JFK assassination, in part because it was so obvious.

The JFK assassination, to me, wasn't quite obvious. I really had to think about it for a while and figure out who was telling the truth and add it all up. It actually took me a few years to be certain what was done, to the extent that there was an institution that was central to killing JFK. That institution was the CIA.

And with 9/11, once I heard about David Ray Griffin's work and took a hard look at it, I was a bit more personally offended.

One thing, I felt stupid for not having seen it for a few years. For just having been suspicious when the evidence was staring me in the face the whole time, and here I am this supposed Islamic studies expert.

I think I was a little annoyed at myself. And then I was also annoyed by the scale of this lie.

It was mainly a lie. The killing of JFK was a crime designed to change policy by changing leadership, but 9/11 was basically designed as a big lie to get the policies they wanted by convincing the people that this grotesque untruth was true, and that I found very offensive, so I've had a kind of bring it on, make my day, kind of attitude.

Iran fighting terrorists created by US, Israel: Academic

Home / Featured / Interviews Tue May 24, 2016 2:46PM

Terrorists prepare artillery shells during clashes with Syrian forces near the village of Om al-Krameel, in Aleppo's southern countryside on May 5, 2016. (Photo by AFP)

Press TV has conducted an interview with James H. Fetzer, professor at the University of Minnesota Duluth from Madison, about remarks made by Leader of the Islamic Revolution Ayatollah Seyyed Ali Khamenei on using all means in fight against terrorism in the Middle East.

Kevin has become a regular feature on PressTV *of Iran, which, along with* Russia Today *and* Sputnik News, *have become more reliable sources of accurate information on world affairs than* The New York Times *or* The Washington Post.

JAMES FETZER, UK assistant professor of philosophy, is a man of many faces and gestures in the classroom. He has been described in this element—here he lectures a freshman class in logic—as a corps commander directing troops or a demonstrative maestro conducting his orchestra.

FETZER

philosophy teacher exudes
n that's contagious to students

—Photos by Bill Wells

Commerce Building which has boards on two walls. Students are sent to the board in waves, typically eight at a time, while each student in another squad of eight prepares to present a critique of one of the problems being solved by the blackboard workers.

As the students work, the professor moves about like a corps commander directing a battle. When the blackboard crew sits down, it is time for critical discussion as those forces on the ground explain to the class whether the problem has been copied or translated correctly, the general strategy to be employed in solving the problem, and whether the problem has been solved correctly step-by-step.

"I have found that this approach keeps my students interested throughout the class period and that it is an effective alternative to homework assignments they often find tedious and boring."

He adds: "This approach also keeps me keenly aware of the problems and difficulties they are encountering with the course material and thus in an appropriate position to clarify and correct misunderstandings."

The Text, he says, is to be used, but "don't let the text be the master of you."

(Continued on page [illegible])

STUDENTS: BARRETT EXCELLENT PROFESSOR

"He seems pretty harmless to me. I don't think he should be fired."

Justin Freeman
UW senior

"You don't have to agree with him, but you have to listen to him and respect his opinions."

Damian Naylor
UW freshman

"He's kept the class free of controversy, and he's an excellent teacher."

Peter Volkmar
UW junior

"It's not like he's trying to force his views on us. He's a great lecturer, and the stuff he teaches us is great."

Ryan Cotant
UW freshman

[Chapter 8] Stephenville, Texas, on a Saturday Night, headed to Mecca

> "... it's almost in the American mind – that of course the government is our parent, our father, and we almost don't want to think that they're bad...
> "... we live in a dysfunctional society, but nobody wants to talk about living in that dysfunctional society [...] they know they're going through the pain, they know it's there, but they don't want to talk about it, so you just do your thing every day ... and it's almost like that's what's happening here in America."
>
> \- Bob McIlvaine

by Mike Palecek

WEATHERFORD, TEXAS – I had hoped to make it to Stephenville tonight, but it's midnight, and I'm about an hour or more short. Stephenville is where there have been a recent rash of UFO sightings.

I'll go outside and smoke a cigarette and look around.

It's the best I can do.

I'm here, UFOs.

Abduct me.

Thursday night I met with the Dallas-Fort Worth 9/11 Truth group at Crystal's Pizza.

Daniel and Dale are from Dallas. They are jailers in the Dallas County Jail.

I mention the old jail and it being in Dealey Plaza and how some inmates said they saw a shooter in the sixth floor window.

Daniel says it's closed now, but they used to hold hangings on the roof.

He says former inmates of the jail and older jailers say it's haunted because of that.

Dale is big and bald and he'll be twenty-one soon.

He's from Arizona and his dream would be to get onto the Dallas police force and then become a resource officer in the schools.

This morning I went to Mecca. I don't think being in Bethlehem could be any more awe-inspiring than where I was today.

Maybe a John Prine concert. Dealey Plaza. 411 Elm Street.

The first day I walked into kindergarten at Lincoln School, Miss Steele had written all across the blackboard in big fluffy yellow teacher handwriting – President John F. Kennedy. In third grade, just after lunch, Sister Ellen floated into the classroom on the invisible nun conveyor belt – and told us the President had been shot and that he was dead.

"Why?" I ask Mike Brown, who is standing on the Grassy Knoll, why he comes here.

"For the truth," says Mike. He is a big, black man wearing black work clothes. He's got a deep voice and he's giving folks the alternative view of history, the op-ed of what they have just heard nearby in the JFK Museum tour.

He has been coming to this place ever since that day forever to tell the truth.

What is the truth?

"Everybody ran here," he says, meaning the Grassy Knoll. "You could smell the gunpowder."

He didn't see any shooters when he arrived, but he pulls out a black and white photo of a man in a suit and a white cowboy hat, behind the fence, carrying something under a jacket or cover that Mike says is a rifle.

There is a police officer in the photo.

Mike knows him, shows the two together in a recent color photo.

The police officer says the man told him he was with the Secret Service and should keep the crowd that was coming up to the fence area away, which the officer then did.

The man disappeared.

Mike was thirteen in 1963.

He shows a color photo of himself in the crowd on Elm Street, a skinny kid in a red and white checkered shirt, wide eyes, leaning forward to see the oncoming motorcade in front of the Dal-Tex building.

He later testified in front of the Warren Commission when it came to Dallas.

It's small. Tiny. So much in so little space. It's like finding out WWII actually took place in the high school gym.

The shot from the Grassy Knoll was point-blank. There is an "X" in the middle lane of the road.

The road angles downward.

The Grassy Knoll fence is still there.

Right there is the overpass where the car disappeared into history with Jackie Kennedy climbing onto the back of the vehicle to retrieve part of her husband's brain.

I walk around to look over the fence.

I would be too short to be a shooter, but you realize that the shot was point-blank. It's all just right-there.

The train whistle blows. Behind, there are the tracks, the overpass.

Mike says it's all just as it was then, the fence is the same. He points to the perch where Abraham Zapruder stood with his camera.

It's right there, just a few feet away.

This hasn't all been a dream. It's real.

On the back of the fence people have written their names, dedications to the president.

"St. John Hunt was here, son of E. Howard Hunt, 1/13/08."

"JFK, God Bless You."

"George Bush Did It/9/11 Truth."

Inside the museum they give you headphones and you go up the elevator to the sixth floor.

You walk around the parts of the exhibit listening to the audio tour. You learn about the Kennedy presidency, and also about the mood in Dallas before his visit, during his visit.

You see amateur film of the event, still-photos. The crowds were ten-deep along Main Street.

You look out those windows on the sixth floor, down Houston Street where the motorcade came before turning sharply left.

There are people all around the area, taking photos, pointing toward the sixth floor, a group is gathered out on the Grassy Knoll.

New carpeting, new shiny displays, but the wooden beams and big steel braces are the same.

You can touch them, lean against them, feel them.

It's family history, genealogy. We want to know where we came from.

It's not like going to see some World War I battlefield. It's now.

There are people alive now who know the truth, who were there. It's a cold, open case.

On the Lincoln School seventh grade history textbook timeline of world history it's still the same day.

It's mostly quiet in the museum because people are walking around with earphones, listening to the audio tour.

But it's also quiet from intensity, like folks are walking in to view the body of a close friend. When they actually get there it's perhaps more than they can handle.

I had meant to walk around in the neighborhood behind the depository where Oswald ran or walked to get away, but in the tour they say that he walked out the front door, took a bus, then a transfer, then a cab, then walked, to get home in the Oak Cliff neighborhood, change clothes, get his gun, then supposedly kill officer J.D. Tippit, then try to hide in the Texas Theater on Jefferson Boulevard, where he was captured by the Dallas police.

Mike points back over the trees to the double McDonald's arches in the distance and says that's where Kennedy was supposed to be going to speak at a luncheon at the Market Hall. He was just a few minutes from there. I ask why Oswald ran. Mike says he didn't run, he just went home, to get his gun. Tippit was supposed to kill him. Oswald was the patsy. Maybe he realized at that moment what was happening to him.

Oswald sounds calm on the earphones saying he didn't kill anybody.

You stand there, in the spot, and hear those words, and I can't see myself being that cool.

I get lost leaving the area as a matter of course – go along an overpass and find myself in Oak Cliff.

... This is where Oswald lived, where Tippit was shot, where the theatre is.

It's now a black neighborhood.

I'll bet it was white middle class back then.

I make a wrong turn and almost hit a white car.

The black woman screams and honks.

I mouth "sorry" and head back toward downtown.

Mike says that Tippit was supposed to kill Oswald the patsy and that Ruby had to be called in to clean up the job.

But who shot Tippit, then. And why?

I can't help but wonder what it would have been like to be Oswald at that time, to be boarding that bus, running, with all this happening around him, walking along a normal city street knowing his life would never be okay ever again.

Well, I go all the way through the downtown along Commerce, finally find Main Street and realize this is the motorcade route right here.

I'm on it.

And it will take me back to Dealey Plaza.

Here it is. I pass the spot at the curb where Mike stood in 1963.

Here I go, down the dip.

There is Mike on the Grassy Knoll with another group, pointing up to the Dal-Tex rooftop, where he says one of the shooters was, along with two behind the fence and one more on the sixth floor.

"Not Oswald." Mike has told me.

Mike has never left Dealey Plaza. He never will.

I'm exiting soon, with President John F. Kennedy still etched into my brain in flaky yellow chalk.

And then – boom – there I am, on the "X".

The knoll is right there. There's the overpass.

I turn right to take 35-E. In a few moments I pass Market Hall, where Kennedy was supposed to speak at a luncheon, then a few moments later the exit for Love Airfield, where the Kennedys landed just before noon that day. And where they left later in the day with the president's body in a box.

[Chapter 9] Jim: Princeton, "Smoke Gets in Your Eyes"

> "When the oppressors succeed with their illegal thefts and depredations, it's called colonialism. When their efforts to colonize indigenous peoples are met with resistance or anything but abject surrender, it's called war. When the colonized peoples attempt to resist their oppressions and defend themselves, we're called criminals."
>
> - Leonard Peltier, *My Life Is My Sundance*

JIM:

I was born in Huntington Memorial Hospital in Pasadena, California.

You can see the Rose Bowl from the hospital.

My father was a pretty average guy. He spent some time in the Army. He was a sergeant. He was in accounting, and when he got out he continued accounting. He'd gone to UCLA. He earned his degree, studying political science.

My mother had also gone to UCLA and believe it or not, I don't know what she majored in.

They got to know each other on North Hill Street in Pasadena because of the proximity of the families and how Eleanor's family had this club with the kids and Jerry and Johnny were in Los Aventureos and Bill joined, and Henry joined and Bill Scott; now Henry was about 5-10, 170 pounds.

He was a very normal, ordinary, affable guy. I don't know that there's any particular trait he had that was so extraordinary. He would later in life, after I'd gone to college, become exasperated with the younger kids, especially Tom, who drove him a bit up the wall.

And while we have funny stories, you know, in the family, about that, it really wasn't so much a part of his character as it was just circumstantial. Eleanor was very sociable, liked to play the piano.

The happiest I ever saw her was a social event at our home, 2379 El Empino Drive, in La Habra when there were lots of friends there and socializing.

She was having a drink and playing this little upright piano and smoking. I've never seen her happier in my life.

So, she's a woman who really depended on a social life but her second husband, Bill Scott, was the strong, silent type. He was probably 6-2 and close to 220 pounds and fairly muscular physique, but he really didn't care about people.

It was a mismatch.

I think because of his time in the Merchant Marines she saw him as a romantic figure, but after years of living with him in this rather isolated existence she came to believe that she had made a mistake.

And of course I've already talked about that.

Princeton was absolutely wonderful for me. It was all men. I believe that an all-male school is actually better for intellectual development because you don't have the distractions of co-education.

Just as I'm fairly convinced, based upon my experience in the Marine Corps, that integrating women into a combat situation is a terrible mistake. It's not that men are going to fight more fiercely, it's that they can be distracted by having women there and they're not going to have as much confidence in women one way or another and they're going to be distracted by sex and all that.

The idea of having women aboard ship in my opinion is completely catastrophic. You're going to have everybody chasing after pussy and nobody, you know, doing what they should be doing.

I think it's a calamity. Political correctness would have the idea that you should have women integrated into the military in all branches. I think actually it's really, completely, ridiculous, and I do not believe Princeton is the better for having been turned co-education.

When I was there it was all men.

My first semester, I took a mix of courses. I would pore through the catalogue and circle the courses that looked interesting to me. The overwhelming majority had to do with methodology and theory and conceptualization.

I realized more and more that the bulk of the courses I was interested in were in philosophy, but I also took other courses that dealt with conceptual and theoretical and methodological issues and other areas. By the end of my freshman year I already knew I intended to major in philosophy.

And indeed that stood me well. I didn't know it at the time, but I gravitated toward the philosophy of science; I wrote my undergraduate thesis for Carl G. Hempel, who it just happened was the leading philosopher of science in the world, not necessarily the most influential among natural scientists – Sir Karl Popper – or among social scientists – that role probably fell to Thomas Kuhn – but among professional philosophers, Hempel was the extraordinary, leading figure in the field.

And I wrote my undergraduate thesis for him and received The Dickenson Prize for the best essay in logic or theory of knowledge.

It was on the logical structure of explanations of human behavior. In other words, I'd given an analysis of the kinds of factors that needed to come together to explain human behavior, something I would eventually return to in my much later work.

In one of my last or most recently published books, *The Evolution of Intelligence*, in particular, I bring together a framework for understanding human behavior in terms of motives, beliefs, ethics, abilities and capabilities, and analyze behavior based upon biological consideration, distinguishing genetic from cultural, and so forth.

So in a way I came home to where I began, with that book, which probably was the best thing I ever wrote in its original carnation. I'll address that by and by.

Princeton at the time was rated number one in the world in physics, mathematics and philosophy, so I really had the benefit of a fantastic education. I was taking a Navy ROTC course each semester.

Princeton was on the semester system. That was part of the contract with the Navy, whereby I agreed to serve a minimum of four years as a commissioned officer in the Marine Corps or in the Navy in return for support for four years of college including tuition, books and fifty dollars a month. Doesn't sound like much, does it? Fifty dollars a month. But there it was. And for doing six weeks as a midshipman each summer.

So that last summer between high school and college, I was a delegate to the 14th World Convention on Christian Education from the Episcopal Diocese of Los Angeles.

My first cruise, between my freshman and sophomore year, was out of Norfolk, Virginia to Halifax, Nova Scotia.

My best friend from Princeton, a fellow named David Ziegler, and I were going to meet at his family home in Norfolk before we went on the cruise, and just before I was to head out there I received a notice – well, actually I think I showed up at the door – there was a note there for me to check with the neighbor.

I discovered to my utter dismay he'd been killed in an automobile crash. He'd been celebrating his sister's graduation from high school, and he'd been in a car with some others who'd been drinking, and they wrapped the car around a tree and David was killed.

It was a great loss for me personally.

He would have been by far my closest friend as an undergraduate. We had many, many common interests, common traits. He had a great sister, whom I drove back from New York, where the funeral was held, to Norfolk. And his father, who was a very stern man, had explained to me how he was entrusting me with her well-being, and that I should adhere to that.

I guess I did my best not to, but I wasn't very successful. She was quite enticing, but our relationship never really developed.

And when I set off on that cruise it was aboard a destroyer escort and I was learning about ships as a midshipman. I remember having a girlfriend by the name of Bobbi who – we kissed and kissed and kissed. I think actually our lips turned black and blue.

I went out there to Bermuda, though, I remember drinking. I really had never drunk in my life, actually. And as I recall I had a lot of scotch and soda, and then there was some drink that Pat – that was David Ziegler's sister's name, Pat Ziegler – that she liked; it was, I don't know, rum and coke. Anyway I switched to rum and coke and I remember, man, I just barfed my brains out after that. I remember going back to the ship from land and just sort of hanging over the side of the boat, barfing.

Anyway, that was my freshman cruise.

Sophomore year I took more philosophy, took physics, a year-long class in physics by a man named Eric Rogers, a very, very good physics class.

I actually had a lab in connection with that course and I conducted my own experiments with Galileo's inclined plane and all that, wonderful, wonderful stuff.

Something that had bothered me the whole time, I was studying this wonderful course in physics, was why we had these very elegant explanations about, say, Galileo's law of free-fall, distance equals one-half rate times time, and that distance fallen was equal to times squared, and what I didn't understand when I did the inclined plane experiments was why they were never quite in conformity with the law. And my lab instructor would explain, well that was due to friction.

But it seemed to me there was a problem there, because, well, this would become more and more obvious to me as I matured as a philosopher of science, but here you had the idealized examples of laws in the classroom, which really talked about what would be the case if certain conditions were to obtain, in other words using subjunctive or what are technically known as counter-factuals, when in fact they aren't the case, such as free-fall in a vacuum.

Well, if the world isn't a vacuum, then how does a law about free-fall in a vacuum help us to understand the world? And the fact is, it's a close approximation, it's what would happen under ideal circumstances, and if you can make a calculation, for example, for air resistance, then you're going to get an accurate prediction of what would occur.

But it would take me years to sort out that what was really going on was the difference between these idealizations that were being advanced in the classroom and the actual experiments that were taking place in the lab, which were inconsistent with them. One of the mistakes I made early on was when I decided what to keep from Princeton when I was packing up to go to the Marine Corps.

I remember debating over my workbook.

And I couldn't imagine what I'd ever do with it and I tossed it.

And ohhh, have I ever agonized over that decision because there were the experiments I actually performed.

I could have used them in innumerableways, as innumerable illustrations in articles on the philosophy of science, talking about the relationship between experiment and theory, and I didn't.

I mean, I let it go.

Anyhow, uh, my brother was also accepted to Princeton. He was a freshman when I was a senior. I was the Class of '62. He was the Class of '65.

Princeton had an eating club system where you went through a process called "bicker," where you'd be interviewed for whether or not you should become a member of an eating club. It was basically a social organization but one on the street by the name of Tower actually had an educational component. That drew me toward Tower.

So that I, in fact, I and my then closest friend Michael Bortman, bickered and were admitted into Tower.

I may be the first person who ever resigned from an eating club after his junior year, because another close friend of mine, by the name of Pete Tredick, was in charge of the common dining hall where all the freshman and sophomores ate at Princeton. And my brother was a waiter. So, you know, the eating club was expensive, comparatively speaking, and I resigned to join my friend Pete Tredick and my brother, Phil, in the common dining hall.

To the best of my knowledge I was the first person who ever did that.

But Tower was a good club, I mean, as clubs go. There was implicit elitism involved in the different rankings of the clubs. Ivy was the most highly rated or most elite and Cap and Gown was good, and Cannon and a couple others, but Tower was, if there were a dozen on the street, Tower was maybe number five, something like that, but it was a good club.

And I didn't resign from Tower because I didn't like Tower, I just resigned from Tower because I wanted to spend the time with my brother and friend in the common dining hall and save some money.

So it went.

In any case, on graduation my mom and dad, that was Henry and Marguerite, came out to Princeton and they saw me commissioned, and there are photographs of me being commissioned as a second lieutenant.

I received my degree magna cum laude, and of course, I'd received The Dickenson Prize.

Years later I would tell Marguerite what an impression she'd made upon me when I was in junior high and high school, and we used to talk about education and college and all that. She'd talk about figures who'd made a significant impact on American education, how she'd attended the University of Chicago; she used to talk about academic degrees and all that.

And I told her how, in Fox Chapel, a very exclusive area of Pittsburgh, where at the time my sister was living with her then husband, who was a vice president for Westinghouse, how much that had meant to me, what an impact. We were drinking margaritas while I was telling her how much it had meant to me and she just casually dismissed it and said, oh, that was just talk.

And I think this had to do with a kind of deep-seated resentment, for, you know, Eleanor taking her life, bringing Phil and me into their family – she'd just had Mark, her oldest, she was pregnant with Tom, and it just turned her and Henry's world upside-down, it seems to me.

They were great. They were really good for us, for me, for Phil. But I think it meant that her own kids, Mark, Tom, Julia, Hal, actually never received the amount of time and attention they would have had.

I mean, we were living in a little tiny house, 1800 Camden Avenue. It was a little Cape Cod. It had two bedrooms and a screened-in porch in the back. And I actually drew the blueprints to convert the screened-in porch in the back into a boys' room with built-in bunk beds and a shower and some bookcases and all that.

I'll never forget. There was a little shelf there, like a quarter circular shelf, by my head, and I had a little radio there and I used to listen to something called Lucky Logger Dance Time, and it had all this great music of the time, like Shaboom and Elvis and "Sincerely".

It really was that music that brought me out of a profound depression over my mother's death. I mean, it just brought me emotionally back to life. Marguerite used to refer to it as my Beer Hour, humorously, but it really made a huge difference to me, so that I advocate, for anyone who is in the state of profound emotional loss, that there's great merit, great wisdom in music.

I'll just never forget. "Smoke Gets In Your Eyes", just a host of those most wonderful songs that we still listen to today, I grew up with. I was listening to the originals, all that great stuff, wonderful.

Here's a little story I didn't mention. When I was in the third grade, I was playing in the jungle gym, and when I looked, there were a couple of little girls, ahead of me, and I could see their underpants.

It had nothing to do with sex, but they would squeal when I looked up at their underpants, so I thought that was kind of funny and I kind of moved around, but it was all completely innocent on my part.

Well, somebody complained about it.

One of the teachers took me off to meet the sixth grade teacher. The third grade teacher was a woman by the name of Stone, but she wasn't the fearsome teacher at this La Habra Heights school. It was this sixth grade teacher, her older sister, who really had a heavy reputation, and I had to report to her, and she asked me what I was doing, and I said something like, I was just playing, and she took me by the ear to the principal's office.

And I remember the secretary, who knew me and liked me, said something like, oh, Jimmy, something like that, ya know. They called my mother. She had to come all that way down and take me home. She never said a single word to me about it.

Never said a single word to me about it.

Another story, when I was growing up there I remember walking into the master bedroom and discovering Bill Scott was already in bed, but Eleanor was standing stark naked, and ya know, I saw her and of course she looked different than a little boy looks and I said, can I pat it? And she said yes, and I went over and just sort of patted her bush and I said, can I tell Phil, and she said yes, and so I got my brother, and I said, Phil, she doesn't have one! She doesn't have one! And you know, she was just wonderful. She was so calm. She was a good mother.

I told Mike Bortman, who would eventually become a screenwriter in Hollywood, that story, and while I've never seen the film, *The Good Mother*", for which he wrote the screenplay, I gather it had something to do with reversal of that situation.

When I once saw him out in Hollywood many, many years later, where my own son, Bret, came out to visit Hollywood to understand what the screen writing business was all about, I asked him about that story and he denied having remembered it, but, I'd be astonished if he didn't remember it.

But I think in Hollywood there's lots of concerns about copyright and authorship and all that. I wasn't interested in any of that, I just thought there had been a carry-over from the story I'd told him, which I believe to this day there was, but no matter.

In any case, after graduation I went through infantry officer training in Quantico. I'd elected to become an artillery officer, so I was sent for eleven weeks to Fort Sill in Lawton, Oklahoma for artillery training.

My first assignment as a second lieutenant would be as a fire direction officer with the Mortar Battery, 1st Battalion, 12th Marines, Third Marine Division, which was base-camped in Okinawa.

But I had two weeks home for R&R before I had to depart from Treasure Island in San Francisco. When I got back to South Pasadena I discovered a girl I dated when I was in high school, actually I'd gotten to know her at St. James Episcopal Church. I'd met her when I played this character in a play who eats raw eggs and leaps over sofas and all this. Her name was Dewey Evans and she was just very dear, very pretty, and I really liked her.

We wound up dating and kissing and all this really innocent stuff, and when I'd gone off to college, she'd actually switched over to South Pasadena High School, I believe, but she was only there for a year.

Her father was a chief engineer for a big heavy construction outfit. L.E. Dixon. He would be the project manager, and because he was so great with labor relations and all that, he would make the company millions by bringing projects in early, like the Chief Joseph Dam, I think it's on the Wenatchee River.

One time I think when I was in college I'd returned back to California; I think she was then living in Spokane, if it wasn't in Wenatchee, and I went to see her, and she was dumbfounded when I just sort of showed up at the door.

Well, when I went home for R&R, believe it or not, she was there, because she'd become involved with a young man that her parents didn't approve of because he belonged to some very extreme conservative religious church.

So, we started going out. We had a whirlwind romance and we eloped to Las Vegas. We flew from LAX to Las Vegas and were married in Fred White's Wedding Chapel, which really was a motel that all had been painted over white.

And we were back in L.A. and nobody even knew what had happened. But like the next day I had to fly to Okinawa. The problem here was I was a bit impetuous, impulsive, and I was smart enough that if I had a plan I knew how to execute it. I will never forget that when we got into the airport in L.A. it was playing "Baby Elephant Walk" and we got into Las Vegas it was playing "Baby Elephant Walk," which we both thought was some kind of sign.

In any case, I'd been on Okinawa, and her parents eventually discovered that we'd gotten married, and they flew her over as a wedding present.

By division regulations she could stay there for two months, but exactly one month after she arrived I was flapped out to cover the evacuation of American civilians in the aftermath of the Diem brothers' assassination, should it become necessary.

And I had written her a long letter before I embarked, telling her that I thought that it was too uncertain, too hazardous; that she should take our dog, Charlie, the only time that I ever had a dog, with her back to California and we'd get together then.

Otherwise we had been planning to meet, to rendezvous, in Hong Kong, which would have been terrific.

Well, I gave this letter to a sergeant who promised me he would deliver it.

I actually talked the communications officer into breaking radio silence and sending her a short note saying ignore my letter, let's wait and see.

So, it was off to sea, and you know, during the whole course of my thirteen months in the Far East we pulled training ops in Korea, which is a fairly god-forsaken place, and in the Philippines and Japan, and in fact when I first arrived, my unit was in Japan, so I actually joined up with the unit in Japan, and the C.O., Captain Hoch, sent me out to set up the fire coordinates, set up a live firing exercise. They went ahead and they used my coordinates.

I mean I had a very good fire direction team.

Anyway, here we were lobbing artillery shells off the base of the sacred mountain, and in the distance you could see pilgrims making their trek, and I turned to one of my fellow officers and said, "and who calls us Ugly Americans?"

So Dewey came out and was there for one month exactly before I was flapped out. We had a wonderful time. My executive officer fell in love with her. He thought she was the greatest thing since sliced bread. Robinson was his name.

In any case I was anchored out aboard the lph, landing platform helicopter, Iwo Jima, which was designed like a carrier, but it has a shallow draft because it's for helicopters, which take off and land vertically, so they don't need that long, stable horizontal runway of fixed-wing aircraft.

And we were anchored out in Kaohsiung Harbor, Formosa, when I was wakened by my then executive officer Fred Rentcshler, who was the officer of the deck, at three-thirty in the morning to tell me that JFK had been shot.

I remember standing on the deck the next morning for formation, but there really was virtually no talk about it.

I mean it was just something that happened. We were on the other side of the world. We had no idea what was going on there. And it wouldn't be until I returned to the United States that I began following up on this and reading a book by a fellow by the name of Josiah Thompson entitled *Six Seconds in Dallas*, which was appealing to me because he was at the time a philosophy professor at Haverford and he'd been in the UDT.

So, here I was, a student of philosophy and in the Marine Corps. When I came back to the states in June of '64 I was assigned as a series commander at the recruit depot in San Diego.

Now, a series commander has fifteen DI's and three hundred recruits under his command, taking them through the training cycle, which at that time was eleven weeks in duration.

So we had a setup where we could train eight thousand recruits every eleven weeks, and it was continuous with new cycles and all that.

The next year they would move me up to regimental headquarters and have me revise the training program. I was now a first lieutenant.

They had me revise the training so we could train eleven thousand recruits in eight weeks using the same facilities, and I was there to see it working in optimal efficiency.

So Dewey and I were there with our dog, Charlie, and we had our son, Bret, who turned out to be a marvelously talented young man.

When time came for Bret to decide where to go to school, to college, there was only one that we all agreed upon, and that was Reed, which was great for Bret because Reed was very tolerant of idiosyncratic kids and Bret was very idiosyncratic. He had a hard spell with Texas Tech, his mother ...

Well, while I was in the Marine Corps I'd given a lot of thought to how I wanted to spend the rest of my career, and the two professions that appealed to me were university teaching and becoming a lawyer.

And I reasoned that if I became a lawyer I would gravitate toward criminal law, I'd win a lot of cases and make a lot of money, but I wouldn't have a lot of time to spend it, and when I lost a case I'd feel that I had been the employee of my client and feel a great sense of remorse and guilt.

And I decided really that college teaching was a much, far better alternative for me. And I wound up following Hempel's advice and going to Indiana where I studied with his leading critic, a fellow by the name of Wesley Salmon. Now, when Dewey and I moved back ...

Oh, I've gotta add this personal comment, I bought my first car after I returned to San Diego. I got an Austin Healey 3000 XL. It was aqua-green, wire wheels, custom-made wooden steering wheel, lamb's wool interior, just a wonderful car. It was only a two-seater of course.

It had a little tiny jump seat, but that was of no real significance. When I was admitted to graduate school and had to return to begin school in the fall of 1966, I sold the car, I actually took a loss on it.

I think I bought it for $1600 and sold it for $1350. But, you know, if I'd driven it across country to Indiana, I could have done one or two spins around the campus and probably sold it for a song because everyone would have wanted to have it.

In any case, while I was in the Marine Corps, there in San Diego, I'd bought what was then known as a square-backed sedan through the grey market. In other words, there was a colonel who was dealing cars, buying automobiles in your own name and then they brought 'em in and they'd have them conformed to department of transportation requirements.

Well, for the square-backed sedan actually I think there wasn't any question about it. It was just fine. So we bought the square-back Volkswagen sedan and took that back to Indiana, I sold the Austin-Healey, with Bret.

We wound up, with Dewey's parents' help, buying a house on South Park Street. I was in Indiana, Bloomington, not that long ago and I remember driving by the house where we lived.

But, we weren't getting along as well, and we decided to get a divorce.

And I'll just never forget how difficult it was for me to tell Bret how his mother and I were going to divorce.

By the time we divorced actually I'd done two years and earned my masters degree in the history and the philosophy of science.

She stayed there in Bloomington and she was starting to date a fellow from Bogotá from a very wealthy family by the name of Alberto Cortes, and I thought it would be great for her to have Bloomington to herself. I took a faculty fellowship to Columbia University and spent a year at Columbia, studying with some of the best people around, I mean I had a seminar with Ernest Nagel who was world famous as a philosopher of science. I had a course with Sidney Morgenbesser, also a very famous guy. I had other courses, a guy named Sidorsky for a course in ethics, a course with Justice Buechler on signification; this had to do with Charles. S. Peirce's theory of signs, that was a very important course for me.

I used my courses at Columbia as my outside minor and came back the next year and finished my Ph.D., wrote my dissertation on the history, probability and explanation for Wesley Salmon and earned the degree.

Jim founded Scholars for 9/11 Truth on 15 December 2005 and invited Steve Jones, Ph.D., a professor of physics from BYU, to serve as co-chiar (at the suggestion of David Ray Griffin).

[Chapter 10] Kevin: “I got my Hush Puppies on”

> “If it is possible for someone to assassinate a President in broad daylight in a major American city, and then have the federal government fake the autopsy evidence and conceal the nature of the crime itself, then those who exercised that kind of power are emboldened to repeat performances of that kind over and over again. The American people are not unreasonable to suspect that that has happened to them many times by now.”
>
> -Paul Kuntzler

KEVIN:

[Left Madison, headed to San Francisco, in a ...]

In a 1955 Chevy half-sized school bus that was converted into a motor home.

With my then-girlfriend.

I’d been out of college for about a year, graduated with a B.A. in journalism.

Did a little freelance writing and poetry and singing in a punk rock band in Madison.

Paid 600 or 700 dollars for it, the bus.

She went and got a job. I stayed living in that vehicle through about 1986 or ‘87 – from about ‘81 to ‘86 or ‘87, then traded it off for a motor home, a ‘64 Dodge Travco.

[How do you park on the street all that time?]

It was easier in those days.

[Lost brakes three times, not great in San Francisco]

Used to park along the edges of Golden Gate Park, which was one of my favorite places. Lower Great Highway along Ocean Beach – favorite places, ‘82 or ‘83 – got interested in film making – was traveling – leave the vehicle in San Francisco and a friend would move it once a week.

Got enrolled in classes by this friend – in City College of San Francisco, in a filmmaking course. Also in French course and English Lit course.

Made some experimental films and spent time hanging around the San Francisco Art Institute, never enrolled because didn't have the money, appeared in friend's films, made my own, using a Super 8 camera.

Enrolled in City College in early '80s – in about '86 or '87 joined the masters program in English at San Francisco State University. Graduated from there in '91. Had been on career track to be English teacher at San Francisco State.

Won competition – funding ran out.

Had to be teaching assistant and still enrolled in a graduate program, and became French graduate assistant while teaching English at San Francisco State.

In 1993 graduated with French Masters, and then taught French and English and later Humanities.

[Spent a year in Seattle]

1984 and 1985.

Going door to door for The Nuclear Freeze campaign.

Not so much just to do that, but also had a friend who was a pretty good rock and roll guitar player from Madison who decided to move out to Seattle and wanted to start a band with me, so we wrote songs and did some more rock 'n roll while I was also working for The Nuclear Freeze and that lasted about a year.

This was just at the birth of Grunge.

The studio we practiced in was in a warehouse near Gas Works Park. Talk about grungy studios. I actually lived in there for a while. I parked my school bus near Gas Works Park and spent the nights sleeping in the studio.

I found that it was nice to have the electric light. There was a light bulb hanging down from the ceiling dangling by an electric wire. There was a rat that would sometimes come down from the ceiling. It would shimmy down the wire to the light bulb and then leap the rest of the way to the floor and when that happened the first time, during our practice, the drummer, who was female, just about jumped through the ceiling.

[Had not done graduate studies at that time]

I hadn't done any graduate studies at that point.

At that point I had just hung around City College making movies and learning French and reading English literature.

So then I left City College, went to Seattle for a year, and it was when I came back that I enrolled in San Francisco State in the graduate program.

[Return to San Francisco from Seattle, why?]

Well, I missed San Francisco.

I still kind of miss San Francisco. The weather is quite a bit nicer than Seattle. It's a bit of a paradise in some ways. Remember, I was parking these vehicles next to Golden Gate Park, which is one of the most beautiful urban parks in the world.

I've seen the parks of Paris, and Central Park in New York, and I don't think they're even close. So here I could have this incredible park as my backyard and pay no rent at all and virtually no utilities, just fill up my propane bottle every once in awhile.

I could also go park next to Ocean Beach, which is just gorgeous. I spent a couple of years there by the Lower Great Highway at the end of the N Judah Train, and I would be body surfing every day, even in the winter. If you go in the cold ocean every day you get used to it.

Which is why they wouldn't allow Alcatraz prisoners to take cold showers.

I kind of had a permanent crust of ocean salt on me.

It was a pretty nice life in a lot of ways for somebody who's young and wants to be free and spend time screwing around making movies and writing poetry and things like that.

[Trip to Paris]

That was in 1988-89.

My official reason for going to Paris was to write a paper on the French reception of science fiction writer Philip K. Dick.

So I got funded just enough to go over there and ... the funding was actually not quite enough to live on. It lasted for maybe half the time I was there and then I had to get a job.

I was teaching French-English translation and American Civilization at L'Institut International de Communications de Paris, and I was living in a small chambre de bonne, or maid's quarters on the seventh floor of a building pretty close to the Bastille.

[MICEFA Program]

It allowed you to just approach any professor in the whole University of Paris system and explain that you were an exchange student and you would like to take their course. I took courses on Bakhtin, and one with Helene Cixous, a feminist writer. And I also had enough time to explore Paris, so that was a fun year.

[Hoax d'Amerique]

I ended up working with some street kids from the south of France; they'd come to Paris, and they were rock and roll musicians playing in the metro for spare change.

And they had hoaxed the French media into believing that they had been discovered by a famous American film director of Australian origin named Christopher Maudson, and cast in his upcoming film called le Paris d'Amerique, which means "The Paris of America" but is also a pun meaning the wager on America. The whole thing was basically a wish fulfillment fantasy of French rockers making it big in the U.S. and in Hollywood, which of course never happened, never will. It's always the British rockers who make it big, the Beatles, the Stones, etc.

But the French public and the French media just ate this up because they wanted it to be true. And these guys had originally selected an Australian kid at the youth hostel to pretend to be the director and then this guy had to go home pretty quickly.

They saw that I looked sort of like him and had similar glasses so they picked me to continue the hoax. We made the lead story in the Paris edition of *The Express Magazine*, which is like the Time Magazine of France. It was quite an experience. We ended up kind of hoaxing the whole country for several months.

[Insight into fooling media]

Yeah, it was quite stunning to see.

My first interview was completely cold. I had run into these kids and given them my phone number. Several days later they just happened to call me and said I had an interview with The Express in a couple hours and so I should go meet them in the Metro. They were lucky they caught me at home. So I went down to the Metro train, knowing nothing about any of this. All I knew was I was supposed to be this director.

The singer tried to yell in my ear the stuff I was supposed to know during this interview as the train went to where the interview was, but I couldn't understand hardly any of it because he had this thick south of France accent, and the band was playing for spare change, loudly, and so I basically knew nothing at all.

I knew my name, Christopher Maudson.

I was originally from Australia and I had supposedly made this film with this band. That was all I knew. And they mentioned that Tom Waits and Willy DeVille were in the film.

We got to this huge rock and roll exposition in this huge warehouse type building. The whole French music industry had set up exhibitions in this place.

We went in there and I got mobbed by journalists and then taken off to a private area by the person from *The Express* and the photographer.

They posed me on a Harley and treated me like some kind of famous Hollywood director. I had to do a whole interview knowing nothing at all, virtually nothing. I didn't even know the name of the movie.

And so when they asked me the title of the film supposedly coming out in just a few months I said, well, I can't really talk about that because there's a dispute with the producers, and sort of pretended my French was a little worse than it was when I had to and somehow got through it. I just couldn't believe they would really be thinking I was a famous Hollywood director. A few weeks later we were the lead story in *The Express*. And I was supposedly a good friend of Francis Ford Coppola.

Yeah, it was obvious that the journalists really don't check their information very well, for the most part. They basically are in the business of telling stories.

And they tell the stories that will sell newspapers or eyeballs or whatever, and they tell the stories that the people are going to want to believe and that they want to believe. Nobody wants to tell a story that's going to make people feel really bad.

This story of a French rock band supposedly making it big in America and in Hollywood is something that all the French people really wanted to believe, because they have a national inferiority complex because they never had these kinds of bands that the British had.

Even the Germans and other countries do better than the French in the rock and roll world. You just tell them this story that fulfills their wish fantasy and boom, they just eat it up. They don't want to check. They don't want to know the truth.

And each of these journalists, when they would find out they were hoaxed,it didn't make them feel good to find out they were hoaxed, and so they would really rather just accept the story.

And likewise, I think, with something like 9/11 or JFK or these other big, ugly political hoaxes, it's so much more pleasant for people to buy into the official story and imagine that they and their country are the good guys, going out to righteously smite the evil enemy.

That is more appealing to people's emotions than facing the fact that they have been duped.

That they are idiots and dupes, and that the whole media is a bunch of idiots and dupes and genocidal liars, and that their whole country is an evil, genocidal empire that the world would probably be better off without.

These are pretty hideous recognitions that you pretty much have to face, if you face the truth about any of these things, and nobody wants to feel that way, so they would rather live with the pleasant lie than the ugly truth.

[Junkets to Mexico, Central America]

Well, I noticed that poor people in Central America and Mexico, for the most part, seemed happier than wealthy people in the U.S.

It's hard to say why, but it almost looked like, the further south you go, the happier people are. Maybe it's the weather, I don't know.

But also, I think that, there's ... I also felt kind of liberated in a way during these trips, living very simply, with whoever I was running into. Sometimes I would hang out with other foreign travelers, and occasionally stay with hosts in these countries.

Morris Berman – he's recently left the U.S. to live in Mexico, because he's just sick of the U.S., where nobody cares about you, where there's no community. He went to Mexico and found there is community. People care about each other. There are human values. His take is that people in the

U.S. have gotten very interested in things more than people, and in Mexico there's still a sense that people are at least as important as things.

And I can relate to that.

I've always felt there's kind of a weird coldness and reserve among North American white people, especially Midwestern Protestant types like I grew up around mostly.

And that people are warmer and more human and more emotionally honest and more interested in other people in southern countries, in Catholic and Islamic cultures. And so I kind of got a taste of that in traveling in Mexico and Central America.

[Logistics of those trips]

I flew to Mexico at least twice and once to Guatemala and I took the train to Mexico once.

The train trip was part of an Amtrak trip around the U.S. – pick three cities and back home for a pretty reasonable price – got off in New York and New Orleans, and from New Orleans I went to El Paso, Texas and crossed over to Ciudad Juarez and took the train from there in Mexico to Chihuahua, and from there took the Chihuahua Los Mochis railway through the Copper Canyon, which is one of the biggest canyons on earth, many times bigger and deeper than the Grand Canyon, actually kind of got lost for a while down in the Barranca de Cobre.

Plane trips – one to Puerto Vallarta, one to Mexico City, and then took buses around Mexico – Oaxaca – spent a bunch of time in Michoacan.

[Reason to go?]

I was just kind of curious. I had taken some Spanish in college and I enjoyed practicing and getting better at Spanish.

I remember during one of those trips I was hauling around a book of Borges stories and a Spanish dictionary. I think I went through there and asterisked just about every word I didn't know and wrote these definitions in the margins, so I had this fully annotated edition of a book of Borges stories, which I then lost on the beach in Oaxaca.

I was on the beach in Oaxaca and I had to get back to fly home the next day from Puerto Vallarta, which is a few hundred miles up the coast.

I went body surfing and left my bag on the beach and when I got out it was all gone, so I was missing my plane ticket, my bus ticket, my wallet, and my I.D., so I basically had nothing to get back, and I had to go two hundred miles the next morning and try to get on a plane after that, so that was a real test of talking your way through things.

The next morning I talked my way on to the bus. I told the bus driver what happened and he let me get on, and then I got back to Puerto Vallarta and somehow had to get my plane ticket replaced that day, so I went over to the, I think I had to go to the U.S. consulate and also some kind of Mexican government building, and I ended up with pieces of paper, including a replacement plane ticket, that were going to get me on, but then I had no money and I had to get across town to the airport, so I had to talk my way onto the bus and get a free bus ride again, which fortunately worked.

And I think this stuff is actually, I think this stuff is easier in Mexico.

So I'm all set now.

Except I discover I have to pay a thirty-dollar departure tax and I don't have a penny. I was carrying a whole bunch of ponchos that I had bought in the highlands of Michoacan.

I went around trying to peddle them – sold one – everybody else felt sorry and gave me change – so I was barely able to get the departure tax. Flew back to San Francisco and had to call a friend to get picked up. That was pretty interesting.

Makes you realize, money and I.D., these worthless pieces of paper and coins of no inherent value are very, very important, and if you try to go some place randomly where nobody knows you and you don't have any of that stuff, you're in trouble.

So I can kind of relate to how it must feel for a poor Mexican who sneaks across the border and is trying to get by in this country, where people are actually, in general, pretty friendly, but not nearly as friendly and helpful, to him, as these Mexican people were to me.

[With all your travels, does that leave you with a feeling of being fulfilled, to have done all that?]

Well, it is what it is. I have feelings both good and bad. I was pretty irresponsible in my relationships with women, prior to getting married, and I feel kind of bad about that.

And that kind of irresponsibility is one aspect of this lifestyle, of trying to be very free, but without commitments, responsibility, or a whole lot of moral seriousness.

So there are good and bad feelings about it, but ultimately it is what it is, and I'm very grateful that God led me through that to a better path.

["Dr. Weirde's Weirde Guide To San Francisco"]

That was based on an idea I had when I was in Paris, there were these books called *La Guide Noire, The Black Guides*, that were tour guides that showed where in Paris all sorts of interesting and bizarre things had happened, and I thought, you know, San Francisco would be a great place for a book sorta like that.

So I did my own version of the weird tour guide, which I believe was the first weird tour guide in America, and it has since been copied in a lot of places, for instance there is a big selling book here in Wisconsin called *Weird Wisconsin*, which is kind of a rip-off of my San Francisco guide, which was published in '94.

It's a tour guide with little maps and things and lots and lots of pictures, that takes you around San Francisco to the place where Allen Ginsburg took peyote buttons and had a vision of Moloch that inspired his poem *Howl*, to where the Grateful Dead lived, where Charles Manson and his family lived, where there have been UFO sightings, serial killers, ghosts.

Emperor Norton is really my favorite San Francisco character, so you can see where he lived.

Emperor Norton was a guy who lost all his money and became a bum on the street and then he started issuing his own currency. He found a printer who was willing to print up Emperor Norton bills in different denominations.

So he went around using his Emperor Norton currency and the whole city humored him, and gave him goods and services in return for his homemade currency with his face on it, and he quickly became a local character and he used to write and issue commands to the President of the United States and Queen Victoria and sign his official letters, "The Emperor of The United States and Protector of Mexico."

So this guy quickly became one of my heroes. He seemed to be parodying the currency system, which I always realized was a joke. This idea that these scraps of paper cause people to jump through hoops, this way?

It's hilarious if you think about it.

[That's a ton of work, putting all that together yourself.]

I designed everything, including the covers.

Took all of the contemporary photographs. Did the whole layout on PC. Drew all the maps in Corel Draw program.

It was a big project, looking back at it. It did very well, sold out two print runs in less than a year, and I quickly became kind of a local celebrity.

I got called up by the radio stations, TV stations and newspapers to do little interviews.

It was originally self-published, the first two editions. I was going to be leaving San Francisco to come back to Wisconsin to learn Arabic and get a Ph.D. and all of that so at that point I sold the book to Last Gasp.

[You had to really want to do it, to put all that work into it.]

I like sculpting words, playing around with words, in a creative way. I always have.

And I originally thought I would do that with journalism, sort of based on the Tom Wolfe, Hunter Thompson model.

There's not a huge market for that, so I went through life just sort of playing around with words and not really caring about selling the product, and then when I did this book, that was just at the point where we were going to have our first child, and I was married, and I'd actually been putting together the idea and collecting the material for some time before that.

But it was actually, partly, wow, I just got married, maybe I should try and sell something, some written product, instead of just scribbling bohemian poems, and here's a project that I know I can sell. I know this is going to be very successful.

So it's a matter of let's see if I can write and sell something.

[Converted to Islam, in 1993, after a train ride from San Francisco to New York, met Fatna in a café]

Transferred from Amtrak train to subway, with a friend, John Mensing, the same guy I went to see Mark Lane with, and headed over to Brooklyn, where we were going to be staying. We got off the L Train in Brooklyn, and there was the café. He said, hey, let's stop in the local café, so we did.

And then Fatna walked in to check the bulletin board.

She needed a job at that point. She had escaped from Disneyworld.

She was very disappointed and disillusioned that the Disney company had not really lived up to what they had advertised when they recruited her, which was they were going to continue her college education and it turned out that what that was, was Disney University, where they teach you how to smile and wear polyester and then when you "graduate" after six weeks they put mouse ears on your head.

Somehow she'd gotten the idea that while she was working at the Epcot Center in Florida she would also be attending a real American university, and it turned out not to be true.

So, she thought she would go back to Morocco, but before she went back to Morocco she wanted to see a little bit of America, so she went to New York, and suddenly she realized her money was low and she was going to have to get a job, so she went into the café to look at the bulletin board.

I heard her accent and tried French on her and it worked, so we started talking in French, and then I actually ran into her by chance, again, a couple of days later, and then I just kind of looked at her and I was captivated. I was actually captivated the first time, but I was too stupid to try to get her phone number.

[You were in New York for a week or so ...]

During that week I got to know Fatna and we spent a lot of time talking in the Path Train Station right below the World Trade Center Towers.

That was kind of a strange coincidence.

It was one of those situations, if I wanted to be with her I was going to have to marry her and be with her for life.

That possibility was kind of frightening and overwhelming, and so I got on the train and went back to San Francisco, and once I was back in San Francisco she stayed in contact, and it was about a month later that she flew out to San Francisco to marry me.

[Left San Francisco in '94]

I left San Francisco in summer of '94, enrolled at UW-Madison in the fall of '94 in the Ph.D. program in African languages and literature.

[To Morocco]

I received a Fulbright Grant to do dissertation research about the paranormal in Morocco.

I was interested in learning more about Islam.

That was one of the reasons I was studying Arabic in this Ph.D. program.

In particular, though, I noticed when I was visiting Fatna's parents and relatives before that – I think the first time we got there was '95, '96, a little after we were married we went back there – I was fascinated by some of the stories.

We call them personal experience narratives.

Classic example: here in the U.S. there are a lot of people with UFO contacts, or Bigfoot contacts for that matter, psychic experiences.

In Morocco there are similar stories, and they have somewhat different patterns of meaning; they tend to be more tied in with religion.

For instance, if you're kidnapped by strange beings here, it's going to take the form of UFOs. If you were kidnapped by the same strange beings in Morocco, it would probably be the Jinn, or you would interpret it as the Jinn, rather than aliens.

So I was interested in the stories I was hearing about these kinds of things, as well as miracle stories. One story told of somebody who fell off a very high cliff and just floated all the way down, cushioned by angels, completely unscratched. And saint stories are tied in with this.

In Moroccan Islam there is a tradition of people who were holy or extremely pious who were believed to be Awliya – which means literally friends or vice regents of God, kind of the equivalent of a saint in Christianity. These people are well-known for working all kinds of miracles.

I'm interested in this stuff because I recognize that, even though you don't want to believe every such story that you hear, there is some reality to some of it. The psi phenomena are very real.

I've known that since I started reading about these things in high school, when I encountered the Encyclopedia of Philosophy and its entries on psychic phenomena or ESP. You will find that the existence of psychic phenomena has been proven seven ways from Sunday. Since the 1950s, it was completely cut and dried.

What this means, if consciousness is in some sense not dependent on the material stratum, which I'm convinced is the case, what this means is that this very strong transformation of consciousness that happens when people die kind of makes waves in the ether or whatever.

Our consciousness is tied in with the consciousness of people who are close to us, and so when those people go through that very intense transformation, it impinges on our consciousness, directly.

It's really just a sort of a fundamentalist ideology to believe that everything is material. The reality is I think pretty clear, that actually consciousness is fundamental and material reality is just an epiphenomenon of consciousness.

And God then becomes sort of the ultimate source of consciousness, the ultimate dreamer that's dreaming all these dreams that we're participating in.

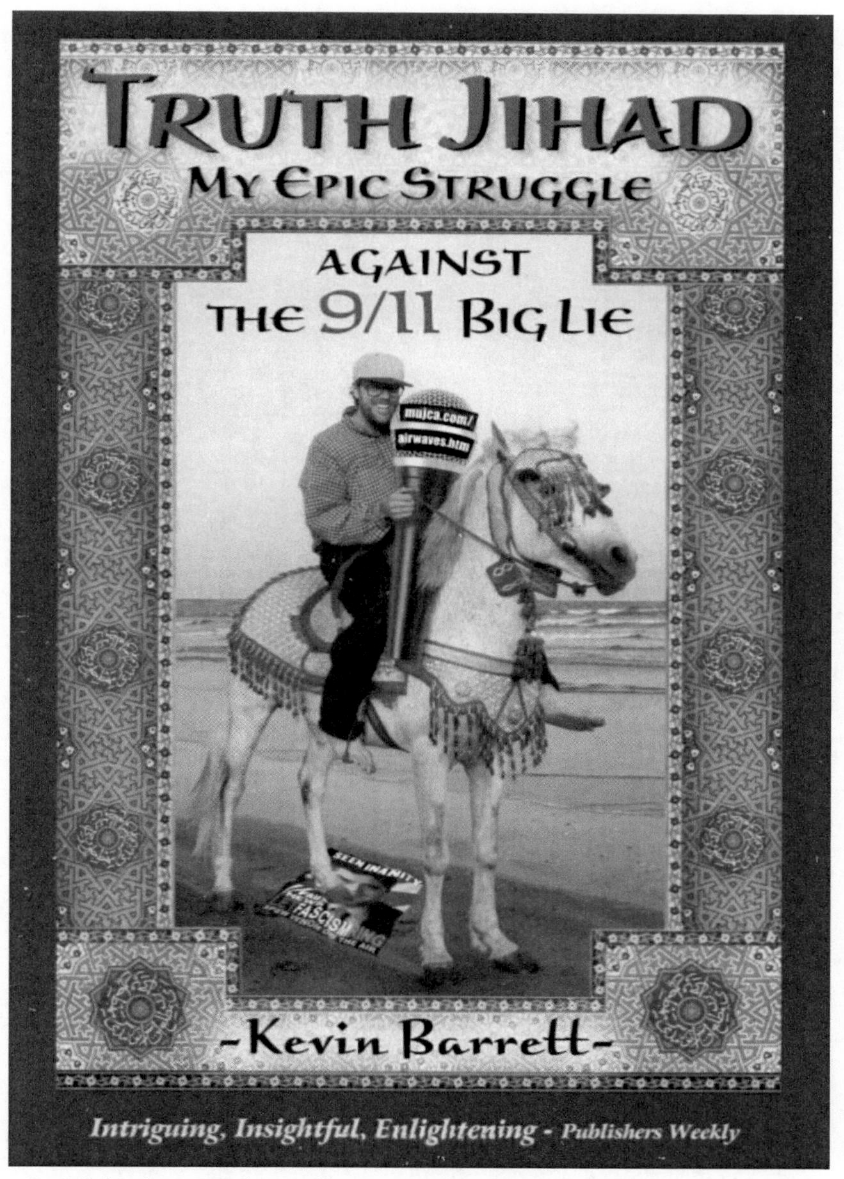

Kevin's book received virtually unanimous praise as a great read and highly informative.

BADGERHERALD

THE UNIVERSITY OF WISCONSIN'S INDEPENDENT STUDENT NEWSPAPER SINCE 1969

Unfair advantage
LSAT gives students with bad GPAs, school records better chance
OPINION, page 5

Flagpole sitting
Interview with Harvey Danger's Sean Nelson reveals new attitude
ARTSETC., page 6

Rocky road
Badgers seek 1st Big Ten victory against resurgent Indiana
SPORTS, page 12

FRIDAY, SEPTEMBER 29, 2006

/11 theorists to
iscuss 'folklore'

rett, Fetzer to voice views in presentation
analyzes attack incongruities of Sept. 11

Wisconsin State Journal

LOCAL

INSIDE: GREEN PARTY CANDIDATE ARRESTED AT SENSENBRENNER HEADQUARTERS

Barrett to talk on 9/11 belief

Barrett

Continued from Page B1

Controversial University of Wisconsin-Madison Islamic studies lecturer Kevin Barrett talks with reporters Friday outside his home in Lone Rock.

Teacher

Continued from Page A1

that he said would be required for anyone teaching at the UW. The questions included, "Do you believe that the Warren Report performed a thorough and unbiased investigation of the murder of JFK?" and "Do you believe that allegations of government involvement in the assassinations of Robert Kennedy, Martin Luther King Jr., Malcolm X, John Lennon, Mel Carnahan, and Paul Wellstone, and the attempted assassination of Ronald Reagan, have been conclusively disproven?"

Anyone answering no to a question could be dismissed, he said, and signed the letter "Steve Nass, Reichschancellor, Thoughtcrime Division, University of Wisconsin-Madison."

Nass is a Republican state representative from Whitewater who has called for Barrett's firing.

David Walsh, president of the Board of Regents at the University of Wisconsin, has characterized the issue as one of academic freedom and is not calling for Barrett's dismissal.

UW-Madison officials have said they are reviewing Barrett's plans for the class and will likely announce their decision on his hiring next week.

Kevin became a figure of local controversy for including a week on 9/11 in a course on the history of Islam, where he presented both the "official account" and a more disturbing alternative.

[Chapter 11] Kevin, Jim, 9/11, and other things

> "Our faith is that human beings only support violence and terror when they have been lied to. And when they learn the truth, as happened in the course of the Vietnam War, they will turn against the government."
>
> - Howard Zinn

KEVIN:

[First influences learning about 9/11 – Meyssan, Griffin, Ahmed ...]

I heard of Thierry Meyssan's study of the Pentagon early on, pretty much when it happened, which would have been four months after 9/11, or less even. I saw it. It was just a chain email. And at that point I wasn't really used to the Internet being used for research on these kinds of topics. My first reaction was this is some kind of crank or disinformation because it sounded too preposterous.

I was already suspicious about 9/11. I wasn't really suspecting that the whole thing would have been faked.

I couldn't imagine that they would bomb the Pentagon and then claim that a plane hit it or whatever they did. I assumed that there must have been actual hijackings of some kind, planes hitting buildings, and I hadn't really heard about the controlled demolition stuff right off, so I was pretty skeptical when I heard about Thierry Meyssan's work.

I was thinking more along the line of maybe Israelis infiltrating and steering an Al-Qaeda cell or something like that, with permission from the American higher-ups.

I think that actually was part of the scenario. But it was actually only when I heard about David Ray Griffin doing his research for *The New Pearl Harbor*," in late 2003, that I sat down and decided to seriously research what happened at the Pentagon and this issue of alleged controlled demolition.

I quickly saw that it was obvious there wasn't a big plane at the Pentagon and that these New York skyscrapers were taken down in controlled demolitions. So that was shocking to me because it just seemed like the media should have been a lot more alert.

It's hard to imagine that they could get away with something that preposterous and not have even a whisper of it in the corporate media.

So it was right around then, right at the end of 2003 that I became fully convinced that it was a complete fabrication. And then when Griffin's book came out a few months later that just confirmed everything I had learned from my own research.

[Influence of David Ray Griffin]

I was convinced to look seriously at it by hearing that David Ray Griffin was arguing that it looked like there was no big plane at the Pentagon and that the towers were demolished with explosives, so I wasn't ever really the first one out there.

I think it was my respect for David Ray Griffin, who I cited several times in my Ph.D. dissertation, that made me do that, so I wasn't one of these people who saw pictures or whatever and figured it out, and so I have no idea what that feels like.

Those people must be pretty independent thinkers.

[When he first become aware of Jim Fetzer]

Well, I heard a little bit about him, because I used to be interested in the JFK assassination question.

I read a lot about that from when I heard Mark Lane speak in high school and saw the Zapruder film.

I kind of drifted away from that after the film *JFK* came out in the early 1990s. I just took that as confirmation that I'd been right.

The film basically got the story right.

And the polls showed that more than two-thirds of the American people believed the CIA killed JFK.

So I kind of thought, okay, case closed, I was right, now everybody admits it, and let's move on and do something else because I don't think any justice is going to happen here.

I heard about Fetzer, he just sort of got involved at about the same time I bowed out. I still kept an eye on things in the JFK research community a little bit, and so I heard of his name, and then it was in '95 that I bought his book *Assassination Science*.

I actually found that at the university bookstore at a discount, so I snapped it up, and was very impressed, and I think I might have briefly looked at a little bit of his work online.

And then, it wasn't until, I think, 2004 or 2005 that I saw his work on the Wellstone assassination online. I saw his website which was then *Assassination Science*, and saw some of the work he was doing on 9/11 and was impressed.

And then in June 2006 I was co-organizer of the Chicago 9/11 Truth Conference, and part of my job was to invite various people, or to say who should be invited, put in my suggestions. I remember there was some controversy about Jim Fetzer, because he's a controversial guy and there are people who really don't like him, as well as a lot of people who really do respect his work. I think I remember saying I thought we should definitely invite him.

Gabriel Day, I believe, actually flew to Los Angeles to meet Jim. Gabriel was another organizer of the conference, and was favorably impressed, so I didn't have too much trouble convincing the committee to invite Jim to the Chicago conference.

And then he gave a great talk.

My first sight of him was his kind of gung-ho rant about 9/11 overthrowing the Constitution, and it was great. It was really very passionate and very eloquent, and so I was immediately captivated by that.

Wow, this guy is amazing!

And he scared the crap out of the writer for the academic magazine for college professors. The *Chronicle of Higher Education* journalist who saw Jim give this rip-roaring talk, calling out the Bush administration for treason and basically saying, we need to hang these guys right now, get some rope, this guy was terrified.

You could even sense his horror in the way he wrote up his article.

[http://chronicle.com/article/Professors-of-Paranoia-/9095, Professors of Paranoia]

But I was very favorably impressed by that so I got to meet Jim there.

And then it turned out, I got an email from Jim shortly later saying he was just in the process of moving to Madison from Duluth, because I think his daughter was in school in Madison and he was looking for a place to retire so they bought their house outside of Madison, in Oregon.

So I thought that was great, here's a very eminent, truth-seeking scholar who's coming down to live near me, so we got to know each other personally at that point and became friends and started doing events together. Shortly after that I got witch-hunted at the university, and suddenly I was all over the news, so some of the events I did Jim would also be speaking at. We did one at the University of Wisconsin-Milwaukee. And I think we've probably traveled around together to well over a dozen events at this point.

[Do you guys hang out?]

Yeah, I cross paths with Jim periodically, both at the local events and we have lunch once in a while together.

[*The Dynamic Duo*]

Well, that was how I got into radio.

I think it started with Jim asking me to guest-host his radio show. It was a pretty interesting show. This was on Republic Broadcasting Service.

The head of Republic Broadcasting is a guy called John Stadtmiller, who's pretty out-there. He's a co-founder of the Michigan militia, which is supposedly where the Oklahoma City bombers got their ideas. He deals precious metals, he's big into guns, he's a take back our Constitution by any means necessary kind of gung-ho character.

So, Jim had a show on Republic at that point and he invited me to guest host.

The guest had been pre-arranged, and it was John Kaminsky, who is a virulently anti-Jewish, former mainstream journalist. He was an early 9/11 Truther.

So I had a two-hour interview with Kaminsky and the first hour went pretty well, but a third of the way into the second hour I finally brought up this topic of well, John, some of the things you say about Jews are pretty extreme, and then he just started ranting about how Jews are the curse of the planet and responsible for all the ills of humanity and so on.

I argued with him for a while and he just got crazier and then during the commercial break John Stadtmiller came in and said, Kevin, I'm worried the ADL is going to come in after me, maybe you should just dump this guy, and so I did, and I just ranted myself for the rest of the show.

So that was a pretty strange introduction to being a radio host, but apparently it went pretty well and then the next thing I know John is offering me my own show.

So I had *Truth Jihad Radio* going on RBN, and then maybe a month after that, I think John fired Jim, because he figured out that Jim was a liberal.

And then Jim moved over to GCN, Genesis Communication Network, which is the network Alex Jones is on. It's based in Minneapolis.

And they offered Jim, I think it was a five-day a week show, and Jim didn't want to do the full five days and so he got me to do maybe two of them I think it was, and so now I ended up with two shows.

I kept the one on RBN and I also had the one on GCN with Jim, which was called *The Dynamic Duo*, and that name, I think Jim thought it up, or somebody did.

I wasn't all that crazy about it, but, hey, it was okay.

[David Ray Griffin on C-Span in Madison – big effect]

I think the original idea was one I came up with along with a fellow teacher at Edgewood College, who had known David Ray Griffin, they went to school together. At that time I was teaching at the University of Wisconsin and I was also co-teaching a class at Edgewood College of Madison.

A friend of mine, a Muslim, had said to him that, well, most of us Muslims think that 9/11 was an inside job, and this guy said, oh, that's ridiculous. And my friend told him well, there's a guy named David Ray Griffin, a pretty eminent professor who's written some pretty great stuff about it; here, you should read this book. And so the Edgewood professor said, wait a minute, David Ray Griffin, I know him; he was my classmate in college.

So he read the book and was pretty amazed. And so I talked to him about bringing David to Madison and finally he decided that would be fine. He was thinking of a smaller event, and I was hoping it would be somewhat bigger. I did almost all of the organizing, including running around the streets putting up a lot of posters. And then a week before the event

C-Span announced they were coming to Madison to broadcast it live and suddenly the media went crazy for it and covered it in the local media, and it became very successful.

It was attended by almost five hundred people, packing one of the biggest rooms on campus, and it was a terrific talk.

We had a bunch of people filming it with video cameras, along with the C-Span camera, but the problem was the light wasn't that great and the people weren't that professional, so the footage we ended up with was in many cases not the best. I ended up sending all the footage we had over to Ken Jenkins, who is a video guy, and he was able to rehabilitate it and stitch it together to make a pretty decent DVD out of.

But it was a big thing because at that time there hadn't been any successful really large 9/11 Truth events and there certainly hadn't been anything getting national TV coverage.

So it was kind of a landmark in the truth movement, sort of legitimizing it, especially because Griffin is so well-credentialed and doing such good work, and then getting it on C-Span I think woke up a lot of people.

[In your autobiography you said that the 9/11 issue offers "a rare opportunity for hope and change".]

I think it's kind of a long-term process. You always hope there's going to be some kind of quick awakening.

Everybody hopes that Jesus or the Mahdi will come back and everybody's consciousness will be transformed and people will wake up to reality and start treating the planet and each other decently and all of that.

There've always been these apocalyptic expectations of a new and better world as part of the whole Middle Eastern monotheistic tradition and the Western tradition.

So I bought into that a little bit, that we're heading into a very, very nightmarish, Orwellian world with the official story of 9/11 being enshrined and carved in stone.

If it could be radically and suddenly overthrown, especially back when it was still fresh in people's memories, I think the change in consciousness would be really profound, because 9/11 did affect human consciousness more powerfully than any event that ever happened on earth. The only remotely close correlations would be maybe the crucifixion or death or resurrection of Jesus or whatever it was. And I guess you could claim that the revelation coming to the Prophet Mohammed, peace upon him, would be up there, too.

But with 9/11, I think it hit a huge slice of the planet's population, which is so much bigger now than it was back then, much more quickly, so it gave this sort of jolt to the nervous system of the whole planet.

And more than half the people turned out to have gotten PTSD from it, since there was this very, very strong effect that basically jolted people's consciousness in the wrong direction towards a kind of primitive fear and hatred kind of mentality, very, very tribalistic. And of course having this happen in the U.S. where it was focused was worst of all, because the U.S. is already completely tribalistic. The U.S. is already doing most of the terrorism and the killing on the planet because it imagines itself to be the good guy.

So here's this event that makes people even more brutal and angry and fearful and aggressive and makes them feel justified in the atrocities that they're already committing on an off-the-charts scale.

It's like the worst possible thing that could ever happen to humanity.

You could even argue, the end of humanity.

If there's a God or alien overseers looking down on this planet and they see this happen, it's like you might as well finish it off and exterminate this species, this was a mistake to have a species like humans ever even come into existence.

So, given the absolute, extreme power for evil of this event, which I think was of course designed actually by people who are in the business of evil, religiously, literally, people who worship Satan and have black Masses and things like that.

That power for evil could be turned into a pretty strong or equally strong power for good if the truth were revealed. So it really did offer this incredible opportunity for changing people's consciousness, not just back to what it was pre-9/11, which was already in some ways getting better, as the average American person's consciousness was becoming less tribalistic and less murderous and full of fear and hatred.

But even beyond that, this could completely undo the entire American imperial mindset.

It could end the empire and get the U.S. to go back to being a normal country.

And since the invention of nuclear weapons it seems that war has been relegated from being a very central activity to being a more marginal activity, and so maybe this could lead to a world in which war continues to be further and further marginalized until it finally disappears.

So it could really make the difference between a completely failed species and a destroyed planet and a successful species and a living planet.

Because consciousness is really the basis of everything. Many people imagine that we're living in a world governed by purely material forces, in a kind of Newtonian materialist paradigm, but obviously human beings now are exerting tremendous physical force on the planet in so many ways, consuming a pretty sizeable fraction of all of the solar energy that's used by life on earth. A pretty big fraction of that is being harvested one way or another by human beings.

We've become sort of the gardeners of planet earth.

We run the place, and what we do to it determines how things grow in this garden.

It could end up being a scorched earth sort of place or it could end up being a really nice garden. Humans are no longer just one little part of nature. Humans have become the dominant influence on what used to be nature. So, given that and given that humans behave the way they do based on the kind of consciousness they have, then the issue of affecting human consciousness for good or ill becomes really the million dollar question.

And so that's why changing consciousness around 9/11, the event that influenced human consciousness the most of any event in all of history, is so crucially important, and so this is kind of an Archimedes lever. He said, give me a big enough lever and I can move the world, and this event had such leverage over human consciousness, especially in the most powerful country and the most powerful civilization, that it was available to be used, to try to change things for the better.

[Are we closer to that now, with recent, perhaps failed, attempts at false flags?]

Yeah, it seems to me that there's sort of an ecological arms race between the predators and the prey.

This happens with like foxes and rabbits where the rabbits get faster and smarter so the foxes get faster. Each side gets a little advantage to outsmart the other.

It's a classic loop that people study in the science of ecology. I think we have the same thing happening with these false flag manipulations.

It's getting harder and harder to control people and to keep their consciousness at a very low level.

All sorts of ways of changing your consciousness for the better are starting to sort of come online.

At the same time the traditional religions, which were a force for changing consciousness for the better, are declining, or even being exterminated, I think, by evil forces, so it's a very interesting and strange kind of time.

But it seems the wicked mind controllers, who can enslave the minds of the masses for the gain of the elite, are having a harder time controlling people now, because there's the spread of mass education, literacy, and improved communications.

So, they have to work harder to control people. Brzezinski has a really interesting quote where he said that it's now harder to control a million people than it is to kill them. Which is kind of frightening. It makes you wonder if they plan to start killing millions of people since they can't control them anymore. But in any case they're resorting to more and more extreme and desperate measures to control people.

And 9/11 being a classic example of an extreme and desperate measure.

And since then, it seems to me that the prey, that is, us, the people, are getting faster and smarter faster than the predator is getting faster and smarter. Looking at this series of false flags post-9/11, these various events that have been arranged to keep the so-called war on terror going and to keep people in a state of fear and mental enslavement, it seems that the people are ahead of the mind controllers.

The mind controllers are really not doing very well post-9/11.

They executed 9/11 well enough and it was so new.

Nobody'd ever gone to that length before, staged something that huge. They made plenty of mistakes.

It was easy to see through it.

It was just so big and so new that a lot of people didn't see through it until they'd been brainwashed.

But since then everything they've been doing, if you add it all up, it's not all that impressive.

They haven't been able to make bin Laden a very plausible villain. They haven't been able to show any real evidence that terrorism is any real threat at all, statistically, to people's health, to their lives. You're more likely to be hit by lightning or drown in your bathtub, or whatever.

And these false flag plots that they're coming up with are really pretty sad. Many of them are relatively small and pathetic, some guy who can't get Sterno lit in his shoe or his underwear. They're giving us these terrifying villains who are so stupid they don't even know that plastic explosives without a detonator are just like Sterno camping fuel, and these guys can't even get it lit to burn their own feet or their own crotches.

We're supposed to be terrified by these villains?

And the FBI has been working overtime trying to round up, to find retarded teenage Muslims that they can somehow convince to say something on tape that makes it sound like they are part of some FBI instigated terror plot.

It's just pathetic.

They're having a terrible time keeping their war on terror going, and this Boston bombing is just the latest example. This was supposed to be something big, spectacular, dominate the news for several news cycles, blame Muslims once again and just keep the whole war on terror concept going.

But the truth movement is way out ahead of them. This has been the biggest week ever for the truth movement with a greater fraction of the population suspecting and sharing this alternative information about the Boston bombing.

So I do think that the truth movement is moving faster and getting smarter than these false flag mind controllers, and that's a good sign. Maybe rather than saving the world all at once by instantly somehow having everybody wake up, I think it's probably going to be more of a slow, gradual awakening, in which ultimately the rulers are no longer able to do these things.

JIM:

[Do you think the jumpers were real?]

I think the jumpers were real. And I think this was done for psychological, emotional, effect, that there had been cases where, in previous fires, occupants of a building had been saved by going to the rooftop and removed by helicopter. The rooftops in this case were locked. That means they were all trapped there. There were little helicopters that you can only see in some footage that were circling there and appear to have been bombarding them with electro-wave radiation.

I mean, it takes something very frightening to cause a person to prefer to leap out of a 110-story building to remaining inside of it. And yet we have photographs of people who were tearing off their clothing to try to get away from whatever it was. I'm convinced this was a psyop aspect of 9/11, particularly horrifying, and that quite a few people, I mean this may even be several hundred, actually leapt to their death to avoid the fact that their skin was on fire. I mean, just think about it. If it hadn't been for that, what in the world would cause one to leap out of a building to their certain death.

I can't imagine.

[Why did Donald Rumsfeld even bother to make the announcement about the missing 2.3 trillion on Sept. 10, 2001?]

Well, it was brilliant.

Because he knew that something was going to intervene that was going to eradicate it from memory, so he gets it out there and it's wiped away and he waltzes into Congress the next day to ask for hundreds of billions more of defense spending, which he got.

[But, why announce it at all?]

Well, because it would eventually show up.

And what they did, they used the announcement to get all of the budget experts, financial analysts, accountants, into the west wing of the Pentagon, with all the documents and records for the missing money. And then they blew it up, killed 'em all and destroyed all the records.

So you were 2.3 trillion to the good by doing that. And that's a lot of motive.

I can just hear Rumsfeld saying to the section chief, "Now, I had to tell the public about this missing money, it's very embarrassing. I want you to get down there with all the records and all the people who know about this to get to the bottom of it."

When he was actually setting them up to be killed and the records destroyed. That's the degree of corruption we're dealing with here.

[What happened to the crews and the passengers?]

Well, they were phantom flights! None of the planes crashed! No passengers died on 9/11! There weren't even any hijackers on any of those planes! In fact, independent analysis has already shown the government had never been able to prove any of those hijackers were aboard any of those planes.

[But, the passengers, made up?]

Oh, yeah, it was a mix, people who were already dead, some fictitious names, it was a mix.

[Planes?]

There are those who insist they made some kind of substitution, some kind of military plane, a remotely controlled plane, but the fact of the matter is no real plane could have entered the south tower, for example, intersecting with eight different floors, consisting of steel trusses, connected at one end to the core columns and at the other to the external steel support columns, filled with four to eight inches of concrete. Each floor represented an acre of concrete.

And it's intersected with eight of them? If we use the average of six inches per floor times eight floors, that's 48 inches of concrete! I mean, that's massive.

We know what happens when a plane hits a tiny bird that weighs a few ounces in flight. It makes a hole in the fuselage. They have to land. You think this plane's going to intersect with eight floors of steel trusses and four to eight inches of concrete and not crumble? Its wings fall off, its body, seats and luggage fall to the ground, its tail break?

The engines might have penetrated the buildings.

The windows on those buildings were designed narrowly, because they didn't want to heat up the building to over-stress the air conditioning, so less than twenty-five percent of the facade was glass. So those who want to insist that well, it's because of all that glass ... I do believe, and this is really important, that in the beginning they wanted to use remotely controlled drones, but they found it wasn't physically possible. This is Newton's Law. This is elementary physics.

Here is the more important point. The plane would have exploded when it hit the building. They had to get the plane all the way inside the building before it exploded to create those massive fireballs and the false claim that the fire burned so hot, so intensely hot, that it caused the steel to weaken or melt and bring about the cascade of floor upon floor.

They had to do that. The only way they could get the plane all the way into the building without exploding was to fake it. The only way they could fake it and have people view what they thought was a real plane was the use of sophisticated holograms. And we now have substantiation that was how it was done.

Now, let me just add this. There are so many members of the 9/11 community that are just peeing their pants over the thought that we should tell the public that this was how it was done. In fact they don't even want to talk about the fact that we already know that none of the planes can have crashed. I mean, I already established that already.

But to explain that they used a form of fakery – frankly, I think the American public would be fascinated. We see Spiderman spinning his web from building to building, Superman flying... We see Iron Man performing all kinds of stunning and impossible feats. Why should we not benefit from realizing that Hollywood-style special effects were used to deceive and mislead us on 9/11?

I believe the American people would be fascinated to know that no plane crashed in Shanksville, no plane hit the Pentagon, and that what we thought we saw in New York was fabricated or faked.

The American people can understand that.

I can explain it to them.

I've explained it many times. But those who are controlling what you might call the mainstream within the 9/11 Truth movement won't allow it to be addressed.

Because they think politically it's going to make us look ridiculous. I say, if it's a truth movement then go for the truth, the whole truth, nothing but the truth. I won't compromise. I won't put politics ahead of science. I say, spell it out, what had to have been done.

There's a dozen ways to prove these claims I'm making, and I've proven it over and over again. But they underestimate, in my opinion, and insult the intelligence of the American public.

Why Doubt 9/11? | Flight Manifests | Who Are We? | Press Releases | Resources | Links | Contact Us | Get Involved! | Login | Search |

Scholars for 9/11 Truth

Exposing Falsehoods and Revealing Truths

Patriots Question 9/11

Home Beginner? Headlines Events Books Papers Articles Media Perspectives Foreign Perspectives New Postings

27 January 2006 - SCHOLARS REPUDIATE OFFICIAL VERSION OF 9/11

SCHOLARS REPUDIATE OFFICIAL VERSION OF 9/11

Claim government's account violates laws of physics and engineering

Duluth, MN (PRWEB) 27 January 2006 -- An influential group of prominent experts and scholars have joined together alleging that senior government officials have covered up crucial facts about what really happened on 9/11. The members of this new non-partisan association, "Scholars for 9/11 Truth" (S9/11T), are convinced their research proves the current administration has been dishonest with the nation about events in New York and Washington, D.C.

These experts contend that books and articles by members and associates have established that the World Trade Center was almost certainly brought down by controlled demolitions and that the available relevant evidence casts grave doubt on the official story about the attack on the Pentagon. They believe that the government not only permitted 9/11 to occur but may even have orchestrated these events to facilitate its political agenda.

The society includes U.S. and international faculty and students of history, science, military affairs, psychology, and even philosophy. According to its spokesmen, S9/11T represents a concerted effort to uphold the standards of truth and justice and to strengthen democracy in this nation, which has taken a terrible hit in the aftermath of 9/11, when "everything changed." Its function is to bring scientific rigor to the study of 9/11 phenomena.

The members of this group are dedicated to exposing falsehoods and to revealing truths behind 9/11, "letting the chips fall where they may." The evidence has become sufficiently strong that they are speaking out. They are actively devoting themselves to reporting the results of their research to the public by means of lectures, articles, and other venues.

Scholars maintained a web site, sponsored conferences, promoted lectures, published articles and distributed videos.
(See 911scholars.org.)

NATION

Teacher's 9/11 views irk lawmakers

Legislators want U. of Wisconsin to fire instructor of class on Islam

Kevin's efforts to present objective differences about the atrocities of 9/11 led to the non-renewal of his contract with UW-Madison.

[Chapter 12] James Manns: Jim Fetzer is ...

> "How many people do you have to kill before you qualify to be described as a mass murderer and a war criminal? One hundred thousand? More than enough, I would have thought. Therefore it is just that Bush and Blair be arraigned before the International Criminal Court of Justice. ...
> "The United States supported and in many cases engendered every right wing military dictatorship in the world after the end of the Second World War. I refer to Indonesia, Greece, Uruguay, Brazil, Paraguay, Haiti, Turkey, the Phillipines, Guatamala, El Salvador, and of course, Chile. The crimes of the United States have been systematic, constant, vicious, remorseless, but very few people have actually talked about them.
> "You have to hand it to America. It has exercised a quite clinical manipulation of power worldwide while masquerading as a force of universal good. It's a brilliant, even witty, highly successful act of hypnosis."
> - Harold Pinter, Nobel Prize for Literature Lecture, Dec. 7, 2005

James Manns on Jim Fetzer

Basically Jim Fetzer is just like any other person, only more so. We all reason; we all feel. We rejoice, we laugh; we regret, we reject. All of us have our preferences and our peeves. These basic elements of human being have simply been painted more vividly – practically in Day-Glo colors – onto Jim's character.

I came to know Jim when we were colleagues at the University of Kentucky Philosophy Department.

That was my first and only academic appointment; for Jim it was the first of many. We got along well, then and thereafter, apparently because – and I venture this after many years of retrospection – we both had sufficient self-respect to feel no personal threat emerging from the other (though as the following pages will suggest, Jim certainly constituted potentially the more threatening figure).

Whatever space Jim happened to be occupying, he filled to the bursting point. When he was amused, everyone on our floor knew it – we heard it; we felt it; his laughter shook the walls!

The same could be said of his anger, or his excitement. To speak of his excitability, he could present a paper to an audience of philosophers on a subject as seemingly dry and arcane as, say, a probabilistic causal calculus. Are you already starting to feel a twinge of passion surge within you at the mention of a probabilistic causal calculus?

I didn't think so.

But by the time Jim approached the conclusion of his presentation, he would no longer be reading, but roaring – his face would be red, his forehead moist. He would hammer at the lectern every so often for emphasis. Somehow, as if by miracle, a sentence like "an object X is a formula of L if, and only if, X belongs to every set S which contains every sentence letter and also contains ..." seemed to become poetic, pulled by its speaker from a thick soup of emotion.

Were those famous lines of Gerard Manley Hopkins to be read aloud by the poet himself:

> ... sheer plod makes plough down sillon
> Shine, and blue-bleak embers, ah my dear,
> Fall, gall themselves, and gash gold-vermilion.

They would likely come across as far drier and more analytic than a whole string of Fetzer's "if and only if"s!

The radical dichotomy between reason and emotion enunciated by the Logical Positivists, refuted by the generation of critics that followed them, then reinstated by la nouvelle vague of armchair neurologists with their right brain-left brain dogma, in fact holds true for none of us – but this fact is nowhere more colorfully apparent than in the person of Jim Fetzer: he is a paragon of reason emotionalized, or emotion rationalized.

Teacher – Student

That fragment of a quote above, incidentally, forms part of the explanation of the fork – or as it was known around the department, the Fetzer Fork. Technically I believe it was an attempt to work the phenomenon of causality into a logical symbolic system that had long been grounded in "mere" truth-functionality (adding to the basic "if X is true, Y is true; X is true: therefore Y is true" a certain causal efficacy in the move from X to Y). I stand correctable on this, of course (I taught Philosophy of Art). Visually, it consisted in a recumbent horseshoe (open to the left, the typical logical symbol for the "if ... then" relationship), with a horizontal line piercing its right flank.

What is more, I don't know if the symbolism ever "caught on" in the broader realm of the Philosophy of Science, i.e., came to be adopted in a variety of texts. Probably not – old habits are hard to break away from. I mention it here to provide a bit of background, in order to bring out a very different point, one having nothing to do with logical vs. ontological symbolism, but everything to do with personal realities.

Jim trotted out this symbolic innovation in the last Philosophy of Science class he was to teach at our university. Again, it would appear that we were drawing our breath in a very rarefied, abstract atmosphere here – hardly the stuff of intense emotions.

And yet as a parting gift from students to professor, a "thanks for the memories" token of their deep esteem and affection, the class presented Jim with ... a branding iron ... in the shape of a Fetzer Fork!! Truly a unique gift in the Halls of Academia! (I suppose being in Lexington, KY – The Heart of the Bluegrass, an agrarian region that rightly thought of itself as the thoroughbred racing capital of the world – brought such a gift within the realm of the reasonable. Blacksmiths were not difficult to come by there.)

Apparently – reportedly (I never attended one of Jim's classes) – the same fire, enthusiasm, and raw power with which he would deliver an academic discourse characterized his classroom presentations, as well. And students appreciate that. Most students arrive in a class with a "Well, let's see what this is all about?" attitude, and when they confront a professor who burns with enthusiasm over what he is professing, the first conclusion they draw is "Whatever it is, it must be something important!"

Given the powerful intellect which Jim never exactly hid behind a bush, the obvious inference is that a mind this strong would not get this worked up over something trivial.

So he managed to gain, and was able to sustain, their attention, and ultimately capture their devotion. That is step one in the teaching process – maybe even step one-and-a-half.

It seems that a special bond grew between teacher and student where Jim was the teacher. Students aren't learning machines, they're people; and when any presentation of abstruse material (for Jim never took on simple-minded issues) is coated with emotional fervor, their own emotions can be summoned forth. It is at the level of emotions that bonds are formed.

Jim cared about more than the material he was discussing – he cared about his students, and he cared that they should absorb this material and be better people for it. Caring – caring, that is, about something and someone other than oneself – is perhaps the most laudatory quality a person can possess and exhibit. (You need both, of course: exhibiting it without possessing it is known as hypocrisy, while possessing it without being able to exhibit it, well, that's the first step down the road to misery.)

So in Jim Fetzer we had someone who cared deeply about the ideas he was expressing, cared deeply about the students with whose education he was entrusted, and this care was heartily reciprocated.

In our school, we had long had a "distinguished professor" award that was awarded each year to a faculty member for the kinds of things we were told we should be doing, which meant teaching well (or at least not objectionably), but which also stirred publication record into the mix, maybe even university service.

The voting body called upon to award this honor was ... other faculty. Who could better know what one of us should be doing than ... the rest of us. Kind of like the Academy Awards, in the end: Hollywood congratulating Hollywood. Well, a moment came when the students themselves decided this wasn't the fairest way to decide what professor should be lauded, so a group of them got together, organized their own distinguished professor survey, collected and counted the ballots themselves – even bought a little plaque to present to the winner.

And the initial winner of this award was James Fetzer.

Indeed it almost appeared (from the outside, looking in) as if the idea of such an award crystallized in the minds of a number of students around Jim, who then set out to reward in some way the efforts he put forward on their behalf.

That is to say, the passion behind the creation of such an award was the very passion Jim imparted to and shared with his students.

The award lingered a bit longer – in fact the winner the year after was also one of us from the Philosophy Department.

Then I don't remember hearing anything further about it (and I was around for another 25 years). It was born in passion; but students move on, and the passion manifested in one year may well not be passed on to the next class, especially when the object of their initial passion is told he should move on.

That is to say, such a cooling of student enthusiasm may well have followed from the sorry fact that Jim was not to be around for the years to come, either. Indeed it is likely that there was a general disillusionment over the fact that the expression of approval of students toward a faculty member had little or no (or perhaps even a negative!) effect on decisions made by the faculty as to who among themselves should stay and who should be let go. I can't get inside the minds of others to see what they really are thinking, what really motivates their actions.

In fact I have come, over these many years, to see that most people have little idea why they do what they do. But it is not at all outside of the realm of possibility that a strong show of support on the part of the students should have been just what was needed to nudge certain faculty members over a psychological edge, and take steps to see that Jim was sent packing.

I do recall how he reacted to news of his selection as if that was the last critical piece of evidence he needed in his bid for tenure. Could it have in fact been the last nail in his coffin?

Loyalty

Among the various human traits that Jim has always possessed to an exaggerated degree is loyalty, and this was very evident – again perhaps to his ultimate undoing – in his relationship with students.

When someone moved from being just one of his students to being one of his students, they entered a special domain of protectedness. A student who for one reason or another came under Jim's wing had found a safe haven. (This is true of more than just students, it bears mentioning – anyone who has done anything to win Jim Fetzer's loyalty has won it for life, and can never doubt of it. t the moment, though, I speak of his relationship with his students.)

Two incidents stand out to me as illustrative both of this special, protective relationship and of how it worked to Jim's "professional" detriment. Of one, the underlying causes are a bit hazy to me now (and I think they were then, too), but they involved questions raised about the fitness of certain of our Logic TAs.

Jim was at the time the overseer of our Introductory Logic classes that were taught by teaching assistants, and perhaps one of our faculty had been trying to find out about someone's performance without going through appropriate channels, i.e., without asking Jim straightforwardly about him.

This produced an enormous explosion in one of our department meetings – perhaps the first I had witnessed, which made it seem all the more explosive (and let's remember who I am writing about here – Jim's explosions were, and probably still are, like no one else's, on the Richter scale).

But the Logic TAs fell within his domain, which meant that they qualified for fight-to-the-death protection. Which they received. Whatever the question was that had been raised, it was quickly dropped and never brought up again. But a mark had been made, and it wasn't a happy one. It seemed to raise in some people's minds the question as to whether our department was big enough to contain this larger-than-life person, capable of these larger-than-life emotional outbursts.

A second telling incident came during the oral examination of one of our students who was defending his master's thesis. Jim had directed the thesis, so naturally it had his fingerprints all over it.

But this was someone with whom he had worked closely for a year or so, hence someone who qualified for full protection under the-law-as-Fetzer-saw-it.

What that meant, it turned out, was that any question posed to the student, however anodyne it may have been, was perceived as a challenge, and as any good father would (I see my own father springing to my defense on various occasions during my life, as I write this), Jim rose up to parry that challenge. And what that meant was that he wound up speaking at considerably greater length than the examinee.

When a moment came where one of the examiners said, showing a bit of persistence, "I'd sort of like to hear the candidate answer the question," another of those Richter-scale explosions occurred. A protectiveness which knew no bounds, in this instance ought to have. I'm sure the candidate could have and would have liked to give his answer, but in fact I forget whether he did; all I still remember is the shaking of the wall during the temblor.

The aftermath of this incident was as surprising to me as the outburst itself. Let us be amused – after many decades have shouldered their way between then and now, and many successes have dimmed unpleasant memories to their vanishing point – that Jim called me at home later that evening, and somewhat hesitatingly, diffidently (the calm that followed the storm), but in complete and humble sincerity asked me "Was I a bit too forceful this afternoon?" A bit too forceful?! Joshua was merely pussyfooting around when he fit that battle and made the walls of Jericho come atumblin' down! I don't recall what I said (whatever it was, it wasn't what I just now said), but this isn't about me.

So allow this account of my own astonishment at the question give indication of the way anyone would have reacted to such a question, at such a time. "He has no idea who he is, what he does, and what effect he can have on people," was the conclusion I came away with following the incident.

The Artist Known as Fetzer

In his book *What is Art?* Leo Tolstoy exemplifies the artistic process not by citing any experiences of his own or of his fellow novelists, but by imagining a boy who had been frightened by a wolf, and who proceeds to relate the experience to fellow townfolk.

In so doing, the boy relives the experience, drawing out of himself the same fears he felt at the time, and eliciting from his listeners similar fears, until through his description all present are aquiver with fright.

This is Tolstoy's model: feel an emotion, recreate that feeling in oneself, communicate (impart) that same feeling to an audience. When teaching this particular (and peculiar) approach to art, the most convincing example I could come up with, hence one that I used in class, was that of Jim Fetzer relating an anecdote.

The anecdote that stood out in my mind involved driving some stranger's Lincoln Continental across country from NY to LA. Imagine – someone posted an ad on a bulletin board at Princeton, looking for someone to drive his car across country for him (while he took the plane), thinking that Princeton would be a good place to find a responsible, conscientious volunteer for the task! And this misguided notion led the gentleman to Jim Fetzer!

The critical sequence in the journey took place somewhere in the Rockies, at night – Jim driving and two other companions resting in the back seat.

At a given point he took it upon himself to pass a truck by sneaking past it on the shoulder of the road, a move which the truck driver seemed not to take favorably to, not yielding his place one bit, and funneling the Fetzer-driven Continental ever closer to a cliff ahead that that formed the terminus of the shoulder. Slow down? Back off? Return to a proper lane in the highway?

Hardly the Fetzer way!

Flooring the accelerator, he raced the truck, both of them at full throttle, and succeeded in ducking in front of the cliff just before obliterating the car, himself, and his two companions against the rocky outcropping. I heard this tale recounted one Thanksgiving evening, about forty years ago. It still stands out so vividly in my mind because of the manner it which it was delivered. One could positively feel the thrill of the challenge, hear the roaring of the engines, see the tires of the Continental spewing gravel behind them, and stare right into the ashen faces of the two companions, stunned deep into silence, as Dostoevsky must have been when his blindfold was removed and he was informed that the execution that supposedly was to have followed was only a charade.

Note: We get two for the price of one in this anecdote – a glimpse into the impulsive, impassioned, literally death-defying personality of the young Jim Fetzer, and a look at how emotions swirl inside him and make their way out, sometimes in very creative ways.

The Character of our Character

I don't believe Jim has a conniving or devious bone in his body. That may well have been a contributing reason behind the difficulties he encountered in gaining tenure within our department. Most generally, he seemed to believe that all one need do to achieve a desired end is present the simple truth of any matter, in terms as clear as possible to the relevant audience, and, being clear-minded rational beings, they will apprehend this simple truth for what it is, and act accordingly. Tch tch; how naive!

Is he still the same in this regard? I can't say, having been separate from his milieu of operation these many years. His primary non-academic interest – to bring to light as much of the truth as possible concerning the assassination of JFK (which involved, as well, casting as much doubt as possible on spurious accounts of that terrible event) – might well have shown him that revealing the truth concerning certain matters is a far trickier business than, well, simply revealing the truth.

When even Rachel Maddow, an intelligent, progressive voice, nonetheless speaks of Lee Harvey Oswald as "the man who killed JFK", (not "one of the men", and certainly not "the patsy offered in place of the men"), we might expect a Fetzer to give out a loud sigh, and retreat in discouragement.

And yet his pursuit of and inquiry into other "suspicious incidents", from the plane crash that took the life of Paul Wellstone to the 9/11 cataclysm itself, shows him to be undaunted in his pursuit of truth, however unhappy or even dangerous the consequences of such an effort might be.

And I say "dangerous" because in taking on the sinister forces behind the Kennedy assassination, who knows when one might reach into a crevice somewhere and latch onto a rattlesnake?

His pursuit of the Wellstone "tragedy" put him squarely and unequivocally in antagonistic opposition to the FBI – an institution it is much more desirable to count on as one's ally.

The challenges he raised concerning the official accounts of the 9/11 cataclysm aim straight at the highest levels of government, and if he should be correct in his allegations, they aim at individuals to whom killing comes naturally.

So in effect, he has never let up seeking traction on the gravelly shoulder of that Colorado highway.

The moral of this brief consideration might be that the years have not led him to make any significant adjustments in his approach to public relations, even though in later years he went on to reach an increasingly large public – one much larger than the confines of a classroom.

Indeed, the last time I saw Jim, he arrived at our house, had a quick drink to unwind a bit from his travels, then went and parked next to our telephone in order to participate in a three-hour discussion of the 9/11 event on a Canadian radio station.

So there, at least, I could listen first hand to the same take-no-prisoners approach to revealing unpleasant truths that I had always been acquainted with.

The Showdown

Only too soon the question of Jim's promotion and tenure arrived. For the benefit of any non-academic readers, I should describe briefly what tenure involves. Faculty are in a manner of speaking "on trial" for the first six years of their career. If they prove themselves over that time to be able teachers, researchers, and university citizens, they can expect to receive tenure, which makes their subsequent dismissal extremely difficult (except for, say, high crimes and misdemeanors).

Those granted tenure can thereafter speak their minds freely, be themselves. People who have chosen to pursue an academic career seem to prefer such security, and the freedoms that come with it, over money, which their education level would surely enable them to earn in other fields of endeavor.

Jim's attitude toward gaining tenure was simple – and naive. He believed that if one accomplishes what he is told he ought to accomplish, then, regardless of whatever else he has done – e.g., embarrass or perhaps even frighten certain colleagues, behave at times in a manner deemed by some to be indecorous, exhibit an overabundance of self-confidence – he will be duly rewarded for it.

And indeed we were always told we should strive to teach our classes effectively, write publishable papers and represent the university well at regional and national conferences, and serve the university in its internal operation when called upon to do so. These have always been the "do's" of gaining tenure.

But there are certain "don'ts" as well – they simply are never formalized in any evaluative checklist.

And high on the list of these "don'ts" is "Don't show up your colleagues, especially in a public venue."

I remember a talk he gave once where in the question and answer period that followed, the line of questioning that was pursued by another professor in our department succeeded in eliciting a testy response from Jim which terminated with a sweep of the hand – as if to erase from the realm of being everything his interlocutor had said – and a stern directive: "Go read your Hempel!"

Well, maybe later on the fellow did go read his Hempel, but he also absorbed a slight that may well have festered within him and poisoned his attitude toward this boisterous colleague. (Funny how, forty years later, I can still see that dismissive gesture and hear that condescending phrase. There's only one other person in the world who might – not Jim, for sure, but the recipient of it.)

Now in our department, it was the tenured faculty alone were empowered to vote, and there wasn't one of them who hadn't at one time or another either felt the sting of one of Jim's upbraidings, or at least witnessed it close enough at hand to fear the possibility of himself being stung at some point. The vote went against Jim.

Prof. Read-your-Hempel did "support" Jim, but wrote a letter on his behalf (a letter that would forever form part of his file on campus) that said, in effect, "I'm casting a vote in the affirmative, but now I'm going to enumerate all the reasons that I shouldn't be doing so." With allies like that, who needs enemies?

Was the matter of tenure thereby settled? Does Jim Fetzer sound like someone willing to "go gently into that good night"? Of course not – "Rage, rage" was the inevitable reaction.

An appeal of the verdict was lodged, a hearing held (I believe the first and maybe the last such hearing ever held in that university), an adjudicatory committee formed, representatives of both sides (in effect, the prosecution and the defense) appointed, witnesses called – and a broader range of witnesses this time than in the simple tenure vote, which involved just a handful of guys (yes, nothing but guys).

This time the untenured faculty as well as the tenured were called upon to give testimony. That made for a ticklish situation for two of us (there were three of us untenured faculty in the department at that time, but the third had the circumspection to be on leave in Europe that year, so only I and another fellow enjoyed the pleasure of cutting our own throats for a nobler cause).

Actually, in the year that intervened between the negative verdict and the committee hearings, I had come up for tenure myself. From "internal sources" I learned that I had been granted tenure, but no formal announcement of it was made. The reasons behind that were clear: (a) the "established powers" wanted to coerce me, out of my own self-interest, to soften what testimony I might give, or perhaps even tilt it in their direction, lest I be at the center of such a hearing the next year – my own! And (b) Jim simply had a stronger dossier than I did, so it would have looked doubly suspicious that I was being tenured while he wasn't. The ploy didn't work. I said what I had to say.

The other untenured colleague who was called upon to testify was in a worse position than I, as his review was to come up the next year. And also, he was a good bit more Fetzer-like than I, made a very strong statement, apparently with a lot of finger pointing and admonishing, and knew at the end of the day that so far as our department was concerned, he was dead in the water. Somehow he managed, straightaway, to secure a position at another university, where he went on to enjoy a long and successful career.

In any case, by the end of the hearing the truth had come out clearly, the evidence of Jim's competence was overwhelming, and the prejudices among the tenured faculty were laid bare for anyone to see who was willing to look.

So naturally the verdict was negative.

The hearing proved to be a marvelous piece of administrative theater and nothing more.

There is an aphorism I once heard, and which has clung to me ever since, to wit: First-rate people hire first-rate people, and second-rate people hire third-rate people. The case of Jim Fetzer tragically illustrates what can happen when this principle is breached, and second-rate people, to their ultimate discomfort, hire someone first-rate.

After Words

In the years that followed Jim's departure, we remained in loose contact. For some time immediately after, I would each year find myself supplying another letter of recommendation for Jim, as he bounced from one-year appointment to one-year appointment.

In each letter I would explain to the best of my ability why this extremely talented, accomplished individual was turned away by our department. At times prospective employers would even call to receive a fuller account of the situation. Skepticism generally prevailed.

Undaunted, ever confident in his ability, Jim soldiered on, and at last some university had the courage to offer him a real contract – one that didn't have a return trip ticket stapled to the bottom of it.

And the rest, as they say, is history.

I laud the good people of Minnesota-Duluth for taking a chance on a risky commodity.

In the end, they proved to be the big winners.

Google
James
Saturday, May 21st, 7:00-8:50 am PST * 10:00-11:50 am EST * 14:00-15:50 GMT
The Fabricated Global War on Terrorism
Speakers: Jim Fetzer, Michael Springmann, Gearóid Ó Colmáin

Jim Fetzer spoke on, "How we know ISIS was 'Made in the USA'", at the Left Forum on 22 May 2016.

[Chapter 13] John Mensing: What I remember is that Kevin ...

> "On television the voices of dissent can't be counted upon to match the studio drapes or serve as tasteful lead-ins to the advertisements for Pantene Pro-V and the U.S. Marine Corps. What we now know as the "news media" serve at the pleasure of the corporate sponsor, their purpose not to tell truth to the powerful but to transmit lies to the powerless."
>
> \- Lewis Lapham

John Mensing on Kevin Barrett

What I remember from High School is that Kevin was one of the brightest kids in our class. I remember being in sort of informal competition with him for having the highest GPA – they posted the top students in the class on board as you came in to the school, and sometimes his name would be on top, and sometimes mine. Whether or not he was aware of this I don't know.

I had a friend who lived down the road from him – Greg Welch – whom I was closer with than Kevin.

I went over occasionally to Kevin's house, and knew his parents and his brother Bruce and his sister Tara. He had a very nice house, on the lake, and his family was relatively more affluent than mine; although children are not as aware of these things, they make some kind of impression.

Kevin was more athletic and popular at school than I was.

I was involved in a lot of extracurricular activities, drama, the school newspaper, the debate club, etc., and so kept myself pretty busy. I had three friends, Greg, Tom, and Chris, that I mostly hung out with. Kevin would join with us sometimes, and sometimes I would go independently to visit Kevin.

I liked him, I guess, because he was intelligent, and sociable, and into reading similar things (like the *Bugle American*, the Milwaukee underground newspaper). Of course we had some of the same classes as well; Pewaukee was a very small school relatively, about 500 students.

The summer of my junior year in High School, I went away to St. Cloud State College (now University) for a Summer Institute in the Experimental Analysis of Behavior, a National Science Foundation sponsored program which brought together high school students from around the country for six weeks of intensive college-type classes. Most of these programs were in the hard sciences, but this was one of the few in the behavioral sciences, and even then it was a very hard, Skinnerian, approach. Nevertheless, the faculty was excellent and it was a really good opportunity for a kid from a small town and cultural backwater to be exposed to the larger world.

Two of the members of that group, Mike London (who's now a film producer in Hollywood) and Gilbert (can't remember his last name) came and visited me after that summer program was over and before school started, and together with Kevin we hitchhiked over to The Farm, which was near Lacrosse, and an offshoot of the commune that Steven Gaskill started (I think in Ohio?). So that was a taste of commune life (albeit for a few days).

I think all of us were kind of enamored of the hippie lifestyle, although we were born too late, on the cusp really, of that social movement/counter-culture lifestyle alternative.

I think Kevin split off after that, while I continued on up to Minneapolis to stay for awhile with Mike's family. I think we had an interesting time at the commune, and it kind of de-romanticized that lifestyle option for us.

For me, anyway. It wasn't a bad visit, and I didn't come away with a negative view of it, but certain limitations in that lifestyle were made manifest by being there in person.

As to Mark Lane, I do remember going there, and being somewhat impressed with the whole thing.

For me, living in essentially a cow pasture, a visit to the city at that age, and going to a movie theatre and hearing a slide show and a lecture, was quite an event. Separate from the content. As to the content, I remember seeing the Zapruder film and being fairly convinced that there was more than one gunman, and that Oswald was probably led into the whole thing quite unwittingly, and that there were dark, sinister, but unspecified forces at work.

I remember hearing that Kennedy had been assassinated, but I was quite young, and the meaning of it didn't really register in the profound way it might have for someone older and more politically aware.

And, perhaps consistent with my later involvements, I didn't see too much relevance there. I have a kind of local bias to my political activism. As to how we got to be there, I think it was at the impetus of Mark Euslin, who organized it – ask Kevin and see if he remembers the same.

When you speak of the evolution of political consciousness in a specific era, reference points are hard to pin down, and it can sometimes be misleading to look at national markers.

What I would identify as my own would be books, like *The Greening of America*, *Growing up Absurd*, *Silent Spring*, *Diet for a Small Planet*, *Looking Back: A Chronicle of Growing up Old in the Sixties*, *The Electric Kool-Aid Acid Test*, and *One Flew Over the Cuckoo's Nest*.

The television program Laugh-In was quite influential, and I watched it religiously, as were The *National Lampoon Radio Hour* and the comedy of *The Firesign Theatre* and George Carlin.

As to the rest of High School – I skipped out of my senior year there at PHS to go to a college accelerated program in Philadelphia. My parents got divorced and I had to quit that program after one semester, and ended up at Marquette University, which admitted me into the journalism college without a high school diploma.

I didn't like Marquette much, and wanted to go to Madison, where Kevin and Greg were and which seemed like more fun.

But the dean there, George Reedy, took a liking to me and arranged for me to get a full scholarship to Marquette from the Milwaukee Journal corporation, and so I was "stuck" (the way I felt at the time) going to Marquette.

In retrospect, and with a broader perspective, it was a kind of lucky break, but it didn't feel that way at the time.

So, I kinda kept in touch with Kevin through the college years, getting together during the holidays sometimes, and was aware that he was out in San Francisco, and doing some kind of organizing trip, living in a school bus, kind of doing the hippie thing, I thought.

Wasn't much for California myself.

Not long after college, I got a job as an Editorial Assistant at Rawson, Wade, working for Jim Wade, George Reedy's editor. They went out of business six months later, but eventually I got another job at Crown Publishers, but left them to work at Shocken, a smaller press more devoted to Anarchist and Scholarly titles.

They eventually got bought out too, and I worked for a year at CARE, and then decided I'd had enough of working in offices, and moved into an abandoned building on the Lower East Side with the thought of starting some kind of social protest housing movement.

I'd been doing some freelance organizing of radical types, writing leaflets and doing demonstrations, some connected with the homelessness issue, which Bob Hayes was also working on. We started this adverse possession movement with about a half dozen of these types, and it quickly mushroomed to several hundred and got itself named "the squatters movement" (a name I didn't much like).

Back to Kevin.

During the winter break between my two semesters at Emory, I went back to Pewaukee, and saw Kevin, also home on break. I persuaded him to accompany me back to NYC. We hung out there for a few days, staying at my old apartment, which my roommate now occupied by herself, and where I still had many of my things.

In the course of hanging out, we visited a new café – I think it was the L café – that had just opened up near the L stop in Williamsburg.

The neighborhood was on the cusp of skyrocket gentrification, but I think I didn't really realize that yet. I've always been a café guy – Billy Sleaze (aka Billy White) and I hung out in Life Café on 10th and B almost every day for about two years running – and chatted up whoever was in there when I was.

A young woman from Morocco, Fatna Bellouchi happened to be in there and in the course of our conversation I guess I asked her out to a movie – anyway, we ended up seeing Tous Les Matin Du Monde (All the

Mornings in the World) together. She kept in touch with Kevin, though, and eventually ended up on his doorstep in S.F. and as I think you know they have two children together.

While I have never had any reason to leave the Lutheran tradition I was raised in, ecumenically appreciating other faiths is axiomatic. Seeing the truth in one tradition helps one to see the truth in another. While I have not had the privilege of studying the faith of the prophet Mohammad, nor known the joy of reading the Koran in Arabic, I truly believe it to be a very sublime religion for those who know it intimately.

Many cultural traditions discourage some Muslims from mingling with those of other faith practices (esp. Buddhists), but I think efforts like Kevin's, along with the inexorable march of post-modernity, may lead to greater tolerance and perhaps fewer restrictions.

Well, when I was going for my Ph.D. at the University in Sri Lanka (in the field of Buddhist Studies) I started corresponding with Kevin again, mostly about politics, and a bit about religion. I think the details of those conversations, or rather, exchanges of e-mails, are lost, as I was on Yahoo at the time.

Also, I visited Kevin a few years back, with my two children, but the visit was not eventful in any way I think would be of interest to your task here.

You asked about my political beliefs or views vis-à-vis Kevin. As a former citizen arson prevention specialist, I recognized the World Trade Center as a potential target for arson. Back when Hugh Carey built it, it was largely regarded as an inane folly, a white elephant, and as near as I've been able to determine, the place never made money – it always lost money, and had high vacancy rates.

After that Van-Bomb, I wouldn't have doubted there was some structural damage that put the place at medium-term risk.

In any event, with building codes being what they were, the place was probably full of asbestos and what-have-you.

Fixing it up would be a losing proposition added on top of an already losing proposition.

Mind you, I liked the place – they had a great $11.99 brunch deal up on the roof there, at the Windows on the World. But can you imagine how much it would have cost to tear down, if all the environmental codes were adhered to? So it seemed a prime target for arson-for-profit.

As to specific policy issues, Kevin and I might be in broad agreement.

I am sympathetic to Iran, for example, and think the way the country and its leaders have gotten treated in the U.S. has been shameful.

I saw reasons to admire their past president, and admit I haven't followed the election results so can't comment on that situation now. I would have hoped that the US intelligensia, as well as perhaps the State Dept. and whoever else was concerned in the government, would have focused on those reasons to admire him. There is so much to admire, and love, and honor in Persian culture.

I applaud Kevin for encouraging rapprochement with Iran, but fear he may be romanticizing the virtues and handicapping the vices. I guess to me, if you're doing organizing, you don't talk big, and you don't talk shit. (We used to joke about knowing the difference between monkey shit, horse shit, elephant shit, etc., when differentiating political rhetoric.) You organize and you get things done, you seek out actionable change. (Right now I'm helping to organize a Burning Man festival in Korea that I feel sorta passionate about.)

But there's nothing, I feel, wrong, per se, with what Kevin is doing. (And I confess that I'm not all that up on what he is doing.)

It may be helpful, and it may be good, to spread the word in the way he is doing. Organizing has many facets, and consciousness building is one of them.

And if he is able to make a living from that, so much the better. I hope in the future I can get back in touch with him, and catch up on what he's been up to, and how he's been feeling about it.

'Neoconservatives take over US academic institutions'

Home / US / Interviews — Mon Feb 8, 2016 7:17PM

"Unfortunately today, these neoconservatives whose philosophy is that intellectuals should be in the service of tyrants who rule using big lies and mass murder," said Kevin Barrett, who has a Ph.D in Arab and Islamic studies.

Neoconservative Zionists have taken over US academic institutions and are promoting Islamophobia while pushing out professors who are sympathetic towards Islam and Muslims, an American scholar says.

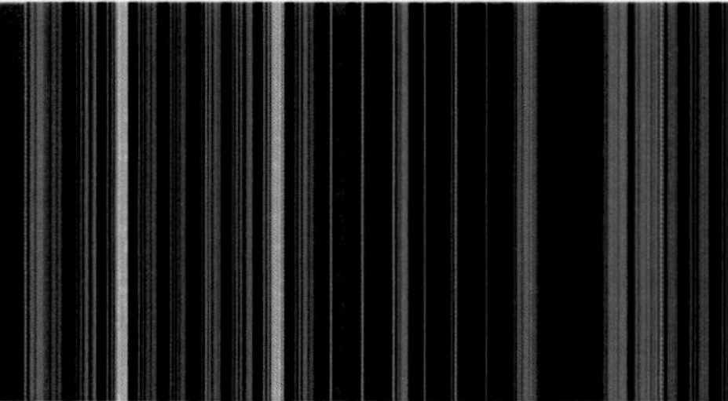

It wasn't a School Massacre.
It was a FEMA Drill.
EVERYONE MUST CHECK IN
Proof it was a drill was right before our eyes:
* the sign, "Everyone must check in!"
* boxes of bottled water & pizza cartons
* Port-a-Potties present from scratch
* many wearing name tags on lanyards
* parents bringing children to the scene
Proof it wasn't a massacre was also there:
* no surge of EMTs in to the building
* no Med-Evac helicopter was called
* no string of ambulances to the school
* no evacuation of 469 other students
* no bodies placed on the triage tarps

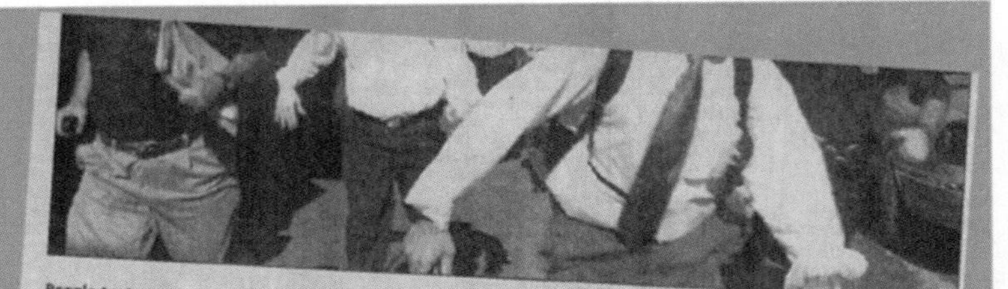

People try to escape as the first of the World Trade Center towers collapses on Sept. 11, 2001.

SUZANNE PLUNKETT – Associated Press archives

GUEST COLUMN

Academic freedom, combined with 9/11 research, is good policy

By KEVIN BARRETT

In the former Soviet Union, the monopoly media acted as cheerleader for a brutal, repressive government. Dissident academics were silenced, fired, or institutionalized.

For two or three years after 9/11, our media served as a megaphone for Bush administration lies, and academics were intimidated into silence. Every Middle East Studies colleague I know understood from the start that Iraq could not possibly threaten the United States with WMDs even if it had them, which it almost certainly did not, and that the Iraqi people would resist a U.S. invasion with every ounce of their strength. The only way Cheney's criminal war of aggression could be sold was by terrorizing the American people with 9/11 and the anthrax attacks, lying about a nonexistent WMD threat to take advantage of the people's fear. . . and intimidating scholarly experts into silence.

Barrett

What if professors had exercised their academic freedom back in 2002 and 2003 and spoken the truth: "The Bush administration is obviously lying about the WMD threat, and invading Iraq would not only be strategically stupid, but also the biggest war crime since Hitler invaded Poland?" We would not be trapped in a hopeless quagmire, and 600,000 Iraqis and thousands of Americans would still be alive.

If, in 2002, a professor had used his academic freedom to speak the truth and help stop the Iraq war before it started, he would have "morphed from teacher into advocate, promoting himself and his view nationwide."

That is what the Wisconsin State Journal accuses me of doing when I explain the results of my research, and express my private political views about the facts and meaning of the 9/11 atrocities, to the media.

Thousands of professors carry on controversial research with political implications and discuss their research, and their views, with the media. UW history professor Alfred McCoy has researched the massive CIA drug dealing that has continued since Vietnam, and the standard, horrific CIA practice of torturing people. He expresses his own views about the inappropriateness of these activities in media interviews and public speaking engagements.

Professors Peter Dale Scott of the University of California, James Fetzer of the University of Minnesota, and many others have researched the JFK assassination and shown that it was an inside job by elements of our own military-industrial-intelligence complex—as the majority of the American people has understood since at least 1990. They report on their research and express their views in books, articles, media interviews, and speaking engagements. Nobody has ever tried to fire them or silence them.

Currently Scholars for 9/11 Truth (st911.org) has over 80 Ph.D. members with university affiliations, many of whom are conducting research on 9/11 and reporting their findings to the public.

Like thousands of other American academics, I will continue to conduct research in my fields of interest, report my findings to the public, and act as a public policy advocate in my areas of expertise. The fact that neither Rep. Steve Nass, R-Whitewater, nor even one of the more than 2,000 professors at UW-Madison dares to debate me about 9/11 suggests that my research and conclusions are sound. The excuse that my position is marginal no longer holds, given that only 16 percent of the American people believe the government is telling the truth about 9/11 (New York Times poll) and 36 percent of Americans, and half of New Yorkers, believe top US officials conspired to commit mass murder and high treason on 9/11 (Scripps-Howard and Zogby polls).

Public policy on questions of war and peace, preserving the Constitution, and related issues will be better served by free and robust debate than by fear-mongering and censorship.

It is long past time for a rational, evidence-based debate on the facts and meaning of 9/11. Any takers?

Barrett is a part-time lecturer at UW-Madison.

11/26/2006
The Capital Times

[Chapter 14] More voices

"You will understand me when I say that my Middle High German was my life. It was all I cared about. I was a scholar, a specialist. Then, suddenly, I was plunged into all the new activity, as the university was drawn into the new situation; meetings, conferences, interviews, ceremonies, and, above all, papers to be filled out, reports, bibliographies, lists, questionnaires. And on top of that were the demands in the community, the things in which one had to, was 'expected to' participate that had not been there or had not been important before. It was all rigmarole, of course, but it consumed all one's energies, coming on top of the work one really wanted to do. You can see how easy it was, then, not to think about fundamental things. One had no time."

- Milton Mayer, 1955,
They Thought They Were Free: The Germans 1933-45

The wayfarer,
Perceiving the pathway to truth,
Was struck with astonishment.
It was thickly grown with weeds.
"Ha," he said,
"I see that no one has passed here
In a long time."
Later he saw that each weed was a singular knife.
"Well," he mumbled at last,
"Doubtless there are other roads."

- Stephen Crane

"What is true of the journalist holds true for the journalist's audience. They do not want a reporter who knows there was a conspiracy and explains it to them. Rather, the typical citizen is much more content to have a journalist who believes there was a conspiracy, but at the same time indicates there is doubt, room for debate, and thus one is not in a position to draw any firm conclusions and there is nothing to be done. The 'powers that be' can count on the fact that the more important the person or institution which commits a crime and the more serious the crime in regard to the system, the more central will be the threat of knowledge of the truth to the ordinary citizen, the more the psychological interest in uncertainty and confusion."

- Martin Schotz, *History Will Not Absolve Us*

"The American people have been called, by numbers of people all over the world, as being the most dumb-downed population in Western Civilization. Certainly they are probably among the least, politically and other ways, sophisticated people in western culture.

"That's no accident.

"And it's no testimony to the lack of intelligence and potential of the citizens of this republic.

"It is a testimony to the control of thinking and the flow of information that people are allowed to have. [...] the effects of the media and the thought control that has been developed in this country is extraordinary, and it's very difficult to overcome. [...] one wonders how long it's going to take for the uprising to occur.

"And I actually think we may be reaching a point, where we're entering a pre-revolutionary stage."

- William Pepper, March 30, 2011, *Truth Jihad Radio*,
hosted by Kevin Barrett

"These two [King-RFK] political assassinations have determined the course of history like no other in our lifetime, indeed perhaps in the history of this republic of ours, they have determined and shaped what has happened and where we are today.

And where we are today in terms of the consolidation of the control of media and information, in terms of the militarization of the police in local towns, cities, across the country, in terms of the disparity between the wealthy, severely wealthy, and the poor people in our country, and in terms of the failing infrastructure and the breakdown of Democracy in America.

All of that has placed us in a worse situation than we were back in 1968 when these two potentially great leaders were alive.

[...] The question is how long will they be able to cover this up. Will they be covered up for all of history? That's really what the goal is. It's really what it is, isn't it?

[...] People today are so busy with their own jobs and try to survive and make a living because of the very dire economic situation that we're in [...] the other reason that people don't want to look at it [available evidence] is that it will shatter their own sense of who they are, which is tied to a government, which is tied to an idea of a nation, and if they ever really understood the degree of evil that sometimes abounds with this government, it would shatter them, and I don't think very often want to be confronted by something like that, particularly when they know and believe there is nothing they can do to change it. [...] nevertheless we have an obligation to our children and grandchildren and to history to try to lay out what has happened and what government has done and what government will continue to do if they can go on unassaulted and unaccused by committing these kinds of crimes."

"[...] you know, the last journalist to whom I spoke from mainstream media about this case had been visited the week before by Gov. Averill Harriman, who came at the request of the President of the United States and that journalist was the publisher, the managing editor of *Look Magazine*, [Bill Atwood] [...] he said you will be pleased perhaps and also saddened to know I had a visit last week [...] and he said, Governor Harriman came at the request of the President [...] he said he wished me well, from the President, and then he asked me to do a favor, and that favor was, never to publish anything, ever, that Bill Pepper wrote.

And he said, what do you think of that?

And I was quite, I guess, thirty years old, a young guy, young journalist, no real credentials in the field, and here the President of the United States doesn't want us to publish.

I said, I'm more interested in what you told him [...] and he said, well, I told him that we're going to meet with you and if I believe what you had to say, we were going to publish. [...] that was an era, 1967, that was a time, when the media wasn't fully controlled and wrapped-up, and Len, do you know how many major anchors and people whom I know, with whom I'm friends, said to me, Bill, we just can't touch this, it's not worth our jobs.

I mean, it's all wrapped up now. And the sad thing about the Atwood story is that a week later, he had a heart attack, and he went from *Look Magazine*, and of course, the story about Vietnam and the whole of my work there was never published, and the associate editor, who was to have worked on the story, was fired.

So, they began wrapping things up, I think, at around that time, and it shouldn't surprise us.

Len, back in 1915 J.P. Morgan said, let's identify the major print publications in this country that we have to control, and let's be about the business of doing it, because that's how we will get mass public opinion where we want it.

So they've been aware of the necessity and they've been about the business, and the other sad thing is that it's not just mainstream media. In the alternative media itself there are a number of gatekeepers who do very good work on a lot of issues, on a wide range of issues, and do inform their audience about specific wrongs and issues that should be heard, but when it comes down to certain matters, certain issues, they will not go there. [...] particular issues, and political assassinations happen to be one, and that's sad, but it's a reality."

- William Pepper, April 4, 2013, on *Black Op Radio*

"There's never no mentally disturbed individuals who do that, from killing the president to blowin' up buildings, that's crap, but the American people buy it, like the Hitler and the Nazi's bought it and the Romans bought it before it fell, all that is a game, and the press is part of it and we buy into it because we part of it."

- Dick Gregory [W.E A.L.L. B.E. TV]

"Would these children know they live in a fascist society? Would their parents know they live in a fascist society? Is it possible to live in a fascist society without realizing it? Of course it's possible ...

"When you talk about fascism people instinctively talk about Hitler and Mussolini and brown shirts and walking goose-step down the streets. That's fascism that's in your face. Of course, it doesn't have to be like that. That's not the defining feature.

"Fascism can be sexy. Fascism can look like American Idol or Monday Night Football, Internet video games, or whatever, it can be the things that distract you the citizen from what's actually going on.

"Fascism, in other words, can be a lot more attractive, than they realize, to people. What we have is invisible fascism. It's fascism that people can't really see, frankly because most people don't have the conceptual tools to understand what's happened.

"Most people have to work, they've got families, they've got things to do, they're not out there to fight the machine, they're not out there to be heroes, they're just out there to live their lives.

"They don't want to have trouble. They haven't really studied this matter. They may feel in their bones that there's something wrong. Sure they do. But it's one thing to feel there's something wrong and it's another to be able to put it all together and to conceptualize it and to see how it's wrong.

"So, I see what has happened is that it's a fascism that you can feel, but you can't see it, because you don't know how to see it, that's why I call it invisible.

"That's what we have. In other words, for us to assume that today fascism is going to look like Hitler's fascism, well that's kind of stupid. We're living in a completely different century, a completely different era. Of course it's not going to look like Hitler's fascism. It's going to look very different.

"9/11 plays a crucial part in allowing that, because what was necessary was to have a legal revolution within the United States.

"And that of course, is what has 9/11 has allowed. It has also allowed a fascist revolution. What else do we call it? It has gone under the radar as such."

- Richard Dolan, Talking about seeing kids at a playground

"The people that run this country wanted both of them dead. They wanted Jack Kennedy dead as well. They wanted Malcolm dead.

"You couldn't let these people live. They were beyond control. Bobby was going to end the oil depletion allowance, the same way Jack was. That's 27 percent of every barrel that goes into the pockets of the oil barons. They couldn't allow that to happen.

"Bobby was going to re-open the investigation of the assassination of his brother. He was going to end the war in Vietnam, which was a huge hit on some of the construction companies, oil and energy companies. There was just no way they could ever allow Bob Kennedy in the White House. Martin King was going to bring half a million people to Washington. That was going to turn into a revolutionary group when they didn't get peacefully what they wanted. They're not going to let that happen."

-Attorney William Pepper, speaking on the killings of Martin King and Robert Kennedy on the *Project Camelot* radio program

The English and Arabic editions of 9/11 and American Empire, *which Kevin Barrett co-edited.*

Green, Nass renew call to UW to fire 9/11 conspiracy professor

Upcoming talk is impetus

Associated Press

Barrett

A Republican lawmaker and a gubernatorial candidate renewed their call Tuesday for the University of Wisconsin-Madison to fire a part-time instructor who believes the U.S. government orchestrated the 9/11 attacks.

The calls by GOP gubernatorial candidate Mark Green and Rep. Steve Nass of Whitewater came after they learned a UW-Madison academic unit was sponsoring a lecture on Sunday by Kevin Barrett titled "9/11: Folklore and Fact."

Barrett said the British Broadcasting Corp. is expected to film the lecture as part of a story on those who share the view that U.S. government officials, not terrorists, were behind the attacks.

The UW-Madison folklore program is sponsoring the lecture. It will also feature 9/11 Truth leader James Fetzer, who has similar views as Barrett.

The university's decision to allow Barrett to teach a course this fall, "Islam: Religion and Culture," touched off a firestorm of controversy over the summer.

UW-Madison Provost Patrick Farrell decided to retain Barrett for the course after reviewing his plans and qualifications, but later warned him to stop seeking publicity for his personal political views.

"Rather than stick to their guns and fire Kevin Barrett for openly defying university policy again, the administrators at UW-Madison have, once again, refused to put a stop to this charade," Green said in a statement.

Farrell said Tuesday that it was appropriate for the folklore program to sponsor the lecture even though it will bring publicity to Barrett's views.

"My understanding is that he's followed the rules, got a sponsor and plans to present something that the department feels is appropriate," he said.

Students have so far enjoyed Barrett's class, Farrell added.

Barrett said his talk would focus on research into how folklore studies methodology can be applied to look at the movement of those who question the official version of the attacks.

Like other folk groups, the movement spreads its message creatively and makes a major distinction between insiders and outsiders, he said.

"What I'll be doing is purely academic and something people can appreciate regardless of their political persuasions," he said.

He said supporters of his views have raised $8,247 and plan to present it to the university during the lecture. That's the amount that Barrett is scheduled to earn this semester — and how much the Ozaukee County Board cut funding for UW-Extension to protest.

Farrell said he would tell them to give the money directly to UW-Extension or to the school's private foundation for student scholarships.

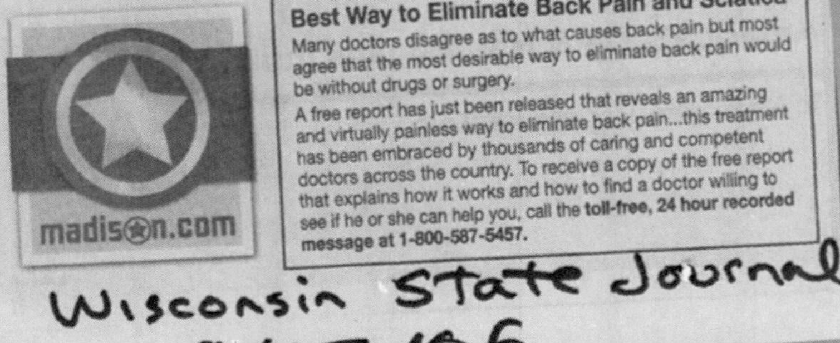

Wisconsin State Journal
9/27/06

[Chapter 15] James Tracy re: False Flags, Conspiracies

"Law shall not stop with the punishment of petty crimes by little people. It must also reach men who possess themselves of great power."
- Robert Jackson, chief prosecutor for the U.S., at the Nuremberg trials

False Flag Terror and Conspiracies of Silence
The *Memory Hole Blog* April 16, 2013

by James Tracy

The news media's readiness to accept official pronouncements and failure to more vigorously analyze and question government authorities in the wake of "domestic terrorist" incidents including mass shootings and bombings contributes to the American public's already acute case of collective historical amnesia, while further rationalizing the twenty-first century police state and continued demise of civil society.

Some may recall "Bugs Raplin" (Giancarlo Espisito), the resolute investigative journalist depicted in Tim Robbins' 1992 political mockumentary Bob Roberts. After being framed as the culprit in a false flag assassination attempt by corrupt political huckster Bob Roberts (Robbins), Raplin delivers a perceptive soliloquy that among other things effectively describes the American public's moribund civic condition and short-circuited democracy. "The reason Iran-Contra happened," Raplin begins,

> is because no one did anything substantial about Watergate. And the reason Watergate happened is because there were no consequences from the Bay of Pigs. They're all the same operatives – the foot soldiers at the Bay of Pigs, the plumbers that got busted at Watergate, the gunrunners in Iran-Contra – all the same people, same faces. Now it doesn't take a genius to figure out the connection here: A secret government beyond the control of the people and accountable to no one. And the closer we are to discovering the connection, the more Congress turns a blind eye to it. "We can't talk about that in open session," they say. "National security reasons." The truth lies dormant in their laps and they stay blind out of choice. A conspiracy of silence.

Twenty years later amidst the vast outsourcing of intelligence and military operations many more events may arguably be added to such a shadow government's achievements – the 1993 World Trade Center bombing, the 1995 Oklahoma City Murrah Federal Building bombing, the September 11 terror attacks, the non-existent weapons of mass destruction prompting the occupation of Iraq, the July 7, 2005 London bombings, the shoe and underwear "bombings" – all of which have contributed to the official justification of imperial wars abroad and an ever-expanding police state at home.

Lacking meaningful contexts with which to understand such events in their totality the general public is incapable of recognizing the road it is being forced down.

The most recent set of events that give pause are the horrific, military-style shootings in Aurora, Colorado and Oak Creek, Wisconsin that authorities maintain were carried out by "lone wolf" gunmen.

Operation Gladio in America?

A potential backdrop and precursor to the Colorado and Wisconsin events is the oft-forgotten Operation Gladio, a campaign involving U.S. and British intelligence-backed paramilitaries anonymously carrying out mass shootings and bombings of civilian targets throughout Europe.

Hundreds of such attacks took place between the late 1960s and early 1980s by "stay behind armies" of right wing and fascist saboteurs in an overall effort to terrorize populations, deploy a "strategy of tension", and thereby maintain a centrist political status quo.[1] In the uncertain environment the petrified citizenry pled for stepped-up security and stood poised to part with personal freedoms.

At the same time the maneuvers allowed for political adversaries – in Gladio's time socialist and Communist groups – to be blamed for the attacks and thereby demonized in the public mind.

The string of still unresolved U.S. political assassinations throughout the 1960s suggests how such practices were not restricted to foreign countries.

Nor were they solely the terrain of intelligence agencies. Along lines similar to Gladio, in the early 1960s the U.S. Joint Chiefs of Staff proposed Operation Northwoods, where terrorist attacks would be initiated against U.S. civilians in American cities and the violence blamed on Cuban combatants to justify war against the island nation.[2]

The Kennedy administration rejected the proposal.

While Northwoods exhibited the capacity for government to conceive and propose such plans, Gladio was demonstrably carried out against Western civilian populations in multiple locations over many years.

Consideration of Gladio and Northwoods might be dismissed were it not for early eyewitness accounts following the Colorado and Wisconsin shootings contending how there were two or more killers present at each incident – testimonies contradicting official government narratives that have accordingly been suppressed in the public mind.[3]

As communications historian Christopher Simpson observes, "The tactics that created the [Gladio] stay-behinds in the first place are still in place and continue to be used today. They are standard operating procedure."[4] Such potential explanations will appear foreign to an American public that is systematically misinformed and easily distracted. And in times of crisis especially that very public is tacitly assured of its safe remove from such practices, looking instead to political authorities and experts to reestablish a stasis to the carefully constructed "reality" major media impose on the mass psyche.

In this alternate reality Gladio has effectively been "memory-holed".

A LexisNexis Academic search for "Operation Gladio" retrieves a mere thirty-one articles in English language news outlets – most in British newspapers. In fact, only four articles discussing Gladio ever appeared in U.S. publications – three in *The New York Times* and one brief mention in the *Tampa Bay Times*. Barring a 2009 BBC documentary [5] no network or cable news broadcasts have ever referenced the maneuver.

Almost all of the articles related to Gladio appeared in 1990 when Italian Prime Minister Giulio Andreotti publicly admitted Italy's participation in the process. *The New York Times* downplayed any U.S. involvement, misleadingly calling Gladio "an Italian creation" in a story buried on page A16.[6] In reality, former CIA director William Colby revealed in his memoirs that covert paramilitaries were a significant agency undertaking set up after World War II, including "the smallest possible coterie of the most reliable people, in Washington [and] NATO."[7]

A Plausible Narrative / Conclusion

Gladio's successful concealment for so many years demonstrates how mass atrocities can be carried out by a shadow network with complete impunity. Most incidents from the Gladio period remain unsolved by authorities. In the U.S., however, a plausible narrative appears to be required for public consumption.

For example, just a few hours after the Wisconsin Sikh temple shooting Bureau of Alcohol, Tobacco, and Firearms (ATF) and Federal Bureau of Investigation (FBI) officials swept in and wrested the case from Oak Creek authorities by classifying it as an act of "domestic terrorism."[8].

Less than twenty four hours later one of the federal government's foremost de facto propaganda and intelligence-gathering arms – the Southern Poverty Law Center (SPLC) – developed a storyline that was unquestioningly lapped up by major news media.[9]

In an August 6, 2012 *Democracy Now* interview with SPLC spokesman Mark Potok and *Milwaukee Journal-Sentinel* reporter Don Walker, Potok explained in unusual detail how the alleged killer was involved in "white supremacist groups", "Nazi skinhead rock bands", and that the SPLC had been "tracking" the groups he was in since 2000. Potok's remarks, which dominate the exchange and steer clear of the suspect's experience in psychological operations, contrasted sharply with Walker's, who more cautiously pointed out that the suspect's "work in [U.S. Army] PsyOps is still a bit of a mystery to all of us ... We talked to a psychiatrist who said that [being promoted to PsyOps is] like going from the lobby to the 20th floor very quickly."[10]

Like the Aurora, Colorado storyline of a crazed shooter who expertly booby-trapped his apartment with exotic explosives, such appealingly sensationalistic narratives serve to sideline the countervailing testimonies of eyewitnesses and are difficult to contest or dislodge once they are driven home by would-be experts through almost every major news outlet.

A similar scenario played out in the wake of the Oklahoma City federal building bombing when the ATF, FBI and SPLC together constructed the dominant frame of Timothy McVeigh as the lone bomber, an account that likewise diverged with the local authorities' initial findings, early news reports of unexploded ordinance and a mysterious accomplice of McVeigh, and the overall conclusions of the Oklahoma City Bombing Investigation Committee's Final Report.[11]

The narrative nevertheless served to maintain the political status quo while securing the Clinton administration's second term in office. To this day most Americans believe McVeigh was solely responsible for the bombing despite overwhelming evidence to the contrary.

For its time Raplin's prognosis was an accurate description of America's cascading socio-political nightmare. Elected officials abdicate their responsibility of oversight for personal gain and thus perpetuate "a conspiracy of silence".

Yet over the past two decades, the quickening pace of "terrorist" events suggests how shadow networks have grown in boldness and strength, while each attack has contributed to the steady erosion of civil society and Constitutional rights.

With this in mind both the mainstream and "alternative" news media, through their overt censorial practices, their consistent failure to place events in meaningful historical contexts, and their overall deliberate obeisance to dubious and unaccountable authorities, compound this conspiracy by ensnaring the public in questionable realities from which it cannot readily escape.

Notes:

[1] Daniele Ganser, NATO's Secret Armies: Operation Gladio and Terrorism in Western Europe, New York: Routledge, 2005; Richard Cottrell, Gladio: NATO's Dagger at the Heart of Europe, Progressive Press, 2012. For a succinct historical overview of false flag terror see Kurt Nimmo,"A Brief History of False Flag Terror Attacks, Or Why Our Government Loves State-Sponsored Terror," Infowars.com, August 14, 2012. See also the BBC Timewatch documentary, "Operation Gladio."

[2] James Bamford, Body of Secrets: Anatomy of the Ultra-Secret National

Security Agency, New York: Anchor Books, 2002, 83. For recent applications see Michel Chossudovsky, Syria: Killing Innocent Civilians as Part of a US Covert Op. Mobilizing Support for a R2P War," GlobalResearch.ca, May 30, 2012, http://www.globalresearch.ca/index.php?context=va&aid=31122. Entire Operation Northwoods document available at http://archive.org/stream/OperationNorthwoods/operation_northwoods#page/n0/mode/2up.

[3] Overall sufficient scrutiny of the Colorado and Wisconsin shootings is entirely lacking save a handful of alternative news media. See Alex Thomas, "Wisconsin Sikh Shooting False Flag: Multiple Shooters, Army Psy-Ops, The FBI, Operation Gladio, and the SPLC," Intellhub.com, August 6, 2012, http://theintelhub.com/2012/08/06/wisconsin-sikh-shooting-false-flag-multiple-shooters-army-psy-ops-the-fbi-operation-gladio-and-the-splc/; Jon Rappoport, "Shooting in Sikh Temple: Who Benefits Big Time?" August 5, 2012, http://jonrappoport.wordpress.com/2012/08/06/shooting-in-sikh-temple-who-benefits-big-time; Kurt Nimmo, "Sikh Shooter a Former Psyop Soldier Linked to FBI's National Alliance," Infowars.com, August 6, 2012, http://www.infowars.com/sikh-shooter-a-former-psyop-soldier-linked-to-fbis-national-alliance/.

[4] NATO's Secret Armies, Andres Pichler, director, 2009. Simpson interview at 46:23, http://www.indybay.org/newsitems/2010/07/09/18653266.php.

[5] NATO's Secret Armies.

[6] Clyde Haberman, "Evolution in Europe: Italy Discloses Its Web of Cold War Guerrillas," New York Times, November 16, 1990, A16.

[7] Stephen Lendman, "NATO's Secret Armies" [A Review of Daniele Ganser, NATO's Secret Armies: Operation Gladio and Terrorism in Western Europe, op cit.] September 15, 2010, http://sjlendman.blogspot.com/2010/09/natos-secret-armies.html.

[8] Steven Yaccino, Michael Schwirtz, and Marc Santora, "Gunman Kills 6 at a Sikh Temple Near Milwaukee," New York Times, August 6, 2012, A1.

[9] For example, Erica Goode and Serge F. Kovaleski, "Wisconsin Killer Was Fueled by Hate-Driven Music," New York Times, August 7, 2012, http://www.nytimes.com/2012/08/07/us/army-veteran-identified-as-suspect-in-wisconsin-shooting.html?_r=1&pagewanted=all; Madison Gray, "Sikh Temple Shooter Identified, Had Ties to White Supremacist Movement," Time News Feed, August 6, 2012, http://newsfeed.time.com/2012/08/06/sikh-temple-shooter-identified-had-ties-to-white-supremacist-movement/; Dinesh Ramde and Todd Richmond, SPLC: 'Frustrated neo-Nazi Opened Fire on Sikh Temple," Associated Press, August 6, 2012, http://minnesota.publicradio.org/display/web/2012/08/06/white-supremacist-opened-fire-on-sikh-temple/.

[10] Amy Goodman, "Neo-Nazi Rampage: Army Psy-Ops Vet, White Power Musician ID'd as Gunman in Sikh Temple Shooting," *Democracy Now*, August 7, 2012, http://www.democracynow.org/2012/8/7/sikh_temple_shooter_wade_michael_page.

[11] Charles Key, The Final Report on the Bombing of the Alfred P. Murrah Federal Building, Oklahoma City: Oklahoma Bombing Investigation Committee, 2001. http://www.okcbombing.net/

[Reprinted here with permission.]

In Search of the Last Liberal Intellectual
Memory Hole Blog March 27, 2013

by James Tracy

In the wake of the Sandy Hook School shooting public incredulity with the official version of events led to numerous speculations on what really happened. In short order corporate media marshaled pundits to disparage such alternative interpretations as "conspiracy theories" and the work of deranged and even malevolent Sandy Hook "truthers".

The now-prevalent phenomenon where only the narratives authorized by law enforcement and government authorities are worthy of serious consideration suggests the unmistakable extent to which public discourse has declined. In such an ideational system journalists and academics are expected to either fall silent or perform the rearguard action of deflecting criticism from the state.

Events such as Aurora or Sandy Hook have profuse informational gaps and a multitude of questions authorities have not begun to adequately address. Regardless of political stripe journalists and academics especially should be instinctively distrustful of such momentous incidents. Unfortunately many put short-term interests of preserving reputation and livelihood above the obligatory search for truth.

Today's project of policing the public sphere for unorthodox thoughts is a form of stealth authoritarianism that combines the weight of academic or journalistic expertise with a phony liberalism (or conservatism) to confirm the often unexamined perspectives of a specific political constituency. Such a technique is most readily employed against the apparently irrational ideas, beliefs and practices of a foreign other. In this regard "conspiracy theorists" and "truthers" typically play the "straw man" role.

For example, a recent piece by Dartmouth political scientist Brendan Nyhan exhibits anxiety over major media's attention toward individuals critical of what authorities have told them to believe about Sandy Hook.[1] Nyhan is fearful that research into the Newtown massacre contradicting the government's official narrative – what he emphatically terms "conspiracy mongering" and "obscure myths" – may be given a platform by more "prominent advocates" from the political realm.

From here the dangerous notions could gain the support of the unenlightened – "credulous believers" and "new adherents who would not otherwise have been exposed to or persuaded by false claims."

Such verboten ideas, Nyhan argues, should instead be allowed to "wither and die."

The problem with this stance is that it consciously paves the way for the official false claims and myths that powerful political entities and corporate news and entertainment media are capable of forcing upon the public mind and collective memory, be they Osama bin Laden masterminding the 9/11 attacks, babies being thrown from incubators in Kuwaiti hospitals, or North Vietnamese forces firing the first shots in the Vietnam War.

Such a position is not unusual from a palace court intellectual; whether it is morally sound and faithful to the liberal tenet of speaking truth to power is a matter for another day.

In reviewing other arguments of those using this form of defamatory innuendo toward the Sandy Hook truth community I encountered numerous poorly reasoned arguments and claims that could not withstand serious scrutiny and amounted to a bulwark for the official narrative – indeed, arguments most appealing to those with a dangerously unexamined faith in state power and lacking the inclination to consider alternative perspectives or investigate the event for themselves.

This prompted me to contact several notable "conspiracy theory" decriers and request an interview with each of them.

Instead of mere name-calling, I remain sincerely interested in better understanding why such apparently intelligent individuals have come to arrive at their conclusions and become the self-appointed guardians of legitimate public exchange.

I thus set about assembling a set of questions on a wide array of "conspiracy"-related issues and phenomena.

I figured I would begin by reaching out in a collegial manner to Professor Nyhan himself. "Sorry, not interested," he replied, rather tersely. I next contacted Ben Smith and C.J. Lotz, staff writers at the popular liberal website Buzzfeed.com, who wrote a piece remarkably similar to Dr. Nyhan's titled, *Sandy Hook Conspiracy Theories Edge Toward the Mainstream*.[2] Smith and Lotz never responded to my emails.

Undeterred, I contacted the operators of the well-known liberal "fact check" website Snopes.com. "I'm sorry, I'm afraid we just can't," Barbara Mikkelson replied. "I fear this is the downside of having a small operation."

Next I dropped Salon.com political writer and ThinkProgress assistant editor Alex Seitz-Wald a line. The youthful Seitz-Wald prides himself as being one of today's foremost "truth" skeptics. Since early January he has written a series of articles generally disparaging Sandy Hook researchers. "I'm writing one more story on this," he said, "but really not interested in getting back into this subject or enduring more hate mail."

I moved on to career anti-conspiracist and former *High Times* editor John Foster "Chip" Berlet.

Calling himself a progressive and champion of liberal democracy, Mr. Berlet wrote profusely on the resurgence of the so-called "new right" throughout the 1990s.[3] "I do not spend time with people promoting crackpot conspiracy theories," he replied, somewhat peevishly. "It is annoying, counterproductive, and gives me a headache. Nevertheless, I support your First Amendment right to waste bandwidth and electricity."

Just when I was about to give up hope Jonathan Kay, editor at Canada's *National Post* and author of *Among the Truthers: A Journey Through America's Conspiracist Underground* [4] responded favorably to my interview request. "Sure," he said, much to my delight. Yet when I provided Kay with the questions he balked. "Just about all the answers to these questions are in my book," he replied.

I countered that very few of the questions were actually addressed in the book. "I get the sense that my perspective wouldn't really be that meaningful to you. I'm going to pass on this."

In the end while skilled at defending the varied machinations of our out-of-control police state by helping to confirm their immediate audiences' prejudices, none of the foremost conspiracy cynics and debunkers opted to have a dialogue – one where they would likely be compelled to interrogate their own claims and assumptions.

Could it be that what these commentators desire in lieu of dialogue is a one-way transmission of their ideas devoid of critique or interpretation – one where the pursuit of "truth" itself is caricatured as a fool's errand?

If liberalism is based in part on a free and open exchange, perhaps some of the foremost figures and media outlets touting themselves as progressive and liberal, and purporting to preserve and defend rational discourse, really aren't so open-minded after all.

The following are the questions I was hoping my would-be interlocutors would address. The main thrust of John Milton's Areopagetica is that in a fair exchange an argument based on the truth will triumph over lies and deception. Do you think that the major media's use of terms such as "truther" or "conspiracy theorist" to designate individuals or groups with ideas and theories that differ from government and/or corporate entities is a productive part of the journey toward truth and enlightenment Milton envisioned?

To what degree do you think citizens and the press should hold government officials accountable for momentous events such as the terror attacks of September 11, 2001?

What characterizes a conspiracy theory? How can we distinguish between a conspiracy theory and a valid assessment of a specific phenomenon, issue, or event?

U.S. political leaders uniformly maintain that Osama bin Laden and the al Qaeda network were the sole agents behind the 9/11 attacks. The 9/11 Commission's report attributed this set of events to "a lack of imagination" in terms of government agencies' preparation. In your view, what are the most compelling pieces of evidence to support this official explanation of the 9/11 events?

Historian Richard Hofstadter argues in his well-known essay, *The*

Paranoid Style of American Politics, that regardless of how much evidence the conspiratorially-minded gather and present on a topic or phenomenon they are not worthy of a hearing as their views may endanger rational political discourse and consensus. Does such a position potentially jeopardize effective and honest journalistic practice?

In your estimation, is the tendency to entertain or proffer conspiracy theories a sign of a potential psychiatric condition? Along these lines, are at least some conspiracy theorists inherently dangerous?

In 1977 Carl Bernstein reported that through "Operation Mockingbird" and related activities many major news organizations were infiltrated by CIA operatives or consciously aided the CIA in intelligence gathering activities and "planting" stories in the press. CIA document 1035-960 suggests how the agency went about thwarting criticism of the Warren Commission's examination of President Kennedy's assassination by utilizing intelligence assets in news outlets to bolster the Warren Commission's legitimacy and labeling critics "conspiracy theorists". In your estimation, is the intelligence community's penetration of the press an ongoing phenomenon? Is it more widespread today or has it subsided to any significant degree?

Political scientist Lance deHaven-Smith cites *The Declaration of Independence* as a conspiratorial document and asserts that the ideology of America's founders was in many ways motivated by paranoia toward British rule. In fact, the notion of conspiracy has been a consistent theme in American politics. With this in mind, what is it about modern forms of governance that render such impulses and worldviews irrational, obsolete, and perhaps even dangerous?

The bombing of the Alfred P. Murrah Federal Building in Oklahoma City brought into public consciousness the notion of "homegrown terrorism". At the same time the event provided the pretext for laws compromising Americans' civil liberties and paved the way for the PATRIOT Act that was enacted in the wake of 9/11. Is it reasonable for the public to conclude that Timothy McVeigh and Terry Nichols were the sole or principal agents in the bombing? Have you examined the Oklahoma Bombing Investigation Committee's 2001 report on the incident? If so, would you consider its findings to be sound and cause for a new judicial interrogation of the event?

The official theory of what transpired at Sandy Hook Elementary School on December 14, 2012 involves 20-year-old Adam Lanza going on a murderous rampage that resulted in the deaths of twenty children and seven adults. Major media outlets appear to have unquestioningly gone forward with this scenario. In your estimation, have law enforcement and medical authorities produced evidence sufficient to support this theory of events?

There are a variety of public figures and websites that deem themselves as "alternative" sources of political news and analysis, such as Alex Jones and Infowars.com, and Dr. Webster Tarpley of Tarpley.

net. Why do you believe such individuals are frequently held up as promoters of conspiracy theories? In your view, what is it that makes these commentators and sources of analysis less reliable than, say, CNN's Piers Morgan, MSNBC's Rachel Maddow and Chris Matthews, or the editorial and op-ed pages of a regional or national newspaper?

Philanthropic foundations contribute large sums to a wide array of non-governmental organizations and media outlets in the United States. What role, if any, do you believe such entities play in shaping public discourse and opinion around controversial issues and events?

Notes:

[1] Brendan Nyhan, "Boosting the Sandy Hook Truther Myth," *Columbia Journalism Review*, January 22, 2013. Dr. Nyhan speaks dismissively of this author yet it is difficult to find a conventional article addressing independent Sandy Hook analysis that does not. I chose this piece to aid in analyzing its argument and a specific sociocultural tendency rather than its author. CJR seeks "to encourage excellence in journalism in the service of a free society" and its "major funders" include George Soros' Open Society Foundations and the Rockefeller Family Fund.

[2] Ben Smith and C J Lotz, "Sandy Hook Conspiracy Theories Edge Toward the Mainstream," *Buzzfeed.com*, January 22, 2013.

[3] For example, see the barely concealed political tracts Chip Berlet (editor), *Eyes Right! Challenging the Right Wing Backlash*, Boston and Somerville MA: Political Research Associates and South End Press, 1995, and the quasi-academic *Too Close for Comfort: Right Wing Populism in America*, New York: Guilford Press, 2000.

[4] Jonathan Kay, Among the Truthers: A Journey Through America's Conspiracist Underground, New York: Harper Collins, 2011.

[Reprinted here with permission.]

James Fetzer, PhD

James Fetzer, PhD – Distinguished McKnight University Professor Emeritus of Philosophy at the University of Minnesota. Former Captain, U.S. Marine Corps. He has published more than 100 articles and reviews and authored, co-authored, and edited over 20 books on the philosophy of science, the theory of knowledge, and the theoretical foundations of computer science, artificial intelligence, and cognitive science, including: *Foundations of Philosophy of Science: Recent Developments* (1993), *Minds and Machines : Journal for Artificial Intelligence, Philosophy, and Cognitive Science* (1997), *Philosophy, Mind, and Cognitive Inquiry, Resources for Understanding Mental Processes* (2001), *Computers and Cognition: Why Minds are not Machines* (2002), *Consciousness Evolving (Advances in Consciousness Research)* (2002), *Science, Explanation, and Rationality: The Philosophy of Carl G. Hempel* (2003), *The Evolution of Intelligence* (2004), *Render Unto Darwin: Philosophical Aspects of the Christian Right's Crusade Against Science* (2007).

- **Essay *9/11: Rational Beliefs are not Paranoid* 12/8/06:**

Kevin and Jim would both become members of Patriots Question 9/11.

[Chapter 16] The Boston bombings

> "What we get on TV is managed news and it's created a truth emergency that's quite severe."
> - Peter Phillips

KEVIN:

[Where were you when you heard about the Boston bombing?]

I think I heard a breaking news alert from *Citizens for Legitimate Government*. [I was then doing a show with Allen Roland – he told me about it – he thought blowback.]

My first reaction was false flag. And since then I think I was probably instinctively right, because there are so many of these tell-tale red flags once again. We're just getting used to it now.

It looks like the real bomber is one of those guys with the skull logo. The official story is that they had pressure cooker bombs in their backpacks and left them, but it's pretty bizarre that all those paramilitary guys are running around with big black backpacks and there's a picture of the exploded backpack that has a white square on it which is identical to the black backpack with a white square on it worn by one of the paramilitary guys, and there's photos showing the surviving brother leaving the scene apparently with his backpack still on.

Why would there be a terror drill going on at the same time, which it turns out there was and why would they be denying it now, and then why would there be all those Craft guys there with big black backpacks just like the bomb was in, including with the white square.

I mean it's really way too much for coincidence, to say the least, so there's got to be – it just looks like another bad false flag. These guys should be getting better at it. It looks like the official story is, they were caught because they tried to carjack somebody and rob a 7-11? It's like Oswald all over again.

And then supposedly they shoot a cop, just like Oswald. All these Lee Harvey Oswald parallels.

It's just one damn thing after another.

Oswald, the FBI was all over him, in fact, he was even reporting to the FBI, and with these brothers, same thing, the FBI's been over them for years, according to their parents ... and they get arrested after killing a cop – get arrested supposedly healthy – tell us it's a shootout – brother critically wounded coming out of boat and then he gets shot up later – then sent to Beth Israel Hospital to be treated by Israeli doctors ... so you add it all up and it stinks to high heaven.

[Re: Recent interview w. Sherwood Ross, where you said something about how we're gaining ground on this whole truth thing, and how maybe that also means they might be lining up the railroad cars and laying down the track to the concentration camps ...]

I'm starting to wonder. I used to think that it was all just contingency planning. They were concerned that with the economy continuing to get worse, at some point there's going to be massive unrest, and they're going to have to use their camps, and so on, then, but I don't know, they sure seem to be practicing.

This Boston lockdown? That's pretty crazy. I never knew that Constitutionally you could force a million people in a city to stay indoors, all day, that's crazy.

[Developments with Boston bombing research]

Far more than just about any event since 9/11, I've concluded that this was obviously a false flag, very early. Because for whatever reason they seem to have either screwed up or done it in such a way as to make it really obvious.

All of the other false flag events or presumed false flag events, such as the shootings in the Aurora, Colorado theater, the Sikh Temple in Wisconsin, and Sandy Hook School, were all, to my mind, somewhat less obvious. I mean, all of them look like false flags.

There's evidence for multiple shooters in all of these cases, there are loose ends that are pretty extreme, but with this Boston event it's just beyond obvious that it's a false flag, they had Craft International paramilitary guys out there planting the bombs in full view, you can see them.

You can see them planting the bombs in the film.

The FBI asks everybody to analyze the photos.

Well we did and we found out who did it.

There's just a mountain of evidence that became available very, very early that this Boston event was a false flag.

[Supposed bombers trained by CIA?]

By "trained" what they're trying to make you think is trained in making bombs, but actually he was probably just brought on board as a CIA asset.

That means they probably paid him a little something, who knows what they did with him, but that just means that they got control of him, which makes him the kind of person they can set up as a patsy. And that's how it works. A lot of the times the patsies are intelligence people.

Lee Harvey Oswald was a classic example. We now know that Oswald was not only reporting to the FBI as an informant right up to the assassination of John F. Kennedy, but he was also an intelligence operative when he was in the Marine Corps.

He was in Japan working at the top-secret U2 spy base and apparently feeding U2 information to the Russians as part of a program actually run by U.S. intelligence designed to give the Russians U2 intelligence that the U.S. wanted the Russians to have.

So Oswald was very deep in the intelligence world and because of this, he had controllers who could get him placed in the right spot to take the blame for the Kennedy assassination, and likewise this accused Boston bomber undoubtedly would be in the same situation. He would have intelligence handlers who were paying him, so he does what they say and they can get him to the right place where he can be blamed.

[The Mother and Father Tsarnaev]

Well, the mother, the father, one of the uncles, one of the uncles was CIA, and so this one uncle who's like a fake convert to Islam is married to the daughter of Graham Fuller. Fuller is this filthy CIA criminal who led the cover-up of 9/11 in Turkey, who went around threatening all of Turkey's leading journalists, basically giving them death threats if they ever breathed a word of truth about 9/11, that they and their families would be dead.

This Fuller creep, as I said, his daughter married one of the uncles of the bombers, and this uncle is a complete criminal.

But every other family member of these guys, mother, father, etc., and neighbors and friends, everyone is convinced that they are innocent and completely incapable of these crimes, and they're all coming right out and calling it a false flag ... and the two accused brothers are 9/11 Truthers.

And the younger brother, who's still alive and being silenced by Israeli doctors, his last Facebook post said that he was set up. He was innocent and he was set up. So they're all 9/11 Truthers, they all know that these guys are innocent.

You know, maybe they picked the wrong patsy this time? Because it's making it harder for the mainstream media to cover these things up. What the media is doing is they're trying to spin it as, oh, these guys are radical Muslims because they're Truthers.

Well the fact is that 80 percent of the world's Muslims are 9/11 Truthers, and it's the other 20 percent that you have to worry about, because the 80 percent who are Truthers know that this kind of attack on civilians is going to be used against Islam, so obviously they would never do it. The 20 percent who are not Truthers include a lot of people who are sympathetic to the ideas of so-called Al Qaeda and those are the people who you have to watch out for.

[The aunt seemed strong.]

She also was saying it was a false flag.

Boston Bombing:
Jim Fetzer vs. New Hampshire

Responses to an article in the *New Hampshire Union Leader* by Garry Rayno ...

> CONCORD – The House voted 312-0 Wednesday to honor the victims and heroes of the Boston Marathon bombing and formally disavowed comments made by one of its members.
> The vote was a rebuke to Rep. Stella Tremblay, R-Auburn, who claimed the attack was the work of a federal government "Black Ops" team and questioned whether bombing victim Jeff Bauman was in pain or shock after the bombing.

Letters to the editor:

Garret Saunders said:

> Don't get me wrong, I fully support this resolution by the house, but couldn't they have taken this time to do something more effective like censure her or move to remove her from her elected position somehow. I don't know what is possible within the rules of our state government but someone so profoundly out of touch with reality should not be allowed to continue to serve.

May 8, 2013 10:26 pm

Carolyn Pillsbury said:

> Garret Saunders, and you think that our government officials are in touch with reality. Ms. Trembly is simply voiceing what many Americans are thinking these days. The United States goverment wants your guns, and soon your freedom of speech, your rights to assembly, your freedom of religion.

May 9, 2013 3:20 am

James Fetzer said:

> As a former Marine Corps officer and retired professor of philosophy, who has devoted himself since his retirement to the study of complex and controversial issues of public importance, I have been astonished at the gullibility of the American people. I have published three articles about the Boston bombing, including my latest, in which I honor Stella Trembly, *Man of the Year: Stella Tremblay, NH Legislator*, http://

www.veteranstoday.com/2013/05/04/man-of-the-year-stella-trimblay-nh-legislator/, where I honor her as "Man of the Year" rather than as "Woman of the Year" or even "Person of the Year" because she is the only one who has the ***** to "tell it like it is".

I have consulted experts on different aspects of the case and, for those of us who have actually analyzed the evidence, the Boston bombing was an obvious staged event, where some bystanders were injured or killed but where the perps were not those two brothers but members of the paramilitary company, Craft International; where the older brother was taken alive and then killed while in police custody; where the scene reeks with fakery, including the absence of spurting blood from Jeff Bauman's leg, the wrong color blood that was used to create false impressions; and a host of other subtle points, including that he had also lost the little finger of his left hand before the bombing. I don't claim to be incapable of making mistakes, but I think those who are praising Bauman for his performance here have missed the boat, big time!

May 9, 2013 3:42 am

Tom Sheffield said:

Carolyn and James – BOO!

May 9, 2013 5:51 am

Chris Kofer said:

James Fetzer, career conspiracy theorist ... or is this just a parody.

May 9, 2013 5:58 am

Chris Kofer said:

Carolyn meant to write "what UNAmericans are thinking.

May 9, 2013 6:00 am

Samantha Stevens said:

Bunch of fruit cakes ... Pillsbury, Fetzer, Little, Young ... absolute fruit cakes. To think our own government would stage such an act. Paranoid. Delusional. It's a wonder you all can sleep at night with your conspiracies of terrorism and fear of loosing your guns. I feel kinda sorry for you all. Sad bunch.

May 9, 2013 7:43 am

Len Cannon said:

312-0 vote to honor the victims. This is news? What a courageous vote! BTW ... where were the other 88? Did they cast the courageous "present" vote? I would love to interview a member of the chamber who voted against the victims. And ... Garret: If we removed all legislators who said something stupid ... well let's just say there would be a lot of "special elections" to fill the posts. And ... James Fetzer: At what vantage point on the grassy knoll were you able to make such astute observations of the "faked" bombings? Good God! It's not even the weekend yet! Did they let you out early? "An obvious staged event!" Do you still write for *PRAVDA*? Or am I confusing you with some other Pulitzer Prize winner? Didn't you write that gem of a piece on the "faked Chernobyl nuclear disaster?" And the "obvious staged Lunar landing in 1969 by NASA, Neil Armstrong and all the other actors in that studio?" Freedom of speech can be a scary thing sometimes!

May 9, 2013 8:28 am

Timothy Phippard said:

Seems the sheeple believe in everything the lame stream media tells them to believe in when there are many questions left unanswered. Why were the Craft International (Corporate Military) all around the bombing sites? Why was there more police and security there then at any other marathon event anywhere at anytime? Bomb sniffing dogs everywhere? Question everything the government tells you! Please look at all the FACTS and see what the real story is, http://www.davidicke.com/5/5/13. See if you believe what the government wants you to believe.

May 9, 2013 8:39 am

Dean Frazier said:

James Fetzer has no idea what happens in the human body after a traumatic injury. Niel Young has no idea what happened in Benghazi. The lunatic fringe is out in force this morning with *The Drudge Report* on their laptops and Conspiracy Theory on their TVs. The voters will take care of Tremblay if she is stupid enough to run.

May 9, 2013 8:40 am

Shirley Munroe said:

@James Fetzer ... just another nutcase!!

May 9, 2013 9:12 am

James Fetzer said:

Fascinating! Those of us who support Stella are "know nothings", "conspiracy theorists" and "ultrawingnuts", even though I have presented ample proof of my points, which none of these critics even discuss. Just for the record, I graduated magna *** laude from Princeton (1962), served as a commissioned officer, US Marine Corps (1962-66), earned my Ph.D. in the history and philosophy of science at Indiana (1970). For 35 years, I offered courses in logic, critical thinking and scientific reasoning. I know better than to draw conclusions without studying the evidence. We have photos of Craft International personnel on the scene with backpacks that, unlike the backpack that Dzhokhar was wearing, were a match for one that exploded. We have videos of Tamerlan being arrested, stark naked, and put into a

police vehicle. We have his brutally damaged body and a witness who reported seening the police run over him repeatedly with an SUV.
Is it too much to expect readers of this newspaper and residents of New Hampshire to take a look at the evidence in this case before you condemn the one voice in the nation who has spoken out about it? We also have close-up photos of Jeff Bauman and what remains of his legs. They are not spurting blood. He is not writhing in pain. He has an accomplice wearing a hood who is assisting him. The blood at the scene is bright red, when it should have been dark red from oxidation. When he is rushed away in a wheelchair, he is sitting upright and alert, when he should be unconscious from the loss of blood. The bone extension appears to be a fabrication that does not even have the physical features of a human tibia. If you don't study the evidence, you would never know. For more, see *Some "hard lessons" from the Boston bombing*, http://www.veteranstoday.com/2013/04/19/some-hard-lessons-from-the-boston-bombing/ and *Welcome to Amerika: No More Truth, Justice or American Way*, http://www.veteranstoday.com/2013/04/22/welcome-to-amerika-no-more-truth-justice-or-american-way/. Or, if you don't want to believe me, try *Russia Today*, which has more accurate information about the Boston bombing than *The New York Times*, assuming it's worth investing 12 minutes of your time: www.youtube.com/watch?v=GcxmAunB4Ck.
May 9, 2013 9:25 am

Joanna Aiken said:
If anyone truly believes your Government is incapable of commiting acts of terror upon its own citizens needs to review the declassfied documents on Operation Northwood.
May 9, 2013 9:55 am

John Shades said:
James Fetzer @ I'll certainly agree with you with respect to the gullibility of some people and the unfortunate number of low-information voters as witnessed in these posts. But you sir, like Ms Tremblay, are quite the anomaly and in need of some serious therapy. With some counseling, effort and time, you can rid yourself of your insecurities and make the world a better place.
May 9, 2013 9:57 am

John Yule said:
Fetzer ... you are a disgrace to the Corp and if you ever really did serve you have tarnished the honor of every other Marine that also served. You are nothing but a psycho who needs serious therapy and is hopefully on a terrorist watch list! Crawl back into whatever little pathetic hole you came out of and stop insulting the good people of this country and especially Mass. and NH who suffered real harm at the hand of the bombers. You and all the other conspiracy nuts out

there are the real danger to this country.
May 9, 2013 10:06 am

Robert Baronas said:

Is this Fetzer guy for real? He can't possibly be serious. Seems like a hopeless cry for attention to me. He is clearly one the gullible American he speaks of and lost all credibility when he came in tooting his own horn. Obviously one of those people with his fingers stuffed firmly in his ears, who has convinced himself that if he screams louder than everyone else it will somehow justify his baseless accusations. Sir, your comments are disgraceful, disgusting, and dishonorable. I agree with John Shades, you need to take a step in a positive direction and move past your insecurities and delusional paranoia. You have severe, severe trust issues ... Craft international, LOL!. How about Civil Support Team Smart guy. Intelligence was clearly wasted on you.
May 9, 2013 10:19 am

Len Cannon said:

Thank you, John Tule. But you forgot to mention Princeton. Somehow we are all supposed to accept his theory of an "obvious staged event" because he graduated Magna from Princeton in 62. Bill Ayers is a "distinguished professor of Education." Ted Kazinski (aka: the Unibomber) is a Harvard graduate.
Dr. Tim Leary taught at Harvard. I don't believe Socrates ever went to college.
Is he less credible than Bill Ayers? How about the fruitcake professor over there at UNH who belongs to a group (and proudly admits to such) that claims George Bush ("the single dumbest President ever elected" according to them) planned and carried out the 9/11 attack and got away with it.
They have voluminous photographic and written "evidence" according to them, that proves this insane proposition. George somehow got the cooperation of tens of thousands of people (Islamists, Christians, Jews, CIA spys, FBI, informants, local NYPD cops, innocent bystanders, etc.) all to do their part in the attack AND to keep quiet about it! Is that good "critical thinking", Dr. Fetzer?
May 9, 2013 10:39 am

James Fetzer said:

These replies are quite pathetic. I mention my education and background because I am most unlikely to qualify as "a conspiracy theorist" or a "wingnut", much less some kind of "psycho" who has disgraced the Marine Corps! Are all of you this stunningly incapable of serious thought? I appreciate the social pressures that may lead to conformity as a community phenomenon, but once attention has been focused on the actual evidence about what really happened, there is no more excuse for name calling and petty ad hominem attacks. And notice: THAT IS ALL THEY HAVE! Those making them could not have passed a course in critical thinking, where I taught freshmen to avoid trivial fallacies of these kinds. Why is no one here LOOKING AT THE EVIDENCE? We know that Craft International was "on the job" in Boston. I have photographs of them in "Some 'hard lessons' from the Boston bombing". We also know that Tamerlan was taken into police custody, because we have videos of it taking place, which I featured in *Welcome to Amerika: No More Truth, Justice or American Way*. We know that Stella is the only political figure to "tell it like it is" given the obvious fakery involving Jeff Bauman, as I explain in "Man of the Year: Stella Trimblay, NH Legislator". Have none of you even spent 12 minutes of your time watching the RT video, *Boston Bombing: What you aren't told*, www.youtube.com/watch?v=GcxmAunB4Ck? Is that too much time for this "brain trust"? Why attack Stella when she is speaking the truth? Just study the Craft photos I have presented. Compare their backpacks with one of those that exploded. Compare both of them with the backpack that Dzhokhar was wearing. Notice that they are not the same. Watch the video of Tamerlan being arrested. Both his mother and his aunt have identified him. Compare his condition being taken into custody with the body thereafter. Can you imagine how it was done? A witness reported watching the police run over him repeatedly with an SUV. Look at the photos of Jeff Bauman. Why are his legs not spurting blood? Why is the blood at the scene bright red when it should be dark? How can he be upright, conscious and alert as he is being rushed off in a wheelchair? Try looking at the evidence for a change! Egad! His fake prosthesis falls off as they are rushing him away, so they stop and reattach it! Just how dumb are the American people? Lots of us in higher education have worried about the pervasive influence of television, cell phones and the like, which reduce the exercise of our higher mental capabilities, such as reading, and reduce the level of our intellectual engagement, which has the effect of reducing our functional intelligence across time. Among my most recent books are *THE EVOLUTION OF INTELLIGENCE* (2005), where latest (co-edited with Ellery Eells) is *THE PLACE OF PROBABILITY IN SCIENCE* (2010). The "official account" of the Boston bombing is preposterous, in light of the evidence, but it seems to make no difference to any of my critics here.

May 9, 2013 11:31 am

Robert Baronas said:

Fetzer is denial in its purest form.

May 9, 2013 11:36 am

William Ducharme said:

James Fetzer, you have a very interesting Curriculum Vitae, but your vitae lack any medical education or training. I am surprised at your medical conclusions just by looking at pictures. I have listed several people each with an impressive Curriculum Vitae. Kaczynski was accepted into Harvard University at the age of 16, where he earned an undergraduate degree. He subsequently earned a Ph.D. in mathematics from the University of Michigan. He became an assistant professor at the University of California, Berkeley at age 25. Holms graduated from Westview High School in the Torrey Highlands community of San Diego in 2006. Holmes attended the University of California, Riverside and, in 2010, received his undergraduate degree in neuroscience with the highest honors. He was a member of several honor societies, including Phi Beta Kappa and Golden Key. According to UCR recommendation letters submitted to the University of Illinois at Urbana-Champaign (UIUC), Holmes graduated in the top 1percent of his class with a 3.949 GPA. The UCR letters also described Holmes as "a very effective group leader" and a person who "takes an active role in his education, and brings a great amount of intellectual and emotional maturity into the classroom". In June 2011, Holmes enrolled as a Ph.D. student in neuroscience at the University of Colorado Anschutz Medical Campus in Aurora.[34] He received a $21,600 grant from the National Institutes of Health, according to agency records, which was disbursed in installments from July 2011 to June 2012. Hasan joined the United States Army immediately after high school, and served eight years as an enlisted soldier while attending college. He graduated from Virginia Tech in 1995 with a bachelor's degree in biochemistry. He gained admission through a selective process for medical school at the Uniformed Services University of the Health Sciences ("USUHS" or "USU"). After earning his medical degree in 2003, Hasan completed his internship and residency in psychiatry at Walter Reed Army Medical Center. Hasan received the Army Service Ribbon as a private in 1988 after completing Advanced Individual Training (AIT), the National Defense Service Medal twice for service during the time periods of the Gulf War and the War on Terrorism, and the Global War on Terrorism Service Medal for support service during the War on Terrorism. One was the Unabomber, another the Aurora Movie Theater Shooter and lastly the Ft Hood Shooter, and like you, seem to have mental issues. The world or the government isn't out to get you and there are people who can help you deal with your paranoia. Good luck to you, sir.

May 9, 2013 11:39 am

C. Edney said:

First, doesn't the NH legislature have anything better to do than waste its time on stupid "bills" like this? Really, this and the white potato? Way to solve NH problems guys and girls. Second, it is sad to see people attack those who have opinions that differ from there own, specifically people like Mr. Fetzer. Personally, I am more afraid of people who put their faith and belief in the government (people like

William Ducharme) than of people like Mr. Fetzer. If you truly believe that our government is actually looking out for "us" – the American citizens – you are frightenly naive when it comes to politics. Retract your claws folks, no need to attack the messenger, but at least be open minded enough to look at all the evidence, you might be surprised. I'm not saying, I'm just saying ...
May 9, 2013 12:15 pm

Carl Sims said:

James,what witness? Don't you think that these witnesses would be all over the news if they were. Even remotely believable? As for Jeff Bauman's legs not spurting blood, luckily bystanders and medical personnel used tourniquets. Plus by then he didn't have enough blood in his system to spurt. The naked man taken into custody was a totally different person which the police acknowledged. And my guess he was in massive shock due to blood loss caused by explosive amputation of his legs. You hit all the spots on the conspiracy theorist bingo card except black helicopters.
May 9, 2013 12:40 pm

William Ducharme said:

C. Edney I never said I had an untethered belief in our government, but I don't have an imaginary fear of a government ghost chasing me either. Hopefully you can find a friend or family member to read my post to you, so you can understand my point. As a Veteran I protected something I believed in which is this Country. My advice for you is the same as for James; you can get help for your paranoia. Good luck, Sir.
May 9, 2013 1:05 pm

John Yule said:

Fetzer ... really, you know Craft Intl was "on the job" becuse of the hats? A hat like that can be bought in dozens of stores ... So can ATF and FBI t-shirts and jackets ... doesnt make them agents now does it. An earpiece is visible? Really ... they are quite common in many forms today from hearing aids to MP3 player earbuds to cell phones ... get a grip boy before the men in white coats come take you away!
May 9, 2013 1:15 pm

James Fetzer said:

God forbid anyone here should ACTUALLY LOOK AT THE EVIDENCE. I would not have believed there were this many mental midgets in the entire state of New Hampshire but for their showing up here en masse. This is embarrassing! How can I be in denial when I am simply pointing out that the evidence contradicts the "official account"? (1) Craft personnel were there in abundance. They were wearing backpacks like one that exploded. It even had a distinctive white square on it. (2) The backpack that Dzhokhar was wearing looked nothing like either of them – and was clearly not packed with a pressure cooker bomb. (By the way, how many here regard a pressure cooker bomb as a WMD? Show of hands.) (3) So Dzhokhar was not the source of either of the bombs. But a Craft guy was observed, first with his backpack with the distinctive white patch, then rushing away without. I wonder whether that makes any impact on this brain trust? (4) The video of Tamerlan being arrested was confirmed by his mother and his aunt. Who would be better positioned to identify him? And after he has been arrested, he turns up dead, where his body has been brutalized and mutilated. Who else could have done this than the police? (5) The case was solved so swiftly by the alternative media that they had to send out an FBI stooge to tell you, "Ignore the man behind the curtain! Look only at our photos of two suspects and no other," which would have made sense only if they had already examined every other photograph and cleared every other possible suspect. (6) They asked for the help of the public in identifying the two young men, but they had had them under surveillance for at least five years. Which means THEY ALREADY KNEW WHO THEY WERE. (7) There was a lock-down of the City of Boston, a massive presence of military force, even though that is in direct conflict with Posse Comitatus. Soldiers were going door-to-door and searching homes without warrants in gross violation of The Fourth Amendment. Doesn't anyone in New Hampshire care about that? I am convinced that there is an all-out disinformation campaign to conceal the truth from the American people. The perps, who appear to have been Craft International working with DHS and the FBI, were caught with their pants down and now they are doing everything they can to cover it up. This is the most obvious "false flag" attack in US history. If we the people can't see through this, there is no hope for truth, justice or the American way. Welcome to Amerika!

May 9, 2013 3:03 pm

Jonathan Christopoulous said:

to James Fetzer: You are a freakin ***** marine philosopher. Obviosly, you wore your helmet too high and tight for too long.

May 9, 2013 3:48 pm

Carolyn Pillsbury said:

People don't like to thinnk abour anything that might take them out of their comfort zone. Just look at the horrible stories that have come out of the Catholic Church sexual abuse scandal. We have not had a pope reitre in centuries, but it has happened now. I wonder why.

May 9, 2013 3:50 pm

James Fetzer said:

What most Americans do not know – principally because the main stream media is controlled by the government, which does not want the public to know – is that a subcommittee of the Senate Committee on Homeland Security and Intelligence issued a report on 3 October 2012 based upon its own study of 680 "fusion center" reports (where fusion centers merge federal, state and local "anti-terrorism" activities) spanning 2009-10 and found no indications of any domestic terrorist activity: NONE! ZIP! ZERO! NADA! That, however, must have come as most unwelcome news to the DHS, which has an agenda of its own to take control.

Which means, given the size of the sample and that those who were conducting the investigations being reported were zealous in its pursuit, that there is virtually no domestic terrorist threat! It is safe to infer that events like the Boston bombing are intended to compensate for that dearth of terrorism in the United States. If they can't find a real reason for DHS, they are going to contrive one. We appear to be living through the reincarnation of "Operation Northwoods", which was a false flag op to conduct terrorist attacks in the US and blame them on Fidel Castro as a justification for the invasion of Cuba, which JFK rebuffed.

But Obama is no JFK – and appears to be complicit. Indeed, what is remarkable in this case is that the "false flag" meme seems to have broken through. There is so much about the outrageous conduct of the FBI and its clumsy attempt to distract attention from the real perps to the patsies in this case that it may be impossible to put the toothpaste back in the tube! As Kevin Barrett has observed, *Yahoo News!* did something astonishing by conducting a poll about who was responsible for the Boston bombing, where the alternatives included the American government: But after the Boston bombings of April 16th, 2013, even the corporate monopoly media could no longer ignore the possibility of a false-flag attack.

Yahoo News asked "Who's behind the Boston Marathon bombings?" and offered 4 theories: (1) Islamic jihadists, (2) Right-wing militia types, (3) the government, and (4) a criminally-insane lone wolf. Numbers (1), (2), and (4), of course, are the usual suspects. But including (3) "the government" on the suspects list is unprecedented for a mainstream news story reporting on a domestic terror incident. The false-flag meme's growing prominence was underlined at Massachusetts governor Deval Patrick's press conference after the bombings. The first question for Governor Patrick came from *Infowars* correspondent Dan Bidondi, who asked whether the bombings were "a false-flag staged event to take away our civil liberties." Patrick, of course, answered "no." Even the *Atlantic Monthly*, a neocon-lite magazine associated with names like Goldberg and Hitchens, felt compelled to publish a story headlined: *What Is a 'False Flag' Attack, and What Does Boston Have to Do with This?*

Amazingly, the *Atlantic* article stated that yes, there is historical precedent for viewing the Boston bombing as a false-flag event. The author, Philip Bump, even admitted: "If the Boston attack had been a 'false flag' attack, Gov. Patrick would have responded 'no' anyway."

Barrett attributes this break through to the success of the 9/11 Truth movement in elevating the consciousness of the American public to the fact that governments, especially the Israeli but including our own, resort to attacks on their own people and their own nation to promote the government's political agenda. A nice example is the attacks on the Israeli Embassy and the Jewish Community Center that took place in Buenos Aires in 1992 and 1994 in apparent retaliation for Argentina's cooperation with Iran in the development of its peaceful atomic energy program, which illustrates the kinds of cases that have occurred, again and again, throughout modern history.

May 9, 2013 5:33 pm

Steve Johnson said:

@James Fetzer, having a PhD does not preclude you from being bat s-h-i-t crazy.

May 9, 2013 5:46 pm

ED MCCARTHY Jr said:

Methinks someone's mother was standing up when they were born.

Joanna Aiken said:

Hey James ... Not sure why you bother trying to educate the sleeping masses that continue to swallow the blue pill so they can stay blissfully ignorant. What you're doing threatens everything they've been brainwashed to believe and most can't handle the truth! It's just too painful. It's called Cognitive dissonance. If people would spend as much time reading history books, reviewing declassified documents (such as Operation Northwoods) and doing their homework instead of watching sports, dancing with the stars and drinking their beer, maybe they'd understand what you're trying to say!!!! Why not listen to the whistle blowers, people from the CIA, FBI, Military personnel.

You know, people like Bradley Manning or Sibel Edwards. The information is out there but you first have to want to know the truth. Most can't handle it! They'd prefer to stay in their blissfully ignorant little world and watch their primetime news to get their daily dose of dumbing down. Yes folks, the MSM is mostly controled by the CIA.

I would highly recommend listening to the testimony of William Schapp in the 1999 King vs Jowers trial (it's on *Youtube*). What he exposed in that trial will blow your mind!! It took Juror's a whole 59 MINUTES to find the US Government guilty of murdering Martin Luther King.

OH but I'm sure you weren't aware of this because the mainstream media didn't tell you, so it can't be true! It's certainly not the "conspiracy theorist" that scare me. It's the lazy people that can't pick up a book and read or capable of doing any research!!! The Federal education system was so successful in the dumbing people down.

These post are a perfect example of it!! George Carlin use to say it best. "They don't want a population capable of critical thinking. They want people just smart enough to run the machines and do the paperwork and just dumb enough to passively accept it!! Just keep eating your GMO's, drinking the flouride and aspirtame in the plastic bottles made out of BPA!! And people wonder why the United States is circling the drain!"

May 9, 2013 7:24 pm

Timothy Phippard said:

The lame stream media tells all of you the night they released the photos "Do not look at any other evidence it is all false." That is exactly when you should start looking. Many of us had days invested in alternative media sources prior to and after the "FBI's news release" *Russia Today* is far more truthful then any lame stream media source. When the lame stream media (State run media) is wrong and there is evidence that the government want seen or known then that evidence becomes "Conspiracy Theory". Wake up and do some google searches, or follow some of the links for the alternative media when posted and all the work is done for you! Try a month withour flouridated water, or do some searches on those effects, and how the Germans used flouride to calm the Jews in the camps. Do some research instead of name calling it is right at your fingertips.

May 9, 2013 7:24 pm

Sharon Omand said:

I have a suggestion to all you conspiracy theorist – as a mental health professional – get yourself to the nearest MH center for an evaluation of your paranoia before it gets out of hand. Including rep. Trembley and I think Mr. Fetzer must me suffering from some sort of PTSD from his service that has manifested into a psychotic paranoid delusion.

May 9, 2013 9:07 pm

John Jenkins said:

My father was a Marine Corp Sgt and I spent forty years in education. Mr. Fetzer I will pay for your next examination by a professional doctor. As the Irish say: "Never leave the opportunity to keep your mouth or written words closed and I think any time is right for you.

May 9, 2013 9:54 pm

William Simpson said:

I would like to remind those on the left who are making hay with the nuts on the right, that you have your own. Those who have delusionally convinced themselves that 9/11 was "an inside job." Those who believe our invasion of Iraq was "a war for oil", which is repudiated by President Obama's praise of President Bush's decency and leadership last week and his embrace of Bush's Afghanistan and Iraq policy. The point in this case is not to make partisan advantage; it

is to make clear that both sides have a loony element and to remind people that those fringes are best left ignored. They will not go away, but painting the entire right or left because of them is absurd. Nuts are nuts regardless of to whom they belong.
May 9, 2013 10:31 pm

Joanna Aiken said:
John ... I don't find the murder of MLK a joke. And you seriously compare the trial to Rodney King or OJ. You are one sick puppy!! There is absolutely no comparision!! You're either a paid troll on this pages to keep people too paranoid of being labeled a conspiracy theorist so they won't research the information provided OR you've drank WAY too much of the kool-aid.
So why no comment on OPERATION NORTHWOOD?? Gee, those are declassfied documents on the Governments plan to commit acts of terror on American citizens. Crashing planes into buildings (hmmm, that sounds awefully familiar). JFK wouldn't allow it. How convenient he got killed. What happened after that? We went to war with Vietnam ... based on a lie. Gulf of Tonkin incident never happened,. How many American soldiers died in that war John? 58k? Just like "Weapons of Mass Destruction!: How many lives have been destroyed in that war, again based on lies? How about you read Smedley Butlers book *War is a Racket* ... guess that would be asking too much wouldn't it? Reading that is and doing some "thinking!"
We are now in a never ending war with "terrorist". An invisible boogie man! This never ending war is a revolving door of profit for the Military Industrial Complex!! Terrorist could be anyone these days, according to Obama!! Including you John!! Better wake up before your town becomes a police state. And just so you all know, a Conspiracy Theory is just that a Theory. However, everything mentioned is declassified FACTS!!! Now go do your homework and take the red pill instead!! Wake your sorry a$$es up!! And let's see some real interviews with the people in Watertown during the police state. Bring in the Gestapo's. Not sure why the police need to physically search people. Did they think the 19 year old was hiding in their pants? It's all a part of your conditioning for what's coming! http://www.youtube.com/watch?v=qxpEoE-UJo&feature=youtu.be.
May 9, 2013 10:52 pm

Joanna Aiken said:
And I have to laugh at the "keep your mouth or written words closed." Really John? So I guess Paul Revere should have kept his mouth shut, huh? I guess our Founding Fathers should have kept their mouths shut too. Just bend over and take it up the *** people AND keep your mouth shut! Everybody be good little boys and girls and follow orders from your Fascist Government!
May 9, 2013 10:58 pm

Len Cannon said:

@John Jenkins: Don't waste your money on that examination offer for Mr. Fetzer. I have a friend in Colorado who emailed me about the Boston bombing and believes there is "ample" evidence that the Tsarnaev boys (the smirking pot smoker and the "stay-at-home" dad) were newbee IA trainees for their uncle who worked for the CIA and who went "rogue" before they could be stopped. He asked, "how else can you explain that a guy on watch list was able to go to Russia for 6 months and be allowed to reenter the US undetected?" I told him it was simple. The DHS, CIA and FBI, although skilled and competent in many areas, are loaded with incompetent, political appointee hacks and affirmative action placements who have no business being in those agencies and who screw up constatnly and scurry like cockroaches to hide when exposed. Janet Nepolitano, dumb as a post in my opinion, is a perfect example. I asked my firend if Maj. Hassan was also just another "inside job" spy who went "rogue" before he could be stopped? People like my friend and Fetzer are free to believe what they will. But they will never explain that photo that shows people scurrying in panic as the second bomb explodes but also shows Dzhokhar just calmly walking away like he was taking a stroll in the Public Gardens. Oh, I know. The CIA and DHS planted that photo on that man's I-Phone after they doctored it. Ya, that must be it!

May 10, 2013 7:13 am

Len Cannon said:

Joanna ... your Paul Revere (aka: Dr. Fetzer) analogy is a stretch. Don't you think?

May 10, 2013 7:42 am

James Fetzer said:

Those who are displaying their incompetence are those who are formed their opinions based upon official accounts but now disregard the actual evidence. Steve Johnson, Ed McCarthy, Jr., and Sharon Omand, for example, attack me for having a few screws, but what could be more blatantly irrational than ignoring relevant available evidence about a matter that counts? (1) We have multiple photos of Craft personnel, who are acting in a manner consistent with their participation in the bombing, including one of them wearing a distinctive backpack with a white square insignia, identical with one of the backpacks that exploded, where we see him rushing off in great haste WITHOUT HIS BACKPACK immediately thereafter.

(2) We have photos of Dzhokhar with his backpack slung over his right shoulder. It does not appear to contain a heavy object, such as a pressure cooker, and it is the wrong color to have been either of the two that exploded. His is silver in color, while one of those that exploded was black with a white square insignia and the other tan or beige.

(3) We have video of Tamerlan being stripped naked and placed into a police car, under arrest. Then next thing we learn is that he is dead, where we have photos of his body, which has been brutalized. A witness reports having seen the police run over him repeatedly with an SUV, probably his own car. He appears to have been murdered by police.
(4) We have photos showing the faking of injuries at the scene, where Jeff Bauman's legs are not spurting blood and he is not in shock. The blood at the scene only shows up later: you can see the alleged bone extension, but there is no blood initially, which is only added later and is bright red when it should have turned dark red from its oxidation.
Those who are attacking me are displaying a complete absence of reason and rationality. Surely the citizens of New Hampshire are not going to be played for suckers, even if some, like these three, turn out to be gullible saps. I am grateful to Timothy Phippard and especially Joanna Aiken for signs of intelligent life in coping with mass deception. The blunder that is being committed here is that of mistaking authority for truth, when truth should be the authority. We need to recall William Colby's observation that the CIA owns everyone of significance in the major media and Bill Casey's remark that the agency's disinformation program will be a success when everything Americans believe is false!

May 10, 2013 9:24 am

John Yule said:

Joanna ... are you mixing your Johns up ... or is that a normal state of your confusion. Oh yea, I know context is hard for you to understand ... I was referring to the trial as a joke BTW, and the believability of the witnesses from the transcripts I read is highly suspect. You know ... kinda like the things Fetzer says LOL!!!

May 10, 2013 10:35 am

The Real Deal Ep # 205 Raising "The Smoke Curtain" on the Pentagon with Dennis Cimino

[Chapter 17] The Second White Rose Leaflet

It is impossible to engage in intellectual discourse with National Socialism because it is not an intellectually defensible program. It is false to speak of a National Socialist philosophy, for if there were such an entity, one would have to try by means of analysis and discussion either to prove its validity or to combat it. In actuality, however, we face a totally different situation.

At its very inception this movement depended on the deception and betrayal of one's fellow man; even at that time it was inwardly corrupt and could support itself only by constant lies. After all, Hitler states in an early edition of "his" book (a book written in the worst German I have ever read, in spite of the fact that it has been elevated to the position of the Bible in this nation of poets and thinkers): "It is unbelievable, to what extent one must betray a people in order to rule it."

If at the start this cancerous growth in the nation was not particularly noticeable, it was only because there were still enough forces at work that operated for the good, so that it was kept under control. As it grew larger, however, and finally in an ultimate spurt of growth attained ruling power, the tumor broke open, as it were, and infected the whole body.

The greater part of its former opponents went into hiding. The German intellectuals fled to their cellars, there, like plants struggling in the dark, away from light and sun, gradually to choke to death.

Now the end is at hand. Now it is our task to find one another again, to spread information from person to person, to keep a steady purpose, and to allow ourselves no rest until the last man in persuaded of the urgent need of his struggle against this system. When thus a wave of unrest goes through the land, when "it is in the air," when many join the cause, then in a great final effort this system can be shaken off. After all, and end in terror is preferable to terror without end.

We are not in a position to draw up a final judgment about the meaning of our history. But if this catastrophe can be used to further the public welfare, it will be only by virtue of the fact that we are cleansed by suffering; that we yearn for the light in the midst of deepest night, summon our strength, and finally help in shaking off the yoke which weighs on our world.

We do not want to discuss here the question of the Jews, nor do we want in this leaflet to compose a defense or apology. No, only by way of example do we want to cite the fact that since the conquest of Poland three hundred thousand Jews have been murdered in this country in the most bestial way.

Here we see the most frightful crime against human dignity, a crime that is unparalleled in the whole of history. For Jews, too, are human beings – no matter what position we take with respect to the Jewish question – and a crime of this dimension has been perpetrated against human beings.

Someone may say that the Jews deserved their fate. This assertion would be a monstrous impertinence but let us assume that someone said this – what position has he then taken toward the fact that the entire Polish aristocratic youth is being annihilated? (May God grant that this program has not fully achieved its aim as yet!) All male offspring of the houses of the nobility between the ages of fifteen and twenty were transported to concentration camps in Germany and sentenced to forced labor, and the girls of this age group were sent to Norway, into the bordellos of the SS!

Why tell you these things, since you are fully aware of them – or if not of these, then of other equally grave crimes committed by this frightful sub-humanity?

Because here we touch on a problem which involves us deeply and forces us all to take thought. Why do the German people behave so apathetically in the face ofall these abominable crimes, crimes so unworthy of the human race? Hardly anyone thinks about that. It is accepted as fact and put out of mind.

The German people slumber on in their dull, stupid sleep and encourage these fascist criminals; they give them the opportunity to carry on their depredations; and of course they do so.

Is this a sign that the Germans are brutalized in their simplest human feelings, that no chord within them cried out at the sight of such deeds, that they have sunk into a fatal consciencelessness from which they will never, never awake?

It seems to be so, and will certainly be so, if the German does not at least start up out of his stupor, if he does not protest wherever and whenever he can against this clique of criminals, if he shows no sympathy for these hundreds of thousands of victims. He must evidence not only sympathy; no, much more: a sense of complicity in guilt.

For through his apathetic behavior he gives these evil men the opportunity to act as they do; he tolerates this "government" which has taken upon itself such an infinitely great burden of guilt; indeed, he himself is to blame for the fact that it came about at all! Each man wants to be exonerated of a guilt of this kind, each one continues on his way with the most placid, the calmest conscience. But he cannot be exonerated; he is guilty, guilty, guilty!

It is not too late, however, to do away with this most reprehensible of all miscarriages of government, so as to avoid being burdened with even greater guilt. Now, when in recent years our eyes have been opened, when we know exactly who our adversary is, it is high time to root out this brown horde.

Up until the outbreak of the war the larger part of the German people were blinded; the Nazis did not show themselves in their true aspect. But now, now that we have recognized them for what they are, it must be the sole and first duty, the holiest duty of every German to destroy these beasts.

> "If the people are barely aware that the government exists, they are happy. When the government is felt to be oppressive, they are broken."
> "Good fortune, alas! builds itself upon misery. Good fortune, alas! is the mask of misery. What will come of this? We cannot foresee the end. Order is upset and turns to disorder, good becomes evil. The people are confused. Is it not so, day in, day out, from the beginning?"
> "The wise man is therefore angular, though he does not injure others: he has sharp corners, though he does not harm; he is upright but not gruff. He is clear-minded, but he does not try to be brilliant."
>
> - Lao Tzu

> "Whoever undertakes to rule the kingdom and to shape it according to his whim – I foresee that he will fail to reach his goal. That is all."
> "The kingdom is a living being. It cannot be constructed, in truth! He who tries to manipulate it will spoil it, he who tries to put it under his power will lose it. "
> "Therefore: Some creatures go out in front, others follow, some have warm breath, others cold, some are strong, some weak, some attain abundance, others succumb. The wise man will accordingly forswear excess, he will avoid arrogance and not overreach."
>
> - Lao Tzu

Please make as many copies as possible of this leaflet and distribute them.

Jim organized the first conference for Scholars for 9/11 Truth in Madison, WI, 1-3 August 2007, and edited the first book from Scholars.

Jim Fetzer
Kevin Barrett
David Ray Griffin
11 DE SEPTIEMBRE 2009
Conferencia Internacional por la Verdad y la Justicia del 11-S
Internacional Conference for 911 Truth and Justice
VANCOUVER 9/11 TRUTH CONFERENCE
9/11, CANADA and the NEW WORLD ORDER
Prof. Kevin Barrett
June 22nd - 24th, 2007
KEVIN
vancouver 9/11 TRUTH
v911truth.org
CONFERENCIA INTERNACIONAL POR LA VERDAD Y LA JUSTICIA: 11-S
Dr. Jim Fetzer

[Chapter 18] Gary Kohls: The White Rose

"People have to understand. It's easy to get a patsy. Get some joker on a plane ... I mean, it's ridiculous. If you travel around the world you realize that we especially in the United States, we live in a bubble ... especially if you talk to people in Russia ... they know it's propaganda ... we still think it's free press ... and that's our biggest darn problem in this country."
- Bob McIlvaine, 9/11 Parent

The White Rose
by Gary Kohls

Seventy years ago, on February 23, 1943, three courageous German college students at the University of Munich were beheaded by the Gestapo after being arrested five days earlier and convicted of treason earlier in the day.

The group included 22-year-old medical student Christoph Probst, 24-year-old Hans Scholl, also a medical student, and Hans's 21-year-old sister Sophie. They were part of a small group of university students whose code name was the White Rose.

As were many other alert Germans, the White Rose was fully aware of the atrocities that were being committed against certain non-Aryan minorities. They had seen clearly the loss of liberty, the shredding of human rights, and the disturbing reality that the war was probably already lost.

By the summer of 1942, these savvy dissenters, who knew that resisting Hitler in any form was a capital crime, were fully aware of the existence of Nazi concentration camps and that hundreds of thousands of Jews had already been murdered in them.

These altruistic young Germans were also alarmed at the fear and apathy that they witnessed in the adults all around them. They were troubled by the fact that no active resistance movements were being organized by anybody that they knew.

The White Rose students, of which there were dozens scattered around Germany, knew that Hitler's aggressive war-making, torture, and state-sponsored terrorism were making Germany the most hated nation in the world. Being real patriots who loved their homeland enough to have an argument with it, they felt that they had to do something to stop Hitler. So, in late 1942, the White Rose started composing and distributing amazingly insightful, well-written leaflets, warning their fellow Germans about the criminal regime that most Germans seemed to be tolerating without objection.

These altruistic students were wise enough to realize that they needed to use nonviolent resistance tactics in their efforts. They had witnessed the brutality of the homeland security agencies, the secret police, and the "see something, say something" policies that encouraged folks to snitch on their neighbors.

These students knew that the liberal printing presses had already been smashed by right-wing fascist thugs during the latter part of the "made-to-fail" 1920s Weimar Republic experiment in democracy and that those thugs, mostly angry World War I veterans, had been aligned with militarized, big-business-subsidized groups such as the Nazi Party.

Even nonviolent resistance to tyranny was a capital crime in Nazi Germany.

The major treasonous "crime" that the White Rose members were accused and convicted of was circulating a series of six "subversive" leaflets whose only purpose was to awaken fellow Germans to the atrocities that were being perpetrated by Hitler's henchmen and to try to motivate them to rise up in resistance.

Of course the major "crime" they may have been guilty of was embarrassing the Gestapo and humiliating the Nazis by successfully evading detection and capture for so many months.

The Nazis thought that the influence of the White Rose ended with their arrest, trial, and beheadings.

The trial, so well portrayed in the powerful movie *Sophie Scholl: The Final Days*, was orchestrated by the notorious Roland Freisler, the shrieking Nazi judge who had been ordered by Hitler to organize the infamous "People's Court" show trials that the Nazis then used for propaganda purposes and to instill fear in the people.

Little did the Nazis realize that the executions of this heroic group, rather than eliminating them from the pages of history, actually made martyrs of them so that their spirits live on, continuing to inspire modern nonviolent resistance movements to this very day.

Excerpts from the *Third Leaflet of the White Rose* – February 1943:

> "But our present 'state' is the dictatorship of evil. 'Oh, we've known that for a long time,' I hear you object, 'and it isn't necessary to bring that to our attention again.' But, I ask you, if you know that, why do you not bestir yourselves, why do you allow these men who are in power to rob you step by step, openly and in secret, of one domain of your rights after another, until one day nothing, nothing at all will be left but a mechanized state system presided over by criminals and drunks? Is your spirit already so crushed by abuse that you forget it is your right – or rather, your moral duty – to eliminate this system?
>
> "Many, perhaps most, of the readers of these leaflets do not see clearly how they can practice an effective opposition. We have no great number of choices ... The only one available is passive [but

active] resistance. At all points we must oppose [fascism], wherever it is open to attack. We must soon bring this monster of a state to an end. A victory of fascist Germany in this war would have immeasurable, frightful consequences... The defeat of the Nazis must unconditionally be the first order of business...

"Sabotage in armament plants and war industries, sabotage at all gatherings, rallies, public ceremonies, and organizations of the National Socialist Party. Obstruction of the smooth functioning of the war machine (a machine for war that goes on solely to shore up and perpetuate the Nazi Party and its dictatorship). Sabotage in all publications, all newspapers, that are in the pay of the [fascist] 'government' and that defend its ideology... The presses run continuously to manufacture any desired amount of paper currency... Try to convince all your acquaintances, including those in the lower social classes, of the senselessness of continuing, of the hopelessness of this war; of our spiritual and economic enslavement at the hands of the National Socialists; of the destruction of all moral and religious values; and urge them to passive resistance!

"Aristotle said it is part [of the nature of tyranny]... that everywhere [the subjects] will be spied upon... and so it is part of these tyrannical measures, to keep the subjects poor, in order to pay the guards and soldiers, and so that they will be occupied with earning their livelihood and will have neither leisure nor opportunity to engage in conspiratorial acts...

"Please duplicate and distribute!"

[Originally published in *The Duluth Reader*, and reprinted here by permission of the author.]

Iran Review > What Others Think

How We Know ISIS Was "MADE IN THE USA"

WEDNESDAY, JANUARY 20, 2016

James H. Fetzer

For those who may have missed the memo, 9/11 was brought to us by the CIA, the Neo-Cons in the Department of Defense (most of whom were dual US-Israel citizens) and the Mossad. Its objective was to transform US foreign policy from one in which we (at least, officially) never attacked any nation that had not attacked us first to one in which we would become the greatest aggressor nation in the world.*[1]*

Wesley Clark, upon his return from serving as Supreme Commander, Allied Forces Europe (the military chief of NATO), learned the plan was to take out the governments of seven nations in the next five years, beginning with Iraq and Libya and ending with Syria and Iran, which he shared with us during a speech at The Commonwealth Club in San Francisco, which may have been the most honorable act of his life.*[2]*

That it has not played out that way has not been from lack of trying. The brilliant intervention of Russia on behalf of Syria and its people and in defense of its maligned president, Bashar al-Assad, a staunch ally, has thrown a monkey wrench into the master plan, which would enable Israel to become "the Greater Israel" and fulfill "its destiny" by dominating the Middle East from the Tigris-Euphrates to the Nile.*[3]*

The massive control of the mainstream media in the United States, however, has obfuscated the grim reality of the situation, where the Obama administration was thwarted in its plan to lob cruise missiles into Syria on the fabricated context that Assad had gassed his own people, which Russia refuted with a 50-page dossier to the United Nations. This required the Neo-Cons who dominate his administration to regroup and contrive a more subtle rationale for attacking Syria.*[4]*

Jim has also published on ISIS in IRAN REVIEW *(20 January 2016).*

Who Killed
JFK?
JAMES FETZER

[Chapter 19] Kevin: Maddow, Moore, Goodman ...

> "A lot of these pieces of information, taken together, prove that the official story, the official conspiracy theory of 9/11 is a bunch of hogwash. It's impossible. ... There's a second group of facts having to do with the cover up. ... Taken together these things prove that high levels of our government don't want us to know what happened and who's responsible."
>
> - Lt. Col. Robert Bowman, Ph.D., U.S. Air Force (ret) – Director of Advanced Space Programs Development under Presidents Ford and Carter. U.S. Air Force fighter pilot with over 100 combat missions. (Ph.D. in Aeronautics and Nuclear Engineering, Cal Tech). Former Head of the Department of Aeronautical Engineering and Assistant Dean at the U.S. Air Force Institute of Technology, 22-year Air Force career.

KEVIN:

[On Rachel Maddow coming out strong against Truthers]

That's her job. That's what she's being paid for. If you want to tell the truth, you don't get paid for it.

Well, it's really not about liberal-conservative.

If anything liberals tend to be suckers for government even more than conservatives do. They're big cheerleaders for big government.

So their whole ideology prevents them from being able to see that these things are being done by government to increase government power. Rachel Maddow, she might actually be sincere in her beliefs, and of course she's going to be more effective if she is sincere, so everybody is going to try to conspire to try to keep her sincere.

And she was I think a victim of a psyop in which they used Glen Beck to poison the well of so-called conspiracy theories.

They put Glen Beck out there yammering about that he was giving Obama until Monday to admit that it was a false flag or he would reveal this information about what a terrible evil terrorist the Saudi guy was who was injured in the bombing.

The following Monday, rather than Beck coming out and naming this guy and explaining what the problem was, Beck kept his mouth shut, but a bunch of other members of the propaganda team, these smaller fake conspiracy websites, astro-turf conspiracy websites started putting out bogus information that the Saudi who was injured at the site of the bombing was Osama bin Laden's son and heir, so this kind of, and that Obama was somehow complicit.

So this kind of right wing fake conspiracy theory with Glen Beck leading the charge is used to poison the well so that people like Rachel Maddow, when they hear about people questioning whether it's a false flag are going to be thinking, oh, idiots like Glen Beck and just instantly dismiss it.

[More on liberal gatekeepers – Michael Moore]

Michael Moore is not as bad as Maddow and Jon Stewart, because Michael Moore is at least not attacking us.

That's a huge difference.

People like Chomsky and Rachel Maddow and other tools of the genocidal criminals that did 9/11 are basically, they should be considered traitors. They need to be prosecuted for treason, which is a capital crime.

Because they are actively blocking the investigation and solution of the biggest crime of all humanity's history, but people like Michael Moore are acting more responsibly, although I wouldn't really defend what he's done.

He is a coward.

I talked to his manager, by the way, when Michael Moore was speaking at the Memorial Union Terrace in Madison, and I spoke with his manager and asked him why, you know, since Michael obviously knows that 9/11 was an inside job, that he never talks about it, in public.

And at that point I don't think he ever really had. And the manager said, well Michael Moore wants to reach the maximum possible audience. That was his answer.

So again, it's a strategic calculation.

Michael Moore thinks, if I speak out too strongly for 9/11 Truth, they're going to blackball me, I'll never get a movie made again, I'll never get a movie distributed again, I won't be invited on *Democracy Now*, I won't ever be allowed access to the foundation funded pseudo-alternative media, *The Nation* magazine, *The Progressive*, etc. etc., I will be completely black-balled and I'll have no more income, I won't be able to do anything.

So Michael decides, he sees where his bread is buttered and he decides to keep his mouth shut, but he hasn't completely kept his mouth shut.

He's made a number of statements, generally kinds of informal situations that can be ignored by most people and by the mainstream.

So he says things like, I know there are at least a hundred cameras that showed what happened at the Pentagon, where are those videos. He's said a lot of things like that, he knows it was an inside job and even if you just look at *Fahrenheit 9/11* between the lines it's obvious that he knows that what happened isn't what we're told.

He's Jewish and not entirely unsympathetic to Israel.

He's a little bit brainwashed on that issue like so many people, and I think that may be a factor as well.

So many people who have been brainwashed into feeling that sympathy for Israel, especially Jewish Americans, but also a lot of really dumb, you know, dumbass Christian Americans, are worried at a sort of unconscious level, they know that if 9/11 comes out, that's curtains for Israel.

And I think that contributes to keeping a lot of these people away from it, but Michael Moore, at the end of the day I would say that his way of dealing with this, even though it's cowardly, it's not criminal, in the way that Rachel Maddow, Amy Goodman and Noam Chomsky have been absolutely criminal in their actions for the cover-up of the worst crime in human history.

[Amy Goodman?]

I've tried to contact her several times.

I helped convince her to bring on David Ray Griffin on her radio show.

She had originally booked David Ray Griffin and Ellen Mariani, which would have been a dynamite one-two punch, but apparently her controllers told her that she couldn't do that, so she backed off at the last minute, cancelled Ellen Mariani, and then put up Chip Berlet, who's a professional CIA propagandist, so-called debunker, another of the worst criminals walking the face of the earth today, a guy who should be executed as soon as possible.

Well, after a fair trial, of course.

Chip Berlet, a very smooth, polished professional liar, just did a hideously bogus job of trying to counter what David Ray Griffith was saying on *Democracy Now*.

And it was just lies, nothing but lies, anyone who knew anything about this issue was tearing their hair out, listening to Berlet's very smooth, slick professional lies, but unfortunately, people who didn't know anything abut the issue might very well be persuaded by those lies because Amy Goodman wasn't playing a fair referee, calling out the lies.

She didn't know anything about the issue either and she didn't want to.

So the net effect of David Ray Griffin's appearance on *Democracy Now* was nil.

It was barely even a positive blip because of the way that Amy Goodman handled it.

So this really pissed me off, and one of the reasons that I turned down a post-doc to go work at the University of California in 2004, 2005, I guess I would have been there in 2006.

I turned down that post-doc because it was funded by the Ford Foundation, which was also funding Amy Goodman, in fact it gave her a special grant of, I forget if it was a few hundred thousand dollars or half a million dollars, in that neighborhood to report on the aftermath of 9/11.

Now, Amy had been broadcasting from the Firehouse Studio, near Ground Zero, so this huge chunk of money from the Ford Foundation was basically hush money, telling her, here's a bunch of money to cover 9/11 without causing trouble.

And then I did some research on the Ford Foundation, discovered that this is par for the course for them, that they're basically a CIA front, and I decided I didn't want to go to the University of California and be paid by the CIA-front Ford Foundation to ... they were going to have me studying African Muslim immigrants, and that would have been like making me a CIA agent, keeping track of Muslim immigrants. Are you kidding? So I turned that down.

I continued to be completely appalled at Amy Goodman's behavior and her continuing efforts to cover up this crime of 9/11 that she had personally witnessed.

She was actually there for the controlled demolition of Building 7 and the reason she was there almost certainly was because that demolition had been pre-announced on the radio, so she went out to watch the building come down, and she was there as a countdown went out over police radio, 10-9-8-7-6-5-4-3-2-1, boom, and the building comes straight down, six and half seconds for forty-seven stories.

Amy Goodman and all the rest of the people who've come out to watch it after hearing that it was going to be demolished on the radio, they turn and run.

So she was there and she knows Seven was a controlled demolition and yet she won't ever talk about this or cover it and that makes her a really seriously complicit war criminal.

First I was just trying to get her to turn around and get on the right side of this issue.

A few years later I finally got tired of that and started sending out some pretty harsh anti-Amy Goodman polemics and when she came to speak at the University of Wisconsin-Madison I went there and asked her about Building 7, and she tried to weasel out of it by saying, well I did not demolish Building 7, and then she called for a new investigation of 9/11, which is nice, only she's never doing anything to make that new investigation happen even though she has a lot of power to do it.

I'm completely disgusted with her and with the whole milieu of morons who trust her.

[Chapter 20] Jim, Kevin: "There he is!"

The ARGO: What is the long, hard night that America must go through that you've spoken of?
Mort Sahl: She has to hang on through a period of the military and the CIA with a blank check trying to sell fascism. If she can hang on long enough, Americans may yet live in the country in which they were born. And that is the country structured by Tom Paine and Tom Jefferson.

- Mort Sahl, interviewed by Perry Adams of *The Argo* on Monday, March 18, 1968

JIM:

[Are you known on the streets of Oregon? Madison?]

No. I'm known to people who know, who have paid attention to research on 9/11, JFK, Paul Wellstone. People like that.

If they pay attention to international news. If they ever watch interviews. I'm known to those people. But that's a fairly intellectual, sophisticated percentage of the population.

I'm not known to the man in the street.

KEVIN:

[Often the outcome that many people are faced with, who do this sort of work, is becoming a non-person. Maybe that is by someone's design, maybe it just happens. It does not seem to have happened to you.]

Yeah, well the Internet is helpful.

So many people saw through the 9/11 false flag that it became a pretty big club including a lot of very respectable people, so rather than being marginalized by my 9/11 Truth work, I've actually gotten to meet all kinds of brilliant and very accomplished people.

Now I have friends like Colonel Bob Bowman who unfortunately is very ill right now with cancer, who's a Cal Tech rocket science Ph.D. who used to run the Star Wars missile defense program, and Paul Craig Roberts who's the architect of Reaganomics, Dorian Sagan, and his late mother Lynn Margulis. Lynn was one of the greatest scientists of all time and Dorian is a genius of a science writer himself, and I could go on like this. Suddenly, thanks to my 9/11 conspiracy work, rather than losing all my friends and sitting on a sidewalk somewhere and scribbling out angry signs to flash at passers-by, I'm hanging out with the world's best people, not just best people, but people who are widely recognized for their talents and accomplishments.

I think this is one of the mistakes they made, with 9/11, making it a little too obvious.

Who knows whether they made it intentionally obvious, or whether it was all just screwups or right hand didn't know what the left hand was doing, but with the Internet there, it was easy for people to find each other, and no matter how hard they tried to poison the well, they really couldn't because there were just too many smart, ethical people who were calling them on it.

Jim's book on Sandy Hook--which has thirteen (13) contributors, including six (6) Ph.D. (current or retired) college professors--was banned by amazon.com less than a month after its appearance on 22 October 2005, where Jay Carney, former White House spokesman, had gone to amazon.com as Senior Vice President. It blows the official narrative out of the water, where the school appears to have been abandoned in 2008.

[Chapter 21] Jim: Teaching at the University of Kentucky, remarrying, Virginia, Cincinnati

> "These fake bin Laden tapes appear to be simply one part of an extensive propaganda operation, in which the U.S. military intelligence is using tax dollars – illegally – to propagandize the American public, with the aim of furthering the militarization of America and its foreign policy."
>
> - David Ray Griffin

JIM:

My first position was at the University of Kentucky, in Lexington.

And, I guess it just wasn't a very good fit, you know, I'd done all this work with Hempel and Salmon, who were the two leading philosophers of science in the world. Nagel might be counted as the third. I hadn't met Sir Karl yet, but I'd been very impressed by Popper's work.

I published a lot at Kentucky. I gave a lot of talks at the invitation of other departments because all my work was so inter-disciplinary. I think I must have given in the first five years, I must have given talks in eight different departments at the University of Kentucky.

Probably never happened to any other faculty member there.

The way tenure is set up, you're reviewed for tenure your sixth year and then you have a seventh year, as it were, to find another job if you're not granted tenure. Tenure is a privilege, not a right. The decision to grant tenure is one that has to be made on the merits.

I had lots of articles. I think I had twelve or thirteen articles, all in very good journals, and I had received the first distinguished teaching award ever presented by the student government at the University of Kentucky, which the student government hoped would contribute to securing tenure for the recipient.

But, my colleagues, I guess I stepped on too many toes. You know, I acted like I belonged there, I remember putting my boots (I was still wearing my combat boots from the Marine Corps) up on the table when we'd have faculty meetings and the head of the department... There were only six tenured faculty at the time and you had to get a majority vote of the tenured faculty.

Well, one of the first things they'd done is put me in charge of the undergraduate logic program, so I had a group of TAs who were in our masters program who worked with me and they were really good students.

And they had their own sections in logic and we were turning out these little logicians who just loved it. It had been the most difficult course I'd had at Princeton, well apart from statistics or calculus; I was not really very good at higher mathematics. But I had a course in logic with Hempel, where Paul Benacerraf who's really quite a brilliant guy had been my classroom instructor, called Preceptors, at Princeton.

But what I hadn't understood about logic was actually very parallel to what I was figuring out about physics, namely that, they introduce a model of logic, it's called Formal Logic, so you have symbols for sentences, initially, and then you break down sentences into their subject-predicate form. And there's an elaborate symbolism to capture the relationship between sentences when they're true and other sentences that must be true or must be false if those sentences are true.

And what I hadn't understood as an undergraduate was how this is a simplified model that doesn't capture all the features of ordinary language, so when I became a teacher of logic, formal logic, I would explain to my students how this is a simplified model. It doesn't capture all the features of ordinary language.

And I'd be very specific about this as related to the conditional, if-then sentences, which are probably the trickiest part of formal logic, and why there's a difference between if-then as it's used in ordinary language and if-then as it's formalized in symbolic logic. I would eventually wind up doing advanced research in this area, about subjunctive and counter-factual conditionals and probabilistic causal conditionals and universal strength causal conditionals, with a fellow by the name of Donald Nute, who earned his philosophy degree at Indiana but in the department of philosophy, whereas I earned mine in the history and philosophy of science.

Don and I would later collaborate on the probabilistic Calculus C. Interestingly, just over the last year, there's a fellow in Australia who has sent me a seemingly interminable series of inquiries about the work that Don and I did together, and I dealt him in.

We responded to all his questions about the probabilistic cause of Calculus C and the nature of what are technically known as single case propensities, which has to do with the interpretation of probability, a subject on which I spent quite a lot of work.

My most recent book actually, co-edited with Ellery Eells, who was on the faculty in the department of philosophy at the University of Wisconsin-Madison, is entitled *The Place of Probability in Science*.

And I had been so looking forward to spending time with Ellery when I moved down here after my retirement, and unfortunately, shades of David Ziegler, Ellery died.

He'd actually been an alcoholic, he became quite a chronic alcoholic.

Something I loved about Ellery, I mean we got along really, really well, but he was an insomniac, and he'd stay up late listening to radio shows like *Coast to Coast AM*, and he'd invariably call me up to tell me how he'd heard me on the radio, ya know, at one o'clock in the morning, he heard me on the radio!

I've been five times on *Coast To Coast*, three times about JFK, once about Paul Wellstone, and once about 9/11.

But they seemed to discontinue inviting me to appear on the show after 2008 when I first began talking about the Israeli complicity in 9/11. I can't say that is the explanation, but is the best I can see.

Some of my shows on *Coast To Coast* about JFK were simply extraordinary, I mean they were just terrific.

I've now done, you know, a thousand radio shows, if you were to actually count them; I've probably given as many as four or five interviews in a single day on some occasions. I've done a tremendous number of interviews about JFK and now more recently about 9/11, and of course, most recently, about Sandy Hook and the Boston bombing and all that.

Wellstone, somehow less. I did recently give a talk at the Wellstone Center in Saint Paul on the 25th of October, 2012, ten years after his death, where I've done a tremendous amount of research on that.

So here I'd received the first distinguished teaching award, I'd published all these articles, but I embarrassed the guy who'd been teaching, running the logic program before I took it over.

He always explained that he got poor course evaluations because his students thought it was inherently difficult, and here I was getting these raving reviews and even the teaching award, which was based largely in my success in getting everyone to understand logic.

And then the head of the logic program was Allen Perreiah. Ironically, Allen had grown up in Alhambra, which is right across Huntington Drive from South Pasadena.

Anyhow, the head of the department was a fellow named Dallas High, who actually had a Ph.D. in religion, but had created the impression with the department when they did the search that he had his Ph.D. in the philosophy of religion, which was untrue.

So that Dallas wanted to have a Ph.D. program at Kentucky. I thought that was really a bad idea, so he wasn't very happy with me on political grounds.

He would later contend that he thought the department needed a different kind of philosopher of science, and the person he suggested that would be was a fellow named Hans Jonas, who actually is a theologian. He's not a philosopher of science at all. But he was the head of the department at the time, and he voted against me.

A split vote could not defeat a reappointment, but could defeat a tenure application – and I had the unanimous support of the department until I got the teaching award, and after that, split three-three. And the third who voted against me was a fellow named Jesse DeBoer, who was an elder in the Presbyterian Church; he earned his Ph.D. at Harvard in like 1941 or 1942, and he would later tell a colleague of mine that he voted against me because I lived with my girlfriend without the benefit of marriage. My girlfriend at the time was a woman named Linda Sartorelli, who had come to Indiana to earn her Ph.D., and she and I had a long, enduring, wonderful relationship. She was from Chelsea in Boston, and I actually spent seven Christmases in a row in Boston.

We had a wonderful relationship.

But at a certain point, you know, I thought we ought to get married, and initially she thought so too, but eventually she decided she couldn't be herself enough with me and she returned to, well, she took another job, whatever, we split.

Now, one of the members of the department who had supported me was a fellow by the name of Michael Bayles, who had done a lot of work in ethics and so forth. And his wife and I, his wife Jan and I, had done a lot of socializing with Linda, and when Linda left we still continued to do some socializing. And actually, Michael and Jan's relationship wasn't everything that Jan wanted, and they split and she and I dated and got married about a year after they divorced, in 1977.

Just in the last month of my appointment at Kentucky, I'd gone through a very hairy case with the AAUP chapter. When I was denied tenure the AAUP chapter had never contested a tenure decision at the university in its history. They wanted a case that was so solid it would set a right precedent. They thought my case was that case. And so they created a hearing. There was a panel. I think there were five on the panel.

But the president at the time, Otis Singletary, had his chief counsel argue the case, so everyone knew that the president was favoring my non-tenure. Both I and the fellow who was helping me, who was on the faculty of the law school, were apparently so good in argument – he'd make the legal points and I'd add the substantic points – that they decided this was too much to deal with and insisted that only one of us could speak.

So, I thought, well, you know, if I get pissed off at these people, that might make a bad impression, so maybe he should do it and I'd just give him information, but I think in retrospect, probably, I knew the people, I should have carried the burden. It was my career, and I should have argued it, rather than he.

Anyway, they split, 4-1, 5-1. I remember there was some piece of information I needed to give them, and I came to the room where they were deliberating, knocked on the door, and when they opened the door I discovered the president's legal counsel was in there discussing it with them. It was completely wrong, a complete violation of my rights, and, you know, very unsettling, and this is one of those cases where the agony of uncertainty, ya know that anguish... I just had no idea at the time what had actually caused me to have this great difficulty in dealing with uncertainty.

After I'd spoken to the head of the committee, he said he was going to investigate and make sure my rights were being upheld; I called him back after a couple of hours – I hesitate to surmise just how long that period of time was – and told him I was sure they were trying to do, ya know, the right thing, and it was immediately ignored, and I got a letter from the vice president explaining I'd had the hearing and I was being dismissed.

Anyway, there were other cases like that where I stumbled, and I think it was due to subconscious influences of which I was not aware and might have been able to deal with had I become conscious of them then as I did only after my retirement.

Anyway, Mike and Jan had two daughters, Melanie and Michele, just terrific girls.

And when Jan and I married, let's see, Mel was on the verge of going to college, she wound up going to Indiana. Mike actually entered his Ph.D. at Indiana.

Michele later would want to go to Indiana, but Mike would tell her because he was then at the University of Florida that he wanted her to go to Florida because no tuition would be charged.

I told Michele how important I thought it was she go to Indiana, and that I was very glad to pick up the tab, to assume the responsibility, and I wish she had, because she felt she should follow her father's preferences, but the only place she ever wanted to go to school was Indiana.

And Mike, I'm sorry to say, was just too selfish. He was just too into himself, and this was a terrible, terrible mistake.

He would, ironically, eventually commit suicide.

He believed that it was a philosophical option for humans to make if they thought most of their productive years were behind them, that they were probably going to experience pain in the future, and that this was something they could elect to do, it was a human freedom.

I appreciated that.

I actually can support that. I mean, obviously, I don't have any constraints of my own about suicide except that people often don't know the influence it's going to have on other people. But Mike was then married to his second wife. Actually, I think they'd already been divorced, married and divorced. I think they had a home in Gainesville. He was at the University of Florida, then he was at Florida State.

He was doing well. I mean Mike had a very successful career. He published about a dozen books, and was well-regarded in the field of ethics and social philosophy, but he obtained a handgun, I think it was a .38. He learned how to shoot it.

He knew how to shoot himself to make sure he'd kill himself, and he went out in the backyard and blew out his brains. So, that was very sad.

I recall calling Mel and Michele with Jan to tell them that Mike had done this, and how my mother had committed suicide, how much I shared their sense of grief.

Because I was denied tenure at Kentucky I spent ten years on a succession of visiting appointments.

In fact, Virginia hired me immediately as visiting associate professor. I mean Kentucky had denied me a promotion to associate, but Virginia, which was the leading public institution in the country, may well still be, hired me as visiting associate professor.

I came back the next year at Cincinnati. I taught a year as a visiting associate professor at Cincinnati, and then I had an NSF and I wrote my first book on the theoretical foundations of scientific knowledge the following year, which was probably my greatest.

We still had the home in Lexington, so Jan was there ... how did we do it at Virginia? ... oh, we rented the house out in Lexington and we moved to Virginia, where our daughter Sarah would be conceived, and I really enjoyed Virginia. I thought it was an absolutely wonderful place, Mr. Jefferson's University.

It was terrific, and I was real proud of Michele, we were having a great time, and the next year I was given a visiting appointment at Cincinnati, and then the second year I had an NSF. I think probably the greatest intellectual achievement of my life was writing my first book on a typewriter. It was about 500 pages.

I wrote it continuously first page to last. I'd use liquid paper to make some corrections as I typed each page, but once it was done, it was done; I'd go on to the next, and the next. They didn't ask me to change a comma.

I think it just reflects how well I knew my subject. I knew what I was doing.

There were many very technical parts of this book. In fact, I've written books at five different levels of difficulty. This was by far at the highest level of difficulty. Eventually it was dedicated to Sir Karl Popper.

And just to give you an indication, Sir Karl wrote me a hand-written letter to tell me how much he liked it and how much he enjoyed reading it and that he hadn't done everything he should do to prove all the theorems, but he thought there was difficulty in my form of exposition, why do I intimidate my readers so?

And he offered as his example of an intimidating sentence the first sentence of the first paragraph of the first chapter!

I thought, well my God, if Sir Karl Popper, one of the most formidable intellects in the world, thinks the first sentence of the first chapter of my first paragraph is intimidating, then perhaps I need to write books at different levels. I would eventually write an introduction to the philosophy of science that was very accessible.

That was probably at the, if five is the most difficult, I think the philosophy of science intro was at the second level of difficulty.

The one book of mine that's gone into a second edition was written at the first level of accessibility. The was *Philosophy and Cognitive Science*. And I have, you know, a couple others, like, *The Evolution of Intelligence*, which is probably at the fourth level of difficulty, but still easier than the fifth.

But the first book was my greatest intellectual accomplishment, I have no doubt.

I remember being in an elevator where Bob Cohen, who was running a program in the history of philosophy of science at Boston University, wanted to publish my book in the series he was editing, *Boston Studies in Philosophy of Science*. He just sort of turned to me in the elevator, and there were other people there, telling me how much he'd like to publish my book, and I said, well, I appreciate that.

And I wound up publishing it with him, but it turns out – this was something I really didn't understand about the profession – that there is a hierarchy among publishers, and that what I should have done, however much I appreciated Bob's gesture, was to have begun with say, Cambridge and then Oxford, go with the publishers who have the greatest prestige. Cambridge, I think, has the greatest prestige in the world, and I think Cambridge probably would have loved this book.

But I didn't.

I published it in *Boston Studies*.

I also made a mistake.

I wound up using most of my grant, but a good friend of mine name of Chuck Dunlop, when we had, I don't know, maybe four or five hundred bucks left, I think, said, why don't I print it up and send it out early as an NSF report.

And I actually did that. I printed out I don't know, forty of these? And I sent them to forty leading philosophers of science in the world. I didn't know it at the time, but this was a huge blunder.

Because it meant these people had actually already read it by the time the book was published, and it takes about two years to get a book into print. They'd already read it, so I didn't get all the reviews I should have got, and it would have made a certain kind of mark.

I mean this is just one of the ways in which I would eventually learn. I don't think it was until my retirement that I've actually looked back upon these points and realized how I'd misplayed my cards.

But there it is. I was doing what I could at the time. I was very naïve.

I assumed that philosophy and academia generally was a meritocracy, and it was largely free from politics and, uh, I think eventually I would learn that that's not quite the case and this was one of those instances where I made a mistake. By far not the only significant mistake I would make, but there it is.

It would be twenty years before Linda would remark to me that at a convention she had overheard a conversation between faculty discussing how important it is to have the right publisher for your books, and she said that the illustration they were discussing was me.

I think if I had had an agent it probably would have made a tremendous difference in my professional career, because managing my decisions in relation to my profession was really one of my short suits, sad to say.

There it is.

In any case, after completing the book at Cincinnati I received an offer for a year appointment at the University of North Carolina Chapel Hill.

Jan and I really enjoyed living in Chapel Hill with Sarah and I recall that the departmental executive secretary, Claire, made the witticism – the University of North Carolina has a Fetzer Gymnasium – she would quip that the university had Fetzer Gym, but the department had Jim Fetzer.

In any case, finding positions from year to year was extremely laborious, so I would be filling out sixty or seventy applications and listing referees and the whole bit from year to year to year, and the next hire was at New College of the University of South Florida, which was the honors college for South Florida.

It's located on a beautiful expanse, the former estate of John Ringling of Ringling Bros. Circus.

I've described it as three pink tents on an enormous green expanse, the buildings were made of marble and brought block by block from Italy to be reconstructed.

All the students had over 600 SATs. There were no grades. Instead it was all narrative evaluations. All the students designed their own course sequence with a faculty advisor, everyone did a thesis, there were about 400 students and forty faculty. It was kind of a paradise for teaching, which I really enjoyed. We had a place in the Whitman Estates in Bradenton very nearby.

There is a story to tell there.

I had initially a two-year stint as replacement for a faculty member who was on a congressional fellowship and was expected not to return. I mean the department was tiny.

There were only actually two and a half members of the department: Douglas Berggren, Doug Langston, who was half religion and half philosophy, and me. I really enjoyed it tremendously and when the guy decided to return I was exiled back into no-mans-land, but the university came through.

A fellow named Jay Moseley, who was the head of the humanities division, arranged for me to receive the offer of a visiting McArthur professorship, where I had what was probably the longest title in history.

I was the "John T. and Katherine D. McArthur Visiting Distinguished Professor in the Arts and Sciences at New College of the University of South Florida."

And would you believe I was so insecure in those days that when I sent out applications and so forth I actually used that whole title? Faintly ridiculous as I look back upon it, but there it was.

After that ran out, they gave me an appointment as a visiting research fellow.

But what was really most important about all this was that a friend of ours in Whitman Estates, he was the assistant principal at the W.D. Sugg Middle School, told me, Jim, I want to have a conversation with you. He told me, you're not going to like what I'm going to say, but I've got an eighth grade science teacher who's taking a maternity leave, and if you would go down to the board of education, because of your Ph.D. they'll give you a teaching certificate, and then you could be hired as a substitute teacher for the first semester.

And I didn't have any other options, really, so, I mean, I told him that I would do it, and walking into that eighth grade science classroom at W.D. Sugg Middle School for the first time in my life was the greatest act of moral courage of my life.

It was very interesting.

You had, you know, four repetitions of the same class, and I used the first couple of weeks to get my feet on the ground by doing basically an introduction to the philosophy of science.

I had been given a choice, because that year for the eighth grade they had an atomic theory of matter section with a very nice book that had two-page assignments.

The lab work involving acids, hydrochloric sulfuric acid and all that, there was no way I was going to get into the laboratory with eighth grade students doing experiments with hydrochloric and sulfuric acid, so I chose the option of doing the atomic theory of matter.

And the book was really quite wonderful, but I began by using a big easel and creating a whole host of outlines in the philosophy of science, I mean, I wasn't calling it that, I was just explaining how scientific reasoning works.

I remember how one student after, I don't know, about a week and a half, said to me, he raised his hand, I said, yes, he said, "Mr. Fetzer, you're not a normal teacher, are you?"

I thought that was very amusing.

And I don't recall exactly what I said, but I conceded that much, you know.

And we went from there.

When it was over I told Jan, "Honey, don't make me go back there."

I'll never forget one day, you know. In these four different classrooms, of course, you had a mix of students. I remember one day this smaller black kid, who, you know, had been very obnoxious, I remember actually grabbing him by his lapel and I think I actually lifted off of the ground.

And then a voice in my head said, Jim, uh, maybe this isn't the smartest thing you ever did.

So, I let him back down. He was actually the head of the black gang in the school and he probably could have had me wasted. Ohhh!

But somehow I survived.

I remember there was one, my God, absolutely gorgeous young woman, who, I mean, eighth grade! She looked like she was going on eighteen. I mean, she was, just terrific looking, and was a big fan of Motley Crew, and I was just glad that I had, uh, enough sense to not commit an indiscretion in what would have been a disastrous situation. She was terrific.

Anyway.

So during all this period of time I was applying for positions and all that. I remember an interview I had at the University of Florida which will give you an illustration, some insight.

I knew someone on the faculty who told me that the way the discussion had gone after I'd been there and they had all their candidates in, was that the head of the department opened by saying that he'd start with me, that I had the best letters of recommendation, that I had the best record of publication, that I'd given the best presentation, but I'd been denied tenure at the University of Kentucky and there must be something wrong with me, so, next candidate.

So, that Kentucky thing, however unjust it may have been, had enduring ramifications.

The following summer I was being considered for two different chairs, one at St. John's in Minnesota, where they really loved me. The dean was a really good guy, loved my work.

My last interview, the morning after I'd given my presentation and all that, and I'd really hit it off with the search committee, was with the vice president.

They had a merger of two schools, there was St. John's and I think St. Catherine's was the name of the women's college, and she was from St. Catherine's; her name was Sister Eva Hooker.

And I just knew that a nun by the name of Hooker was going to be bad news.

And as we began our interview she was very interested in my having been denied tenure at Kentucky, and started writing notes furiously and made a big deal about it, and that was very unsettling to me.

So when I got out of the interview and it was just about lunch time, I was walking across the parking lot and I saw the dean in the distance, and I called to him and we had a brief conversation during which I explained I'd been very upset about this, because everyone surely knew, and yet Sister Hooker seemed to be making a big deal out of this.

I told him, by the way, that since I didn't have other options, that if I wasn't going to get this position he should let me know. He eventually, I mean, it was like pulling teeth, told me they'd hired some fellow who did critical thinking out of, I don't know, San Bernardino State.

He told me how difficult the decision had been, and I said, well, did he have any books, and, this was in email correspondence, and the answer was no. Did he have any publications? The answer was no.

So, you know, I knew that, uh, the whole interaction with Sister Hooker had been a complete and utter disaster.

I would later be contacted by Chuck Dunlop, my friend I'd met at Cincinnati, who said that he was going to go into a program for Ph.D.s in philosophy and linguistics at the University of Dayton in – no, it was Wright State, in Dayton, Ohio, and that he would like to know if I would consider it, and I began contemplating the possibility, I mean, it would be quite a considerable change in direction, or so it would appear, by going into a program where I would earn a masters degree in computer science, but it was intriguing to me, and I certainly felt I needed to do something different, so that when I received a contact from Davidson College inviting me to do another visiting appointment I explained that I had, you know, a whole raft of visiting appointments.

I really had to do something different, though I appreciated their invitation, you know, the answer was no.

And I went into this program in computer science and artificial intelligence at Wright State.

We moved up to a lovely town in Ohio, Springs, Yellow Springs, Ohio. It was not a bad commute. At that time, this was like 1986.

They were using a main computer, there was a main computer, and each of us had, you know, terminals from our office.

I remember when we got up there, because it began in the summer, so it was a summer, a year, and a summer to do the whole program. And they actually had given me a fellowship for doing it, which offset tuition and all that, which was, of course, a very nice gesture, and which I greatly appreciated.

So, during the years 1986-87, beginning with the summer, I was a post-doctoral fellow in computer science at Wright State University in Dayton, Ohio.

And for months I left the packaged computer terminal I'd been provided to connect back to the mainframe at the university in the living room of our home in Yellow Springs.

Before I'd enlisted in the program, before I'd applied for and been admitted to pursue a masters degree in computer science, I had never used a computer.

The one time, the one interaction I had, had been going down in Sarasota to some display that IBM had set up, where you could print in a word in the spaces provided, and it would give you a point count for the success you had in your typing. And I printed in a word like passenger, that had a double "s".

But it was one space off, in other words, I didn't begin with the very first space, I began with the second space, so instead of the first space having a "p", it was the second space with a "p", preceded by a blank.

I would get a point for each letter I had correct, but I had only one point. Because of the double "s", one "s" wound up in the right spot, which convinced me – I remember thinking how stupid this machine was, because anyone who looked at it would see that I had entered the word correctly, it was simply offset by one spot.

I think subconsciously that had a great impact on me, because eventually I would become a leading critic of what's known as the computational theory of the mind, according to which, minds are like computers.

And I've explained multiple, three different, major reasons why minds are not computers, and it's become a major theme of my work, but at the time, of course, I had no idea what the future would hold. In any case, it took me a very long time to even take the computer out of the box.

And the fact of the matter is, that many people thought that because of my success with logic and teaching logic that I was a natural to be a programmer, because programming processes of reasoning involves, you know, steps like the construction of proofs in logic.

But the fact of the matter was that for some reason, I still can't explain it, I really never got the hang of it. The whole time I was in the program I don't believe I ever completed a single programming project.

What happened, and why it was so important, I noticed all these philosophical issues that computer scientists hadn't appreciated that were just lying all over the place.

I mean it was like a veritable minefield. One of the first courses I took that fall semester on programming languages, I picked up on and wrote my term paper on an argument that had been in the literature between the formalists and their critics. The formalists maintain that programming is exactly like logic, and that you can guarantee what a computer will do when it executes a program by conducting a proof, which they called a verification, technically better a validation but they call it a verification, that the program is correct, which is a purely formal procedure.

Well, I had spent a lot of time in the philosophy of science distinguishing between analytic and synthetic knowledge.

Knowledge that is analytic is true, cannot be false because it reflects syntactical trivialities like a rose is a rose as long as you mean the same thing by both phrases. That something that is a rose is something that is a rose is a triviality and cannot be false given grammar and language alone, or more formally, syntax.

So, when I encountered this thesis, rooted in a debate in computer science between the formalists and their critics, I knew something was terribly wrong, but that the critics had the wrong argument.

The critics were arguing that determining whether a proof is correct or not is a social process involving an interaction between different referees, where they could be making a mistake in what technically could be validating the proof, so that you can't be certain that the program is correct.

But I knew that if I were to argue with the computer science community about this on the basis of a philosophical distinction with which they were unfamiliar it would be a mistake, so instead I argued the case in this paper, twenty-page term paper.

My instructor loved it.

He wrote on it: "Fascinating".

And I thought, well, gee, if my instructor in this graduate program at Wright State thinks this is fascinating, maybe it's worth submitting. So I actually submitted the paper to the *Communications of the ACM*, which is the principal professional journal of the *Association For Computing Machinery*.

And as luck would have it, my paper fell into the right hands, because the title had something to do with social processing.

The editor who processed it had me undertake three different revisions to explain more clearly for their audience what I meant by all these points, and each time I revised it, it grew by about seven pages, so it went from the original twenty or twenty-one pages to forty-two pages.

They started sending me letters to the editor they were receiving about it.

And one of the first was signed by seven prominent computer scientists, all of whom were verificationists, who were saying I knew nothing about computer science, blah, blah, blah, blah, blah. It was an insult to the profession and to the journal that the article had even been published.

So they gave me a chance to write a response and when I wrote my response I just took them apart. I just dismantled it. I mean this was a wonderful, wonderful, wonderful response, maybe the best I ever gave. I have done plenty.

But the letters continued to pour in from all over the world. I remember it became a huge matter. Several other journals picked up on it.

Jon Barwise, who is regarded as kind of a god among computer scientists, picked up and reflected very favorably on the article.

He would later write that he thought that the world slept just a bit safer at night because of my having published that article. And in the end I think it had a tremendous impact.

I would be invited to contribute entries to two encyclopedias of computer science about program verification. I would write other articles about it, and all in all, it's probably one of the most important contributions I have made in my professional career as a philosopher.

Some, like Tim Colburn, who would become the book review editor for *Minds and Machines*, which was a journal of philosophy of artificial intelligence and cognitive science, which I founded and edited for the first ten years, would describe me as the founder of the philosophy of computer science, and I think that there must be something to that. I think that's probably right.

Because what I was doing was getting into the deep epistemological and ontological issues that computer technology provides or presents, including what are, what kinds of things are, computers.

You know, what's their standing in the world?

In any case, I had this difficult juggling act to perform while I was in the program, because I was a disaster at programming, and I needed to keep my fellowship.

They warned me that they were going to withdraw, you know, if I didn't complete my programming assignments. But the fact of the matter is, being in that computer science program made a huge difference.

The year before I had received seven invitations for interviews at The Eastern APA, the annual meeting of the Eastern Division of the American Philosophical Association, all for junior positions.

I'll never forget the one I had with Georgia State, where the head had a private meeting with me and asked me, Fetzer, he said, are you a troublemaker?

I said, no, I'm not a troublemaker.

But I added, I will speak out if I think something's wrong.

So that was the end of that.

Once again, where's that agent to manage my career?

Curriculum Vitae

James H. Fetzer

Personal

Born: 6 December 1940; Pasadena, California. Married.
Home: 800 Violet Lane, Oregon, WI, 53575; (608) 835-2707
Office: Department of Philosophy, University of Minnesota, Duluth, MN 55812

Education

Indiana University, Ph.D., 1970, History and Philosophy of Science
Columbia University, 1968-69, Philosophy
Indiana University, M.A., 1968, History and Philosophy of Science
Princeton University, A.B., 1962, Philosophy

Military Service

Commissioned Officer, United States Marine Corps, 1962-66

Current Position

Distinguished McKnight University Professor Emeritus, University of Minnesota, 2006-

Professional Experience

Distinguished McKnight University Professor, University of Minnesota, 1996-2006
Director, Master of Liberal Studies Program, University of Minnesota, Duluth, 1996-2006
Department Chairman, University of Minnesota, Duluth, 1988-92
Professor of Philosophy, University of Minnesota, Duluth, 1987-96
Research Scholar, New College, University of South Florida, 1985-86
Visiting Professor, University of Virginia, Spring Semester, 1984-85
Adjunct Professor, University of South Florida, Fall Semester, 1984-85
MacArthur Visiting Distinguished Professor in the Arts and Sciences,
New College, University of South Florida, 1983-84
Visiting Associate Professor, New College, University of South Florida,1981-83
Visiting Lecturer, University of North Carolina at Chapel Hill, 1980-81
Visiting NSF Research Professor, University of Cincinnati, 1979-80
Visiting Associate Professor, University of Cincinnati, 1978-79
Visiting Associate Professor, University of Virginia, 1977-78
Assistant Professor, University of Kentucky, 1970-77

After his denial of tenure at Kentucky (for stepping on too many toes), Jim spent ten years on visiting appointments, where the turning point came when he entered a program in computer science and AI for Ph.D.s in linguists and philosophy during 1986-87. He had been interviewed for seven jobs (all junior) the preceding year, but that December he was interviewed for seven jobs (all senior) and was hired as full professor with tenure on the Duluth Campus of the University of Minnesota, where he would spend 19 years to complete a 35-year career as a professor of philosophy.

[Chapter 22] More Voices

"You see," my colleague went on, "one doesn't see exactly where or how to move. Believe me, this is true. Each act, each occasion, is worse than the last, but only a little worse. You wait for the next and the next.

"You wait for one great shocking occasion, thinking that others, when such a shock comes, will join with you in resisting somehow. You don't want to act, or even talk, alone; you don't want to 'go out of your way to make trouble.' Why not? Well, you are not in the habit of doing it. And it is not just fear, fear of standing alone, that restrains you; it is also genuine uncertainty. ...

... "But the one great shocking occasion, when tens or hundreds or thousands will join with you, never comes. That's the difficulty. If the last and worst act of the whole regime had come immediately after the first and smallest, thousands, yes, millions would have been sufficiently shocked – if, let us say, the gassing of the Jews in '43 had come immediately after the 'German Firm' stickers on the windows of non-Jewish shops in '33.

"But of course this isn't the way it happens. In between come all the hundreds of little steps, some of them imperceptible, each of them preparing you not to be shocked by the next. Step C is not so much worse than Step B, and, if you did not make a stand at Step B, why should you at Step C? And so on to Step D."

- Milton Mayer, 1955, *They Thought They Were Free: The Germans 1933-45*

"... if any of you have been watching footage, which was not shown on any major media, of the Bradley tanks shooting fire into the compound, which I think went against the party line story, which was that they shot teargas in order to help the mothers and children to get out [...] the major news said it was the Branch Davidians who started the fire, and yet I've seen footage of a Bradley tank shooting fire into the compound [...] isn't that odd that no major news source has picked up on that [...] because that basically means that the government, from the FBI, the ATF, up to Janet Reno and Clinton are liars and murderers. [...]

"... the Branch Davidians did not start the fire ... they were murdered in cold blood by the pussies, the liars, the scumbags, the ATF [...] they burned these fucking people alive, because the message they want to convey to you is state power will always win [...] we'll say anything we want over the major media, our propaganda machine, and we'll burn you and your children in your fuckin' homes [...] so you just be apathetic America, you stay docile, and don't you ever forget, you're free to do what we tell you."

- Bill Hicks, on Waco

"One year after 9/11, we still don't know by whom we were struck that infamous Tuesday, or for what true purpose. But it is fairly plain to many civil-libertarians that 9/11 applied not only to much of our fragile Bill of Rights but also to our once-envied system of government which had taken a mortal blow the previous year when the Supreme Court did a little dance in 5/4 time and replaced a popularly elected president with the oil and gas Cheney/Bush junta. [...]

"Afghanistan is the gateway to all these riches. Will we fight to seize them? It should never be forgotten that the American people did not want to fight in either of the twentieth century's world wars, but President Wilson maneuvered us into the First while President Roosevelt maneuvered the Japanese into striking the first blow at Pearl Harbor, causing us to enter the Second as the result of a massive external attack. Brzezinski understands all this and, in 1997, he is thinking ahead – as well as backward. `Moreover, as America becomes an increasingly multicultural society, it may find it more difficult to fashion a consensus on foreign policy issues, except in the circumstance of a truly massive and widely perceived direct external threat.' Thus was the symbolic gun produced that belched black smoke over Manhattan and the Pentagon.

"Complicity. The behavior of President George W. Bush on 11 September certainly gives rise to all sorts of not unnatural suspicions. I can think of no other modern chief of state who would continue to pose for `warm' pictures of himself listening to a young girl telling stories about her pet goat while hijacked planes were into three buildings.

"... The media, never much good at analysis, are more and more breathless and incoherent. On CNN, even the stolid Jim Clancy started to hyperventilate when an Indian academic tried to explain how Iraq was once our ally and `friend' in its war against our Satanic enemy Iran. `None of that conspiracy stuff,' snuffed Clancy. Apparently, `conspiracy stuff' is now shorthand for unspeakable truth.

"... It is interesting how often in our history, when disaster strikes, incompetence is considered a better alibi than [...] well, yes, there are worse things. After Pearl Harbor, Congress moved to find out why Hawaii's two military commanders, General Short and Admiral Kimmel, had not anticipated the Japanese attack. But President Roosevelt pre-empted that investigation with one of his own. Short and Kimmel were broken for incompetence. The `truth' is still obscure to this day.

"... Bush personally asked Senate Majority Leader Tom Daschle to limit the Congressional investigation into the events of 11 September [...] The request was made at a private meeting with Congressional leaders [...] Sources said Bush initiated the conversation."

- Gore Vidal, "The Enemy Within", Oct. 27, 2002, *The Observer*

"No one could have been happier than I was when the Berlin Wall came down on November the 9th, 1989. The elation on our side of the curtain was near universal and very significant on the other side as one country after another regained its freedom. Nearly everyone believed that it was the dawn of a new era of peace and prosperity for people everywhere. There was much talk of a peace dividend. The prospects were dazzling, dazzling in their scope and diversity. It was a unique and god-given opportunity for a new braver and fairer world.

"We blew it. We blew the chance of a lifetime to do good things. A small group of zealots undermined our golden opportunity to pursue peace, not war, and little did we dream that they had a vastly different vision of the new world order.

"Their plan, which is now commonly known as 'The Project for A New American Century', included preventive wars in clear violation of international law, regime change wherever and whenever the U.S. desires, and if they can get away with it without excessive casualties, the establishment of a kind of economic and cultural hegemony with America acting as 'constabulary' (that was their word) globally.

"This was to be accomplished without authority of the United Nations and without the restrain of existing international treaties.

"It would involve a military buildup unprecedented in peacetime history. It could trigger an arms race which is precisely the opposite of the peace dividend that the world had rightly looked forward to.

"The Machiavellian scheme involved secret police, the curtailment of civil liberties, defiance of the U.S. Constitution, and a moribund economy, operating way below its potential.

"Exactly those features for which the Soviet Union was held in contempt. The initial draft of the document was so controversial when it was leaked in *The New York Times* that it had to be rewritten, but it was not changed very much, just cosmetics. Enough to make it politically acceptable.

"The document said this. [Reads from book] While it may have been easy to persuade President Bush to abandon his stated policy of not getting America more deeply involved in international affairs, persuading the American people would be more difficult.

Sophisticated Americans would question such a giant sea change in policy.

"The authors of *Rebuilding America's Defenses, Strategy, Forces and Resources for a New Century* recognized this difficulty from the outset because their document contained the following sentence: 'Further, the process of transformation, even if it brings revolutionary changes, is likely to be a long one, absent some catastrophic and catalyzing event, like a new Pearl Harbor.'

"And it wasn't too long before they got their catastrophic and catalyzing event. Terrorists struck the World Trade Center in New York and the Pentagon in Washington on September the 11th, 2001."

- Paul Hellyer, at The Citizen Hearing on Disclosure, April 29-May 3, 2013, Washington, D.C.

"I think they (the government) know who John Doe #2 is, and they are protecting him.

This is because John Doe #2 is either a government agent or informant and they can't afford for that to get out."

- Hoppy Heidelberg

(Hoppy Heidelberg was a grand juror empaneled by the federal government to gather evidence following the attack on the Alfred P. Murrah Federal Building in downtown Oklahoma City on April 19, 1995. He was dismissed from the grand jury after writing a letter to the judge with the above statement included in that letter.)

More from Hoppy Heidelberg:

"It was just too important, for the American people to know what happened there, for me to speak up, because nobody else was going to speak up."

"The bombing was designed to get the anti-terrorist bill passed. The bill had been written and was before Congress in 1992, but they couldn't get it passed. So in '93 they had the first World Trade Center bombing, and had it been successful they would have been able to get the anti-terrorist bill passed, but it was not successful, so they had to come to Oklahoma City in '95, and they killed enough people there, big enough body count in '95, that they got the anti-terrorist bill passed.

There were three buildings in consideration and we "won", because we had the only federal building with a daycare center in it. And they correctly figured that it was the pictures of those little babies' bodies in the paper every morning and on the six o'clock news that would get the anti-terrorist bill passed."

Sherwood Ross, interview with Kevin Barrett, *American Freedom Radio*, April 17, 2013:

[Sherwood Ross] There is no disaster that can happen in the United States now where people should not suspect the federal government in one way or another. I'm sorry to have to say that. It really grieves me to say that. But that is how it looks. You can't exclude the United States government from the list of usual suspects. You know they were involved in the anthrax scare of October 2001. You know it came from Fort Dietrich, Maryland, that's been established, and if they would do that, what would they not do?

[...] One judge hearing a "terrorism" case, Colleen McMahon, of the U.S. District Court for the Southern District of New York, said it was "beyond question that the government created the crime here" and criticized the FBI for sending informants "trolling along the citizens of a troubled community, offering very poor people money if they will play some role – any role – in criminal activity."

And this is typical of the entire war on terrorism. This is a false, manufactured war by the military industrial complex. Think about it, seven hundred men put in Guantanamo, and of those seven hundred only two or three were brought to trial. Secretary of Defense Rumsfeld said they were the worst of the worst. Why were only so few brought to trial? 500 were returned to their countries of origin. The fact is, that they were all virtually innocent.

But if you release 500 of the worst of the worst and you only bring two or three to trial, what does that tell you about your operation? It tells you that it's a manufactured crisis.

[...] This is a fascist operation or a communist operation if there ever was one. In Russia under Stalin you could go to the gulag for five or ten years, serve your sentence and on the day you walk out, they re-arrest you.

[...] I think you have a population that is uninformed and those who are informed feel that they have no redress. There is a big disconnect between them and what they can get done with members of Congress.

Barrett: The spread of the truth I think is responsible for polls showing that more than two-thirds of the American people no longer trust the federal government and Congress' approval rating is down to ten percent or less. We're seeing an erosion of the powers that were, as some folks are calling them now. You think they're ever going to have to really clamp down with serious fascism, locking up all their opponents, and so on.

Sherwood Ross: Well that may yet happen. Everything is in place for that. President Obama, on New Year's Eve, 2011, signed into law the National Defense Authorization Act. And that gives him the power to arrest any American and hold them indefinitely, throw away the key, and if you do that to a person the Constitution is meaningless. I don't understand why we don't close down every law school in America, because the law no longer exists when you have a king on the throne who signs into law legislation giving him more power than King George ever had.

[...] You have this despicable individual, I mean, he's brilliant, a very capable President. He may be the smartest man to ever be in the White House, but he is certainly not one of the more ethical presidents we've had.

[Chapter 23] Kevin: Islam ... Is there a God? ... the 9/11 Report and the study of folklore

> "It is the United States which is perpetrating every maltreatment on women, children and common people.
> "I have already said that I am not involved in the 11 September attacks in the United States. As a Muslim, I try my best to avoid telling a lie. I had no knowledge of these attacks, nor do I consider the killing of innocent women, children and other humans as an appreciable act. Islam strictly forbids causing harm to innocent women, children and other people. Such a practice is forbidden even in the course of a battle."
>
> -Osama bin Laden

KEVIN:

[On converting to Islam at the age of 35. Is there a God? Using folklore background to study the 9/11 Commission Report.]

In San Francisco with Fatna and a couple of friends.

At that time I was not particularly interested in the sort of clerical aspect of Islam. The thing that appealed to me about Islam is there is no priesthood, no clergy.

Anybody can lead the prayer, and so when you convert to Islam you just recite a particular prayer, the *Shahada*, in front of witnesses.

So at that time it was kind of a revelation to me that there could be this religion, with these very cool rituals, very powerful rituals, this very clear sense of God, and that basically it corrects the same mistake that Unitarianism corrects.

I grew up with a very light Unitarian background and I guess that shaped my view that the Christian concept of God just really doesn't make sense to me.

Or at least aspects of it don't.

In all of these ways Islam seems so much more common sense, and not having this priesthood or clergy telling you what to think.

I'm still the product of the Protestant Reformation, and so this really appealed to me. Just being able to be with Fatna and a couple of friends and recite that prayer to convert.

It was very liberating.

[Is there a God?]

One of my touchstones on this is the Koran. A lot of the Koranic passages on this tell you to just kind of look around.

Look at the heavens and the earth, the water and the land, the sun and the moon, that's the kind of imagery and rhetoric that's used.

You just kind of open your eyes and think and be conscious of what you see, and have taqwa, which is translated as kind of God-Consciousness or sometimes God-Fearingness, a kind of awe.

So basically looking at natural phenomena, and particularly these gorgeous, huge, perfectly balanced phenomena like, lets say, the sun and the moon, and the kind of awed appreciation that you feel at such things, is knowledge of God or knowledge of the existence of God.

How can you explain that?

A lot of people I think have had that experience where at certain moments of their lives they have this kind of perception of this awesome reality and this perfect balance and creation, and they recognized that this means there is a creator, and they appreciate the work of the creator, a little like you would appreciate the work of a truly great artist.

I guess if we're going to translate this into the language of science or philosophy we might say that science is increasingly rewriting everything in terms of information theory.

Physics and biology are both starting to get rewritten in terms of information theory. What is information? Information is a kind of order.

A very highly, intricately ordered phenomenon has more information than a kind of random, entropic phenomenon. That is, information is the opposite of entropy. And there is this tendency in the created universe for things, if they're unguided by consciousness, to disintegrate into entropy or disorder. And if you look at something that's got a lot of disorder, it's often not as beautiful; at least certain kinds of order are very beautiful, and beauty seems to be based on certain kinds of very intricate order.

So if indeed the universe that we witness and experience has an extremely high level of order, that means that at some level, just like a work of art with a really high level of order, it's the product of a mind. It can't be the product of randomness. Randomness is the absence of mind, because that always degenerates into entropy.

It's a little like the monkeys at the typewriter producing Shakespeare; that is, you recognize that a Shakespeare play is the product of a mind, even an extraordinary mind, and no matter how many monkeys you had at no matter how many typewriters for how long, it would never produce that.

So consciousness is an integral part of recognizing the order of a Shakespeare play, both that there is an author and that we are the witnesses, and I think that's true also of creation.

This incredible order, this awesome beauty that the Koran reminds us of, this perfect balance that we witness in creation, can't be there as just the product of randomness, because randomness always leads to disorder, and so order has to be the product of a mind. A mind has to always be selecting in order to create and perceive order.

There's a sense in which the creation and the perception of order are almost the same thing.

What that means is, given that there is this astonishing, beautiful order in the universe, it must be the product of a mind.

And the word God is the word we use to describe that ultimate mind that is, you could call it dreaming it all up, or ordering it all, shaping it, etc., etc.

And many of the religious sacred stories do talk about this.

In Genesis we have the mind of God dividing night from day, the waters from the earth, and so on. And the same type of description is also there in the Koran.

That is how I would translate it into the language of science and philosophy. This experience you have, of recognizing that there has to be a creator behind this highly ordered and beautiful cosmos, is the real proof of God.

And of course this doesn't mean necessarily that there is a God that is particularly humanlike, but there is an analogy in that God has to be a consciousness, and humans, we're blessed with a pretty intense kind of consciousness, perhaps a little more intense than the grass and the trees and the bugs have.

So in that sense I think there's sort of an analogy between human consciousness and God consciousness.

A lot of the popular descriptions of God have to be in language that people can understand, and that language is obviously inadequate to the reality.

[*The 9/11 Commission Report*, the Keen-Hamilton report – sacred myth ... did Kevin's study of folklore help him in referring to that report?]

Well, yeah and I'm sure Phil Zelikow's study of folklore gave him a unique perspective in preparing it.

Folklore studies all sorts of things, unofficial knowledge, and unofficial knowledge includes all sorts of things from the characteristic ways that we tell stories.

Certain kinds of stories get repeated in certain kinds of patterned ways across cultures, and this unofficial knowledge can be opposed to official knowledge.

The whole idea of the discipline of folklore came about as intellectuals started looking at their own cultures, particularly the unofficial and popular dimensions of their own cultures.

Anthropologists, who do virtually the same things as folklorists, got started by looking at other cultures. The folklorists and the anthropologists like to imagine themselves as intellectuals in the privileged position of knowing, as they looked at people who were somehow less than themselves, that is the primitives the anthropologists studied, or the folk that the folklorists studied. But the folklorists tended to champion the popular cultures that they studied to some extent, and that's gotten even stronger; now, today we have all kinds of ethnic folklorists who champion their own ethnic group and its folklore.

Anyway, with [*The 9/11 Commission Report*, one way of looking at it from a folklore perspective is that actually the people, as Paul Craig Roberts said, are the ones who are understanding 9/11; that is, the unofficial discourse on 9/11, which is the skeptical discourse, doesn't believe the government's story.

That's a very unofficial kind of knowledge, and I guarantee you that in the black community, on Sept. 11 and even for the next few days, there was a lot of this popular level skepticism. People who have not been fully brainwashed by the official culture are able to see through these things better than professors and academics and intellectuals who have spent so much time being brainwashed into their cultural pre-conceptions.

So that's one angle of folklore telling us that this story of Phil Zelikow's 9/11 Commission Report, in a sense, is an artifact of official culture that folk cultures are going to dispute. Folk cultures are always making fun of their betters. It's one of the great things about them.

And from another angle, the study of mythology gives you an insight into the way that Zelikow constructed that report. Mythology, you could call it a branch of folklore and anthropology, is about sacred stories, that is the stories that a particular culture holds to be sacred; and you can figure out which stories those are, because they are the stories you'd better not make fun of or openly doubt.

If you do, you're a heretic.

So, the whole story of 9/11 was, I believe, worked up by professionals long ago, at least decades probably in advance, and worked out with various permutations; in a way it's based on the primordial creation myths, because each sacred creation myth divides time into a before and an after.

The creation myth is kind of a grounding myth for a particular culture. It says, once this thing happened that our story is about, that was the creation of the culture that we all belong to.

One example is the Christian myth of Jesus, his birth and his death, and of course when I say myth I don't mean it's not true, I'm just saying that it's a sacred story.

So for Christians the story of Jesus is a sacred myth, and it divides time into a before and an after, in this case A.D. and B.C. For Muslims, the sacred myth is the story of Mohammed getting the revelation and then creating a community.

And the date at which that community was created, which was the flight from Mecca to Medina, is the moment that divides time into a before and an after.

Before that moment was the jahiliyah, the time of ignorance, and after that moment is the time of Islam.

And every other religion, every other culture has this, has a sacred myth, or many sacred myths.

Another one is the founding of America. George Washington cut down the cherry tree and said I cannot tell a lie. All these stories of the American Revolution are part of the myth of 1776, which divides time into a before and an after.

Before is before there was an America, the after is the world we know today, the world of our community, the United States. So the Christian community, the Muslim community, and the American community all have these myths that divide time into before and after.

The people that did 9/11 wanted to create that kind of world-forming, world-shaping event.

They are Straussian neo-conservatives and they believe that the political community of the United States of America, as it existed before 9/11, was not adequate to the tasks that they wanted to accomplish, which I believe are to perpetuate and expand the American Empire for the next century, as the title "Project for A New American Century" suggests, and also to perpetuate and expand the Israeli empire in the Middle East, because all of these people are extreme Zionists.

So, they scripted the events of 9/11 to create a whole new world and divide time into a before and an after.

And Philip Zelikow actually states in a 1998 article published in *Foreign Affairs* that that's precisely what a giant Pearl Harbor style terrorist attack, such as the destruction of the World Trade Center, would do.

So, he's basically giving the game away in his 1998 *Foreign Affairs* article.

Zelikow says that if there was a new Pearl Harbor, such as the destruction of The World Trade Center, time would be split into a before and an after. That's a virtually direct quote from that article by Zelikow in 1998. This is the guy they picked to write the 9/11 Commission Report.

Zelikow, being an expert in what he calls "the creation and maintenance of public myths", understands how this myth making capacity works.

And so 9/11 was designed to create a sacred myth, the good Americans and Israelis who are now cemented together in blood versus the evil Arabs and Muslims and basically anyone else that they don't like – the "terrorists".

So this is all very carefully worked up and scripted, and of course 9/11 has created a split in time into a before and an after. People can hardly remember what life was like before 9/11, back when we had a Constitution that actually meant something.

In this new world that we're living in, the President can order people murdered by drone assassinations or any other means without any judicial review or any kind of due process of law, directly contravening the Constitution in a blatantly impeachable or even treasonous way.

Any eight-year-old that's taken a course on American government for eight-year-olds knows that the President is a traitor who should be executed.

You don't even need a trial at this point, it's so obvious. He's saying it. They're all saying it, yeah we're going to order people killed with no judicial review or due process of law.

Well, sorry, you're a traitor, you must be executed.

But we're in this whole new world, so people just accept it.

And this new world was created by experts like Phil Zelikow, the self-proclaimed expert at the creation and maintenance of public myths.

[Chapter 24] Looking For Bigfoot and The Truth, in America

> "Robert Kennedy was assassinated within seconds after moving decisively towards the presidency by winning the California Democratic primary. Kennedy was committed to ending the Vietnam War, which after his death would continue for seven more years under presidents Nixon and Ford. He was also dedicated to abolishing poverty by forming a uniquely reconciling coalition of blacks, white, Hispanics and Native Americans.
> "This radical vision of transformation would have been in harmony with the vision of the already gunned-down Martin Luther King, Jr. It is astonishing that such a man almost became president and not surprising that he was assassinated the moment that it became apparent that he might."
> -Jim Douglas, *Catholic Peace Voice*, Spring-Summer 1998

[Jack Robert King, on Looking For Bigfoot Internet radio, from *Looking For Bigfoot*, by Mike Palecek, Howling Dog Press]

Good morning, dear people.

And good morning, Oakland, California, home of the Black Panther Party. The Panthers are a group that this Midwest boy does not know much about, not supposed to. I have heard that they, the Chicago police and FBI, killed Fred Hampton and Mark Clark in a morning raid in Chicago. The Panthers were an actual threat to power and that meant they could not exist.

Is there anything or anybody out there these days that is an actual threat to these criminals today? I heard Dick Gregory speaking one day in Omaha. He said he did not believe we landed on the moon.

And then he said, "They will roll tanks on your ass."

That was an epiphany for me. I did not believe it at first. If you become effective, if you really challenge them, there will be tanks in your zinnias by morning.

I believe we are about to see just how right Mr. Gregory was.

Is this Heaven?

No, it's Iowa.

This is *Bigfoot Radio*, streaming to you on the Internet.

Hello.

My name is Jack Robert King.

They killed Paul Wellstone.

I can feel it all around me, like ninety-eight percent humidity, like the feeling there is someone in the house who shouldn't be there.

They attacked the World Trade Center to put out the Patriot Act, to steal the oil, to rule the world, to impress their long-lost junior high sweethearts, who knows why.

I suddenly realize it and reach behind me into the backseat to snatch the bad guy who I know is there, but all I grab is air. I can still hear it breathing, catch a shadow in the rearview.

They killed the Kennedys and Martin and now we've got the books and testimony, but before that all I had to do was walk down to the SuperValue for Mom to buy bread and stand on a milk crate to look into the eyes of the checkout lady as she counted my change.

I might have guessed Vietnam was a lie by the glare in Father Tom's eye and the way Sister Margaret rushed by, like she was always on her way somewhere to cry.

Someone once said that violence is as American as apple pie and now I know why. Just some small kid from a small town, thinking nothing ever happens here, when actually I was right in the middle of the action.

The baker bombed Iraq.

The barber gunned down Bobby.

And the four little grandmothers in blue flower dresses and green metal chairs in that row of white porches on Sarah Street sliced the throats of children in El Salvador in their spare time during the summer in the 1980s.

You can see it in their eyes, dull and dead.

Not from seeing too much of the world, but too little.

The robins are tweet-tweeting on the front lawn, puffing their red chests into the sun. Their song: Hang the niggers.

On the days we bombed Iraq, the Farmers Coop Elevator dryers hummed a happy tune. The coffee-drinkers smiled across Formica tables and asked for more cream, please.

And for the ten years in between, while children died from the sanctions from no food or light or heat or love or prayers or Hardee's – Mr. Johnson and Mr. Smith went to work each day, drove on the right side of the road, smiled, kept their desks in order, and were not considered suspects.

They really, truly stole a presidential election in the United States and our response was to wave at the limousines as they passed by on the TV atop the kitchen counter, next to the toaster.

They shot down or lasered-down Wellstone's plane and they really did attack their own Pentagon.

I see this and I have zero documentation. I don't care. I have all the proof I need from the glazed look in your eye as you struggle to attach the American flag to your car antenna.

I understand America by watching you.

I know it from growing up in the Midwest of America, from playing baseball and football and riding down the middle of the street with no hands eating an ice cream cone.

The strawberry drips on my white T-shirt and I don't care.

Mom will wash it, clean it up, just as she rinses the blood of a thousand Chileans from her hands.

A lemony spray makes everything smell fresh.

I see more than I want to in the referee's face as he prepares the jump-ball toss and the smile of the drive-up teller as she helps another customer.

Would evil men and women kill in order to gain absolute power?

Pretty darn near impossible to believe when they look just like us and sound like us, tell the same tired jokes and watch the same TV shows.

I do know, because I saw it myself over the top of my SuperSize Diet Pepsi – that while children are being bombed to gooey bits – the mail still arrives at our house at ten and the garbage is picked up at one, school dismisses at three-thirty, and Raymond comes on at seven.

I see the banality of evil old Mrs. Schwartz using her tongs to set another fish square into a slot on a lunch tray at St. Mark's elementary as a child in Baghdad has his nose blown away by a small bomb he thought was a toy.

I do not have a leaked file or a tidbit of information or an inside source. I know all I need to know from seeing your guilty face staring out into the night while you wash dishes, or leaning out the car window to order an A&W root beer, or chasing your children into the school house with one last admonition.

I don't need to know Barack Obama or George Bush or Karl Rove.

I know you.

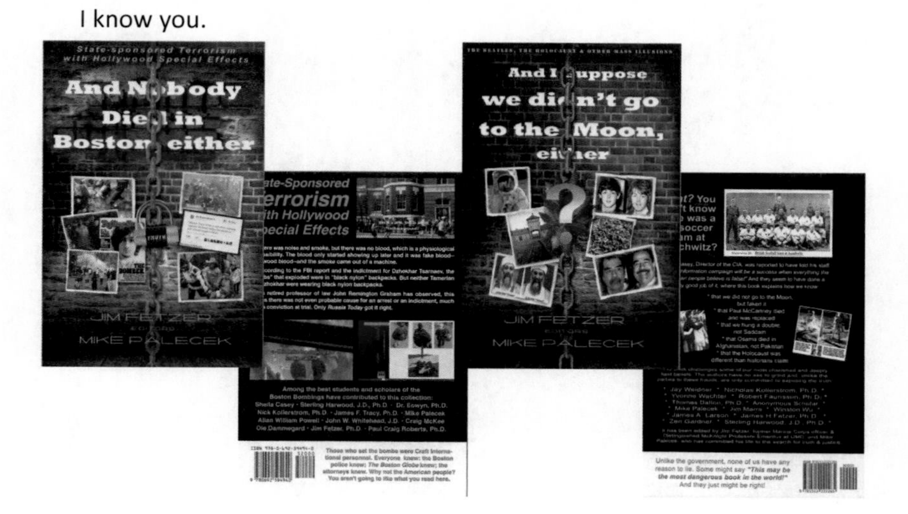

Jim continues to pursue the complex and controversial issues of our time, bringing together experts on different aspects of each case.

Jesse Ventura
Vince Bugliosi
Jim Fetzer
Andy Klemer
Jim Fetzer
Mike Lynn
Jim Fetzer
Stewart Galanor
David W. Mantik

[Chapter 25] Wellstone

"There's so many things about this that don't add up. We're going to get to the bottom of this."
- Paul Wellstone, talking to a group of Veterans in Wilmar, Minnesota about 9/11 after being threatened by Vice President Dick Cheney

JIM:

[Wellstone – where were you when you heard? What did you think right at that moment? What was the first piece of evidence that made you think it was an assassination? Have you ever heard anything from the Wellstone family? Have you ever heard anything to make you doubt your conclusions?]

I was being interviewed by a writer for an alternative newspaper in Duluth, which [interview] was later published in the book, *Gonzo Science*. Nothing about it sounded right to me from the beginning. He said that the black box would tell us what happened and I replied, "There won't be any." False claims about the weather, the timing in relation to the election, and other factors told me something was wrong.

[When you wrote about Wellstone, what was that like? On a personal level. Did people approach you?]

Well, I had met the man and admired him greatly. What has dumbfounded me is that those who profess to have been his most devoted followers have shown no inclination or interest in what happened to the plane and how he died.

This appears to be another nice example of cognitive dissonance, suppressing or denying information that conflicts with your most dearly-held beliefs, no matter how strong the evidence. And in this case, the proof of assassination is simply overwhelming.

[What is it like to be the front man for questioning the death of Paul Wellstone? That takes some kind of courage and real confidence. Where do you think that comes from?]

Well, I have experienced enough injustice in my own life that I am no longer willing to tolerate it. During the twilight of my life, I want to do whatever I can to set the record straight about at least some of the monstrous lies that the government has fed the American people to promote its own political agenda – about JFK, 9/11, Wellstone, Sandy Hook, the Boston bombing, and even more.

[I think you presented on the Wellstone case at The National Press Club? Talk about that in detail, getting there, getting situated, who invited you, anecdotes.]

When the government doesn't want something out, they cover it up.

Practically no reporters showed up. We made our presentation, which was a significant historical event, and then went out for lunch.

[What's it like looking out at the "sea" of reporters? What response did you get?]

It didn't happen that way, alas.

When the Wellstone plane went down I was being interviewed by an alternative newspaper in Duluth, and I told the reporter, when he said, "we'll have to see what the black box tells us," that there wouldn't be one. There would be exaggerated claims about the weather even on national news.

Wolf Blitzer was talking about how there'd been freezing rain and snow and the NTSB had closed the airport, and that told you all you needed to know, but in fact the NTSB routinely closes airports in relation to crashes, because it doesn't know if something about the airport might have contributed to the problem.

Blitzer was wrong.

There was not only no snow, there wasn't even any rain, much less freezing rain.

I got photographs from a pilot who was on the ground there, showing how clear it was across water, no rain. And other pilots landed there without any problems that day.

The plane was like the Rolls Royce of small aircraft, the whole situation was completely absurd, even trying to pin the tale on the pilots.

Following up on Wellstone I think was a fairly obvious thing to do. Duluth was very supportive of Wellstone. I admired the man beyond words, and to me – I just wanted to get to the truth of the matter.

I believe the American people are entitled to know the truth about their own history, and I've been dumbfounded that no one in Duluth or in the Wellstone organization has picked up on our findings, which have been multiply confirmed now, including by a brilliant documentary by SnowShoe Films entitled *Wellstone: They Killed Him*, which confirmed in spades everything that my research had shown, including my collaboration with Don "Four Arrows" Jacobs and John P. Costella, a Ph.D. in electromagnetism, whom I flew up from Australia for us to tramp around at the crash site in thirty-five-degree-below-zero weather.

John was superlative. And the results of our efforts would be published in Michael Ruperts's *From The Wilderness* under the heading, "The NTSB Failed Wellstone."

KEVIN:

I was living in Madison I think. I had been going out to Lone Rock, working on building my house at that point, but I was living and teaching in Madison.

I don't remember where I was, but I remember just throwing up my hands and saying, my God, something is rotten in Denmark. At this point I hadn't really figured out the extent of the 9/11 deception, I was just suspicious about it, could see it looked like a Reichstag fire but had not really figured out that the evidence was as overwhelming as it turned out to be.

But, when this Wellstone assassination happened, I thought, you know, something really stinks about this; he was Cheney's biggest enemy, he'd just been doing really well in the polls. It looked like the anti-Iraq war movement was going to succeed, thanks to Wellstone winning a landslide re-election, and suddenly this happens.

I was very angry. Actually it kind of made me feel committed.

Before that I was kind of just drifting along, you know, and kind of looking askance at what was happening, but not exactly committed to trying to do anything about it.

But after that Wellstone assassination I remember being really pissed off, and feeling I want to try to do something about this. Whatever it takes, at this point, if they're going to do this.

They killed his family, too. They killed a bunch of other people who weren't even their targets, including his wife, and this is really disgusting.

So, it really pissed me off, in a way that 9/11 didn't when it happened, because I was still, I didn't really know what was up with 9/11, but from the second the Wellstone assassination happened I was just lividly angry. And then the head-in-the-sand attitude of Wellstone's supporters, these liberal morons, just pissed me off even more, so I think that kind of primed me for getting into the 9/11 Truth fight.

I'm not sure I even maybe would have if I didn't have that sense of commitment to do something about what happened to Wellstone.

[So, you think he was murdered?]

I know he was murdered.

I'd stake my life on it.

Former lecturer Kevin Barrett discusses his trip to Morocco, hoping to find a 9/11 hijacker.
Kevin Barrett, an instructor at the University of Wisconsin-Madison, holds a 9/11
Vol. II
9/11 and American Empire
Muslims, Jews, and Christians Speak Out
edited by Kevin Barrett, John Cobb, and Sandra Lubarsky

[Chapter 26] "Wisconsin Girl Guillotined by Hitler"

> "Unfortunately, you've grown up hearing voices that incessantly warn of government as nothing more than some separate, sinister entity that's at the root of all our problems. Some of these same voices also do their best to gum up the works. They'll warn that tyranny is always lurking just around the corner. You should reject these voices. Because what they suggest is that our brave, and creative, and unique experiment in self-rule is somehow just a sham with which we can't be trusted."
>
> - President Barack Obama, address to graduates at The Ohio State University, May 5, 2013

Wisconsin Girl Guillotined by Hitler

Wisconsinology http://Wisconsinology.blogspot.com/
Sunday, February 17, 2013
Frank Anderson

Here's a favorite post of mine from a few years back. I've updated it and posted a new picture. It shows Mildred Fish-Harnack and her husband, Arvid.

Berlin, 1942.

Milwaukee born UW grad Mildred Fish-Harnack led a double life. She and her husband Arvid Harnack, a German national who she met while attending the University of Wisconsin, were respected academics at Berlin University. They also led The Red Orchestra, an anti-Hitler resistance group that included Greta Lork Kuckhoff, a UW grad student from Germany who had met Mildred and Arvid in Madison during the 1920s.

In early 1942, the Red Orchestra was rounded up and put on trial. Arvid Harnack was sentenced to death and Mildred was sentenced to six years in prison.

The defense argued well in her favor, convincing the German judges that because of her job at the University translating great German works into English, she was an asset to the German cause. The decision angered a Fish-Harnack obsessed Hitler. He now took a personal interest in her case. Arvid Harnack and many other members of the Red Orchestra were quickly hung with a short rope, a technique meant to prolong the agony of the victims.

For Mildred, there was to be a retrial. On Jan. 16, 1942, she was sentenced to death and transferred to prison.

Five months of interrogation left her broken, unable to stand upright.

On February 16, 1943, she was led into a courtyard and inside a red brick building that housed a guillotine.

She would be the only American woman to be executed on direct orders from Hitler.

In a cemetery in the Zehlendorf neighborhood of Berlin is Arvid and Mildred's headstone.

It was only by luck that Mildred was buried there. After execution, her headless body was put in a wooden crate and sent to an anatomical institute for dissection.

But, as it turned out, a professor that Mildred knew recognized her remains and secretly cremated her. He kept her ashes in an urn and, after the war, returned them to the Harnack family.

On the night before their trial, Arvid wrote a farewell letter to Mildred, he wrote of Wisconsin.

"Do you remember picnic point, when we became engaged? Before that our first serious conversation in the restaurant on State Street? That conversation became my guiding star, and has remained so. You are in my heart. You shall be in there forever. My greatest wish is for you to be happy when you think of me. I am when I think of you."

Lovely.
On Wisconsin.

[Reprinted here with permission.]

[Chapter 27] The Nuremberg tribunal and the role of the media

"Actually, God bless the people, they're getting wise to these false flag attacks, and they're not liking being lied to! But the people need to wake up. The American people have got to wake up. Otherwise, America is gone. Only the people waking up could possibly save America."
- Bishop Richard Williamson on Kevin Barrett's radio show

U.S. prosecuted Nazi propagandists as war criminals: The Nuremberg tribunal and the role of the media

World Socialist Web Site

by David Walsh, 16 April 2003

The ongoing U.S. aggression in the Middle East raises the most serious questions about the role of the mass media in modern society.

In the period leading up to the invasion, the American media uncritically advanced the Bush administration's arguments, rooted in lies, distortions and half-truths, for an attack on Iraq.

It virtually excluded all critical viewpoints, to the point of blacking out news of mass anti-war demonstrations and any other facts that contradicted the propaganda from the White House and Pentagon.

The obvious aim was to misinform and manipulate public opinion, and convince the tens of millions within the U.S. who were opposed to the administration's war policy that they constituted a small and helpless minority.

Now, as if on cue, the U.S. media has obediently turned its attention to Syria, evidently the next target of the U.S. military. If the focus of the White House and Pentagon should shift to North Korea or Iran, the appropriate items will begin to appear about the dire threat represented by those regimes to the security of the American people.

In the American media there is barely a trace of serious analysis concerning the political and social realities of the Middle East. It long ago abandoned any sense of responsibility for educating and informing the public or carrying out the critical democratic function traditionally assigned to the "Fourth Estate", i.e., serving as a watchdog and check on government abuses and falsifications.

Instead it slavishly carries out the function assigned it by the ruling elite: to confuse, terrorize and intimidate the American public, rendering it less able to resist the reactionary program of the right-wing clique in Washington.

The television networks and leading newspapers are the prime source of news and information for tens of millions of people in the U.S. However, these public resources are in the hands of giant firms, controlled by fabulously wealthy individuals who will stop at nothing to defend their profits and property. The corpses of thousands, or, if necessary, millions of Iraqis, Syrians, Iranians and others are a small price to pay, as far as the media billionaires are concerned, for achieving American military and economic domination of the globe.

This makes the U.S. media an accessory before and after the fact to crimes carried out in Iraq and future crimes against other peoples in the region and around the world.

Sitting far from the ravaged Iraqi cities, in well-appointed boardrooms, the media moguls may believe they will never face such charges.

There are, however, historical parallels and precedents to the contrary.

The Nuremberg precedent

The role of propaganda and propagandists figured prominently at the Nuremberg war crimes tribunal, convened to render judgment on the Nazi leaders following World War II.

The tribunal was an institution organized by the victorious Allied governments, serving in the final analysis the ruling classes of those countries.

Nonetheless, in their arguments U.S. prosecutors set forth a democratic legal principle derived from the international experience of a half-century of carnage: that planning and launching an aggressive war constituted a criminal act and that those who helped prepare such a war through their propaganda efforts were as culpable as those who drew up the battle plans or manufactured the munitions.

The case made against Hans Fritzsche, one of the individuals chiefly responsible for Nazi newspaper and radio propaganda, is particularly significant.

Fritzsche, born in Bochum, Westphalia in 1900, served in the German army in World War I and studied liberal arts at university, but left without a degree. He began a career as a journalist working for the Hugenberg Press, a newspaper chain that supported the right-wing "national" parties, including the Nazis.

Fritzsche began commenting on radio in September 1932, discussing political events on his own weekly program, "Hans Fritzsche Speaks".

That same year the regime of Franz von Papen appointed him head of the Wireless [Radio] News Department, a government agency. Fritzsche was generally sympathetic to the Nazi cause, but not a member of the party.

Underlining the importance with which the Hitlerites viewed radio as an instrument of propaganda, on the evening that the Nazis came to power, January 30, 1933, two emissaries of Joseph Goebbels, soon to be minister of propaganda and enlightenment, paid Fritzsche a visit.

The latter was allowed to stay on as head of the Wireless Radio Department despite his rejection of certain conditions set by Goebbels, including the immediate firing of all Jews and all those who refused to join the Nazi Party.

The Nuremberg prosecution case against Fritzsche notes: "Fritzsche continued to make radio broadcasts during this period in which he supported the National Socialist [Nazi] coalition government then still existing."

In April 1933, Goebbels paid Fritzsche a personal visit and informed him of the decision to place the Wireless News Service under the jurisdiction of the newly created Propaganda Ministry as of May 1, 1933.

Apparently satisfied with the results of the first meeting, Goebbels arranged a second at which Fritzsche informed the propaganda minister of the steps he had taken to "reorganize and modernize" the agency, including ridding it of Jewish employees.

"Goebbels thereupon informed Fritzsche that he would like to have him reorganize and modernize the entire news services of Germany within the control of the Propaganda Ministry. ... He [Fritzsche] proceeded to conclude the Goebbels-inspired reorganization of the Wireless News Service and, on 1 May 1933, together with the remaining members of his staff, he joined the Propaganda Ministry. On this same day he joined the NSDAP [Nazi Party] and took the customary oath of unconditional loyalty to the Fuehrer."

After entering the Propaganda Ministry, Fritzsche went to work for its "German Press Division".

From 1933 to 1942 Fritzsche held various positions in that department, heading it for the four years during which the Nazi regime launched its invasions of neighboring countries.

The Nuremberg prosecution argued: "By virtue of its functions, the German Press Division became an important and unique instrument of the Nazi conspirators, not only in dominating the minds and psychology of Germans, but also as an instrument of foreign policy and psychological warfare against other nations."

According to Fritzsche's own affidavit: "During the whole period from 1933 to 1945 it was the task of the German Press Division to supervise the entire domestic press and to provide it with directives by which this division became an efficient instrument in the hands of the German State leadership. More than 2,300 German daily newspapers were subject to this control. [...]

"The head of the German Press Division held daily press conferences in the Ministry for the representatives of all German newspapers. Hereby all instructions were given to the representatives of the press."

The prosecution case: propaganda as an instrument of aggression

The prosecution case, argued by Drexel Sprecher, an American, placed considerable stress on the role of media propaganda in enabling the Hitler regime to prepare and carry out aggressive wars.

"The use made by the Nazi conspirators of psychological warfare is well known. Before each major aggression, with some few exceptions based on expediency, they initiated a press campaign calculated to weaken their victims and to prepare the German people psychologically for the attack.

"They used the press, after their earlier conquests, as a means for further influencing foreign politics and in maneuvering for the following aggression."

Fritzsche was named head of the German Press Division in 1938 after the "primitive military-like" methods of his predecessor, Alfred Ingemar Berndt, created "a noticeable crisis in confidence of the German people in the trustworthiness of its press," in Fritzsche's words.

The Nuremberg prosecutor detailed the propaganda campaigns taken up by the German media, under Fritzsche's immediate supervision, in relation to various acts of foreign aggression, including the incorporation of Bohemia and Moravia (1939) and the invasions of Poland (1939) and Yugoslavia and the USSR (1941).

The Nazi press propaganda campaign preceding the invasion of Poland involved manufacturing or manipulating complaints of the German minority in that country.

Fritzsche explains: "Concerning this the leading German newspapers, upon the basis of directions given out in the so-called 'daily parole,' brought out the following publicity with great emphasis: (1) cruelty and terror against Germans and the extermination of Germans in Poland; (2) forced labor of thousands of German men and women in Poland; (3) Poland, land of servitude and disorder; the desertion of Polish soldiers; the increased inflation in Poland; (4) provocation of frontier clashes upon direction of the Polish Government; the Polish lust to conquer; (5) persecution of Czechs and Ukrainians by Poland."

In regard to the Nazi propaganda surrounding the Yugoslav events, the prosecutor noted the "customary definitions, lies, incitement and threats, and the usual attempt to divide and weaken the victim."

Fritzsche describes how he received instructions on the eve of the invasion of the Soviet Union in June 1941:

> [Foreign Minister Joachim von] Ribbentrop informed us that the war against the Soviet Union would start that same day and asked the German press to present the war against the Soviet Union as a preventative war for the defense of the Fatherland, as a war which was forced upon us through the immediate danger of an attack of the Soviet Union against Germany. The claim that this was a preventative war was later repeated by the newspapers which received their instructions from me during the usual daily parole of the Reich Press Chief. I, myself, have also given this presentation of the cause of the war in my regular broadcasts.

Thus, the presentation of an illegal invasion of a foreign country as a "preventative" or pre-emptive war did not originate with Bush, Cheney or Rumsfeld.

The prosecution in the Fritzsche case raised an issue that is of the greatest relevance today: the role of Nazi media propaganda in inuring the German population to the sufferings of other peoples and, indeed, urging Germans to commit war crimes.

It argued: "Fritzsche incited atrocities and encouraged a ruthless occupation policy. The results of propaganda as a weapon of the Nazi conspirators reaches into every aspect of this conspiracy, including the atrocities and ruthless exploitation in occupied countries.

It is likely that many ordinary Germans would never have participated in or tolerated he atrocities committed throughout Europe, had they not been conditioned and goaded by the constant Nazi propaganda. The callousness and zeal of the people who actually committed the atrocities was in large part due to the constant and corrosive propaganda of Fritzsche and his official associates."

The American media today reports poll results indicating that 60 or 70 percent of the population supports the war against Iraq. Such polls are not conducted by disinterested bodies for the purpose of advancing sociological knowledge.

The manner in which the interviewees are selected and the questions formulated has a considerable impact on the results obtained.

The powers that be in America have every interest in maintaining the fiction of a nation united behind its president and armed forces.

In reality, there is widespread hostility and opposition to the war and to the Bush administration, which finds no expression in the media, the Democratic Party or any other official American institution.

Nonetheless, there is a constituency for war among the more backward layers of the population. Aside from the relatively small number of right-wing fanatics, who would be in favor of war against almost anyone, including a good section of their fellow Americans, those in favor of the assault on Iraq believe a) that the Saddam Hussein regime had a hand in the September 11, 2001 terrorist attack on New York City and Washington; b) that the Iraqis possessed "weapons of mass destruction," which they intended to use against their neighbors or the U.S. at some future point; and/or c) that the Iraqi population desired "liberation" at the hands of the U.S. military.

While it is outside the scope of this article to expound on this, all three claims have been proven to be lies by the events of the war itself and will be further exposed by future developments. If many Americans, however, believe these arguments, with all the tragic consequences for the Iraqi and other peoples, how is that to be accounted for?

Clearly, by "the constant and corrosive propaganda" of the U.S. media over the course of months and even years, dating back to the first Gulf War.

The media's very success in manipulating public opinion is one of the strongest proofs of its culpability in the commission of war crimes.

It is worth quoting extensively from the Fritzsche prosecutor's conclusion, for it sheds considerable light on the role of the media in the modern age, as well as the democratic sensibilities of those pursuing the Nazi war criminals, sensibilities that no longer carry any weight within U.S. ruling circles.

> Fritzsche was not the type of conspirator who signed decrees, or who sat in the inner councils planning the overall grand strategy. The function of propaganda is, for the most part, apart from the field of such planning. The function of a propaganda agency is somewhat more analogous to an advertising agency or public relations department, the job of which is to sell the product and to win the market for the enterprise in question. Here the enterprise was the Nazi conspiracy. In a conspiracy which depends upon fraud as a means, the salesmen of the conspiratorial group are quite as essential and culpable as the master planners, even though they may not have contributed substantially to the formulation of all the basic strategy, but rather concentrated on making the execution of this strategy possible. In this case, propaganda was a weapon of tremendous importance to this conspiracy. Furthermore, the leading propagandists were major accomplices in this conspiracy, and Fritzsche was one of them [...]
>
> Fritzsche learned a lesson from his predecessor, Berndt, who fell from the leadership of the German Press Division partly because he over-played his hand by blunt and excessive manipulation of the Sudetenland propaganda. Fritzsche stepped into the gap caused by the loss of confidence of both the editors and the German people, and did his job with more skill and subtlety. His shrewdness and ability to be more assuring and "to find," as Goebbels said, "willing ears of the

whole nation" – these things made him the more useful accomplice of the conspirators [...]

Fritzsche is not in the dock as a free journalist but as a propagandist who helped substantially to tighten the Nazi stranglehold over the German people, who made the excesses of the conspirators palatable to the German people, who goaded the German nation to fury and crime against people they were told by him were subhuman.

Without the propaganda apparatus of the Nazi State, the world would not have suffered the catastrophe of these years, and it is because of Fritzsche's role in behalf of the Nazi conspirators, and their deceitful and barbarous practices, that he is called to account before the International Military Tribunal.

The tribunal found Fritzsche not guilty on the dubious grounds that he had not had sufficient stature to formulate or originate the propaganda campaigns undertaken by the Nazi regime.

It also asserted that the prosecution had not proven that Fritzsche was aware of the extermination of the Jews or had spread news he knew to be false. (Fritzsche was immediately rearrested and charged by German courts with various crimes. He was sentenced to nine years at hard labor, left prison in 1950 and died of cancer three years later.)

The prosecution, in its reply to the "Unfounded Acquittal of Defendant Fritzsche", returned insistently and pointedly to its arguments. It noted that the verdict failed to take into account that Fritzsche was until 1942 "the Director de facto of the Reich Press, and that, according to himself, subsequent to 1942, he became the 'Commander-in-Chief of the German radio.'"

The prosecution went on: "For the correct definition of the role of defendant Hans Fritzsche it is necessary, firstly, to keep clearly in mind the importance attached by Hitler and his closest associates (as Goering, for example) to propaganda in general and to radio propaganda in particular. This was considered one of the most important and essential factors in the success of conducting an aggressive war."

In Hitler's Germany, the reply to the verdict continues, "propaganda was invariably a factor in preparing and conducting acts of aggression and in training the German populace to accept obediently the criminal enterprises of German fascism. [...]

"The basic method of the Nazi propagandistic activity lay in the false presentation of facts. [...]

"The dissemination of provocative lies and the systematic deception of public opinion were as necessary to the Hitlerites for the realization of their plans as were the production of armaments and the drafting of military plans. Without propaganda, founded on the total eclipse of the freedom of press and of speech, it would not have been possible for German Fascism to realize its aggressive intentions, to lay the groundwork and then to put to practice the war crimes and the crimes against humanity. In the propaganda system of the Hitler State it was the daily press and the radio that were the most important weapons.

"There is little to be added to this condemnation.

"While all historical analogies have their limits, the indictment of the German media chief for war crimes speaks with great force to the role of the U.S. media barons in contemporary world affairs."

[Reprinted here with permission.]

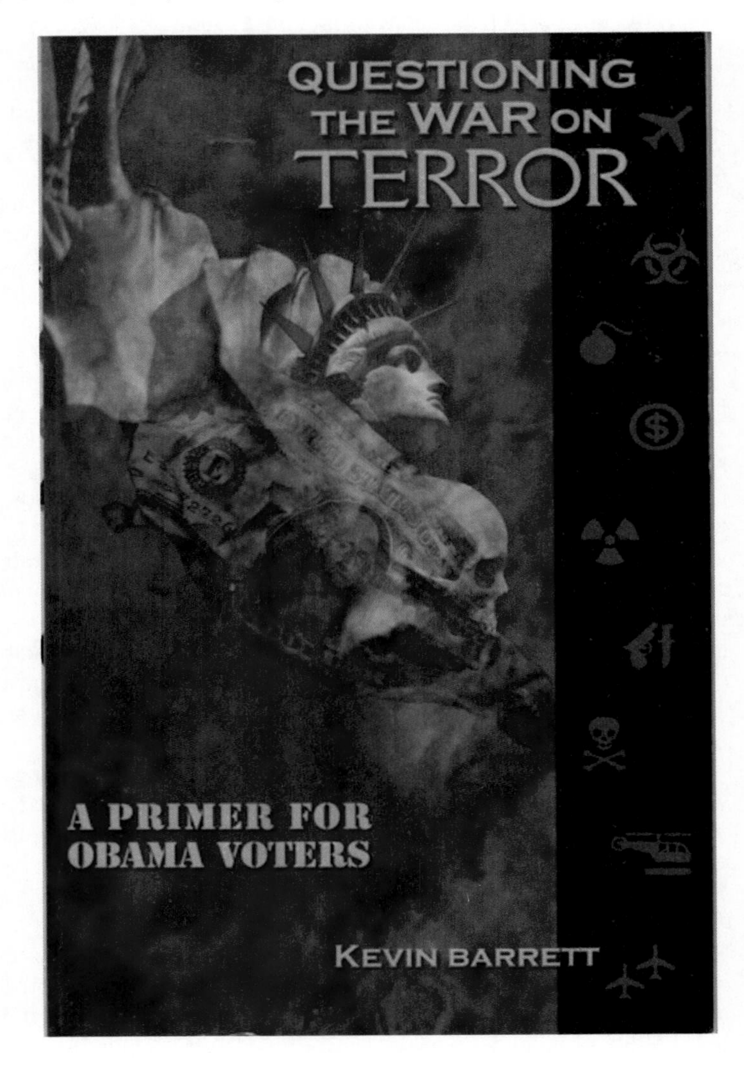

[Chapter 28] Regarding Jim Fetzer

Dr. Ralph Cinque:

Jim Fetzer is a modern American hero, and he is a leader in the truth movement. In fact, he was involved in it before it became known as "truthing". I have been involved with him mostly with JFK assassination truth, but Jim has been active on many fronts. I consider us lucky to have someone so accomplished and credentialed at the helm.

And Jim takes a lot of heat for what he does. The rancor and animosity hurled at Jim on the forums is unparalleled. But, Jim is made of armor, and he fends it off – undaunted.

It doesn't even slow him down. Regarding JFK, no one has assembled more data and more conclusive evidence than Jim has. Jim Fetzer is the one who put the Fritz notes on the front page – and you cannot overstate the importance of those notes.

Whenever someone says, "Why didn't Oswald say he was outside?" we can say, "He did." Jim Fetzer is the one who first started talking about "Obfuscated Man" in the doorway of the Altgens photo – which is proof of alteration.

The high placement of the Oswald Innocence Campaign on the search engines is due entirely to Jim Fetzer. I should add that many of our most prominent members were brought in directly by Jim, including Peter Janney (author of *Mary's Mosaic*) and Phillip F. Nelson (author of *LBJ: Mastermind of the JFK Assassination*) and naval airman Dennis Cimino.

As we approach the 50th anniversary of the JFK assassination, there is no greater "spoiler" to the government propagandists than Jim Fetzer. They know it; we know it; and through our continued diligent efforts, the whole world is going to know it. As for faults, Jim is a Type A personality, and he can be pretty darn insistent and unyielding. He can bark loudly, even to his friends.

It can be grating at times, but the truth is that Jim has saved us from mistakes, and here's an example: We have seen plenty of examples of photographic alterations in the JFK case.

Basically, they altered everything they could get their hands on. But, I was slow in seeing that even the FBI photos of Lovelady taken in February 1964 were altered.

They used shadow and other techniques to soften Lovelady's face to make him look more like Oswald – and hence like Doorman. Jim saw it before I did, and he insisted that we say so on the OIC site. He pressured me about it, put his foot down, and I am darn glad he did, even though at the time I was resisting it.

There is no longer any doubt that they "softened" Lovelady. In fact, we have found the "hard" versions of those pictures. So, even Jim's faults have been a blessing in disguise, and they have served us well. Jim is a leader, our leader, and he is going to lead us to victory for JFK truth.

Thomas Farrell:

In addition to being a well-published scholar in philosophy, Princeton-educated Jim Fetzer is an intellectual gadfly in the tradition of Socrates. As is well known, in the restored experiment of participatory democracy of male citizens in ancient Athens, Socrates' fellow Athenians finally voted the death penalty against him.

It remains to be seen if Jim Fetzer's fellow Americans will consign him to a similar fate for being an intellectual gadfly.

To be sure, Jim has far more than his fair share of political views, not all of which are of equal value. However, he is in no danger of ever being elected to elective office in the United States, because he simply does not have the talents that politicians must have to woo American voters into voting for them. (Neither do I.) In short, he is not a politician. He is strictly an idea guy – an intellectual gadfly in the tradition of Socrates.

Gordon Duff:

Fetzer is one of the most interesting characters of our time. I find him a total joy to work with. The key aspect of Jim is his openness. His fault is that he gets so much energy from the dynamic of crushing the fools sent against him. Jim is a "work in progress," continually getting better at what he does.

I consider him our "junkyard dog".

Thomas Farrell:

Yes, Gordon Duff, Jim Fetzer is characterized by his openness, as you say.

To be sure, in my experience of Jim, he has never appeared to believe that a word to the wise is sufficient. On the contrary, he appeared to believe that he was not speaking to anybody who might be wise. Evidently, because of this apparent presupposition, he characteristically fights to have the last word.

Yes, he often appears to find it satisfying to verbally demolish his real or imagined adversaries.

But you also say that he appears to you to draw energy from verbally crushing his real or imagined adversaries

Wow! This characterization of Jim makes him sound like a sadist – in short, sadistic.

Now, the Jungian theorist Robert L. Moore of Chicago Theological Seminary has written and spoken extensively about the Warrior archetype in the male psyche. (He claims that there is also a Warrior archetype in the female psyche.)

Moore writes explicitly about drawing energies of the Warrior archetype. (He also writes about drawing energies from the other archetypes of maturity that he discusses.)

Moore refers to two "shadow" forms of the Warrior archetype: (1) the Sadist and (2) the Masochist.

In addition, Moore writes about the optimal form of the Warrior archetype. (He also writes about two "shadow" forms of each of the other archetypes of maturity that he discusses and about the optimal form of each of those as well.)

Based on my experience of Jim Fetzer over the years (since we both began teaching at UMD in September 1987), I would characterize him as embodying and manifesting the optimal form of the Warrior archetype, not the Sadist "shadow" form.

I would also characterize Jim as also drawing energies of the optimal form of the Magician archetype.

Two out of four optimal forms is outstanding.

However, as you say, Gordon Duff, Jim Fetzer is a work in progress.

In my estimate, he still needs to work on drawing on the optimal forms of the King archetype and the Lover archetype in the archetypal level of his psyche. For further discussion of the archetypes of masculine maturity, see the revised and expanded edition of Robert Moore and Douglas Gillette's book *The King Within: Accessing The King [Archetype] In The Male Psyche* (Chicago: Exploration Press, 2007).

Larry Rivera:

It has now been a year since I have known, corresponded, been interviewed by, and collaborated with the Honorable Jim Fetzer. His indomitable spirit has crossed many boundaries of investigation. By applying his vast experience in logic and philosophy, scientific methods of hypothesis and investigation, he has surpassed all of his peers in deciphering how our government keeps the masses in line. The mystique he now projects is second to none.

I have vastly enjoyed his many areas of expertise, which I am only now aware of from reading his many *Veterans Today* articles and his radio programs and interviews on the Internet. Whenever he lags behind in answering emails it is because he is always involved in some interview, article, radio or TV program which I'm sure spreads him thin and makes one wonder how he is able to maintain this pace.

To paraphrase his radio shows, he IS the Real Deal and I am extremely proud to know the man. He is our venerable Obi Wan Kenobi (because of his knowledge, not age), and I am sure when all is said and done, he will be there to protect us with his light saber.

Dennis Cimino:

One thing about Jim is that he is an indomitable spirit, and all of the epithets and pathetic zio bleating to discredit him have done little damage to the man who keeps pushing to get what he believes is the TRUTH out to the world.

Decades ago I remember seeing his name in the MCRD roster there in San Diego, and now it has been a very rare pleasure and opportunity to co-author work with him.

In the so-called, and wholly infiltrated by zio scum, TRUTH movement, he's almost the SOLE VOICE, with the exception of Nick Kollerstrom in London and a small cadre of others at O.I.C. now, who are not too likely to hang up their keyboards.

Paul Craig Roberts, Jim Fetzer, Nick Kollerstrom, and a mere handful are all that remain in a world full of deceit and zio lies.

We have done what we can to carry the torch of TRUTH without dropping it on our quest for resolution, and it is my hope we press on and keep the flame burning and illuminate the minds of those seeking the immutable, non-negotiable, and oh so very precious commodity we know as VERITAS.

We will continue to pass that fiery baton as we keep the sun from setting on humanity in dark ages to come.

I owe a debt to all of you, not just Jim Fetzer, but to all who have so selflessly served this task to put TRUTH before all deceit and obfuscation, as perhaps more than ever, not unlike that tiny gas flame on JFK's tomb in Arlington, the bright white light of TRUTH shall not be extinguished nor perish into the pages of history, being blown out by the last gasp of global zionism.

Richard Hooke:

Well, I second all that others have said about Jim Fetzer. Last Thanksgiving (11/22/2012), Jim Fetzer came to San Francisco to give a talk at The Roxie Theater, on the anniversary of the JFK assassination, along with Judyth Vary Baker. I had explained to Jim I regretted I was not able to make Jim's presentation, in lieu of my wife Roxie's sumptuous, home cooked, Thanksgiving dinner.

Anyway, Jim met me for coffee, on Market Street, at the Coffee Bean & Tea leaf, earlier that day. Jim called my house and had my wife call the coffee shop to track me down, because I had my cell turned off; was zoned-out doing some research on Lee Harvey Oswald, out of my backpack, with a pile of books & notebooks & empty latte containers in a remote corner. Jim walked ten blocks from Union Square to track me down. I spotted Jim as he came through the door he was calling me on his cell, saying, "Richard where are you?" I heard Jim, loud and clear, and stood up saying, "JIM, I AM OVER HERE!!!"

And Jim came over, and he was very nice, not as big as I thought he was going to be, and we shook hands, sat down, and I showed him my research. Jim was very complementary, and gracious, a gentleman and, of course, the scholar that he is. So, then we walked further down Market Street to the Ferry Building, with the big clock tower, by San Francisco Bay, and then south on Embarcadero, toward AT&T Park, in search of an open restaurant for lunch. The two of us went into Sinbad's and got a table overlooking the choppy, blue-green, salt water of the bay, with white sailboats tacking into it, in front of Treasure Island, and the massive grey-girders of the Bay Bridge. Jim and I had lunch as he explained that was his Thanksgiving dinner because he was in San Francisco alone.

And we talked about many things and I thought Jim is kind of like the older brother I never had ... I told him the story of how I had gotten into JFK research about five years prior, after my dad had gotten killed in a robbery. We looked out the large wall-of-windows, across the bay, at Treasure Island and Jim said, "There's T I," and I said, yes, my dad used to take me there, when I was a boy, for Thanksgiving dinner, in the officer's club (dad was retired Navy), and Jim pulled out his old military I.D. and showed me; you know the type; like those pictures of Oswald's I.D.

Of course, Jim picked up the tab and, as we walked back up Market Street, we passed a homeless man, in bad shape, lying in his dirty tattered clothing, with his hat upside down in front. Not wanting to look like I was trying to impress Jim, I walked on by, but Jim stopped and gave the guy all the change in his pockets; then, not wanting to appear like a cheapskate, I doubled back and gave the man some also.

We arrived at BART (the subway), it was time for me to say goodbye, and I think I surprised Jim as I stretched my right arm out and patted my right hand down on Jim's left shoulder. Even though this was the first time I had met Jim personally I felt an affinity; he was my good friend, and I said, "Thanks man, I'll talk to you later." And Jim said, "Happy Thanksgiving Richard," and then I disappeared down the subway tunnel.

Jim Viken:

Jim Fetzer has the brightest, quickest mind and best memory for details of any top truth researcher I know of.

He chews up misinformation sock puppets like gumdrops and is a prolific and gifted writer. He cuts through USG propaganda and lies like a red hot knife through butter.

USG apologists, liars and cover-uppers need to stay clear of Professor Fetzer. He will shred them and expose them for all to see in a few minutes and in some cases pound them so hard they will never appear in public again to argue as USG dupes.

His dynamic groundbreaking work on the JFK assassination set the standard for truthers in general and laid a basis for cracking many of the numerous false narratives supplied by a deceptive, lying USG.

His ability to think on his feet and debate any professional psyops and win hands down in only a few minutes is why none will even try to debate him any more. He shredded Ollie North on Fox news in only few minutes despite Ollie's handling by a psyops handler by earphone. Fetzer is a formidable debater and will shred anyone foolish enough to try and speak lies in front of him. He will disassemble them in mere minutes.

Watch Fetzer pound Colmes and John Cathey to pieces on Fox News in this classic video clip.

http://www.youtube.com/watch?v=08va1i6LYPc&feature=player_detailpage.

Now you know why no major mass media will dare have Prof. Fetzer on for any more attempts to set him up. The USG does not have anyone near as skilled as Professor Fetzer anywhere – at Langley or anywhere else – that can match him. And they know it and avoid him like the plague.

Prof. Fetzer is clearly one of the world's top experts on logic and critical thinking if not the top. When someone violates the rules of logic, which is usually necessary for arguing cover-ups, Fetzer shreds 'em in a instant because he catches the flawed logic in their arguments immediately and hits back fast and hard.

Yes, Jim Fetzer has literally cracked the JFK case with a huge collection of grand jury ready evidence that could convict many beyond any reasonable doubt of murder, misprision of felonies and treason, sedition, RICO, fraud, and accessories after the crime, as well as numerous criminal conspiracy offenses. But because the USG is so corrupt and infiltrated and owned at every level by IZCS operatives who have unlimited funds, nothing has been done to prosecute. However, I know for a fact that millions of dollars are spent each year by American Intel to keep pumping out misinformation to keep the JFK crime buried. This is because the regime responsible is still in power today. As always, if the JFK thread was pulled all the way, the whole USG would collapse and that is why they still work so hard to keep the cover-up going.

The continuing JFK cover-up is expensive and sophisticated. A good example is the numerous ghost written books and dupe books written by folks such as Bugliosi, Mailer, Posner and many more who have received little "not to worry" visits which encourage them to cooperate and be part of such blatant crap.

Fetzer shreds these folks like cheese through a grater. He turns their work into an expensive paperweight and makes them a perpetual joke in a very short time. He literally dissects them point by point and throws them into the trash heap of history.

Another example of the continuing JFK cover-up which Fetzer exposed has been the reservation of Dealey Plaza by U.S. intel cutouts, to prevent any real commemoration of JFK on the 50th year anniversary of his murder.

Jim Fetzer's main fault is not completely counterproductive. That fault is his commitment to discuss any event or issue with anyone, even sock puppets or misinformation artists. He gives everyone a chance to be heard, and quickly exposes their errors of fact and logic while acknowledging any good ideas too. Some would view this as a waste of time and an energy parasite, but strangely Prof. Fetzer seems to become even more energized by such actions.

Professor Fetzer has done more to get the truth movement going than anyone else, and has shredded so many USG lies and propaganda spyops and psyops it would fill a very thick book to list them. Rather than backing off since his retirement as a tenured full professor at the University of Minnesota, he is coming on stronger than ever and clearly in prime form. USG BS'ers and apologist liars associated with big govt lies and corruption had best beware. Professor Fetzer will expose you and shred your lies and deceit.

Rich Parker:

Thank you for the reminder.

And please thank Jim for including me in the list of people he gave you, so that I would have this opportunity to provide some "brief reflections" to you.

I don't normally do "brief" very well at all, as Jim can verify, and when the subject is Jim himself, it's even harder for me to be brief, since I have known him so long and in so many different contexts.

But I will endeavor to be brief.

So I will share with you a single story that I think captures Jim's caring side.

Jim and I were friends and neighbors, growing up together in junior high and high school in an admirable, if conventional, small suburb of Los Angeles, South Pasadena. Our high school class was small, about 200, and we were both student body officers. I recall that we took pleasure from the fact that we were both rather low in the final class rankings – at least by the usual standards – and that we actually tied! By then it was known that he had been admitted to Princeton, and I to Stanford, so we could laugh about the rankings.

Neither he nor I were a part of any particularly close group of friends; there were plenty of cliques, but we did not belong to any of them. We did share a number of mutual friends, and one of them I will call Robert. Jim and I had known Robert for many years. Robert was (and remains) bright, articulate, interesting, and passionate about many things.

But Robert was also rather effeminate and, this being the mid-to-late 1950's, in high school he was teased and badgered and harassed about it, constantly. He did have friends, but the atmosphere for him was unpleasant and stressful, even poisonous. As a result, Robert does not look back on his high school days with much pleasure or nostalgia. So he was never interested in attending high school reunions, even after he moved back into the community, following his retirement from a long and successful career with IBM. Jim and I had tried over the years to interest Robert in coming to a reunion, because we thought he might enjoy it, and also because we would enjoy having him there. (We guessed that maybe he had forgotten how many friends he did have.) But he was never interested.

Robert discovered he was gay in his thirties. He and his long-standing partner (they have now been together for perhaps twenty-five years) had been living in South Pasadena for years, when Jim traveled there from Minnesota for a major class reunion. Jim made a point of visiting Robert the day before the main reunion event, so that he could try to entice him into attending the event the following evening. Jim worked hard to convince him to give it a try.

Jim can be very persuasive at times, and persistent, like a bulldog. And he was successful, because Robert did show up the following evening, and we all had an evocative and rewarding evening, especially Robert, who loved it. He had, indeed, forgotten or not fully realized how many classmates cared about him, and he enjoyed rekindling those friendships. It was a special time for Robert, and it quite changed his outlook. The reunion made a significant impact on his life.

And it was due entirely to Jim.

James Tracy:

I have only known Jim for a year or so because of my own increasing outspokenness on deep events. He had me as a guest on his radio program, *The Real Deal*, in spring 2012, and I've since been on several times to discuss the Sandy Hook massacre and Boston Marathon bombing. We are regularly in touch and both members of a small research collective that is presently investigating Newtown and Boston.

In my view, Jim is one of the most principled researchers, academics, and commentators in the world today. He is a competent researcher addressing pivotal events impacting the trajectory of national and international history. Jim has a brain like a computer and it's amazing how he can recollect historical events and actors. With his attention to minute details he reminds me of a cross between Sergeant Joe Friday and a nineteenth century barrister. In other words, when he goes after something he's relentless. With these things in mind, Jim is also representative of an era, and I'm afraid they don't make many like him anymore.

Jim has an international reputation for good reason. He is also more productive in retirement than most professors who are still full time faculty at their institutions. At his age if he didn't have such a keen sense of responsibility to remain engaged he could easily be sipping cactus coolers on the links or kicking back in the La-Z-Boy with the remote. This, after all, is the standard mode for most of his contemporaries.

Jim is also a bouyant and gregarious man with a great sense of humor who always makes time for those involved in meaningful research. If there were more intellectuals who had the morality, courage, sociological imagination and overall talent to produce the work he has, we would see a significant transformation in public opinion and discourse in this country and beyond.

I have also greatly appreciated his encouragement and willingness to defend me by writing a public letter to my employer, Florida Atlantic University, when I was under fire from the university administration and major news media because I publicly suggested that the Newtown massacre may have been staged.

John Costella:

Without Jim Fetzer, I would never have investigated the authenticity of the Zapruder film, and even if I had, almost no one would have heard of the results.

I don't agree with Jim Fetzer on all topics – or even most topics, for that matter. Even within the small domain of the alteration of the photographic evidence of the JFK assassination, we remain on opposite sides of the fence on some issues (e.g. "Moorman in the Street"); and away from the JFK assassination, and the NTSB's investigation of the Wellstone crash, we agree on far less.

But regardless of how many times he has been right or wrong (a tally that few of us civilians are honestly in any place to sensibly assess), Jim has been one of a select few public figures to draw attention to alternative explanations of important events (or, in the case of JFK, alternatives to the "standard alternative"), long before that became fashionable and commonplace; and, most importantly, he has demanded that the scientific process be brought to bear on those issues.

Far more important than his opinions on world history is the collection of experts, researchers, and commentators that he has exposed his readers and listeners to, the contemplation of which gives each of us a much better chance of forming a more accurate view of what really happened – or, at least, a richer understanding of the palette of possible truths – than what we would have blindly believed if we had never heard of this crazy conspiracy theory professor from Duluth, Minnesota. He is imperfect; we love him to death.

Ron White:

Jim was the first professor I had at UK.

I was working on a Masters degree in philosophy. I was a teaching assistant in logic.

Jim was in charge of the logic sections and the logic TAs. Before Jim arrived most those sections were taught in huge lecture with the professor doing the lectures, and TAs did mostly grading. Jim taught us all how to teach logic, then gave us the classes to teach ourselves. His teaching method consisted of sending students to the board to do logic problems and assigning one or two students to check the "proof". The idea was to create more student participation in class and get students to teach each other. TAs still did lectures, but they were fewer and shorter. Students loved these courses.

All of us TAs earned excellent student evaluations and Jim won UK's distinguished teaching award for the whole university! Later I adapted this "collaborative teaching style" to all of my classes with similar success ... long before the rest of academe caught on.

Jim was also very forthright in sharing his scholarly research with us and often solicited our input. Because of Jim I went on to focus on the philosophy of science, and I wrote my thesis on Charles Sanders Peirce's *Epistemology*. Later I earned a Ph.D. in the history of science and medicine. When Jim was denied tenure for sociopolitical reasons we were all devastated.

Even today I harbor a deep distrust of committees and the politics of tenure and promotion. Jim's basic problem was that he alienated many of his colleagues by ardently arguing not only philosophy but departmental policies.

A skilled logician and a passionate quick-thinking philosopher, Jim tended to make enemies. He also has a loud and boisterous laugh that can be heard throughout a building. And ... he laughed a lot in classes, meetings, and private conversations. So despite the fact that he won the distinguished teaching award and had 19 articles published in top-notch journals, Jim was denied tenure, which left him with one to two year appointments for many years.

Here's a story for you ... years ago drove up to visit Jim and Jan. About an eight-hour drive as I recall. After feeding me, giving me a couple of glasses of wine, he handed me a twenty-five-page paper that he had just finished on Peirce's Theory of Signs and asked me to read it. I read it and we talked about it the rest of the night. In short, Jim is an intense guy ... He is also intimidating at scholarly meetings and will argue very heatedly (and loudly) with others ... then afterward ... he always makes friends. It's important to note that Jim often defends views that are outside of orthodoxy, therefore he often faces many critics. And ... as you know ... he's good at it. He's also a "true blue" friend and more than a "good person" in the moral sense. He's a Kantian ... which enlightens all of his moral views. Years ago I was contemplating defaulting on my student loan. I had two young kids and no job ... Jim convinced me to pay it off ... which I did. In short, Jim has been a major influence on my life.

I've also worked with Jim on many scholarly projects. I wrote the "Epilogue" for *Assassination Science*. We've done several panel discussions together for the Association for Politics and the Life Sciences. I also have some insight into Jim's penchant for conspiracies.

We can talk about that later.

David Mantik:

Jim is a force of nature. When he decides to do something, nothing else matters.

He is always enthusiastic, brimming with energy, and commited to his goals. He is extremely loyal and generous, and will do anything for his friends (sometimes too much, according to his wife).

Since Jim always has the last word, he is a remarkably good bulldog to send into intellectual combat.
And he has never lost a battle.
After all, he was a U.S. Marine.

There is no one like him, but perhaps one is enough.
Life would have been infinitely more boring without him.
I am deeply grateful to have known Jim.

The NTSB Failed Wellstone

IGNORED EVIDENCE AND SUPPRESSED INVESTIGATIONS

By

Jim Fetzer and John Costella

Special to *From The Wilderness*

When Senator Paul Wellstone's plane crashed near Eveleth, Minnesota on Friday, October 25, 2002, killing him, his wife, his daughter, three aides, the pilot, and the co-pilot, a casual observer might have forecast a simple investigation by the National Transportation Safety Board (NTSB). The mass media widely reported bad weather in the area—freezing rain, snow, icing, and fog, with poor visibility—and implied that the weather had caused the crash.

All that remained of the fuselage of Senator Wellstone's plane: little more than ash. This photograph looks back from the cockpit (foreground) into the fuselage. (The yellow numbered markers are NTSB identification points.)

BABY'S • FAMILY • TREE

FATHER'S • SIDE

FATHER Henry Fetzer
PLACE OF BIRTH Winchester, Va.
DATE OF BIRTH Dec 1, 1913
GRANDFATHER Henry Fetzer
PLACE OF BIRTH Frederick Co, Va.
DATE OF BIRTH April 11, 1854
GRANDMOTHER Julia E. Fetzer
PLACE OF BIRTH Woodstock [illegible]
DATE OF BIRTH [illegible]

MOTHER'S • SIDE

MOTHER [illegible] Watchman Fetzer
PLACE OF BIRTH Pomona, California
DATE OF BIRTH February 10th 1917
GRANDFATHER [illegible] Watchman
PLACE OF BIRTH Cedar Rapids, Iowa
DATE OF BIRTH February [illegible]
GRANDMOTHER Bessie A. Watchman
PLACE OF BIRTH Chicago, Illinois
DATE OF BIRTH March 17 – ?

[Chapter 29] Regarding Kevin Barrett

There's a reason

by Kevin Barrett

There's a reason we're all doin' what we're doin'
But what that reason is I just can't say
Maybe we're all crazy
Maybe we're just lazy
Maybe we were all born yesterday

There's a reason we're all doin' what we're doin'
But what that reason is, I have no clue
Maybe we're all nuts, or just can't get off our butts
We're just doin' what other people do
Just doin' what other people do

We just keep right on payin' our taxes
We should have quit payin' long ago
And told the bastards where to go.
Now, when they kill, we too are to blame.

We just keep workin' for the rich man
Though all our real wages get smaller every year
We sure must be dolts, not to revolt
They've got our minds chained up with greed and fear ...

My Brother Kevin

by Bruce Barrett on July 14, 2013

Kevin is my brother, both in the sense of having the same parents, but also as a fraternal comrade in the journey of life, and in the struggle to make the world a better place.

As young children we lived first in Newport Beach, California, and then grew to maturity in Pewaukee, Wisconsin.

With mother Laurie, father Pete, and sister Tara, we shared many of the common experiences of our generation: TV shows laden with consumerist advertisements, Christmas holidaze with too many presents, the growing hegemony of corporatized fast food and throw-away purchases, and auto-tour vacations across America's iconic landscapes.

To their credit, our parents were intellectually inquisitive, open-minded, and liberal, influenced by the civil rights movement and Vietnam war protests, but also caught up in the American Dream, which for them centered on sailing but also included canoes, motor boats, downhill skiing, hiking and camping, and gradually moving up the socioeconomic ladder.

Kevin has always been a rebel. From an early age, his in-born drive towards autonomy tested our parents, his teachers, and any adult foolish enough to try to impose conventions or rules that didn't pass muster with Kevin's increasingly analytical critique.

A voracious reader, my brother turned me on to the writings of Abbie Hoffman and Malcom X, and to the tunes of the *Rolling Stone*s, Frank Zappa, and Country Joe MacDonald. Underground comics featuring the Furry Freak Brothers complemented *Steal This Book* and *The Power Elite* as writings that Kevin discovered, then passed on to me.

As I recall, Kevin studied the Kennedy assassinations at an early age, then sought to educate his teachers at Pewaukee High School about the "inside job" nature of that crime, and about the unholy alliance of the national security state and the military industrial complex with organized crime, both licit and illicit.

I learned about the Tri-Lateral Commission and the Knights of Malta from Kevin, and joined the growing ranks of Americans who despised the meta-system based on greed, lies and violence, and hoped for a revolutionary transition towards democracy, equality, and justice.

Kevin is one of the smartest people I know. I am a physician, a scientist, and a tenured professor at the great University of Wisconsin. As such, I interact regularly with a considerable number of very smart people.

Yet I believe that Kevin may be the brightest and best read of all, both in terms of having studied the classic writings of Western "civilization", and in terms of the intellectual critique of such writings. Philosophy, sociology, economics, anthropology, and political science, Kevin has been there, done that, read the seminal works of the great authors, and is always ready with critique and commentary.

Kevin is one of the bravest people I know.

On the day that the twin towers went down, I wept.

My tears were for that day's victims and their loved ones, but also for the all the victims to come. Within seconds of hearing the news I knew instinctively that 9/11 would be used as justification for war, and that the victims would come mostly from the Muslim world.

It was no secret that neocons such as Cheney, Rumsfeld, Wolfowitz and Feith wanted to escalate the war on Iraq. American control of Iraqi oil was a central plank in their bid for a New American Century. With the Bush the Lesser in the White House, U.S.-led war in the Middle East was not a difficult prediction. What was unknown at the time, of course, was that the true and full nature of the September 11 events was not being told by the mass media.

Pursuit of 9/11 Truth and dissemination of related knowledge has been Kevin's main mission for several years now, and it is for this role that he is most widely known.

In my humble and perhaps brotherly-biased opinion, Kevin's track record demonstrates a degree of fearlessness and unrelenting intellectual drive rarely seen in today's world of mediocrity, timidity, and complacency.

A hero to some and a scoundrel to others, Kevin is one of the more interesting people you'll ever have a chance to meet, or to learn about through radio or written words, if an in-person meeting is not in your cards.

Kevin is my brother and I love him. Sometimes I fear for him, as I know that there any number of people who do not wish him well. And sometimes I worry for him. I imagine that the life he has lived has not always been easy. But in the end I realize that we each have only one life to live, and that while speaking truth to power may not be the calling of all heroes, it is more than most scoundrels can manage, and is certainly a laudable endeavor.

Rock on, brother Kevin!

May your life be long and satisfying, and may your work contribute to a better world for all.

Dr. Kevin Barrett is an extraordinarilly courageous person of absolutely exceptional integrity whose commitment to the search for Truth, to explain and broadcast the Truth without regard for consequences, to struggle to advance the cause of Truth in a world dominated by those whose raison d'etre is based on the propagation of lies, falsehood and deception, has raised him head and shoulders above the multitudes who today lack the qualities necessary to stand up for Truth.

- Imran N. Hosein

-

In my capacity as a professor of philosophy at the University of Michigan, I have known of Kevin Barrett for several years. I was always intrigued at the idea of a professional academician who had the guts to challenge the conventional 9/11 story, and who unjustly suffered for it. In 2010, I ran a topics course called "Hoaxes, Frauds, and Conspiracies," during which I had Kevin participate live via Skype – the first such classroom interview done on my campus. We had two student groups exploring the 9/11 conspiracy, and it was very enlightening to hear directly from someone so knowledgeable. He was a big "hit" with the students.

Then in both 2011 and 2012, I was a guest on Kevin's *Truth Jihad* web radio program. We discussed the aftermath of my Hoaxes course, and the general topic of academic freedom. He is a great radio host, and really allows the guests to have their say.

In general, I would say that I very much respect Kevin's diligence and perseverance regarding 9/11 Truth. From my perspective, he is a leading figure in the field, and a great resource. He has paid a price for confronting the powers that be – especially the Jewish Lobby – and he is to be commended for holding strong and not giving in. Very few people of his caliber are willing and able to pursue the "inconvenient truth" about 9/11, Zionist terrorism, the war on Islam, the Holocaust, and related topics.

We need more people like him!

- David Skrbina

Dr. Kevin Barrett's ordeal is a glimpse into the unfolding American Tragedy. Barrett, a spectacular intellect and a promising academic, has been subject [to] an ongoing harassment campaign led by the notorious Zionist ADL as well as some institutional elements within the Jewish Left.

Barrett's crime is obvious – he is committed to the notion of *Truth Jihad* – the belief that the search for truth is the real meaning of self-perfection.

In contemporary America, a brilliant curious mind such as Barrett is spit out of academia due to the pressure of a notorious Zionist lobby, yet a banal spin-doctor such as Alan Dershowitz is safely settled at Harvard.

In the last few years I exchanged with Barrett numerous times; I have been guesting on his radio show. Every encounter with Barrett is an unforgettable experience. Barrett possesses a unique and rare scholarly capacity to examine history and politics from a theoretical perspective.

He transcends himself beyond the actual and the factual and delves into the deep cultural and ideological substances that drive our reality.

In the last few years Barrett has been scrutinizing the work of Neocon mentor Leo Strauss. Barrett is now at the forefront of the research into the philosophy and the spirit that lead Neoconservative thinking. He identifies the thoughts and the characters that push the English Speaking Empire into global conflicts.

Dr. Barrett is clearly a severe threat to American warmongers.

And it is hardly a big surprise that the enemies of peace are united and dedicated to his destruction.

- Gilad Atzmon

[Chapter 30] Jim: "Who wants to live in Duluth?" ... "He was a magnificent human being"

> "In George Orwell's *1984*, it is perhaps Emmanuel Goldstein who is the pivotal character. Orwell's Goldstein is a Jewish revolutionary, a fictional Leon Trotsky. He is depicted as the head of a mysterious anti-party organization called "The Brotherhood" and is also the author of the most subversive revolutionary text ("The Theory and Practice of Oligarchical Collectivism"). Goldstein is the 'dissenting voice', the one who actually tells the truth. Yet, as we delve into Orwell's text, we find out from Party's 'Inner Circle' O'Brien that Goldstein was actually invented by Big Brother in a clear attempt to control the opposition and the possible boundaries of dissidence."
>
> \- Gilad Atzmon

JIM:

[I would like to talk about how you keep going.]

I know that, like everyone else, I am not going to live forever. I am doing what I can as long as I can.

[Talk about your family. Has it been hard for them, your work? Examples of times it has not been easy.]

They have not universally shared my enthusiasm for exposing corruption by our own government. It is too stressful for them to become immersed in my efforts. So they appreciate them from a distance.

[What still needs to be done?]

The American people need to wake up and realize that this nation is turning into a fascist police state – and it is taking place with breathtaking rapidity.

When the U.S. Senate can vote to support an attack by Israel on Iran – when Iran is a peaceful nation that has not attacked anyone for 300 years, has no nuclear weapons program, and has signed the NPT and allows inspectors, none of which is true of Israel – even though it violates international law, the UN Charter and even the U.S. Constitution by a vote of 99-0, something is terribly wrong.

We really are "The United States of Israel", sad to say.

[Would you like to be able to stop? What would you do if you did not "have" to do this?]

Probably develop Alzheimer's from lack of brain exertion. But then, as Jan likes to say (given my tendencies toward absent-mindedness), if I were to acquire Alzheimer's, how could anyone tell?

[Talk about this quote. I don't think most people feel this much confidence and I would be interested to know where it comes from in you. When asked, how you wrote and published so much, you replied, "I just know what I'm doing. I'm extremely efficient."]

Well, it's true. I am well-organized, generally thorough and painstaking, and know what I am doing. I wrote my (very technical) first book sequentially from page 1 to 500 without any revisions. I finished one page and turned to the next 500 and the publisher did not ask me to change a comma.

[Talk about this quote. I might believe this of your writings, but I think it is unusual that a person would, again, have the confidence to say that about one's own work. You said, "These books I have published are the most important in establishing the objective and scientific evidence of the existence of conspiracy and cover-up in the assassination of JFK. Bar none. No other books come close. Remotely. None. They're in a category by themselves. This shattered the whole goddamn cover-up!"]

They are edited books in which I brought together the best qualified experts I could find on different aspects of the assassination. One of my strengths is that I know my own limitations with regard to domain-specific knowledge (of medicine, ballistics, radiology and so forth) and compensate for that by creating research groups in relation to JFK, 9/11 and (on a smaller scale) the Wellstone crash. I said to Mike Mosedale immediately after I said that to be sure to add what I have just explained (that it was because I was working with other experts that we accomplished so much), but he left that out.

["Who wants to live in Duluth?" ... In the masters program for computer science, also applying for teaching jobs, eventually ... Headed to Duluth, Athens, Madison, Bill O'Reilly, The McKnight]

I was interviewed for seven positions again, all senior. And the fact of the matter is I would be interviewed at the Eastern Division meeting of the American Philosophical Association by several representatives from the University of Minnesota-Duluth. And you know, there's an irony to this. I was applying for all those vast number of jobs, you know, and going through this publication called *Jobs In Philosophy*, and I actually think I made a direct contribution to the creation of that by my interaction with the head of the department at Columbia, whom I knew because of the year I'd spent there. A story for another day, but the fact is that Jan would look through the ads to make sure I hadn't overlooked anything. And she asked me, why haven't you applied for this position?

And I said, well, who wants to live in Duluth? And she says, oh, no, she'd been through Duluth several times on the way to Canada. It was a beautiful city and I really ought to apply so I figured, well, what's one more thirteen-cent stamp?

So I applied and in fact of course that would turn out to be quite fateful. I think it's another case where I haven't always known where my best interests lay, and here it was.

So I was interviewed. Had a real good interview. But I had a lot of good interviews that year.

They would eventually invite me up to the campus to a talk about the history of logical empiricism, logical positivism, Carnap, Reichenbach, Hempel, all this stuff which I knew backwards and forwards.

And, they hired me. Full professor with tenure. That was going to make a huge difference.

Meanwhile I was back at Wright State and I was just soaking up everything I was learning about computer science. But I knew they were going to forfeit my fellowship, which they did. I think it was actually not until the end of the second semester, meaning spring semester.

But the fact was, it didn't make a difference any longer, because I'd already been hired as a full professor with tenure. There were five of us in the program. The other four got their masters degrees, including, of course, Chuck Dunlop. I was the only one who did not. But of course I would go on to do all this work in the area of computer science and artificial intelligence, cognitive science.

Subconsciously it's very interesting. Dallas High, going all the way back to Kentucky, had complained that he thought I was too narrow.

I was actually doing all this classic work on the nature of laws, scientific explanation, scientific knowledge, and all that, which Kentucky didn't appreciate, especially a guy whose background was in religion, couldn't comprehend, actually.

But, by going into this computer science program, I enormously broadened the scope of my research. I mean, I wound up doing all this work on the theoretical foundations of computer science, artificial intelligence, cognitive science, and eventually, evolution and mentality.

But once at Duluth it was as though it unleashed all of my creative capabilities, and in the first couple of years I must have published, I don't know, 13 new books in the first couple of years.

A lot of them were edited or co-edited, 29 books, but there were seven or more co-authored books, 10 or 12 more edited books, and then several other co-edited books, so it's been a variety of different forms of contribution that I've been making.

In addition to founding *Minds and Machines*, I also founded "The Society For Machines and Mentality", and I was invited to become the series editor of a professional library entitled *Studies in Cognitive Systems*, which would eventually have thirty different volumes.

In any case, I liked my students at UMD. They [the department] had a merit matrix, which means an objective set of criteria for determining who would receive merit raises in the department, which I liked tremendously. It's one of the invariable sources of friction in departments. In most places this is done in a highly subjective manner upon the head's recommendation to the dean.

And there's often discontent among faculty not believing they received the appropriate raise and that others received too much. I've never heard anyone argue that others received too little and they received too much.

But the fact is that Duluth made an objective matrix, which I thought was sensational.

It heavily favored people who published books, you know. I was racking up tremendous point totals because I was also so proficient in my publication, and wound up receiving raises that were the highest in the department.

I would eventually become the highest-paid faculty member in the college of liberal arts at the University of Minnesota-Duluth.

And some of my colleagues, you know, were not happy campers, feeling as they did that I had somehow gamed the system, which was ridiculous. So that eventually, this is a long time down the pike, they would actually revise their criteria to down-weight books and articles, where I was so proficient, and to upgrade other areas where the other faculty were proficient.

By and large, in the end, if you assume that for each book I had more than other faculty I was entitled to a thousand dollars more per year, then that's about the way it played out.

[The McKnight Award]

I continued with my research on JFK, but I didn't publish my first book on JFK until 1998. So, I was hired in the department in 1987 and in 1996 the University of Minnesota introduced a new program for new full professors, and it was a wonderful award.

You got the title of Distinguished McKnight University Professor, which I liked even better than John D. and Katherine T. McArthur, that title.

Plus a hundred thousand dollar research grant, and the title was permanent.

I was just dumbfounded when I was selected. I received actually two phone calls in my office. One was congratulating me, but I didn't know what for. And another said they just wanted to give their congratulations to the McKnight Professor.

And, sitting there in my office, I felt it was like the layers of an onion were peeling off, all these layers of defense that I'd acquired over all these years were just peeling right off of me.

I just felt completely different.

I think that was probably the single most important event in my professional career.

I'd received other forms of recognition including, for example, the medal of the University of Helsinki for my contributions to the philosophy of science, and I'd traveled to Finland to receive it, and given a series of lectures at Finnish universities. That was marvelous.

This McKnight Professorship was absolutely sensational and made a huge difference.

Intellectually, I've always been a problem solver and, though I would like to deny it, a bit of a perfectionist.

Philosophy involves resolving heretofore unresolved conceptual and theoretical problems, especially about the meaning of words and the methods that are most appropriate for dealing with newly emerging disciplines. I have focused on the meaning of "probability", "laws of nature" and the conditions of adequacy for explanations.

In relation to computer science, AI, and cognitive science, I have focused on the nature of mind and the differences between minds and machines. Eventually my work expanded to encompass evolution and the emergence of mind from animal mind, primate mind, and the higher primates.

I do not doubt that I have been driven to study JFK, 9/11, and other events because they represent heretofore unresolved historical problems of enormous interest and importance to understanding our own history. And I have had the good sense to bring together experts and scholars across a wide range of backgrounds and disciplines in collaboration.

I received the McKnight in 1996 and the first book I published on JFK, a collection of expert studies, would appear in 1998.

It just so happened there was an associate dean in the graduate school who loved my work on JFK, and he was always very supportive of it, which may have given me, you know, a layer of defense against some ordinary faculty who might have looked askance at research on a subject like the assassination.

In the end, probably my work on JFK will prove to be the most enduring; I mean, I would like to believe a lot of my work in other areas, computer science, artificial intelligence, cognitive science, evolution, and mentality, will also endure. But that's a matter over which it's impossible to calculate.

It's all dependent upon the community appreciating your work.

I remember an early article I wrote for the behavorial and brain sciences about creativity.

It was a commentary on an article they were featuring ... and I explained there were three dimensions to creativity. One is doing something no one else has ever done, which is relatively trivial.

The second is doing something no one else that has ever done that is important. I think a lot of my contributions actually fall into that category.

But the third is doing something that no one else has ever done that's important, and that becomes influential.

And there, I think, time and time again I have somehow not understood how important it is to get your work into the right venue, presented in the right forum, receiving attention from the right parties, to make a difference.

So, there it is.

I retired from UMD in 2006 after a 35-year career, teaching principally courses in logic, critical thinking, and scientific reasoning. Of course, subsequently I have continued the work on JFK, publishing many articles … After my retirement I've had, I'm now with my fourth different radio show, which is Monday-Wednesday-Friday for two hours: in-depth interviews with experts or people who know more than I, or who at least have an interesting take on the most complex and controversial issues of our time, entitled *The Real Deal*.

And I published more than forty articles in *Op-Ed News* before I had a falling-out with the editor, Rob Kall, who I now regard as some kind of left-wing gatekeeper, who has actually taken the incredibly unprofessional, unethical move of removing my articles. I've written him to ask what's going on here and he will not reply, but it's clear this is a vendetta.

I mean if others who contribute to journals knew that if they were ever to tick off the editor he might erase all of their publications, I think they would be dumbfounded.

But in addition to that I've done all these interviews, made all these public presentations. I make trips … *Scholars for 9/11 Truth* conferences … books, 60 articles or more on VT …

Jan has observed that I'm actually busier now than I was when I was teaching full-time and that's probably true, especially because my colleagues for the most part didn't like longer courses, Tuesday-Thursday courses are longer courses.

Well, I love longer courses, because in a normal, say 50-minute class I can barely take a breath, so these were all at least an hour and 15, and I love that, so for nearly 35 years I had all my courses on Tuesday-Thursday, not beginning before 11. No doubt, you know, that freed up my time to do research.

I'd have long weekends. I could work on an article Friday-Saturday-Sunday-Monday, and I think that was a tremendous benefit.

[Moving to Madison, the Dynamic Duo is re-united]

In June 2006 I would retire and in anticipation, I hadn't really thought about doing that, but my daughter had called us to say if I were thinking about retiring that they'd love it if we were to move down to Madison to be near them, because they wanted to start a family and they'd like for us to help raise their kids, and I was so touched that I began looking into it. So that must have been in the fall of 2005.

And actually in June 2006 I'd be completing a 35-year career of college teaching. I'd be 65½, which meant I'd be eligible for Social Security, and I'd receive some retirement arrangement with the university.

And I was just very touched by Sarah's request.

So we spent six months going through all the little towns outside of Madison, Black Earth, Mount Horeb, and a host of others, and worked our way 'round to Oregon. Just a couple hours before we were to fly to Las Vegas for a family wedding, we visited this house in Oregon, Wisconsin, and I said to Jan, I'm not leaving here without buying it. We've loved the house. It fit us perfectly.

[Also, you have a son, Bret, and then Melanie and Michele are step-daughters. Do I have that right?]

Yes, you have that right.

Mel lives in Bloomington, Indiana; Michele in Bradenton, Florida; and Bret in Seattle, Washington.

[Traveling for Truth]

I've done a fair amount of traveling of course, but probably the most important events have been, well, let's see, I organized the first *Scholars for 9/11 Truth* in Madison in 20 ... oh, okay, here. In 2006 I was invited to Athens, Greece.

My wife and I were flown over all expenses paid and put on a television program that was broadcast worldwide for 3½ hours, about 9/11 Truth, it was quite wonderful.

The host told me as we were walking in that while there were twelve panelists most of them typically wouldn't ask questions. I said, not today.

And of course I was right.

And every one of them asked questions. And when I pointed out to a friend of mine in New York by the name of Paula Gloria that I'd suspected one fellow there who was dressed as a publisher, three-piece suit and all that, that I suspected he was CIA, when she looked at the video she said that she had an uncle that they always thought was CIA and that was who it was!

It was that very guy. So I think Paula has the DVD of that, I don't believe I ever got it back. That was 2006.

In 2007 I organized the first conference for *Scholars for 9/11 Truth* right here in Madison. I did my best to bring together representatives of all the different 9/11 groups.

I invited Steve Jones and Kevin Ryan, for example, to speak. I had several people from their side who already were planning to attend, but they black-balled it, pulled 'em out, wouldn't let them participate. I gave Judy Wood an unprecedented three hours to speak and a number of her supporters and fans, of whom I was one at the time, including Morgan Reynolds, Jerry Leaphart, and Ace Baker, also spoke, and so forth.

It's amazing to me how our views can change over the years.

In 2008 I was flown down to Buenos Aires to give talks on 9/11 and JFK. And to my astonishment while I presented those talks in a very small room above a theater, I got a lot of news coverage.

I mean, they'd have a quarter page or half a page in a newspaper, with photographs from 9/11, really big play, and I was also put on television for an interview about 9/11 that was broadcast all over South America.

The following year, 2009, I was flown down to Buenos Aires again for an international symposium on 9/11 Truth and justice where I was the principal speaker, and where I met the FEMA videographer who was subsequently accused of murder in what appears to have been a trumped-up charge, and his wife, who was just wonderful.

She was a translator for me. The room was packed. It was held in the national library of the Republic of Argentina, which just shows how differently, you know, the more intellectual audiences, more sophisticated audiences, more knowledgeable audiences respond to scholars and intellectuals who are dealing with these subjects. And it was sponsored by the Minister of Culture.

In 2010 I organized a 9/11 event at Friend's House in London, debunking the war on terror, where I invited Kevin Barrett and Gilad Atzmon, the celebrated Israeli Jewish saxophone player, who is very much a critic of Jewish identity politics, to speak.

Also, Kevin O'Keefe, the hero of The Freedom Flotilla, who had single-handedly disarmed several Israeli commandos when they embarked upon their ship and killed several pre-targeted Turkish-Americans, really an outrageous act. He was our master of ceremonies.

That was a wonderful event.

And in 2012 I organized the Vancouver Hearings in British Columbia, which was a wonderful event, with a very large array. And once again it was black-balled. I invited Richard Gage and Steven Jones, I think perhaps even Neils Harrit, and even Judy Wood, to speak; none of them participated, and Richard Gage tried to subvert the whole thing. We wound up getting a miniscule attendance. The electronics for the conference were abysmal. But if you go to the Vancouver Hearings, our webpage, I think you'll find we did some spectacular work, the consequences of which are still being felt today. So.

Those I believe are the most important conferences in which I participated, two of which I organized. The most sensational of which, no doubt, was the visit to Athens, back in 2006.

And of course I was invited on national television several times, first on *Hannity & Colmes* on the twenty-second of June 2006, where Ollie North was sitting in, and I'll never forget telling my wife, Jan, that since Ollie was sitting in and he's a former Marine Corps officer as am I, that it would be a casual conversation between two former Marine Corps officers. "Don't kid yourself," she said, "they're going to try to kill you!"

And I had them bring in a TV before I went on, into the studio, and I observed that shortly before I came on, they announced that "you're not going to believe what your professors are teaching your children."

But I knew they didn't know enough to get it right, and indeed the first words out of Alan Colmes' mouth were, "Is this a required course?" And I explained to him that I didn't teach any such course, that I organized a research group to conduct research on 9/11, but not to offer any courses, and that they seemed to have their "facts Foxed." And I knew I had to pronounce it carefully.

And it went from there. I really was able to seize control. And a friend of mine has often remarked that he can't recall seeing Oliver North on television since that encounter, which everyone can find on YouTube.

Then a couple months later I was invited back when Sean Hannity was actually in the house, and they tried to set me up again.

I mean, in these cases they're trying to find people they can use as foils, as props. I'd been told for example before the first event that they were going to ask, try to solicit information of what *Scholars for 9/11 Truth* had discovered about 9/11, but of course that wasn't the case at all.

I should add, by the way, that was shortly before the American Scholars Conference, organized by Alex Jones, where Scholars provided many of the speakers. For example, C-Span filmed a press conference that was held on Sunday of four speakers, moderated by Alex Jones, and the four speakers were Steve Jones, physicist from BYU, whom I had made my co-chair, Bob Bowman, who has a Ph.D. in nuclear engineering from Cal-Tech and was the scientific director of the Star Wars program under Carter and Ford, or Reagan and Ford. Webster Tarpley, the author of *9/11, Synthetic Terror, Made in the USA*, one of our foremost experts on covert activities, and myself as the founder of *Scholars for 9/11 Truth*. I gave my top-ten list, the top ten reasons the Islamic hijackers are fake, which you can find on YouTube and which many regard as their favorite all-time presentation.

In any case it ran an hour and 45 minutes, and C-Span would subsequently broadcast it seven or eight times in very good time slots, and I think it actually had the effect of shattering the kind of glass ceiling that had curtailed public discussion on 9/11, so I think that was a great event. It was a huge hall. It had at least twelve hundred people there. Alex had made me the keynote speaker.

And then as I mentioned I was invited back on *Hannity & Colmes* a couple months later.

That didn't go a whole lot better for them and I was even able to work in my phrase, "facts Foxed", again, and I was able to tell the story of Norman Mineta, about how he'd been in an underground bunker with Dick Cheney when an aide had come up to Cheney and said, sir, it's fifty miles out, sir, it's forty miles out, do the orders still stand? Which is a classic impugning of the government, because Alan Colmes had even asked me during the first interview whether I had any evidence whatsoever to implicate the government, such as if Dick Cheney had been involved, and I said, absolutely! And I told him the story! It was great.

And then months later I'd be invited on by Bill O'Reilly on *The Factor*, who's a different kind of case altogether.

I sat in the studio waiting, staring at a blank screen, I was being televised from a local studio here in Madison, for about thirty minutes, just looking at a blank screen before O'Reilly came on moments before I went on the air and told me, "I'm going to tell the country you're a nut and you hate your country."

And then, bling! I'm on the air.

And he gives a massive ad hominem assault, and then he says, well, we'll let the audience figure that out, and then he gives another assault, so, you know, you're hamstrung as to how to go back and deal with the first assault.

In any case, it was really, on my part, a rope-a-dope strategy, such as Mohammad Ali adopted in his fight with Frazier, the thriller in Manila, the thrilla in Manila.

And I thought it hadn't gone terribly well, but, at one point, at one of the two occasions I spoke at Cooper Union Hall, in New York City, for a major 9/11 event, my wife and I, and Paula Gloria, and some others, had gone to an event Alex Jones was holding in another theater in town. They put me right up on the stage with First Responders, they just treated us wonderfully.

And as I was sitting there, one of these guys sitting right next to me, leaned over and said to me, watching me on O'Reilly convinced him that 9/11 had been an inside job. And I figured, well, maybe it was worth it. Maybe it was worth it.

As far as what keeps me going, well, much of my motivation has to do with the fact that I can't stand, I can't abide liars, cheats, and frauds, and to me, discovering that our government is among the world's most-practiced and skilled in lying, cheating, and deceiving the American people is simply ... it offends me ... profoundly.

I believe that the American people are entitled to know the truth about their own history and I'm simply doing all that I can with the resources I have to make sure they have that opportunity, and I must say, as Jan has observed, I've been busier since my retirement in 2006 than I was when I was teaching full-time, probably.

I think the fact is, that I just love to write and publish, and I have been continuing that, especially in regard to the more perplexing, complex, and controversial public issues of our time, such as JFK, 9/11, the plane crash that killed Paul Wellstone, and more recently the events in the Middle East, the war on terror, Sandy Hook, and the Boston bombing, the beat goes on.

["A devastating intellectual machine"]

I once described myself as having been at a certain point in my career a devastating intellectual machine, but that's the fact of the matter. I received a first-rate education, especially in philosophy in Princeton, which was ranked at the time I was an undergraduate number one in the world in math, physics and philosophy. I spent four years in the Marine Corps, which had a way, as it were, of honing my disciplined aggression.

When I went to graduate school I was in a program in the history and philosophy of science, and it gave me insights and skills and knowledge that most of us don't have the opportunity to acquire.

It just meant that I was prepared when I was in the position of tackling other issues, in philosophy they're mostly rather abstract, conceptual, and theoretical problems. What philosophers do when they're doing philosophy is try to make manageable issues that haven't been manageable, especially in clarifying the meaning of certain phrases and expressions in language.

I've done a huge amount on the nature of probability and distinguishing it as a physical magnitude. You might talk about the probability of events, or the strength of a causal process and so forth, versus the mere frequency with which things happen, which is a weak sense of probability, or other senses in which we might ask about the strength of the evidence, how probable is A versus B; but, when you have a background like mine, I mean, and I'm placed in the position of addressing issues that have been dealt with heretofore by persons who don't have a professional background as a scholar, it makes a huge difference.

So the way I approach JFK, for example, is to bring together the best qualified experts in different areas, because it's essential, to do good work, that you know your own limitations.

And I knew how good I was at reasoning and putting together relationships between evidence and conclusions and fashioning arguments, but that did not mean I was an expert on the human brain, or an authority on ballistics, or an expert on the interpretation of X-rays, or a Ph.D. in electro-magnetism, the properties of light, and the images of moving objects.

So I brought together the best qualified people I could, and we re-constructed the case of JFK from the ground up, and managed to really take it apart and put it back together again with devastating results.

And I've continued to do that with another group of experts in relation to *Scholars for 9/11 Truth*. Pilots and physicists and engineers, structural, aeronautical, mechanical, and so forth, all joining together to do our best. And then with a new group in relation to JFK, a group with different backgrounds and abilities, including a chiropractor for example, which has made a tremendous difference, as it turns out, analyzing the Altgens 6, this very famous photograph [offers proof that Oswald was in the doorway during the shooting].

The books that I have published on JFK, by the way, have been the most important in shattering the coverup. Even Vince Bugliosi, who supports the government's official account, including the lone assassin and the magic bullet, has described these books as the only exclusively scientific work ever published on the assassination.

And they include some absolutely sensational stuff, including David W. Mantik, Ph.D., M.D.'s studies of the autopsy X-rays, Bob Livingston, M.D., world authority on the human brain, an expert on wound ballistics, analysis of the diagrams and photographs of the brain in the national archives, observing that it can't possibly be the brain of JFK that's being portrayed.

Other studies by multiple experts, but especially David Mantik raising questions about the authenticity of the Zapruder film, that's all in *Assassination Science*, 1988, probably the most important book published in the history of the assassination because of the extent to which it shatters the cover-up.

And then in the year 2000 I published *Murder in Dealey Plaza*, a title suggested to me by David Mantik, which is very suitable, very appropriate, because he contributed three absolutely fantastic essays to that collection. There are a lot of people that think that is the best book published on the assassination, to distinguish it from the first as the most important.

I would chair or co-chair four national conferences on the death of JFK (Minneapolis 1999, Dallas 2000, Dallas 2001, and Duluth 2003), and I have a fifth in Santa Barbara for the 50th.

In Duluth, I brought together the best experts on the film – David Mantik, John Costella, Jack White, David Healy and David Lifton – and we held a two-day conference – which is available on YouTube – and produced a wonderful, wonderful book.

I introduced the issues with the assistance of my son-in-law, Scott Lederer, who did a brilliant comparison of four different versions of the Zapruder film, which show the same sequence of events but have different areas of information as you do when you crop a photo and reduce its image content. Scott made very discerning, subtle observations about the number of pixels in the frames, that some versions were missing frames and others had frames in the wrong order.

I don't know if I have ever told him this, but I was simply blown away – astonished! – when he exposed a lot of problems with (what was widely regarded as) "the gold standard" among JFK researchers, the MPI version, which turns out to have missing frames, at least one repetition and others in the wrong order. John Costella has produced the best available version by replacing the missing frames, re-ordering the frames, and eliminating aspect-ratio and pincushion distortion. But Scott was new to the film and did this essentially without any coaching from me – completely brilliant!

So the best version of the film is now free and accessible to the public at assassination.com.

Included in this conference was David Healy, who is an expert in film and video production talking about what was available technologically back then; Jack White, who'd been doing decades and decades of studies on the photos and the films; David Mantik, who is reporting his research on the Zapruder film; David Lifton, who had done a great deal of work on the Zapruder film, and knew a lot about its history through his own contacts; and John Costella, of course, who is the leading expert on the Zapruder film in the world today, just as David Mantik is the leading expert on the medical evidence in the world today.

I front-loaded these books by making the most important arguments in the beginning of each of the books, so that by the time you finish the introduction, the preface and prologue, in particular, you should be already convinced, and then going through the rest of the articles is picking up all the details and confirming everything I explained at the beginning of the book. So I did quite a lot there about deceit and deception in the assassination and many demonstrations of fakery in the medical evidence and the photographic record and so forth.

[The Big Picture ... Ruby, LBJ ... Oswald in the doorway]

As far as the big picture is concerned, I think Jack Ruby got it right when he told reporters this would never have happened if someone else had been vice president.

He suggested that if Adlai Stevenson, for example, had been vice president instead of LBJ ... he was very explicit about all this.

What Jack Ruby told us that day has been corroborated by, for example, Madeline Duncan Brown, who was a mistress of Lyndon Johnson. Not his only mistress, but she bore him a child, not his only child out of wedlock, but his only male offspring, Steven, in 1950, with whom I had over a hundred conversations. Madeline confirmed the events at the Murchison, the Clint Murchison Sr. home the night before, which was a ratification meeting, attended by J. Edgar Hoover, H.L. Hunt, Richard Nixon, John J. McCloy, George Brown.

Lyndon Johnson showed up late.

They disappeared into a board meeting, and after fifteen or twenty minutes he strode over toward her and she thought he was going to whisper sweet nothings in her ear; instead, in a hateful tone of voice he told her that after tomorrow he wasn't going to have to put up with embarrassment from those Kennedy boys any longer.

Six weeks later they had a rendezvous in the Driskill Hotel, New Year's Eve, 1964, and she confronted Lyndon with rumors rampant in Dallas that he'd been involved, since no one stood to gain more personally.

He blew up at her and told her the CIA and the oil boys had decided that Jack had to be taken out.

She published all this in her book, *Texas In The Morning*, named after Lyndon's tendency, when they'd get out of bed, to throw open the windows and say, "God! I love Texas in the morning!"

Billy Sol Estes, who knew these guys up close and personal, confirmed what Madeline had to say, in his book, *A Texas Legend*, characteristically modestly titled after himself, and how Lyndon had sent his chief administrative assistant, Cliff Carter, down to Dallas to make sure all the arrangements were in place for the assassination. And he knew from his conversation with Cliff Carter and with Malcolm "Mac" Wallace, who was Lyndon's personal hit man, who murdered at least a dozen people for Lyndon including one of his own sisters, that they'd been involved in the assassination.

You can find more in the book by Barr McClellan, *Blood, Money, Power*. And E. Howard Hunt, in his last confession to his son, Saint John, identified the chain of command as extending from Lyndon to Cord Meyer to David Atlee Phillips to William Harvey to David Sanchez Morales.

Lee Oswald's whole history was working for intel agencies for the United States.

I've said a lot about this but the fact is, the fact that we've been able to prove that Lee was in the doorway just confirms that he was just what he said he was, namely, a patsy. He was where he said he was, out front with Bill Shelley, and the backyard photographs, as he observed, were fake, so, Lee was one of the good guys.

[9/11, everything phony about it]

Everything about 9/11 was fraudulent.

There was a massive stand-down by the U.S Air Force that morning to ensure there would be no fighter aircraft to interdict. It was a change in standard operating procedure. All of the crashes were faked, phony.

None of them were real. Two of the planes weren't even in the air that day, Flights 11 and 77.

There was lots of clever manipulation and deception. While Flights 93 and 175 were in the air that day, Pilots For 9/11 Truth has established that 93 was over Champaign-Urbana after it had purportedly crashed in Shanksville. Flight 175 was also in the air but it was over Harrisburg and Pittsburgh, Pennsylvania long after it allegedly hit the south tower.

We even have FAA registration data showing that the planes corresponding to Flights 93 and 175 were not formally taken out of service until 28 September 2005, which raises the question, how can planes that weren't even in the air that day have crashed on 9/11, and how can planes that crashed on 9/11 have still been in the air four years later?

It was a quite elaborate fraud that originated with the demise of the Soviet Union in 1990-91, where the military industrial complex needed a new boogeyman to keep all that money flowing, and settled on Muslims.

This benefited Israel tremendously, which was very instrumental in fabricating the whole war on terror because they wanted the dismantling of the modern sophisticated Arab states, so that Israel could have undisputed domination of the Middle East.

And together with their friends among the neo-cons, especially Dick Cheney, Donald Rumsfeld, Donald Feith, Paul Wolfowitz, Richard Perle, William Kristol, Charles Krauthammer, Gen. Richard Myers, Rudy Giulliani, Larry Silverstein, these were among the principals.

It was organized by the CIA in collaboration with the Department of Defense and the Mossad. There's lots and lots more about it.

We have plenty of research by other experts. Elias Davidsson has shown the government was never able to prove any of the hijackers were aboard any of the planes.

These appear to have been classic moves, fabricated events intended to create fear in the American people, to support a transformation in our avowed foreign policy from one where we never attacked any nation that hadn't attacked us first to one in which we became an aggressor nation, which we have been in Afghanistan, in Iraq, through NATO in Libya, now possibly getting involved in Syria, though I'm very optimistic that Putin having put his foot down after the Israeli attack and sending more missiles to Assad is going to salvage the situation there. And I'm hoping there will be a defensive alliance between Russia and Iran and China, where an attack on one is treated as an attack on all, because there's absolutely no justification at all for an attack on Iran.

[Secret Service Hit]

As we approach the 50th observance I'll just say the short take on JFK is we have more than fifteen indications of Secret Service complicity in setting him up for the hit, including most strikingly that the driver, William Greer, pulled the limousine to the left and to a halt after the bullets began to be fired to make sure he would be killed.

All the vehicles were in the wrong order, with the Presidential limousine set out front when it should have been in the middle.

The flatbed truck that would have preceded it was cancelled, and instead of having the mayor and vice president ahead of JFK he was put out front. All the vehicles were of different makes, models and colors to make it more conspicuous who was where.

It was a gross abuse of authority when the Assassination Records Review Board, created by an act of Congress, asked the Secret Service for their Presidential protection records for previous motorcades for JFK and instead of producing them, they destroyed them.

So while the AARB has managed to release 60,000 documents and records we didn't have before, there's no telling what remains behind.

We do know there are records by George Joannides, who was a CIA psyop expert who appears to have been involved in both the assassination of JFK and Bobby, that those have not been released, and where the AARB described the ONI, Office of Naval Intelligence, which appears to have recruited Oswald, as a black hole.

Two agents were left behind in Dealey Plaza, the manhole covers were not welded shut, the open windows were not covered, the crowd was allowed to spill eight, ten, twelve into the street. The 112th military intelligence unit was ordered to stand down, over the adamant opposition of its commanding officer.

The motorcycle escort was cut down to four, and instructed not to ride forward of the rear wheels, which one of the officers said was the damnedest formation he'd ever encountered.

The motorcade route was changed four days before, apparently by John Connally faking a phone call from Kenny O'Donnell in the White House to get it changed from a location where JFK would speak from the Women's

Forum, which was a very secure building which the Secret Service had approved, to the Trade Mart, which was not, lots of balconies and exits and so forth.

In order to justify the turn from Main Street on to Houston, and then back one hundred and ten degrees onto Elm without alarming the occupants – that was another violation of Secret Service protocol. And of course when the limousine got to Parkland Hospital with a moribund President, they got a bucket and sponge and started washing the blood and brains out, and when spectators noticed a through and through bullet hole in the windshield they moved the limousine.

It was taken back to the Ford Motor Company and completely stripped down to bare metal and rebuilt on Monday the 25th, which was the day of the formal state funeral.

He was a magnificent human being.

The events in Dallas represented the assassination of America, not just the death of JFK, but our last true American President, because as Jack Ruby observed, a whole new form of government is going to take over the country, and that, alas, is precisely what has come to pass.

The famous photograph taken by Mary Moorman on 22 November 1963.

[Chapter 31] Tucson, Aurora, Sandy Hook

"When a leader allows himself to break the rules of humanity, it is the duty of every citizen to break the leader's rules."
- Franz Jagerstatter

The Nexus of Tyranny: The Strategy Behind Tucson, Aurora and Sandy Hook

by Dennis Cimino, with Jim Fetzer
Veterans Today
Jan. 30, 2013

Sandy Hook poses so many uncertainties and even contradictions that it should come as no surprise that virtually every aspect of whatever happened is being subjected to the most minute scrutiny.

I have now published multiple articles about it here at *Veterans Today*, including "Sandy Hook: Huge Hoax and anti-Gun 'Psy Op'", where others, such as historian of science and expert on 7/7, Nicholas Kollerstrom, have addressed the parallels between those events. On one web site, I have even been asked by a serious but skeptical reader whether it is even possible that none of the children were actually killed.

The question is not as unwarranted as most of the public might believe. If this had been a real shooting of children, there would have been a sense of panic and of hysteria. EMTs would have rushed into the school building. The children would have been rushed out on stretchers and into ambulances and other vehicles and rushed to a hospital for doctors to treat them and formally pronounce the death of those who had been killed. Nothing remotely like this happened. The police cordoned off everyone from the school.

No one was allowed to see the bodies. They were transported in the dead of night. It was simply bizarre beyond belief.

These considerations already indicate that Sandy Hook was a fabricated or staged event. I wish it were not the case, but that conclusion is reinforced by multiple peculiarities about photographs and other matters, extending to conflicting reports about whether the alleged shooter, Adam Lanza, was a student at the school or not; whether his mother was a teacher there or not; police radio reports in real time of two perps heading toward the reporting officer, one of whom was apprehended, the other fled into the woods and was tracked in helicopter footage.

Concerns that this is an elaborate "psyop" to create hysteria in the hearts of the American people and bring about a stampede of public support for the confiscation of every semi-automatic weapon in the country, as Sen. Diane Feinstein's bill would impose, are open to serious question in light of the discovery that, in the Social Security Death Index, Adam Lanza is reported to have died on the 13th, the day before the "massacre."

After all, if Adam died the day before, he cannot have slaughtered those twenty children and six adults (seven, including his mother) on the following day. And the matter has been compounded by the rediscovery that all three of the major networks – ABC, NBC and CBS – reported that his body had been found accompanied by hand guns (whose numbers range from two to four), while the alleged "assault rifle" was left in the car!

As a former Marine Corps officer who qualified with a .45 and a rifle four years in a row (from 1962-66) and occasionally shot expert with the M-14, I have found it very difficult to imagine how this young man of slight build, who appears to have had little or even no marksmanship training, could possibly have pulled it off.

I supervised marksmanship at Edson Range, Camp Pendleton, as a Series Commander at the USMC Recruit Depot, San Diego, Calif., and the ratio of target to kills strikes me as not merely extremely improbable but virtually impossible, especially if he was using hand guns, but even with a Bushmaster.

And the probability that he killed anyone on the 14th when he appears to have died on the 13th does not require emphasis.

The New York Times has entered the fray by publishing "Reliving Horror and Faint Hope at Massacre Site" (28 January 2013), in which it recounts the horrific experiences of five law enforcement officers who were among the first on the scene at Sandy Hook. Like many other articles about the shooting, it makes a strong appeal to the emotions but is short on proof:

> NEWTOWN, Conn. – The gunfire ended; it was so quiet they could hear the broken glass and bullet casings scraping under their boots. The smell of gunpowder filled the air. The officers turned down their radios; they did not want to give away their positions if there was still a gunman present.
>
> They found the two women first, their bodies lying on the lobby floor. Now they knew it was real. But nothing, no amount of training, could prepare them for what they found next, inside those two classrooms.
>
> One look, and your life was absolutely changed," said Michael McGowan, one of the first police officers to arrive at Sandy Hook Elementary School on Dec. 14, as a gunman, in the space of minutes, killed 20 first graders and 6 adults.

Questions that are not explored by *The New York Times* include why there were no EMTs rushing to aide the victims, why there was no rash of ambulances to transport them to the hospital, why the officers on the scene were the ones to declare them dead, and why not even their parents were allowed to identify their children. Too tough for The Times, it appears.

As Miles Mathis has observed in *Sandy Hook Conspiracy Theories debunked? No*, the government likes to hire people to run this gambit:

> They publish some ridiculously weak response as a debunking, it utterly fails to debunk anything, but then simply because it got published by top outlets they claim the theory has been debunked.
>
> Go study just about any tragedy or big news story of the past 50 years, and you will see the same progression. [Specifically, you can study *Popular Mechanics*' pathetic efforts to debunk 9/11 Truth by this method.]
>
> But I have news for them, publishing an article with the title Debunked does not automatically mean the theory has been debunked. You actually have to make a strong argument. Blowing smoke for a couple of pages isn't a debunking, it is just more propaganda, and most people who read these things can see that.
>
> The debunking of 9/11 didn't work, because the debunking was exponentially weaker than the data it was trying to debunk. Most people now recognize that fact. We are seeing the same thing here with Sandy Hook.

To prove this, Miles Mathis goes "point for point" through the debunking of *Salon* writer Alex Seitz-Wald, demonstrating that he has done no more than deploy "3rd-string debating tricks and cold cabbage" and that his title constitutes a case of false advertising, "Your comprehensive answer to every Sandy Hook conspiracy theory".

Indeed, as he also explains, there are also multiple indications that photos have been shopped, including the "Christmas pose" by the Robbie Parker family, whose daughter, Emily, appears to have posted with President Obama when he visited Newtown to convey his sympathies.

In the following essay, Dennis Cimino does his best to sort out what has been going on across the country, because Sandy Hook appears to be the latest in a series of contrived events of increasing violence, which may be designed to motivate the American people to surrender their Second Amendment rights and embrace all-encompassing forms of gun control, which has already happened in New York.

The Nexus of Tyranny: The strategy behind Tucson, Aurora and Sandy Hook

by Dennis Cimino

In the immediate aftermath of the Newtown staged hoax in Connecticut, many of us began to finally take harder looks at the hoaxes staged in Tucson, Arizona, and in Aurora, Colorado, to see if we could find links connecting them.

They appear to have been carried out by Attorney General Eric Holder and POTUS (aka Barry Soetoro) as a calculated and nationwide smattering of "terrorist attacks" of an OPERATION GLADIO variety, plotted and carried out to strike fear into the American public and create an hysterical response against the 2nd Amendment.

Their secondary purpose seems to have been to further demonize 9/11 Truth, as was evident in the closure of Facebook accounts of most of the prominent 9/11 Truth figures who were involved in publicizing Israel's role in the mass murders of 9/11, which occurred in the immediate aftermath of the Newtown hoax.

The key begins in Tucson where the acting sheriff, Clarence Dupnik, and his auxiliaries, staged the elaborate hoax that a federal judge and a Congress woman named "Gabby Giffords" were shot, the judge fatally. While Gabby may have been seriously wounded, I have found multiple indications that suggest this, too, may have been a hoax.

Evidence of purely FEMA-staged acting was apparent in the fact that, when you do careful analysis of the photos of the scene, you can find many significant clues.

One striking one is a FEMA coach, kneeling by a stretcher, cue-card in his non-gloved hands, reading that, with a small plastic cup of fake blood there, at a site where allegedly real human beings were shot by an orange hair whacko named 'Holmes' that is so psychologically goofy looking you can barely stand to look at him, let alone realize he is like the rest, another Greenberg Zionist actor, participating in one of a series of hoaxes. What is particularly telling in the photo of Giffords with an allegedly grave head wound, nobody seems concerned. All backs are turned.

In real life if you had a potentially mortally wounded person being taken by an ambulance to a hospital, every one of those people would have been focused on her.

Nobody cares. Nobody is concerned. Not one person seems in a hurry to move her to the ambulance, either. You know this is a drill, because of the lack of concern and urgency in these people around this simulated victim or "VicSIM".

Closer examination of the stretcher that Giffords is on, is that no blood is present, and her aide who stated he had "used his own hands to pressure point stop a head wound bleed" oddly has no blood on his gloved hands at all.

Neither do any of the EMT personnel transporting her to the ambulance. As many of you might know, head wounds bleed profusely. Yet Giffords has no blood on her except a small red patch on a rag wrapped around her skull.

If the lightbulb hasn't gone on for you yet, it should when you see photos of two of Dupnik's elderly sheriff's auxiliary pretending to be victim relatives at the alleged but simulated crime scene.

They appear to be accomplices to an act of treason by Clarence W. Dupnik, the Pima County Sheriff.

In the case of the Aurora, Colorado hoax staged fraud, we have an FBI agent standing behind the Chief of Police of Aurora, watching the Chief read his cue card in his head, while Special Agent Jim Yacone smirks in satisfaction when the Chief says he is not prepared to comment about how the shooter may have gotten into the theatre.

In the immediate aftermath of this shooting hoax, we have a number of witnesses talk about at least two individuals being involved and flash-bang grenades being thrown into the theatre from different directions by two individuals.

Clearly, on a day like this, no FBI agent has the right to 'smirk' about anything the chief of police might divulge, nor would there be any reason for many witnesses to talk about the fact that clearly the assault on the theatre, all staged and a hoax, came from both sides of the theatre and was carried out by more than one person.

So, here again, if Holmes was the man, who were his accomplices? We know someone came in from both sides and threw flash bang grenades into the small theatre. One man could not do that.

In the Newtown, Connecticut shooting, where we have been told twenty children and six adults were slaughtered, many very big and inexplicable similarities were evident, looking rather like a repetition from Tucson and Aurora, least with the use of Greenberg's actor cadre, the Crisis actors from FEMA.

We have Dawn Hochsprung, who was allegedly killed shielding children from the lone gunman, giving an interview to *The Newtown Bee* newspaper that morning.

Clearly this is not merely a misunderstanding here: no reporter would give an interview and not clarify who that was they were talking to. Yet Hochsprung was alive enough to give that interview in the aftermath of a shooting in which she died trying to shield children from bullets.

Not possible.

The CNN SWAT TEAM Video

We have CNN video of SWAT team members running to the school door through a column of previously arranged orange traffic cones.

Expecting someone important that day, were they? Especially since this was footage intentionally shown by CNN of a drill that had actually been staged at the school months before.

A bigger clue is that the crack sealant used to seal the driveway in some of the shots was nice and shiny and fresh, but not long thereafter, it's dull and dirty and aged.

That cannot happen in one day. So we now know that the earlier drill was used by CNN (actually shot at St. Rose of Lima Elementary School, approximately fourteen miles southwest of the Sandy Hook closed school, based upon information we now have that has matched up the helicopter vs. Google Earth view and beyond a reasonable doubt shows CNN effectively had to be in on the scam!) in more than one non-live shot of what allegedly took place on December 14th, but clearly did not, as it was obviously a hoax.

All of it. Purposely staged to deceive the American public to grab our guns.

In the helicopter footage which is now disappearing from YouTube, you see at around 7 a.m. a helicopter hovering over the scene with a Detroit fire truck in the footage.

EMS is staged far back at the Fire Station and almost nobody is closer than one-hundred yards or so from the school, and with this video being about two hours before shooting happened, it elicits many questions again about 'how' and 'why' we are able to see it on a day when we were told that a kid got the drop on a security door and nobody was forewarned that he was attempting to gain entry.

Crisis Actors and the Coroner's Press Conference

Now it has been firmly established that many Crisis Actors were used in Newtown, the most notable one is Robbie Parker, who is told 'just read the card' and has to get into character to act 'distraught' when moments before he is seen smirking and laughing, very much like FBI agent Yacone had in Aurora at the Chief of Police press conference.

I don't know about you, but nobody can explain away his very poor acting here, and nobody can explain the "just read the card" scenario, either.

In virtually all of the follow up interviews of parents, they are all dry eyed and not puffy faced, although they are said to have lost their children.

This is acting. By Crisis Actors. By Greenberg Crisis Actors.

Later that day we have the coroner, Wayne Carver, who is oddly out of character, telling us that all of the vicSIMS were shot using the long rifle, the .223 caliber one, and that some vicSIMS had been shot more than ten times.

Nobody bothered to ask Wayne why nobody was air-lifted to Danbury General for possible salvation as it is not possible that nobody would survive any shooting involving twenty-seven people, under any remote stretch of the imagination.

Someone would have been found clinging to life, yet no triage existed that day to ascertain this, and someone mysteriously, not this flakey-acting coroner, had decreed that all were "dead" on the scene.

This again is not possible. That is not proper code blue protocol. You triage. You air lift. You try to save people.

Not at Newtown, where they all died instantaneously and were declared dead by someone other than the medical examiner that day. By whom? By what authority?

James Tracy has a brilliant critique of Carver's performance where, if ABC/NBC/CBS are correct in their reporting (that the body was found with only handguns and the rifle had been left in the car), then what precisely are we to make of Carver's contention that they were all shot with the Bushmaster? What is more likely: that ABC/NBC/CBS, who confirmed their report with federal and state officials, are wrong about the body having been found with only handguns in the vicinity? Or that Carver – who did not even know how many of the dead were boys and how many were girls – is wrong about them all having been shot with the Bushmaster?

Bear in mind, if multiple shooters had been involved, then both reports could be true, where Adam Lanza's body was placed with handguns in the vicinity and other shooters slaughtered the children, if, indeed, any children were actually murdered at all.

There is even a report that Carver himself has admitted that it was "a hoax".

More Fraud and Fakery

United Way forgot to check the schedule before they had set up the fraudulent "fleece America" site to get money from bleeding hearts who wanted to donate to the hoax fund to pay these crisis actors.

Yep, on 11 December this donation site was set up by United Way. That's mighty clairvoyant thinking there to be so prepped. And the brochure for telling families how to talk to their kids just happened to be released that day, when anyone in the brochure printing business knows that the laying up of a brochure and the production takes days not just an hour or two.

Yet it was done on December 14th.

And there is evidence it was produced on 12 December, two days before the shooting, meaning again, this was a hoax! An act of premeditated high treason.

We have photoshopped photos by FEMA presumably or the FBI, showing Robbie Parker's fake family all sitting in a Christmas card scene that do not make sense. Ironically, the same dress is worn by the vicSIM girl – although some maintain that she is actually her sister – when being photographed with President Obama, but we are told that dresses can be used by any child.

By the way, all of them are smiling, possibly because that photo was taken during the drill months before not on the day alleged. This, in turn, raises serious questions as to whether President Obama himself is complicit in this case of apparent hoax and high treason.

Add to the fact that two weeks before this, Eric Holder, the U.S. Attorney General, met with the Lt. Governor and Governor of the State of Connecticut and during a press conference held by the Governor with his Lt. Governor there, they admit this freely, implicating themselves in this hoax and lie perpetrated on the American public on not just this occasion, but in Tucson and Aurora.

What we have is a series of hoaxes all staged by the department of JUST U.S. here, which were interspersed across various parts of the Continental U.S. to do two things: a.) grab guns and end the 2nd amendment. b.) demonize all independent 9/11 investigators and others who would so decry these as being elaborately staged hoaxes using crisis actors!

A Multiplicity of Hoax Shootings

The evidence bears this out that not only was the government involved, but by virtue of CNN airing the drill video months before as live video they too are implicated, as is Anderson Cooper and many others in MSM, including a British scumball gun grabber named Piers Morgan who demands we disarm.

We have proven these hoaxes were purposely staged by FEMA and crisis actors strictly, and that no people were truly harmed or killed in any of these events.

We know that Gabrielle Giffords and a federal judge were not shot in Tucson without blood being everywhere, yet not one EMS person on the scene there had any blood.

You can pretty much rest assured that nobody died in Aurora either, that crisis actors were again used, and per the smirking FBI agent and treasonous snake named James Yacone, behind the chief of police, this too was a hoax and lie.

We can prove the long rifle alleged by Wayne 'fake coroner' Carver in Newtown was found in the trunk of a black Honda that evening, and we can prove that rifle rounds not shotgun shells were ejected onto the pavement behind that car by someone not in law enforcement, by the manhandling and grandstanding of the weapon that night on the helicopter video we all have. We can prove that per their own admission now that authorities have now morphed this weapon into an exotic and odd foreign made shotgun when it clearly was not a shotgun.

It's not relevant any longer whether it was a shotgun, a zip gun, or a BB gun, because the likes of Lt. Paul Vance of the Connecticut State Patrol, has now said that both long guns that were taken to the crime scene had been locked in a vehicle and outside of the reach of a shooter who died the day before, and could not have used them because they were found in the vehicle long after any rational person could so justify this cordoned off with crime scene tape, search hours and hours later in darkness.

That was not by accident.

It was on purpose, filmed from the roof of the school using just enough flood lighting to make positive identification of the weapon almost impossible other than it was not a pistol.

In summary regarding the weapons in the car, they could not have been used by any shooter that day, so they are now excluded forever!

Add to this the incredible threat by the Connecticut State Patrol to charge and incarcerate any individuals debunking these hoaxes, and a lying snake POTUS without tears on his face, decrying we need to give up our Second Amendment rights as citizens. ...

We have the goods.

We can prove these are hoaxes staged to grab guns.

I ask you to indict these traitors and treasonous liars, including the Attorney General, the FBI, and the President of the United States as well as Clarence W. Dupnik, the Chief of Police of Aurora, Colorado, and the Lt. Governor and the Governor of Connecticut, for taking part in these hoaxes. And, yes, every single crisis actor who participated in these frauds perpetrated on America in these three staged hoaxes.

Now is the time for every single American to come to grips with the hard reality, which is that our own federal government has become an internal enemy, which has been hijacked by powerful interests who will cover up any degree of mass murder, treason, and looting that is committed here, especially by Zionists who are promoting the interests of Israel and not those of the United States.

Each and every one of us has a choice, which is simple: RESIST!

[Chapter 32] "Hallelujah!"

> "For those of us who were alive on 22 November 1963, it remains forever a current event embedded in our memories. I was a 10-year-old boy at the time. That fall day defined the beginning of a turbulent era whose ripples continue to be felt today throughout our government and the nation's psyche. A faith and trust in government was lost that the truth can only restore."
>
> - Douglas Weldon, J.D.

[Hallelujah]

by Mike Palecek

A couple on their way out to eat heard the top of the hour CBS news theme music and turned up their radio.

"Seven Iraqis were vaporized as they slept early this morning when a United States Cruise missile hit their home."

"We are more free!"

The couple turned to each other and exclaimed.

On that same morning a middle school government teacher stood in front of his first period class. Together they watched the television set in the corner.

"Two Iraq children were shredded today when they picked up a bomb fragment they mistook for a toy."

"They died that we could be more free," said the instructor.

"U.S.A.! U.S.A.! U.S.A.!" the children chanted. The teacher bid them to be quiet by raising his hands. With another familiar hand motion he told them to rise to say the Pledge of Allegiance.

The next Sunday the minister at the brick church around the corner marched to the podium and announced to the congregation that he had found time to watch the news before coming to the late service.

"My brothers and sisters, God Bless Our Troops, who earlier this morning destroyed an Iraqi unit, killing dozens of the enemy. They have courageously made it safe for us to worship our merciful, awesome God here this morning, as we choose, in freedom.

"Let us pray."

"Hallelujah."

"Hallelujah."
"Hallelujah."

Four businessmen seated themselves at their regular middle table for morning coffee. Before the drinks arrived, one of the men read aloud from the newspaper, as was his custom. He read that three fishermen had been lost off the coast of West Africa and were feared dead.

"We are that much more free," said one of the men while examining his tie.

The reader continued to scan the international news briefs.

"A woman in an east London suburb last evening stepped on a nail and bled to death before she could reach home after work."

"God Bless our Freedoms," said one of the four while the others nodded and moved their hands off the table to make room for the cups.

"Six men in Canada were feared drowned when their fishing house plunged through the ice in eastern Saskatchewan."

"I am proud to be an American."
"We are No. 1!"

The couple sat together in the evening watching the news.

"Three skiers in the Swiss Alps were buried alive by a mid-afternoon avalanche," said the announcer.

"God Bless the USA," said the man.

"These colors don't run," said the woman, reaching to scoop bean dip with a tortilla chip.

Kevin has been prolific in publishing articles on Veterans Today.

[Chapter 33] Jim: The biggest mistake

JIM:

["The biggest mistake"]

The year before my adventure at W.D. Sugg Middle School I was invited the second semester to return to Virginia as visiting full professor, where perhaps the most important role I played was to review a stack of submissions, applications they had for a permanent position they had in the philosophy of science.

I went through a very large number, sixty or seventy, and explained that none of them were appropriately qualified, when the then chair of the department showed me one more, from a fellow who had earned his Ph.D. from Stanford and had a background in physics and statistics as well as the philosophy of science and who had actually published on propensities, on which I had done so much of my own work, whom I recommended as the person they ought to hire.

His name was Paul Humphreys.

He would become my closest friend within the profession for more than, hmm, twenty years.

And I occasionally rib him about having made his career by getting him the job!

Which he never really appreciated.

Paul would later try to save me from one of my career management mistakes when I had a two-book deal with MIT Press for a collection of my essays on computers and cognition, and then for a second book on biology and behavior.

I had said to Betty Stanton, who was the key player there, who had made MIT world famous in the area of cognitive science, that there was one person – they could use any referees they wanted, but there was one person – I recommended they not use, a fellow with whom I'd had conflicts in the past and I knew disliked me intensely.

I think that was a blunder on my part, because the name stuck in Betty Stanton's mind, he was among the very first whose book she'd published, and she used him here. And on the basis of a couple of words I had used in the introduction [he recommended its rejection].

I mean, this sounds incredible, but it's true; he had talked them into rejecting the book after I'd already been given a contract. I mean, the book was just fine. The collection is excellent though I would make one substitution. There was a review I had included ...

Well, when they rejected the book I really was thrown for a loss, and I stewed about it and thought, you know, well, what are they going to do about *Biology and Behavior*?

And I actually reasoned it through, though no one else has actually heard me explain this before, that if they rejected *Computers and Cognition*, that *Biology and Behavior* had the same theory of mind, so they would reject it too.

So I sent to Betty Stanton a one-sentence email, the biggest mistake of my professional career, that said, "I hereby withdraw *Biology and Behavior* from consideration for publication by MIT Press."

And I thought of adding, "Call me," but I thought it was so obvious that if she wanted the book she would call me, that I didn't. And I sent it, and the next thing I knew Paul Humphreys was calling to tell me that the book would make me famous, and I said, well, I'm already famous. He said, really famous, and he went on to say, ya know, how he thought, he gave a series of arguments, which I rebutted. Did I never want to be published?

I said, why would I not have it published, if MIT wanted to publish it? And other points he made.

I explained how I was upset because they'd rejected my book, *Computers and Cognition*, even after I'd been issued a contract, and I regarded it as a corrupt press. And I think Paul went back to Betty and told her that it was hopeless.

A different argument would have worked. I'm not faulting Paul for this. I should have thought it through myself. But here was probably the best book I ever wrote with the best possible publisher and if I wanted my book to become influential I should have gone with it.

The fact that Betty never called me to tell me how much they liked it, meant I had never actually had a direct response from the publisher about the book and I felt that since they hadn't called me even though Paul had, that it must have been the case that it didn't make that much difference.

I think actually it would have been a very big deal.

MIT actually ran a series of ads, which is unheard of, asking for a book that did what my book did, kind of from A to Z, beginning really with issues of the origin of the universe and the role of God as a creator and so forth and arguments about creationism and creation science, which were at that point the introductory part of the book.

They eventually sent me, intermittently, three referee's reports, which were all very favorable. One observed that I hadn't talked about intelligent design, but that he did not think that was a significant omission.

And another wrote when he was in graduate school he used to joke about a book talking about A to Z, the creation of the universe to the end, and he thought this actually did it. And when the book included a considerable discussion about the evolution of intelligence, and why blacks in the United States have a stunningly lower I.Q. as measured by I.Q. tests than do whites, he was observing that I had explained how evolution had got them into this situation and that evolution would get them out.

I submitted it to another press and the editor there took a great long time thinking about it and told me he believed I had two books here.

So I actually would substitute the two books, and publish them separately as *The Evolution of Intelligence*, in 2005, and as *Render Unto Darwin*, in 2007.

But I think actually the genius of the book in part was the combination, and those who said, you know, that this was so masterful from beginning to end had it right, and that I simply blew the opportunity.

I would eventually attempt to put the book back together again, but, you know, since it had already been published as two separate books, that really wasn't a very feasible idea.

And I did publish it online, including a chapter about intelligent design, under the heading *Evolution Mentality and Morality*, which anyone who wants to see the original version of *Biology and Behavior* can find by accessing it using the title.

And if they can think of the book without the chapter on intelligent design, then that's basically how *Biology and Behavior* would have looked. Among all the decisions I made – there were probably half a dozen that were fairly fateful – that were wrong, this was undoubtedly my greatest mistake. And unfortunately, you know, there's nothing that can be done other than to suck it up and acknowledge that as you live your life you're gonna make mistakes and the best thing to do is simply accept your fallibility in that regard. In fact it's ironic that it is an empirical criterion for the possession of mentality, on the theory of minds semiotic or sign using systems that I developed on the basis of Charles Peirce's work, that the commission of mistakes, the ability to make mistakes, to mistake something for something else, is a reliable evidential indicator of the possession of mentality.

So, I've made my share of mistakes.

And somehow I can't find great comfort in recognizing that is a sure indication that I have a mind, because I would like to have believed that I have the capacity to reason these things through more adequately and arrive at better decisions.

Jim Fetzer

Bill Scott, Jr., Phil Fetzer and Jim Fetzer

Jim Fetzer

David W. Mantik

Phil, Henry, and Jim Fetzer

[Chapter 34] The Third White Rose Leaflet

"Salus publica suprema lex"

All ideal forms of government are utopias. A state cannot be constructed on a purely theoretical basis; rather, it must grow and ripen in the way an individual human being matures. But we must not forget that at the starting point of every civilization the state was already there in rudimentary form.

The family is as old as man himself, and out of this initial bond man, endowed with reason, created for himself a state founded on justice, whose highest law was the common good. The state should exist as a parallel to the divine order, and the highest of all utopias, "the civitas dei", is the model which in the end it should approximate.

Here we will not pass judgment on the many possible forms of the state – democracy, Constitutional monarchy, and so on. But one matter needs to be brought out clearly and unambiguously. Every individual human being has a claim to a useful and just state, a state which secures the freedom of the individual as well as the good of the whole.

For, according to God's will, man is intended to pursue his natural goal, his earthly happiness, in self-reliance and self-chosen activity, freely and independently within the community of life and work of the nation.

But our present "state" is the dictatorship of evil. "Oh, we've known that for a long time," I hear you object, "and it isn't necessary to bring that to our attention again."

But, I ask you, if you know that, why do you not bestir yourselves, why do you allow these men who are in power to rob you step by step, openly and in secret, of one domain of your rights after another, until one day nothing, nothing at all will be left but a mechanized state system presided over by criminals and drunks?

Is your spirit already so crushed by abuse that you forget it is your right – or rather, your "moral duty" – to eliminate this system?

But if a man no longer can summon the strength to demand his right, then it is absolutely certain that he will perish. We would deserve to be dispersed through the earth like dust before the wind if we do not muster our powers at this late hour and finally find the courage which up to now we have lacked.

Do not hide your cowardice behind a cloak of expediency, for with every new day that you hesitate, failing to oppose this offspring of Hell, your guilt, as in a parabolic curve, grows higher and higher. Many, perhaps most, of the readers of these leaflets do not see clearly how they can practice an effective opposition. They do not see any avenues open to them. We want to try to show them that everyone is in a position to contribute to the overthrow of this system.

It is not possible through solitary withdrawal, in the manner of embittered hermits, to prepare the ground for the overturn of this "government" or bring about the revolution at the earliest possible moment.

No, it can be done only by the cooperation of many convinced, energetic people – people who are agreed as to the means they must use to attain their goal.

We have no great number of choices as to these means.

The only one available is "passive resistance".

The meaning and the goal of passive resistance is to topple National Socialism, and in this struggle we must not recoil from any course, any action, whatever its nature.

At "all" points we must oppose National Socialism, wherever it is open to attack. We must soon bring this monster of a state to an end. A victory of fascist Germany in this war would have immeasurable, frightful consequences. The military victory over Bolshevism dare not become the primary concern of the Germans.

The defeat of the Nazis must "unconditionally" be the first order of business. The greater necessity of this latter requirement will be discussed in one of our forthcoming leaflets.

And now every convinced opponent of National Socialism must ask himself how he can fight against the present "state" in the most effective way, how he can strike it the most telling blows.

Through passive resistance, without a doubt. We cannot provide each man with the blueprint for his acts, we can only suggest them in general terms, and he alone will find the way of achieving this end:

> "Sabotage" in armament plants and war industries, sabotage at all gatherings, rallies, public ceremonies, and organizations of the National Socialist Party. Obstruction of the smooth functioning of the war machine (a machine for war that goes on solely to shore up and perpetuate the National Socialist Party and its dictatorship).
>
> "Sabotage" in all the areas of science and scholarship which further the continuation of the war – whether in universities, technical schools, laboratories, research institutions, or technical bureaus. "Sabotage" in all cultural institutions which could potentially enhance the "prestige" of the fascists among the people.
>
> "Sabotage" in all branches of the arts which have even the slightest dependence on National Socialism or render it service. "Sabotage" in all publications, all newspapers, that are in the pay of the "government" and that defend its ideology and aid in disseminating the brown lie.

Do not give a penny to the public drives (even when they are conducted under the pretense of charity). For this is only a disguise. In reality the proceeds aid neither the Red Cross nor the needy. The government does not need this money; it is not financially interested in these money drives.

After all, the presses run continuously to manufacture any desired amount of paper currency.

But the populace must be kept constantly under tension, the pressure of the bit must not be allowed to slacken! Do not contribute to the collections of metal, textiles and the like.

Try to convince all your acquaintances, including those in the lower social classes, of the senselessness of continuing, of the hopelessness of this war; of our spiritual and economic enslavement at the hands of the National Socialists; of the destruction of all moral and religious values; and urge them to "passive resistance"!

Aristotle: 'Politics":

> "... and further, it is part [of the nature of tyranny] to strive to see to it that nothing is kept hidden of that which any subject says or does, but that everywhere he will be spied upon,... and further, to set man against man and friend against friend, and the common people against the privileged and the wealthy.
>
> "Also it is part of these tyrannical measures, to keep the subjects poor, in order to pay the guards and the soldiers, and so that they will be occupied with earning their livelihood and will have neither leisure nor opportunity to engage in conspiratorial acts ... Further, [to levy] such taxes on income as were imposed in Syracuse, for under Dionysius the citizens gladly paid out their whole fortunes in taxes within five years. Also, the tyrant is inclined constantly to foment wars."

Please duplicate and distribute!

Obama surrenders to Bibi & Bachmann, will bomb Iran

By Kevin Barrett on November 29, 2013

by Kevin Barrett

President Obama has announced that due to the interminable whining, nagging, and complaining from Israeli PM Netanyahu and US Congress clown Michele Bachmann, he has decided to go ahead and bomb Iran with them – despite the P5+1 nuclear agreement.

"Michele Bachmann – I hesitate to use the word 'Congresswoman' out of respect for that once-great legislative body – insists that Iran absolutely must be bombed, agreement or no agreement," Obama said Friday. "Her commander-in-chief, the Israeli Prime Minister, agrees. So just to shut them up, I have decided to launch a really ugly-looking bat-winged Northrop-Grumman B-2 to drop a truly vicious load on the Iranian nuclear facilities at Arak. And I have decided to honor dear Michele and my good friend Bibi by making them an integral part of the mission."

Obama has ordered the Strategic Air Command to prepare a place for Netanyahu and Bachmann in the B-2's bomb bay atop a moth-eaten mattress beside an ice bucket of cheap champagne. The pair will ride in comfort from Whiteman Air Force Base in Missouri until the aircraft is approaching the Iranian nuclear facility at Arak. As "preparation to launch" orders are issued, the bomb bay doors will open and Netanyahu and Bachmann will be dangled by their heels, stark naked, outside the aircraft. At "launch," the pair will be released to plummet head first toward strategic targets at the Iranian nuclear site.

Kevin has proven himself to be the master of satire, which he deploys with devastating effect, as in this example of 29 November 2013.

Page 8B Pine County Courier Thursday, May 4, 2006

Conspiracy theorist visits county, calls reasons behind 9/11 a hoax

By Blair Nelson
Pine County Courier

James H. Fetzer says the events of Sept. 11, 2001 are a mirage.

The professor at the University of Minnesota-Duluth gave a lecture called "Conspiracy Theories: JFK, 9/11, and Wellstone" at Tobies in Hinckley Saturday.

He said the Sept. 11 terrorist attacks were a hoax orchestrated by our own government in an attempt to instill fear and terror in order to launch a "war on terror" and eventually the war in Iraq.

"The American government has been practicing terrorism on its own people," he said. "That is the way things appear to be in this country." He suggested removing every member of Congress and starting anew.

With Steven Jones, a professor of physics at Brigham Young University, Fetzer founded a group called "Scholars for 9/11 Truth" dedicated to "exposing falsehoods and revealing truths …" … the group's Web site, www.scholarsfor911truth.org. Members of the group conclude that there is a conspiracy theory regarding the real truth of 9/11. Fetzer and others believe the World Trade Center twin towers and Building 7 were destroyed by controlled demolition.

Fetzer showed a tape of the south tower falling and floors being blown out, evidence of demolition, he said. He said the steel left from tower wreckage had a sulfur residue that can't be accounted for. Fetzer said based on his research, the towers could have been brought down by a chemical agent known as thermite, which can turn steel to molten metal quickly. Fetzer said jet fuel could not have caused the same effect.

Fetzer said a key player in the government conspiracy is President Bush's brother, Marvin Bush. He heads Securacom, which provided security for the W…

JFK

Fetzer and his colleagues believe the theory that President John F. Kennedy was killed by the government for essentially not playing along. Fetzer said JFK was shot in a "high-level operation within the government" that involved collusion from the CIA, FBI, Vice President Lyndon Johnson, the mafia and oil companies. He said it went as deep as the Secret Service, sworn to protect the president.

"They felt Jack was betraying the country and that he threatened the CIA's power," Fetzer said.

He said there were six shots on Kennedy from three different directions. He talked at length on the legendary "Zapruder" film taken of the assassination.

Because no one talked then, conspiracy theories were shrugged off. In recent decades, though, that has changed, Fetzzer said. "People have talked, they haven't kept silent."

He said there were "alterations and substitutions in the …ennedy case." Evidence, …cluding forensic evidence from the limousine, was obstructed and the vehicles riding with Kennedy in the motorcade procession were completely out of order.

Fetzer ended his talk with the "conditioning" of the American people through the process of cognitive dissonance. Proof of its power is the seemingly unchallenged acceptance of a Patriot Act that violates the freedoms of the people and voting machines that are obviously fraudulent, he said.

"Incompetence and corruption are the greatest they've ever been," Fetzer said, leading to the unfortunate American image as "the biggest bully in the world."

Fetzer ran out of time to discuss his theories on the death of Minnesota Sen. Paul Wellstone. He believes he was purposely killed to sway the 2002 elections.

UMD professor James Fetzer gave his talk to about 40 people in Hinckley.

JFK, 9/11, Wellstone – were they all conspiracies?

Come listen to author James Fetzer at Cambridge Campus on March 1 to find out.

For all you conspiracy theorizers, don't miss reknowned author James Fetzer's lecture at the Anoka-Ramsey Community College Cambridge Campus on Wednesday, March 1 from 6 to 9 p.m. in the food court.

Fetzer – who has written three books on President John F. Kennedy's assassination – will spend the first hour of his lecture talking about his finding pointing directly to a conspiracy.

In the second hour, Fetzer will discuss the government's conspiracy related to the terrorist attacks on Sept. 11, 2001.

In the final hour, the topic will be the conspiracy behind Senator Paul Wellstone's plane crash. Fetzer's latest book – American Assassination – goes indepth about the strange death of the Minnesota senator.

For more information on Fetzer's lecture, please contact Holly Olson at 651-235-3751.

Fetzer will also be on KBEK, 95.5 FM, on Monday afternoon.

AMERICAN ASSASSINATION
THE STRANGE DEATH OF SENATOR PAUL WELLSTONE

Fire Trail on which white van flees from scene minutes after the King Air A 100 crash.

John P. Costella and Jim Fetzer

[Chapter 35] Palecek: A license to drive slow

"I'm not concerned about all hell breaking loose – but that a PART of hell will break loose. It'll be that much harder to detect."
- George Carlin

DRIVING TO DES MOINES – It's sixty-three songs from Sheldon, Iowa to Rochester, Minnesota. I got my iPod back up and running. I won't be alone anymore.

Got the Dixie Chicks, John Prine, Guy Clark, Jerry Jeff Walker, Mary-Chapin Carpenter, John Denver, The Clash, Bill Hicks, Cat Stevens, The Soggy Bottom Boys, Alison Krause, The Eagles, Green Day, Greg Brown, Woody Guthrie, Steve Forbert, Harry McClintock, all squeezed into the brown Honda.

Austin, Minnesota is thirty-four songs from Rochester.

It is the home of the Spam Museum. I'm probably in there somewhere, maybe in the hall of fame with all my emails over the past ten years trying to hawk my books.

In the early 1990s, Ruth, Sam, Emily and I lived in Byron, eight miles west of Rochester.

We owned the tiny Byron Review, ran it out of the north side of our home on Byron Avenue.

We scrimped and saved and hustled and fought with the city council, school board, lumber yard, elevator, fire department, and won the newspaper of the year award from the MNA in 1994. We went out of business later in the year.

Sitting in traffic in Rochester was the first time I felt kind of vulnerable with my bumper stickers: 9-11 Was An Inside Job, Jail Bush, Impeach Bush. Rochester is a conservative island in Minnesota. But it wasn't really that. I think I was just tired, depressed a little from having to leave home and think of three months ahead of me on the road, and so maybe I was poking along a little and getting some looks from my fellow Americans.

But I've got a license to drive slow – Iowa plates.

And now I remember how fast people in southeast Minnesota drive. They are busy people, getting things done, going places. I try not to get in the way.

Sitting in heavy traffic on Broadway Avenue in Rochester I kept an eye on the fat blonde woman behind me with no neck driving the forest green Dodge Caravan. Had my hand on the auto-lock in case she opened her door. Once when I was a seminarian at the College of St. Thomas in Saint Paul in

1979 I flipped a trucker the bird as I drove past him in my 1959 brown and white Chevy. Just because I thought I could, and get away with it.

As I sang along with an Eagles song I could see a familiar truck getting bigger in the rearview mirror.

I had to stop and the trucker pulled up next to me, got out of his truck, came around to my door and pounded on the door and the window, saying somebody should teach me a lesson.

I did learn a lesson.

Don't stop.

Or if you have to stop, keep one eye on the lady in the fur-lined jacket in the side mirror.

When we were in Byron in the early '90s I did a story on the Leonard Peltier case, and interviewed an FBI agent in the Rochester office.

One of them, David Price, was mentioned in the book, *In The Spirit of Crazy Horse*, and had been accused by some in the American Indian Movement of having murdered Anna Mae Aquash. He wasn't in the office the day I was there, so I did not get to meet him.

The other, Don Dealing, did visit with me.

He talked about Peltier, Jack Coler, Ronald Williams, Wounded Knee.

He had been at Wounded Knee as a member of some sort of FBI special forces team.

By searching Google for Don Dealing tonight I found that he testified in 2004 in a trial regarding the death of Anna Mae Aquash. He says he was the first FBI agent on the scene. I don't recall talking to him about that. In the 2004 testimony he also says that his only knowledge of COINTELPRO is through what he has seen "through media and that sort of a thing."

Have you ever met an FBI agent? I have talked to a few, while in custody, as a reporter, watching a friend be arrested by a boatload of them once in Omaha. They don't seem human.

They have a non-terrestrial aura. Stay away from them if you can. Your life will be richer for it.

Anyway, I spoke last night to the southeast Minnesota peacemakers group in Rochester, perhaps the most organized peace group in the continental USA. They have name tags and agendas and motions and seconds, and non-acidic tea.

In my talk I raise the question of whether Senator Paul Wellstone was assassinated by the Bush government. I really didn't know what to expect in giving the talk in Minnesota. But during and afterwards some said they agreed, and some thanked me for saying out loud what was on people's minds.

They were not aware of Jim Fetzer's book, *American Assassination*.

And so when someone asked what additional information I had about the Wellstone affair, I told them about the book.

And I said that an electro-magnetic weapon was a possibility, and told how the FBI was on the scene too soon not to have left Minneapolis before the plane crashed. And the fire burned blue-white, which is how an electrical fire burns.

These are things I found out from reading Fetzer's book.

I have to admit, out loud, that a lot of what I say comes not from knowing, but from feeling.

I don't apologize for that.

I don't think there is anything wrong with saying what you feel. I would actually like to have someone show me, to my satisfaction, that I am wrong about Bush and 9/11, Bush and Wellstone. That would be fine with me.

To have to imagine the alternative, that persons within our own government did these things, is not particularly easy to live with. I would be glad to let it go.

I first found out about Wellstone's death when I turned on my computer that day and went to "Common Dreams" and there was Wellstone's photo. I then went over to run on the treadmill at nearby Dordt College, and the Wellstone news was on the TV in the corner. A couple of college girls were snickering, implying that he got what he deserved. Gotta love those pro-lifers.

The timing of the death of Wellstone was perfect for the Bush administration. They needed that seat to control the Senate.

Wellstone stood in the way of a lot of things.

Think how excited they would be at about that time, after pulling off 9/11, and set up perfectly to run the table, to take over the world. Would people like this let one guy stand in their way after all the work and struggle they had committed to become rich and powerful?

Not likely.

There was an investigation. The National Transportation Safety Board determined that pilot error was responsible for the plane not maintaining adequate air speed, which led to a stall from which they could not recover.

And so we can be certain Wellstone was not murdered, because a commission said he was not.

Well, I don't agree.

I think these things can be rigged: the Warren Commission and the 9/11 Commission come to mind.

I just think someone like Wellstone, who had heart, who was twice the man, twice the human being, that George W. Bush is, deserved better. He deserves justice. He deserves a real investigation.

He deserves to not be forgotten.

CAYMAN
TURTLE
FARM

[Chapter 36] The Dude & 9/11 ...

Things that make you go WTF?

> "Duct tape reinforced by aluminum foil held together the black and white drone's wood wings. The wooden propellers and tiny engines were fastened to a well-worn fuselage, fashioned from the fuel tank of a larger aircraft. The words "God is Great" were hand painted in red ink on both sides. Perched on a sawhorse at a military research base twenty miles north of Baghdad, the drone looked more like a large school science project than a vehicle capable of delivering chemical and biological weapons. Iraqi officials denied the airplane had any strategic use."
>
> \- *Boston Globe*

"An Iraqi drone found by UN weapons inspectors is of "very primitive" design and is definitely not capable of flying 500 km as suggested by U.S. Secretary of State Colin Powell, *Jane's Defence Weekly* said today.

"On Feb. 5, Powell told the UN Security Council that the Iraqis possessed a drone that could fly 500 km, violating UN rules that limit the range of Iraq weapons to 150km."

9/11 psychic interview

In an article that was published on *Veterans Today* on April 10, 2013, and later in an interview with Kevin Barrett on *American Freedom Radio*, James and Sandy Duncan talked about how Sandy, a psychic, has had contact with a victim of the attacks of Sept. 11, 2001.

Sandy said she had contact with David Angell, one of the writers for the sitcom *Cheers*, and the co-creator of *Frasier* and *Wings.*

In the article, James tells the story of how he was sitting there, at their living room table, as his wife spoke with David Angell and relayed what he was saying.

"He died at the airport," she said. "He did not get on a plane. Everything was normal, he says. He was waiting for his plane with a few other people. He was told there would be a delay and was called into a lounge. There were two men and two women. They could look out and see the runway. At one point, someone noticed that there was no activity. They tried the door, which was locked. They then began banging on the door. People then burst in wearing all black outfits and carrying guns. They wore gas masks over their face. They were not dark skinned.

"They put hoods over our heads and herded us to another room. They were bound," Sandy said, sometimes relaying his actual words and sometimes interpreting for me. "I wanted to take my briefcase, but they wouldn't let me. They took us to a nearby room," Sandy stated again. "It was near the runway. I could smell jet fuel. I was worried they were going to set us on fire. I tried to feel for a window to try to break it, but could not find one.

"I was strangled from behind with a wire. Then he slit my throat."

They had been told to sit quietly. He couldn't tell how long he was there – it could have been ten minutes, it could have been hours. He didn't have a sense of time.

He didn't hear anyone else cry out, so he thought he was the first person murdered. They had taken the women into another room. It was very hard for any of them to believe.

In relating the story, James tells of how he came to believe in Sandy's psychic abilities, that she was able to tell him things about family members that he had never talked to her about previously.

Conspiracy Theory term invented by CIA

> Mark Crispin Miller, professor of media studies at New York University,from a talk delivered at the "How 9/11 Changed The World" conference, New York City, Sept. 12, 2010.
>
> Conspiracy theory functions as a most effective cudgel against anyone who tries even to discuss a certain range of stories. You call somebody a conspiracy theorist and you have very effectively neutralized them. Once a journalist, for example, gets defined as a conspiracy theorist, or a professor, public intellectual, anybody, that person has been neutralized. And I would suggest that it's a much more efficient way to silence people than to have some goon come to their house at night and pop them, ya know?
>
> It's a really clean, safe way to prevent people from listening to what you have to say. Now the other day I was privileged to moderate a press conference on the 9/11 subject and one of our speakers was Lt. Col. Shelton Lankford, who was a Lt. Colonel in the Marines, flew a lot of missions in Vietnam, he's part of the military community speaking out for a new investigation of 9/11, and he began by noting that his personal hero was Smedley Darlington Butler, who was a Marine general who is famous for having blown the whistle on the so-called Business Plot in the '30s, as a group of plutocrats, rich people, who asked him to function as the man on the white horse to lead an army

of outraged veterans to Washington and depose Franklin Roosevelt and take over as dictator.

And he actually blew the whistle on this, went to Congress and talked about it. Now, Lt. Col. Lankford's point was that if Butler stepped forward and said this today, he'd be dismissed as a conspiracy theorist. I think that's obviously true, but that raises the crucial question, when did this phrase suddenly become the means of choice for defining the all-important boundary line between conspiracy theories that we can all believe in, right?

Like the official explanation of 9/11, or the international communist conspiracy, and those conspiracy theories, that, ya know, by definition we just aren't supposed to talk about? When did this happen? So I did some research and I can tell you exactly when it happened. It happened in the mid-to-late '60s.

If you do a search on the phrase 'conspiracy theory'" in *The New York Times* archives you find that it's rarely used until that moment. And if you do a search at Time.com, *Time* magazine, you'll find that it's never used until that moment. Then it's used all the time. Okay?

And I would suggest to you that the reason it becomes so frequent in journalistic circles is [...] that there is a declassified CIA memo that you can all get online [...] dated Jan. 4, 1967, and it's sent out to all station chiefs, worldwide, about our concern. Our concern is, that from the day of President Kennedy's assassination there has been speculation about the responsibility of his murder. Specifically, there were a number of books that had just come out or were about to come out questioning the conclusions of the Warren Commission Report.

And the two books that most concerned the CIA were Mark Lane's *Rush To Judgment* and Edward J. Epstein's *Inquest*.

CIA Document 1035-960

Concerning Criticism of the Warren Report

1. Our Concern. From the day of President Kennedy's assassination on, there has been speculation about the responsibility for his murder. Although this was stemmed for a time by the Warren Commission Report, (which appeared at the end of September 1964), various writers have now had time to scan the Commission's published report and documents for new pretexts for questioning, and there has been a new wave of books and articles criticizing the Commission's findings. In most cases the critics have speculated as to the existence of some kind of conspiracy, and often they have implied that the Commission itself was involved. Presumably as a result of the increasing challenge to the Warren Commission's report, a public opinion poll recently indicated that 46 percent of the American public did not think that Oswald acted alone, while more than half of those polled thought

that the Commission had left some questions unresolved. Doubtless polls abroad would show similar, or possibly more adverse results.

2. This trend of opinion is a matter of concern to the U.S. government, including our organization. The members of the Warren Commission were naturally chosen for their integrity, experience and prominence.

They represented both major parties, and they and their staff were deliberately drawn from all sections of the country. Just because of the standing of the Commissioners, efforts to impugn their rectitude and wisdom tend to cast doubt on the whole leadership of American society. Moreover, there seems to be an increasing tendency to hint that President Johnson himself, as the one person who might be said to have benefited, was in some way responsible for the assassination.

Innuendo of such seriousness affects not only the individual concerned, but also the whole reputation of the American government. Our organization itself is directly involved: among other facts, we contributed information to the investigation. Conspiracy theories have frequently thrown suspicion on our organization, for example by falsely alleging that Lee Harvey Oswald worked for us.

The aim of this dispatch is to provide material countering and discrediting the claims of the conspiracy theorists, so as to inhibit the circulation of such claims in other countries. Background information is supplied in a classified section and in a number of unclassified attachments.

3. Action. We do not recommend that discussion of the assassination question be initiated where it is not already taking place. Where discussion is active [business] addresses are requested:

a. To discuss the publicity problem with [?] and friendly elite contacts (especially politicians and editors), pointing out that the Warren Commission made as thorough an investigation as humanly possible, that the charges of the critics are without serious foundation, and that further speculative discussion only plays into the hands of the opposition.

Point out also that parts of the conspiracy talk appear to be deliberately generated by Communist propagandists. Urge them to use their influence to discourage unfounded and irresponsible speculation.

b. To employ propaganda assets to [negate] and refute the attacks of the critics. Book reviews and feature articles are particularly appropriate for this purpose. The unclassified attachments to this guidance should provide useful background material for passing to assets. Our ploy should point out, as applicable, that the critics are

(I) wedded to theories adopted before the evidence was in,

(I) politically interested, (III) financially interested,

(IV) hasty and inaccurate in their research, or

(V) infatuated with their own theories. In the course of discussions of the whole phenomenon of criticism, a useful strategy may be to single out Epstein's theory for attack, using the attached Fletcher [?] article and Spectator piece for background.

(Although Mark Lane's book is much less convincing that Epstein's and comes off badly where confronted by knowledgeable critics, it is also much more difficult to answer as a whole, as one becomes lost in a morass of unrelated details.)

4. In private to media discussions not directed at any particular writer, or in attacking publications which may be yet forthcoming, the following arguments should be useful:

a. No significant new evidence has emerged which the Commission did not consider. The assassination is sometimes compared (e.g., by Joachim Joesten and Bertrand Russell) with the Dreyfus case; however, unlike that case, the attack on the Warren Commission have produced no new evidence, no new culprits have been convincingly identified, and there is no agreement among the critics.

(A better parallel, though an imperfect one, might be with the Reichstag fire of 1933, which some competent historians (Fritz Tobias, AJ.P. Taylor, D.C. Watt) now believe was set by Vander Lubbe on his own initiative, without acting for either Nazis or Communists; the Nazis tried to pin the blame on the Communists, but the latter have been more successful in convincing the world that the Nazis were to blame.)

b. Critics usually overvalue particular items and ignore others. They tend to place more emphasis on the recollections of individual witnesses (which are less reliable and more divergent--and hence offer more hand-holds for criticism) and less on ballistics, autopsy, and photographic evidence. A close examination of the Commission's records will usually show that the conflicting eyewitness accounts are quoted out of context, or were discarded by the Commission for good and sufficient reason.

c. Conspiracy on the large scale often suggested would be impossible to conceal in the United States, esp. since informants could expect to receive large royalties, etc. Note that Robert Kennedy, Attorney General at the time and John F. Kennedy's brother, would be the last man to overlook or conceal any conspiracy. And as one reviewer pointed out, Congressman Gerald R. Ford would hardly have held his tongue for the sake of the Democratic administration, and Senator Russell would have had every political interest in exposing any misdeeds on the part of Chief Justice Warren. A conspirator moreover would hardly choose a location for a shooting where so much depended on conditions beyond his control: the route, the speed of the cars, the moving target, the risk that the assassin would be discovered. A group of wealthy conspirators could have arranged much more secure conditions.

d. Critics have often been enticed by a form of intellectual pride: they light on some theory and fall in love with it; they also scoff at the Commission because it did not always answer every question with a flat decision one way or the other. Actually, the make-up of the Commission and its staff was an excellent safeguard against over-commitment to any one theory, or against the illicit transformation of probabilities into certainties.

e. Oswald would not have been any sensible person's choice for a co-conspirator. He was a "loner," mixed up, of questionable reliability and an unknown quantity to any professional intelligence service.

f. As to charges that the Commission's report was a rush job, it emerged three months after the deadline originally set. But to the degree that the Commission tried to speed up its reporting, this was largely due to the pressure of irresponsible speculation already appearing, in some cases coming from the same critics who, refusing to admit their errors, are now putting out new criticisms.

g. Such vague accusations as that "more than ten people have died mysteriously" can always be explained in some natural way e.g.: the individuals concerned have for the most part died of natural causes; the Commission staff questioned 418 witnesses (the FBI interviewed far more people, conduction 25,000 interviews and re interviews), and in such a large group, a certain number of deaths are to be expected.

(When Penn Jones, one of the originators of the "ten mysterious deaths" line, appeared on television, it emerged that two of the deaths on his list were from heart attacks, one from cancer, one was from a head-on collision on a bridge, and one occurred when a driver drifted into a bridge abutment.)

5. Where possible, counter speculation by encouraging reference to the Commission's Report itself.

Open-minded foreign readers should still be impressed by the care, thoroughness, objectivity and speed with which the Commission worked. Reviewers of other books might be encouraged to add to their account the idea that, checking back with the report itself, they found it far superior to the work of its critics.

"This will not stand, man"

In *The Big Lebowski*, in the opening shot in Ralph's, The Dude is purchasing a carton of half & half, and is writing out a check for sixty-nine cents. The date he writes is September 11, 1991.

As he is signing the check, President George H.W. Bush is shown on the little black and white TV in the store giving a speech about how aggression against Kuwait "will not stand."

And ...

- In *The Matrix*, Neo's passport expires on 9/11/01.
- In *The Dark Knight Rises*, a map is shown bearing the words "Sandy Hook."
- The Aurora, Colorado shooting took place on opening night of *The Dark Knight Rises*.

- In the 1986 *Dark Knight* comic, a crazed, gun-toting loner walks into a movie theater and starts shooting it up.
- Six months before 9/11, Fox TV aired the pilot for *The Lone Gunmen* series, depicting a U.S. government plot to crash a hijacked airliner into the World Trade Center.

Martin Keating wrote *The Final Jihad* in 1991, four years before the bombing of the federal building in Oklahoma City.

He did not find a publisher until 1996.

The Final Jihad is a story in which terrorists in Oklahoma City decide to blow up a federal building.

One of the main terrorists is named "Tom McVey."

The terrorists are stopped by an Oklahoma highway patrolman for having a broken tail light.

On April 19, 1995, the day of the Oklahoma City bombing, Timothy McVeigh was stopped by an Oklahoma state patrolman because of a missing license plate.

In *The Final Jihad* Keating also predicts the TWA downing and the World Trade Center bombing.

Martin Keating's brother is Frank Keating.

Frank Keating served as Governor of Oklahoma from 1995-2003.

He is a former FBI agent and assistant secretary of the Treasury who supervised the Secret Service, U.S. Customs, and the Bureau of Alcohol, Tobacco and Firearms. Keating's uncle, Barney Martin, was a career intelligence officer who headed the U.S. Navy's worldwide foreign intelligence collection operations and counterintelligence activities.

Susan Serrano

RFK Must Die: The Assassination of Robert Kennedy
The Girl in the Polka-Dot Dress

Sandra Serrano's Video Testimony

[Narrator] There was also evidence of another conspirator:

the girl in the polka dot dress.

Twenty-year-old Kennedy volunteer Sandra Serrano was sitting outside on a fire escape.

After seeing the picture of Sirhan in the newspaper, she felt certain this was the same person.

[Sandra Serrano, Kennedy Volunteer] That's what it was, seeing the photograph in the L.A. Times, that I said, "Wow, it really does look like that guy."

[Narrator] The FBI asked why she hadn't mentioned Sirhan on TV, even though Sirhan hadn't been identified at that point.

[Sandra Serrano, Kennedy Volunteer] I distinctly remember feeling like they were trying to drive me crazy, to say that I was mentally unstable. They had hung ten to twelve polka dot dresses in a room, and left me there in this room with all these polka dot dresses all hanging around. And then coming in and asking me, "What dress most looks like the dress that the girl wore? Were the polka dots the size of a nickel? Were they the size of a dime? Where they the size of a quarter?" You know, it was like you're trying to confuse the person.

[Narrator] As Serrano stuck to her story, Sergeant Enrique "Hank" Hernandez was brought in to give her a polygraph test.

[Sandra Serrano, Kennedy Volunteer] He was a very frightening person, and he was like some Dr. Jekyll/Mr. Hyde type. One minute he was just like really, really nice and soft-spoken, like a wonderful big brother. And then the next minute he was like, "You know, you're an awful person, and you're hurting the Kennedys." I seen those people.

[Sergeant Enrique "Hank" Hernandez] No. No. No. No. Sandy, remember what I told you about that? You can't say you saw something when you didn't see it. Sandy, look ... I can explain this to the investigators where you don't even have to talk to them ... and they won't talk to you. I can do this ... but please in the name of Kennedy!

[Sandra Serrano, Kennedy Volunteer] I remember seeing a girl!

[Sergeant Enrique "Hank" Hernandez] No. No ... I'm talking about what you have told here about seeing a person tell you "We have shot Kennedy." And that's wrong.

[Sandra Serrano, Kennedy Volunteer] That's what she said.

[Sergeant Enrique "Hank" Hernandez] No, it isn't, Sandy! Look, I love this man ...

[Sandra Serrano, Kennedy Volunteer] So do I!

[Sergeant Enrique "Hank" Hernandez] And you're shaming him. If, right now ...

[Sandra Serrano, Kennedy Volunteer] Don't shout at me!

[Sergeant Enrique "Hank" Hernandez] Well, I'm trying not to shout, but this is a very emotional thing with me, too, you see ... If you love the man, the least you owe him ... the least you owe him is the courtesy of letting him rest in peace.

[Sandra Serrano, Kennedy Volunteer] I felt like I was a criminal. That's my best description. I felt like I was a criminal, and I had done something wrong. "You didn't do that. You didn't see that. You weren't there. You're making all of this up. Why are you doing this?" Just a lot of browbeating. So, you know, during later years it crosses your mind, "Why did they invest so much in beating you up? If there was nothing there, why did they beat you up so much?" I remember thinking that he was lying, and then thinking, "No, he can't lie; he's the police. The police don't lie."

- *Who Killed Bobby Kennedy?: The Unsolved Murder of Robert F. Kennedy*, by Shane O'Sullivan

Kevin Barrett with Bill O'Reilly on "The Factor" (19 December 2006).

Kevin Barrett with Sean Hannity on "Hannity & Colmes" (11 July 2006).

GLOBE CRIME UPDATE

BLOCKBUSTER new technology will prove once and for all that Lee Harvey Oswald was not the lone assassin of John F. Kennedy and that more than three shots were fired at the president on that horrific day in Dallas, reveal sources.

"Not only can the analysis prove that more than three shots were fired, but it may reveal as many as eight to 10 shots felled the president," says professor James H. Fetzer of the University of Minnesota Duluth, who has investigated the Nov. 22, 1963 assassination for more than a decade.

The new equipment is a digital scanning device at Lawrence Berkeley Laboratory. Amazingly, it can detect the sounds of shots fired from a rifle with a silencer – and it's being used to analyze an audiotape recorded through a microphone on a police motorcycle in the president's motorcade.

JFK investigator Mark Lane – author of the 1966 book *Rush to Judgement* and one-time colleague of former New Orleans district attorney Jim Garrison, who probed the president's shooting – tells GLOBE the new audio equipment is like DNA tests in rape cases.

"It's a little like someone's found a new way to prove the world is round," Lane tells GLOBE. He also maintains that more than three shots were fired on that grim day.

"The results of five shots can be demonstrated," Lane says.

The controversial official explanation of JFK's shooting is that Lee Harvey Oswald fired three shots at the president from a window in the schoolbook depository building, while Kennedy was riding in an open car past a grassy knoll in Dallas' Dealey Plaza.

But Fetzer and many others believe the damage inflicted on the president had to have been caused by more than three bullets.

"Jack was hit at least four different times," says Fetzer. "He was hit in the throat from the front by a shot that passed through the windshield. He was hit in the back about 51/2 inches below the collar by a shot fired from a high trajectory, probably the top of the county records building.

"He was hit twice in the head – once in the back of the head and the other in the right temple by an exploding bullet, the shockwaves of which blew half his brains out the back of his head with such force that a motorcycle patrolman to the left rear thought he himself had been hit."

Professor Fetzer notes that a House committee in the '70s also disputed the three-shot Oswald theory. "A House committee 15 years later concluded that there might have been a fourth shot, based on acoustical evidence," says Fetzer, who has edited three books on the assassination.

"They actually set out an array of microphones in Dealey Plaza to ascertain whether shots fired from the vicinity of the book depository or the grassy knoll would show up the way some did in the audio recording.

"They did, which led the committee to conclude that there had been at least a fourth shot."

And Fetzer says it's been discovered that "all the basic evidence in the case has been subject to manipulation" and even films taken of the shooting have been altered.

"This analysis may show how many shots were fired and where they came from," says Lane, "but it's not going to show who pulled the trigger." – STEVE HERZ

Bee, Tim, and Hunk Barrett

NEWS

Barrett plans trip to Morocco to seek 9/11 hijacker

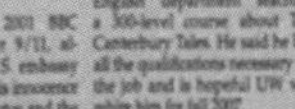

Conspiracy theorist also hopes to teach again at UW this fall

By Pedro Oliveira Jr.
State Reporter

Former University of Wisconsin lecturer Kevin Barrett said Thursday he will travel to Morocco in an attempt to find and interview a man accused of hijacking an airplane and flying it into the World Trade Center.

Barrett, widely known and criticized for his 9/11 conspiracy theory, announced at the state Capitol that he will head to Casablanca this Sunday and try to locate Saudi Arabian pilot Waleed al-Shehri.

The 9/11 Commission has said al-Shehri stabbed two unarmed flight attendants and crashed a plane into the World Trade Center five and a half years ago. According to Barrett, al-Shehri is alive and working in Morocco as a pilot.

"Since our government won't do its job and investigate what really happened on 9/11, I, as a U.S. citizen, will fly to Morocco and try to find out what's going on," said Barrett, who taught an introductory-level Islam course at UW in fall 2006.

According to a 2001 BBC report, a week after 9/11, al-Shehri visited the U.S. embassy in Morocco to claim his innocence and admitted the photos and the biography of the suicide hijacker were indeed his.

"Indications are that he was hired by the CIA to play a role and be a patsy for 9/11," Barrett said.

He intends to bring al-Shehri back to the U.S. or at least interview him and try to find out his true involvement with 9/11.

Despite criticism, Barrett said he is still hopeful he will prove his conspiracy theory and al-Shehri will come to the U.S. to testify in his favor.

Barrett is publicly associated with Scholars for 9/11 Truth, a private organization that believes the Sept. 11, 2001 terrorist attacks on the World Trade Center and Pentagon were an inside U.S. military job.

"I hope that in 10 years I'll be offered a chair in conspiracy theory studies at the University of Wisconsin," Barrett said. "But for now I'm just an unemployed Ph.D."

Barrett said he has applied for a position as a lecturer in UW's English department teachin[g] a 300-level course about Th[e] Canterbury Tales. He said he h[as] all the qualifications necessary f[or] the job and is hopeful UW w[ill] rehire him for fall 2007.

"The class has nothing to d[o] with Islam and there is no wa[y] I would be able to mention an[y] theories," Barrett added.

However, university officia[ls] said they have not receive[d] Barrett's application.

English department cha[ir] Michael Bernard-Donals denie[d] any knowledge regarding th[e] matter, adding he would be th[e] person to know if Barrett ha[d] indeed applied.

UW Assistant Director of Sta[te] Relations Don Nelson confirme[d] Bernard-Donals' account an[d] added UW "currently has n[o] intention to hire Kevin Barrett."

During the Thursday mornin[g] press conference, Barre[tt] challenged Rep. Stephen Nass, R-Whitewater, to a debate regardin[g] 9/11, but the representative wa[s] out of the office for the day.

"Barrett's action today prov[es] again why he should not b[e] employed by any university i[n] this state," said Mike Mikalse[n], a spokesperson for Nass. "He [is] only looking for media coverage

Former lecturer Kevin Barrett discusses his trip to Morocco, hoping to find a 9/11 hijacker.

[Chapter 37] Kevin: OBL buried at sea, Obama in the CIA

"When you know that governments are capable of doing this, one shouldn't be surprised about anything that governments do."
- William Pepper, attorney for the King family, commenting on "Operation Northwoods," in which the U.S. government planned an attack on United States civilians in order to instigate the rage for an attack on Cuba

KEVIN:

[On Obama announcing the killing of Osama bin Laden]

I was here at my house in Wisconsin, in Lone Rock, and I got the news on the Internet and was able to respond very, very quickly, and so I put up what I still think is a really good post at my *Truth Jihad* blog about that, pointing out that the information we were being given at that point was contradictory and completely insane. We threw him in the ocean according to Islamic burial custom. It doesn't get crazier than that.

There's no such thing.

The Islamic, it's true there is a kind of Islamic way of dealing with people's bodies when they die, which is that you immediately wash the body and immediately bury them in the earth. Anything other than that, throwing in the ocean, or cremating, is very bad.

So when they announced that they threw him in the ocean according to Islamic burial custom, this was a gratuitous thumbing their nose at Muslims or anyone who knows anything about Islam.

[What about Obama?]

I'm sure Obama's been groomed by the CIA for a long time. Webster Tarpley has two books out on Obama that are must reading. One is called *The Postmodern Coup*, the other is the unauthorized biography.

It's pretty obvious that Obama, if he wasn't CIA all his life, which is quite possible because it looks like his mother and stepfather were CIA, but, if he wasn't, he certainly was by the time he got to Columbia University.

At Columbia University he was living quite mysteriously, not being seen by anybody, even his roommate. Who knows what kind of training he was getting. He was in contact with Dr. Zbigniew Brzezinski, who was his Russian teacher.

Obama was majoring in Russian studies and Brzezinski was head of the Russian program at Columbia. Brzezinski, of course, is one of the leading national security strategy figures in the world, so Obama was obviously recruited, and his first job out of college was as a CIA agent.

He went to Pakistan probably under some kind of fake I.D., possibly including his Indonesian passport, and as Wayne Madsen points out, this is a real citizenship issue with Obama; it's not so much the birth certificate issue, but the real issue is Obama almost certainly has Indonesian citizenship, and as a dual citizen, I don't believe he's eligible to be President.

Of course that doesn't stop all of the Israeli dual citizens who are infesting our government, but I don't think any of them has ever been President.

I guess Lieberman probably would have been the closest if he had been, if Gore had been allowed to claim his victory in 2000.

So, Obama is obviously CIA.

His whole path has been greased by these people. After he did his CIA work with that CIA front company out of Columbia University, he went to Harvard and was just given the position as president of the *Law Review*.

He's like a made man.

Then they move him to Chicago to be a "community organizer". And when he starts running for office everything goes his way.

His opponents just start dropping out and bowing out and these scandals show up that knock the opponents aside.

It's like he's in a video game racing down the street and everybody's just diving out of his way. Everything's been arranged for him.

His whole path has been set out and greased by his intelligence world contacts, so he's been a made man, probably from the day of his birth, but certainly since his days at Columbia.

He's America's fourth consecutive CIA President, because both of the Presidents Bush have been CIA, and of course they're not only CIA they're also ultra-corrupt drug smuggling mafiosi CIA, and then Bill Clinton is also drug smuggling mafiosi CIA.

Bill Clinton ran the cocaine import end of the CIA's Central American coke-smuggling business that went through Mena, Arkansas and all of that; the vast amounts of cash at play during that period probably have a lot to do with the whole Whitewater investigation and the death of Vince Foster and all these scandals that dog Bill Clinton. People on the left quickly dismissed all this as a giant right-wing conspiracy theory.

These were all probably pretty much true, and the real issue was that Bill Clinton was a CIA cocaine smuggler. So, basically, every President since Reagan has been a CIA agent, and of course Reagan's White House was heavily controlled by Bush the vice president, who was a CIA agent. So we have to go all the way back to Jimmy Carter to find a President who was not a CIA agent and placed in the Oval Office by the CIA.

[Chapter 38] Jim: Thinking About "Conspiracy Theories"

"Anyone who has proclaimed violence his method inexorably must choose lying as his principle."

- Aleksander Solzhenitsyn

-

THINKING ABOUT "CONSPIRACY THEORIES": 9/11 and JFK
by James H. Fetzer, Ph.D.

ABSTRACT

The phrase "conspiracy theory" harbors an ambiguity, since conspiracies are widespread and theories about them need not be mere speculations. The application of scientific reasoning in the form of inference to the best explanation, applied to the relevant evidence, establishes that the official account of the events of 9/11 cannot be sustained. Likelihood measures of evidential support establish that the WTC was brought down through the use of controlled demolition and that the Pentagon was not hit by a Boeing 757. Since these hypotheses have high likelihoods and the only alternatives have likelihoods that range from zero to null (because they are not even physically possible), assuming that sufficient evidence has become available and "settled down", these conclusions not only provide better explanations for the data but are proven beyond reasonable doubt.

1. "Conspiracy Theories"

We need to come to grips with conspiracies. Conspiracies are as American as apple pie. All they require is that two or more persons collaborate in actions to bring about illegal ends. When two guys knock off a 7/11 store, they are engaged in a conspiracy. Most conspiracies in our country are economic, such as Enron, WorldCom, and now Halliburton as it exploits the opportunities for amassing profits in Iraq. Insider trading is a simple example, since investors and brokers collaborate to benefit from privileged information. Ordinarily, however, the media does not describe them as "conspiracies".[1] The two most important conspiracies in our history are surely those involving JFK and 9/11.

One fascinating aspect of 9/11 is that the official story involves collaboration between some nineteen persons in order to bring about illegal ends and thus obviously qualifies as a "conspiracy theory". When critics of the government offer an alternative account that implicates key figures of the government in 9/11, that obviously qualifies as a "conspiracy theory", too. But what matters now is that we are confronted by alternative accounts of what happened on 9/11, both of which qualify as "conspiracy theories". It is therefore no longer rational to dismiss one of them as a "conspiracy theory" in favor of the other. The question becomes, Which of two "conspiracy theories" is more defensible?

There is a certain ingenuity in combining "conspiracy" with "theory", because the word "theory" can be used in the weak sense of a speculation, conjecture, or guess to denigrate one account or another for political or ideological reasons without acknowledging that "theory" can also be used in the stronger sense of an empirically testable, explanatory hypothesis. Consider Newton's theory of gravitation or Einstein's theory of relativity as instances. The psychological ploy is to speak as though all "theories" were guesses, none of which ought to be taken seriously. Various different cases, however, can present very different problems. Evidence can be scarce, for example, or alternatives might be difficult to imagine.

Moreover, there are several reasons why different persons might arrive at very different conclusions in a given case. These include that they are not considering the same set of alternative explanations or that they are not employing the same rules of reasoning. The objectivity of science derives, not from transcending our human frailties, but from its inter-subjectivity.[2] Different scientists confronting the same alternatives, the same evidence, and the same rules of reasoning should arrive at all and only the same conclusions about which hypotheses are acceptable, which are rejectable, and which should be held in suspense. And, in the search for truth, scientific reasoning must be based upon all the available relevant evidence, a condition called the requirement of total evidence, and is otherwise fallacious.[3]

2. Scientific Reasoning

Scientific reasoning characterizes a systematic pattern of thought involving four stages or steps, namely: puzzlement, speculation, adaptation, and explanation.[4] Something occurs that does not fit comfortably into our background knowledge and expectations and thus becomes a source of puzzlement. Alternative theories that might possibly explain that occurrence are advanced for consideration. The available relevant evidence is brought to bear upon those hypotheses and their measures of evidential support are ascertained, where additional evidence may be obtained on the basis of observation, measurement, and experiment. The weight of the evidence is assessed, where the hypothesis with the strongest support is the preferable hypothesis. When sufficient evidence becomes available, the preferable hypothesis also becomes acceptable in the tentative and fallible fashion of science.[5]

Among the most important distinctions that need to be drawn in reasoning about alternative scenarios for historical events of the kind that matter here are those between different kinds of necessity, possibility and impossibility. [6] Our language imposes some constraints upon the possible as functions of grammar and meaning. In ordinary English, for example, a freshman is a student, necessarily, because to be a freshman is to be a student in the first year of a four-year curriculum. By the same token, it is impossible to be a freshman and not be a student.

The first is a logical necessity, the second a logical impossibility. Since a conspiracy requires at least two conspirators, if there were not at least two conspirators, it is not logically possible that a conspiracy was involved; if there were, then necessarily there was.

More interesting than logical necessities, possibilities and impossibilities, however, are physical necessities, possibilities and impossibilities.[7] These are determined in relation to the laws of nature, which, unlike laws of society, cannot be violated, cannot be changed, and require no enforcement. If (pure) water freezes at 32° F at sea level atmospheric pressure, for example, then it is physically necessary for a sample of (pure) water to freeze when its temperature falls below 32° F at that pressure.

Analogously, under those same conditions, that a sample of (pure) water would not freeze when its temperature falls below 32° F is physically impossible. And when a sample of (pure) water is not frozen at that pressure, it is justifiable to infer that it is therefore not at a temperature below its freezing point of 32° F.[8]

Laws of nature are the core of science and provide the principles on the basis of which the occurrence of events can be systematically explained, predicted, and retrodicted.[9] They therefore have an important role to play in reasoning about specific cases in which those principles make a difference. In legal reasoning, for example, the phrase, "beyond a reasonable doubt", means a standard of proof that requires subjective conviction that is equal to "moral certainty".[10]

In the context of scientific reasoning, the meaning of that same phrase is better captured by the objective standard that an explanation is "beyond a reasonable doubt" when no alternative is reasonable. Notice that the falsity of hypotheses that describe the occurrence of events that are physically impossible is beyond a reasonable doubt.[11]

3. Probabilities and Likelihoods

An appropriate measure of the weight of the evidence is provided by likelihoods, where the likelihood of an hypothesis h, given evidence e, is determined by the probability of evidence e, if that hypothesis were true. [12] Hypotheses should be tested in pairs, h1 and h2, where the relationship between the hypotheses and the evidence may be regarded as that between possible causes and effects. Thus, suppose in a game of chance, you were confronted with a long series of outcomes that would have been highly improbable if the coin were symmetrical (if the dice were fair, or if the deck was normal). If such a run would be far more probable if the coin were bent (if the dice were loaded, if the deck was stacked), then the likelihood that the coin is bent (the dice are loaded, the deck is stacked) is much higher than the likelihood the coin is symmetrical (dice are fair, deck is normal).

A better grasp of probabilistic reasoning follows from distinguishing between two kinds of probabilities as properties of the world. The first is relative frequencies, which simply represent "how often" things of one kind occur in relation to things of another kind.

This includes averages of many different varieties, such as the average grade on a philosophy exam in a course on critical thinking. The second is causal propensities, which reflect "how strong" the tendencies are for outcomes of a certain kind to be brought about under specific conditions.[13]

Frequencies are brought about by propensities, which may differ from one case to another. When the class averages 85 on the first exam, that does not mean every student scored 85 on the exam. It might even be the case that no student actually had that score. But each student's own score was an effect of his propensity to score on that exam.

It can be easy to confuse "how often" with "how strong", but some examples help to bring their difference home. Canoeing on the Brule River in Wisconsin is not a hazardous pastime, but a 76-year old woman was killed on 15 July 1993 when a tree that had been gnawed by a beaver fell and landed on her.

The tree fell and hit the woman on the head, as she and her daughter paddled past it.[14] The tree was about 18 inches in diameter and 30 to 40 feet tall and stood about 10 to 20 feet up the river bank. So while hundreds and hundreds of canoeists had paddled down the Brule River before and escaped completely unscathed, this woman had the misfortune to be killed during "a freak accident".

It was improbable in terms of its relative frequency of occurrence yet, given those particular conditions, the causal propensity for death to result as an effect of that specific event was great.

When the same causally relevant conditions are subject to replication, then the relative frequencies that result tend to be reliable evidence of the strength of the causal propensity that produced them. But when those conditions can vary, how often an outcome occurs may not indicate the strength of that tendency on any specific trial.

We commonly assume smoking diminishes life spans, which is usually true. But a 21-year old man was confronted by three thugs who, when he failed to respond quickly enough, shot him.

He might have been killed, but a metal cigarette lighter deflected the .25-caliber bullet and he lived.[15]

Once you appreciate the difference, three principles that relate probabilities of these kinds become apparent, namely: that propensities cause frequencies; that frequencies are evidence for propensities; and that propensities can explain frequencies. But it depends on the constancy of the relevant conditions from one trial to another.[16]

4. The Case of JFK

Conspiracy theories have to be assessed using principles of scientific reasoning. In the case of JFK, the difficulty has not been a dearth of evidence but sorting through the superabundance of conflicting and even contradictory physical, medical, witness, and photographic "evidence" to ascertain which is authentic and which is not. Something qualifies as evidence in relation to an hypothesis just in case its presence or absence or its truth or falsity makes a difference to the truth or falsity of that hypothesis. But "evidence" can be planted, faked, or fabricated to provide a false foundation for reasoning.[17]

That has proven to be true here. Once the task of sorting things out has been performed, it becomes relatively simple to draw appropriate inferences about the general character of the assassination on the basis of what we have learned about the cover-up,

Early studies by Harold Weisberg, Mark Lane, and Sylvia Meagher, for example, were instrumental in establishing that *The Warren Report* (1964) could not be sustained on the basis of evidence available even then (Weisberg 1965, Lane 1966, Meagher 1967). According to the official account, a lone assassin fired three shots from the sixth floor of the Texas School Book Depositor Building, scoring two hits.

One of those hits is supposed to have entered at the base of the President's neck, passed through without hitting any bony structures and exited just above his tie. It then entered the back of Governor John Connally, who was seated in front of him, shattered a rib, exited his chest and injured his right wrist before being deflected into his left thigh. The bullet alleged to have followed this trajectory was later "found" in virtually pristine condition.

This sequence of events appears so improbable that the missile that caused all of this damage has come to be known as the "magic bullet".[18] The jacket and the shirt JFK was wearing both have holes about 5½ inches below the collar. An autopsy diagram verified by the President's personal physician shows a wound at that same location. A second diagram prepared by an FBI observer shows the wound to the back below the wound to the throat. The death certificate executed by the President's personal physician also places that wound at the level of the third thoracic vertebra, about 5½ inches below the collar. Even photographs taken during re-enactments of the shooting show patches on stand-ins for the President at that location.[19]

Although *The Warren Report* tries to imply that the "magic bullet" theory is not indispensable to its conclusions, that is a gross misrepresentation. No less an authority than Michael Baden, M.D., who chaired the forensic panel that reviewed the medical evidence when the case was reinvestigated by the House Select Committee on Assassinations in 1977-78, has remarked that, if the "magic bullet" theory is false, then there had to have been at least six shots from three different directions.[20] An especially disturbing aspect of this situation is that all the evidence described here was not only available to the HSCA in 1977-78 but had been discussed quite extensively in those early books by Weisberg, Lane, and Meagher (Weisberg 1965, Lane 1966, Meagher 1967). The government has simply ignored their discoveries.[21]

5. Recent Scientific Studies

Since the release of Oliver Stone's film, *JFK*, in 1992, research on the assassination evidence (conducted by the best qualified persons who have ever studied the case)[22] has revealed that the autopsy X-rays have been altered in several ways, that another brain was substituted for that of JFK during its examination, and that the home movie ostensibly taken by a spectator named Abraham Zapruder has not only been extensively edited but actually recreated by reshooting each of its frames (Fetzer 1998, 2002, 2003).[23]

The film was redone using techniques of optical printing and special effects, which allow combining any background with any foreground to create any impression that one desires, which included removing series of frames that would have given the plot away, such as that the driver pulled the limousine to the left and stopped after shots began to be fired.[24]

The alterations of the medical evidence include "patching" a massive defect in the back of the head caused by a shot from in front, in the case of the lateral cranial X-ray, and adding a 6.5 mm metallic slice to the anterior/posterior X-ray, in an evident attempt to implicate a 6.5 mm weapon in the assassination, which have been exposed by means of optical density studies.[25]

Adapting a simple technique from physics, David W. Mantik, M.D., Ph.D., on the basis of objective measurements and repeatable experiments, has been able to prove that the JFK autopsy X-rays are not authentic. And, by even simpler comparisons between descriptions from experienced and professional physicians at Parkland Hospital describing extensive damage to the brain of JFK, Robert Livingston, M.D., a world authority on the human brain, has concluded that the diagrams and photographs of a brain that are stored in the National Archives must be of a brain other than that of John Fitzgerald Kennedy.[26]

The evidence establishing the recreation of the Zapruder film comes from diverse sources, including that frame 232 was published in LIFE with physically impossible features; that a mistake was made in introducing the Stemmons Freeway sign into the recreated version; that the "blob" and blood spray was added on to frame 313; that the driver's head turns occur too rapidly to even be humanly possible; that the Governor's left turn has been edited out of the film; that Erwin Swartz, an associate of Abraham Zapruder, reported having observed blood and brains blown out to the back and left when he viewed the original film; that several Secret Service agents observed brains and blood on the trunk of the limousine; that others have viewed another and more complete version of the film; and that Homer McMahon, an expert at the National Photographic Interpretation Center, studied a very different film on that very night.[27]

Other evidence that has long been available to serious students of the death of JFK includes multiple indications of Secret Service complicity in setting him up for the hit.[28] There was no welding of the manhole covers; no coverage of open windows; the motorcycles were placed in a non-protective formation; agents did not ride on the limousine; an improper route, including a turn of more than 90°, was utilized; the vehicles were in an improper sequence; the limousine slowed nearly to a halt at Houston and Elm; the limousine was actually brought to a stop after bullets began to be fired; the agents were non-responsive; brains and blood were washed from the limousine at Parkland before the President was even pronounced dead; the autopsy X-rays and photographs were taken from the morgue; and the limousine was sent to

Ford Motor Company, stripped down and completely rebuilt, on 25 November 1963.[29]

6. Patterns of Reasoning

Records released by the ARRB have shown that Gerald Ford (R-MI), a member of the commission, had the description of the wound changed from "his uppermost back", which was already an exaggeration, to "the base of the back of his neck" to make the "magic bullet" theory more plausible (Fetzer 1998, p. 177). And Mantik has now proven that no bullet could have taken the trajectory ascribed to the "magic bullet" because cervical vertebrae intervene (Fetzer 2000, pp. 3-4). So the vastly influential accounts of the death of JFK that take it for granted as their foundation – *The Warren Report*, *The House Select Committee on Assassinations Report*, and Gerald Posner's *Case Closed* – are not only false but provably false and not even anatomically possible.

The wound to his throat and the wounds to Connally have to be explained on the basis of other shots and other shooters. We now know that JFK was hit four times – in the throat from in front; in the back from behind; and twice in the head: in the back of the head from behind and then in the right temple from in front.[30] We know Connally was hit at least once and another shot missed and injured a bystander. It thus turns out that Michael Baden, M.D., was correct when he observed that, if the "magic bullet" theory is false, then there had to have been at least six shots from at least three different directions. The theory is not even anatomically possible and, with at least one to Connally and one miss, there had to have been at least six shots.[31]

Anatomical impossibility, of course, is one kind of physical impossibility, insofar as humans are vertebrates with vertebrae, including those of the cervical variety.

The wound observations of the attending physicians at Parkland and at Bethesda were cleverly concealed by Arlen Specter, now a United States Senator from Pennsylvania, but then a junior counsel to the Warren Commission. Specter did not ask the doctors what they had observed or what they had inferred from what they had observed, but instead posed a hypothetical question: "If we assume that the bullet entered the base of the back of the neck, traversed the neck without impacting any bony structures, and came out just above the level of the tie", he asked, "would that be consistent with describing the neck wound as a wound of exit?"

In response to this trivial question, they dutifully replied that it would be, but Malcolm Perry, M.D., who had performed a tracheotomy through the wound and had described it three times as a wound of entry during a press conference, added that he was not in the position to vouch for or to verify the assumptions he had been asked to make, which of course was true.[32]

The discoveries about the X-rays, the brain, and the Zapruder film are also powerful. What makes these discoveries so significant as evidence is that none of these things could possibly have been done by Lee Harvey Oswald, the alleged assassin, who was either incarcerated or already dead. Other theories, moreover, can be rejected on similar grounds.

The Mafia, for example, could not have extended its reach into the Bethesda Naval Hospital to alter X-rays under the control of agents of the Secret Service, medical officers of the United States Navy, and the President's personal physician. Neither pro nor anti-Castro Cubans could have substituted one brain for another.

Nor could the KGB, which probably had the same ability as Hollywood and the CIA to fabricate movies, have been able to gain possession of the Zapruder film to subject it to alteration. Which raises the question, who had the power to make these things happen? Given what we know now, the answer is no longer difficult to discern. It required involvement at the highest levels of the American government.

Insofar as the "magic bullet" theory describes the occurrence of events that are not only provably false but actually physically impossible, that it cannot possibly be true is beyond reasonable doubt. Moreover, the discovery that the autopsy X-rays have been altered, that another brain has been substituted, and that the Zapruder film has been recreated imply a very meticulous and carefully planned cover-up in which the alleged assassin could not have been involved. The identification of more than a dozen indications of Secret Service complicity means that the evidence has "settled down".[33]

The probability of the evidence on the lone-assassin hypothesis does not even rise to zero, since it posits a physically impossible sequence, whose value is better set at null.[34]

The probability of the evidence on a conspiracy scenario, by comparison, is extremely high, depending upon the competence and the power of those who carried it out. There is in fact no reasonable alternative to a fairly large-scale conspiracy in the death of our 35th President, which means that it has been established beyond a reasonable doubt.[35]

7. The Case of 9/11

It has taken nearly 40 years for the deception to have been decisively settled on the basis of objective scientific evidence. In the case of 9/11, however, we are vastly more fortunate. As a consequence of inquiries by Nafeez Ahmed (2002), Thierry Meyssan (2002), Paul Thompson (2004), Michael Ruppert (2004), and David Ray Griffin (2004, 2005), among others, we already know that the official account of 9/11 cannot possibly be correct. That account contends that 19 Arabs, with feeble ability to pilot aircraft, hijacked four airliners and then executed demanding maneuvers in order to impact the World Trade Center and the Pentagon;[36] that the damage created by their impact combined with the heat from burning jet fuel brought down WTC1 and WTC2; that WTC7 was the first building in history to be brought down by fire alone; and that the Pentagon was struck by United Flight 77, which was a Boeing 757.[37] The basic problem with this "conspiracy theory", as in the case of JFK, is that its truth would violate laws of physics and engineering that cannot be transgressed.

The extremely high melting point of structural steel (about 2,800° F) is far above the maximum (around 1,700° F) that could have been produced by jet fuel under optimal conditions. Underwriters Laboratories had certified the steel used in the World Trade Center to 2,000° F for up to six hours.[38] Even lower maximum temperatures result after factoring in insulation, such as asbestos, and the availability of oxygen.[39] Since steel is a good conductor, any heat applied to one part of the structure would have been dissipated to other parts. WTC1, the North Tower, was hit first at 8:46 AM/ET and collapsed at 10:29 AM/ET, whereas the South Tower, hit second at 9:03 AM/ET, collapsed at 9:59 AM/ET. They were exposed to fires for roughly an hour and a half and an hour, respectively. Insofar as most of the fuel was burned off in the gigantic fireballs that accompanied the initial impacts, that these towers were brought down by fuel fires that melted the steel is not just improbable but physically impossible.[40]

Most Americans may not realize that no steel-structure high-rise building has ever collapsed from fire in the history of civil engineering, either before or after 9/11. If we assume that those fires have occurred in a wide variety of buildings under a broad range of conditions, that evidence suggests that these buildings do not have a propensity to collapse as an effect of fire. That makes an alternative explanation, especially the use of powerful explosives in a controlled demolition, an hypothesis that must be taken seriously. Indeed, there appear to be at least ten features of the collapse of the Twin Towers that are expectable effects of controlled demolitions but not from fires following aircraft impacts.[41] They include that the buildings fell about the rate of free fall; that they both collapsed virtually straight down (and into their own "footprints"); that almost all the concrete was turned into very fine dust; that the collapses were complete, leaving virtually no steel support columns standing; that photographic records of their collapse show "demolition waves" occurring just ahead of the collapsing floors; that most of the beams and columns fell in sections of 30' to 40' in length; that firemen reported hearing sequences of explosions as they took place; that seismological events were recorded coincident with aircraft impacts and again when the buildings collapsed; and that pools of molten metal were observed in the subbasements for weeks after.[42]

The situation here is analogous to what we encountered with multiple indications of Secret Service complicity in setting up JFK for the hit. Suppose, as before, we adopt a value of 1 time in 10 for any one of these features to occur as a causal consequence of an aircraft impact and ensuing fire. We know that is a fantastically high number, since this has never occurred before or since. But, for the sake of argument, let us assume it. Then if we treat these features as having propensities that are independent and equal, for those ten features to have occurred on any single event of this kind would have a propensity equal to 1 over 1 followed by ten zeros, that is, 1/10,000,000,000, which is one chance in ten billion! Of course, since there were two such events – given TWC1 and TWC2 – the probability that they would both display these same ten features on the very same occasion is equal to the product of one in ten billion times one in ten billion, which is 1 over 1 followed by twenty zeros, or 1/100,000,000,000,000,000,000. This is a very small number. And these calculations assume values that are far too high.[43]

8. 9/11: The Pentagon

The Pentagon case should be the most accessible to study, since it only depends upon observations and measurements, which are the most basic elements available for any scientific investigation. Indeed, photos taken prior to the collapse of the Pentagon's upper floors supply evidence that, whatever hit the Pentagon, it cannot possibly have been a Boeing 757.[44] The plane was 155' long, with a wing span of 125' and stood 36' high with its wheels retracted. The initial point of impact (prior to the collapse of the floors above) was only about 10' high and 16-17' wide, about the size of the double-doors on a mansion. A meticulous engineering study with careful measurements has been conducted that offers powerful evidence that the official story cannot possibly be correct. The damage done appears to have been inflicted by a smaller aircraft, such as an F-16, or by the impact of a cruise missile, as an alternative possibility.[45] The amount of damage is simply not consistent with what would have occurred had the building been hit by a plane with the mass and the dimensions of a Boeing 757.

Unofficial variations on the official account include that the Boeing 757 first hit the ground and then bounced into the building, that the plane's engines plowed across the lawn before it entered the building, or that its right wing-tip hit and caused it to "cartwheel" into the Pentagon.[46]

None of these accounts is remotely consistent with the smooth, green, and unblemished lawn. It is all the more remarkable, therefore, that the Secretary of Defense had the lawn resurfaced as though it had been damaged during the attack. Photographs of the lawn were taken immediately after the attack that demonstrate it was not damaged at all.[47] Anyone who only viewed the lawn after its reconstruction, however, would be more likely to accept the official account. And it is of more than passing interest that far more damage could have been caused by less demanding maneuvers if the plane had been crashed through the roof of the building as opposed to hitting a newly reconstructed wing that was largely bereft of personnel and records – as though the "terrorists" wanted to inflict minimal damage.

Had a Boeing 757 hit the Pentagon, it would have left massive debris from the wings, the fuselage, the engines, the seats, the luggage, the bodies, and the tail. Take a look at photographs taken shortly after the impact before the upper floors fell, however, and you will observe none of the above: no wings, no engines, no seats, no luggage, no bodies, no tail. It does not require rocket science – or even the calculation of any probabilities – to recognize that something that large cannot possibly have fit through an opening that small and left no remnants in the form of wings sheared off, debris scattered about, and so on.

One piece of fuselage alleged to have come from the plane appears to have been planted evidence, which was moved around and photographed in more than one location.[48] But if massive debris from the fuselage, wings, engines, seats, luggage, bodies, and tail were not present at the scene, the scene cannot have been of the crash of a 757. The argument involved is about as simple as they come. The principle of logic involved is known as modus tollens, which states that, if p then q, but not q, then not p. If q must be true when p is true, but q is not true, then p is not true, either. This is an elementary rule of deductive reasoning, employment of which is fundamental to scientific investigations.

If you want to test an hypothesis, deduce what must be true if that hypothesis is true and attempt to ascertain whether those consequences are true. If they are not true, then the hypothesis is false. Q.E.D. If a Boeing 757 had hit the Pentagon, as the government has alleged, it would have left debris of specific kinds and quantities.

Photographs and measurements show no debris of those kinds and quantities. As long as these photographs are authentic and those measurements are correct – which concerns the quality of the evidence for not q and appears to be rather difficult to dispute – then no Boeing 757 hit the Pentagon.[49] Q.E.D.

9. What really happened?

The remnants of the single engine found inside offer clues as to what actually hit the Pentagon. Boeing 757s are powered by two Pratt & Whitney turbofan engines, with front-rotor elements about 42" in diameter and high-pressure rear stages that are less than 21" in diameter.

The part found was less than 24" in diameter and, it turns out, actually matches, not the turbofan engine, but the front-hub assembly of the front compressor for the JT8D turbojet engine used in the A-3 Sky Warrior jet fighter.[50] Since cruise missiles have a 20" diameter, moreover, they appear to be too small to accommodate this component. It follows that the Pentagon was not hit by a Boeing 757 or by a cruise missile but, given this evidence, was probably struck by an A-3 Sky Warrior instead.

The available relevant evidence is not even consistent with the government's official account, which deserves to be rejected. Its likelihood given the evidence is actually null, while the alternative A-3 hypothesis makes the relevant evidence highly probable and has high likelihood as a clearly preferable explanation.

This conjecture, which the evidence suggests, receives additional support from other sources. Two civilian defense contract employees, for example, have reported that A-3 Sky Warriors were covertly retrofitted with remote control systems and missile-firing systems at the Ft. Collins-Loveland Municipal Airport, a small civilian airport in Colorado, during the months prior to 9/11.

According to information they supplied, "separate military contractors – working independently at different times – retrofitted Douglas A-3 Sky Warriors with updated missiles, Raytheon's Global Hawk unmanned aerial vehicle (UAV) remote control systems, new engines and fire control systems, transponders, and radio-radar-navigation systems – a total makeover – seemingly for an operation more important than their use as a simple missile testing platform for defense contractor Hughes-Raytheon."[51] These reports substantiate the alternative.

If a small fighter jet rather than a Boeing 757 had hit the Pentagon, that would tend to explain the small impact point, the lack of massive external debris, and a hole in the inner ring of the building, which the fragile nose of a Boeing 757 could not have created. It would also suggest why parts of a plane were carried off by servicemen, since they might have made the identification of the aircraft by type apparent and falsified the official account.[52] A small fighter also accommodates the report from Danielle O'Brien, an air traffic controller, who said of the aircraft that hit, "Its speed, maneuverability, the way that it turned, we all thought in the radar room – all of us experienced air traffic controllers – that it was a military plane."[53]

Nothing moves or maneuvers more like a military plane, such as a jet fighter, than a military plane or a jet fighter, which could also explain how it was able to penetrate some of the most strongly defended air space in the world – by emitting a friendly transponder signal.

Another line of argument suggests that the evidence has "settled down". Confirming that the engine found at the Pentagon was indeed a JT8D, Jon Carlson has proposed that the plane used in the attack must have been a Boeing 737, which also uses them.[54]

That contradicts the use of a 757, of course, but it would also be vulnerable to a parallel argument about the absence of debris of the right kinds and quantities. Interestingly, both are incompatible with the smooth and unblemished landscape, which should have been massively disrupted by the wake turbulence that would have been generated by any plane of those dimensions at that low height, a phenomenon even known to rip tiles off roofs at ordinary altitudes.[55]

These and still other lines of argument establish that, whatever hit the Pentagon, it cannot have been a Boeing 757 (or a 737). It may be that controversy over this specific point has been so strenuous because it offers such a clear and obvious indication of the government's complicity.

10. Preferability vs. Acceptability

New York events require only slightly more sophisticated analysis. We know that the government's account posits a physically impossible sequence of events whose probability is null. So a probability of zero is merely a close approximation to null. If the buildings were brought down by controlled demolition, by contrast, then the steel would not have had to have melted or to be significantly weakened from heat, but would have been blown apart by the precise placement of explosives. And the propensity that the building would have collapsed at about the rate of free fall and that there would have been enough energy to pulverize concrete would have been very high.

Since the buildings did fall at approximately the rate of free fall and there was enough energy to convert concrete into fine dust, the evidential support for this alternative is very high. It would have been quite easily confirmed by metallurgical study of what remained of the structural steel, but it was rapidly removed and sent to China by an extremely efficient company that's named "Controlled Demolition, Inc."

The measure of evidential support here can be captured more precisely by the use of likelihoods. The likelihood of an hypothesis (h1), the official account, on the basis of the available evidence e, is equal to the probability of e, if that hypothesis were true. The probability of the evidence as an effect of the official account of the cause, we have found, is approximately zero. The likelihood of the alternative, (h2), the demolition hypothesis, on the available evidence e, by contrast, is extremely high. One hypothesis is preferable to another when the likelihood of that hypothesis on the available evidence is higher than the likelihood of its alternative. Insofar as the likelihood of (h1) on e is very low, while the likelihood of (h2) on e is very high, the demolition hypothesis (h2) is obviously preferable to alternative (h1), based upon e.

A preferable hypothesis is not acceptable until sufficient evidence becomes available, which occurs when the evidence "settles down" or points in the same direction. Any concerns on this score are resolvable by adding that there were vast pools of molten metal in the sub-basements of WTC1 and WTC2 for weeks after their collapse.[56] This would be inexplicable on (h1) but highly probable on (h2).

If any more proof were necessary, we know that Larry Silverstein, who leased the WTC, said that WTC7 was "pulled", which means it was brought down using explosives.[57] This occurred hours after the other buildings came down. No plane ever hit WTC7 and its collapse was perfectly symmetrical and again occurred at virtually free-fall speed. The building could not have been "pulled" without prior placement of explosives. The collapses of WTC1 and of WTC2 were very similar and equally suggestive of controlled demolition.

A new documentary, *Loose Change*, includes a photographic record that offers very powerful substantiation of the controlled demolition of WTC1 and WTC2 by providing additional evidence that explosives were used to bring them down. The videotape includes eyewitness reports of firemen and other first responders, who heard what they reported to be the sounds of sequences of explosions in rapid sequence ("Boom! Boom! Boom!").[58] It displays the effects of massive explosions that occurred at the subbasement level just before the aircraft impacts, recorded at 0.9 and 0.7 on the Richter scale, and events of magnitudes of 2.1 and 2.3 of 10 and of 8 seconds duration, respectively, concurrent with their collapse.[59] And it also explores a remarkable, odd series of "security related" interruptions of security cameras and other safeguards, which involved vacating large portions of WTC1 and of WTC2 for intervals that would have allowed for the placement of explosives to have occurred. This remarkable documentary dramatically contradicts the government's account.

11. "Beyond a Reasonable Doubt"

A conclusion may be described as having been established "beyond a reasonable doubt" when no alternative conclusion is reasonable. In this case, hypothesis (h2), controlled demolition, can explain the available evidence with high probability and consequently possesses a corresponding high likelihood.60 But hypothesis (h1), the government's account, can explain virtually none of the available evidence and has an extremely low likelihood.

Indeed, strictly speaking, given that it even requires violations of laws of physics and engineering, the likelihood of (h1) is actually null. When seismic, molten metal, and eyewitness evidence – and especially the collapse of WTC7, which was never hit by any plane – are taken into account, the evidence also appears to have "settled down". Thus, a scientific analysis of the alternatives on the basis of the available evidence demonstrates that the government's account of the collapse due to heat from fires cannot be sustained and that the alternative of a controlled demolition has been objectively established beyond a reasonable doubt.

This conclusion receives support from other directions, moreover, since the project manager who was responsible for supervising the construction of these buildings has observed that they were constructed to withstand the impact from the largest commercial airplanes then available – namely, Boeing 707s – and that the structural design was so sophisticated airplane crashes would have been analogous to sticking pencils through mosquito netting.[61] It's not as though the possibility of events of this kind had never been given consideration in the construction of 110 story buildings! This observation reinforces the conclusion that the government's account is not just "less defensible" than the alternative. The likelihood of the demolition hypothesis is very high, while the likelihood of the government's account is actually null, which is a value that is less than zero. This means that the official story cannot possibly be true.

It follows that, when these "theories" are subject to the kinds of systematic appraisal appropriate to empirically testable alternative explanations, one of them turns out to be overwhelmingly preferable to the other. Since they are both "conspiracy theories", however, we have discovered that at least some "conspiracy theories" are subject to empirical test and that, based upon likelihood measures of evidential support, one of them is strongly confirmed while the other is decisively disproven. Indeed, strictly speaking, the inconsistency of the government's account with natural laws makes it physically impossible, a nice example of the falsification of a theory on the basis of its incompatibility with scientific knowledge. So some "conspiracy theories" are not only subject to empirical test but have actually been falsified by the available evidence.[62]

The fact that the government's "conspiracy theory" cannot be sustained needs to be widely disseminated to the American people. Not all "theories" are mere guesses and many of them are empirically testable. In this case, elementary considerations have proven that one "conspiracy theory" is false (indeed, as we have discovered, it cannot possibly be true), while the alternative appears to be true (on the basis of measures of probability and likelihood). Since the (h1) alternative to (h2) is unreasonable and no other alternative appears remotely plausible, the demolition hypothesis (h2) has actually been established beyond a reasonable doubt. That, I believe, is something that the American people need to understand. With only slight exaggeration, this government makes a practice of lying to us all the time. It has lied about tax cuts, minimized the threat of global warming, offered a series of lies about the reasons for going to war in Iraq, and on dozens of other major issues. Some lies are bigger than others. This one – about the causes and the effects of 9/11 – counts as a monstrosity!

12. Who had the Power?

The observation that the government's official account cannot be sustained and that the alternative has been established beyond a reasonable doubt is not tantamount to an assertion of omniscience. Scientific reasoning in the form of inference to the best explanation applied to the available relevant evidence yields the result that, in the case of JFK, the official account of Lee Harvey Oswald as a lone assassin is not even physically possible, which means that it has null probability. It cannot possibly be true. And, in the case of 9/11, the same principles applied to the available relevant evidence yields the result that the official account of the events of that day are not even physically possible, which means that they have null probabilities, too. These conclusions are objective discoveries that anyone using the same rules of reasoning applied to the same evidence and considering the same alternatives would reach.[63]

Conclusions in science are always tentative and fallible, which means the discovery of new evidence or new alternatives may require reconsideration of the inferential situation. The suggestion could be made, for example, that the South Tower fell first because it was hit on a lower floor and to one side of the building, where the lack of symmetry caused it to fall. But that ignores the load-redistribution capabilities built into the towers, which would have precluded that outcome.

The claim has also been advanced that the steel only had to weaken, not melt. But the heat generated by the fuel fires never reached temperatures that would weaken the steel and, if it had, the buildings would have sagged asymmetrically, not completely collapsed all at once, as in fact was the case. The buildings both fell abruptly, completely, and symmetrically into their own footprints, which is explicable on the controlled demolition hypothesis but not on the official account. Similar considerations apply to the Pentagon hit.

Even if the wings had been shorn off, a Boeing 757 – which weighed 100 tons! – cannot have entered the building through that tiny opening and not have left massive debris. Both the government's "explanations" violate laws of nature. They cannot possibly be true.

Which raises the question, Who had the power to make these things happen and to cover it up? Once the evidence has been sorted out and appropriately appraised, the answer is no longer very difficult to find. Like the assassination of JFK, the events of 9/11 required involvement at the highest levels of the American government.

This conclusion, moreover, receives confirmation from the conduct of our highest elected officials, who took extraordinary steps to prevent any formal investigation of 9/11 and, when it was forced upon them by tremendous political pressure, especially from the survivors of victims of these crimes, they did whatever they could to subvert them. There are good reasons for viewing *The 9/11 Commission Report* (2004) as the historical successor to and functional equivalent of the Warren Report (1964).[64]

I therefore believe that those of us who care about the truth and the restoration of responsible government in the United States have an obligation to make use of every possible media venue from talk radio and the Internet to newspapers and television whenever possible.

The American people can act wisely only when they know the truth. So, while the truth is said to "make us free", the truth only matters when the American people are able to discover what is true. Obstacles here that are posed by the government-dominated mass media, including the use of stooge "reporters" and of prepackaged "news releases", only make matters that much more difficult. As John Dean asks in *Worse than Watergate* (2004), If there has ever been an administration more prone to deceiving the American people in our history, which one could it be?

13. Ubiquitous Conspiracies

Moreover, we must overcome the inhibition to talk openly about conspiracies. That the United States is now engaged in a conspiracy to control the world's oil in relation to Afghanistan, Iraq, Iran, and Venezuela comes as no surprise.[65] Read John Perkins' *Confessions of an Economic Hitman* (2004) or Robert Barnett's *The Pentagon's New Map* (2004) for modern extensions of the predominant attitudes of the recent past elaborated by Peter Dale Scott in *Deep Politics and the Death of JFK* (1993). But not all conspiracies are global in character and many are more limited in scope, such as the effort to keep an Italian journalist from returning to Italy from her captivity in Iraq, which seems to have been deliberately contrived to contain information about war crimes committed by American forces in Fallujah.[66]

If anyone doubts the ubiquitous presence of conspiracies, let them take a look at any newspaper of substance and evaluate the stories that are reported there. During an appearance on *Black Op Radio*, for example, I went through a single issue of *The New York Times* (Wednesday, 18 March 2005), which I chose as suitable for a case study. Multiple conspiracies are addressed throughout, including the WorldCom scandal, atrocities in Iraq and in Afghanistan (involving the murder of at least twenty-six inmates), the assassination of Refik Hariri in Lebanon, the use of counterfeit news by our own government, an SEC suit against Qwest for fraud, the 125 bank accounts of Augusto Pinochet, on and on.[67]

Efforts to promote the view that "conspiracy theories" must never be taken seriously continue unabated. A recent example of my acquaintance appears in the December 2004 issue of *Scientific American Mind* (December 2004), its "premiere issue". This issue features an article, "Secret Powers Everywhere", whose author is identified as Thomas Gruter of the University of Munster in Germany.[68] Its theme is that, while "most individuals who revel in tales of conspiracies are sane," they tend to "border on delusion."

This is a very unscientific article for a publication that, like its sibling, Scientific American, focuses on science. We have discovered that conspiracies are ubiquitous and amenable to scientific investigation. This article thus appears to be only the latest in an ongoing series of propagandistic assaults upon our rationality.[69]

Although it ought to go without saying, no "conspiracy theory" should be accepted or rejected without research. Each case of a possible conspiracy has to be evaluated independently based on the principles of logic and the available relevant evidence. Conspiracies flourish and time is fleeting. We lack the resources to confront them all.

But we need the intelligence and the courage to promote truth in matters of the highest importance to our country and to the world at large. We must do whatever we can to uncover and publish the truth and to expose the techniques so skillfully deployed to defeat us. History cannot be understood – even remotely! – without grasping the prevalence of conspiracies. And American history is no exception.

NOTES

1 The recent indictment of former Speaker of the House Tom DeLay for money laundering and the investigation of Senate Majority Leader Bill Frist for insider trading are even being referred to as "conspiracies". See "Big money, big influence, big trouble", Duluth News Tribune (4 December 2005). See also Section 13 below.

2 Properties whose presence or absence depends upon and varies with different observers or thinkers are said to be "subjective" (Fetzer and Almeder 1993, p. 99). Beliefs are "rational" when they satisfy suitable standards of evidential support with regard to acceptance, rejection, and suspension (Fetzer and Almeder 1993, pp. 13-14).

3 Some relevant evidence may not be available and some available evidence may not be relevant (Fetzer and Almeder 1993, p. 133). The fallacy that results from picking and choosing your evidence (call it "selection and elimination") is known as "special pleading", a common practice by editorial writers, politicians, and used-car salesmen.

4 Some alternative models of science include Inductivism, Deductivism, Hypothetico-Deductivism, Bayesianism (which comes in many different variations), and Abductivism, whose alternative strengths and weaknesses are assessed in Fetzer (1981), (1993), and (2002). The most defensible appears to be Abductivism, which is adopted here.

5 Acceptance within scientific contexts is "tentative and fallible" because new evidence or new hypotheses may require reconsideration of inferential situations. Conclusions that were once accepted as true may have to be rejected as false and conclusions once rejected as false may have to be accepted as true, as the history of science progresses.

6 In philosophical discourse, differences like these are known as "modal" distinctions.

7 And an event is historically possible (relative to time t) when its occurrence does not violate the history of the world (relative to t). Historical possibility implies both physical and logical, and physical implies logical, but not conversely. See Fetzer and Almeder (1993). For a detailed technical elaboration, see Fetzer (1981), pp. 54-55.

8 The example ignores the phenomena of supercooling. Some natural laws are causal and others are non-causal, while causal laws can be deterministic or indeterministic (or probabilistic). On the differences between kinds of laws, see Fetzer (1981), (1993), and (2002). Laws of society, such as speed limits on highways, of course, can be violated, can be changed, and require enforcement.

9 Scientific explanations of specific events explain why those events occur through their subsumption by means of covering laws. Predictions and retrodictions offer

a basis for inferring that an event will occur or has occurred but, depending upon their specific form, may or may not explain why. See Fetzer (1981), (1993), and (2002).

10 The term "proof" sometimes simply refers to specific evidence or an illustration of a principle or theorem, as in the case of a laboratory experiment. For a discussion of the meaning of "proof" in legal contexts, abstract contexts, and scientific contexts, see James H. Fetzer, "Assassination Science and the Language of Proof", in Fetzer (1998).

11 Thus, the stage of adaptation (of hypotheses to evidence) entails the exclusion of hypotheses that are inconsistent with the evidence. Like acceptance, rejection in science is also tentative and fallible, since the discovery of new alternatives or new evidence may require rejecting previously accepted alternatives, and conversely.

12 Formally, L(h/e) = P(e/h), that is, the likelihood of h, given e, is equal to the probability of e, given h. For propensities as opposed to frequencies, the formula may be expressed as NL(h/e) = NP(e/h), that is, the nomic likelihood of h, given e, equals the nomic probability of e, given h. See Fetzer (1981), (1993), and (2002).

13 Strictly speaking, relative frequencies are collective properties that do not belong to its individual members, while propensities are distributive properties that belong to each of its members, but may not be the same for every member in the collective. Under constant conditions, relative frequencies are evidence for causal propensities.

14 "Woman canoeing Brule River is killed in freak accident", *Duluth News Tribune* (16 July 1993), p. 1A. If those same unusual conditions were to be replicated over and over, of course, the relative frequency for death while canoeing would become extremely high. Enthusiasm for paddling the Brule River would no doubt diminish.

15 "Cigarette lighter saves man from a bullet", National Enquirer (6 July 1993), p. 21. In another case, a man who walked away unharmed after his truck hit a utility pole was killed as he left the crash scene, stepped on two downed power lines, and was electrocuted. His luck had run out. *Duluth News Tribune* (11 October 1993), p. 2D.

16 The sequences of cases that make up collectives are properly envisioned as sets of single cases, where the cause of each single case is the propensity that was present on that occasion. Laws of nature describe what would happen for any single case of the kind to which it applies up to the values of its propensities (Fetzer 1982, 1991, 2002).

17 The discovery that the autopsy X-rays have been altered, that someone else's brain was substituted for that of JFK, and that the Zapruder film has been recreated thus afford striking examples of the tentative and fallible status of scientific knowledge, where conclusions previously regarded as true must be rejected as false. See below.

18 Rather like the beaver on the Brule River, it seems to have been responsible for what would otherwise have appeared to have been a most improbable outcome. The difference, however, is that the Brule River incident actually occurred, while the "magic bullet" phenomenon cannot have occurred. It is not physically possible.

19 Warren Commission drawings of the alleged path of the "magic bullet" along with photographs of the holes in the jacket and shirt, the autopsy diagram, the death certificate, and some re-enactment photographs may be found in Galanor (1998), which presents available and relevant evidence contradicting *The Warren Report*.

20 Baden no doubt meant to imply that, since it would be absurd to suppose there had been as many as six shots from three directions, the "magic bullet" theory must be true. Recent scientific research has not only established that the "magic bullet" theory is physically impossible but that there had to have been at least six shots.

21 When the available relevant evidence proves that *The Warren Report*, which is the official government account of the assassination of JFK, the 35th President of United States, is false, yet the government refuses to revise its phony "explanation" of the cause of his death, it is abusive to demean the serious investigators as "buffs".

22 These include Robert B. Livingston, M.D., a world authority on the human brain, who was also an expert on wound ballistics; David W. Mantik, M.D., Ph.D., a Ph.D. in physics who is also an M.D. and board-certified in radiation oncology; and John P. Costella, Ph.D., an expert in electromagnetism and the physics of moving objects.

23 The authenticity of the Zapruder film has dedicated proponents, such as Josiah Thompson, the author of an early study (Thompson 1967), and David Wrone, the author of a recent study (Wrone 2003). For a critique of the critics' arguments, go to "*The Great Zapruder Film Hoax Debate*", http://www.assassinationscience.com. Some of their arguments were already refuted by the "Preface" to Fetzer (2003).

24 The witnesses to the limousine stop range from Roy Truly, Oswald's supervisor in the Texas School Book Depository, to Richard DellaRosa, who has viewed another and more complete film that includes the limo stop. See, for example, David W. Mantik, M.D., Ph.D., "How the Film of the Century was Edited", in Fetzer (1998), pp. 274-275; Vince Palamara, "59 Witnesses: Delay on Elm Street", in Fetzer (2000), pp. 119-128; and Richard DellaRosa, "The DellaRosa Report", in Fetzer (2003), Appendix E. This was such an obvious indication of Secret Service complicity that it had to be taken out.

25 With respect to the medical evidence, see David W. Mantik, M.D., Ph.D., "The JFK Assassination: Cause for Doubt", with its "Postscript: The President John F. Kennedy Skull X-Rays", in Fetzer (1998), pp. 93-139; and Robert Livingston, M.D., "Statement 18 November 1993", in Fetzer (1998), pp. 161-166. See also Fetzer (2000), (2003). Blunders were committed along the way. For example, while the 6.5 mm metallic slice was intended to implicate an obscure 6.5 mm weapon, the weapon itself only has a muzzle velocity of 2,000 fps and is not a high-velocity weapon. So if JFK was killed by the impact of high-velocity bullets, as his death certificates, the Warren Commission and the HSCA supposed, then he was not killed by Lee Harvey Oswald. See Weisberg (1965), Model and Groden (1976), and Groden and Livingstone (1989).

26 Livingston's conclusion has now been reinforced by the recent discovery that two supplemental brain examinations were conducted, one with the real brain, the other with the substitute. See Douglas Horne, "Evidence of a Government Cover-Up: Two Different Brain Specimens in President Kennedy's Autopsy", Fetzer (2000), pp. 299-310.

27 A summary of evidence for alteration may be found in James H. Fetzer, "Fraud and Fabrication in the Death of JFK", in Fetzer (2003), pp. 1-28. See especially John P. Costella, Ph.D., "A Scientist's Verdict: The Film is a Fabrication", in Fetzer (2003), pp. 145-238. It had to be recreated by reshooting the frames for technical

reasons related to sprocket hole images that have the effect of linking one frame to another. That the cinematic techniques for recreating the film were available in 1963 has been established by David Healy, "Technical Aspects of Film Alteration", in Fetzer (2003), pp. 113-144. The Disney film, *Mary Poppins*, for example, with its elaborate special effects, was completed in 1963 and released in 1964. For easy access to the evidence, see John P. Costella, "The JFK Assassination Film Hoax: An Introduction", at http://www.assassinationscience.com.

28 See, for example, Vincent Palamara, "Secret Service Agents who believed there was a conspiracy", http://www.geocities.com/zzzmail/palamara.htm?20054; Vincent Palamara, "The Secret Service: On the Job in Dallas", in Fetzer (2000); and Vincent Palamara, *Survivor's Guilt: The Secret Service and the Failure to Protect the President* (1995); Lifton (1980); Marrs (1989); Livingstone (1992); and Fetzer (1998, 2003).

29 When the Assassination Records Review Board (ARRB), which was established by Congress to declassify documents and records held by the CIA, the FBI, the NSA, and other agencies in the wake of the surge of interest generated by Oliver Stone's "JFK", was drafting requests for copies of its presidential protection reports for some of his trips during 1963, the Secret Service destroyed them. See Fetzer (2000), pp. 12-13.

30 Even the mortician observed that the deceased had a massive defect to the back of his head, a small entry wound to the right temple, several small puncture wounds to the face, and a wound to the back about five to six inches below the collar. (See, for example, Fetzer (2003), pp. 8-9.) This information should have been easily available. Even the Warren Report describes the holes in the shirt and jacket he was wearing as "5 3/8 inches below the top of the collar" in the jacket and as "5 3/4 inches below the top of the collar" in the shirt, contradicting its own declared conclusions (Warren 1964, p. 92). David W. Mantik, M.D., Ph.D., believes that the small puncture wounds were caused by shards of glass when the bullet that hit his throat passed through the windshield.

31 There appear to have been eight, nine, or ten shots from six locations. See, for example, Richard F. Sprague, "The Assassination of President John F. Kennedy", Computers and Automation (May 1970), pp. 29-60; James H. Fetzer, "Assassination Science and the Language of Proof", in Fetzer (1998), pp. 349-372; and David W. Mantik, M.D., Ph.D., "Paradoxes of the JFK Assassination: The Medical Evidence Decoded", in Fetzer (2000), pp. 219-297.

32 Lane already noticed this deceptive performance (Lane 1966, "The Hypothetical Medical Questions", Appendix II). Perry, who had performed the tracheostomy, was not in the position to vouch for or to verify the assumptions that he had been asked to make, because he knew they were false! The press conference transcript, where he described the wound three times as a wound of entry, was not provided to the Warren Commission, but has been published in Fetzer (1998) as Appendix C.

33 There were others, including that the crowd was allowed to spill into the street, the 112th Military Intelligence Group was ordered to "stand down", and a flatbed truck that would normally precede the limo for camermen to film was cancelled. Even on the unreasonable assumption that, say, one time in ten, the Secret Service "forgets" to weld the manhole covers, to cover the open windows, and such, then the probability that there would be a dozen independent events of this kind

is equal to 1 over 1 followed by a dozen zeros, 1/1,000,000,000,000, or one in a trillion. Even if we arbitrarily discount half of them, the probability that there would be a half-dozen independent events of this kind is equal to 1 over 1 followed by a half-dozen zeros, 1/1,000,000, or one in a million. Since hypotheses in science are rejected when they have improbabilities of 1 in twenty or more, these alternatives must be rejected.

34 The difference is that between events that, while extremely rare, can in fact occur and those that are impossible because their occurrence would violate laws of nature. The accidental death of the woman canoeing on the Brule River had a probability of zero, but it was not physically impossible or it could never have occurred. The prime numbers occur with diminishing relative frequency among the natural numbers and have a limiting frequency of zero, but there are infinitely many of them, nonetheless. It is therefore important, as a point of logic, to distinguish between "zero" and "null".

35 Those who make a last-ditch stand on behalf of the government's position often insist that, if there had a been a large-scale conspiracy, then some of those involved would have talked – and no one has talked! Proof that they don't know what they are talking about may be found in many places, including Noel Twyman's Bloody Treason (1997), where on a single page he lists eight prominent figures who talked (page 285)! None of this inhibits late night MSNBC-show hosts from fawning over Gerald Posners.

36 The identity of the alleged hijackers remains very much in doubt. Nila Sagadevan, *9/11 – The Real Report* (forthcoming), has observed that none of the names of the Arabs who are supposed to have committed these crimes are included in the flight manifests for any of the planes. Others, such as Griffin (2004, 2005), have observed that not only were fifteen of the nineteen from Saudi Arabia and none from Iraq, where at least six of those alleged to have been involved have turned up alive and well and living in Saudi Arabia. The FBI has not bothered to revise its list, but it should be apparent that the probability that they died in the crash, yet are still alive, is null.

37 A French human-rights activist and an investigative journalist, Thierry Meyssan, was among the first to observe that the government's account of the attack upon the Pentagon did not comport with the evidence. He published two of the earliest books on 9/11, *Pentagate* (2002a) and *9/11: The Big Lie* (2002b). Meyssan has been the target of many attacks, including by James S. Robbins, *9/11 Denial* (2002), whose rebuttal consists of two assertions, "I was there. I saw it." Whatever he may have thought he saw does not affect the evidence Meyssan emphasizes. See, for example, the web site http://www.asile.org/citoyens/numero13/pentaone/erreurs_en.htm.

38 Notice that the magnitude of the differences that are involved here is very large (http://reopen9/11.org/Core.htm). The melting point of iron is 2795° F, but steel as a mixture has a melting point dependent upon its composition. Thus, typical structural steel has a melting point of about 2,750° F. The maximum temperature of air-aspirated, hydrocarbon fires without pre-heating or pressurization is about 1,700° F. Even if the temperatures of those fires had reached as high as 1,700-2,000° F, as FEMA suggests, there was not enough time for sufficient heat to have been produced to have caused the steel to melt (Hufschmid 2002, pp. 32-40).

Underwriters Laboratories had in fact certified that the steel used in construction could withstand temperatures of 2,000° F several hours before even any significant softening would have occurred. (http://www.prisonplanet.com/articles/november2004/121104.easilywithstood.htm)

39 It certainly would not have melted at the lower temperatures of around 500° F to which, UL estimated, they were exposed, given the conditions present in the towers. (http://www.prisonplanet.com/articles/november2004/121104.easilywithstood.htm) Nor would they have melted at temperatures as high as 1,200° or 1,300° F, as other estimates suggest (Griffin 2004, p. 13). The hottest temperatures measured in the South Tower were about 1,375° F, far too low to cause the steel to melt, even if the exposure time had been much longer than 56 minutes. (See below.)

40 In the case of 9/11, as in the case of JFK, physical impossibilities lie at the core of the cover-up. What is impossible cannot happen, but many people are able to believe impossible things, especially when they are unaware of the laws that are involved and the specific conditions that were present. Gullibility tends to be a function of ignorance.

41 Griffin (2004), pp. 26-27. Griffin's latest study, "The Destruction of the World Trade Center: A Christian Theologian's Analysis" (forthcoming), adds even more. As Frank A. DeMartini, who was project manager for the construction of World Trade Center, during an interview recorded in January 2001, explained, "The building was designed to have a fully loaded 707 crash into it – that was the largest plane at the time. I believe that the building could probably sustain multiple impacts of jet liners because this structure is like mosquito netting on your screen door – this intense grid – and the plane is just a pencil puncturing that screen netting. It really does nothing to the screen netting." (http://www.prisonplanet.com/articles/november2004/121104designedtotake.htm). Three other engineers involved in the project – Lee Robertson, Aaron Swirski, and Hyman Brown – offered similar opinions (http://www.rense.com/ general17/eyewitnessreportspersist.htm). DeMartini died at the towers on 9/11.

42 See the discussion of seismic phenomena in Section 10. Peter Tully, President of Tully Construction, who was involved in the process of clearing the site, reported seeing pools of "molten steel", an observation that was confirmed by Mark Loizeaux, President of Controlled Demolition, Inc., who said they had been found at the subbasement level as low as seven levels down. Moreover, those pools remained "three, four, and five weeks later, when the rubble was being removed" (http://www.americanfreepress.net/09_03_02/NEW_SEISMIC_/new_seismic_.html). These extreme temperatures would not result from either burning fuel or collapse due to the "pancake effect", which would have propensities of zero or null, but would be expectable effects of the use of powerful explosives to bring them down.

43 Indeed, most of these features would have a null propensity on the official account. Suppose, for example, that the collapse was brought about by a "pancake" effect, with one floor falling and overwhelming the capacity of the lower floor to support it. Suppose, further, that the collapse of one floor onto another occurred at an average speed of 1/2 second per floor. (Try dropping a set of keys from various heights and measure the time!) Even if the initial collapse occurred

more slowly and increased with the increase in falling mass, an assumption that is not unreasonable, for all 110 floors to collapse – using averages, it would not matter which collapsed first or where the planes hit! – would have taken about 55 seconds. The buildings actually fell in about 10 seconds, as even *The 9/11 Report* itself concedes (Zelikow 2004, p. 305). That, however, is about the speed of free fall through air for objects encountering no resistance at all. If these assumptions are even remotely correct, then that the buildings should have collapsed so much faster than 55 seconds would appear to be physically impossible on a "pancake" account. Eric Hufschmid, in *Painful Deceptions* (2003), a video he produced, has shown that seismic data has confirmed that towers came down in about 10 seconds.

44 See, for example, http://www.assassinationscience.com/9/11links.html. This site includes many important studies of the Pentagon crash, such as a set of PowerPoint studies by Jack White. It also includes the links to many of the reports cited in this chapter, including "Hunt the Boeing!", which presents Meyssan's analysis in a series of photographs. I have found that links to evidence that tends to contradict the government's account do not always work normally, however, and sometimes just simply disappear. Similar photographs are found in Meyssan (2002a), color photo section, pp. VI-VII. The same conclusion is drawn by Eric Hufschmid (Hufschmid 2002).

45 A photograph is archived at http://www.assassinationscience.com/9/11links.html. The opening appears to be about 10 feet high and roughly 16 or 17 feet wide, or not much larger than the double-doors on a mansion. Another photograph suggests that the width may even be considerably less than 16-17 feet, perhaps much closer to 10 feet, but it appears to be of two windows that were blown out of the second floor instead (http://www.serendipity.li/wot/crash_site.htm). Notice several unbroken windows in the impact area and the lack of collateral damage. According to A. K. Dewdney and G. W. Longspaugh, the maximum diameter of the fuselage is about 12 feet, 4 inches, with a wingspan of 125 feet (http://www.physics9/11.net/missingwings.htm). They found, "The initial (pre-collapse) hole made by the alleged impact on the ground floor of Wedge One of the building is too small to admit an entire Boeing 757"" and "Wings that should have been sheered off by the impact are entirely absent. There is also substantial debris from a much smaller jet-powered aircraft inside the building." They conclude with a "high degree" of certainty that no Boeing 757 struck the Pentagon and with a "substantial degree" of certainty that it was struck by a small jet, like an F-16.

46 Bloggers observed the proliferation of inconsistent stories about what happened at the Pentagon, where some were saying that the wing hit the grass and it "cartwheeled" into the Pentagon, others saying that it "nose dived" into the Pentagon, others saying that it flew "straight into" the Pentagon, others saying that it hit the helicopter pad and the wreckage flew into the Pentagon: "Why so many different stories? Are these people seeing different things?" (http://www.abovetopsecret.com/forum/thread71124/pg11). The Pentagon said the crew of a C-130 had watched the attack take place while circling Washington, D.C. (http://www.ratical.org/ratville/CAH/linkscopy/C130sawF772P.html).

47 Go to http://www.asile.org/citoyens/numero13/pentagone/erreurs_en.htm for a photograph of the construction. Compare it with other photographs of the lawn,

which can be found at http://www.assassinationscience.com/9/11links.html, including in the PowerPoint studies of Jack White. The lawn seems to be as smooth as a putting green.

48 Slide 20 of Jack White's PowerPoint studies displays two photographs of the same piece of "aircraft debris" with two different backgrounds (http://www.assassination-science.com/9/11links.html). Another study supporting the impossibility of a Boeing 757 having passed through that entry point includes photos not only of the same piece of alleged debris but others showing two men in suits carrying what appears to be the same or similar pieces and, interestingly, an enormous box being carried from the site by six or eight servicemen, who have covered it up completely by using blue and white plastic tarps (http://www.geocities.com/s9/11surprise3b/american_airlines_flight_77/).

49 Hufschmid (Hufschmid 2002, Chapter 9), concludes that the building may have been hit by a Predator drone, which could have been painted to resemble an American Airlines aircraft. Most arguments for the official government account tend to emphasize eyewitnesses who said that they saw a Boeing 757 hit the Pentagon. (See note 37 above.) But the physical evidence overwhelmingly outweighs the contrary eyewitness evidence, since it is not physically possible that an aircraft of those dimensions hit the building at that location and left no evidence. Think of driving a car through your front door for a comparison. The air controller's report, by contrast, was a group response by professional experts.

50 See http://www.simmeringfrogs.com/articles/jt8d.html, which includes photos of a JT8D turbojet engine and the remnant found at the crash site. A similar conclusion is drawn by http://www.physics9/11.net/missingwings.htm., which concludes that this part cannot have come from a Boeing 757 but was probably from a small fighter jet, such as an F-16. The F-16 and the A-3 Sky Warrior are both small fighter jets. Both pages are also accessible from http://www.assassinationscience.com/9/11links.html.

51 The workers' reports about these activities may be read at "Secret Global Hawk Refit for Sky Warrior!" (http://portland.indymedia.org/en/2005/05/318250.shtml).

52 See http://www.geocities.com/s9/11surprise3b/american_airlines_flight_77/.

53 She is quoted by Meyssan (2002a) on p. I and on pp. 96-97. The original source is http://www.abcnews.go.com/sections/2020/2020/2020_011014_atc.feature.htm.

54 The JT8D, however, was superceded in 737s by CFM56 engines in the early 1980s. A new study by Russell Pickering, however, raises serious questions about the JT8D evidence, leaving me more certain that there was no 757 than confident that it was an A-3. See "The JT8D & A3 Skywarrior Pentagon Theory: What is it and where did it come from?", http://www.rense.com/general70/jt.htm. Jon Carlson, "FBI Hides 85 Pentagon Videos and 9/11 Truth", http://www.rense.com/general69/9/1185.htm, relates that, "the Power Hour has found that Pentagon 9/11 'witnesses' were given prepared written statements to say that a commercial airliner hit the Pentagon." As a former Marine Corps officer, I can confirm that it would have been effortless to acquire the testimony of any number of enlisted that they personally observed Bruce Wayne drive the Batmobile into the Pentagon that morning. I wonder how many of us could tell the difference between a 767, a 757, or a 737, for example, especially when whatever hit was only observable for a brief span of time? AA Flight 77 left the radar screen in the vicinity of the Kentucky/Ohio border.

One possible explanation for what became of it is that it went down and the bodies were transported back to a make-shift morgue in Washington, D.C., an hypothesis that may merit more investigation.

55 Wake turbulence occurs as an unavoidable effect of aircraft operation and "is generated when the difference in air pressure above and below the wings of an aircraft causes the air to spiral at the aircraft's wing tips." It dissipates rapidly in windy conditions, but in still conditions, "the spirals sink toward the ground and degrade slowly" (http://www.aeru.com/au/pages/page189.asp). Pilots are offered instructions for avoiding the problem (see "FAA Advisory Circular, AC-90-23E: CAUTION WAKE TURBULANCE", http://www.fcitraining.com/article14_fci_training_jul04.htm). The effects can be substantial, which gives rise to the following dilemma: if a 757 was flying low enough to impact the hit point on the ground floor with the official trajectory, then it should have massively disrupted the grass and lawn; but the grass and law were not massively disrupted. And if it was not flying low enough to massively disrupt the grass and lawn, then it was not flying low enough on that trajectory to hit that point on the ground floor. Indeed, at heights low enough to impact the ground floor, the engines or even fuselage would have been expected to plow the ground, which clearly did not occur.

56 See note 42 above and the discussion of this important point that may be found at http://www.americanfreepress.net/09_03_02/NEW_SEISMIC_/new_seismic_.html.

57 During a PBS documentary, "America Rebuilds", broadcast 10 September 2002, Larry Silverstein remarks, "I remember getting a call from the, er, fire department commander, telling me that they were not sure they were gonna be able to contain the fire, and I said, 'We've had such terrible loss of life, maybe the smartest thing to do is pull it.' They made that decision to pull and we watched the building collapse." (http://9/11research.wtc7.net/wtc/evidence/pullit.html). That, however, could not have occurred unless the building contained prepositioned explosives. If WTC7 had prepositioned explosives, that strongly suggests WTC1 and WTC2 had them as well.

58 In this respect, "Loose Change" corroborates earlier reports from eyewitnesses to explosions, such as http://www.chiefengineer.org/article.cfm?seqnum1=1029 and http://www.resne.com/general17/eyewitnessreortspersist.htm. See also note 21.

59 WTC1, hit first but falling second, had events of 0.9 and of 2.3 on the Richter scale, while WTC2, hit second but falling first, had events of 0.7 and 2.1 on the Richter scale. These differences may be important. See, for example, http://www.americanfreepress.net/09_03_02/NEW_SEISMIC_/new_seismic_.html and http://www.democraticunderground.com/duforum/DCForumID43/5189.html, which includes the seismic record of Columbia's observatory.

60 For additional discussion, including many more links, see, for example, http://.www.propagandamatrix.com/articles/july2005/060705controlleddemolition.htm.

61 See note 41. The properties of Boeing 707s and Boeing 767s are very similar.

62 United Flight 93, which went down in Pennsylvania, may be an easy case. Persons living in the area at the time have contacted me and told me they heard an explosion before the plane crashed, but the FBI would not record it. Others told me that they had been taken to an area far larger than the official crash scene to search for debris and body parts, but the Sheriff who accompanied them told them that, if they were to repeat this, he would deny he had said that. A former

Inspector General who used to supervise air crashes for the Air Force told me that, if the plane had crashed as it was officially described, it should have occupied an area about the size of a city block; but the debris is actually scattered over an area of some eight square miles. There is also a report the plane was shot down by a "Happy Hooligans" Air National Guard officer, one Major Rick Gibney, at http://www.letsroll9/11.org/articles/flight93shotdown.html.

63 On the objectivity of scientific reasoning, see Fetzer (1981), (1993), and (2002).

64 For more discussion and evidence, see Ahmed (2002), Meyssan (2002), Griffin (2004), Thompson (2004), Ruppert (2004), and Griffin (2005) and (forthcoming).

65 See "Mission Accomplished: Big Oil's Occupation of Iraq", BUZZFLASH.COM (2 December 2005), http;//www.buzzflash.com/contributors/05/12/con05464.html.

66 See "Hostage's shooting 'no accident'" (http://news.bbc.co.uk/go/fr/-/2/hi/europe/4323361.stm) and "Dead Messengers: How the U.S. Military Threatens Journalists" (http://www.truthout.org/docs_2005/030605.shtml). *The New York Times* has recently lost one of its own, "Reporter Working for Times Abducted and Slain in Iraq", *The New York Times* (20 September 2005), although The Times has not suggested that he was deliberately targeted by the American military. See, for example, "The Twilight World of the Iraqi News Stringer", *The New York Times* (25 September 2005). For another troubling report, see "U.S. forces 'out of control', says Reuters chief", http://www.guardian.co.uk/Iraq/Story/0,2763,1580244,00.html.

67 The discussion is archived at http://www.blackopradio.com/. Go to "archived shows 2005" and scroll down to Part 2, Archived Show #213. Other examples of probable conspiracies making their way into the national media include financing propaganda in Iraqi ("U.S. Is Said to Pay to Plant Articles in Iraq Papers", *The New York Times*, 1 December 2005) and the DeLay-inspired G.O.P. redistricting of Texas ("Lawyer's Voting Rights Memo Overruled", *The New York Times*, 3 December 2005).

68 I have received an email from "Dr. med. Thomas Gruter" (25 January 2005) in which he advises me that he has not been a member of the faculty at Munster for nearly 20 years and never was a professor. He is a medical doctor and journalist writing on scientific subjects. He asked Scientific American Mind to correct this, but it never did. He faulted the magazine's translation of his German, which, he wrote, should have said, "Most conspiracy believers are certainly sane, even if the dividing line to a delusional disorder of thinking may be ill-defined (or fluent)." So the problem could have arisen from an editor's decision to publish an English translation without verification from the author.

69 A distinction must be drawn between rationality of belief and rationality of action. Rationality of belief involves accepting, rejecting, and holding beliefs in suspense on the basis of the available relevant evidence and appropriate principles of reasoning. Rationality of action involves adopting means that are efficient, effective, or reliable to attain your aims, objective, or goals. Lying about tax cuts (global warming, Iraq) can be a rational act if it is an efficient, effective, or reliable means to attaining goals, which may be political, economic, or personal. And they can attain their aims even if they are ultimately discovered. Assessments of comparative rationality with respect to belief must take into account that persons are rational in their beliefs when they incorporate the principles that define it.

Since the "community of scientists" can be littered with phonys, charlatans, and frauds, "scientists" are those who adhere to the principles of science. Analogously, "rational persons" are those who adhere to the principles of rationality. They tend to converge. See Fetzer (1981), (1993), (2002).

BOOK REFERENCES

Ahmed, N. M. (2002), The War on Freedom: How and Why America was Attacked, September 11th, 2001 (Joshua Tree, CA: Tree of Life Publications, 2002).

Barnett, T. P. M. (2004), *The Pentagon's New Map: War and Peace in the Twenty- first Century* (New York, NY: G. P. Putnam's Sons, 2004).

Dean, J. (2004), *Worse than Watergate: The Secret Presidency of George W. Bush* (New York, NY: Little, Brown, and Company, 2004).

Fetzer, J. H. (1981), Scientific Knowledge: Causation, Explanation, and Corroboration (Dordrecht, Holland: D. Reidel, 1981).

Fetzer, J. H. (1993), *Philosophy of Science* (New York, NY: Paragon House, 1990).

Fetzer, J. H. (2002), *Propensities and Frequencies: Inference to the Best Explanation*, Synthese 132/1-2 (July/August 2002), pp. 27-61.

Fetzer, J. H., ed. (1998), *Assassination Science: Experts Speak Out on the Death of JFK* (Chicago, IL: Catfeet Press/Open Court, 1998).

Fetzer, J. H., ed. (2000), *Murder in Dealey Plaza: What We Know Now that We Didn't Know Then* (Chicago, IL: Catfeet Press/Open Court, 2000).

Fetzer, J. H., ed. (2003), *The Great Zapruder film Hoax: Deceit and Deception in the Death of JFK* (Chicago, IL: Catfeet Press/Open Court, 2003).

Fetzer, J. H. and R. F. Almeder (1993), *Glossary of Epistemology/Philosophy of Science* (New York: Paragon House, 1993).

Galanor, S. (1998), *Cover-Up* (New York, NY: Kestrel Books, 1998).

Griffin, D. R. (2004), *The New Pearl Harbor* (Northampton, MA: Olive Branch Press, 2004).

Griffin, D. R. (2005), *The 9/11 Commission Report: Omissions and Distortions* (Northampton, MA: Olive Branch Press, 2005).

Groden, R. and H. Livingstone (1989), High Treason: The Assassination of President Kennedy and the New Evidence of Conspiracy (Boothywyn, PA: The Conservatory Press, 1989).

Hacking, I. (1965), *Logic of Statistical Inference* (Cambridge, UK: Cambridge University Press, 1965).

Hufschmid, E. (2002), *Painful Questions: An Analysis of the September 11th Attack* (Goleta, CA: Endpoint Software, 2002).

Lane, M. (1966), *Rush to Judgment* (New York, NY: Holt, Rinehart, & Winston, 1966).

Lifton, D. (1980), Best Evidence: Disguise and Deception in the Assassination of John F. Kennedy (New York, NY: Macmillan, 1980).

Livingstone, H. (1992), *High Treason 2: The Great Cover-Up* (New York, NY: Carroll & Graf, 1992).

Marrs, J. (1989), *Crossfire: The Plot that Killed Kennedy* (New York, NY: Carroll & Graf, 1989).

Meagher, S. (1967), *Accessories after the Fact* (Indianapolis, IN: Bobbs-Merrill, 1967).

Meyssan, T. (2002a), *Pentagate* (London, UK: Carnot Publishing, Ltd., 2002).

Meyssan, T. (2002b), *9/11: The Big Lie* (London, UK: Carnot Publishing, Ltd., 2002).

Model, P. and R. Groden (1976), *JFK: The Case for Conspiracy* (New York, NY: Manor Books, Inc., 1976)

Palamara, V. (1995), Survivor's Guilt: The Secret Service and the Failure to Protect the President (Self-Published: Xerox, 1995).

Perkins, J. (2004), *Confessions of an Economic Hitman* (San Francisco, CA: Berrett-Koehler Publishers, 2004).

Posner, G. (1993), Case Closed: Lee Harvey Oswald and the Assassination of JFK (New York, NY: Random House, 1993).

Robbins, J. S. (2002), *9/11 Denial, The National Review On-Line* (9 April 2002), http://nationalreview.com/robbins/robbins040902.asp.

Ruppert, M. (2004), Crossing the Rubicon: The Decline of the American Empire at the End of the Age of Oil (Garbiola Island, BC: New Society Publishers, 2004).

Scott, P. D. (1993), *Deep Politics and the Death of JFK* (Berkeley, CA: University of California Press, 1993).

Thompson, J. (1967), *Six Seconds in Dallas* (New York, NY: Bernard Geis, 1967).

Thompson, P. (2004), The Terror Timeline: Year by Year, Day by Day, Minute by Minute (New York, NY: Regan Books, 2004).

Twyman, N. (1998), Bloody Treason: On Solving History's Greatest Murder Mystery: The Assassination of John F. Kennedy (Rancho Santa Fe, CA: Laurel Publishing, 1997).

Warren, E. et al. (1964), Report of the President's Commission on the Assassination of President John F. Kennedy (New York, NY: St. Martin's Press, 1964).

Weisberg, H. (1965), *Whitewash: The Report on the Warren Report* (New York, NY: Dell Publishing, 1965).

Wrone, D. (2003), *The Zapruder film: Reframing JFK's Assassination* (Lawrence, KS: University Press of Kansas, 2003).

Zelikow, P., et al. (2004), The 9/11 Commission Report: Final Report of the National Commission on Terrorist Attacks Upon the United States (New York, NY: W. W. Norton, 2004).

JAMES H. FETZER, McKnight University Professor of Philosophy at the University of Minnesota, teaches on its Duluth campus. He has authored or edited more than twenty books in the philosophy of science and on the theoretical foundations of computer science, artificial intelligence, cognitive science, and the evolution of mentality. He has also published widely on the death of JFK. Fetzer has received many honors and awards for distinguished research in the philosophy of science.

[Chapter 39] The Big Split

> "After Sept. 11 CLEARCHANNEL issued a list of 150 songs to its member stations that it deemed too sensitive to play in the wake of the terrorist attack. Many were related to peace, "Bridge Over Troubled Water," "Imagine." The list also included all songs by the political rock group RAGE AGAINST THE MACHINE.
> "One month later, the CLEAR CHANNEL-owned radio station KMEL in San Francisco fired its popular community affairs director, David "Davey D" Cook, shortly after his show aired the anti-war views of Rep. Barbara Lee, the lone member of Congress to vote against military action in Afghanistan."
>
> - *BuzzFlash*

The Big Split
by Preston James
Veterans Today May 12, 2013

A very Big Split is now occurring in the Hived, American Group Mind.

Even though the American Group Mind (AGM) has been successfully "Hived", it's hard for the Big Lies of the U.S. Government (USG) to last forever thanks to the advent of the alternative news provided by the worldwide Internet.

As more and more USG Big Lies are exposed, the USG reacts by staging additional Gladio-style false-flag attacks (GFFA) in desperate attempts to bombard the American Group Mind back into submission and compliance with their completely false narratives which are dispensed through their Controlled Major Mass Media (CMMM).

Although an obviously very painful personal experience, more and more average Americans are waking up each day thanks to the Internet and are personally starting to connect the dots for themselves and are failing to accept these false narratives designed to recondition or re-hypnotize them back into the hived American Group Mind (AGM).

What is the hived AGM? It is a perversion of normal community solidarity which was recognized by French sociologist Emile Durkheim as the conscience-collective (CC), or also known as the "moral density" of a society which results from folks living together in a community.

The Conscience-Collective (CC) is the set of normal, expected common moral beliefs of the community, the force which can arise to form vigilante actions when law enforcement is corrupt or unwilling to act. It is the common community normative outrage that results from anti-social or criminal acts that threaten the community's solidarity.

When functional, the conscience-collective (CC) is typically quite useful to the general community at large, but when hijacked and perverted by very crafty covert operators serving a corrupt central government, it can be transformed into a mechanism to hive the AGM and produce an environment that supports fascism, tyranny and suspension of normal rights which are supposed to be guaranteed by the U.S. Constitution and its Bill of Rights.

The quickest way for any central government to elicit this transformation of the normal CC into a hived AGP which allows and supports tyranny by the USG is to institute major staged Gladio-style false-flag attacks (GFFA's) like the Nazis did with their staged Reichstag fire and their false flag attack on their radio station at Gleiwitz, Germany.

This worked well for the Nazis to create a false but believable pretext for their invasion of Poland just as the staged 9-11 GFFA provided a new Pearl Harbor type incident which also served as a false but believable pretext for numerous unprovoked, illegal, unConstitutional, undeclared wars.

Now thanks to the advent of the Internet provided alternative news, many folks are now able to detach themselves from this hived AGM and begin to think independently. These folks are now attuned to the obvious facts readily available that the USG has been very busing criminally conspiring to defraud the American People, stage these GFFA's and create an internal police state that rivals the East German Stasi.

True-Believers who learn the truth about deep black covert operations and staged GFFA's and become open-minded Truth-Seekers usually suffer strong and immediate rejection from others who refuse to listen because they are closed minded and cloned members of the hived AGM.

When a person who has been a true-believer in the false USG narratives begins to understand all the Big Government Lies and creeping police state tyranny inside the beltway and tries to share it with other peers, such individual is usually quickly met with put downs, discounting and a label of being a conspiracy theorist which is a nice term for being viewed as a whacky conspiracy nutcase.

Yes, in reaction to their awareness that many of the populace are catching on to these Big Government Lies, USG continues to stage more and more GFFA's in attempts to counter this splitting off of more and more folks from the hived AGM, and by doing so has hoped to successfully re-strengthen the hive mentality of the populace. But alas, this strategy is now starting to fail and thanks to the extremely botched GFFA at the Boston Marathon by the DHS, many folks are catching on and waking up for the first time.

Sophisticated and deniable multi-level, layered trade-craft is used in the deployment of these staged GFFA's.

Of course intel agencies have developed very sophisticated fall-back strategies and the "sting-gone-bad" one can be invoked as needed, since almost all these GFFA's are usually embedded in training exercises in the first place which are then covertly taken live (as was done at the Boston Marathon by DHS).

If too much incriminating evidence comes forth, they let things shift to a "sting gone bad" position based on usual USG incompetence rather than very skillful deep black covert stage GFFA-type operations.

It's like the little boy crying wolf too many times, the power of these staged Gladio-style False-flag Attacks (SGFA) is lessening and the USG is progressively losing its ability to re-hypnotize the collective American mass Mind. So to counteract this, once again, the USG is likely to stage even more frequent GFFA's and even perhaps more serious ones like the use of small nuclear weapon detonations in major U.S. cities or dirty bombs.

Let's face it, if the USG will murder about 3,000 innocent Americans on 9-11-01, they are evil and capable enough to do the most evil additional GFFA's unless stopped cold by a major mass awakening of the masses or a very high level, effective coup de etat from the high military command.

With the advent of HD video devices in so many hands and instantly available from so many sources, the Big USG Lies are now being quite easily unraveled within mere hours and days of these GFFA's.

Thanks to the worldwide Internet, a major split in the hived AGM is now well under way and cannot be stopped without instituting complete martial law, something which would undoubtedly trigger a serious armed rebellion.

Despite the use of these coordinated USG GFFA's on the rising American Spirit to re-establish the hive mind in full strength as before, a major split in the American Group Mind (AGM) has now occurred and can be expected to increase and intensify as the economy crumbles in open view.

The American Group Mind (AGM), a sophisticated "hive-mind" or conscious-collective of the American group psyche, was constructed by the Secret Shadow Government (SSG) using sophisticated mindkontrol technology known as the ancient Babylonian or medieval "Black Arts" allegedly based on luciferian, demonic or dark side spiritual influences.

Experts in these matters who have had contacts with "insiders" have claimed that the overall purpose is to seize and "hive" the whole world for Lucifer into one mass of group thinking mental clones, create a luciferian Globalist NWO one-world Government system and bring all this about through a process of first creating massive worldwide chaos, death and destruction, the ashes from which their NWO Phoenix will arise.

Along the way the game plan is to instill this hive mind through thought cloning, engaging in "soul snatching" of the average person and replacing their soul with the demonic group hive-mind.

Yes, such a concept as the "hiving of society" seems absurd at face value, but becomes more believable when one fully examines the evidence for it which suggests that the USG has engaged in massive long term Mindwar against the American people based on highly sophisticated mindkontrol technologies including the mass persuasion Madison Avenue techniques of Edward Bernays as well as a Controlled Major Mass media (CMMM) and use of ultra-high tech psychotronics through the police radio system and cell phone systems as well as other even more sophisticated psychotronic means (1).

It is easy to diagnose when a person has been "hived" or cloned into the American group Mind (AGP). All one has to do is ask them about key litmus test questions, such as do they believe Oswald was a lone-nut assassin of JFK and do they think the Warren Report was correct, or "do you think 9/11 was an inside job" done by the USG with help from foreign and domestic Intel?

Breaking free of the hived AGM requires learning the truth about at least one major staged Gladio-style false-flag attack (GFFA).

It is almost impossible for a person to know the truth about the JFK Assassination, who did it, and who ran the cover-up, and still remain part of the AGP, the hived group-mind or perverted Conscience-Collective (CC) of American society. And that is why ever since American intel and the JCS assassinated JFK they have spent millions of dollars each year working hard to keep their treason completely covered up and withheld from the American people.

Thanks to Professor James Fetzer and numerous other such highly respected JFK Assassination researchers, folks like Jim Marrs, Noel Twyman, Harrison Edward Livingstone and many others, this crime of the 20th century has been completely cracked and a great deal of significant valid Grand Jury ready evidence exists which could be used to indict and try numerous surviving folks who were part of the plot and those who have continued to be major accessories after the crime even today. The names of all those still alive are now known and the evidence is readily available, but for the massive cover-up remaining in place today by the SSG and American intel. And of course there is never any statute of limitations on murder or crimes involving fraud. (2)

Once a person become informed and is "hip" to the reality of USG staged Gladio style inside-job false-flag terror, it is impossible for them to ever trust any news from the CMMM ever again or almost anything any politician says. They have truly been broken out of the Information Control Matrix (ICM) which is a by-product of the hived American Group Mind (AGP).

Another recent phenomenon is the formation of the USG hive concept "the Federal Family". This concoction is a special attempt to create a new political class of the law enforcement protected and privileged actually quite like the German SS or the East German Stasi, both of which were constructed and managed by the hidden but quite real International Zionist Crime Syndicate (IZCS).

If you are federalized Law Enforcement or work in any capacity of the Department of Homeland Security (DHS) you are considered to be "oh so special" and treated with privileges not available to ordinary citizens, such as fat paychecks, liberal benefits, great retirement and lots of slack as far as disobeying the laws that ordinary citizens must. You are also engendered with a superior authoritarian attitude that breeds disrespect of the citizens who pay your way, folks you are supposed to work for and serve rather than tyrannize as many of you do, while rationalizing it under "national security" or "fighting terrorism" or "keeping the homeland safe" which is exactly what you are NOT doing.

This current American hive-mind aka the American Group Mind (AGM) was constructed by the USG concocting and dispensing propaganda through the Controlled Major Mass Media (CMMM) under the well-financed long term Operation Mockingbird which Bill Colby once stated was the CIA's greatest achievement. Obviously the CMMM has become little more than a dispenser of USG propaganda and serves as the USG's jumping jack.

The Vietnam war was the first time a large proportion of the public began to fully realize that the USG was seriously corrupt and engaging in war profiteering for the large defense contractors, as was warned about by President Eisenhower in his last speech in political office.

Obviously the Vietnam War was for some Americans the first time they were able to break out of the AGM hive thinking and see that something was very, very wrong with the USG dispensed narrative about the claimed reasons for the war. A classic song by Marvin Gaye in 1970 reflected this recognition by some whom could no longer accept the USG narratives which were comprised of lies, realizing that things were terribly wrong in society.

Perhaps a great deal of the blame for the recent accelerated cloning or hiving of America can be attributed to establishment of a national policy of "political correctness" which is the always the main enforcement system for elicited perversions which are thus forced to be accepted as normal.

So we see kindergartners taught that obscene perversions are normal and cannot be reacted to negatively. And we see adults forced to accept various types of perversions and deviance that obviously are destructive to normal society but quite useful in the establishment of a hived American Group Mind (AGM).

And at the same time we see the emergence and high level promotion of "twisted sisters" with obvious AIS and numerous closeted politicians and judges blackmailed into submission by crafty foreign and domestic intelligence agencies who specialize in the "fine art of human compromise". Of course these teachings are actually trademarks of the International Zionist Crime Syndicate IZCS's Bolshevism which has been used for about 100 years to debase a society and soften it up for hijacking, disarmament, invasion and take-down before the "red terror" style mass murdering begins.

All tyranny and mass murder of war the last 100 years appears to have originated from the IZCS who are the main enforcement arm of the Old Black nobility (OBN). For whatever reasons those that run the IZCS have an out of control blood lust and love to mass murder millions of civilians. This has been their pattern for at least 100 years. Some have claimed that the IZCS is actually the main action arm of the world luciferian system of interlinked cults who work secretly behind many organizations which present themselves as public servants.

Political correctness is a cancer on the body politic and a sure means of eventual descent into a central police state tyranny and mass murder of the populace by central government.

Political Correctness is the flip-side and enforcer of the highly dysfunctional, community destroying "perversion and diversity is normal" narrative which is being force fed to folks at all levels of American Society including inside the public school systems.

Political correctness was the fear-force that kept East Germans "under the boot" of the greatly feared and highly murderous and abusive Stasi. Folks there lived in constant fear of neighborhood snitches "dropping a dime" on them, which often would mean their sudden disappearance to a work camp or prison for years.

Since DHS was designed and built by IZCS choice Markus Wolfe, who was hired as a consultant two years before he died, one can easily understand why DHS is a clone of the East German Stasi which he ran on behalf of the IZCS, which is a well-known fact in the higher echelons of intel.

Yes, DHS was designed to create an internal American police state tyranny for terrorizing normal law abiding citizens. And each years the U.S. Congress, which is filled with bought, owned and deeply compromised public non-servants, passes hundreds of unConstitutional Liberty and Rights robbing so-called laws.

These laws are all invalid from the get-go based on the famous Supreme Court decision of Marbury vs. Madison, and are obvious and clear cut violations of common law as well as completely unConstitutional despite what a bought, owned and highly compromised Supreme Court rules.

Political Correctness robs personal Freedom and Liberty and breeds totalitarianism and central government police state tyranny

Political correctness allows little freedom of thought and truth-seeking.

It is a hard slave driver and demands near 100-percent cohesiveness of beliefs to the hived AGM.

And if that was not enough, now we have the Director of Homeland Security, Janet Napolitano, calling for community snitching as a way of life with her absurd Stasi paranoid program "If you see something say something", another attempt to erode basic community trust, the glue that holds society together.

It's obvious to anyone that understands history the true purpose of DHS is to destroy the American Republic, and beat American citizens down into complete childlike submission so they can be completely asset stripped and then mass murdered by red terror.

It's obvious to anyone that does some basic research that DHS is little more than an agent for the International Zionist Crime Syndicate (IZCS) and its associated central Banksters run out of the City of London Financial District, a separate country with its own ambassadors and police.

It is the enforcement arm of the ADL and the SPLC which are constantly identifying normal mainstream American groups and organizations as hate groups, when this is all psychological projection because they are the real hate groups and progenitors of hate and tyranny in America as well as agents of foreign intel hidden in plain sight.

So we have the ADL and SPLC indoctrinating and training our police with biased, incorrect information that leads to tyranny against the ordinary law abiding citizen. How's this for hypocrisy and irony? How's that for a real threat to our national security, freedom, Liberty, Constitution, Bill of Rights and way of life?

Accusing others of what one is doing themselves even more is one of the oldest deflection tricks of history. Once it is exposed, the cat is out of the bag and the jig is up.

This big trick of accusing others of what is one's mainstream activity is the oldest game used to justify tyranny in history. It is taken right out of the Bolshevik, Nazi and Stasi playbooks which were actually created by the IZCS, although few realize this since it seems to counter-intuitive.

Sometimes fact is stranger than fiction and it is in this case. If you think this is perhaps one of the greatest dark secrets of history, you are perhaps getting warm.

Keep peeling the onion and you will understand "their plan" to bring about worldwide chaos, death and destruction and create "hell on earth", mass murder about 80 percent of the world's population through eugenics, soft-kill, war and red-terror, in order to bring about their Globalist NWO to rise as a Phoenix from the ashes of a destroyed world. Of course this is why we see history moving ahead to clear signs of a future World War 3 based on massive nuclear exchanges.

The folks who hijacked America and much of the world are a hidden but very real worldwide "death cult" that worships the ministering of death to the world as a means to purify the race and create their own interlocked massive power systems.

Destroying basic community trust is one of the key goals of DHS under Janet Napolitano, key action agent for the IZCS

How's this for helping to destroy basic community trust which is needed to keep any society cohesive? Can any normal well adjusted person take this obvious absurd propaganda seriously. It completely discredits DHS as it should and shows it for what it really is, nothing but a doofus tool of tyranny for the IZCS.

If you like the idea of Bolshevik Red Terror, you are going to love what DHS has planned for the sheeple. Unless stopped they plan to mass murder most of us as the IZCS finishes asset stripping America, and all major institutions of America fail.

DHS will provide the final stop to protect the super-elite deviants who run the SSG and the USG while they set up and move into secure compounds or leave America for South America.

Of course anyone who checks knows that Homeland Security is basically a foreign spy apparatus that has hijacked and organized American intel and Law Enforcement including the alphabets into a single group that is now much easier to control and use as an agent of the IZCS. (3).

So basically we have a foreign based intel service serving as a main

Cutout for the IZCS and its London Banksters that has hijacked almost all of our American LE and Intel. How's that for the gross misuse of the staged terror of 9/11 to hijack the essence of the USG?

Propaganda is an essential requirement in constructing the hived AGM. In 1928, Edward Bernays, "the father of public relations," wrote in his book "Propaganda":

> The conscious and intelligent manipulation of the organized habits and opinions of the masses is an important element in a democratic society. Those who manipulate this unseen mechanism of society constitute an invisible government which is the true ruling power in our country.

The SSG has worked very hard to successfully establish the hived AGM over the last 100 years.

The Secret Shadow Government (SSG) has worked very hard to create this unitary, collective and hived American group Mind (AGM) over the last 100 years to be comprised of "true believers" who have accepted these false narratives supplied by the USG through the CMMM as Gospel Truth, when even a superficial examination of the actual related facts shows them to be bald faced lies.

The Problem is that most folks are so mindkontrolled they are unwilling to even examine or discuss any of the background facts and details of these false narratives which would easily expose them as phony. Normal disbelief must be suspended.

In order for Americans to be successfully hived, they must be conned into suspending normal disbelief that would ordinarily occur when inconsistent or contradictory statements which are made by the USG and communicated by the CMMM.

The habitual ability to suspend disbelief has been facilitated by a lifetime of TV and movie watching for a strong social need to escape reality and temporary suspension of belief and reality is necessary in order to project oneself into the plot for the duration of the shows.

When most folks watch TV and movies and get deeply into a show this is actually a type of self-hypnosis and resembles what happens when folks read, hear and believe phony USG narratives dispensed through the CMMM without any critical evaluation from those with actual factual knowledge and serious research skills.

Hiving folks to create the AGP involves Pavlovian and operant conditioning as well as the dispensing of sophisticated propaganda by the CMMM.

Yes, the use of these Pavlovian and operant-conditioning techniques to mindkontrol the American populace and produce a hived AGM has been so successful that most folks quickly exhibit a recoil response when confronted with any real facts which show any USG narratives are likely to be false.

This of course prevents almost any real conversation about the real facts or issues of any of these staged terror matters or any questioning of the official narrative dispensed by the CMMM.

Denial and the Knee-jerk reaction to label Truth-Seekers as conspiracy theorists and whackos

When confronted with the basic facts of USG staged GFFA's, the typical hived American shuts down and rejects the message and the messenger with no critical consideration of any of the evidence.

When the average "hived" person who is part of the AGP is confronted with even basic minimal facts, their typical response is to shut down and react like mindkontrolled dummies, typically labeling any such person who present such facts as a "Conspiracy Theorist", when they are actually a Truth-Seeker and a free thinker, able to examine all evidence and claims.

This automatic recoil response to any intrusion into their accepted narrative in a hived individual is typically an unconscious and conditioned knee-jerk reaction instilled by USG based mindkontrolled technology based on frequent repetition of false narratives dispensed from CMMM sources regarded as credible by most viewers when actually comprised of well rationalized lies, deception and clearly false narratives.

One wonders, how did it ever get to this?

Here's how.

Classically in American early times, truth was a product socially constructed by one's immediate nuclear family, local community and the church. This was Gemeinschaft society based on homogeneity where common interests resulted in common group morals and beliefs.

With urbanization, mass production the society shifted to a Gesellschaft model based on heterogeneity, where many businesses make money off of other people's trouble.

Central Government became based on this principal and found that it could generate big revenues and gain more and more centralized power by capitalizing on the people's trouble and thus became interested in generating more and more "people's trouble" to increase power and tax revenues, since they found that the naive public could be easily manipulated into seeking increased safety and help from the central government, wrongly assuming that the government gave a damn about them.

So poverty was capitalized on and transformed into a very expensive centralized war on poverty which helped the enrichen and empower the politicians while doing a very good job spreading poverty.

And the drug problem which was small and controlled was capitalized on and transformed into the War on Drugs, also helping to enrichen and empower the USG while providing huge off-the-books funding for deep black covert operations to assassinate leaders, take down foreign governments, provoke foreign wars, and bribe and compromise American politicians.

This phony war on drugs has resulted in dramatic increases in drug abuse and addiction and huge growth of the drug cartels which are all in business one way or another with the USG, the CIA and the major Wall Street Banks.

It keeps the private prisons profitable and filled with harmless non-violent offenders who would be better served by medical supervision in a state with legalized and controlled drugs and appropriate treatment made available.

Certainly as shown in the book "Underground Empire" by James Mills the CIA was involved in the background of every major drug cartel supplying illegal drugs to America. There were several intel attempts to discredit the book, but senior insiders say that Dennis Dayle of Centac told his story accurately.

And a sensitive, little known Congressional hearing many years ago showed conclusively that many high ranking U.S. Customs officials were on the taker and allowing intel to traffic the cartel's drugs into America across border inspection points.

And the new and equally phony War on Terror is a concocted cover narrative, a big lie dispensed to the American People by the USG in the CMMM as a tool of state to increase central police state power just like the Nazis did during the 1930's.

Government Staged terror can be used to gain the passage on draconian, freedom robbing laws which would never otherwise be possible

If a government can secretly elicit massive subconscious primal fear in a populace, it is really quite easy to sell them the idea of increased police state powers for the central government in order to promise more protection and safety, when of course just the opposite will occur as Tyranny ensues. And so, instead of the Reichstag Fire, we have 9/11, and instead of the Enabling Act we now have the Patriot Act, the Military Commissions Act and NDAA, all of which are completely illegal, completely unConstitutional and actually constitute international war crimes and crimes against humanity just like those prosecuted at Nuremberg.

So the USG entered a phase where its main objective was to become as big and powerful as possible in order to further the interests of those offshore Banksters who hijacked it in 1913.

To do this these folks knew that they would have to engage in perpetual, illegal, unprovoked, unConstitutional, undeclared wars to attain these goals and that is exactly what they have done. And the back-up plan was as the public started to catch on, to bring the war home by waging it against the groups outlined, defined and accused by the intel agencies of the IZCS such as the ADL and SPLC.

And an essential part of the SSG plan to do this was to destroy the classical American family and replace it with a Globalist NWO one. In the NWO Globalist American Family, the new Daddy is the USG, the new Mommy is the Controlled Major Mainstream Mass Media (CMMM) and the new church is the public school indoctrination system. This is the reason so many adults seem so childlike and suggestible after the 9/11 attacks and the phony War on Terror ensued.

Breaking up is hard to do, very, very hard to do

In years past before the advent of the worldwide Internet, when folks try to expose the Big Lies of the USG dispensed in the CMMM it was typically an uphill battle, since any True-Believer" who decided to "jump-ship" from the hived AGM sensed and feared unconsciously that they would suffer rejection from mainstream society which is hived and substantially mindkontrolled by the CMMM.

Naturally this has classically been almost always an uphill battle, until the advent of the worldwide Internet, which is a major game changer on many fronts.

It's hard work for any government to set up the pretext for wars they deem necessary in order to maintain and expand power and this where the effective use of covert black ops is essential and staged terror is essential.

If the public was actually 100 percent informed of what the real truth was of that the USG had been doing in the background almost every top USG official would be tried under RICO or for Treason and Sedition, convicted and hung on a military gallows like the assassins of Abe Lincoln.

Thus we have the fake Gulf of Tonkin incident used to wage a criminal war in Vietnam. We have Operation Northwoods which fortunately was stopped by JFK before it could be used to start WW3 over Cuba. Of course the JCS tried again with the JFK Assassination and that too failed but they did get to continue their war in Vietnam which JFK was withdrawing from.

"All warfare is based on deception," wrote Chinese General Sun Tzu in The Art of War more than twenty-five hundred years ago

And it has now been completely established that the so-called terror attacks of 9-11-01 were actually staged by the NeoCons, the USAF and the International Zionist Criminal Syndicate as a pretext for the American people to willingly to give up many Constitutional rights for promises of more safety and to enter expensive, criminal wars in the Mideast under false pretenses which were unprovoked, undeclared, unConstitutional and clearly war crimes like the Nazis invading Poland (4).

This was all possible because it is well known by USG propaganda planners that any such major blood shock such as the twin towers collapse of 9/11 produces incredible suggestibility in the populace, allowing deep programming to occur. This is a well-established principle of mindkontrol and is exactly what happened.

Thus the American Group Mind (AGM) was programmed collectively to falsely blame the Arabs in the Mideast and to be willing to attack them in a clearly illegal war which constituted clear cut war crimes and crimes against humanity. This would have not been possible without the elicitation of massive primal fear at a deep subconscious psychological level and the stage terror of 9-11-01 attained this in spades.

Once a True-Believer understands the truth about any USG staged GFFA, the game is over and they become Truth-Seekers and are no longer part of the hived AGM.

Now, thanks to the first time penetration of the alternative "truth" media via the worldwide Internet, many folks are gaining access to the basic facts which quickly expose many recent USG narratives reported in the major mainstream media, making them "truth seekers" rather than the usual cloned "True-Believers" which most Americans have been.

So essentially there is a new internal information/truth Civil War now going on inside America between the old guard True-Believers and the new Truth-Seekers.

Truth-Seekers can no longer accept the phony war on terror or the numerous USG narratives which are Big Lies once they fully comprehend at least one staged GFFA (i.e. any U.S. Intel covert operation inside America) such as the Murrah Bombing, First World Trade center Basement Bombing, or 9/11, or any of the staged mass shootings such as Aurora, Sikh Temple or Sandy Hook.

Once a person understands even one of these the "jig is up" and they have knocked themselves out of the hived AGM forever.

Truth-Seekers know they do not have all the facts behinds these so-called Terror Events, but they have accessed enough truth that the official USG narrative supplied through the major mainstream media are based on "big lies" and that somehow the USG is deeply involved and responsible.

Some Truth-Seekers have inside information from many years of experience and firsthand knowledge about the various USG covert operations behinds these events and are coming forth and disclosing those facts for the first time.

And various former USG officials and experts who are highly credible have now come forth and provided massive amounts of facts showing complete USG complicity and responsibility for these acts of terror which are now known to be Gladio style, indie job, staged terror event to induce the public to give up more and more of their Constitutionally guaranteed rights.

As many truth seekers now realize when they attempt to inform others of the facts of the matters of the recent so-called "terror attacks" to show them they are staged terror done by the USG itself, the typical reactions is "oh, you are a conspiracy theorist", and their minds quickly close off from any truth input.

Reality is always a socially constructed phenomena

Reality is a socially constructed phenomena and the SSG gained control over the major mass media via Operation Mockingbird, a sophisticated and quite expensive covert operation of American Intel.

This has allowed near complete control over the narratives supplied to the public by the major mainstream mass media to construct this American Collective Consciousness or Group Mind, thereby constructing a nation of True-Believers in almost everything the USG claims.

When you have the means to print or issue all the money you want or can raise black funds from the massive sale of illegal drugs and weapons, it is not too difficult to buy up and control almost every politician and media editor you desire, thereby making complete control of the major mainstream mass media attainable.

True-Believers who break away from the hived AGM become Truth-Seekers and marginal men and it is best for them to socialize with others truth-Seekers who have left the hive too.

There are always "marginal men" who are resistant to the installation of this artificially constructed reality from the SSG's media propaganda dispensers. These folks are then free and independent thinkers (Truth-Seekers) who walk to their own beat and are far too skeptical to ever sell out to any group or ever become "true believers" of any USG dispensed propaganda.

The worldwide Internet has provided these free thinkers (Truth-Seekers) unbridled access to the facts of the matters behind major world events as never before.

Classically such truth was limited to late night talk radio and occasional paperback books. Now it is widely available for all and many who have been good USDG mindkontrolled clones are now seeing it and reading it for the first time. And some are quickly realizing they have been fed a pack of lies and mindkontrolled by false media dispensed USG narratives, thus starting to "wake up" for the very first time.

And once a person wakes up and gains the knowledge that the USG lied to them about one major assassination or terror event, the jig is up and these folks will no longer believe a known liar anymore such as the USG or their propaganda mouthpiece the major mainstream mass media. This quickly splits them off from the rest of the American group mind which has been cloned or "hived".

This of course can create some stress and separation conflicts with peers and other family members who refuse to examine or even listen to the real evidence which exposes the USG "Big Lies".

When folks fully realize for the first time that the USG is the world biggest liar and has fed them nothing but Big Lies, obviously this is a major life changing realization and one that has major future ramifications (5).

Until one breaks free from the hived AGM, one is remains a victim of numerous false USG narratives dispensed by the CMMM

The collective group mind of the average American which has been provided by the narratives of the USG via their controlled major mainstream media has served to create a complete firewall and cover for the SSG's long term criminal and unConstitutional activities, creating an instant wall of denial to any folks who discover and try to expose any of these activities.

But now thanks to the Internet, major cracks in this unitary American group Mind which is an artificial construct to control minds and limit truth, is now developing major cracks and splits.

And as the economy continues to worsen and the numerous BIG Lies of the USG are starting to unravel in the controlled major mass media for the first time as with the Benghazi affair, a major split is now beginning to occur in the American Group Mind, which offers great hope for real change for the first time in a very long time.

Induction of important suppressed stories into the CMMM by the Internet provided alternative media is becoming a common occurrence, as the CMMM is becoming less and less popular. And for the first time, there are now cases where the coverage of certain forbidden stories in the Alternative media on the Internet has raised so much attention that these stories have been driven into the major media.

One example is the massive procurement orders of DHS for ammo as a ploy to deny the citizen any. At first the USG vehemently denied this, but the alternative media has become so prominent that its exposure of the actual DHS documents has driven this case into the public spotlight and even into congressional hearings and proposed laws to prevent this.

Even though the JFK assassination attained many of the SSG's goals, it also began an actual process of splitting off folks from the hived American Group Mind which has continued and intensified with each of the staged Gladio false flag covert operations such as Murrah, the first NYC Trade Towers Basement Bombing, the 9/11 attacks, Aurora, Sikh Temple, Sandy Hook and now the Boston Bombing op.

And as folks are split away from the AGM, itself initially a painful event, they typically become very angry at the USG which has fed them years of constant media dispensed Big lies and pretty much duped them across the board. Once an entity such as the USG and its main partner in crime, the controlled mainstream major mass media (CMMM) is fully understood to be based completely on USG dispensed propaganda and Big Lies, these entities must never trusted again, ever. Anyone who examines their ownership quickly comes to an understanding why those comprising the CMMM are habitual liars and USG propaganda dispensers.

Litmus Tests for truth

There are important Litmus Tests which will clearly indicate whether an individual is part of the hived American Group Mind (AGM), a True-Believer, or whether someone who has broken free of the hive-mind of the AGP, a Truth-Seeker and Free Thinker.

The first and best Litmus Test is whether or not the person thinks Oswald was a lone-nut assassin of JFK and the Warren Commission was correct.

Hived AGP folks typically believe that Oswald did it alone and the Warren Commission was correct despite the fact this crime of the 20th Century was completely solved and proven beyond any reasonable doubt to have been done from deep within the USG, and the American Military and Intel with the FBI working overtime to cover it up.

Another key Litmus Test concerns the 9-11-01 attacks.

Folks who fully believe the phony USG narrative and the 9/11 report are clearly still hived members of the AGP and are unable to process truth and are seriously effected mindkontrolled victims or chumps without knowing it. The evidence available now clearly shows that 9/11 was a Gladio-style inside job false-flag attack beyond any reasonable doubt. Each of the following was a USG covert deep black op despite what the USG and the CMMM and the hived members of the AGP claim:

The Murrah Bombing, the first World Trade Center Bombing, the 9-11-01 attacks at the Twin Towers and the Pentagon, the Aurora Mass shooting,

The Sikh Temple mass shooting, the Sandy Hook mass shooting, and the Boston Marathon Bombing. The USG, state government and CMMM claims about these events are all blatant bald-faced lies and based on phony, concocted narratives which serve to support the public's willingness to give up more rights and support a blatant Nazi/Stasi style police state.

Fortunately, numerous high ranking American military have now realized that 9/11 was a USG staged Gladio style False Flag attack and know which elements inside and outside of the USG did it.

This of course is going to result in the eventual complete exposure and disempowerment of the International Zionist Crime Syndicate (IZCS) and many of those NeoCons and dual citizenship alliances responsible as well as their intel assets who serve the IZCS such as Aipac, the ADL and the SPLC.

And with the deep penetration of the Internet and the facts about these deep cover covert black ops now being revealed in the alternative media, it's only a matter of time that we will see the complete collapse of the IZCS, the SSG and the world wide secret Babylonian central bank "money-magick" fiat based usury system. It is a house of cards that will be trashed by the Third Force who has been using it to obtain its own secret goals.

Yes, it's pretty obvious from all the signs which suggest a complete central bank collapse is coming when one considers the massive issuing of too many U.S. Dollars, the BRICS nations clear damage to the U.S. Petro-Dollar system, and the secret centuries long plan of the Third Force to use and then dispose of their main cutouts, the IZCS and the central Banksters when finished with them (and that time is quickly approaching).

As Mystery Babylon Falls, the great City of Commerce, London, and its whole worldwide Central banking system will go down the tubes with it much to the surprise of these USG/SSG/IZCS entities which are now cornered, desperate and hanging on for dear life.

As this all occurs it can be expected that the Big Split within the hived American Group Mind (AGM) will continue to occur and will increase in intensity, liberating many from the USG dispensed lies and phony narratives, and from the homogeneous group-think of the cloned and hived AGM. It's always a somewhat painful process to break free from the hive, but once well underway there is a new found Freedom of thought which is exhilarating.

[Reprinted here with permission.]

References:

(1) http://www.veteranstoday.com/2012/06/11/mass-mindkontrol-final-nwo-assault-on-the-american-people-and-their-republic/

(2) http://www.assassinationscience.com/

(3) http://www.veteranstoday.com/2013/04/10/kingpins-and-cutouts-aliens-and-hybrids/

(4) http://www.veteranstoday.com/2011/08/14/peeling-the-9/11-onion-layers-of-plots-within-plots/

(5) http://www.veteranstoday.com/2013/03/10/belt-way-whoppers/

JAMES FETZER

KAREN PFANKU

Two Students Win School Carver Award

★ SOUTH PASADENA

Selected for high scholarship and Christian ideals, two seniors instead of one from South Pasadena High School are recipients of the annual Carver Award this year.

They are Karen Pfanku of 270 St. Albans Ave., and James Fetzer of 1800 Camden Ave. Karen served this year as president of the Tri-Hi-Y Council, secretary of Bengals, president of Huntington Auxiliary and president of the council of Pilgram Fellowship at Oneonta Congregational Church. In addition to the Carver Award she received other honors, including the Alcoa Award.

Fetzer was commissioner of finance, had a leading role in the senior play and has been active in St. James Episcopal Church. This summer he will go to Japan as delegate from the church to the World Council of Churches. In addition to the Carver Award he is recipient of the 4-year ROTC scholarship to Princeton.

Both students were speakers at baccalaureate services

[Chapter 40] Jim, Kevin: On Israel

"You cannot criticize Israel in this country (USA) and survive."

- Helen Thomas

JIM:

[Israel involved in the 9/11 attacks?]

Absolutely.

There's no question about it.

Israel was involved.

A lot of Zionist powerful real estate people were involved in the transfer. They were members of the Port Authority. The transfer of the World Trade Authority from public possession to private possession to Silverstein Properties was completely unnecessary. This was contrived. He took ownership just six weeks in advance. He fired the security firm that had been looking after the towers, the whole World Trade Center, since 1970 when it first opened.

He insured the buildings, now, against terrorist attack, and because there were allegedly two planes, got double indemnities, so he makes something in excess of $4.4 billion on a $114 million investment.

Larry Silverstein always had breakfast at Windows of the World at the top of the north tower, typically with his daughter, who also worked in the building. That day, however, he did not show up, nor did his daughter.

Israel had everything to gain here.

Israel wanted to use the United States to bring about the destruction of the sophisticated Arab states that posed counterweights to Israeli domination of the Middle East, and that's what they brought about.

KEVIN:

[Israeli involvement in 9/11]

I think Israel or the Israeli intelligence and Zionists in general were a major force behind 9/11, probably the major force.

I think that ultimately 9/11 served only the interest of extremist right wing Zionism. It didn't really serve any other interests in the long-term. It did allow certain people and certain industries to get rich in the short run but I don't think that simply getting rich in the short term would be enough of a reason to take such risks.

So I think that the only party that had a motive to take the kind of extreme risk that 9/11 represented was Israel, because the state of Israel is not legitimate and its neighbors are very strongly convinced that that's the case and that it's just not really going to be there in the medium term future.

The state of Israel is completely illegitimate. We're told in our lying mass media that the United Nations authorized the creating of Israel, well that's just not true.

The United Nations General Assembly, which had absolutely no power to do anything like that simply passed a resolution recommending the partition of Palestine along certain lines, but the Security Council, which could have made it legitimate, never did, so what happened was, the Zionists in Palestine just launched this brutal war to seize territory and ethnically cleanse that area.

So they went into villages and just butchered men, women, and children, a lot of them with bayonets, they would just go in and stab and slice women and children and kids and any men that couldn't get away with their bayonets.

So they had bayonet murders of many, many thousands of Palestinians in villages all over Palestine, and this wave of genocidal murders by what later became the Israeli defense forces led most of the rest of the Palestinians to flee. And many were mowed down by airplane gunfire, their ships were sunk and fired at, but a total of maybe a little less than a million Palestinian refugees did survive.

So at that point the Zionists just seized that territory and unilaterally just declared themselves to be the state of Israel, but they've never been legitimate.

The U.N. has never made that legitimate, and the U.N. actually passed resolutions saying all of the Palestinian ethnic cleansing victims had to be allowed to return, reclaim their land, and be paid a significant compensation for the crimes against them, and these resolutions have been repeated ever since.

And of course, the so-called Israelis, who really are just the Zionist occupiers of the legitimate state of Palestine, have never gone along with any of these resolutions.

So it's just been one case of aggression after another, including the war of 1967, in which they seized even more territory. Nobody in the region expects so-called Israel to be there in thirty years, and virtually everybody in the region as well as probably close to a billion people around the world, including myself, would do anything, including sacrificing our lives or the lives of our families' children or as many lives as it takes to make sure that Israel is not there in thirty years.

So, they're in a terrible situation, and that's one reason that they're so insane. They've got their Samson Option, they're threatening to blow up every capital in Europe and the Middle East with their nuclear weapons when the time comes for them to step down and let Palestine be Palestine. So they're in a terrible situation strategically, they're fanatically committed to their genocidal project, yet that project faces an extremely uncertain future at best.

So they have the motive to pull off 9/11, in order to brainwash the American people into perpetually going to war, for a hundred years or more, against the entire Islamic world.

That's really the only way that Israel could possibly try to save itself; it would be essentially the murder of every Muslim in the world and most of the Third World as well.

So, that's what I think 9/11 was really all about.

But I think they convinced a bunch of Americans, who might not have had Zionism as their first priority.

And that of course does not include people like Perle and Wolfowitz.

Those people are loyal, fanatical, genocidal Israelis, they are not Americans.

But people like Rumsfeld and Cheney and Bush are not great fanatical partisans of Israel, although I think Bush did get brainwashed to some extent by Wolfowitz.

But those guys, who were very corrupt and not terribly bright Americans, I think, got suckered into going along with this Zionist 9/11 plan.

They fed them a bunch of different lines.

They fed them this New American Century line that only something like a new Pearl Harbor would allow the U.S. to rule the world for the next hundred years, and of course this document, *Rebuilding America's Defenses*, called for this New American Century built on the back of a New Pearl Harbor was published on Sept. 11, 2000, exactly one year before 9/11 by the people that we now know did 9/11.

So I think these Zionists convinced the non-Zionists that what it was really about was American empire and possibly inoculating the world against terrorism.

Cheney is a lunatic and Cheney believes that if there's a one in a million chance that something terrible like a nuclear bomb going off in an American city could happen, we have to assume that it will happen and take appropriate counter-measures.

So that's exactly the line that the Zionists would have fed Cheney in order to make Cheney think that, well, if we're going to stop the possibility now, we have to consider the likelihood or the inevitability of a nuclear bomb, a terrorist nuclear bomb, going off in an American city. The best way to rally the nation's defenses to make sure that this doesn't happen is to inoculate the nation with a spectacular terrorist attack that doesn't really do much damage, that actually removes white elephant buildings and accomplishes urban renewal by other means at a very, very good price, actually makes everybody a bunch of money. Only kills a couple thousand people, which is nothing, you know. We plan to lose fifty million in a nuclear shootout every second of the day as we go over all our strategic plans for fighting the next big war, so three thousand people is nothing.

So, yeah, we'll go ahead and sacrifice these people as part of a sort of inoculation against future terrorism.

So I think the Israelis – or the Zionists we should say, because a lot of them are dual citizens, citizens of the USA – basically conceived and developed this whole plan for their own interests, and sold it to defense intellectuals and anti-terror people who were not necessarily fanatical Zionists, using a number of false pretenses.

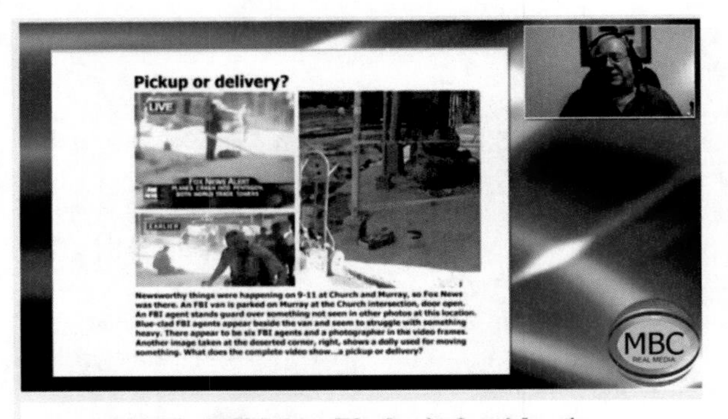

The Real Deal Ep # 205 Raising "The Smoke Curtain" on the Pentagon with Dennis Cimino

Iran fighting terrorists created by US, Israel: Academic

Home / Featured / Interviews   Tue May 24, 2016 2:46PM

MADISON

PRESSTV

Terrorists prepare artillery shells during clashes with Syrian forces near the village of Om al-Krameel, in Aleppo's southern countryside on May 5, 2016. (Photo by AFP)

Press TV has conducted an interview with James H. Fetzer, professor at the University of Minnesota Duluth from Madison, about remarks made by Leader of the Islamic Revolution Ayatollah Seyyed Ali Khamenei on using all means in fight against terrorism in the Middle East.

Jim and Kevin have continued to make their views know over a wide range of books and articles, radio shows and television appearances.

[Chapter 41] Kevin on Sandy Hook

"It's one big lie, not one word of it is true."
- Seymour Hersh on the U.S. Navy Seals raid that supposedly killed Osama bin Laden in 2011

KEVIN:

I was able to see a lot of the mainstream coverage of Sandy Hook because I just happened to be in the hospital getting a hip replacement at the time, so I had a TV in front of me.

I don't own a TV at home, so I would never have gotten to see the actual TV coverage, which is of course what most people see, and actually I do think that the manipulation of news events for propaganda purposes is done probably first and foremost through TV.

TV is the main mind control device out there, the most influential one, so everything they do they try to calculate it for the effect it's going to have through TV. And of course you really see this with 9/11, where the whole thing was like a Hollywood film and the purpose was to produce those TV images that were used to brainwash people on Sept. 11, 2001.

They story-boarded it, they had a script, they did a story-board out of the script, they did special effects, with "blast-code" software to see what different kinds of demolitions would look like so they could get the most spectacular TV images.

The propaganda aspect of news, which is of course the dominant aspect these days at least, is done primarily with the purpose of producing the right kinds of TV images and sounds to brainwash the population.

So anyway, I was in the hospital during the Sandy Hook coverage and got to watch it, and what I really noticed was that it was obviously pushing a gun control agenda.

I'm not a right-wing gun person by any means, but even from my lack of affection for guns, I could see that the way they were reporting this event was 100 percent pushing gun control.

It was like a PR stunt for gun control. You could just see the way it was being discussed, the way the images were being shown, the way they would bring on some guy from the NRA, who's of course off-script, and they would beat him up the same way they would try to bring me on *Hannity & Colmes* and beat me up to stop 9/11 Truth, they were doing the same thing to the so-called pro-gun zealot ... So it was a 100 percent choreographed pro-gun-control reaction at Sandy Hook, and that made me wonder if it wasn't scripted.

You never really know whether these events just happened, and they very easily could have these kinds of media scripts to push gun control, and just bring them out when some kind of shooting happens, because shootings happen all the time.

There's, I forget how many hundreds of school shootings every single year in the U.S., but rarely are there that many people killed. So that's one possibility, kind of the Naomi Klein Shock Doctrine hypothesis, that generally what happens is that the powers that be take advantage of naturally occurring events.

But of course we know that they often make the events happen, as they did with 9/11, so that's the other possibility, that Sandy Hook was staged in order to push this gun control agenda.

Either way you slice it, they obviously had a choreographed gun control agenda to try to brainwash the population through television.

Whenever something like this happens, where the so-called terrorist attack or violent incident creates a lot more damage and a lot more casualties than a normal one does, it becomes a candidate for an inside job.

Because what they want to do with these events is to maximize the propaganda impact of whatever they're going to put out, and to do that they need big spectacular-looking events. Theoretically the event wouldn't have to actually be spectacular, but it has to look spectacular and have a huge impact.

So the impact of those nearly three thousand deaths on 9/11 was all televised live in such a way as to induce PTSD in half the population.

Those 3,000 deaths have a huge impact, way more than the subsequent millions of deaths in the wars that were triggered by this event. So I think when they actually want to create a public relations kind of event to sell something, then one way to do it is to use an existing situation or problem, like the fact that we have these hundreds of school shootings every year, most of which don't kill anybody.

And then stage one, and make sure that lots and lots of people get killed and it gets wall-to-wall coverage, and the pre-scripted, orchestrated response is put out immediately afterwards.

We can see that in so many cases these big spectacular events are basically selling the fight against something that's normally – the normal incidents are not nearly that big or spectacular.

There really is a certain amount of terrorism, meaning non-governmental forces go out and try to do something to try to get attention for their cause, but it tends to be pretty small-time, you're more likely to get hit by lightning or drown in your bathtub than be killed by a terrorist. It's really hard to get the public to focus on it, so if they want to get the public focused on terrorism they have to do something like blow up the twin towers with three thousand people inside, which is something so far beyond the capabilities of any actual non-government terrorist group that it's a complete joke. And, likewise with these other types of terrorist events, these exaggerated events, like Oklahoma City, where the bombing was vastly larger than could have been done by a truck bomb; the Fort Hood shooting is a good candidate for a false-flag, because he managed to kill thirty people or something.

It is kind of ridiculous, killing that many people on a military base; there are a lot of military base shootings, but usually they would kill a couple of people. If they want to have an evil Muslim attack American military people, and make it a big spectacular media event, they have to make sure that a whole lot more people get killed than would be in a naturally occurring event.

So for that reason, I would suspect that this Connecticut school shooting could very well have been an orchestrated event. What they would be doing is saying, look, we've got all these school shootings that happen, we could easily use one of these to push the gun control agenda.

So let's send in our special forces guys, professional killers, and make sure that enough people get killed that we can turn it into a massive wall-to-wall media event. And we can orchestrate the coverage ahead of time, we can sit down and have our experts figure out exactly what tricks of coverage will have the desired effect, and so we'll be all ready to go with the whole reaction to the event.

Just like with 9/11.

If 9/11 had just happened naturally as an actual foreign attack, it would have been chaos and confusion afterward, and no one would really get it until someone actually took the responsibility and the reaction wouldn't be well-orchestrated, well-organized, choreographed to kind of galvanize public opinion.

Public opinion would not be galvanized by a naturally occurring event like that, in the way it was by the fake one, because they had the whole reaction ready to go ahead of time. Experts had spent probably years, if not decades, working out exactly how the government should respond to 9/11. So, even a buffoon like Bush was able to take charge and get 90 percent approval ratings, and people were sort of salivating on command like Pavlov's dog every time Bush said some idiotic thing, like, you're either with us or against us.

All of this had been scripted. The whole reaction was well planned.

So, I wouldn't be surprised if Sandy Hook turns out to have been one of these public relations stunts designed to push a public agenda, in this case gun control.

[Were they actors, was anyone killed?]

I'm pretty confused about that.

If they did do Sandy Hook as a false flag, it seems to me that they covered it up a little better than they covered up 9/11, in that there's all kinds of anomalies around Sandy Hook, but they're not the obvious, they don't reveal the truth, in and of themselves, as easily as the anomalies on

9/11 do. Obviously no plane hit the Pentagon, obviously the three towers are blown up, and the towers are exploding, they're not falling.

These things are just in-your-face obvious, and it takes about two seconds to put two and two together and figure out what really happened.

But with Sandy Hook, it's kind of hard to figure out. A lot of these anomalies don't point really obviously at exactly how it was done and so on, and so I'm still kind of agnostic about that.

I lean toward thinking it was an orchestrated, special forces type of event, but how it would have been done, I'm not really sure.

[How could people do this, though?]

They do it all the time, Mike.

What do you think they do in Iraq and Afghanistan?

Those people are psychopaths.

They do psychological testing on people in the military, and the ones with a certain I.Q., who test in a top two percent for psychopathy, get the special forces jobs, or at least the sensitive special forces jobs. Like the guys they brought into Waco to burn all those kids alive were obviously elite psychopaths.

[Now they say that yes, The Underwear Bomber was working for the CIA. Isn't that at least a little validation for the truth movement and yourself?]

When they do these propaganda events, they want to create a really spectacular effect on people as it's perceived through the media. Sometimes they do that by actually killing a whole lot of people, as apparently happened on 9/11.

And other times they might create kind of a fizzle, a bomb that doesn't go off, it's just a dud, but somehow they're able to spin that into a big story anyway.

You can see the way they think. It would be, you know, we can get an effect that would be similar to having a city nuked, but we can do it by just blowing up these Twin Towers on TV and having these people-eating pyroclastic clouds chasing people down the street. It's going to be such a powerful image that it'll have more psychological impact than if we actually nuked a city and killed a million people, so we're actually getting a lot of bang for our buck in terms of 3,000 lives, that's nothing in terms of what you sacrifice for wartime advantage.

And so the way they're thinking is how to maximize their impact on the public for, you know, the minimum of outlay or expense or whatever.

[... The Underwear Bomber]

It turns out nobody was even in danger because the so-called plastic explosives he had – well, they were plastic explosives, which is just Sterno, which is the same thing you heat your beans with when you're camping –

as campers know, Sterno isn't going to explode, you would have to get a blasting cap to make it explode.

So, there was never any danger whatsoever to any of those people on the plane, and so they had this idiot on the plane trying to light his Sterno underwear on fire.

It's just so bizarre to imagine that anyone would take seriously a terrorist trying to bring down a plane by, you know, putting Sterno in his underwear and trying to light it on fire.

It's kind of a joke, but somehow they were able to have the media put out a choreographed response, and to turn this into a gigantic incident to terrify people about the evil Muslims.

[How about self-doubt? When can we give permission to ourselves to say "we know it" without TV and newspaper validation.]

Well, for me the TV and newspaper validation doesn't mean much anymore. I learned about the JFK thing early on. I think I was about fifteen, so I have to think back a long way.

Also I learned that the Vietnam war was based on lies and evil back when I was, I think, twelve, or maybe eleven, so I'd have to go back to childhood in my memory to find a time when I didn't realize that we were being sold a lot of lies for nefarious purposes by the powers that be. So, for me, thinking of anything that the mainstream media says is validation, only in the sense that, ha, they actually admitted this.

[How about slipping between worlds, speaking with people "in the know" and then watching TV news at the fitness center on twelve TVs on the wall and rediscovering that probably 95 percent of the country believes something totally different?]

I don't watch TV news.

When I was in the hospital, it was just too stupid, for me, watching this stuff.

It's – I'm kind of just constantly rolling my eyeballs at the idiocy of everyone involved in making this stuff, and the idiocy of anyone who would actually watch it.

Call me an elitist, but that's just my emotional reaction to watching mainstream TV.

SWAT team present, windows undamaged, Wayne Carver present, crime scene tape up for a crime that has yet to be committed.

Unreal shooting caused by drilling holes to simulate gunshot trajectories, with perps caught in the act, Nobody Died at Sandy Hook *(2015), Ch. 7.*

[Chapter 42] "And I Laugh"

"The Russians, I think, say it best in one of their proverbs: 'There is no news in the Truth and no truth in the News.'"
"There are two well-known newspapers in Russia; Pravda and Izvestia. Pravda translates as 'truth'. Izvestia means 'news'."
- Edgar J. Steele

And I Laugh
by Mike Palecek

There's a photo on the Internet that makes me laugh.

A little brown boy holding a silent scream forever in four-color. Ha.

The horrified little fellow now has no arms or legs, or brothers, sisters or parents, and I laugh out loud.
I laugh at the Marines, being all they could possibly be in God's creation, at their tough-man commercials.

The Army of One. What a hoot.

The rough-guy coaches and players who let this boy die – what comedy watching them feel strong while letting the real battles be fought by little guys with sticks and bicycles.

The boy has a bandaged head.
He looks so scared his hair might turn white, as in a Hitchcock film, and it sort of makes me chuckle.

I laugh at the ministers here in town and here on this TV saying bless our troops as they defend our freedom.
I laugh at the well-schooled and coifed newspaper columnists with their earnest close-cropped photos in four hundred papers read by forty million people in forty million cities.
And I laugh.

The boy is flat on his back on dirty cement, with his stubs hastily wrapped in Ace bandages, surrounded by the world trying to get a look, by photographers and people on their way to work and out to dinner.

We are nothing. Nothing. Nothing!
Because this boy now has no arms. No legs.

Nothing we do today will mean a thing because we have ripped the arms and legs from this boy as if he was a fly and we are us.

This boy who could be my boy, lying there at the feet of the world and the world looking the other way.

Goddamn us.

Please.

Give us what we deserve.

If you are a just God, rain down fire and hell upon our heads. Lighting bolts upon our backyard decks and rivers of excrement down our smooth, well-scrubbed streets.

Please, dear God we pray.

When I awoke this morning I thought it essential to the world order and being right, and a good person, that I shave, help out with the dishes, be on time, and drive on the right side of the road.

Do a good job. Be pleasant. Smile.

But now I just can't stop laughing.

The world thinks it still matters, and that's kind of funny in a way.

There, the flag flying over the Catholic elementary school and the yellow ribbons tied to the light poles on both sides of Main Street. Stray cats wearing yellow ribbons around their necks, roaming the night, looking both ways before crossing the street, as if it mattered.

You are never so wrong as when you damage a young boy.

We sit down here like the Who's in Whoville celebrating the coming of War Season while this boy lies on the cold floor.

Tee. Hee-hee.

[Chapter 43] Jim: Top Ten Reasons; Kevin: Madison radio, Steve Nass, Fox News, Congress

> "But nobody reads. Don't believe people read in this country. There will be a few professors who will read the record. The public will read very little."
>
> - Allen Dulles, Warren Commission meeting, July 9, 1964

JIM:

June 25, 2006, L.A. 9/11 Symposium

Essentially, everything the government has told us about 9/11 is false. Let me offer an illustration. I've always been very suspicious of this scenario in which a rag-tag group of terrorists with box cutters could overtake four commercial airliners. In my opinion any group of American passengers confronted with a couple of terrorists with box cutters would have beaten them to death with their luggage.

So, let me offer you my Top Ten Reasons for thinking they [hijackers] are fake:

10. Their names do not appear on any passenger manifest.
9. None of them were subject to any autopsy.
8. Five to seven of them have turned up alive and well and living in the Middle East.
7. The FBI, nevertheless, has not revised its list.
6. A special agent of the FBI, by the name of Flagg, has explained that the FBI knew almost immediately the names of all 19 hijackers because of a piece of luggage left by Mohamed Atta, when he had driven up to Portland and then turned around and rushed down to Logan, just in time to participate in a hijacking from that airport. According to Flagg, this piece of luggage included not only a terrorist manual, but a very convenient list of the 19 hijackers.
5. They could not have flown the planes.
4. Those cell phone calls that we've heard so much about could not have been made at the altitudes and speeds these planes were flying.
3. During the trial of alleged 20th hijacker, Zacharius Moussaoui, a tape was played, a tape allegedly from Flight 93, which included the passengers discussing how they were going to attempt to break down

the cabin door using a drink cart. One astute student of the case wrote me to point out that this was ostensibly a cockpit voice recording, and that cockpit voice recorders do not record voices in the passenger compartment.

2. The last words attributed, on that tape, to hijackers, who were facing imminent death, was, "Allah Akbar, Allah Akbar", which is Arabic for "God is Great, God is Great". According to a Muslim member of *Scholars for 9/11 Truth*, the last words that a devout follower of Islam should say when confronting imminent death are not those words, but rather, in Arabic, "There is but one God, Allah, and Mohammed is his prophet." I therefore suggest that the writers assigned to this script simply didn't know enough to get it right.
1. Zacharius Moussaoui, this April, was subjected to a trial to determine whether he should be punished by life imprisonment or even death, for not coming forward to reveal the plot. The government maintained that, had he done so, he would have enabled the government to intervene and saved lives. I make three observations:

– A year before, April last, Zacharius Moussaoui, confessed to a different plot. He had knowledge that he had been involved in a plot to fly a plane into The White House in order to extort release of a terrorist, a sheikh, who had been in prison for terrorist activities in 1993. He denied that he had anything to do with 9/11.

– A year later, the federal government has played a shell game. And now they're insinuating and implying he had something to do with 9/11. As my good friend Webster Tarpley has observed, his man had no obligation to come forward and to confess his involvement in a plot, even if he had been involved in 9/11. We still have something here known as the Fifth Amendment. He had no obligation to incriminate himself.

– Third, and most tellingly, and this must have been incredibly embarrassing to the government, an FBI agent testified he'd been following Moussaoui. He'd been observing him taking this flight training. He had suspected he might be involved in a terrorist plot, even to fly planes into the trade towers, though he suggested later that was merely a lucky guess. He testified, under oath, that he had told his superiors about his suspicions. Not once, not twice – seventy times. And I say to you, five or six might be excused as ordinary incompetence; twenty or twenty-five may be criminal neglect; seventy times has to have been a matter of direct policy, deliberate policy. They were keeping these guys in reserve, so they could use them as their cover story when the government itself perpetrated these dastardly terrorist acts!

KEVIN:

[Madison radio interview, Steve Nass, the university]

Apparently, Steve Nass and Jessica McBride – probably with the help of Jessica McBride's husband, who was a Republican DA running for Wisconsin Attorney General, very much plugged into the Wisconsin Republican Party – cooked up this attempt to turn me into what they called Wisconsin's Ward Churchill.

And who knows whether somebody like Karl Rove would have been behind that, I don't know.

I assume so, because I assume that this whole thing was about a kind of an attempt to preempt the truth movement as it was growing, and specifically to try to scare away scholars and professors who had been joining *Scholars for 9/11 Truth* at a rapid rate at that point.

So in order to strike back I think they were looking for a whipping boy to show the other scholars what might happen to them if they went public or did any major work for 9/11 Truth.

So at some point in mid to late June 2006, Jessica McBride called me up and requested an interview that evening, and also requested that I send her a copy of my syllabus. So I did. I sent her my syllabus, which was for a 16-week course on Introduction to Islam.

And one of those weeks was about conflicting interpretations of the war on terror. And one of those interpretations that would be looked at would be the inside job interpretation, which is held by about 80 percent of the world's Muslims.

And we would be looking at other interpretations as well, including the neo-con interpretation of Bernard Lewis, and the kind of moderate mainstream interpretation of John Esposito.

So I sent her that syllabus, and that evening did the interview with her, pretty late, I think it was like 9 to 10 or something.

And she opened the interview by introducing me as this wicked professor, Wisconsin's Ward Churchill, who is inflicting these terrible, dangerous ideas on the poor, innocent students.

Her show continued for a couple hours after the interview was over. I think her show went on to 11 p.m. or midnight.

And then the next morning, apparently at 9 a.m. in the morning, Steve Nass issued a press release calling on the university to fire me because of the outrageous statements on 9/11 that I had made on this radio show the night before.

It's pretty unlikely that Steve Nass just happened to catch that radio broadcast and somehow get his press release written in time to be issued by 9 a.m. in the morning.

So, it's obvious to anybody who thinks about it that this was a pre-planned setup, an ambush attack for political purposes.

The next morning I went to Milwaukee for an interview with a TV station.

I'd done a few interviews about 9/11 before and it was just by coincidence that my friend Robb over in Milwaukee had managed to set up a TV interview, and so I drove over there having no idea that Steve Nass had just called for me to be fired.

And when I did the TV interview, apparently the TV people didn't know that either. They didn't make the connection between me and this news story that was just starting to go out.

It was kind of weird.

Driving back from Milwaukee to Madison after having done that interview, this is gonna sound pretty strange, but it's the truth.

An unmarked black helicopter, a proverbial black helicopter, came down from the north, right, side of my car as I was driving back to Madison, and like flew right over my vehicle.

It turned around then and made a loop on the south side of the freeway, and came back and flew straight back directly overhead over my car across my path again, flying back north. It was not all that close, it was up in the air several hundred feet probably, but what was kind of weird was the path it chose intersected perfectly with my car, twice.

It was like it flew down from the north, flew over me, and then quickly turned around and flew over me again, back to where it was going or where it had come from. I didn't think that much of it at the time, although it seemed a little weird given the whole black helicopter meme that the paranoid conspiracy theorists have talked about.

But then when I got home, this is what was really weird, as I was pulling into this graduate student and professors housing complex on the university grounds, where I lived ... just as I was pulling up the hill where you enter that complex, at the exact point where you go into the gates of that complex, a black helicopter, looked just like the same one, suddenly appeared from the left side, and once again flew right over the car. It was buzzing me for thirty seconds and then flew off.

And this was really strange, because I'd never seen that kind of helicopter in the skies of Madison ever before in my life. The only helicopters I'd ever seen were the red and white university hospital medical rescue helicopters.

So here's an unmarked black helicopter and now it's shown up to buzz me twice during one drive, a seventy-five mile drive from Milwaukee to Madison.

And that got me feeling a little strange because here I'd just been on television in Milwaukee talking about 9/11 being an inside job, but at this point I wasn't yet a public figure.

So I went to my apartment and Fatna said, some media's trying to get hold of you or something, they called here. I said, really, why is that? She said, I don't know.

So then the phone rang, and it was, who was the first one? I think it was a local TV channel, either Channel 27 or Channel 3, that was asking for my reaction to Steve Nass' statement calling for me to be fired.

I didn't know anything about that statement, but I said whatever I said, reacting to it, not having heard of it before. And then the phone just kept ringing, and it was one journalist after another asking for my reaction.

So I knew something big was going on. And then suddenly it was all over Fox and CNN and the newspapers and so on.

Right around that time Jim Fetzer had been on *Hannity & Colmes* and they brought in the substitute host Oliver North and Jim made mincemeat of Ollie North.

It's one of the all-time great 9/11 interviews, so now that I'm suddenly hitting this media buzzsaw, one of the invitations that came in was from Fox. They sent a limousine to take me from Madison over to Milwaukee to do the interview in the studio in Shorewood, north of Milwaukee.

And it was kind of an uncomfortable situation. I was sitting on a very high stool in the middle of a room with quite a few people around, sort of, all of the edges of the room.

And I was looking into a camera, and I couldn't see the people I was talking to, and I'd never really heard of *Hannity & Colmes*, except maybe vaguely. I hadn't been watching TV. I'd been focusing on learning Arabic and doing my dissertation.

I barely even knew who they were, and so I didn't really know who I was talking to. So it was kind of a surreal experience, sitting there staring into a camera, can't see who I'm talking to, can just hear their voices on the headphones.

But I was kind of juiced up about it, because I'd been putting out this 9/11 Truth information for years and was annoyed at the absolute stupidity of so many people on this, and they annoyed me, and so I had a pretty spirited exchange with them.

But I kind of thought I'd been too excitable and hadn't performed all that well. And the people in the studio actually looked pretty glum afterwards. One of them, said, huh, that went well, didn't it. I was taking that as meaning that my performance hadn't really been very good.

So I got in the limousine to go back to Madison, and the phone rang and the first call was from Faiz Kahn, and he was an old Muslim 9/11 Truth friend. He's a medical doctor and one of the original Muslims for 9/11 Truth.

He was very excited. He said, I just flew back from India. I'm in the airport. I saw you annihilating Sean Hannity on the airport TV. I can't believe it! Am I dreaming? He hadn't ever imagined we were going to get that kind of exposure.

And then I got a bunch of other phone calls on the ride back, too, and people seemed to be very happy with the interview from the 9/11 Truth side.

And then the next morning I got a call from the provost of the university, Patrick Farrell. And he said, Kevin, you're killing us! Don't do this!

So then we negotiated, and I said, well, I'm not going to shut up. He wanted me to just go off. He said, don't you have a cabin in the woods somewhere? Can't you just go off and hide and not communicate with these media people?

I said, no, I've been waiting for years to get this message out, so I can't do that, but is there any particular type of media exposure that you find more objectionable than some other type? He said, yes, the right wing media. Stay off of Fox. Stay away from these right wing lunatics.

I don't know if he quite put it in those terms, but pretty close. It was obvious that he ... Patrick Farrell is not a stupid guy. He's an engineer too, so I wouldn't be surprised if he actually gets 9/11 Truth.

But he had to do his job and protect the university. So we negotiated and I told him, I won't go on Fox, I won't debate on Fox while I'm still teaching, and then once I'm done teaching I might go back on.

I kept doing other media, but I waited. O'Reilly was bugging me to go on his show from that point on. I think there were more than ten times I got called by O'Reilly's people trying to talk me into going on his show.

So finally I agreed with them and went on his show in like December, after the semester ended, so I could keep my promise to Patrick Farrell.

[On O'Reilly]

That time it was in Madison.

I think I drove my own car that time.

With O'Reilly it was kind of weird, because O'Reilly, I don't know if he was mad at me because I wouldn't go on his show, but shortly after the Hannity show, after I turned down O'Reilly, he made what sounded to a lot of people like a death threat against me.

The quote was something like, "Well, my old chancellor at Boston University, John Silver, knew what to do with people like Barrett. If he'd been there he would have been found floating in the river down to the harbor."

So it sounded like he was thinking that the university should call out the mafia to assassinate me or something. So that got a lot of play. And then since O'Reilly couldn't get me, he brought on my student, a student from my class, defending me. And he very surreptitiously and underhandedly humiliated her on his show, and made a complete fool of himself in doing so. It's actually a great episode of O'Reilly.

So that's what led up to it, and then in December when I finally went on his show, it was a bit of an anti-climax, but I got in a good joke at the end of the interview, so it's not too bad of an interview.

[What happened with your job?]

The whole controversy was about whether I should be allowed to teach the class, the Intro to Islam class, that fall, 2006.

And the university refused to fire me, and Nass and most of the Republicans in the state legislature kept urging them to fire me. And then I would shoot back at Nass in the media, which would irritate him and he would shoot back at me.

I was doing this on purpose because I just wanted to get as much 9/11 Truth information into the media as possible.

So that kind of went on through the semester. The university, I pushed it as hard as I could without giving them any excuse to fire me. So they didn't fire me and the class was very popular.

I had like 180 students. And these classes usually had 20 or 30. And I got very high ratings from the students. It was a very successful class and there were people in there monitoring the class from the university.

There were occasionally TV crews, and there were a couple of like young Republican snitches who were trying to find something outrageous that I did, to tell to Campus Watch and Daniel Pipes.

But the snitches were basically disappointed and the class went very well. But the problem was that I had a semester by semester contract, and they didn't renew the contract.

They don't have to give any reason for that.

Had they renewed the contract, there would have been more controversy, more lost money and so on, so you can see why they didn't, but it was still obviously a case of a political blacklisting.

[So, the next semester – beginning in January – you had no teaching to do?]

That's right.

No, I think that semester I was teaching still at Edgewood.

Edgewood College is a Catholic College in Madison.

Teaching Intro to Islam.

[Do you feel you are blacklisted to teach anywhere now? Feel or know?]

Well, I know I'm blacklisted at the University of Wisconsin, because I have sources on the hiring committee.

At Madison my source on the hiring committee has told me that the subject came up, and it was made clear that it would be politically impossible to hire me. That was in the Asian Program at the University of Wisconsin-Madison.

I also have a source, who went public, actually. His name is Howard Ross. And he was the source on the hiring committee for the University of Wisconsin-Whitewater.

And he has testified in public, and even on my radio show, that I was discriminated against, and that I was by far the best candidate of the three finalists for their tenure track job there.

And then I became the only candidate when the other two went elsewhere. And they were all set to hire me when someone on the committee started ranting, brought up the issue of my 9/11 work, and basically stopped the hiring process cold.

So Howard Ross was the Dean of Humanities at the time and he was part of that hiring process and so he became a whistleblower.

He had his own fight with the university, and so he went public about that. So it's very clear that I've been blacklisted at the University of Wisconsin-Madison and the University of Wisconsin-Whitewater, which presumably means the University of Wisconsin system.

And there are some other applications that I've made that were treated in ways that make it obvious that I was blacklisted as well.

I applied for an Islam job at the University of Illinois Champaign-Urbana, for which I was eminently qualified, and they closed the position without hiring anyone, which is what happened at Whitewater also.

[Is that frustrating? Isn't the purpose of a university to dig down deep, to question, in order learn?]

Especially if you're teaching about Islam today.

The fact is that 80 percent of the world's Muslims think 9/11 was in inside job, and it's over 60 percent here in the U.S. And those polls probably understate the case. So if you're going to teach about Islam and say anything at all about any kind of current events whatsoever, this is a huge fact that has to be discussed.

Once you discuss the fact that 80 percent of the world's Muslims think that 9/11 was an inside job designed to launch a war on Islam, then you have to ask, why do they think that?

Among the many answers to why do they think that are some empirical facts. So there's just no way anyone could honestly avoid that topic. I think that when you're teaching in this kind of situation, you should not selectively present facts, but just try to cover the different points of view of informed people, which is what I did in my teaching.

I would never really come down on one opinion; the students wouldn't necessarily know what point of view I tended to believe. I would say, well, these people think this and these people think that, make up your own mind.

But you have to at least point out that the vast majority of Muslims are convinced 9/11 was an inside job. Basically introduce students to the perspectives of people who have been debating that question. If you don't do that, how could you – you could teach medieval Islamic studies or something, or you could teach theology, but you can't really do an Intro to Islam course without at least touching on that.

And if the students want to follow up and really learn something about it, they can, or if they don't, they don't have to.

[You ran for office in 2008 for the U.S. House of Representatives as Libertarian. How did that go?]

I was doing it mainly as a way to try to introduce some truthful views into the debate.

I wasn't really expecting to win.

In fact, I would be horrified if I were actually convicted and sentenced and forced to serve a term in Washington, D.C. I really would not be all that eager to move to Washington, D.C. and hang out with those Congress critters. So it was never really meant to try to win, although that's always a possibility to be dreaded. It was mostly just a platform to get media exposure for 9/11 Truth and other important issues, including the bankster bailout fraud.

That was the year, 2008, that the bankster bailout happened. The New World Order banksters crashed the economy on September 11, 2008, obviously sending a kind of a message. I was out there hammering at the incumbent, Ron Kind, who was in favor of the bankster bailout and voted for it, even though he admitted that every single one of the calls, many, many calls from his constituents, was adamantly against it. It was interesting. The problem of course, was that I was wildly underfunded, virtually unfunded.

I never hit the $5,000 threshold where you have to report. But I did get a little extra media exposure, like on Wisconsin public radio, I think, I did three or four radio interviews.

It's normally impossible to get a word of 9/11 Truth onto Wisconsin public radio. They cut you off. They have orders to hang up on anybody who brings it up. But here was a way to make sure they covered it, because they have to cover political candidates.

[So, you were on the ballot, had to go get the signatures to get on the ballot, right?]

I got the signatures to be on the ballot. I had some helpers, but I got the majority of signatures myself. I went to places like parades and fairs and supermarkets. There was actually one supermarket in Prairie du Chien that was incredibly productive as a place to get signatures.

My favorite place to hang out asking for signatures was the co-op in Viroqua, because Viroqua is really a very enlightened kind of place.

People are very aware. It's like the most rural place in Wisconsin, probably one of the most rural places in America. It's full of back to the land hippie types, organic vegetable growers, and things like that, family farmers, and they're all very up on just how nasty the federal government is. And unlike some of the rural folks like in Texas and Kansas and places like that, these Viroqua people are not really coming at it from a right-wing perspective.

There's a lot of right wing Tea Party populism in a lot of places, but in Viroqua, along with that, there's also a fair bit of sort of the progressive era type of left wing populism. That was where I got most of my votes, both in the primary election and in the general election.

[Did you ride in parades?]

No.

[How many votes?]

Won the primary with 60 percent of the votes. Which was a surprise because I was the unorthodox Libertarian. The other guy was a much more orthodox Libertarian. I was the left-wing Libertarian calling for single-payer health care, which is totally hated by most Libertarians, so everybody was really shocked when I won the primary. In the general election it was like three percent or something. The total number was over 8,000.

[What is your general feeling about having done that, running for office?]

I think people should do it more often.

I think people who are unhappy with the state of affairs should run, not necessarily because we have such a wonderful free and democratic system where we can just change things through the electoral system, but I think it's just one of the tools for change.

And it's a very good way to get that media exposure, and to try to change the conversation and if more people did it, it would at least noticeably change the conversation.

Jim Fetzer with Ollie North on "Hannity & Colmes" (22 June 2006).

Jim Fetzer with Sean Hannity on "Hannity & Colmes" (28 September 2006)

[Chapter 44] Jim: Conspiracies and conspiracism

> "This nation must have a revolution every twenty years in order to cleanse it from the control of the special interests who will inevitably exercise power beyond their numbers."
>
> - Thomas Jefferson

Conspiracies And Conspiracism
by Jim Fetzer
Online Journal 28 June 2010

MADISON, Wisc. – A new study from Political Research Associates entitled *Toxic To Democracy: Conspiracy Theories, Demonization, & Scapegoating*, by Chip Berlet, now proclaims that conspiracy theories are "toxic to democracy" because they share some portion of moral responsibility for irresponsible acts, such as the shooting of the abortion provider, Dr. George Tiller, which some have associated with Rush Limbaugh and other pro-life zealots.

By adopting a sweeping stance that does not discriminate between different cases on the basis of logic and evidence, Berlet discredits himself. Since conspiracies only require collaboration between two or more individuals in illegal acts, they are as American as apple pie.

Perhaps Berlet didn't get the memo, but according to the government, the U.S. was attacked on 9/11 by 19 Islamic fundamentalists who used box cutters to hijack four airplanes, outfox the most sophisticated air defense system in the world, and commit multiple atrocities under the control of a guy in a cave in Afghanistan.

When I published a critique of the "official account", which suggests the facts contradict it, I used the title, *THE 9/11 CONSPIRACY*, in the knowledge that either way a conspiracy was involved – either one told by the government using *THE 9/11 COMMISSION REPORT*, or something far more sinister, which involved key members of the Bush administration with a little help from their friends.

(See, for example, *9/11 and the Neo-Con Agenda,* and the PowerPoint presentation, *Was 9/11 an "inside job?"*, both archived at 911scholars.org.)

According to Berlet, belief in a conspiracy turns out to be the manifestation of a "belief system" that violates the principles of logic. Having taught logic, critical thinking, and scientific reasoning for 35 years, however, the violations of logic seem to be committed by the author.

Berlet commits many fallacies in the course of his study, including some stunning, easily disprovable generalizations about reasoning:

> Conspiracism is neither a healthy expression of skepticism nor a valid form of criticism; rather it is a belief system that refuses to obey the rules of logic. These theories operate from a pre-existing premise of a conspiracy based upon careless collection of facts and flawed assumptions. What constitutes 'proof' for a conspiracist is often more accurately described as circumstance, rumor, and hearsay; and the allegations often use the tools of fear – dualism, demonization, scapegoating, and aggressively apocalyptic stories – which all too often are commandeered by demagogues. (Toxic to Democracy)

No one would deny that a certain proportion of the American public may be vulnerable to "conspiracism" in this sense, which represents the modus operandi of Rush Limbaugh and other right-wing zealots who find conspiracies to be a ubiquitous part of public life, from left-wing efforts to spend the country into oblivion, to encouraging illegal immigrants to flow into the country unabated, to questioning whether Barack Obama has the qualification for office of being "native born".

These are the kinds of "conspiracy theories" that are a dime a dozen, that find gullible followers across the country by the bushel basket.

But so what? If conspiracy theories like these are supposed to be "toxic to democracy", then democracy needs to be made of sterner stuff. Circumstance, rumor, and hearsay, after all, tend to be the starting point for more serious studies of specific events. The BP oil disaster in the Gulf of Mexico is a case in point. Who has not heard swirling rumors about Halliburton having cut corners, the BP practice of putting profits before safety, and the further catastrophes that await those who reside along the coast of the states that are most directly affected? Puzzlement over phenomena that do not readily fit into our background knowledge and preliminary understanding is the point of departure for scientific investigations that may better reveal the truth.

Suppose we were prohibited from speculation and rumor in relation to the events that have made the most difference to American history in recent time? The most important aspect of reasoning is comparison between different theories to measure which best explains the data. Indeed, Jesse Ventura's *AMERICAN CONSPIRACIES* advances no less than 14 illustrations of the collaboration between two or more individuals to bring about illegal ends, from the assassination of Abraham Lincoln (where four co-conspirators were hanged from the same gallows at the very same time), to the big-money conspiracy to overthrow the government in 1934, on to Watergate, the Jonestown Massacre, the Iran-scam that gave the presidency to Ronald Reagan, drug-dealing by the CIA, and many more – a list that can be readily expanded by the assassinations of JFK, RFK, MLK, and Malcolm X (see, for example, *JFK and RFK: The Plots that Killed Them, The Patsies that Didn't*).

Berlet claims (what he calls) conspiracism "must be confronted as a flawed analytical model, rather than a legitimate mode of criticism of inequitable systems, structures, and institutions of power." He claims it suffers from four debilitating features as "metaframes" of the model:

dualism, according to which the world is – presumably simplistically – divided into the forces of good and the forces of evil;

scapegoating, according to which an individual or group of people is wrongly stereotyped with negative characteristics;

demonization, according to which an individual or a group is taken to be the personification of evil; and,

apocalyptic aggression, which occurs when scapegoats are targeted as enemies of the "common good" and may be subjected to violence.

What is fascinating about these categories is how well they fit many of the government's own campaigns to convince the American people to support an unpopular course of action. After 9/11, for example, the world was divided into the forces of good (the Americans) and those of evil (the Mulsims). Members of the Muslim community were said to be fanatical and violent, contrary to the principles of the Koran. 19 alleged hijackers and al Qaeda were scapegoated as responsible for those atrocities. And wars of aggression would be launched against Iraq and Afghanistan, which continue to this day.

Berlet tells us that what "conspiracy theorists lack is the desire or ability to follow the basic rules of logic and investigative research." We can all remember being told Saddam Hussein was responsible for 9/11, but eventually even George W. Bush acknowledged that Saddam had nothing to do with 9/11. We were told that Iraq was in cahoots with al Qaeda, but investigations by the Senate and the Pentagon showed that that was not the case. And when Ed Haas of *The Muckraker Report* questioned Rex Tomb of the FBI about why 9/11 received no mention on a "wanted poster" for Osama bid Laden, he was told the reason was the FBI had "no hard evidence" connecting Osama bin Laden to the events of 9/11. But if Saddam was not responsible and if Osama was not responsible, then who was responsible for 9/11?

Indeed, according to *THE 9/11 COMMISSION*, 15 of the 19 alleged hijackers were from Saudi Arabia. The number from Iraq was zero. So why did we attack Iraq instead of Saudi Arabia? That looks like a stunning illustration of the failure to follow basic rules of logic or investigative research. As Ron Suskind, *THE PRICE OF LOYALTY*, reported, George W. Bush's first secretary of the Treasury, Paul O'Neil, was astonished that war with Iraq was discussed at the first meeting of the cabinet, nearly nine months before the events of 9/11. Which means 9/11 was used as a fabricated rationale to support a predetermined conclusion, which appears to have been a policy that was adopted by Bush and Cheney before their formal inauguration.

While Berlet insists that "conspiracism" fails to follow the basic rules of logic and investigative journalism, he should have explained that rumor and conjecture represent the second stage of scientific modes of reasoning, where it is crucial to elaborate all possible alternative explanations to insure that the true hypothesis is not excluded from scratch. Thus, the first stages of puzzlement and of speculation are followed by those of adaptation (of hypothesis to evidence, using likelihood measures of evidential support) and of explanation (when the evidence has "settled down" and the best supported hypothesis is entitled to acceptance in the tentative and fallible fashion distinctive of science (see *Thinking about 'Conspiracy Theories: 9/11 and JFK*).

The essence of Berlet's book, however, is that he believes conspiracy theories come out of psychological needs of prejudiced people, which makes them INTERNAL FANTASIES. He is thereby throwing the crime baby out with the conspiracy bath water. Conspiracies really do happen in the EXTERNAL WORLD. They are not merely internal figments of the imagination. It is true that some people embrace conspiracy theories and reveal themselves by the inability to improve or adjust their views in light of new evidence or new hypotheses. If they are scapegoating, then the internal origin of their conspiracy need is manifest. However, conspiracy crimes are commonplace and external to us. When they are the subjects of objective investigations, those who study them are governed by logic and evidence, which are basic to rationality.

Ultimately, Berlet has defined a belief system called "conspiracism" that has only tenuous connections with conspiracies. While some gullible persons may satisfy its constraints, there are vastly more conspiracies than there are examples of conspiracism. Ask what Shakespeare would have had to write about if not for plots against the kings and queens of England. How many victims of conspiracies have died in the 20th century alone? In his brilliant study, *The Silence of the Historians*, for example, David W. Mantik, M.D., Ph.D., lists the names of more than two dozen prominent political figures – from Franz Ferdinand and Czar Nicholas II to Salvadore Allende and Fidel Castro – who were targeted for assassination by multiple conspirators, on a single page of *MURDER IN DEALEY PLAZA* (page 402).

The ultimate failure of Berlet's study is that it succumbs to the kind of simplistic thinking that he condemns. The world is divided into forces of good (the rational thinkers) and evil (the conspiracy theorists). The evil conspiracy theorists are stereotyped as trading in circumstance, rumor, and hearsay, while the rational thinkers follow the rules of logic and investigative journalism. Their careless collections of facts and flawed assumptions are often commandeered by demagogues. And of course they can be used to incite unjustified violence against innocent parties. But this presumes knowledge of which claims are true and which assumptions are flawed. Simplistic thinking of Berlet's kind does not advance understanding. As Michael Moore said, when asked if he was into conspiracy theories, "Only those that are true." Each case must be evaluated on its merits using logic and evidence.

Thanks to Mike Sparks for inviting my attention to Berlet's study and more.

James H. Fetzer is the editor of assassinationscience.com and co-editor of assassinationresearch.com. He has a blog at jamesfetzer.blogspot.com. His academic web site is found at www.d.umn.edu/~jfetzer.

- Posted by Jim Fetzer at 3:24 a.m.

REACTIONS:
3 comments:

Dr Stuart Jeanne Bramhall June 29, 2010 at 12:09 a.m.

There are some on the left who speculate that Berlet is possibly getting paid (by you know who) to refute carefully documented U.S. intelligence crimes by labeling them as "conspiracy theories". I have always believed that most creatures that walk and quack like ducks are usually ducks. I write about my own unpleasant experiences (with ducks) in my recent memoir *THE MOST REVOUTIONARY ACT: MEMOIR OF AN AMERICAN REFUGEE* (I currently live in exile in New Zealand).

Reply Republic Constitution December 22, 2010 at 7:50 p.m.

Berlet is a small fry compared to Dr. Michael Shermer. Shermer, like all skeptics, is a self-proclaimed expert on just about any field of study that one can imagine. Thus, is self-appointed position of debunking ghosts, aliens, ufos, 9/11 Truth, JFK research, telepathy, parapsychology, telekinesis, cryptozoology, and anything else you can think of that goes against his personal beliefs or government propaganda.

Reply Jim Fetzer April 8, 2012 at 8:10 a.m.

Actually, I had a relatively brief exchange with Michael Shermer on the *Free Beer and Hot Wings* show back in 2007 (which is archived on the *Scholars for 9/11 Truth* home page at http://9/11scholars.org) and a prolonged exchange with some of his defenders in relation to a piece he published in Scientific American in 2010 (which is lengthy but easily accessible at http://www.scientificamerican.com/article.cfm?id=the-conspiracy-theory-director). I am distressed that this guy gets so much press, since he is clearly obfuscating truths and not revealing them.

Iconic photo of policewoman leading string of children from Sandy Hook to safety.

Taken earlier, there are parents present with their arms folded looking on as the policewoman rearranges the children to get a better shot, Nobody Died at Sandy Hook *(2015), Prologue.*

[Chapter 45] More voices

"You can't wait around for someone else to act. I had been looking for leaders, but I realized that leadership is about being the first to act."

- Edward Snowden, NSA, CIA whistleblower

"The pattern is becoming too, too familiar. So, Boston cops were having a bomb squad drill the same days at the Boston bombing just like the attacks of September 11 in New York and the 7/7 attacks in London."

- Cynthia McKinney

"Suddenly it all comes down, all at once. You see what you are, what you have done, or, more accurately, what you haven't done (for that was all that was required of most of us: that we do nothing). You remember those early meetings of your department in the university when, if one had stood, others would have stood, perhaps, but no one stood.

"A small matter, a matter of hiring this man or that, and you hired this one rather than that. You remember everything now, and your heart breaks. Too late. You are compromised beyond repair.

"What then? You must then shoot yourself. A few did. Or 'adjust' your principles. Many tried, and some, I suppose, succeeded; not I, however. Or learn to live the rest of your life with your shame.

"This last is the nearest there is, under the circumstances, to heroism: shame. Many Germans became this poor kind of hero, many more, I think, than the world knows or cares to know.

"I said nothing. I thought of nothing to say."

- Milton Mayer, 1955, *They Thought They Were Free: The Germans 1933-45*

Reichstag Fire

The police conducted a thorough search inside the building and found Marinus van der Lubbe, a young, Dutch council communist and unemployed bricklayer who had recently arrived in Germany, ostensibly to carry out political activities. The fire was used as evidence by the Nazis that the Communists were beginning a plot against the German government. Van der Lubbe and four Communist leaders were subsequently arrested. Adolf Hitler, who was sworn in as Chancellor of Germany four weeks before, on 30 January, urged President Paul von Hindenburg to pass an emergency decree to counter the "ruthless confrontation of the Communist Party of Germany".

With civil liberties suspended, the government instituted mass arrests of Communists, including all of the Communist parliamentary delegates. With them gone and their seats empty, the Nazis went from being a plurality party to the majority; subsequent elections confirmed this position and thus allowed Hitler to consolidate his power.

- Wikipedia

"But while the story of the Communist plot to set the Reichstag on fire proved an enormous success in Germany and gave Hitler all the political leverage he hoped for, it was beginning to prove a liability abroad. No-one outside Germany would believe that the fire was not a put up job. The shirtless man who had been captured in the Reichstag while he was trying to spread the flames still further – a young Dutch hitch-hiker named Marinus van der Lubbe – was assumed by the world at large to be a tool of the Nazis."

- Sefton Delmer

[Sefton Delmer was a British journalist and propagandist for the British government. During World War II he led a black propaganda campaign against Hitler by radio from England. – *Wikipedia*]

William Shirer: *The Rise and Fall of the Third Reich*
The Reichstag Fire

That it was a crime, a Communist crime, they proclaimed at once on arrival at the fire. Goering, sweating and puffing and quite beside himself with excitement, was already there ahead of them declaiming to heaven, as Papen later recalled, that "this is a Communist crime against the new government." To the new Gestapo chief, Rudolf Diels, Goering shouted, "This is the beginning of the Communist revolution! We must not wait a minute. We will show no mercy. Every Communist official must be shot, where he is found. Every Communist deputy must this very night be strung up."

The whole truth about the Reichstag fire will probably never be known. Nearly all those who knew it are now dead, most of them slain by Hitler in the months that followed. Even at Nuremberg the mystery could not be entirely unraveled, though there is enough evidence to establish beyond a reasonable doubt that it was the Nazis who planned the arson and carried it out for their own political ends.

From Goering's Reichstag President's Palace an underground passage, built to carry the central heating system, ran to the Reichstag building. Through this tunnel Karl Ernst, a former hotel bellhop who had become the Berlin S.A. leader, led a small detachment of storm troopers on the night of February 27 to the Reichstag, where they scattered gasoline and self-igniting chemicals and then made their way quickly back to the palace the way they had come.

At the same time a half-witted Dutch Communist with a passion for arson, Marinus van der Lubbe, had made his way into the huge, darkened and to him unfamiliar building and set some small fires of his own. This feeble-minded pyromaniac was a godsend to the Nazis.

He had been picked up by the S.A. a few days before after having been overheard in a bar boasting that he had attempted to set fire to several public buildings and that he was going to try the Reichstag next.

The coincidence that the Nazis had found a demented Communist arsonist who was out to do exactly what they themselves had determined to do seems incredible but is nevertheless supported by the evidence. The idea for the fire almost certainly originated with Goebbels and Goering.

On the day following the fire, February 28, he prevailed on President Hindenburg to sign a decree "for the Protection of the People and the State" suspending the seven sections of the Constitution which guaranteed individual and civil liberties. Described as a "defensive measure against Communist acts of violence endangering the state", the decree laid down that:

> Restrictions on personal liberty, on the right of free expression of opinion, including freedom of the press; on the rights of assembly and association; and violations of the privacy of postal, telegraphic and telephonic communications; and warrants for house searchers, orders for confiscations as well as restrictions on property, are also permissible beyond the legal limits otherwise prescribed.
>
> In addition, the decree authorized the Reich government to take over complete power in the federal states when necessary and imposed the death sentence for a number of crimes, including "serious disturbances of the peace" by armed persons.

Thus with one stroke Hitler was able not only to legally gag his opponents and arrest them at his will but, by making the trumped-up Communist threat "official", as it were, to throw millions of the middle class and the peasantry into a frenzy of fear that unless they voted for National Socialism at the elections a week hence, the Bolsheviks might take over. Some four thousand Communist officials and a great many Social Democrat and liberal leaders were arrested, including members of the Reichstag, who, according to the law, were immune from arrest.

This was the first experience Germans had had with Nazi terror backed up by the government. Truckloads of storm troopers roared through the streets all over Germany, breaking into homes, rounding up victims and carting them off to S.A. barracks, where they were tortured and beaten. The Communist press and political meetings were suppressed; the Social Democrat newspapers and many liberal journals were suspended and the meetings of the democratic parties either banned or broken up. Only the Nazis and their Nationalist allies were permitted to campaign unmolested.

Paul Craig Roberts, on Kevin Barrett's *Truth Jihad Radio*:

I'm absolutely confident from my time in Washington, if something like that had actually happened, that if a few Arabs had achieved this type of devastating attack, there would have been every kind of demand for an investigation, but there never was. Congress didn't say, how did this happen? The White House didn't say.

The Pentagon didn't say. Nobody wanted to know. All they wanted to do was put out a report that Mohamed Atta did it, and that somehow it had something to do with bin Laden. So that's not an investigation of the most dramatic defeat of a superpower in world history.

[...] It's easy to see why Obama is worse. First of all, he didn't hold Bush and Cheney and the rest of them accountable for their crimes. They committed a lot of crimes, just under U.S. statutory law. For example, they violated the FISA law, they spied on people without warrants.

Each time you do that is a felony. It carries a fine and a five-year prison sentence. And he didn't do anything about the fact that they tortured people, which is also against United States statutory law, as well as international law. He didn't do anything about the fact that they went to war based on lies, intentional lies, fabrications, which is a war crime under the Nuremburg standing. So he let them all off the hook. He didn't hold anyone accountable for probably the greatest crimes that have ever been committed in the United States.

[...] So we now see the United States behaving the way the Soviet Union did at the height of the Cold War, and we see increasingly a move away from using the powers that they had justified on the basis of terrorism against ordinary people.

For example, it was a couple of years ago, the head of Homeland Security said they are no longer focusing on terrorism. They are focusing on domestic extremists. What is a domestic extremist? It's whoever the government doesn't like or who criticizes the government. I think the transition is happening. And as to whether or not they're bothered by the Internet, I think they have to go slow. They have to go piecemeal.

They can't just all of a sudden behave like Hitler or Stalin. They have to work into it, and it's accepted in stages. My own view is, that, if, I don't know how many people the Internet reaches or how many people use it for serious information as opposed to entertainment, but if you could get maybe 20 percent of the people aware, you would have a sea-change.

It never takes a very large percentage of the population. Five percent can't do it. 10 percent is probably not enough. But if you had 20 percent with us, or 30, then it becomes an effective constraint on the government. That's just too many people.

So, I wouldn't say that they don't watch the Internet or don't think the Internet can hurt them, it's just they haven't figured out how they're going to deal with it yet, and they have to come at it in stages, they can't just all of a sudden reveal themselves.

Francis Boyle, on Kevin Barrett's *Truth Jihad Radio*:

Barrett: There seems to be a direct link between the Nazi philosophy of Karl Schmitt and the neo-conservative philosophy of his top student, Leo Strauss, who brought it to the U.S. and trained Wolfowitz, Perle and this new generation of neo-conservatives in this kind of Nazi philosophy.

Actually, Strauss was even more radical than Schmitt. Do you think those guys were actually sitting down and plotting a takeover or coup d'etat in the United States.

We've heard from Stanley Hilton, who was a classmate of these guys at the University of Chicago, which you also attended. Hilton said that Strauss and his top students would sit around all night in bull sessions about how to stage a coup d'etat and overthrow the U.S. government and create the kind of government that they wanted. You think it goes back to a neo-conservative like sort of long-term plan to transform the country?

Francis Boyle: I think you're right, uh, Kevin. I went through the same program at the University of Chicago, in political science, where Strauss taught.

But he had just retired there so I did not study with him personally, but I did study with his foremost student protégé, co-author and executor of his literary estate, Joseph Cropsey.

So, yes, this was neo-Nazi type training. Strauss' mentor in Germany was Carl Schmitt, the law professor who justified hideous atrocities the Nazis inflicted on anyone, even the Jews. Not sure why Schmitt was never prosecuted after World War II, certainly there were grounds to do so.

But in any event, yes, these people are neo-Nazis. There's no question about it. Wolfowitz was there to get his Ph.D. while I was there. The whole institution is like that, right-wing, racist, bigoted, reactionary, war-mongering, you name it. [...] They are in fact neo-Nazis. We have to understand that. This has been an infiltration of neo-Nazi principles, values, philosophies, strategy, etc., into the American republic. There's no question about it. I've been fighting these people since I was at the University of Chicago.

WEDNESDAY, JUNE 1, 2016

9/11: The Who, the How and the Why

by Jim Fetzer

"(All) the wise people in the world who are experts on American policy and who analyze the images and the videos [of 9/11] agree unanimously that what happened in the [Twin] Towers was a purely American action, planned and carried out within the U.S"--Saudi Arabian Press

Saudi Press Just Accused US Govt Of Blowing Up World Trade Centers As Pretext To Perpetual War

Saudi Arabia has blown the whistle on the US over 9/11

It was only a matter of time. Once the infamous 28 suppressed pages of *The 9/11 Commission Report* (2004), which report on Saudi Arabian funding for several of the 19 alleged 9/11 hijackers--15 of whom were from Saudi Arabia, none of which were from Iraq--became the focus of public attention in the mass media and a bill had been introduced to allow US citizens to sue Saudi Arabia for its complicity in the atrocities of 9/11, it was only a matter of time before Saudi Arabia struck back by revealing that, on 9/11, the US had attacked the US in order to provide the pretext for perpetual war in the Middle East.

Jim also maintains a personal blog at jamesfetzer.blogspot.com.

[Chapter 46] George H.W. Bush & the JFK Murder

> "The whole aim of practical politics is to keep the populace alarmed – and hence clamorous to be led to safety – by menacing it with an endless series of hobgoblins, all of them imaginary."
> - H.L. Mencken

Did George H.W. Bush Coordinate a JFK Hit Team?

by Richard Hooke [with Jim Fetzer]
Veterans Today
March 30, 2013

George H.W. Bush was working for the CIA at least as early as 1961; more than likely he was recruited in his college days, at Yale, when he was in the Skull and Bones Society.

He and his wife Barbara moved to Houston where he ran an offshore oil drilling business, Zapata Offshore Co., which was a CIA front company with rigs located all over the world, making it very convenient for him to vanish for weeks at a time on CIA business where one would suspect what he was doing.

Bush was a major organizer and recruiter for the Bay of Pigs invasion, which was codenamed Operation ZAPATA. Col. Fletcher Prouty, former Pentagon high ranking official, who was the basis for the "Col. X" character in Oliver Stone's *JFK*, obtained two Navy ships for the operation that were repainted to non-Navy colors and then renamed HOUSTON and BARBARA.

George H.W. "Poppy" Bush is one of the few who could never recall where he was or what he was doing when JFK was assassinated; as a matter of fact, for over 20 years, he could not recall any details at all. He was 39 years old at the time and chairman of the Harris County (Houston) Republican Party and an outspoken critic of JFK. But on 21 November 1963, GHWB was staying at the Sheraton Hotel in downtown Dallas and spoke that very evening to the American Association of Oil Drilling Contractors.

Some time later, he was reportedly at "the ratification meeting" at the home of Clint Murchison, Sr., receiving last minute instructions and toasting JFK's murder the night before it happened. Deputy Sheriff Roger Craig reported to Jim Garrison he knew of twelve arrests made in Dealey Plaza that day. One, in particular, was made by R.E. Vaughn of the Dallas Police Department, was of a man coming out of the Dal-Tex Building, who said he was "an independent oil operator from Houston, Texas."

The prisoner was taken from Vaughn by Dallas Police detectives, and that was the last he saw of him: no mug shot, no interview, no fingerprints, or name is in existence of this mystery man. "Independent oil operator from Houston" was always George Bush's (CIA) cover. Exactly why was he arrested?

Garrison reported the man came running out of the Dal-Tex building and authorities could hardly avoid arresting him because of the clamor of onlookers. He was taken to the sheriff's office for questioning, although there is no record of it. Afterward, two officers escorted him out of the building to the jeers of the waiting crowd.

They put him in a police car and he was driven away; presumably right back to Dealey Plaza, because that is where he would be photographed with USAF Gen. Edward Lansdale.

Ed Lansdale was identified walking past "the three tramps" by no less authorities than L. Fletcher Prouty, the liaison between the Pentagon and the CIA for covert activities – who was the basis for the figure, "Col. X", in Oliver Stone's *JFK*, and Victor Krulak, who was a legend in the Marine Corps, both of whom knew him well.

As for the identity of GHWB, we have these observations from Ralph Cinque, a professional chiropractor, who is an expert in dealing with person's bodies and clothing:

> The case for George HW being there is cinched.
>
> What's the serious alternative?
>
> That a simply amazing coincidence occurred in which a man who looked strikingly like him just happened to be there?
>
> How many times does V (for Vendetta in the film, *V for Vendetta*) have to tell us that he, like God, does not play dice and does not believe in coincidences? Neither do I or any other serious student of murder, especially not when it involves the JFK assassination.

We have a photo of him standing in front of the Texas School Book Depository; we have photos of Ed Lansdale in Dealey Plaza at the time; and we have yet another in which Lansdale, who was famous for arranging assassinations around the world, is waiting to speak to him. In this case, it may justifiably be said that "these pictures really are worth more than a thousand words."

The Phony Alibi

The next that we hear of George H.W. Bush on 22 November 1963 comes from an FBI Memorandum according to which GHWB, having been cut loose from his anonymous interrogation at the Dallas Sheriff's Office, called into SAC Graham W. Kitchel of the FBI Office in Houston establishing a phony alibi in saying he recalled hearing, in recent weeks, a man named James Parrott talking of killing the President when he came to Houston. Shortly after Bush made this call, FBI agents were dispatched to the Parrot house. In another FBI memo, Parrot's mother said James, who was not home when the FBI arrived, had been home all day helping her care for her son Gary.

Mrs. Parrot advised that shortly after 1 p.m. a Mr. Reynolds came by and talked to her son about painting some signs at Republican Headquarters on Waugh Drive. The net effect was Kerney Reynolds, George Bush's assistant, gave Parrot an alibi, and Parrot was Bush's alibi; everyone's ass was covered.

A bogus phone call reporting a would-be assassin, who was one of Bush's Republican Party sign-painters, who himself is also freed by an alibi from one of Bush's buddies, really doesn't cut it; this is CIA Alibi 101. This type of stuff cannot be allowed to stand in history; if Bush was so concerned about his sign painter, why didn't he call in to alert the FBI before President Kennedy came to Dallas?

Bush has handed us his head on a silver platter with this memo; that's why he always said he didn't remember what he was doing on 11/22/63; he was hoping this incredibly stupid memo never surfaced.

Bush was worried he had been seen, and subsequently panicked and stupidly called the FBI, thinking he was being clever by providing evidence that it wasn't him that was arrested in front of the Dal-Tex building that day. It seemed like a good idea, at the time, but he was actually creating a permanent record of his involvement.

The memo identifies Bush as an oil man from Houston placing a long distance call from Tyler, Texas.

Bush was trying to establish he was not in Dallas during, or shortly after, the assassination. He must had been worried that someone would identify him as the oil man detained running out of the Dal-Tex building and being ushered in and out of the Dallas Sheriff's office.

This FBI memo, dated 22 November 1963, states that Bush called from Tyler, Texas but there is no proof he was actually there.

For over 20 years after the assassination, Bush said he did not remember where he was when the assassination took place at 12:30 p.m. in Dallas. The only other person of whom I have heard such a story was Richard Nixon, who flew out of Love Field just two hours before JFK flew in.

Conspicuously, this FBI memo fails to provide an answer to where George Bush actually was. The memo, however, does tell us that the first moment Bush was free to create a phony alibi was at 1:45 p.m. Bush was staying in downtown Dallas at the Sheraton Hotel, just few blocks from Dealey Plaza, yet he's trying to tell us he was in Tyler, Texas at 1:45 p.m.

George Bush's CIA assignment was obviously in Dallas, that's why he was staying there, so what would he have been doing in Tyler? JFK had just been shot at 12:30 p.m.

Would Bush not have been in Dallas at 12:30 p.m. as well, like everyone else, which was presumably the reason for him having been in town at the Dallas Sheraton Hotel? Would Bush not have driven down the road to Parkland Hospital, to check on the President's condition; like everyone else? Except Bush was being interrogated at the Sheriff's Office.

The FBI Memorandum

Bush appears to be a candidate for prosecution for treason: his alibis for 22 November 1963 are fabricated and we have evidence that shows he was there.

An FBI memo of a call from Tyler Texas does not prove his location, except that he had concocted a textbook CIA alibi, that he was lying and probably was an accessory to JFK's murder.

Bush maintained for over twenty years after the assassination that he simply did not remember what he was doing at the time of the assassination. As a matter of fact, he had no explanation even in his autobiography; and then, all of a sudden, he concocted a story that he was speaking in Tyler, Texas to The Rotary Club. Aubrey Irby said Bush was speaking when the bellhop came over and informed Aubrey that JFK was dead.

Mr. Aubrey passed the info on to Mr. Wendell Cherry Irby, who passed it on to Bush, who stopped his speech. According to Irby, Bush explained he thought a political speech was inappropriate under the circumstances, concluded speaking and simply sat down.

It is inconceivable that George Bush could not have recollected this event for more than 20 years. Walter Cronkite's announcement to the world that JFK was dead came on TV at 1:38 p.m.

Does anyone think that Bush was making a speech at that time, in Tyler, Texas, to the Rotary Club, after the President and Governor Connally were known to have been shot at 12:30 p.m.? President Kennedy had been scheduled to give a speech for lunch at the Dallas Trade Mart, after he passed through Dealey Plaza.

Everyone who was anyone around Dallas was going to attend that speech; and after JFK was shot, most rushed to Parkland Hospital to find out the latest news concerning the gravely wounded President and Governor. A speech being given in Tyler, Texas, inside a building owned by right wingers, to a group of Republican JFK haters, hardly qualities as evidence Bush was not in Dallas, where the available evidence suggests that he was on assignment for the CIA and was supervising the Dal-Tex hit team, from which three shots appear to have been fired with a Mannlicher-Carcano, which appears to have been the the only non-silenced weapon that was used.

Next, George Bush can be seen in photos of Dealey Plaza, next to the TSBD doorway and Ed Lansdale, shortly following the assassination. These photos, unmistakably George Bush, tell us where he went after he left the Dallas Sheriff's Office: back to the crime scene to get an update on all that he had missed.

He must have made his call to the FBI reporting James Parrot from the Dallas Sheriff's Office, at 1:45 p.m., because Bush is seen in Dealey Plaza with Lansdale, who would leave the plaza at about 2 p.m. and walk past "the three tramps" toward the parking lot.

Bush obviously had to go straight back to Dealey Plaza for him to be photographed with Lansdale, who remained around Dealey Plaza until

Oswald was arrested at the Texas Theater at 1:50 p.m. If Lee had not been arrested, then Lansdale, as "Plan B", might have framed the three tramps – Charles Rogers, Charles Harrelson and Chauncey Marvin Holt (often misidentified as E. Howard Hunt) – who had been directed to go to a boxcar, and the assassination have been blamed on them. Holt (CIA), the tramp with the hat, reported that they were found in the box car and taken through the plaza right after Oswald was arrested, which he knew because he was listening in on a CIA-provided radio concealed inside the paper bag that he is carrying in the familiar photos.

An Incriminating Memorandum

An FBI Memo from director J. Edgar Hoover, discovered by John McBride in 1988 but written just seven days after the assassination, provides verification that George H.W. Bush was an officer of the CIA in 1963, and was provided updates on the anti-Castro Cubans.

George Bush has said this memo was referring to another "George Bush" because he wasn't in the CIA at the time. But while there was another man by that name, he was a file clerk, and would not have been receiving a memorandum about the Bay of Pigs operation.

And other information has surfaced showing the George Bush in the document was indeed George H.W. Bush and had the same address. In 1976, President Ford appointed George Bush as the Director of the CIA, replacing William Colby. Bush served in this role for 357 days, from 30 January 1976 to 20 January 1977.

Bush falsely testified before Congress that he had never worked for the CIA, and it was widely reported that this was the first time that a civilian would be appointed to run the agency. But that was more poppycock from Poppy. George Bush appears to have been a CIA lifer, probably recruited right out of Yale.

George H.W. Bush (CIA) was also a close friend with George De Mohrenschildt (CIA); they were both members of the Dallas Petroleum Club. After De Mohrenschildt was found shot to death, the day before he was to be questioned by Gaeton Fonzi for the HSCA reinvestigation of the deaths of JFK and MLK in the late 1970s, Bush's name and address were found in De Mohrenschildt's address book: "Bush, George H.W. (Poppy) 1412 W. Ohio also Zapata Petroleum Midland."

CIA documents reveal that during the planning of the Bay of Pigs Operation (Operation Zapata), De Mohrenschildt made frequent trips to Mexico and Panama and gave reports to the CIA. His son-in-law also told the Warren Commission that he believed De Mohrenschildt was spying for the planned Cuban invasion.

George De Mohrenschildt, notably, was Lee Harvey Oswald's best friend, and appears to have been his handler after Oswald was brought to Dallas in the fall of 1963 and would find work at the TSBD.

Was Bush in the Window?

In *The Killing of a President* (1994), Robert Groden observes that a dark-complected man was seen in the window, whom James Richards has identified to Jim Fetzer as having been Nestor "Tony" Izquierdo, for whom there is a statue in Freedom Park, "Little Havana", Miami, Florida.

He was an anti-Castro Cuban, whom GHWB may have known from the Bay of Pigs. I have built upon the prior research of Duncan MacRae, *Dal-Tex Shooter 2nd floor*, which provides the most suggestive interpretation of the location from which three rifle shots appear to have been fired:

Given that Bush was in the building at the time, I infer that he was there in the background, inside the window of a broom closet of a uranium mining company on the second floor of the Dal-Tex building (which was a CIA asset).

My interpretation is that someone with GHWB's preppy haircut, large left ear, tall height, body language (head tilt), hairline part, and forehead profile was supervising the Dal-Tex hit team.

He was in Dallas for a reason, which was not to watch the presidential motorcade, and appears to have been a supervisor rather than a shooter, where it is very likely he was communicating using a radio device with a spotter. That spotter may have been Danny Arce (CIA), who can be seen speaking into a walkie-talkie out on Houston Street (in the Altgens6 photo above), standing next to Johnny Roselli (CIA/Mafia). Arce was talking with someone as multiple shots were fired. Ruth Ann (CIA) was reported (by complicit witness Loy Factor) to have been counting down a cadence, and to have been receiving information by walkie-talkie from the 6th floor of the TSBD.

Umbrella Man's companion, possibly Orlando Bosch (CIA) [NOTE: or Filipe Vidal Santiago], was not talking on his radio as the limousine passed the Stemmons Freeway sign and the Umbrella man pumped his umbrella up and down, which appears to have been a signal to "keep firing" because the target was still alive. [NOTE: It was at a location that was visible from all of the shooting locations that I have identified above.]

Chauncey Holt (CIA), the oldest of the tramps, said he had a CIA-supplied radio concealed in his brown paper bag that kept him updated on events even from inside the Rock Island Railroad boxcar. Holt had delivered 15 sets of fake Secret Service ID, and left them in a red pick-up truck parked in the lot behind the grassy knoll, which was used by the Dallas Police Department, earlier that morning, facilitating the escape of the grassy knoll shooters.

And Lee Bowers, the railway tower switchman, also testified to the Warren Commission that he observed strange people driving behind the picket fence and noticed one using a walkie-talkie.

Proof Sketch GWHB was there

(1) The FBI report (memo) Bush called in at 11/22/63 1:45 p.m. identified him as an oil business man from Houston, Texas, and the FBI office he called was the Houston office.
(2) The man arrested running out of the Dal-Tex building at approximately 12:35 p.m. on 11/22 was said (per Deputy Sheriff Roger Craig) to have identified himself as "an oil man from Houston". Bush was arrested by R.E. Vaughn of the Dallas Police Department.
(3) Bush called his FBI warning about James Parrot by long distance to his friend, FBI Special Agent Graham W. Kitchel, at the FBI office in Houston.
(4) James Parrot had no history as a subversive, but was a sign painter for George Bush's Republican Senate campaign.
(5) James Parrot was quickly provided an alibi by another friend, who was also an assistant of Bush, Kerney Reynolds.
(6) George Bush was staying in Dallas at the downtown Sheraton Hotel, and had spent the previous night (the 21st) there.
(7) There are at least two photos of George Bush (CIA) in Dealey Plaza speaking with police shortly after JFK was shot at 12:30 p.m.
(8) One of those photos has Bush (CIA) standing next to Ed Lansdale (CIA).
(9) One of the photos shows Bush near the TSBD doorway in a zone police had cordoned off, which would have taken special ID (CIA).
(10) The photo next to Lansdale most likely was taken between 1:45 p.m., when Bush called in his bogus FBI memo, and 2 p.m., when Lansdale is pictured exiting the plaza passing the three tramps. The tramps were taken from the boxcar at approximately 1:50 p.m., when Oswald was arrested at the Texas Theater.
(11) For over 20 years, George H.W. Bush said he did not remember what he was doing during the assassination; then he suddenly remembered he was giving a speech to the Rotary Club in Tyler at 1:38 p.m., while his FBI call reporting James Parrot was placed at 1:45 p.m.
(12) His attendance with Malcolm "Mac" Wallace at Yale, when "Mac" was LBJ's personal hit man, and his attendance at the ratification meeting at the home of Clint Murchison, Sr., are powerful circumstantial evidence of his complicity in the assassination of JFK.

POSTSCRIPT

Remarkably, there is a figure (in the DCA film) walking off the corner of Houston & Elm and toward the Dal-Tex building, where "the oil man from Houston" (George H.W. Bush) had been arrested minutes earlier, who looks a great deal like his son, 17-year-old George W. Bush. This figure's ear, nose (where a crude effort to change the nose has been made in the second of these three images), bridge indent, and jawline are a very close match to George W. Bush, where the preppy loafers and white socks he's wearing are cheerleader appropriate. It looks like W. was there, too.

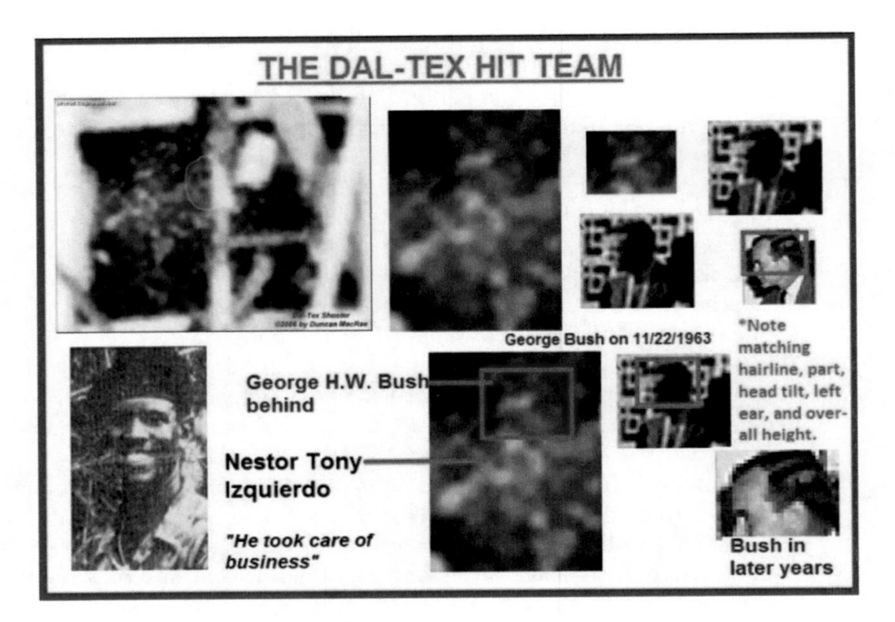

Figures in the Dal-Tex window from which three shots were fired with a Mannlicher-Carcano, the only unsilenced shots fired in Dealey Plaza.

CIA GEORGE BUSH DEALEY PLAZA COORDINATOR

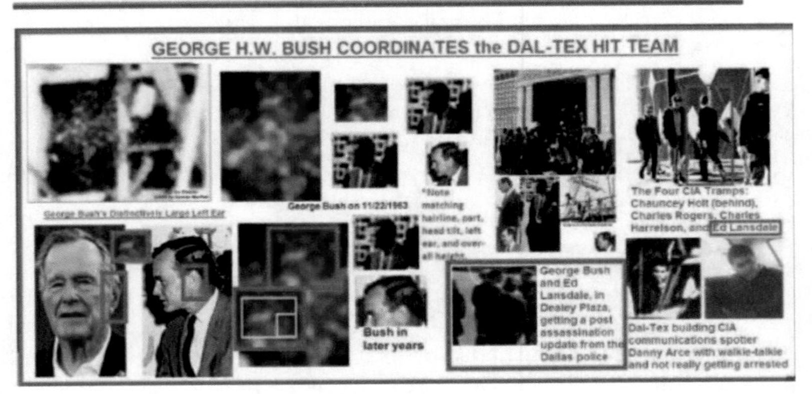

CIA George Bush coordinates the Dal-Tex hit team.

[Chapter 47] JFK & The Unspeakable

"Forget about democracy, forget about any ideology.

"This opposition to Martin King, this growing enmity to him, was based on money and the loss of money. The second aspect of his work that also dealt with money that caused a great deal of consternation to the circles of power in this land had to do with his commitment to take a massive group of people to Washington and there to encamp them in the shadow of the Washington Memorial for as long as it took.

"For as long as it took, they would make daily trips to the halls of Congress and they would try to compel the Congress to act, as they had previously acted in terms of civil rights legislation, now to act in terms of social legislation ... now, he began to talk about a redistribution of wealth, in this the wealthiest county in the world that had such a large group of poor people, of people living then and now, by the way, in poverty. [...]

"They were afraid that mob would overrun the capital.

"They were afraid that what Mr. Jefferson had urged many, many times, that the body politic can only be cleansed by a revolution every twenty years. They were afraid that Mr. Jefferson would be listened to and that that revolution would take place. Because of that, those factors, Martin King was not going to be allowed, not going to be allowed to bring that group of people to Washington."

- William Pepper

JFK and the Unspeakable, by James W. Douglass

a review by Mike Palecek

I waited my whole life to read James W. Douglass' new book, *JFK and the Unspeakable*.

The wait was not worth it. I should not have had to wait, at all.

This is supposed to be America, but it is not.

That is why I was made to wait. Americans should not have to wait.

We like to have it right now.

We want what we want when we want it.

Now. Please.

Sister Ellen walked into our third grade classroom, hands tucked neatly into the opposite brown sleeve.

She was the principal at Sacred Heart elementary, and she only came to the classrooms to announce that the poorest kid in our class and his large family had run off a bridge this morning on the way to school, or to lead us down to the gym for the Christmas movie and extra chocolate milk.

So on November 22, 1963, when lean, tall, straight Ellen floated in just after lunch recess – pre-Vatican II sisters had no feet, legs, arms, nor hair – we saw the Franciscan specter of death.

Later, Mom ironed while she watched the caisson and "Black Jack", the riderless horse, on the black and white television in the front room.

This was Norfolk, Nebraska.

The *Norfolk Daily News* and WJAG told us it was Oswald. We just assumed, along with the *Omaha World-Herald*, that the Warren Commission had been commissioned by God.

Hometown hero Johnny Carson grilled an actual hero, attorney Jim Garrison, because Garrison had the gall to think for himself.

Then followed days and decades of lies.

My mother and I watched out the back door at the turn of the '70s, toward the railroad track, to see if Dad might go past, while grandma Josie sat in her room in the dark, afraid to speak at all.

My dad died to open the '80s, the day before Ruth and I were married.

Football on TV, and lies.

Pot roast on Sunday, with lies.

Turkey and dressing for Thanksgiving. White lies? Dark lies?

Most recently Peter Jennings and ABC News felt the need to cement the lies some forty years after the Kennedy coup.

The program includes a computer-generated reconstruction of the shooting that confirms that Oswald was the lone gunman. And it finds no persuasive evidence of a conspiracy to kill the president.

Through it all, through the fog of American cultural propaganda, some persisted, some wanted the truth, some like Oliver Stone in *JFK* in 1991, hit hard enough to make the ground quiver for a moment, crack in some places.

But the cracks were quickly filled by volunteers with footballs, turkey, dressing, cranberries, credulity.

Now comes James W. Douglass, long-time peace activist, professor, Catholic Worker.

Why is his book the one I've been waiting for?

Maybe it's because of the flood of new information, at least new to me. Maybe it's the way Douglass lays it out, on the line, straight and true, brick by brick, looking us in the eye and telling us it was the CIA who killed John F. Kennedy.

And that it was because of money.

Of course.

Is there something else?

I'm not an assassination expert.

I am an expert in living in America.

I am a Ph.D. in suffering through America, its propaganda, its holiday dinners, football afternoons, coffee conversations, newspaper articles, television news shows, entertainment shows.

If there were one thing worth listening to or hearing out of all those, there would be no need to excuse oneself to go stand in the garage smoking hidden cigarettes, holding the knife at your neck, then putting the cigarettes back into the hiding spot and the knife as well, and going back, to try once more to think and live and act as an American.

I happen to hold several advanced degrees in American Culture – years and decades spent sitting in comfortable chairs wearing new Christmas pajamas, balancing a Jethro Bowl of cherry black walnut ice cream in my lap, seeking enlightenment by watching Johnny Carson, Don Rickles, Dean Martin, Ed McMahon.

And then going to bed convinced beyond any reasonable doubt there is nothing more.

This is what there is.

This is life.

All there is to see and know is what I can see in my peripheral vision while watching Big Red Football, *Gunsmoke*, *Mayberry RFD*, *Happy Days*, *Survivor*.

That is all our Norfolk High School "U.S. History" books, all my parents, Isabel and Milosh, the parish priests, mailman have to tell us.

They were my Socrates and I was their Plato, and in our daily discourse I learned not to ask certain questions.

Over the years and decades I had it drilled into me, the beauty and wonderment and majesty that the rain was good for the farmers and that it would get cold again this winter.

In the Athens that I imagined Norfolk to be, with its Central Park band pavilion and its "world's largest stockyard", which was also a lie, I learned not to learn.

But now ... an unknown stone falls from the sky.

Well ... someone pick it up.

What's this?

There is more?

A lot more.

The land of the free and the home of the brave murders its own presidents when they threaten the men with the money, like the ones who contributed to the schools we grew up in and the newspapers and the ...

Oh, my.

The amber waves of grain will roll right over you, your children, your house if you stand in their path in any meaningful way.

Murder, Inc.

The business of America is business.

To protect and to serve.

We will kill you and you and your sons and daughters, grandmothers, to get what we want.

What we want is to eat and watch television in the dark.

While we grow wrinkles trying to figure out two plus two, those who have made that their profession, manipulate ... everything.

We vote and we work and we study and we worry about our children having Ho Ho's in their lunchbox and friends on the bus.

And we pay money earned on our knees to hire men and women to kill leaders and overthrow governments to make more money for those who built our schools and run our newspapers, and ...

And if those people also decide that our president should die, then we can do that too.

And we pay to have that done. Like having the carpet cleaned, the lawn mowed, the oil changed.

And no newspaper or radio station or TV station will ever talk about it. Unless telling us that it never happened.

And we will believe them.

Because not believing them means figuring out something else to believe.

And we have things to do. We have lives ... to live.

And those lives mean nothing, less than nothing, because they are built, constructed ... days laid down unevenly, brick by brick ... on lies and murder.

Lies. Murder. Lies. Killing. Lies. Death.

And it goes on and on as if it will never stop.

And then one unexpected day, along comes a brave man, like those brave men murdered, who is not like the weak men with the lies.

And everything changes.

A revolution without guns.

A cultural revolution, an indelicate purging of turkey and cranberries, a detoxification.

A new enlightenment, like the one that spawned the men who made this country – that the recent men have destroyed.

And the time does not seem quite so long.

Then and now are connected. Brought together.

Come together.

And now maybe.

Maybe our children will not live within lies, houses of lies, schools of lies, lives of lies.

Just maybe.

[Chapter 48] Jim, Kevin, on MLK, RFK, OKC, Waco

> "To do evil a human being must first of all believe that what he's doing is good. [...] Ideology – that is what gives evil-doing its long-sought justification and gives the evil-doer the necessary steadfastness and determination. That is the social theory which helps to make his acts seem good instead of bad in his own and others' eyes, so that he won't hear reproaches and curses but will receive praises and honors."
>
> - Alexander Solzhenitsyn

JIM:

[Oklahoma City, Waco]

Oklahoma City was such a blatant, fraudulent case, because this fertilizer bomb in this truck that was some distance from the building couldn't have possibly have brought about the devastation and destruction.

Obviously, Timothy McVeigh played a very peripheral role there.

[Did you see that right away?]

Pretty fast.

And, you're talking about the Branch Davidian compound in Waco?

Well, I saw footage from the satellites where you could see the FBI was firing into the building. They ran a tank in there and set it on fire.

It was very nasty. They were bombarding all those people with music to make it impossible to sleep. It was completely unjustifiable. They deliberately slaughtered all those people. It was grotesque.

It was one of a whole series of events that has convinced me that our government has been on a long course of corruption and decent into fascism.

KEVIN:

[MLK, RFK, Oklahoma City, Waco]

The killings of the Kennedys and Dr. King were a tragedy on a global scale because these were the best leaders of the West; I mean, they were the leading figures who could have turned history in a better direction, and they were killed by these dark forces that didn't want to go in that direction, and it's really an epic tragedy.

Dr. King was working on a plan to bring a million Americans to Washington, D.C., and not leave until his two demands were met. One was complete withdrawal from Vietnam, and the second was a serious attempt to end poverty.

Had that happened it could have been the revolution that people were waiting for in the Sixties.

And his charisma was such that he could motivate millions of people, and that's why they had to take him out. So those assassinations really, I think, in some ways, are the root of all of the problems we've been facing ever since then. We took the wrong path. We let them kill the leaders who might have taken us down a much better path.

And Oklahoma City is a major step toward this post-9/11 Orwellian fascism that we're now living under. It was obviously a false flag. There's all kinds of evidence, and people who are interested in evidence that OKC was a false flag should see the movie *A Noble Lie* by the Oklahoma City Bombing Committee. It's a terrific film.

And it seems that Oklahoma City was kind of a dry run for 9/11. They wondered, can we use completely unrealistic means to destroy a building and get away with it?

And they did.

They blew up this building in such a way that it was just beyond obvious that a truck bomb couldn't have done anything remotely like that, and yet they got away with it.

So then they did the same thing on 9/11 and blew up these three skyscrapers, actually they blew up the whole World Trade Center because they bombed the crap out of all the other buildings too, every single WTC prefix building was totaled and not one building without a WTC prefix was totaled.

They just blatantly blew up these buildings and tried to blame it on plane crashes, which were not even remotely close to being an adequate cause, and they got away with that, too.

So OKC was sort of a dry-run in that respect.

And it may have killed many birds with one stone, just like 9/11 did. OKC may very well have destroyed the Whitewater evidence, which was in that building. And it brought vast amounts of money into the incipient Homeland Security complex, and at that time the FBI and international police agencies, and got them the money they could use to start setting up 9/11.

And it got them the fear of terrorism that they could use to rally the people behind the government, and of course there was a huge rally-the-people-behind-Clinton effect with that event.

So I would say the Oklahoma City bombing was basically a step towards

9/11, it was obviously done by the same people that did 9/11 with the same agenda. It's another case that needs to be re-opened.

[Waco]

Well, at the time I didn't know much about it.

It seemed like – at the time I sort of bought the idea that David Koresh and his people were a crazy cult, and that there had been some kind of real shootout. Even though it was tragic and maybe the government used too much force and killed these people when it shouldn't have, I wasn't paying that much attention.

I think when it happened, like OKC, I was still pretty busy with my teaching and scholarship in totally unrelated fields, so I wasn't paying that much attention to this kind of news. And it was really only after 9/11 that I went back and saw the film *Waco, Rules of Engagement*, and did some reading about Waco, and discovered that this had been the cold-blooded execution of these men, women, and children.

Our government had just burned them all to death, and the guys that did it were just a bunch of these psychopathic special forces types.

And of course not all special forces people are psychopathic by any means. There's some good special forces people as well as some bad ones, but these guys they sent into Waco were complete criminals, and it was just another case of mass murder by the U.S. government. In this case it happened here on U.S. soil, and the victims were U.S. citizens.

Usually when they kill people, and they kill millions, they are brown people somewhere abroad.

But these kinds of cases should alert us to the fact that we Americans, of whatever ethnicity, are the victims of this murderous empire, just as much as the people that they murder by the millions abroad.

They're just as happy to kill us as anybody else, and we should be joining the millions of brown people around the world, and people of whatever color and ethnicity, in rising up against this evil empire.

A truck-borne fertilizer bomb cannot possibly have done this.

The Davidian compound was burned completely to the ground.

FBI assaults Waco, TX, Branch Davidian compound.

[Chapter 49] Waco

"If you will study over the reports I've provided for you and the exhibits, think about all the testimony that has been given here and what really happened, ladies and gentlemen, your verdict would have to be that the United States government, the FBI, the Memphis Police Department and others were involved in this conspiracy to murder Dr. King."

- William Pepper, attorney, closing argument in case, Coretta Scott King et al. vs. Loyd Jowers. Memphis, Tenn. Dec. 8, 1999

David Koresh's Revenge: Waco and 20 Years of State Terror
by Anthony Gregory

There is something about April.

From Columbine to Virginia Tech, from Oklahoma City to Boston, mid-to-late April occasions some of the most infamous massacres on U.S. soil.

At least, these are the ones we are told to focus on.

The killers are called terrorists.

Unless they wear uniforms, as they did on April 19, 1993, just outside Waco, Texas.

That time, as we are urged to believe, the terrorists were the ones who died. In all these massacres, regardless of specifics, the government portrays itself as all that keeps chaos at bay.

The state claims to stand against terrorism, but killing people is its stock in trade. Slaughters come in various forms, almost all of which feed the health of the state. The state conducts much killing outright.

The state officially poses against other killing, while nevertheless encouraging it through its own violence. Even the killing that the state has no hand in serves as a pretext for the state to grow.

In Boston this Monday, someone left bombs that murdered three people, including an eight-year-old boy, and injured 176 others. President Obama called the crime an "act of terrorism".

The establishment definition of "terrorism" was always flawed, in that it categorically absolved the government, but at least it specified the targeting of civilians for political goals. Yet these days, even before the motive is known, such as at Boston, or when the targets are not civilians, such as American soldiers abroad, the U.S. government calls any dramatic acts of violence of which it disapproves "terrorism".

This February, they called ex-cop Chris Dorner a terrorist. Then the police surrounded him in a cabin to burn him alive, asking the media to cover its eyes like at Waco. Everyone who knew how the state operates had no reason to expect he would get due process.

They were going to hunt him down and kill him no matter what. The media dropped the formality of calling him an "alleged" murderer. The LAPD tried and convicted and executed him all on the same day, and no one batted an eye. Meanwhile, liberals say all talk of American tyranny is irresponsible, and conservatives continue to worship law enforcement.

Today, violent resistance to the state is called terrorism. Many of the "terrorists" rounded up and imprisoned at Guantánamo Bay were at most guilty of defending their country against an invading army.

Some of these people continue to languish in that dungeon, seeing their desperate hunger strike in protest of declining conditions go unanswered, except by an administration willing to cut off their water.

From February 28 to April 19, 1993, the Branch Davidians resisted.

On the morning of February 28, about one hundred ATF agents, concealed in livestock trailers, descended upon their property.

The agents had planned and trained for eight months, having practiced their histrionic assault on model buildings. There was no reason for all this other than publicity.

The agents could have easily arrested Koresh, whom they had befriended. The agents had conducted an investigation of weapons violations and found nothing. Koresh had cooperated with them.

60 Minutes had recently focused on an ATF sexual harassment scandal, and the agency was accused of racial discrimination during a House subcommittee meeting.

The bureau wanted to improve its public image. Officials reached out to the press to make sure reporters could witness their heroics on the last February morning of 1993.

Unlike the vast majority of the hundreds of daily domestic militarized raids in America, the ATF's surprise raid "Operation Showtime" faced resistance.

When the agents ran out of ammo, the Davidians ceased fire.

There were casualties on both sides, although one anonymous agent told *The Dallas Morning News* that he suspected some agents had fallen from friendly fire. Once the raid became a clear disaster, the ATF forced the press away.

Then came the standoff. The FBI took over, and turned it into a full-blown military operation on American soil.

Psychological warfare came down hard on Koresh's followers. The FBI blared loud, obnoxious music, and sounds of animal slaughter, while shining blinding lights through the night. Agents gratuitously drove a vehicle to defile a Davidian grave.

The government cut off this group's access to family, media, and lawyers. It destroyed their water supply.

The media demonized the Davidians as a heavily armed cult that abused its children. Journalists tended to report government claims as fact, but they became increasingly critical of the ATF and FBI as well.

After weeks of looking like fools in the mainstream press, particularly after a critical exposé in *The New York Times* on March 28 revealed the initial raid's bad planning and recklessness, government officials became increasingly hostile to the media. On April 11, ATF intelligence chief David Troy stopped holding his regular press conferences altogether.

Attorney General Janet Reno, who took office in the middle of the standoff, finally decided to put an end to it.

At about 6 a.m. on April 19, the FBI began pumping flammable and poisonous CS gas, banned in international warfare, into the Davidian home. Officials knew that women and children were holed up in the section of the home exposed to this gas. The government continued to deploy gas for almost six hours.

Chemistry professor George F. Uhlig testified in congressional hearings that he estimated there was a 60 percent chance that the gassing alone killed some children.

"Turning loose excessive quantities of CS definitely was not in the best interests of the children," Uhlig said. "Gas masks do not fit children very well, if at all." He said that the gassing could have transformed their surroundings "into an area similar to one of the gas chambers used by the Nazis at Auschwitz."

The FBI brought out an Abrams tank, the Army's heaviest armored vehicle, to replace its Bradley fighting vehicles. Agents drove the tank, which Attorney General Janet Reno later obscenely compared to "a good rent-a-car", into the building.

FBI sniper Lon Horiuchi, who had shot and killed Vicki Weaver in August 1992 at Ruby Ridge as she held her infant in her arms, was at the scene. FBI agents launched incendiary tear gas canisters.

Justice Department spokesman Myron Marlin later declared, "We know of no evidence to support that any incendiary device was fired into the compound on April 19, 1993." The FBI finally admitted six years later it had indeed used such projectiles at Waco.

The Davidian home went up in flames in the early afternoon. More than 70 people died, all of them civilian targets, many of them Americans, others hailing from other countries, more than 20 of them children and close to half of them people of color, although somehow the Davidians are often smeared, along with the so-called militia movement, as white supremacists. As the fire raged, the FBI turned back the local fire department.

Special agent Jeffrey Jamar claimed that he feared for firefighters' safety – presumably, the Davidians might shoot at the very people trying to stop the fire that was burning them to death. When it was all over, the ATF hoisted its flag atop the conquered ruins.

The trial of the survivors was a sham. Confused jurors intended to convict survivors of weapons offenses, but not murder charges. The judge sided with the prosecution and defied the jurors' intentions. By 1999, polling indicated that a strong majority of Americans blamed the FBI for setting the fire.

Special counsel John Danforth, a Republican, released a report the next year whitewashing the Clinton administration of all guilt in this atrocity.

After Sandy Hook, liberals regurgitated every tired gun control argument, but one of the most interesting is that an armed populace fails as a brake on tyranny because the government has the military hardware to win any confrontation.

And indeed it's true: most who resist government are swatted down like bugs.

Some resist violently, like the Lakota Indians at Wounded Knee in December 1890, and are slaughtered.

Others are shot for daring to resist even by throwing rocks at armed troops, like the four students murdered and the nine wounded at Kent State in May 1970. Others are targeted after a few years of relative calm, like the Philadelphia MOVE radicals in May 1985.

Liberals are correct that the government has the means and the willingness to crush Americans who dare to resist. This fact never seems to convince liberals that the state is way too powerful and menacing to begin with, and maybe the last thing we should want is to give it more law enforcement powers, such as the monopolization of firearms through a war on guns.

About once a day police kill an American, but it's often a criminal and no one cares; or at least a marginalized person, like the homeless Kelly Thomas, beaten in July 2011 by five officers in Southern California, dying of complications five days later.

Or they are veterans, like Jose Guerena, at whom Tuscon police fired 71 rounds in the middle of the night in May 2011, innocent of any crime, just in his own house at the wrong time. The state saves most of its killing for abroad, where killing is its very policy. And now, thanks to the war on terror, Obama calls America his battlefield and the world his jurisdiction. He has made it official doctrine that the president can order anyone's death unilaterally.

Twenty years ago, Waco showed Americans the truth about law enforcement, the U.S. government, and the state itself.

It revealed what reality was like for foreigners overseas. Yet most Americans seem totally indifferent to the mass murder the U.S. government has perpetrated and unleashed in the Middle East.

On the day three were murdered in Boston, 75 died in Iraq. Violence in Iraq nine years ago was called terrorism, unless it was committed by U.S. troops. Today, violence in Iraq hardly makes the news. The state decides whose lives are worth caring about, and when.

Some critics of state violence dislike the very word "terrorism", calling it meaningless, but I disagree. The state perverts most words it uses, but these words can still hold value.

Terrorism refers to violence intentionally inflicted on the innocent to instill fear and advance political goals.

American officials commit terrorism all the time.

In the 20 years since Waco, state terrorism has escalated, from the anti-civilian sanctions on Iraq, to the double-tap drone attacks on foreign first responders, all the way down to the constant domestic police raids. Even the more pedestrian police measures, such as the systematic groping of New York City residents known as "stop and frisk", are there to "instill fear", as police commissioner Raymond Kelly boasted was the intention, according to former NYPD captain Eric Adams's testimony. From top to bottom, at home and abroad, the post-Waco American state seems intent on instilling fear in all of us.

Every April since 2003, I've written a piece about Waco.

I think Americans should never forget what happened. LRC published most of these articles. They each have a little bit of something different, and discuss contemporary events. I also wrote my undergraduate thesis on Waco, and the relationship between the media and the police state.

I might take a break from revisiting Waco next April, not because I've forgotten the victims – I never will – but simply because I feel like I've done enough writing about this particular atrocity for a little while, given that the state has raged on in so many directions, making Branch Davidians out of so many foreigners and Americans caught on the wrong side of the U.S. government's never-ending siege of the world.

Many Davidians died, and others suffered injustice at trial, but tragically these victims are not so unusual. There are also the many thousands slaughtered abroad in the last 20 years. There are the thousands shot by law enforcement since then. There is Abdulrahman al-Awlaki, the 16-year-old from Denver whom Obama snuffed out with a drone, whose death was justified on the grounds that he had a bad father.

Before the rapid rise of the surveillance state and the post-9/11 terror war, Waco was the best opportunity to turn things around. Instead, most Americans turned their backs, and now our country is becoming one big playground for the police state.

We might call the situation David Koresh's revenge.

[Reprinted here with permission.]

James H. Fetzer

Distinguished McKnight University
Professor Emeritus
University of Minnesota Duluth

Department of Philosophy
University of Minnesota
10 University Drive
Duluth, MN 55812

jfetzer@d.umn.edu

James H. Fetzer was born in Pasadena, California, on 6 December 1940. At graduation from South Pasadena High School in 1958, he was presented The Carver Award for leadership. He was magna cum laude in philosophy at Princeton University in 1962, where his senior thesis for Carl G. Hempel on the logical structure of explanations of human behavior won The Dickinson Prize. After being commissioned a 2nd Lieutenant in the Marine Corps, he became an artillery officer and served in the Far East. After a tour supervising recruit training in San Diego, he resigned his commission as a Captain to begin graduate work in the history and philosophy of science at Indiana in 1966. He completed his Ph.D. with a dissertation on probability and explanation for Wesley C. Salmon in 1970.

His initial faculty appointment was at the University of Kentucky, where he received the first Distinguished Teaching Award presented by the Student Government to 1 of 135 assistant professors. Since 1977, he has taught at a wide range of institutions of higher learning, including the Universities of Virginia (twice), Cincinnati, North Carolina at Chapel Hill, New College of the University of South Florida, and now the Duluth campus of the University of Minnesota, where he served from 1987 until his retirement in 2006. His honors include a research fellowship from the National Science Foundation and The Medal of the University of Helsinki. In 1996, he became one of the first ten faculty at the University of Minnesota to be appointed a Distinguished McKnight University Professor.

He has published more than 100 articles and reviews and 20 books in the philosophy of science and on the theoretical foundations of computer science, artificial intelligence, and cognitive science. On this web page, his publications have been divided by area, including special vitae for computer science, artificial intelligence, cognitive science, evolution and cognition, and his applied philosophical research on the death of JFK. His biographical sketch has appeared in many reference works, including the DIRECTORY OF AMERICAN SCHOLARS, WHO'S WHO IN THE MIDWEST, WHO'S WHO IN AMERICA, and WHO'S WHO IN THE WORLD. It may be found, for example, in the DIRECTORY OF AMERICAN SCHOLARS, 10th edition, WHO'S WHO IN AMERICA, 55th edition (2001), and WHO'S WHO IN THE WORLD, 18th edition (2001).

[Chapter 50] Kevin: "He's an alien!" ... High school teaching in San Francisco ... more on 9/11

> "How free are we as a people and a culture when the truth cannot be told? How free are we when evidence and news is managed and withheld? How far our separation from the body of laws we celebrate in our flag, anthems, hymns and pledges. Dare I whisper: far."
>
> - Bob Lupo, author of *A Buffalo's Revenge*

KEVIN:

[Kevin's Alien Experience (?) in Keyhole State Park, Wyoming]

We left Montana a couple of days before that in the middle of these huge wildfires that had just turned the sky black. We even drove through one area where there was burning wildfire on both sides of the freeway and we were barely able to get through before they closed the freeway.

So we were escaping western Montana through all these wildfires. It was very strange.

Just before we left, up by Kalispell, Dayton ... And just before we left there was a big front page headline in the newspaper – cattle mutilations resume.

This is August of 2001.

And the story said there had been this huge wave of cattle mutilations in the 1970s where livestock had apparently been captured by some flying vehicle, carried through the air, various parts of the livestock such as the lips, tongue, eyes, ears and genitals had been surgically removed with incredible surgical precision and then these beasts had been drained of blood and then dropped from a high place and then found lying in the middle of a mud flat with no tracks.

And then it had kind of died down, there were still cattle mutilations, but not on the scale of the '70s; but then in August of 2001 according to this story in the Montana paper that we read right before we left, this was picking up again in a big way in Montana.

So that was kind of eerie to say the least, and then as we were driving back through these wildfires, we ended up camping in Keyhole State Park in Wyoming, which is by the Black Hills and Devils Tower Monument, and of course Devils Tower is associated with UFOs by the Speilberg Film *Close Encounters*. So we pulled into the park.

There was a ticket booth, and the guy in the ticket booth was kind of an old, really weird looking guy who had very creaky, clumsy movements, as if he were moving in a film going eight frames per second instead of twenty-four frames per second, very jerky, very clumsy.

And he spoke in a very clumsy jerky way too. It was like eight dollars, and I tried to give him a ten, something like that.

It took him a long time to take my money, and he was just rambling on with these weird non sequiturs, and the things we remember him saying: we are back, we were away for a long time, but now we are back.

I took the change, kind of rolling my eyeballs, and as I was driving away from the booth, Fatna started saying, that was an alien, that guy was an alien!

I said, no I think they're just hiring the handicapped at the park.

So we went to the campsite and set up camp, and I took a walk before going to bed, and as I walked off through this sort of desert sagebrush type of landscape I came to a place that was a perfect circle, where the vegetation just diminished quickly into nothing in the shape of this perfect circle.

In the middle of this circle, it was totally barren, nothing growing, there were just bones littered everywhere, and that kind of creeped me out. So I walked back just before dusk, as a thunder storm was brewing, and told the kids a bedtime story involving UFOs.

And I said goodnight to the kids and Fatna, who were sleeping in the van, and I went and slept in the tent about thirty or forty feet from the van. And as I was going to sleep this thunderstorm came in with heat lightning, and there were these really powerful flashes.

The flashes corresponded with weird howling and barking of a dog at the neighboring campsite, and hysterical laughter of the people. This kind of kept me from falling asleep right away. And then as I was just about to drift off to sleep I heard the neighboring car peeling out, rrrooom!

And a little later I heard Fatna screaming, Kevin, save us! So I ran from the tent back to the van, which was locked. Fatna was on the inside.

What's wrong, Fatna?

Speak French to me if you're really Kevin, prove to me you're not an alien.

So I spoke French to her, and she let me in, and I asked her what was wrong, and she said that each of those flashes that had been driving the neighboring campers and their dog crazy was a moving star swooping down, brightly, at them.

Did you see them? Did you see the moving stars? No, I didn't see any moving stars.

Oh, there's one now! She pointed and I looked up and yes, it was what looked like a star except it was moving across the sky, and it moved behind a tree and then I didn't see it anymore.

So, that was that. I didn't know what to make of it.

KEVIN:

[On teaching at community college and high schools in San Francisco]

I was taking film, French, and English Lit. classes, and to make some money I was teaching ESL, throughout the '80s.

And then I got over to San Francisco State – '90 to '92 teaching English and French at San Francisco State, '93 teaching at Contra Costa college, Humanities, in San Pablo, California. Substitute teacher in San Francisco public high schools in the early '80s, before I was doing the other stuff. It was actually pretty nice.

There wasn't a whole lot of responsibility for doing lesson plans and things like that. Usually you just follow a script that's already there, and they usually know what to do. It was actually fun.

The San Francisco high schools are wildly diverse in terms of ethnic communities and social class and all that. There are all kinds of different schools.

It was fun getting to know the city, because I was bicycling to the schools where I was teaching; so they would tell me to go to such and such a school that I've never heard of, and I'd end up in some neighborhood I'd never visited, and sometimes coming home afterward I could hang out and check out the neighborhood, so it was fun.

I was living closest to Mission High School, so I told them that was my first choice, so I did get more visits to Mission High School than anything else. It's a beautiful spot, right across from a park, this old sort of Spanish style building. It's a really neat place, by Delores Park.

[Travels doing 9/11 work]

I have done 9/11 talks in all of the regions of the U.S. I go back to New York almost every year for the anniversary, and I've been to Canada several times. I was the M.C. of the *Vancouver Conference* of 2007 and was back in Vancouver for the conference last year. I've done 9/11 events in London, did many, many events and talks in Turkey, spent three weeks there a couple years ago.

I was in Iran just this year for a big event that included 9/11 Truth, and also there was a trip to Belgium, Netherlands, and Germany a year and a half ago. That's most of it.

[Do you enjoy the traveling?]

I kind of enjoy it. Part of the satisfaction comes from doing something useful. I don't normally so much enjoy traveling just for the sake of traveling.

Like if somebody just handed me a free ticket and said I could go fly – I really don't like flying, I really wouldn't want to do it, unless there was a good reason to. Although I did just do a trip to San Francisco with Fatna. It was a two and half day getaway vacation that we got ostensibly for free. It turned out it cost $400 in various kinds of fees. It was wonderful, we had a wonderful time, but just because it was a romantic thing with Fatna. Being with her in San Francisco and seeing my old haunts was really fun. If I travel for any kind of pleasure I much prefer to do it on the train.

[Able Danger – were they the handlers of the so-called hijackers?]

No, I don't think so. Able Danger was a program to keep track of alleged potential Muslim terrorist threats, so they had lots and lots of little names and faces on their boards and charts and they collected data and they tapped their phones and followed them around and stuff.

Colonel Anthony Shaeffer is our source for this. He was one of the higher ups in Able Danger, he might have even been running it. But he was told at one point, they noticed that Mohamed Atta and some of the other people who would become the alleged 9/11 terrorists were doing a lot of strange, bizarre and menacing stuff and sort of setting themselves up, so Colonel Shaeffer got very concerned and headquarters moved in and told him to ignore those people, forget that you ever saw them.

They ordered him to literally put a yellow sticky pad over the face of Atta and the other people who would become the 9/11 hijackers and to forget that he had ever seen their faces or names.

So of course when he blew the whistle on this he got threatened pretty badly. He went to Congressman Curt Weldon of Pennsylvania, who tried to make an issue of this post-9/11, and Weldon then was targeted for all kinds of political destruction that culminated in his being tossed out of the House.

But Able Danger in itself I don't think was the program that ran the hijackers. I think Able Danger was a program, it may have been used in part by the people who set up the patsies as fake hijackers, but I don't think it was actually doing that. I think an Israeli and organized crime element was probably more directly involved in setting up the patsies.

[Did the hijackers actually exist?]

There were originally these 19 people they were telling us about. Most of them or all of them did at one point exist with the identities that we're told about. But then a whole bunch of these guys suffered identity theft, which means that some intelligence agency or criminal network stole their I.D.s, found someone who looked like them, or maybe even created somebody to look like them using plastic surgery, etc. They started running doubles of them.

This happened most blatantly with Ziad Jarrah. There were three Ziad Jarrah's, they were running at least two doubles of the original Ziad Jarrah. Ziad Jarrah is from Lebanon, and his family is a family of Israeli collaborators, basically the whole family is run by the Israelis.

Who knows whether he was actually, consciously, complicit of being involved with the Israelis, but he probably was, just like Oswald was CIA, just like the Boston bombers are CIA. They get their patsies from in-house. This guy Jarrah was probably in-house Mossad, but they were running doubles of him, and they were also running doubles of other hijackers or alleged hijackers, including Atta.

The Atta that we hear about in Florida almost certainly cannot have been the original Mohamed Atta. The original Mohamed Atta was a very, very timid, shy, pious, sensitive person.

The guy in Florida was very outgoing, loud, brash, psychopathic, spoke fluent Hebrew; according to his stripper girlfriend, he was a big cocaine user, a big whiskey drinker, chased prostitutes, gambled. He went to Las Vegas to gamble, spent a lot of time on Jack Abramoff's casino boats – Abramoff of course being a person of interest in 9/11 – so Atta was probably, there were probably two Atta's, the original and somebody they replaced him with.

The guy taking flying lessons in Florida was probably the fake Atta, or at least one of them. They may have had two guys running around Florida. In any case, yes, they were originally real people, and then they had their identities stolen, they were doubled. In some cases they may have been intelligence agency patsies from the get-go; the Saudis appear to have all come to the U.S. on snitch visas, which are the visas the CIA gives to Saudi Arabians who snitch to the CIA.

If you spy for the CIA in Saudi Arabia, the way that you get rewarded is they give you a special kind of visa to come to the U.S., and they may even pay your way if they like you.

So that's how all these Saudi hijackers, which were 15 out of 19 – Jarrah was Lebanese, Atta Egyptian, and I think the other seventeen were all Saudis – every one of those guys was brought over to the U.S. on a snitch visa, meaning that they were all CIA agents. And their lifestyles would indicate this, they were not Muslim fanatics, they weren't even pious Muslims at all.

They didn't pray, didn't fast for Ramadan, didn't visit the Mosque, they just partied like crazy, and of course they partied on your taxpayer money probably. They were getting money from drug smuggling, intelligence-agency-connected criminal networks, pretending to learn how to fly even though they weren't actually taking serious flying lessons, and otherwise just going through the motions.

It's really a pathetic attempt to set up patsies. If you read Hopsicker's book, *Welcome To Terrorland*, it goes into the details about what these guys were actually doing, and not doing, in Florida, prior to 9/11.

You just have to shake your head at the complete ineptitude of the people who set these guys up to be the patsies, because they did such a lousy job. Nobody with the slightest ability to think things through would ever imagine that these guys actually did 9/11. It's a complete joke.

[What about the bin Laden family chartered plane?]

Well, the bin Laden family is known as the Saudi face of the U.S. Army Corps of Engineers. It's a billionaire family and they're very, very tight with the U.S. Very tight with the U.S. government, very tight with the U.S. military, so they're friendlies. The Saudi regime is a U.S. puppet regime, and to some extent a Zionist puppet regime. The Saudi government is the single biggest tool of the Zionist money monopoly. The Rothschild banksters run the world on the Saudi petro dollar.

The way they're able to float the U.S. dollar, which they control through their control of the U.S. Federal Reserve, is by having Saudi Arabia be the world's swing oil producer. And Saudi Arabia prices oil in dollars, so everybody has to stockpile dollars to buy oil, which is the basis for the value of the petro dollar. The Saudis are basically U.S. occupied. They have been since President Roosevelt cut a deal with Ibn Saud in 1945.

The deal was, your family can be billionaires with billions in Swiss bank accounts, just let us run the place, and let us control the way the oil is sold and at what price. So that's been the deal ever since. The Saudi government can't even fly or maintain its own airplanes.

They've spent fortunes on overpriced U.S. military equipment, and they can't operate any of it themselves, so they have Americans over there operating their equipment for them.

It's beyond pathetic, and these Saudi leaders are a bunch of playboys who waste all their money on gambling junkets and women and high life. Drugs. And they run a country? They can't fly their airplanes, they can't do anything, it's completely occupied. Saudi Arabia is just as occupied as Gaza is, only the people have a little bit higher standard of living.

Although not all of them.

You'd be surprised. There is still a lot of poverty in this incredibly wealthy country.

So anyway, the Saudi regime is a complete puppet of the U.S. regime, and the bin Laden family is very, very tight, the bin Laden family is one of the biggest puppets over there.

So, naturally these bin Ladens were going to be taken care of, and flown out of the country post-9/11 to protect them from the repercussions of the official big lie, which is that these hijackers did 9/11. Of course they didn't, but since that was the big lie that was going to be promulgated, they had to get their good friends, the bin Ladens, out of the way.

[What happened at Shanksville?]

Well, there's that 15-foot hole in the ground where they told us that entire plane disappeared into the soft ground. It was soft and partly hollow thanks to coal mining shafts, so that's the official story, and it's a joke, of course. As for what really happened, we just don't know. I'm inclined to think that – even though the simplest way that 9/11 could have been done would have been by sort of automatically hijacking these airliners by remote control and flying actual airliners with their passengers in them into their targets – I don't think they did it that way.

I'm not sure why, possibly because they were trying to strike very, very precise targets, especially in the Pentagon where they had certain groups of people they wanted to kill, certain files they wanted to destroy; maybe they couldn't have been absolutely certain of targeting what they wanted to hit with a jetliner, and maybe the chances of trouble would be greater with a jetliner.

If the jetliners that hit the towers had been flying at the speeds they should have been flying, maybe 250 mph, max, then it wouldn't have been very spectacular, you know. Most parts of the planes would have bounced right off the buildings, there may not even been enough penetration to start any major fires, and of course the fires were what would have to be deemed the official cause of the demolition of these towers.

So they had to create this illusion of jetliners smashing into these buildings at 500-plus miles an hour, which is a joke, these planes can't even go that fast at sea level. That's their cruising speed, but it's not their speed at sea level, because the air's too thick. It's like saying a sprinter could run 30 miles an hour standing in water up to his chest.

It's a complete joke.

If you saw a film of a sprinter setting a world speed record in the 100-meter dash, racing through chest-deep water at that speed, you would say, this is fake.

And that's the same situation that we face when we look at these videos of planes. The south tower plane supposedly was going 570 miles an hour hitting the south tower.

It's a joke.

So that can't possibly have been a Boeing 767 like we were told. So, rather than remote hijacking commercial airliners, which seemingly would have been the simplest way to do this, I think they did some kind of plane switcheroo.

They set up commercial flights, or bogus commercial flights, to take the blame, but they actually did the damage with military means, including bombings at the Pentagon and maybe a missile strike, who knows? And of course explosive demolitions at the Trade Center.

And so to create this illusion of plane hits, they probably used military planes. Or there are other suggestions, Jim Fetzer thinks there may have been some kind of holograph technology used, to maybe cloak a missile with the image of a big plane and fly that into the tower or something. I don't know. But maybe Jim can explain that better than I can.

And he's also, I'm sure, more convinced that he has the answer than I am. All I can say is that we certainly don't have any reason to believe that there were real passenger flights that day. These alleged passenger flights were all mostly empty. Four coast-to-coast flights averaging about one-quarter full? You know, this is ridiculous.

The coast-to-coast flights are never that empty, much less all four of the alleged attack aircraft being that empty. What a joke. So I kind of think the most likely scenario is that they probably had a bunch of complicit people or fake identities, but they only had a very small number.

They averaged like 50 passengers per plane, and of those, maybe 40 would be fake identities and/or people in the military-industrial-complex that they could claim were on the planes and possibly complicit people they would pay off.

So they maybe only had like 10 innocent people that they had to kill. And those 10 people would show up at the airport, wait in the lounge and then be taken away. I'm sorry we have to take you off over to here, go to this place. They would be led to some place and there they would be killed and disposed of.

So as for what happened in Shanksville.

The hole in the ground in Shanksville was probably just made by a bomb or a missile. There are some indications of debris scattered over a wide area, but what that debris is, I don't know.

It's possible that there were planes running drills; maybe there was some kind of a shoot-down over Shanksville because there was that wide debris field of something. Something appears to have been blown up in the air, but we just don't know what.

At this point all we can say is that this was a very carefully organized military operation. It was a deception. It was like a play or a movie more than like an actual terrorist attack.

[Was it all planned out ahead of time, they just had to make sure George W. Bush won Florida?]

Well, I had an interesting discussion about that with John Nichols, who ran into me at the post office, like right after I was suddenly all over the news and screaming headlines and Fox News and stuff.

The next day I was at the post office and ran into him, and so we sat down outside the post office and had a long talk, in which he basically admitted that he knew I was right about 9/11, but that it was a hard thing for people to admit to in public.

He said that he'd been on top of this ever since Gore Vidal wrote about it, and he had been following *The Complete 9/11 Timeline*.

He said that he wondered whether the election in Florida had made this possible. Had Gore actually been able to claim his victory in Florida, that 9/11 would never have happened.

So I thought that was in interesting hypothesis, but I think that it may very well have been designed to happen no matter who was in office. And remember, the vice president would have been Lieberman, and Joe Lieberman is exactly like Dick Cheney, even worse in some ways.

Cheney was a captive of the hard-line militarist-Zionists, but Lieberman is like the chairman of the board of that group. He's America's answer to Netanyahu.

So, had Lieberman been the vice president, they could have easily done 9/11, they could have ran it out of the vice president's office in exactly the way they ran it out of Cheney's office. Instead they would have run it out of Lieberman's office.

Now the question is, would Gore have gone along with it? Well, we have some precedents here. In the past John F. Kennedy was presented with the plan for Operation Northwoods, which was the plan to trigger a war on Cuba by a fake plane shoot down, the murder of hundreds of Americans in bombings around the country, and the sinking of a ship.

All of this would have been attributed to the Cubans. It was a big false-flag 9/11-style event in 1962. It was all set to go. They were going to do it in less than a month. They sent the plan to Kennedy.

The plan was signed by every member of the Joint Chiefs, drafted by General Lemnitzer, and Kennedy turned it down. And so, what happened? Pretty soon Kennedy, a year and a half later Kennedy's gone, he's been killed, and the president is Johnson, who is willing to do what the military wants to do. Which has now changed – now they want to go into Vietnam, and Johnson's in power.

So, even if Gore was not willing to go along with 9/11, if they made that judgment – you know, they might not even ask him directly.

The way that these intel agencies would work, they would study him and talk to him and broach certain subjects, but it would all be very coy, and then they would make a judgment. Will he do what he needs to do or won't he?

And if he wouldn't, then President Gore would have been assassinated, and Vice President Lieberman would take over. In fact, they might very well have assassinated Gore as part of 9/11.

That way, somebody would have killed the President as part of this so-called Islamic terror attack, putting Lieberman in the White House, where Lieberman probably would have done at least as good a job as Bush did of being the liar-in-chief.

That's how I think it probably would have gone down, although maybe Gore would have gone along with it for all I know.

It's interesting that there was a dress rehearsal for the assassination of the President on Sept. 11.

That morning as he was going jogging, George W. Bush was approached by a bunch of Somalis in a van with cameras. And they were in a position to kill Bush if they wanted to.

They didn't. It was supposedly a huge breach of security. But it was obviously an organized breach of security. And these Somalis were basically CIA Muslim terrorist patsies.

So, the morning of 9/11, a bunch of CIA Muslim terrorist patsies were brought right into position to assassinate the President of the United States, but they held back, because apparently they had made the judgment that the President would be willing to go along with this false flag event that was organized out of the vice president's office.

And I think the same kind of judgment might have gone the other way if Gore had been in power.

I think they might have decided to have Gore killed by the Somali terrorists, and then they would have had Lieberman directly running everything as the new president, rather than having Cheney running everything as the ostensible vice president under Bush but as the real power behind the throne.

["Angel is next"]

Yeah, I think this is all a reflection of the fact that the 9/11 plan was designed to be run out of the vice president's office and there was a potential assassination of the president to be used in the case that the President wasn't reliable.

[Rudy Giuliani – on a personal level – how would they get these guys to go along, and so faithfully and for so long, same as with Apollo astronauts?]

I don't know too much about the moon landings, so I'll stay away from that, but in the case of Giuliani, I mean Giuliani is a criminal. He's a made-man. Basically you just have to think of these guys as Mafiosi.

Mafiosi people are not like you and me, they're not going to be concerned whether the truth comes out or not, they could give a shit.

All they care about is their money and their power and playing by their little Mafiosi rules.

Every now and then some Mafiosi will go and squeal, even though it's so much against the code. And they get put in witness protection and, you know, some of them survive.

But I don't think keeping people like this quiet is very hard, especially now that they have such sophisticated techniques of profiling people.

The mob is way behind the intelligence community in terms of its ability to successfully profile people and predict how they'll act in a variety of circumstances and situations.

So, anybody who's going to play a role in 9/11, like Giuliani did, is obviously going to be profiled, and they'll figure out how to make him do what they want him to do.

If a person is completely impossible, like if Giuliani had been somebody with a lot of integrity that was going to be in the way, well, they would find a way to get him out of the way or they would redesign a plan around him. So that's just how these things are designed.

John Perkins gives us a sense of this in his book *Confessions of an Economic Hit Man*.

He describes how he was selected to be an economic hit man based on a bunch of factors. One of the important factors was that he had successfully lied to cover-up the minor crime of a friend of his.

And that was partly what brought him to the attention of the people who selected him. So he was a little bit psychopathic and willing to lie, and good at it, to protect his team member.

So they picked him to be an economic hit man. Now, if he'd been a little more psychopathic, and a little more interested in killing people, they probably would have made him a regular hit man, an asteroid, instead of an economic hit man.

An interesting example of how they can profile people, the people who run these kinds of organizations, and Perkins wasn't working for the CIA.

He was working for the World Bank. So he was part of a parallel intelligence agency run by this private entity, the biggest world bankers, and they probably hire the best guys, the best people, they're able to pay these guys vastly more than the CIA pays. Perkins made many, many millions during his years as an economic hit man. Had he been working for the CIA, he would have been on government salary.

He never would have made remotely that much money. So, these banksters are able to hire a much more talented group of people than the CIA can, and then they profile those people. They've got these techniques of profiling, they can listen to their phone calls and read their email and keep an eye on them.

They've got a sophisticated mechanism for profiling and determining how the person's going to act under whatever circumstances, and so that's how they can make sure that the people they need to stay quiet are going to stay quiet.

The hole in the ground at Shanksville, PA.

Real crash sites vs. Shanksville, PA.

Here are four of the five frames from the Pentagon, which have the wrong dates and times (probably to allow the government to disavow them, if challenged). The first is conveniently labeled "plane".

But it shows an image that is far too small to be a Boeing 757, which means that the government's own evidence contradicts the government's official story; and, Where's the Boeing? As in the case of Shanksville, where is the debris from a 100-ton airliner? Where are the parts of the plane? Where are the bodies, seats and luggage? Not even the engines, which are virtually indestructible, were recovered from either scene.

[Chapter 51] Death to Dissidents: The Fourth White Rose Leaflet

The fourth leaflet of the German anti-Nazi group the White Rose, produced between 1942 and early 1943.

Though we know that National Socialist power must be broken by military means, we are trying to achieve a renewal from within of the severely wounded German spirit. This rebirth must be preceded, however, by the clear recognition of all the guilt with which the German people have burdened themselves, and by an uncompromising battle against Hitler and his all too many minions, party members, Quislings, and the like...

There is an ancient maxim that we repeat to our children: "He who won't listen will have to feel." But a wise child will not burn his fingers the second time on a hot stove. In the past weeks Hitler has choked up successes in Africa and in Russia. In consequence, optimism on the one hand and distress and pessimism on the other have grown within the German people with a rapidity quite inconsistent with traditional German apathy. On all sides one hears among Hitler's opponents – the better segments of the population – exclamations of despair, words of disappointment and discouragement, often ending with the question: "Will Hitler now, after all...?"

Meanwhile, the German offensive against Egypt has ground to a halt. Rommel has to bide his time in a dangerously exposed position. But the push into the East proceeds. This apparent success has been purchased at the most horrible expense of human life, and so it can no longer be counted an advantage. Therefore we must warn against all optimism.

Neither Hitler nor Goebbels can have counted the dead. In Russia thousands are lost daily. It is the time of the harvest, and the reaper cuts into the ripe grain with wide strokes. Mourning takes up her abode in the country cottages, and there is no one to dry the tears of the mothers. Yet Hitler feeds with lies those people whose most precious belongings he has stolen and whom he has driven to a meaningless death.

Every word that comes from Hitler's mouth is a lie. When he says peace, he means war, and when he blasphemously uses the name of the Almighty, he means the power of evil, the fallen angel, Satan. His mouth is the foul-smelling maw of Hell, and his might is at bottom accursed. True, we must conduct a struggle against the National Socialist terrorist state with rational means; but whoever today still doubts the reality, the existence of demonic powers, has failed by a wide margin to understand the metaphysical background of this war.

Behind the concrete, the visible events, behind all objective, logical considerations, we find the irrational element: The struggle against the demon, against the servants of the Antichrist. Everywhere and at all times demons have been lurking in the dark, waiting for the moment when man is weak; when of his own volition he leaves his place in the order of Creation as founded for him by God in freedom; when he yields to the force of evil, separates himself from the powers of a higher order; and after voluntarily taking the first step, he is driven on to the next and the next at a furiously accelerating rate.

Everywhere and at all times of greatest trial men have appeared, prophets and saints who cherished their freedom, who preached the One God and who [with] His help brought the people to a reversal of their downward course. Man is free, to be sure, but without the true God he is defenceless against the principle of evil. He is a like rudderless ship, at the mercy of the storm, an infant without his mother, a cloud dissolving into thin air.

I ask you, you as a Christian wrestling for the preservation of your greatest treasure, whether you hesitate, whether you incline toward intrigue, calculation, or procrastination in the hope that someone else will raise his arm in your defence? Has God not given you the strength, the will to fight? We must attack evil where it is strongest, and it is strongest in the power of Hitler.

> "So I returned, and considered all the oppressions that are done under the sun: and behold the tears of such as were oppressed, and they had no comforter; and on the side of their oppressors there was power; but they had no comforter. Wherefore I praised the dead which are already dead than the living which are yet alive."
>
> - Ecclesiastes 4
>
> "True anarchy is the generative element of religion. Out of the annihilation of every positive element she lifts her gloriously radiant countenance as the founder of a new world [...] If Europe were about to awaken again, if a state of states, a teaching of political science were at hand! Should hierarchy then [...] be the principle of the union of states? Blood will stream over Europe until the nations become aware of the frightful madness which drives them in circles. And then, struck by celestial music and made gentle, they approach their former altars all together, hear about the works of peace, and hold a great celebration of peace with fervent tears before the smoking altars. Only religion can reawaken Europe, establish the rights of the peoples, and install Christianity in new splendour visibly on earth in its office as guarantor of peace."
>
> - Novalis

We wish expressly to point out that the White Rose is not in the pay of any foreign power. Though we know that National Socialist power must be broken by military means, we are trying to achieve a renewal from within of the severely wounded German spirit. This rebirth must be preceded, however, by the clear recognition of all the guilt with which the German people have burdened themselves, and by an uncompromising battle against Hitler and his all too many minions, party members, Quislings, and the like.

With total brutality the chasm separates the better portion of the nation from everything that is opened wide. For Hitler and his followers there is no punishment on this Earth commensurate with their crimes. But out of love for coming generations we must make an example after the conclusion of the war, so that no one will ever again have the slightest urge to try a similar action.

And do not forget the petty scoundrels in this regime; note their names, so that none will go free! They should not find it possible, having had their part in these abominable crimes, at the last minute to rally to another flag and then act as if nothing had happened!

To set you at rest, we add that the addresses of the readers of the White Rose are not recorded in writing. They were picked at random from directories.

We will not be silent. We are your bad conscience. The White Rose will not leave you in peace!

Jim Fetzer on the Sen. Wellstone Assassination at UMD (16 November 2005).

United States Senator Paul Wellstone (D-MN).

[Chapter 52] Death to Dissidents?

> "Hence it is that all armed prophets have conquered, and the unarmed ones have been destroyed. Besides the reasons mentioned, the nature of the people is variable, and whilst it is easy to persuade them, it is difficult to fix them in that persuasion.
>
> "And thus it is necessary to take such measures that, when they believe no longer, it may be possible to make them believe by force."
>
> - Machiavelli, *The Prince*

KEVIN:

[Why are you and others not also killed for speaking out, like the JFK witnesses, Gary Webb, Jack Ruby, Roger Craig, Jennings, Chavez, Kilgallen, Philip Marshall?]

I kind of think that most of the names on the list were people who posed some kind of, what they might call, an actionable threat. I think this is how they think, in organized crime circles and intelligence circles, which are pretty much the same circles.

The Godfather will normally only take you out if you pose an actionable threat to his business.

If you simply write, "I don't like the Godfather," on bathroom walls, or publish articles that, while they may influence public opinion, are not going to destroy the Godfather's business, he probably won't think it's worth it to take the risk and spend the resources.

Having to pay whatever it would cost to hire a hit man, and take the risk that that guy gets caught, problems could ensue that have to be, could be, very costly to cover up.

So every time they kill somebody they're taking a risk, and they're expending a lot of resources, so they don't want to.

You know, my editor over at *Veterans Today*, Gordon Duff, a former intelligence professional, has confessed to having killed people. He was in the Marines in Vietnam of course; he says it's not professional to kill anyone you don't have to, and I think that's not just Gordon speaking. Gordon is probably more ethical than the average person who's been in the institutions he's been in, but I think that's pretty much the institutional motto of most of them, even organized crime.

One of the reasons that guys like Gordon don't like the Israeli Mossad is that the Mossad is reckless, crazy, and runs around killing a lot of people that they don't have to, so they're unprofessional. I suppose the Mossad could always take out somebody like me or Jim just for the heck of it, because they're so insane, but even the Mossad is not that unprofessional.

So, we may be losing a few months of life expectancy by doing what we're doing, but it's not that great.

If we were ever really successful, to the extent of posing an actionable threat ... like when Jimmy Walter was putting millions of dollars into 9/11 Truth, they harassed him, drove him out of the country, and shut him up.

Actionable threats will be dealt with by action, and I'm sure I'm at the level where they may screw around with me a little bit, to try to limit my credibility and limit my audience, but just thinking the way they would think, strategically they probably wouldn't have a good reason to go very far beyond that.

[But, do you think about it?]

Not so much.

I think Jim is maybe a little more aware or concerned than I am. I remember when we were flying to London for the event that we did with Ken O'Keefe and Gilad Atzmon a couple of years ago, Jim was sort of joking about, boy, I don't think we should be on the same plane. But I don't think we're anywhere near that level.

[Have you received death threats?]

Well, lots of them, but they're all from idiots.

When I was in the limelight in 2006 and fighting back, I think they tried to discourage me from fighting back by putting out my university email address to a list of right wing, Fox-News-watching morons, a huge list.

I forget what the group was, but it was one of these astroturf political action groups that gets support from Fox News and people like that, so it had a lot of names.

And they put out a request for action to have them email the university and email me. And so I got many, many death threats among those emails, but they were all from complete idiots, and none of them seemed particularly actionable.

I got one from this crazy guy who poses as an ex-military Truther, and that had me a little worried for a while, because it seemed like he was unbalanced, and, if they were going to try to do anything to me, having some crazy Truther do it would probably be good, to make Truthers look crazy.

So that was the one situation where I was a little concerned, because there was kind of an unbalanced guy rather than just right-wing morons, you know, yapping.

JIM:

[Have you ever been visited or talked to by law enforcement regarding your writings?]

No.

[Do you ever fear for your safety?]

Well, that's a risk you have to accept when you become involved in complex and controversial issues like these. You only hope that if something happens that it will happen to you, and there will be no "collateral damage" as occurred in the Wellstone plane crash, which also killed his wife, his daughter, three of his aides, and of course the two pilots.

My understanding is that the program being run out of Vice President Cheney's office was terminated because of excessive "collateral damage". But I am not convinced that the government is not still assassinating American citizens.

In fact, we know it is.

KEVIN:

[Story of being interviewed by FBI in airport, 2009]

I was going to New York for the anniversary of the 9/11 attacks, and as I left the house I grabbed an old notebook to write my talk in, on the plane. And then on the plane I met a very interesting guy and had a good conversation and forgot all about my notebook, which was in the jacket pocket in front of the seat.

So I went about my business in New York and gave my talk. I was staying with Rev. Frank Morales at St. Mark's Church, and had a very good time in New York, and then went back to the New Jersey airport to fly home to Wisconsin.

And there at the airport when I checked in at the counter I noticed the check-in people were looking at me kind of funny. I went out to the gate and as I was waiting there by the gate I started dozing off, and then somebody tapped me on the shoulder.

I looked up and there were two FBI agents flashing their badges at me. There was a man and a woman, and I think there was a third guy like standing back or something, I forget.

They identified themselves. Are you Kevin Barrett? I said, yeah. Could you come with us, we'd just like to ask a few questions. I said, okay.

So we went to a little room they had. Who knows, maybe this was the kind of room where the passengers got killed, but it was kind of small for that, and it was not very far from the gate. We sat down in this little room and they produced the notebook that I had left on the plane when I'd arrived in New York. They said, is this yours, and I said, yes. And they said, well, do you know why there's Arabic in it? And then I remembered that this notebook was an old Arabic notebook from my Arabic classes when I got my Ph.D. in African languages and my main language was Arabic.

So I explained that, and then they actually made me read some of the Arabic to them. So I did that and then they made me translate it, and it was all this kind of goofy stuff.

There was also some other weird stuff in that notebook. I'd been writing a play. It was called *A Murder of Crows*. It was about the death of Vincent van Gogh, and it was very surreal in the writing style, and so I thought, these guys must think I'm crazy, you know.

So anyway, they kind of realized that this was ridiculous, and so the guy slammed down the notebook and he tried to look really tough and he kind of barked at me, "Are you a terrorist!"

I said, no, but I'm actually trying to help you guys catch the terrorists.

And that disarmed them. I could see there was just an effort to pretend to be tough. These guys had actually been really friendly. When they first tapped me on the shoulder they had been like, oh, yeah, we saw you on Hannity, treating me like I was a celebrity almost.

So that was the one moment where the guy tried to play tough and it lasted about five seconds.

And then they said, tell us what you think about 9/11.

So I did. And I spent the next 10, 15 minutes or however long it was, you know, telling them the things that they should be investigating. And they didn't look particularly like they disagreed with me at all, and they took notes, and they're nodding along.

So when they said, okay, that's fine, you better go to catch your plane, and they shook hands with me, and the lead guy wished me good luck with getting my job back and it looked like he had a sincere feeling of friendship and admiration for what I was doing. So that was pretty interesting.

It made me realize that these national security state cops are not necessarily the enemy and I've seen that ever since then.

You know, the people I work with at *Veterans Today* include a bunch of former national security state types, and many of those guys are actually our most important allies rather than our enemies, so we have to watch out for this kind of left wing reflex of just automatically imagining that everybody in the uniform has got to be an evil person.

[Kevin, have your truth activities cost you personally?]

Well, my family has been supportive most of the time, in most ways.

Fatna in particular has been very much on board, understanding what I'm doing and why I'm doing it and seeing that it's right.

A lot of 9/11 advocates have had relationship problems and divorces even in some cases, because their spouse didn't even accept what they're saying as true.

That would be a really tough situation to be in. I know some people like that.

I have a friend in Canada, Richard, who is married to somebody who is fanatically anti-truth, who has an anti-truth website even, so I think he must be something of a saint to manage to keep that going.

In my case, with my family relationship, the hard thing has not been so much fighting about the issues at all, because we pretty much see these issues the same way. But it's more that it's kind of hard on Fatna to have to deal with the stress of it.

It became very, very stressful starting in June 2006, when suddenly I was made into a public figure and witch-hunted out of the university.

So that led to kind of a media circus. Having to be constantly working and thinking and talking about these kinds of disturbing issues was very stressful, and the kids at times were frightened and ... I really don't want to go into all those details though. Some of it, the kids probably don't really want, it wouldn't be desirable, to have some of their personal issues in a book. The kids are home-schooled, in part because their dealing with this rabid, anti-Muslim brainwashed population in school was not working out.

Sometimes I have to take time to get out of the work and focus on the family. I stopped doing conference calls a long time ago, in 2006, I think. Fatna at that point was feeling like I was spending my whole life on these calls. And actually I haven't missed them that much.

[What would you, Kevin, like to do if this was someday over?]

It's a weird parallel with David Ray Griffin, who has always said he wanted to get 9/11 solved so he could work on his *Summa Theologica*, his grand statement about theology. And I can relate to that, because I would like to work on a Koranic commentary, actually.

I've studied literary theory for quite awhile, and the literary theory that impressed me the most was called dialogism. Bakhtin is the name associated with that, and I'm thinking of how to do a book called the *Dialogic Koran*, discussing the Koran as a dialogue rather than a monologue where God's word is final.

It's all just the word of God and that's it, but that actually doesn't get at the real meaning, because there are these so-called occasions of revelation, so various verses are actually coming into a particular context. Each passage seems to be directed from the voice of God through the voice of the angel Gabriel, through the consciousness of Mohamed, peace upon him, to the companions who heard him, to the larger Muslim community. But what God says through that chain of listeners and speakers is actually an answer to some kind of question that was raised by one of the participants, like a member of the community or the community as a whole.

You hear God saying, they ask you about this, they ask you about that, well tell them.

There's a level of these multiple dialogues happening all at once. Just a few words can have nuances of meaning that are reflections of all these multiple dialogues that are happening at once in the text, and it's pretty wonderful. It's a dialogue between humans and God, and that's the human level. A lot of people misunderstand Islam. They think Christianity is sort of more human, because in Christianity God becomes a human being, Jesus, or this human being Jesus becomes a God; there's a kind of confusion between the divine and the human, and Islam erases that.

Islam says God is God and humans, like Jesus, are humans. He's a prophet, not a God. And so some people think this totally ineffable God is impossible to relate to, but the human-God connection in Islam comes through this dialogue in the Koran, and it's a very powerful dialogue.

The humans are having a hard time trying to act right and to follow the truth, and spreading the truth is costing them. They're all being persecuted, and this dialogue, between this community that's trying to hold to the words of the truth and behave morally in a tough situation and God, is what you really see when you actually sit down and read Koran. It's very, very profound and beautiful.

The whole idea of trying to use a modern literary theory is a little dubious. I'm sure it's been done a little bit, but doing it in a way that really helps with the understanding of the sacred text I think is probably pretty unusual.

I think this would be a really interesting project. So this is what I would like to do. I also would like to try writing fiction. Fiction takes tremendous concentration. You have to just focus on that for a while. So if I weren't being harassed by three interviews per day I would be in a better position to try to write some fiction.

[You have an extensive education, experience, travels. But, in a way that also limits how you are going to be able to relate to Al American. Where do you find friends, peers?]

Well that's one of the nice things about this truth movement. Even though it might alienate you from the larger community of sheeple ... you know I've always been pretty alienated by the larger community of sheeple anyway, and so I've always had friends who share my interests and who are usually kind of deprogrammed.

So that's just even more so now. I have several friends right around this area and, well, pretty much all of the friends I see on a regular basis now are somehow people who are involved, even to a slight extent, in the truth movement, or congenial to it.

Some of my friends from the university period moved away, and then there are a couple I kind of lost as friends – well, I can really only think of two, maybe three, who were just not on board with the 9/11 Truth thing.

So I guess I've lost three friends over this and gained a whole bunch more. I have a couple of friends who are very hip to Islam, and maybe less knowledgeable but generally supportive of the truth movement. I have other friends who are truthers, who are not very aware of Islam. It is hard to find both.

It's been great, though, to meet these amazing people like Imran Hosein, who I interviewed for yesterday's show, who is one of the world's top Muslim scholars, and he's also absolutely on top of what's going on in the world.

So even getting to be kind of a tangential friend of Imran Hosein is something that is so much greater than anything I ever imagined before.

Overall it's been a pretty positive thing, in fact the social life is a little overly active at this point. I've also lost track of people I didn't want to lose track of. I just learned that a friend of mine passed away last October. I didn't even know it, so being so insanely busy with all of these people and the work I'm doing does have that kind of drawback.

[What do you really like to do? Cooking? Fishing? Bowling?]

A little bit of cooking when necessary. Fatna is such a good cook. I'll cook when there's a reason to.

Like if she's off at work. Even then she likes to leave me the recipe and the ingredients and everything, so it's pretty easy to make something really good.

Mostly gardening is the thing, getting outdoors. I'm doing a lot of permaculture here. In fact, we have a non-profit that's actually sponsoring this permaculture project on our property, so I'm doing a lot of work growing vegetables and growing a sort of permaculture guild.

[You don't have a teaching job anymore. Your radio show host thing is probably mostly volunteer. How do you get by, day to day?]

Well, my last academic job ended a couple of years ago, after I was chased out of Wisconsin and then Edgewood. Well, I wasn't really fired at Edgewood.

Then I taught at Kaplan University in Milwaukee for a while. So, I left Wisconsin, I was on unemployment for a couple of years, worked at Kaplan for awhile, was on unemployment for a couple more years, and things gradually developed. I've had some very generous donors who've donated to help continue the radio show and publish the book and everything.

And I've also managed to get some paying writing jobs, so occasionally I get to publish things, actually get paid for it, so that's been nice, too. And I translate. From Arabic.

[You and Fatna ran the Casablanca Deli for a while. How did that go?]

One summer.

[Fun?]

Maybe for a very brief time. But it was not really what I wanted to be working on 24 hours a day, which is what you have to do, with just two people, trying to run a restaurant.

[You said, after the David Ray Griffin talk in Madison that got on C-Span, that that success made it impossible to quit, even if you had wanted to. Can you talk about that?]

Probably an exaggeration, but I had a lot of people, now, wanting me to be helping them with the truth movement. Suddenly I was deluged by people who were working on that issue.

I guess I could have just said no to them and kept saying no, and after awhile they would have gone away, but given the fact that I cared about the issue that much, it was impossible, really, to say no to them.

[How did you come to live in Lone Rock?]

My grandparents bought two plots of land in Lone Rock in the 1950s. And one of those plots, the bigger one, got sold off to pay for my grandmother's nursing home care. And the smaller plot we inherited when she passed away.

And the smaller plot is really nice. It's on a spring-fed lake.

It's in a pine forest, and by the lake it's a deciduous forest, a very, very nice spot, so I was able to build a modest log house here in 2003. And I'd been coming out here to camp in an old 1964 motor home we had parked out here before that.

That was the same motor home I had lived in, in San Francisco. It was on the property until just a few months ago, actually last November, when we finally had it hauled away.

[Are you known on the streets of Madison or Lone Rock? Are you that guy!]

Nobody really treats me as a celebrity, or at least it's rare, which I appreciate. Once in awhile people come up to me and fortunately it's virtually always supporters. I don't think I've had any obnoxious anti-truthers just approach me out of the blue, almost ever, which is great.

You kind of think that people would be afraid of being in my position, thinking that, wow, you couldn't go out in public without some right-wing lunatic accosting you, but that's not been the case at all.

[Sometimes you use violent rhetoric. Can you talk about that?]

That was made an issue by one of the full time propagandists working against me and some other 9/11 Truth people.

There's a guy in San Francisco who, it's hard to tell if he's like mind controlled or what. But he's been a 9/11 Truth movement troublemaker from the get-go.

So this guy, Brian Good, made a huge stink. Basically, he just tries to find anything I say or anything I write, and take it out of context and spread it, in order to try to influence public opinion against me. He does this to other key people as well. He's also a stalker of William Rodriguez. So he's the one who's mostly responsible for various kinds of Internet stuff, like, this crazy Barrett wants to hang people, blah, blah, blah.

In fact, that kind of sort of populist rhetoric, actually, is all over the place on the Internet, I mean, I'm the least of it.

But I don't use it that much. If you wanted to randomly listen to my shows until you heard a reference to hanging somebody, you'd probably have to listen for a very long time. You'd probably be stuck with a hundred hours of radio before you finally got to one.

So it's not a big part of what I do, but the fact remains that the people that we're talking about are mass murderers, traitors, perpetrators of genocide, really the worst war criminals, meaning the worst criminals period in the history of humanity.

Sure, I would be happy to just arrest them and keep them locked up or re-educate them or somehow have them come to a spiritual awakening. That would be fine, too.

But the whole idea of, like, ruling out using strong language about dealing out justice to people like that, is kind of playing with one hand tied behind your back, because the other side – nobody questions really in the mainstream discourse when people say, oh, that evil terrorist bin Laden who killed 3,000 Americans on 9/11 should be hanged.

In fact, not only that, but according to the official story, the official discourse, they hunted him down and shot him like a dog, which is absurd of course, because if you were really a terrorist mastermind they would do everything to capture him alive so they could interrogate him.

But we're in this culture now where the authorities delegate themselves the right to just kill anybody they want, and in doing that they've committed the crime of treason against the Constitution of the United States as well as murder.

So those people technically have committed a capital crime and done it in an extremely outrageous fashion, and for that reason I think calling for their execution is eminently reasonable. In fact, it's kind of an understatement.

If someone started ranting and spent three hours describing the torture that should be meted out to these people before they were executed, I would say, okay, stop after two hours, you've gone too far. But why in the world would it even be controversial to say that the worst war criminals in the history of humanity should be executed.

Well I guess there's the anti-capital punishment argument, which is fine. In the world we live in, capital punishment is reserved mostly for poor black people, many of them innocent, and so, yeah, I'm against capital punishment, too. But there's also just basic justice.

In the case of these extreme monstrous war criminals, I don't think, necessarily, that locking them up for life is any better than just hanging them. I think that pacifists, or people who follow a kind of pacifist line, are often unconsciously brainwashed to accept the violence of the state and of the ruling class and of the world's worst criminals even. They do not really find it strange or disturbing and they kind of accept that it's there; oh, it'd be nice if it wasn't, let's try and build a peaceful world, blah, blah, blah.

But they're not standing up and saying, this is just completely absurd that there's a military, which is an organization based on killing, ya know.

And so, some of these people, sort of left-leaning with vaguely pacifist ideas, are the targets of propaganda against people like me when we talk about the desirability of executing the world's worst war criminals. These people can be swayed by pushing their emotional buttons.

No, no, this Kevin Barrett guy, he's not a pacifist. He's in favor of capital punishment! Which actually I'm not – but in the verbal struggle I am, and I've had a really interesting discussion with Ken Jenkins over this. Ken Jenkins, I view him as an advocate of extremist pacifist language. He wants to purge the English language of any kind of violence.

Which I think is pretty absurd.

I would go along with Sigmund Freud, he said that civilization began on the day that the first cave man hurled an insult instead of a rock. So violent language is an artifact of civilized behavior, but violent action not so much. Although on rare occasions it may be justified, primarily in self-defense.

So, this idea of policing people's language is also I think a product of this kind of Protestant culture.

The kind-of-Protestant liberal middle classes have been so alienated from their true natures and human nature that they're trying to kind of sterilize their language, just like they're trying to sterilize their lives by using a lot of disinfectants and antibiotics to wash their dishes, that kind of anal-retentive pave the earth, clip your grass to a certain length kind of mentality, reacting against their own human nature.

And I think we're better off admitting our human nature and saying it's good, all of it's good, even the violent part is good, you know. Killing an animal and eating it is good.

There's a bad side to it too, maybe we should stop killing animals and eating them, but it's all basically good. The good God created creation and it's all good.

So being at ease with our human nature, including our anger and our violent impulses, is much, much better than repressing them, because once we are at ease with them, and can feel them exactly as they are, then we're free to not be violent in reality.

And it's often people who repress their violence in their minds that end up bursting and becoming violent in reality. And I think that a certain amount of hard language is good, and I'm also I'm a big fan of Rabelais, was the greatest user of hyperbole in history, the author of *Gargantua*.

So, calling something gargantuan – in a sense all language is hyperbolic; when you single something out to describe it, your're exaggerating that quality, because everything else is still there. If I point at a tree and say green, I'm exaggerating the greenness of reality, because the sky is blue and the ground is ....

There are other colors out there. When I point at the tree and say green, I'm making it sound like everything is green. So that is what language does. Language singles stuff out and exaggerates whatever you say. So everything you say is already an exaggeration, no matter how much you try to understate it.

And knowing that and admitting that, and then using hyperbole, which is exaggerated language for a purpose, to communicate, is a noble endeavor. That's what Rabelais did and that's what many great writers have done. Also hyperbole is a huge part of folkloric expressive culture.

Mark Twain borrowed from the folkloric traditions, from the way people are talking in a very artistic or interesting way. You go down to the bar or wherever people are talking, or listen to a southern stump speech, there's going to be a lot of hyperbole, because we like it, because it's effective communication.

So in a sense when you start ranting about hanging the world's worst war criminals, you're engaging in a kind of hyperbole, and I'm conscious of that. Usually when I do that, normally it's in some kind of context where there's some kind of humor, dark humor, irony, or whatever. In other words, I'm conscious of my own hyperbole when I'm doing it, and you can hear it in the tone of voice.

But it's always possible to take that out of context, and try to make it sound as if, oh, this Barrett, he's a lunatic, he's probably going to go and hang somebody. It's kind of hilarious and hyperbolic itself.

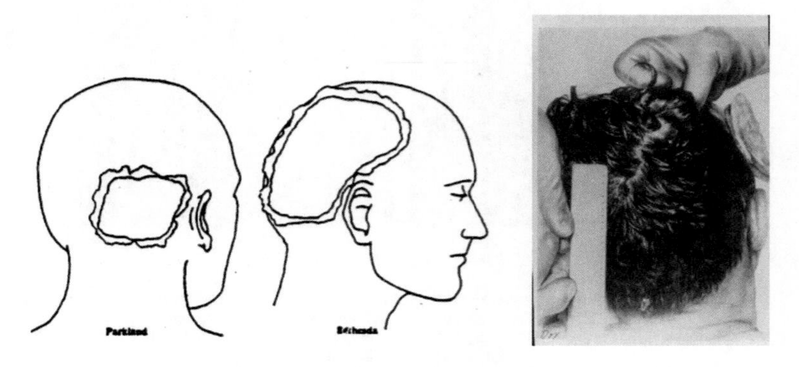

David Lifton, *Best Evidence* (1980), Expanded

The Parkland description of the wound was very different than that at Bethesda, where it was enlarged by James Humes to make it look more like the effect of a shot from the rear; and when the House Select Committed on Assassinations reviewed the case, it contracted to a small entry wound at the top of the head, which was absurd. The wound was blacked out in the Zapruder film, one of many alterations that were done to conceal the true causes of the death of our 35th President.

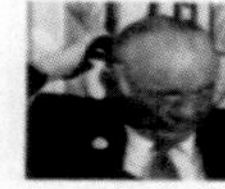

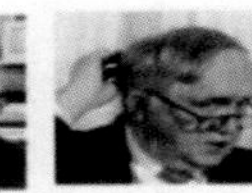

Robert Groden, *The Killing of a President* (1994), Expanded

Some forty witnesses from Dealey Plaza, from Parkland and from Bethesda--including bystanders, physicians, medical technicians, and agents of the FBI--reported that JFK had a massive blow-out to the back of the head, the location of which they demonstrated with their hands.

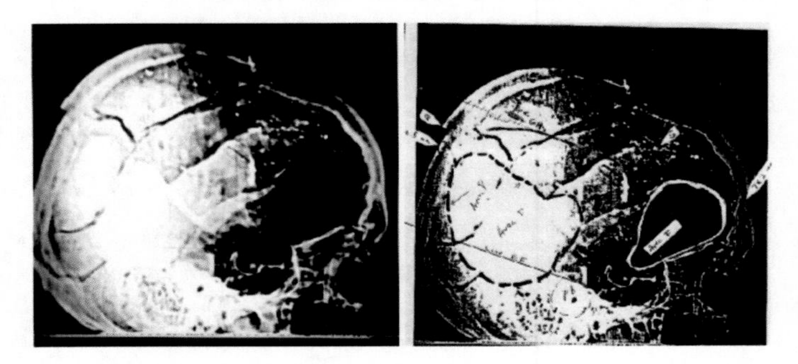

David W. Mantik, *Assassination Science* (1998)

These reports were discounted on the grounds that the autopsy X-rays don't show it. Mantik, a Ph.D. in physics, used the simple technique of optical densitometry to prove that an area--identified here as "Area P"--had been "patched" using material far too dense to be human bone.

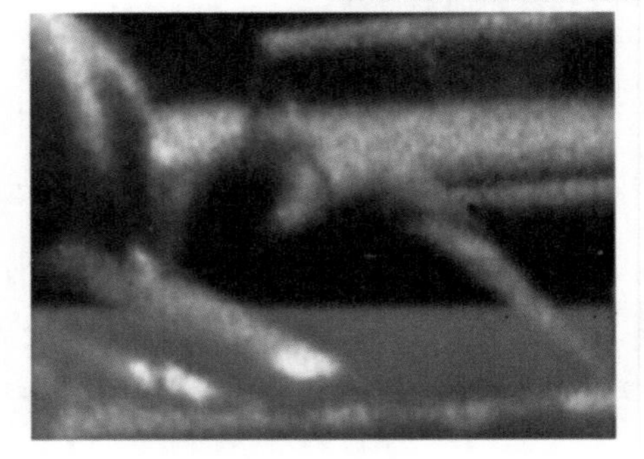

Zapruder Frame 374

It was my suspicion that those who were involved in reconstructing home movies of the assassination, including the Zapruder film, might have overlooked frames past 313-316 that display the wound to the back of the head. I found this image of the blow-out in frame 374.

[Chapter 53] Disappearing Witnesses; We Get The Message

Disappearing Witnesses
by Penn Jones, Jr.

first appeared in Rebel Magazine
Nov. 22, 1983

Shortly after dark on Sunday night November 24, 1963, after Ruby had killed Lee Harvey Oswald, a meeting took place in Jack Ruby's apartment in Oak Cliff, a suburb of Dallas, Texas. Five persons were present. George Senator and Attorney Tom Howard were present and having a drink in the apartment when two newsmen arrived.

The newsmen were Bill Hunter of the *Long Beach California Press Telegram*, and Jim Koethe of the *Dallas Times Herald*. Attorney C.A. Droby of Dallas arranged the meeting for the two newsmen. Jim Martin, a close friend of George Senator's, was also present at the apartment meeting.

This writer asked Martin if he thought it was unusual for Senator to forget the meeting while testifying in Washington on April 22, 1964, since Bill Hunter, who was a newsman present at the meeting, was shot to death that very night. Martin grinned and said: "Oh, you're looking for a conspiracy."

I nodded yes and he grinned and said, "You will never find it."

I asked soberly, "Never find it, or not there?"

He added soberly, "Not there."

Bill Hunter, a native of Dallas and an award winning newsman in Long Beach, was on duty and reading a book in the police station called "Public Safety Building". Two policemen going off duty came into the press room, and one policeman shot Hunter through the heart at a range officially ruled to be "no more than three feet".

The policeman said he dropped his gun, and it fired as he picked it up, but the angle of the bullet caused him to change his story. He finally said he was playing a game of quick draw with his fellow officer. The other officer testified he had his back turned when the shooting took place.

Hunter, who covered the assassination for his paper, the *Long Beach Press Telegram*, had written: "Within minutes of Ruby's execution of Oswald, before the eyes of millions watching television, at least two Dallas attorneys appeared to talk with him."

Hunter was quoting Tom Howard who died of a heart attack in Dallas a few months after Hunter's own death. Lawyer Tom Howard was observed acting strangely to his friends two days before his death. Howard was taken to the hospital by a "friend" according to the newspapers. No autopsy was performed.

Dallas Times Herald reporter Jim Koethe was killed by a karate chop to the throat just as he emerged from a shower in his apartment on September 21, 1964. His murderer was not indicted.

What went on in that significant meeting in Ruby's and Senator's apartment?

Few are left to tell. There is no one in authority to ask the question, since the Warren Commission has made its final report, and The House Select Committee has closed its investigation.

Dorothy Kilgallen was another reporter who died strangely and suddenly after her involvement in the Kennedy assassination. Miss Kilgallen is the only journalist who was granted a private interview with Jack Ruby after he killed Lee Harvey Oswald. Judge Joe B. Brown granted the interview during the course of the Ruby trial in Dallas – to the intense anger of the hundreds of other newspeople present.

We will not divulge exactly what Miss Kilgallen did to obtain the interview with Ruby. But Judge Brown bragged about the price paid. Only that was not the real price Miss Kilgallen paid. She gave her life for the interview. Miss Kilgallen stated that she was "going to break this case wide open."

She died on November 8, 1965. Her autopsy report took eight days. She was 52 years old. Two days later Mrs. Earl T. Smith, a close friend of Miss Kilgallen's died of undetermined causes.

Tom Howard, who died of a heart attack, was a good friend of District Attorney Henry Wade, although they often opposed each other in court. Howard was close to Ruby and other fringes of the Dallas underworld.

Like Ruby, Howard's life revolved around the police station, and it was not surprising when he and Ruby (toting his gun) showed up at the station on the evening of the assassination of President Kennedy. Nor was it unusual when Howard arrived at the jail shortly after Ruby shot Oswald, asking to see his old friend.

Howard was shown into a meeting room to see a bewildered Ruby who had not asked for a lawyer. For the next two days – until Ruby's brother, Earl, soured on him, and had Howard relieved – he was Jack Ruby's chief attorney and public spokesman.

Howard took to the publicity with alacrity, called a press conference, wheeled and dealed. He told newsmen the case was a "once-in-a-lifetime chance", and that "speaking as a private citizen", he thought Ruby deserved a Congressional medal. He told the *Houston Post* that Ruby had been in the police station Friday night (November 22, 1963) with a gun. Howard dickered with a national magazine for an Oswald murder story. He got hold of a picture showing the President's brains flying out of the car, and tried to sell it to *Life Magazine*. Ruby's sister, Eva Grant, even accused Howard of leaking information to the DA. It was never quite clear whether Howard was working for Ruby or against him.

On March 27, 1965, Howard was taken to a hospital by an unidentified person and died there. He was 48. The doctor, without benefit of an autopsy, said he had suffered a heart attack. Some reporters and friends of Howard's were not so certain. Some said he was "bumped off".

Earlene Roberts was the plump widow who managed the rooming house where Lee Harvey Oswald was living under the name O. H. Lee. She testified before the Warren Commission that she saw Oswald come home around one o'clock, go to his room for three or four minutes and walk out zipping his light weight jacket. A few minutes later, a mile away, officer J. D. Tippit was shot dead.

Mrs. Roberts testified that while Oswald was in his room, two uniformed cops pulled up in front of the rooming house and honked twice.

"Just tit tit," she said.

The police department issued a report saying all patrol cars in the area, except Tippit's, were accounted for. The Warren Commission let it go at that.

After testifying in Dallas in April 1964, Mrs. Roberts was subjected to intensive police harassment. They visited her at all hours of the day and night. Earlene complained of being "worried to death" by the police. She died on January 9, 1966 in Parkland Hospital (the hospital where President Kennedy was taken). Police said she suffered a heart attack in her home. No autopsy was performed.

Warren Reynolds was minding his used car lot on East Jefferson Street in Oak Cliff in Dallas, when he heard shots two blocks away. He thought it was a marital quarrel. Then he saw a man having a great difficulty tucking "a pistol or an automatic" in his belt, and running at the same time. Reynolds gave chase for a short piece being careful to keep his distance, then lost the fleeing man.

He didn't know it then, but he had apparently witnessed the flight of the killer (or one of the killers) of patrolman Jefferson David Tippit. Feeling helpful, he gave his name to a passing policeman and offered his cooperation. Television cameras zeroed in on him, got his story, and made him well known. Warren Reynolds, the amiable used car man, was making history.

Reynolds was not questioned until two months after the event. The FBI finally talked to him in January 1964. The FBI interview report said, " ... he was hesitant to definitely identify Oswald as the individual." Then it added, "He advised he is of the opinion Oswald is the person."

Two days after Reynolds talked to the FBI, he was shot in the head. He was closing up his used car lot for the night at the time. Nothing was stolen. Later after consulting retired General Edwin Walker (the man Oswald allegedly shot at before he assassinated President Kennedy), he told the Warren Commission Counsel that Oswald was definitely the man he saw fleeing the Tippit murder scene.

A young hood was arrested for the murder attempt. Darrell Wayne Garner had called a relative bragging that he shot Reynolds. But Garner had an alibi, Nancy Jane Mooney, alias Betty McDonald, who said Garner was in bed with her at the time he was supposed to have shot Reynolds. Nancy Jane had worked at Jack Ruby's Carousel Club. Garner was freed.

Nancy Jane was picked up a week later for fighting with a girlfriend. She was arrested for disturbing the peace. The girlfriend was not arrested. Within hours after her arrest, Nancy Jane was dead. Police reports said she hanged herself with her toreador pants.

Reynolds and his family were harassed and threatened. But upon giving the Warren Commission a firm identification of Oswald as being the Tippit murder fugitive, he said, "I don't think they are going to bother me any more."

Hank Killam was a house painter who lived at Mrs. A.C. Johnson's rooming house at the same time Lee Harvey Oswald lived there. His wife, Wanda, once pushed cigarettes and drinks at Jack Ruby's club.

Hank was a big man, over six feet and weighing over 200 pounds. After the assassination, federal agents visited him repeatedly causing him to lose one job after another.

Killam was absorbed by the assassination, even obsessed. Hours after the event, he came home, "white as a sheet".

Wanda said he stayed up all night watching the television accounts of the assassination. Later he bought all the papers and clipped the stories about Kennedy's death.

Before Christmas, Killam left for Florida. Wanda confessed where he was. Federal agents hounded him in Tampa, Florida where he was working selling cars at his brother-in-law's car lot. He lost his job.

Killam wrote Wanda that he would be sending for her soon. He received a phone call on St. Patrick's day. He left the house immediately. He was found later on a sidewalk in front of a broken window. His jugular vein was cut. He bled to death en route to the hospital.

There is no mention of Killam by the Warren Commission. A number of FBI documents on Killam relating to the assassination were withheld, along with documents prepared by the CIA. What is clear is that SOMEBODY considered Hank Killam a very important guy.

William Whaley was known as the "Oswald Cabbie". He was one of the few who had the opportunity to talk alone with the accused killer of President Kennedy. He testified that Oswald hailed him at the Dallas Greyhound bus station.

Whaley said he drove Oswald to the intersection of Beckley and Neches – half a block from the rooming house – and collected a dollar. Later he identified Oswald as his fare in a questionable police line-up.

Whaley was killed in a head-on collision on a bridge over the Trinity River, December 18, 1965; his passenger was critically injured. The 83-year-old driver of the other car was also killed.

Whaley had been with the City Transportation Company since 1936 and had a perfect driving record. He was the first Dallas cabbie to be killed on duty since 1937. When I went to interview the manager of the cab company about Whaley's death, he literally pushed me out of the office, "If you're smart, you won't be coming around here asking questions."

Domingo Benavides, an auto mechanic, was witness to the murder of Officer Tippit. Benavides testified he got a "really good view of the slayer".

Benavides said the killer resembled newspaper pictures of Oswald, but he described him differently, "I remember the back of his head seemed like his hairline went square instead of tapered off ..."

Benavides reported he was repeatedly threatened by the police who advised him not to talk about what he saw.

In mid-February 1964, his brother Eddy, who resembled him, was fatally shot in the back of the head at a beer joint on Second Avenue in Dallas. The case was marked "unsolved".

Benavides's father-in-law J. W. Jackson was not impressed by the investigation. He began his own inquiry. Two weeks later, J.W. Jackson was shot at his home. As the gunman escaped, a police car came around the block. It made no attempt to follow the speeding car with the gunman.

The police advised that Jackson should "lay off this business." "Don't go around asking questions; that's our job." Jackson and Benavides are both convinced that Eddy's murder was a case of mistaken identity and that Domingo Benavides, the Tippit witness was the intended victim.

Lee Bowers's testimony is perhaps as explosive as any recorded by the Warren Commission. He was one of the 65 witnesses who saw the President's assassination, and who thought shots were fired from the area of the Grassy Knoll. (The Knoll is west of the Texas School Book Depository Building.) But more than that, he was in a unique position to observe some pretty strange behavior in the Knoll area before and during the assassination.

Bowers, then a towerman for the Union Terminal Co., was stationed in his 14-foot tower directly behind the Grassy Knoll. He faced the scene of the assassination. He could see the railroad overpass to his right. Directly in front of him was a parking lot and a wooden stockade fence, and a row of trees running along the top of the Grassy Knoll. The Knoll sloped down to the spot on Elm Street where the President was killed. Police had "cut off" traffic into the parking lot, Bowers said, "so that anyone moving around could actually be observed."

Bowers made two significant observations which he revealed to the Warren Commission. First, he saw three unfamiliar cars slowly cruising around the parking area in the 35 minutes before the assassination; the first two left after a few minutes.

The driver of the second car appeared to be talking into a "mic or telephone"; "he was holding something up to his mouth with one hand and he was driving with the other." A third car with out-of-state license plates and mud up to the windows, probed all around the parking area. Bowers last remembered seeing it about eight minutes before the shooting, pausing "just above the assassination site".

Bowers also observed two unfamiliar men standing on the top of the Knoll at the edge of the parking lot, within 10 or 15 feet of each other. "One man, middle aged or slightly older, fairly heavy set, in a white shirt, fairly dark trousers. Another man, younger, about mid-twenties, in either a plaid shirt or plaid coat or jacket." Both were facing toward Elm and Houston in anticipation of the motorcade. The two were the only strangers he remembered seeing. His description shows a remarkable similarity to Julia Ann Mercer's description of two unidentified men climbing the Knoll.

When the shots rang out, Bowers's attention was drawn to the area where he had seen the two men; he could still make out the one in the white shirt: "The darker dressed man was too hard to distinguish from the trees."

Bowers observed "some commotion" at that spot ... , "something out of the ordinary, a sort of milling around ... which attracted my eye for some reason which I could not identify." At that moment, a motorcycle policeman left the Presidential motorcade and roared up the Grassy Knoll, straight to where the two mysterious gentlemen were standing. Later, Bowers testified that the "commotion" that caught his eye may have been a "flash of light or smoke."

On the morning of August 9, 1966, Lee Bowers, vice president of a construction firm, was driving south of Dallas on business. He was two miles south of Midlothian, Texas when his brand new company car veered from the road and hit a bridge abutment. A farmer who saw it said the car was going about 50 miles an hour, a slow speed for that road.

Bowers died in a Dallas hospital. He was 41. There was no autopsy and he was cremated. A doctor from Midlothian who rode to Dallas in the ambulance with Bowers, noticed something peculiar about the victim. "He was in some strange sort of shock." The doctor said, "A different kind of shock than an accident victim experiences. I can't explain it. I've never seen anything like it."

When I questioned his widow, she insisted there was nothing suspicious, but then became flustered and said, "They told him not to talk."

Harold Russell was with Warren Reynolds when the Tippit shooting took place. Both men saw the Tippit killer escape. Russel was interviewed in January 1964, and signed a statement that the fleeing man was Oswald.

A few months after the assassination, Russell went back to his home near David, Oklahoma. In July of 1965, Russell went to a party with a female friend.

He seemingly went out of his mind at the party and started telling everyone he was going to be killed. He begged friends to hide him. Someone called the police. When the policemen arrived, one of them hit Russell on the head with his pistol. Russell was then taken to a hospital where he was pronounced dead a few hours later: cause of death was listed as "heart failure".

Among others who died strangely were James Worrell, who died in a motorcycle accident on November 9, 1966. He saw a strange man run from the back door of the Texas School Book Depository shortly after the assassination.

Gary Underhill was shot. This death was ruled suicide on May 8, 1964. Underhill was a former CIA agent and claimed he knew who was responsible for killing President Kennedy.

Delilah Walle was a worker at Ruby's club. She was married only 24 days when her new husband shot her. She had been working on a book of what she supposedly knew about the assassination.

William "Bill" Waters died May 20, 1967. Police said he died of a drug overdose (demerol). No autopsy was performed. His mother said Oswald and Killam came to her home before the assassination and her son tried to talk Oswald and Killam out of being involved. Waters called FBI agents after the assassination. The FBI told him he knew too much and to keep his mouth shut. He was arrested and kept in Memphis in a county jail for eight months on a misdemeanor charge.

Albert Guy Bogard, an automobile salesman who worked for Downtown Lincoln Mercury, showed a new Mercury to a man using the name "Lee Oswald".

Shortly after Bogard gave his testimony to a Commission attorney in Dallas, he was badly beaten and had to be hospitalized. Upon his release, he was fearful for his safety.

Bogard was from Hallsville, La. He was found dead in his car at the Hallsville Cemetery on St. Valentine's day in 1966. A rubber hose was attached to the exhaust and the other end extending into the car. The ruling was suicide. He was just 41 years old.

Jack Ruby died of cancer. He was taken into the hospital with Pneumonia. Twenty eight days later, he was dead from cancer.

David Ferrie of New Orleans, before he could be brought to trial for his involvement in the Kennedy assassination, died of brain hemorrhage. Just what caused his brain hemorrhage has not been established. Ferrie was to testify in the famous Jim Garrison trial, but death prevented him.

Dr. Mary Stults Sherman, age 51, was found stabbed and burned in her apartment in New Orleans. Dr. Sherman had been working on a cancer experiment with Ferrie.

Another Ferrie associate, Eladio Cerefine de Valle, 43, died on the same day as Ferrie. His skull was split open; he was then shot. DeValle had used Ferrie as a pilot. DeValle had been identifying some men in a photo taken in New Orleans for Jim Garrison. One of the men in the photo was Lee Harvey Oswald.

Paul Dyer, of the New Orleans Police force died of cancer. He was the first police officer to interview Ferrie. Martin got sick on the job and died a month later of cancer. He had just interviewed David Ferrie.

News reporters were not exempt either. Two lady reporters died strangely. Lisa Howard supposedly committed suicide. She knew a great deal about the "understanding" which was in the making after the Bay of Pigs, between President Kennedy and the Cubans.

Marguerite Higgins bluntly accused the American authorities of the November 2nd, 1963 killing of Premier Diem and his brother Nhu. A few months after her accusation, she died in a landmine explosion in Vietnam.

On Saturday November 23, 1963, Jack Zangetty, the manager of a $150,000 modular motel complex near Lake Lugert, Oklahoma, remarked to some friends that "Three other men – not Oswald – killed the President."

He also stated that "A man named Ruby will kill Oswald tomorrow and in a few days a member of the Frank Sinatra family will be kidnapped just to take some of the attention away from the assassination."

Two weeks later, Jack Zangetty was found floating in Lake Lugert with bullet holes in his chest. It appeared to witnesses he had been in the water one to two weeks.

Lou Staples, a radio announcer who was doing a good many of his radio shows on the Kennedy assassination, lost his life sometime on Friday night May 13, 1977.

This was near Yukon, Oklahoma. He had been having radio shows on the assassination since 1973 and the response to his programs was overwhelming.

Lou's death was termed suicide, but the bullet ending his life entered behind his right temple and Lou was left handed. He joined Gary Underhill, William Pitzer and Joe Cooper whose "suicides" were all done with the "wrong hand" shots to the head.

Lou had been stating that he wanted to purchase some property to build a home. He was lured out to a wheat field and his life ended there. I have been to the spot where Lou died.

Karyn Kupcinet, daughter of Irv Kupcinet, was trying to make a long distance call from Los Angeles. According to reports, the operator heard Miss Kupcinet scream into the phone that President Kennedy was going to be killed.

Two days after the assassination, she was found murdered in her apartment. The case is unsolved. She was 23.

Rose Cherami, 40, was an employee of Jack Ruby's club. She was riding with two men on a return trip from Florida carrying a load of narcotics. She was thrown from the car when an argument began between her and one of the men.

She was hospitalized for injuries and drug withdrawal. She told authorities that President Kennedy was going to be killed in Dallas. After her release from the hospital, she was a victim of a hit and run accident on September 4, 1965 near Big Sandy, Texas.

Robert L. Perrin was a gun-runner for Jack Ruby. His wife, Nancy testified before the Warren Commission that Robert took a dose of arsenic in August 1962.

Guy Bannister was a private detective who was closely involved in the Jim Garrison trial. Guy and his partner, Hugh Ward, died within a 10-day period as the Warren Commission was closing its hearings. Guy supposedly died of a heart attack, but witnesses said he had a bullet hole in his body.

George deMohrenschildt was another man who was to give testimony but never made it. DeMohrenschildt, in his final days, became suspicious of everyone around him, even his wife, and was nearing a nervous breakdown some thought.

He died of gun shot wounds. The verdict was suicide. But deMohrenschildt was a member of the White Russian society and very wealthy. He visited Lee Harvey Oswald and Marina Oswald when they lived on Neely Street. Marina visited the deMohrenschildts when she and Lee Harvey Oswald were having some of their disagreements.

Cliff Carter, LBJ's aide who rode in the Vice President's follow up car in the motorcade in Dealey Plaza where President Kennedy was gunned down, was LBJ's top aide during his first administration.

Carter died of mysterious circumstances. Carter died of pneumonia when no penicillin could be located in Washington, D.C. in September 1971. This was supposedly the cause of death.

Buddy Walthers, Deputy Sheriff, was at the kill site of President Kennedy He picked up a bullet in a hunk of brain matter blown from the President's head. Walthers never produced the bullet for evidence.

Walthers was also at the Texas Theater when Oswald was arrested. In a January 10th, 1969 shooting, Walthers was shot through the heart. In a shootout Walthers and his companion Deputy Alvin Maddox, were fired upon by Cherry, an escaped prisoner.

Walthers and Maddox were trying to capture Cherry when Walthers was shot through the heart. Walthers's widow received $10,000.00 for her husband dying in the line of duty.

Clay Shaw, age 60, died five years after he was charged by Jim Garrison for his involvement in the Kennedy assassination. Some reports have it that he had been ill for months after surgery for removing a blood clot.

Other newspaper reports of his death stated he had cancer. It was revealed that Shaw was a paid contact for the CIA. A neighbor reported that an ambulance was seen pulling up to the Shaw home. Then a body was carried in and an empty stretcher brought out.

A few hours later, Shaw was reportedly found dead in his home. Then he was given a quick embalming before a Coroner could be notified. It was then impossible to determine the cause of death.

On May 15, 1975, Roger Dean Craig died of a massive gun shot wound to the chest. Supposedly, it was his second try at suicide and a success. Craig was a witness to the slaughter of President Kennedy. Only Craig's story was different from the one the police told.

Craig testified in the Jim Garrison trial. Before this, Craig had lost his job with the Dallas Police Dept. In 1961, he had been "Man of the Year." Because he would not change his story of the assassination, he was harassed and threatened, stabbed, shot at, and his wife left him.

Craig wrote two manuscripts of what he witnessed. *When They Kill A President* and *The Patient Is Dying*.

Craig's father was out mowing the lawn when Craig supposedly shot himself. Considering the hardships, Craig very well could have committed suicide. But no one will ever know.

John M. Crawford, 46, died in a mysterious plane crash near Huntsville, Texas on April 15, 1969. It appeared from witnesses that Crawford had left in a rush.

Crawford was a homosexual and a close friend of Jack Ruby's. Ruby supposedly carried Crawford's phone number in his pocket at all times. Crawford was also a friend of Buell Wesley Frazier's, the neighbor who took

Lee Harvey Oswald to work on that fatal morning of November 22, 1963.

Hale Boggs was the only member of the Warren Commission who disagreed with the conclusions. Hale Boggs did not follow Earl Warren and his disciples. He totally disagreed. Hale Boggs was in a plane crash lost over frozen Alaska.

Nicholas J. Chetta, M.D. age 50, Orleans Parish coroner since 1950, died at Mercy Hospital on May 25, 1968. Newspaper reports were sketchy. It was said he suffered a heart attack.

Dr. Chetta was the coroner who served at the death of David Ferrie.

Dr. Chetta was the key witness regarding Perry Russo against Clay Shaw. Shaw's attorney went into federal court only after Dr. Chetta was dead.

Dr. Martin Luther King was murdered, then his assassin not captured until over a year later. Dr. King was the only hope this country had for bringing about equality.

The death of Robert Kennedy, only shortly after Dr. King's death on June 5th, 1968, was a brazen act which gave notice to this entire nation. It became imperative, when Senator Kennedy became a threat as a Presidential candidate, that he had to be killed.

There is evidence that two persons, a man, and a woman were with the accused killer, but authorities have found no trace of them. Coroner, Dr. Thomas Noguchi told the Grand Jury the powder burns indicated the murder gun was fired not more than two to three inches from Kennedy's right ear. Witnesses testified that Sirhan was never closer than four or five feet to the Senator.

I have not, by any means, listed "all" of the strange deaths. I have a complete list in my books. I have listed the most significant ones that occurred after the assassination. The strange deaths after the assassination of President John F. Kennedy, in my estimate, numbered over 100, but I am certain I know of only a fraction.

Many strange deaths occurred after the assassinations of Dr. Martin Luther King, and Senator Robert F. Kennedy. No one knows the exact number.

HASTINGS "BOSTON BRAKES" KILLING A WARNING?

by Gordon Duff, *Veterans Today* Senior Editor

Imagine a new "E Class" Mercedes exploding in flames, burning to a cinder. 220 km/hr crashes on the Autobahn are often survived, certainly without a fire.

There is a reason to own a Mercedes, in normal circumstances the chances of dying in one are quite remote unless you are Lady Di or heir to the presidency of Syria or, just perhaps, wrote a scathing expose that dismembered part of one of the greatest drug empires of all time.

"Yes, you got Michael Hastings. We are warned. Lots of journalists are killed each year. *Veterans Today* loses its share, perhaps a bit more. "

For those who didn't watch the entire video, go back. Catch the last few seconds. I was flabbergasted.

Those of us who have "been there and done that," and come back with more than the T-shirt say goodbye to one of ours.

RIP Michael from "g" and the gang at "VT".

"BOSTON BRAKES" ASSASSINATION TECHNIQUE BECOMES BIG "PROBLEM SOLVER"

by Gordon Duff

Veterans Today
July 25, 2010

I had never heard of "Boston Brakes" until two days ago. I had been on the Kevin Barrett radio show yesterday, discussing, among other things, the endless ways to gain control of an aircraft and plow it into a building, something I had been briefed on by my Air Force buddies. There are a dozen ways to gain control of a plane, in fact, the more "fly by wire" a plane is, the more ways to control it remotely. Now I am told the same thing works for cars, not exactly the same but close enough.

Nothing particularly clever is required, especially when the plane is capable of landing itself or, with a bit of hacking, making an inconvenient stop in the side of a building. I am told this game started with the CIA back in Boston, not with planes but cars. Car wrecks were mechanically staged using the "Boston Brakes" method, not always fatal but always a good way of communicating to someone your displeasure. Sending a college age daughter into a light pole, reporting her speedometer was stuck at 200 mph, and fudging her blood test to show she was "double drunk" has been done countless times.

It isn't just the crash that makes it "Boston Brakes" but the speedometer stuck at some outrageous speed and the blood acohol level, always from a sample that is mysteriously misplaced later. Oh, and I almost forgot, no skidmarks, something accident investigators only see at suicides or murder. Remember, always no skidmarks.

The trail that led me to look into "Boston Brakes" involved the suicide in 2003 of Dr. David Kelly, a suicide now ruled a murder. Kelly was believed to have killed himself because he had been attacked in the press by Prime Minister Tony Blair. Kelly, a prominent weapons scientist had claimed, as we all know is true today, that Tony Blair had falsified intelligence to force Britain into what Deputy Prime Minister Nick Clegg has called "the illegal invasion of Iraq."

With evidence finally, years later, piling in showing that Kelly's body had been moved and a suicide scene staged, pathologist records falsified and that Kelly was murdered with broad complicity by more than one government agency, things have started to take on a life of their own.

The assassination of Dr. David Kelly if prosecuted, and it is now under full criminal investigation, could lead to the highest levels of the British and American governments, the absolute highest.

Kelly was that important and the secrets they thought they had silenced when he was murdered point to the heads of state of several countries, not just Britain and America but Israel, North Korea, South Africa and maybe a few more.

This was a stupid and clumsy murder of a good and decent man. Selling nuclear weapons to North Korea isn't a joke, not at least to Dr. David Kelly. This is what cost him his life.

The suicide is now a murder and the wheels of justice have begun to turn. When that happens, nobody can control the outcome, almost nobody anyway.

First of all, even the reason for the supposed suicide was totally false. Kelly was a whistleblower, yes, but not about falsified intelligence regarding Tony Blair and "sexed up" weapons reports. Kelly was spilling the beans on missing nuclear weapons that he, himself, was involved in, weapons involving Israel and South Africa, a big secret that is now at the root of a major investigation in the United Kingdom, an investigation that went critical when one of the missing bombs exploded in North Korea in 2009. This is why that mysterious "Iraq Enquiry" has come back to life but we are not told why.

Kelly was murdered, not just because he was going to rat out members of both political parties for failing to act in the national interest but because tons of money was spent by mysterious parties to cover this up, money that has shown up on the public record as campaign contributions in amounts not even seen in the United States, from bad sources, unimaginably bad sources, the worst.

The question isn't as much why Kelly was murdered, all this is out now, with a cover story being released, one with no missing nuclear weapons, no Israel and no North Korea for sure, but at least insiders in Britain, key members of the government, the judiciary and the intelligence services will know, some properly informed, some properly castigated and the ones who belong in prison for life, running scott free along with their Yank counterparts, Cheney, Rumsfeld and Bush.

The problem is the pattern of killings, that 9/11 signature that we call "Boston Brakes". The mysterious death of Richard Waddington, relative of a potential witness in the Chilcot Inquiry that could have opened an unimaginable "can of worms".

Waddington was to be subjected to an intimidating show of power, an arranged car accident, not a murder as it ended up. Waddington was killed to prevent someone else from confirming Israel's complicity in building 10 nuclear weapons. The "secret world" says "6". Keeping an Israeli nuclear test secret, keeping a nuke sold to North Korea secret, keeping an "under the table" deal involving the Thatcher government and gun runners secret cost a life.

In 2008, Jorg Haider, the anti-Zionist ready to take power as Prime Minister of Austria got the "Boston Brakes" treatment when his Volkswagen Phaeton, one of the world's finest road cars, as with Waddinton, Princess Di and others, rammed into a concrete abutment, "no skidmarks." I keep going back in my mind to the "dancing Israeli's" when I think of Lady Di's death. How does she tie in? The money that flowed into Tony Blair's political coffers came from the pockets of "Mr. Landmine," a Rhodesian arms merchant Lady Di may have given her life to stop. Tied to Israel, North Korea and the missing nukes, this trail heads to Paris and perhaps even the white Fiat Uno seen next to the ill fated Mercedes. Was it filled with "dancing Israeli's"?

Jon King, writing of these incidents, says the following:

> According to former SAS officer and world-famous explorer, Sir Ranulph Feinnes, it is not beyond reason that both Princess Diana's Mercedes and Jorg Haider's Volkswagen were remotely hijacked.
>
> In his book, *The Feather Men*, Feinnes recounts in some detail a highly sophisticated assassination technique which he says has been employed by the world's intelligence agencies for decades.
>
> A microchip transceiver, he explains, is fitted to the target vehicle's on-board computer, allowing the vehicle to be controlled remotely. He says this technique was first deployed by the CIA in Boston, hence its name: the "Boston brakes".
>
> Feinnes also recounts an instance of the "Boston brakes" being successfully deployed in England in 1986, which resulted in the assassination of SAS Major, Michael Marman, and the near-death of a former equerry to the Queen, Sir Peter Horsley.
>
> According to Sir Ranuplh Feinnes, the "Boston brakes" is all fact, no fiction. Certainly evidence John and I present in our new book, *Princess Diana: The Evidence*, shows clearly enough that Diana was almost certainly the victim of the "Boston brakes".
>
> And given the startling correlations presented above, one has to wonder if Jorg Haider might also have suffered this same premeditated fate."
>
> I remember the first time I stood out in the road, Dealey Plaza in Dallas, Texas, staring up at the Texas School Book Depository, supposed sight of Lee Harvey Oswald, once believed involved in the Kennedy assassination. Holding a photo from 1963 in my hand, I could see the Texas live oak was the same size, totally blocking the view from the window, blocking any potential shot on Kennedy. Even without the obfuscations of Arlen Specter and his "magic bullet" it all fell apart then as it does now.
>
> Similarly, I have walked the route of Princess Di's Mercedes also, walked it when the road is closed for the summer Paris Plages festival and have driven it dozens of times. As with all the "Boston Brakes" killings, no skidmarks. I drive the BMW version of the 12 cylinder Mercedes 600, a car you can dance around curves like a Porsche.

> The Volkswagen Phaeton is much of the same ilk, powerful engine, race car brakes and suspension and incredible handling. I have driven hours above 150 mph on European roads. Drivers do that all the time, you seldom see a "fender bender".
>
> Is there a great conspiracy out there, one that kills minor computer programmers in Ohio like Mike Connell, who threatened to put George "W" Bush in prison for election rigging, one of the endless mysterious plane crashes that clean Democrats out of the United States Senate? Does anyone remember when Ross Perot, a certainty for the oval office, dropped out of the election?
>
> Truth is, we live in a world where it is cheaper sometimes to use simple thuggery, than to go to the bother of rigging a Boeing 767 or running a car into a concrete abutment. When a member of congress is bribed to support a war, vote for a special tax break for a gangster or to submit to some Israeli abuse, did someone send him a photo of his children playing in a school yard or was his brother's wife raped and beaten recently? This is how the game is played.

Between 1995 and 2005, 50 scientists that we know of, all WMD specialists, germ warfare, bio weapons, chemical warfare, died under circumstances, some as plain as an unexpected heart attack in an otherwise healthy young adult to the inevitable "Boston Brakes" crash.

Find this a bit overwhelming? This is only one of several lists. If you wondered what intelligence services do, the answer is simple, they murder people. If you wonder who they work for, the answer is simple also, crooked arms dealers, drug cartels and power mad politicians.

How many people will be murdered, how many kids threatened, how many poisonings, how much in bribes before America agrees to attack Iran? How many billions are being paid to keep America in Afghanistan, supporting Karzai and immune to knowlege of the $65 billion dollar a year drug trade? If you don't think members of congress are at the heart of the conspiracy, you aren't very good at using the Freedom of Information Act to track travel schedules or see who belongs to what organization along with drug lords and thugs.

Ask Sibel Edmonds.

If, like everyone else, you have come to expect terrorist acts, of late almost comedy routines, the "crotch bomber" and the Times Square Fizzler as potential Vegas headliners, expect that "dirty bomb" we have been warned about. If our "bestest buddies in the whole world" can sell submarines to North Korea or give them atom bombs, don't be surprised if, in order to push that Iran war we are hearing so much about, you don't wake up some morning to an American city glowing in the dark.

Within seconds, Fox News will have the whole story, Iranian suspects, airport footage, everything. It is all a game, everything is a game. Everything is a business and our businessmen today are all gangsters, same as our government.

[Reprinted here with permission.]

[Chapter 54] Along a long road ...

> CLEVELAND (AP) March 19, 2003 – Supreme Court Justice Antonin Scalia has banned broadcast media from an appearance Wednesday where he will receive an award for supporting free speech.

It's been a long road
by Mike Palecek

... It's been a long road.

From a stolen election, to a government-planned attack on Sept. 11, 2001, to two invasions based on lies, based on power, on money.

To a murdered Senator, the one standing in their way, who would not be moved.

We didn't want it to come. We marched. We e-mailed, we sang, we wrote, we got arrested.

But it came anyway.

And it is still here.

The New American Dream, a radio program I co-host along with Chuck Gregory, is a "Yellow Ribbon Free Zone".

We do not support the troops.

The troops are not defending our freedom. They are thugs for the empire.

We heard all about "putting a boot up their ass" from Toby Keith.

He's a brave man, to encourage other men to kill men, women and children – for no reason.

The real patriots were the Dixie Chicks. We all know that now.

Protesters protect our freedom.

That's the truth.

Think Cynthia McKinney and Cindy Sheehan not George Bush and John McCain.

A hero does not drop bombs on people who are trying to live their lives.

C'mon ... Teachers, priests, ministers, coaches, parents, please start telling the truth.

We can handle the truth. In fact, without the truth, we cannot live.

We will die.

Slowly, and then all at once.

We will collapse and that will be that.

It will be over.

A dusty pile of rubble and Ho Ho's and lies.

We need a new dream, something real, solid to believe in.

Truth in our history books.

Bread on the table of the poor.

We have many heroes from which to draw inspiration.

People who gave and are giving their lives to the truth.

Patriots, if you will, hard workers, whatever you want to call it. They are there.

They have always been there, even if we don't see them.

Even if they are not famous.

They don't give a damn about that. They are driven by something inside of them. And we can draw hope from the absolute fact that that same thing is also inside of us.

David W. Mantik, M.D., Ph.D., who is board certified in radiation oncology, took a CAT scan of a patient with chest and neck dimensions similar to those of JFK. When he plotted the official trajectory, it turned out to be anatomically impossible. Cervical vertebrae intervene.

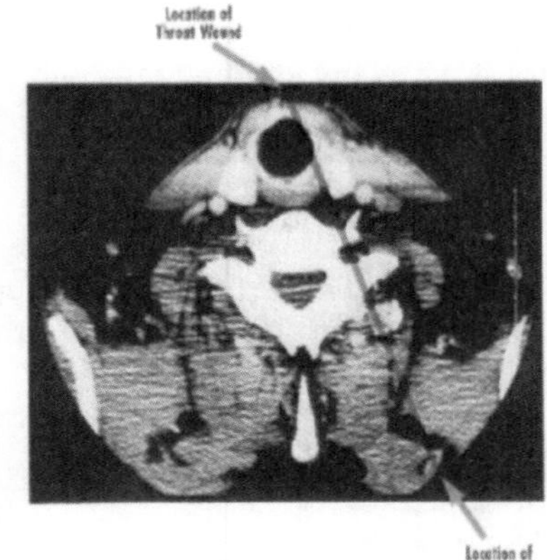

Stewart Galanor, *Cover-Up* (1998)

[Chapter 55] The Last Word

> "I suppose really the only two dates that most people remember where they were was Pearl Harbor and the death of president Franklin Roosevelt."
>
> - John F. Kennedy

Reflections on *The Dynamic Duo*
by Jim Fetzer

Dear Mike,

I have a great affection for Jim but I have no desire to be associated with his conspiracy theories (or to discuss them), so I'll have to decline.

Regards,
Paul Humphreys
Professor of Philosophy
University of Virginia

I find it difficult to express my appreciation to Mike Palecek for having the inspiration and dedication to do this volume on Kevin and me. My gratitude knows no bounds. A few of the themes that emerge here may be worthy of further reflection. One of those is that most faculty – including the tenured faculty – are reluctant to come to grips with politically-loaded complex and controversial issues like JFK and 9/11.

After 35 years of college teaching, I have come to realize that what faculty fear most is being embarrassed: by a question from a student they cannot answer; by being put on the spot when they are unprepared; by having to respond to issues in the public domain they would prefer not to tackle. Tenure was created to protect them in speaking out about issues of that kind – but almost none of them rise to the challenge.

That was conspicuous in the response of Paul Humphreys, Chair of the Department of Philosophy at the University of Virginia. He was my closest friend for more than 20 years, yet – while he holds great affection for me, as he puts it – he does not want to be "associated with [my] conspiracy theories". I am afraid academicians need to be made of sterner stuff. "All that is necessary for evil to triumph ... "

Another illustration comes from the treatment of James Tracy, who is among the few academicians who dare to speak out – in his case, especially about the fabricated events of Sandy Hook and the Boston bombing – yet he is pilloried by the FAU administration and even by other faculty, who succumb to social pressure and adopt conventional views, even though anyone who actually studied the evidence would know that he is right – and be grateful that he has been speaking out.

The most stunning case we currently confront comes from Edward Snowden's revelations about the massive NSA surveillance program.

The espionage charges against him for informing the American people and the world that the NSA has been conducting the most massive spying operation in history are completely baseless and absurd. Snowden is not revealing information that places the national security of the nation at stake but information revealing the NSA has instead been tracking enemies of the national security state.

Those who seem to be the real targets of this surveillance program include veterans, Constitutionalists, NRA members, 9/11 Truthers, Ron Paul supporters, and any one else who might have the courage, the integrity, and the ability to resist the imposition of a new military police state under DHS.

The latest figures about the "Main Core" list of political dissidents stand at around 8,000,000 today.

We know from a report released by a subcommittee of the Senate Committee on Homeland Security and Intelligence, on 3 October 2012, that, after surveying 680 "fusion center" reports gathered from 2009-2010, it had discovered that there were no indications of any terrorist activity: NONE. ZILCH. NADA. NOT ONE! Yet this astounding data has yet to be broadcast or published by ABC, NBC, CBS, or CNN.

This sample, which was obtained under conditions that insured if any domestic terrorist activity had been taking place it would have been revealed, supports the statistical extrapolation that domestic terrorist activity in the United States is virtually non-existent. It also explains why DHS and the FBI have had to fabricate phony events such as those at Sandy Hook and the Boston bombing, which were staged.

Even the claim by General Alexander, the head of the NSA, that this program had foiled 50 terrorist plots appears to be hokum. Ron Paul, for example, explained that it was an ad hoc exaggeration and that it included some 40 trivial events that were alleged to have occurred not in the United States but abroad and a story of an attempt to blow up Wall Street that has all the signs of another FBI fabricated event.

So the existence of a bona-fide domestic terrorist threat appears to be a cover story to justify the most massive spying undertaking ever, using enormous computer capabilities to accumulate information on our emails, our phone calls, our financial transactions, and even (no doubt) our medical records. They want to know everything there is to know about each and every one of us to promote their own agenda.

Everyone must know by now that DHS has acquired 2 billion rounds of .40 caliber hollow-point ammunition, which is not ever permissible in combat under the Hague Convention of 1899. It has also obtained 2,700 light tanks of the kind deployed in Boston (in violation of Posse Comitatus) and 7,000 assault weapons (of the kind that gun control legislation has been proposed to ban). They are preparing for war.

DHS has even made special arrangements with funeral homes and mortuaries to handle "an excess of casualties" should hospitals and emergency care facilities be overwhelmed. This can only be because the government is planning to take out or otherwise "neutralize" the enemies of the state that are being identified by means of its massive surveillance program, which Edward Snowden has revealed to us all.

(1) The violation of the 4th amendment

The first problem with this program is that it blatantly violates the 4th amendment's guarantee to freedom from unreasonable searches and seizures and a history of lower court decisions decreeing the right of citizens to privacy.

Rand Paul has spoken out eloquently about this and Snowden appears to have secret FISA court decisions that rule against the legality of the program that Obama is trying to defend.

Most Americans and others worldwide naively assume that the NSA scandal represents an excess of zeal in attempting to track down domestic terrorists who want to attack targets in America.

What they do not appreciate is that this has nothing to do with national security and everything to do with the national security state. They are not the same. From the perspective of DHS, veterans are potential terrorists.

(2) The potential for blackmail and manipulation

Those who say, "I have nothing to hide," are being extremely naïve, because this surveillance program is complete. It was not designated as "Total Information Awareness" for nothing when first introduced by Admiral Poindexter.

The public outcry led to its re-designation as "Terrorist Information Awareness", but that did not mean that anything had changed. The NSA wants to know everything about everyone so it can selectively use the information to control or modify our actions.

Its use for the purpose of political blackmail ought to be obvious to anyone who knows, for example, that J. Edgar Hoover maintained sex dossiers on the members of Congress, while the Mafia kept one on him.

Relationships with girlfriends and mistresses, watching porn, or having had an abortion are illustrations of the kinds of information that could be used to manipulate Senators, Presidents, or the Courts.

(3) These surveillance programs are privatized

Practically no one in the mass media has observed that Snowden had access to these records because he was working for a private firm, Booz Allen, which gave him opportunities to obtain data that a normal government program would not have allowed. And most of our security and surveillance programs are run by Israeli companies, which is one of the mechanisms by which it controls our leaders.

When the U.S. Senate voted 99-0 to support Israel, should it decide to attack Iran in its own self-defense, without adding that that would have to be in accordance with international law, it thereby violated not only the UN Charter but the U.S. Constitution, which grants treaties, such as ours with the UN, the same status under the Constitution as the Constitution itself. It was a completely unjustifiable act given that Iran has no nuclear weapons program. But it was also an act of treason.

When Rep. Ileana Ros-Lehtinen (R-FL) declares that the revelations by Edward Snowden are "not going to play out well for the national security interests of the United States," she is not talking about the interests of the American people, who are entitled to have their privacy preserved and to be safe-guarded from blackmail and embarrassment. There is no legitimate national security interest than could not be better served by traditional procedures with warrants.

When Sen. Diane Feinstein (D-CA), Sen. Charles Schumer (D-NY), and Sens. John McCain and Lindsey Graham condemn Snowden for treason, they themselves are the ones who are in fact violating the Constitution, their oaths of office, and betraying the American people. Snowden is an American and international hero for speaking out against tyranny and the conversion of America into a fascist state. Edward Snowden, like James Tracy, deserves commendation, not persecution.

The future of democracy hinges upon patriots like them.

THE LAST WORD

by Kevin Barrett

With this book, Mike Palecek has done something brilliant, brave, and beautiful. He's done that before in his novels. But this is different.

In a way, this is the first real book of the Internet age.

The Internet and the 9/11 Truth movement came of age at the same time, during the decade after 9/11.

But people just kept on writing the same old type of pre-Internet books as if nothing had happened.

Even the 9/11 Truth books are pre-Internet artifacts. I know, because I've written two and edited one.

All other books except the one you hold in your hands are like hand-copied manuscripts post-Gutenberg. They're relics – throwback to an earlier era when a tiny handful of people controlled the written word.

Today, the truth is on the Internet. Everyone owns it. It comes in a jumble of bite-size pieces. It's chaotic. It's messy. There are mistakes. There's disinfo. It's a crazy-quilt that you have to sew together yourself.

Mike Palecek put it all together and figured out – as so many of us have – that something is rotten, and not just in Denmark.

He realized that that the U.S. Empire, or the U.S.-Israeli Empire, or the Bankster Empire, or whatever you want to call it, is a horror show. He came to realize that just about everything in the mainstream media is lies – that when the truth shows up on dead trees, it means that someone isn't doing their job.

Because the job of the people who control what gets printed on dead trees is to suppress the truth, and peddle the lies.

So to hell with dead trees.

But wait a minute ... what if we tried to document the truth, as it has emerged on the Internet, preserving the immediacy, the whole style and flavor, of the get-it-out-quick-and-dirty gonzo truth-seeking generation of truly alternative journalists? And printed it on dead trees?

That would be a whole lot like what the White Rose resistance group did in Nazi Germany.

The White Rose pioneered what later became known as samizdat in the Soviet Union, then red-pill journalism in the post-9/11 USA. They were on a suicide mission for truth and justice. Their audience wasn't just their fellow Germans, the good Germans who went along with all the fascist war-mongering bullshit. They were really writing for posterity.

In a sense they were transcribing oral rants ... stump speeches ... heartfelt snippets of oration. In that sense they weren't writing at all. They were speaking. And their voices rise from their graves and ring out more and more clearly every day.

And that is what Mike Palecek is doing here. He is collecting and preserving authentic voices of real dissent, so that some day, people will be able to look back at the post-9/11 USA the way we look back at Nazi Germany today and say: Yes, almost everyone went crazy and became complicit in the most atrocious crimes against humanity imaginable ... but a few people somehow preserved their sanity and spoke out against it.

Rather than just selecting and assembling the best Internet samizdat, Mike decided to intersperse it with transcripts of interviews with me and Jim Fetzer.

Why me and Jim? I guess Mike thinks we're two of the best Internet samizdat artists. Can't argue with him there. And we both happen to live in the same region as Mike, the Upper Midwest. The land of bowling. That's why Mike put the bowling alley picture on the cover.

I've hardly set foot in a bowling alley since I signed up for Bowling 101 to satisfy my high school gym class requirement. And even then, I never wore a Batman mask when I bowled. But hey, it's a cool picture.

And I see what Mike is getting at. In some ways, Jim and I are actually just ordinary Midwestern guys who saw a chance to do the right thing, and decided to go for it.

Jim could have brown-nosed his way to the top of the Philosophy of Science profession. Instead, he sidetracked his brilliant career and put a big asterisk next to his reputation by championing JFK truth, and later Wellstone truth and 9/11 Truth. He did that that because despite his sometimes obtrusive ego, at heart he is a simple ordinary guy (with an unusually good mind) who has somehow retained the simple ordinary ability to know right from wrong, and just do what's right.

And that's why I wound up sacrificing my academic career on the altar of 9/11 Truth. Not because I'm some kind of hero. I'm just simple and ordinary enough to know right from wrong.

I'm so simple and ordinary and unimaginative that I honestly cannot imagine why every professor at every university in America hasn't done exactly what Jim and I have done. Whatever ivory towers they're sitting in, they're obviously way, way above me. They must have some elaborate and compelling reasons for making themselves complicit in the worst crimes against humanity ever committed. I'm just too dumb to understand what those reasons could possibly be.

So Mike sees us as representative of the American everyman and everywoman who hasn't gone along with the genocidal charade, in the same way the voices of the White Rose represent the "bad Germans" who didn't go along with the Nazi program. I guess he wanted to get a little bit up-close and personal, get a sense of the human beings behind the samizdat-artist masks. So he tape recorded and transcribed all those interviews with us.

I think Mike is the real samizdat-artist hero here.

Even if an EMP pulse weapon or solar flare fries every computer on earth and takes down the Internet permanently, this book will still exist, somewhere, in some post-apocalyptic version of a monastic library. Maybe it will even be hand-copied and illuminated à la *Canticle for Liebowitz*, who knows.

And until every last hand-copied illuminated manuscript version finally rots, and the dead trees are broken down by bacteria and returned to the earth to nourish living wood, the existence of this book will prove that quite a few ordinary American men and women stood up against the genocidal 9/11 charade, the political assassinations, the torture, the perpetual murder of truth and justice and decency that passes for public life at the beginning of the 21st century.

God bless Mike Palecek.

NSA spy scandal: It's even worse than Snowden says
by Kevin Barrett

Like Julian Assange, Edward Snowden is a media-trumpeted whistleblower hero. Like Assange, Snowden has striking, TV-star good looks. Like Assange, Snowden is involved in a dramatic TV-style chase across countries and continents.

It's almost like Assange and Snowden are starring in their own reality-TV shows.

With all the hoopla about Snowden (and before him, Assange), it's easy to forget all of the other whistleblowers who have revealed even more explosive information.

Consider two other NSA whistleblowers: Russ Tice and James Bamford.

Russ Tice is a former NSA intelligence analyst who has also worked for the U.S. Air Force, the Office of Naval Intelligence, and the Defense Intelligence Agency. He was a real U.S. intelligence insider, many pay grades above rookie contractor Edward Snowden.

In 2005, Tice blew the whistle on the NSA's illegal spying on Americans. Tice and other NSA sources revealed that the NSA's computerized spy program ECHELON was reading and filtering over 100,000 emails and phone calls per second. That is an even worse abuse of Americans' Constitutional rights than the programs that Snowden has revealed, which store copies of emails and phone calls but (allegedly) do not read them except when legally authorized to do so.

Worse yet, Tice's revelations raise even more troubling issues. Tice and his NSA whistleblower colleagues revealed that the NSA's massive, illegal spy-on-Americans program began in February, 2001 – seven months BEFORE the 9/11 attacks! As Andrew Harris reported for Bloomberg in July, 2006:

> The U.S. National Security Agency asked AT&T Inc. to help it set up a domestic call monitoring site seven months before the Sept. 11, 2001 attacks, lawyers claimed June 23 in court papers filed in New York federal court [...] "The Bush Administration asserted this became necessary after 9/11," plaintiff's lawyer Carl Mayer said in a telephone interview. "This undermines that assertion."

The illegal NSA spy-on-Americans program apparently "became necessary" several months before 9/11, not after 9/11. Why?

In an interview entitled "NSA Whistleblower Russ Tice Alleges NSA Wiretapped Barack Obama as Senate Candidate" Russ Tice recently explained to FBI whistleblower Sibel Edmonds the real purpose of the NSA's illegal spying on Americans: To collect blackmail material and other information that can be used to control influential citizens.

In short: The whole purpose of the NSA spy program was to enable 9/11, protect the perpetrators, and maintain the 9/11-triggered covert dictatorship.

Before 9/11, the neoconservatives of the Bush-Cheney Administration needed to ensure that no influential Americans would dare to stand up against the coming coup d'état. So they directed the NSA to begin wiretapping the American people.

From the billions of intercepted communications, the 9/11 plotters focused on those of extremely influential Americans: Politicians, wealthy people, military and intelligence officers, media figures, and other well-connected individuals. All of these people were profiled: Were they likely to resist the coming 9/11 operation? If so, how could they be stopped?

In some cases, blackmail material was collected. In others, more intensive surveillance was instituted.

Two "actionable threats" to the 9/11 coup were Senators Tom Daschle and Patrick Leahy. After 9/11, they received U.S. government anthrax in the mail. Frightened, Daschle and Leahy quickly stopped questioning 9/11 and opposing the Constitution-shredding USA Patriot Act.

If any influential Americans wanted to expose 9/11, and could not be blackmailed or controlled, they would have to be assassinated. The most illustrious victim was Senator Paul Wellstone, who was murdered, along with his family members and campaign staff, on October 25th, 2002, shortly after being threatened by then-Vice President Dick Cheney.

Senator Barbara Boxer (D-CA) spoke out against the murder of Senator Wellstone, calling it "a message to us all."

She added that if quoted, she would deny her statement. Apparently she was not anxious to get anthrax in the mail, or to have herself and her family members murdered. Another Senator from Minnesota, Mark Dayton, was also threatened by the 9/11 perpetrators. Senator Dayton fled Washington, DC and evacuated his entire staff to Minnesota in August 2004 – then announced his retirement from national politics – after receiving death threats due to his speech on the Senate floor attacking the 9/11 Commission Report as a pack of lies.

So as far back as 2005, Russ Tice and his colleagues revealed that the NSA spy program was used to murder almost 3,000 Americans in an act of bloody treason, and to kill or terrorize anyone who stood in the way. Compared to that, Edward Snowden's revelations are relatively tame.

Another NSA whistleblower is James Bamford, the Agency's quasi-official biographer. Bamford alerted Americans back in 2001 to a plot called Operation Northwoods. Like 9/11, Operation Northwoods was a fake "attack on America" designed to brainwash Americans into marching off to war. And like 9/11, it involved the murder of large numbers of Americans.

Operation Northwoods was designed to trigger war against Cuba and

Russia in 1962. It called for U.S. forces to bomb American cities and sink American ships. The CIA-controlled "Operation Mockingbird" mainstream media would blame Cuba for these murders.

Operation Northwoods was planned by Gen. Lyman Lemnitzer, head of the Joint Chiefs of Staff. Every member of the Joint Chiefs signed off on the proposal. It was one month away from happening, when President John F. Kennedy and Defense Secretary Robert McNamara vetoed it.

In his book *Mary's Mosaic*, author Peter Janney discusses evidence that the Operation Northwoods plan was not just aimed at Cuba. Its deeper purpose was to trigger a pre-emptive U.S. nuclear strike against the Soviet Union. Such a strike would have led to tens of millions of Russian and American deaths.

Every member of the U.S. Joint Chiefs of Staff in 1962 wanted to murder thousands of Americans in a false-flag operation designed to trigger a war that would have killed millions. In 2001, it finally happened.

So the truth is much worse than Edward Snowden is telling us. Our rulers are not just criminals – they are madmen, psychopathic liars, and mass murderers of the worst imaginable sort.

If the mainstream media publicized the most dangerous whistleblowers, the American National Security State would come crashing down.

Let us hope and pray that Edward Snowden's example will inspire other whistleblowers to come forward ... and that the most powerful and dangerous truths will finally be revealed.

JFK appears to have been hit four times: once in the throat (from in front); once in the back (from behind); and twice in the head (once from behind and once from in front). The shots to his throat and to his right temple appear to have been fired from above-ground-level sewer openings on the south and north sides of the Triple Underpass.

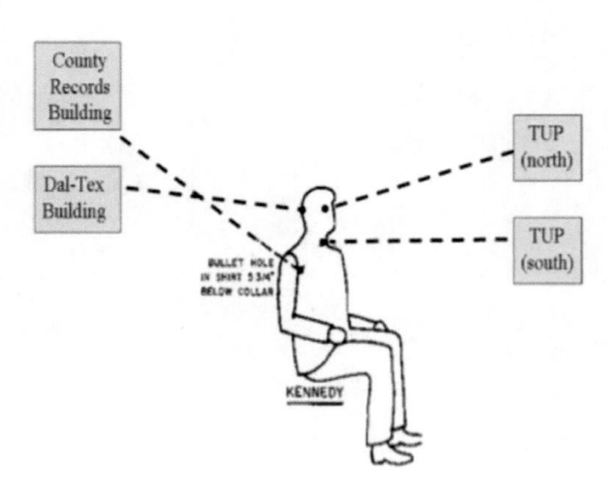

CLASS OF 1962
Carl G. Hempel
Jim Fetzer
David Ziegler
Clark Montgomery
Jim Fetzer
RECRUIT TRAINING REGIMENT
HEADQUARTERS
Jim Fetzer
Marine promoted
Jim Fetzer
Family friend
Henry Fetzer
Marguerite Fetzer
JAMES H. FETZER (JIM)
800 Violet Lane
Oregon, WI 53575-3320
(608) 835-2707
(608) 354-4280 (cell)
jfetzer@d.umn.edu
MAJOR: Philosophy
GRADUATE SCHOOL: Indiana University, M.A., History and Philosophy of Science, 1968; Indiana University, Ph.D., History and Philosophy of Science, 1970
HONORS & AWARDS: Distinguished McKnight University Professor, 1996-2006; The Outstanding Research Award, College of Liberal
269

Arts, University of Minnesota, Duluth, 2000-01; McKnight Endowment Fellow, University of Minnesota, 1996; Summer Faculty Research Fellow, University of Minnesota, 1996; The Outstanding Research Award, College of Liberal Arts, U.M. Duluth, 1992-93; Lansdowne Lecturer, University of Victoria, Victoria, B.C., 1992
President, The Minnesota Philosophical Society, 1991-92, Vice-President, 1990-91
The Medal of the University of Helsinki, Helsinki, Finland, 1990
Summer Faculty Research Fellow, University of Minnesota, 1988; Postdoctoral Fellow in Computer Science, Wright State University, 1986-87; Postdoctoral Research Fellow, National Science Foundation, 1979-80; Distinguished Teaching Award, University of Kentucky, 1973-74; Summer Faculty Research Fellow, University of Kentucky, 1972; Graduate Research Assistant, Indiana University, 1969-70; Fellow of the Faculty, Columbia University, 1968-69; NEA Title IV Fellow, Indiana University, 1966-68;
The Dickinson Prize, Princeton University, 1962; Magna Cum Laude, Princeton, 1962
Hobbies & Interests: Academic Web Site, http://www.d.umn.edu/~jfetzer/
Assassination Science, http://assassination-science.com Assassination Research, http://assassinationresearch.com
Scholars for 9/11 Truth, http://911scholars.org; Scholars for 9/11 Truth Forum, http://911scholars.ning.com
"The Real Deal" Archive, http://radiofetzer.blogspot.com; "James Fetzer" blog, http://jamesfetzer.blogspot.com
Columnist, Veterans Today, http://www.veteranstoday.com/author/fetzer/

Work Status: Retired
McKnight Professor Emeritus
University of Minnesota Duluth

Marital Status: Married
Spouse/Partner: Janice Morgan Fetzer (Jan), June 12, 1977
S/P Occupation: Housewife of Infinite Patience
Children: Bret Lee Fetzer, 1965, Playwright, director, author, critic, actor; Sarah Fetzer Lederer, 1979, Program administrator, housewife, mother

Unlike old soldiers, old McKnight Professors do not "just fade away." Not, at least, if they are named Jim Fetzer, one of the first ten to be selected for that distinction in 1996. Jim graduated magna cum laude from Princeton in 1962, served as an officer in the U.S. Marine Corps for four years, and earned his Ph.D. in the history and the philosophy of science in 1970, eventually joining the UM faculty on the Duluth campus, where he taught from 1987-2006; he retired in June 2006 after a 35-year career offering courses in logic, critical thinking, and scientific reasoning.

Jim has continued with his scholarly research in philosophy. In his last book prior to retirement, "The Evolution of Intelligence" (2005), he argued that humans are not the only animals with minds. This has been complemented by "Render Unto Darwin" (2007), where he tackles sensitive social issues in society today, such as the difference between creationism, creation science, and intelligent design compared to evolutionary theories from a scientific point of view.

Family Wedding, Las Vegas (2009)

It also explains why morality does not require religion and offers a spirited defense of abortion, stem-cell research, and cloning.

He also co-edited a special issue of Synthese (January 2011), on "Evolution and its Rivals" with Glenn Branch of the National Center for Science Education, including his own study, "Evolution and Atheism: Has Griffin reconciled science and religion?" Another on "Limits of Simulations of Thought and Action" just appeared in the premiere issue of the International Journal of Signs and Semiotic Systems (2011), a natural extension of his work in cognitive science and in relation to Minds and Machines, the journal he founded in 1991 and edited for 10 years.

Not one to take half-way measures, when he became involved in 9/11 at the suggestion of David Ray Griffin, Jim founded Scholars for 9/11 Truth that December and has managed its site since. In 2007, he edited its first book, "The 9/11 Conspiracy" (2007), organized its first conference in Madison, WI, and produced its first DVD, "The Science and Politics of 9/11." He has been making an impact, since the BBC has produced two documentaries on 9/11 featuring him as a leading representative of the movement. He has given hundreds of interviews and lectures about 9/11; his latest research on 9/11 has appeared at Veterans Today, including a critique of "The BBC's instrument of 9/11 misinformation."

Griffin had become aware of Fetzer because of Jim's publications on JFK, where he had organized a research group of the best-qualified individuals to ever study the case, including a world authority on the human brain who was also an expert on wound ballistics; an M.D. who is also a Ph.D. and board-certified in radiation oncology; a physician who was present when JFK was brought into Parkland Hospital and two days later was responsible for the treatment of his alleged assassin, Lee Harvey Oswald; a legendary photo and film analyst; and another Ph.D. in electromagnetism, the properties of light and images of moving objects.

Their research led to the discovery that the autopsy X-rays had been altered to conceal a massive blow-out to the back of his head, that another person's brain was substituted for that

On BBC's "Conspiracy Files" (2008)

of JFK, and that the home movies of the assassination were revised prior to their release, which shattered the cover-up. Jim has chaired or co-chaired four national conferences and has edited three books on JFK, "Assassination Science" (1998), "Murder in Dealey Plaza" (2000) and "The Great Zapruder Film Hoax" (2003). Even Vincent Bugliosi, who prosecuted Charles Manson and is a leading proponent of the "lone gunman theory," has described them as the only "exclusively scientific" books on the death of JFK.

The research produced by Scholars and others within the 9/11 movement has created quite a sensation. Jim presented the principal lecture at the American Scholars Conference in Los Angeles the same month he retired from UMD. C-SPAN filmed the panel discussion, which featured him with three other members of Scholars, Steven Jones, Bob Bowman and Webster Tarpley, and their moderator, Alex Jones. C-SPAN broadcast this 1:45:00 session seven or eight times, which had considerable influence in shattering the glass ceiling that had inhibited public discussion of 9/11.

Jim has been featured on "Hannity & Colmes" (twice) and on "The Factor," with Bill O'Reilly, who wanted to trivialize the truth movement, but without success. He has recently appeared on PressTV (Iran) and dozens of his presentations are archived on YouTube. Today there are many other research societies—Pilots for 9/11 Truth, Architects and Engineers for 9/11 Truth, and other groups—a sampling of which may be found at patriotsquestion911.com where more than 2,000 photos, bio sketches, and state-

PRINCETON UNIVERSITY

ments from scholars and experts across a broad range of professions may be found.

His reception abroad has been even more striking. In December 2006, Jim and his wife, Jan, visited Athens, where he was the featured guest on a 3.5-hour television program broadcast world-wide by satellite. He has been flown to Buenos Aires twice (2008 and 2009), where, on September 11, 2009, he presented the principal lecture during The International Symposium on 9/11 Truth and Justice at The National Library of The Republic of Argentina. He organized a symposium on "Debunking the 'War on Terror'" on July 14, 2010, in London (archived at noliesradio.org/archives/21621/). He has been featured hundreds of times on radio programs, including "Talk Radio Europe"; one of his most memorable remains "Howard Hughes (of the UK) interviews Jim Fetzer".

Jim also co-authored (with Don "Four Arrows" Jacobs) a book on the death of Sen. Paul Wellstone, "American Assassination" (2004). His final public lecture at UMD, a three-parter on JFK, 9/11, and Wellstone in November 2005, can be found archived at the bottom of the menu bar of assassinationscience.com, his public issues web site. Jim followed up with additional research in collaboration with John P. Costella, Ph.D., which they published as "The NTSB Failed Wellstone" in Michael Ruppert's "From the Wilderness" newsletter (2006). A new documentary, "Wellstone: They Killed Him," in 15 segments, substantiates their research on Wellstone's death.

Jim continues to contribute to conventional philosophical research; his 29th book, "The Place of Probability in Science" (2010), was co-edited with the late Ellery Eells. He has devoted himself, with great energy and enthusiasm, to what he takes to be the most pressing controversies confronting our society. In retirement, he has become a "public intellectual" who is doing what he can with what he has to convey to the public the kinds of knowledge it needs to move the nation something just a bit closer to the right direction.

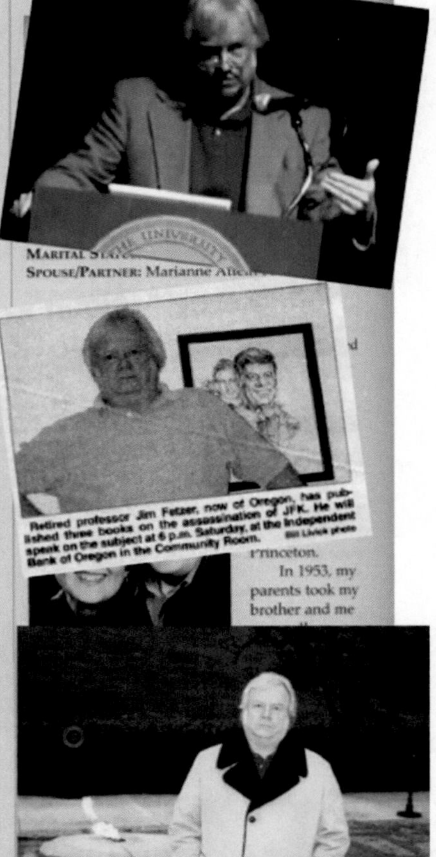

272

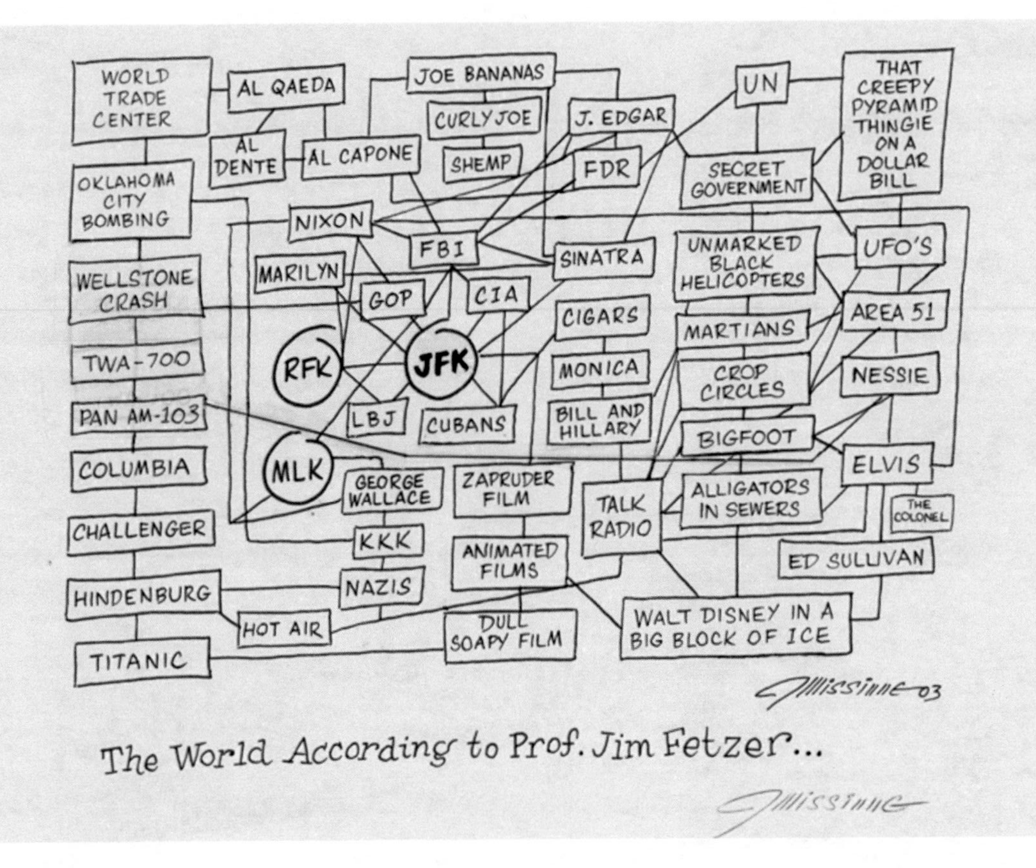
WORLD TRADE CENTER
AL QAEDA
AL DENTE
AL CAPONE
JOE BANANAS
CURLY JOE
SHEMP
J. EDGAR
FDR
UN
THAT CREEPY PYRAMID THINGIE ON A DOLLAR BILL
SECRET GOVERNMENT
OKLAHOMA CITY BOMBING
NIXON
FBI
SINATRA
UNMARKED BLACK HELICOPTERS
UFO'S
WELLSTONE CRASH
MARILYN
GOP
CIA
CIGARS
MARTIANS
AREA 51
TWA-700
RFK
JFK
MONICA
CROP CIRCLES
NESSIE
PAN AM-103
LBJ
CUBANS
BILL AND HILLARY
BIGFOOT
COLUMBIA
MLK
GEORGE WALLACE
ZAPRUDER FILM
TALK RADIO
ALLIGATORS IN SEWERS
ELVIS
THE COLONEL
CHALLENGER
KKK
ANIMATED FILMS
ED SULLIVAN
HINDENBURG
NAZIS
HOT AIR
DULL SOAPY FILM
WALT DISNEY IN A BIG BLOCK OF ICE
TITANIC
The World According to Prof. Jim Fetzer...

[Epilogue]

I believe that everything our government tells us is a conspiracy unless they prove different.

I certainly didn't begin my radio show in 1999 thinking that. At the time, I was a consummate "patriot" and my country could do no wrong.

As the title of my first book, *The Awakening of An American, How My Country Broke My Heart*, showed, once I did the homework I was aghast at the real truths. Perhaps, like you the reader, I too didn't want to know the ugly truths my research and guests all these years have done to expose what our shadow government became and is.

It was extremely painful and disheartening to me. It made my work all the more important as it wasn't a path to the world I wanted my grandchildren to grow up in.

I co-host a monthly show with Jim Fetzer, *Roaring Truth*, and he is one of the most beloved of my co-hosts. I had the pleasure of working with him in Virginia at a truth conference in 2006.

I met Kevin Barrett at a 9/11 Truth Conference in Chicago and his sincerity and softness touched me. I remembered a saying I was taught years ago "sometimes real power can be a very quiet thing".

I see Jim Fetzer and Kevin Barrett as modern day incarnations of Ben Franklin and John Adams, respectively.

Neither man has a secret agenda to what they do, except to educate people and ring the warning bell as Paul Revere did. I highly recommend their work.

You may balk at what you have read in this book, but do the research and prove it to yourselves.

Jim Fetzer is the premier expert in America (as far as I am concerned) on the assassinations of JFK, RFK, Paul Wellstone and many more. He has the credentials and the rare ability of critical thinking to put it all together.

Both of these men have put in countless hours of investigation and study on the topics they present as have most of my excellent guests.

I have met and worked with both of these men personally, and they are loving, compassionate patriots working on behalf of truth. They suffer a lot for what they do and present, and realize that if they don't do it, who will?

When it comes to truth about false flags, our shadow-corporate-fascist government and 9/11/01, they are heroes. True patriots put it ALL on the line for truth and future generations. As I always say, "9/11 happened and we all got convicted." The beginning of the end of the American "experiment" started one fateful day in Dallas a long time ago. The end happened on September 11, 2001. That is the day our Constitution, Bill of Rights, Declaration of Independence, and freedom were taken away from all of us.

As you now know thanks to a "leak", the NSA has been spying on all of our phone calls, emails, snail mail, and computers for years now. We now live in a militarized police state. If you don't know that, you haven't been paying attention. Perhaps America DOES get the government it deserves.

When I rang the warning bell during the reign of George W, people laughed, and called me, Kevin, and Jim "conspiracy theorists". No, we were talking "conspiracy facts". These men still fearlessly expose the criminal cabal that has succeeded in a coup d'etat of our government and should be applauded for it.

This book assures that their names will go down in history. Hopefully as the men who helped get America back on track because of their dedication, fearlessness and most of all – love.

"Peace, we can have it if we want it" – John Lennon

- Meria Heller

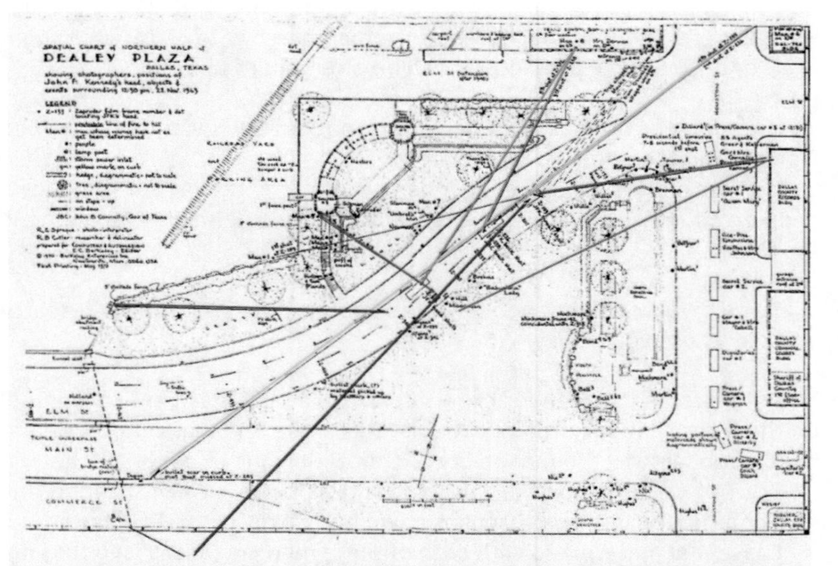

Richard Sprague, *Computers and Automation* (May 1970), Expanded

There appear to have been at least 8, 9 or 10 shots from at least six locations. See "Six JFK Shooters Named, Three with ties to CIA--Oswald not among them", jamesfetzer.blogspot.com (28 December 2013).

[A word from the editor]

CWG Press: A small publisher with big ideas

I started CWG Press in 2006 with the publication of Mike Palecek's novel *The American Dream;* now, eight years later. I'm publishing his new nonfiction book. I think of it as a "dual biography" or perhaps a history book. Imagine that, real history, in a book published in the U.S.A.

This is the 19th book published by CWG Press. Since that first one, they've all used a print-on-demand service.

The cost of printing and storing books, and then fulfilling orders manually, was not easy to deal with; compounded with bookstores wanting money back for unsold books shipped to them for a tour, my press almost failed before getting off the ground. But since then, I've been able to bring quite a few more books to the public, and there has been critical acclaim if not a plethora of actual sales.

I've continued to work with Mike Palecek, and ended up reprinting many of his earlier books as well as publishing *Speak English* and *Johnny Moon* under the CWG Press imprint. I also co-host The New American Dream Radio Show with Mike; you might call us dynamic duo two, but that wouldn't be showing enough respect to the originals, Jim Fetzer and Kevin Barrett. We pale in comparison. But we do our bit to get the word out.

This book was Mike's idea. He saw these two amazing guys just working and working to find out what really has happened and is happening in our country. He saw the controversy, and noted the parallels with the White Rose movement in Germany.

He started to think about that, and wrote some things down, and before long he found a way to interview Jim and Kevin over the phone, and not long after that he had hours and hours of interview recordings. And then he transcribed them to text and started to put this book together.

I was initially just going to be the publisher. Then the guy working on the cover bailed out, and I took that over. And Mike said, oh, by the way, Chuck, there are these sections of photos that the cover guy was going to do, how about picking up that part? And naturally I agreed.

And then there was this big brouhaha over some style issues, and which photos should really be a part of it, and was it too long. The real problem was that there were these three incredibly talented people, all of them very intelligent, and all of them having their own ideas of exactly how things should look or sound. And the visions were not identical.

So I jumped in to the fray, because I've somehow learned to hear the things that are important to people when they are disagreeing, and I knew that all three of these guys really wanted the project to succeed. So I ended up as the editor, and Mike is recognized as the author, because that really is the closest description possible to the role he played in this project. He thought of it, he got all the materials together, he organized it, and he wrote significant parts of it.

It's a book that transcends any one of the four of us who are part of it.

I am honored to have become an integral part of such an endeavor. In years to come, I'll look back at *The Dynamic Duo: White Rose Blooms in Wisconsin,* and I'll think, that was the one where it all came together. That was the one that people will remember.

It is of course because of Kevin Barrett and Jim Fetzer, working tirelessly to find truth and make it known, that there is any basis for a book.

It is because of Mike Palecek's vision, determination, and hard work that the book came into being.

And I think that I provided the computer skills that made everything work together, and the people skills that made everyone work together.

Thanks for listening.

- Chuck Gregory, editor/publisher, CWG Press.

Index

B

C

O

P

Q

R